The Future of Religion

THE FUTURE OF *Religion*

SECULARIZATION, REVIVAL AND CULT FORMATION

Rodney Stark and William Sims Bainbridge

University of California Press   *Berkeley*   *Los Angeles*   *London*

University of California Press
Berkeley and Los Angeles, California

University of California Press, Ltd.
London, England

© 1985 by
The Regents of the University of California

Printed in the United States of America
2   3   4   5   6   7   8   9

Library of Congress Cataloging in Publication Data

Stark, Rodney.
  The future of religion.

  Bibliography: p.
  Includes index.
  1. Religion. 2. Sects. 3. Cults. 4. Secularism.
I. Bainbridge, William Sims. II. Title.
BL48.S72   1984   200   83-18221
ISBN 0-520-04854-7
ISBN 0-520-05731-7 (pbk.)

Contents

Acknowledgments

Of the chapters that follow, four were written with colleagues and friends whom we especially want to thank, not only for their labors on those chapters but also for the encouragement and insights they offered during the entire project: Daniel P. Doyle, Daniel H. Jackson, Lori Kent, and Lynne Roberts. We have also enjoyed the help of a number of social scientists, editors, and students: Grant Barnes, Curtis C. Fuller, William R. Garrett, Jeffrey K. Hadden, Phillip E. Hammond, Benton Johnson, Cynthia E. Keen, Mary Lamprech, Theodore E. Long, Armand Mauss, Charlie Millington, Hart M. Nelsen, Christine A. Norell, Jane Allen Piliavin, George Psathas, Sylvia E. Stein, and Bryan Wilson. Without the treasure of solid data and spiritual energy offered us so freely by J. Gordon Melton, this book would be much the poorer. Finally, we thank with special warmth and respect our principal mentors in the scientific study of religion, Charles Y. Glock and George C. Homans.

1 *The Nature of Religion*

At least since the Enlightenment, most Western intellectuals have anticipated the death of religion as eagerly as ancient Israel awaited the messiah. Social scientists have particularly excelled in predicting the impending triumph of reason over "superstition." The most illustrious figures in sociology, anthropology, and psychology have unanimously expressed confidence that their children, or surely their grandchildren, would live to see the dawn of a new era in which, to paraphrase Freud, the infantile illusions of religion would be outgrown.

But, as one generation has followed another, religion has persisted. A third of Americans claim they are "born again" Christians, and 90 percent pray regularly. During the nationwide strikes in Poland, the workers did not raise the red flag, but the blue banner of Our Lady. The Soviet press angrily admits that 70 years of intensive education in atheism and severe repression of religion are a resounding failure. Nevertheless, most intellectuals remain confident that religion lives on borrowed time, and every sign of weakness in major religious organizations is diagnosed as terminal. All contrary indications, be they revivals of conventional religion or a lush growth of new religions, are dismissed as superficial. Fashionable opinion holds the trend toward secularism to be rapid and inevitable.

The argument developed in this book is very unfashionable. With Daniel Bell (1971, 1980), we think the vision of a religionless future is but illusion. We acknowledge that secularization is a major trend in modern times, but argue that this is not a modern development and does not presage the demise of religion. Rather, as we attempt to demonstrate throughout this book, secularization is a process found in all religious economies; it is something that is always going on in all societies. While secularization progresses in some parts of a society, a countervailing intensification of religion goes on in other parts. Sometimes the pace of secularization speeds or slows, but the dominant religious organizations in any society are always becoming progressively more worldly, which is to say, more secularized. The result of this trend has never been the end of religion, but merely a shift in fortunes among religions as faiths that have become too worldly are supplanted by more vigorous and less worldly religions.

In this book, we demonstrate that secularization is only one of three fundamental and interrelated processes that constantly occur in all religious economies. The process of secularization is self-limiting and generates two countervailing processes. One of these is *revival*. Religious organizations that are eroded by secularization abandon a substantial market demand for less worldly religion, a demand that produces breakaway sect movements. Thus, out of secularization is born revival as protest groups form to restore vigorous otherworldliness to a conventional faith.

Secularization also stimulates *religious innovation*. Not only do worldly churches prompt new religious groups, which seek to revive faith, but secularization also prompts the formation of new religious traditions. New religions constantly appear in societies. Whether they make any headway depends on the vigor of conventional religious organizations. When new faiths that are better adapted to current market demand spring up, older faiths are eclipsed. Thus did Christianity, Islam, Buddhism, and the other great world faiths wrest dominant market positions from older faiths.

In the beginning, all religions are obscure, tiny, deviant cult movements. Caught at the right moment, Jesus would have been found leading a handful of ragtag followers in a remote corner of the mighty Roman Empire. How laughable it would have seemed to Roman intellectuals that this obscure cult could pose a threat to the great pagan temples. In similar fashion, Western intellectuals scorn contemporary cults. Yet, if major new faiths are aborning, they will not be found by consulting the directory of the National Council of Churches. Rather, they will be found in lists of obscure cult movements. Thus, to assess the future of religion, one must always pay close attention to the fringes of religious economies (cf. Tiryakian, 1972; Yinger, 1977).

Social scientists have misread the future of religion, not only because they so fervently desire religion to disappear, but also because they have failed to recognize the dynamic character of religious economies. To focus only on secularization is to fail to see how this process is part of a much larger and reciprocal structure. Having erroneously equated religion with a particular set of religious organizations, Western intellectuals have misread the secularization of these groups as the doom of religion in general. But it is foolish to look only at sunsets and never observe the dawn: the history of religion is not only a pattern of decline; it is equally a portrait of birth and growth. We argue that the sources of religion are shifting constantly in societies but that the amount of religion remains relatively constant.

DEFINING RELIGION

Most scholars limit the term *religion* to those systems of thought embodied in social organizations that posit the existence of the supernatural (Goody, 1961; Stark, 1965b; Spiro, 1966; Berger, 1967). But an articulate minority demands the definition of religion to be broad enough to include scientific humanism, Marxism, and other nonsupernatural philosophies (Luckmann, 1967; Bellah, 1970b; Yinger, 1970). This is a critical dispute. Unless it is resolved, we cannot determine whether a theory of religious movements ought also to include movements such as those inspired by intense, but antisupernatural, political creeds.

Elsewhere (Stark, 1965b; Stark and Bainbridge, 1980) we have argued against lumping supernatural and naturalistic faiths under the common term *religion*—that to do so makes it needlessly difficult to explore conflicts between these contrary systems of thought or to identify the rather different capacities present in each. Now we are prepared to go much further. As Emile Durkheim (1915) correctly proclaimed, there can be no church of magic (see Chapter 2). We are prepared to assert that there can be no wholly naturalistic religion; that a religion lacking supernatural assumptions is no religion at all. Throughout this book, we demonstrate that the differences between supernatural and nonsupernatural (or naturalistic) systems are so profound that it makes no more sense to equate them than to equate totem poles and telephone poles. Indeed, in Part V, we demonstrate that naturalistic meaning systems, be they scientific rationalism, established religions shorn of their conceptions of an active supernatural, or militantly irreligious political elites in control of repressive states, cannot supplant supernaturalism. That is, naturalistic systems cannot replace supernaturalistic systems in the hearts of most human beings. If they cannot function as religious, then they must not be religions.

Scrutiny of the immense literature on the proper definition of religion reveals two key problems. First, the definition must be general. As Georg Simmel (1905: 359) pointed out long ago, we need "a definition which, without vagueness and yet with sufficient comprehensiveness, has told once for all what religion is in its essence, in that which is common alike to the religions of Christians and South Sea islanders, to Buddhism and Mexican idolatry." Clearly, it will not serve sociology to define religion as belief in Christ or even belief in a supreme being. Many groups that obviously are religious do not even know the Christ story and worship an array of supernatural powers of whom no single god is superior to others. Yet the definition of religion must not be too broad. In our judgment, this is the pit into which many modern scholars have fallen. They propose definitions that easily accommodate the vast numbers of faiths we would like to include as religions, but their definitions apply as easily to ideologies that seem better excluded.

The first powerful proponent of an overbroad definition of religion was Emile Durkheim, who is considered one of the founders of modern sociology. In his classic work *The Elementary Forms of the Religious Life* (1915), Durkheim heaped scorn and ridicule on those eminent 19th-century scholars who held that religions must possess some conception of the supernatural, or what the great anthropologist Sir E. B. Tylor called "Spiritual Beings." Durkheim scolded Tylor and others for failing to realize that Buddhism lacks all traces of supernatural belief, yet it must be counted as a religion. Later scholars recognized that Durkheim was simply wrong about Buddhism — that he mistook the "religious" views of a small group of philosophers and court intellectuals for popular Buddhism (Spiro, 1966).

Durkheim (1915: 273) noted that "there is no known society without a religion," and he (1915: 466) asserted that "religion has given birth to all that is essential in society." He also assumed that all healthy cultures are unitary, all members sharing a single creed. From this perspective, evidence that some philosophers in a Buddhist society were atheistic would imply that Buddhist societies were atheistic, and thus that there exist atheist religions. From this logic, it is a short step to abandon popular definitions of religion and to define it without reference to the supernatural. Of course, a definition derived in this way is a poor conceptual tool for measuring variations in religiosity and of little use for understanding such processes of change as secularization and revival.

Durkheim sought to explain the ubiquity of religion by asserting that it performs the essential function of representing the society to its members in the form of sacred symbols that support a moral code and a sense of tribal unity. But if a culture contains several different doctrines, one cannot assume without good evidence that each doctrine serves these functions and deserves to be called a religion. In societies such as ours and that of classical India, there exist schools of thought, promulgated by professional scholars and intellectuals, that recast traditional religious ideas as philosophical systems having no reference to supernatural deities. Far from representing the dominant religious thinking of their societies, these philosophical systems are the extreme in secularization. Perhaps some members of the intellectual elite favor them, but they may have little impact on social behavior.

As Berger (1967: 177) points out about Luckmann's (1967) too-inclusive definition of religion, if one defines all "self-transcendent symbolic universes" as religions, then one immediately is forced to say how science, for example, is "*different* from what has been called religion by everyone else . . . which poses the definitional problem all over again." Or, as Swanson (1960) suggests, if members of the American Association of Atheists, the Lutheran Church in America, and the Revolutionary Communist Youth Brigade are all defined as members of religious organizations, we lose the conceptual tools we need to explore the constant and profound conflicts among them.

How can we distinguish between religions and other ideological systems? In our judgment, the answer was correctly given by the 19th-century founders of the social scientific study of religion, those men whose position Durkheim attempted to bury: *religions involve some conception of a supernatural being, world, or force, and the notion that the supernatural is active, that events and conditions here on earth are influenced by the supernatural.* Or, as Sir James G. Frazer (1922: 58) put it, "religion consists of two elements . . . a belief in powers higher than man and an attempt to propitiate or please them."

EXPANDING THE DEFINITION OF RELIGION

Our studies of religious movements are based on an effort to test empirically our deductive theory of religion. Our basic theory leads us to a definition that attempts to isolate the fundamental features of how religion serves human needs. We shall sketch the logical chain by which our definition arises, and we gave a more formal statement in one of our technical essays (Stark and Bainbridge, 1980).

We begin with a mundane axiom about human behavior: *Humans seek what they perceive to be rewards and try to avoid what they perceive to be costs.* In various forms, this is one of the oldest and still most central propositions about human behavior. It is the starting point for microeconomics, learning psychology, and sociological theories (Homans,

1950, 1961). However, when we inspect more closely this human tendency to seek rewards, we see two important points:

1. In all societies, many rewards are scarce and unequally distributed. Substantial proportions of any population have far less of some rewards than they would like to have and less of these rewards than some other people actually possess. Scarcity, both absolute and relative, is a social universal.

2. Some intensely desired rewards seem not to be available at all. For example, no one can demonstrate whether there is life after death, but everyone can see that immortality cannot be gained in the here and now, in the natural world available to our senses. But the simple unavailability of the reward of eternal life has not caused people to cease wanting it. To the contrary, it is probably the single most urgent human desire.

Noting the strong desires for rewards that are available to many, as well as those that seem not to be directly available to anyone, we can recognize another characteristic human action: the creation and exchange of *compensators*. People may experience rewards, but they can only have faith in compensators. *A compensator is the belief that a reward will be obtained in the distant future or in some other context which cannot be immediately verified.*

We do not use the word *compensator* in any pejorative sense. By it we simply mean to recognize that, when highly desired rewards seem unavailable through direct means, persons tend to develop explanations about how they can gain this reward later or elsewhere. Compensators are a form of IOU. They promise that, in return for value surrendered now, the desired rewards will be obtained eventually. Often people must make regular payments to keep a compensator valid, which makes it possible to bind them to long-term involvement in an organization that serves as a source of compensators. Put another way, humans will often exchange rewards of considerable value over a long period of time in return for compensators in the hope that a reward of immense value will be forthcoming in return.

Compensators are by no means exclusively, or even primarily, religious in nature. They are generated and exchanged throughout the range of human institutions. When a radical political movement instructs followers to work for the revolution now, in return for material rewards later, compensators have been exchanged for rewards. The party receives direct rewards; the followers receive an IOU. Or a compensator is exchanged for a reward when people have their bodies frozen in a cryogenic vault until science discovers how to cure their disease or overcome the aging process. Similarly, when a parent tells a child, "Be good; work hard; one day you will be rich and famous," a compensator-reward exchange is proposed. Sometimes, of course, compensators are redeemed — the promised reward is obtained. But, unless or until they are redeemed, compensators figure in exchange processes as IOUs; that is, they are easily distinguished from the actual reward that is being promised.

In our system, compensators fall along a continuum from the specific to the general. Specific compensators promise a specific, limited reward. The most general compensators promise a great array of rewards or rewards of vast scope. A shaman's promise that, if certain ritual procedures are followed, a person will be cured of warts is a specific compensator. The promise of a happy life is a general compensator. In Chapter 2 and elsewhere in this book, we have found the distinction between general and specific compensators vital in distinguishing between magic and religion, which in turn makes it possible to deduce Durkheim's claim that there can be no church of magic.

When we examine human desires, we see that people often seek rewards of such magnitude and apparent unavailability that *only by assuming the existence of an active supernatural can credible compensators be created.* For example, since time immemorial, humans have desired to know the meaning of existence. Why are we here? What is the purpose of life? Where will it all end? Moreover, people have not just wanted answers to these questions; they have desired particular kinds of answers — that life have meaning. But for life to have a great design, for there to be intention behind history, one must posit the existence of a designer or intender of such power, duration, and scale as to be outside or beyond the natural world of our senses. Similarly, for humans to survive death, it is, at least thus far in history, necessary to posit supernatural agencies. Indeed, to accept that earthly suffering gains meaning as prelude to everlasting glory is to embrace the supernatural. Archeological evidence that our rude Neanderthal ancestors buried their dead with elaborate ceremony and with food and possessions to be used in the next world suggests that such concerns typify humans far back into prehistory.

Although in our more technical essays we are able to derive this line of reasoning from our theory, surely the point can stand on its own merit: Some common human desires are so beyond direct, this-worldly satisfaction that only the gods can provide them. This simple point has profound implications.

So long as humans intensely seek certain rewards of great magnitude that remain unavailable through direct actions, they will be able to obtain credible compensators only from sources predicated on the supernatural. In this market, no purely naturalistic ideologies can compete. Systems of thought that reject the supernatural lack all means to credibly promise such rewards as eternal life in any fashion. Similarly, naturalistic philosophies can argue that statements such as "What is the meaning of life?" or "What is the purpose of the universe?" are meaningless utterances. But they cannot provide answers to these questions in the terms in which they are asked.

This profound difference in compensator-generating capacity is why we have chosen to define religions as *human organizations primarily engaged in providing general compensators based on supernatural assumptions.* Our intention is to isolate those systems of thought that have the capacity to deal with human desires of maximum scope, intensity, and scarcity from those systems lacking such a capacity. The fact that this definition parallels what the term *religion* has always meant in everyday speech is probably not accidental. Social scientists are not uniquely qualified to recognize fundamental features of human societies. Indeed, we suspect that only by letting his social scientific rhetoric obscure real life could Durkheim have failed to notice that religions are a unique source of maximum compensators. This was clear in that atheistic versions of Buddhist philosophy failed to attract any substantial mass following despite being sponsored by powerful and eloquent intellectuals.

These theoretical considerations lead to many dramatic conclusions we shall explore in later chapters. Consider but one of these, which is the major theme pursued in Part V: Movements lacking supernatural assumptions cannot successfully compete, over the long run, in generating mass commitment when confronted by movements that accept the supernatural. To be more specific: So long as humans persist in desires not directly satisfiable, the eventual fate of "demythologized" religious organizations is sealed. Or one can conclude that, although modern-day Communism is in conflict with religion, it is not itself a religion and remains permanently vulnerable to religious competitors, especially once Communist regimes come to power (see Chapter 22). To sum up, our analysis suggests that not only is the notion of a nonsupernatural or naturalistic religion a logical contradiction, but in fact efforts to create such "religions" will fail for want of that vital resource that always has been the sine qua non of religions: the gods.

Thus, the study of religious movements is restricted to organized groups that offer general compensators based on supernatural assumptions. In Chapter 2, we elaborate this definition of religious movements to recognize several different varieties.

DIMENSIONS OF RELIGIOUS COMMITMENT

Thus far in defining religion, we have focused on the unique capacity of supernatural belief systems to provide people with compensators for scarce or wholly unavailable rewards. Another way to examine religion is to observe how people express their religiousness, how they manifest their commitment to religious organizations. Charles Y. Glock (1959, 1962) made the first important attempt to distinguish the variety of ways people can be religious. Glock wanted to resolve a dispute between those who thought a major religious revival had occurred in the United States after World War II because rates of church membership and attendance rose rapidly and those who lamented the loss of faith they believed had taken place during this same time. Glock recognized that people often mean different things by a term such as *religiousness* and that these different modes may vary independently.

Glock began by asking university students to write answers to the question, "When someone is described as a religious person, what do you assume about them?" In attempting to classify the many answers he received, Glock found that five distinct *dimensions* (or modes) of religious expression were invoked. He used these five dimensions to point out that it was possible both for religious participation to increase and for religious belief to decrease — hence that those debating about a religious revival were talking past one another (Glock, 1959).

In later work, Stark and Glock (1968) further refined and measured these five dimensions. Although religious organizations differ in the emphasis they place on various aspects of religious commitment, all expect members to display some commitment in each of these ways: belief, practice, experience, knowledge, and consequences.

1. The *belief* dimension of commitment consists of the expectation that the religious person will accept certain doctrines as true.

2. The *practice* dimension includes acts of worship and devotion directed toward the supernatural. Two important subtypes exist here. *Ritual* practices refer to formal ceremonies, rites, and sacred activities — such things as baptism, attending worship services, and taking communion. *Devotional* practices are informal, often spontaneous, and frequently done in private. Bible reading and private prayer are common examples.

3. The *experience* dimension takes into account that individuals often believe they have achieved direct, subjective contact with the supernatural. Often these are no more than intense but diffuse feelings of special awareness of divine existence — the "born again" experience, for exam-

ple. But sometimes, too, people experience what they define as direct communication with the supernatural; they may even gain new revelations of divine intention and meaning.

4. The *knowledge* dimension indicates that people are expected to know and understand central elements of their religious culture — in the case of Christians, who preached the Sermon on the Mount or the name of the town in which Jesus was born.

5. *Consequences* refer to religious actions in everyday life. All religions direct people to behave in certain ways (to tell the truth, to give alms to the poor) and not to behave in certain other ways (not to drink or fornicate).

Research has found that, empirically, there is much independence among these different dimensions of religious commitment. People who are high on one are not necessarily high on any others (Stark and Glock, 1968). Initially, the recognition that there may be multiple dimensions of religion alerted sociologists of religion to base their research on many measures of religious commitment, rather than on only one. And, indeed, it often turned out that very contradictory findings were produced when results using one dimension were compared with results based on another. The clearest example is research exploring the relationship between religious commitment and social class.

Social Class and Modes of Faith

For a long time, sociologists of religion took it for granted that a primary function of religion was to comfort the poor for their relative deprivations. In so doing, they echoed not only Marx's condemnation of religion as nothing but "an opium of the people" but also St. Paul's belief that religion has greatest appeal to the "weak things of the world." Then, with the development of empirical social research in the 1940s, a series of investigators found the lower classes noticeably absent from church (cf. Stark, 1964). It is the wealthy, not the poor, who are most likely to be found in the pews on Sunday morning. This discovery threatened a major sociological proposition, for if the poor get the most out of religion, they must be doing so without benefit of clergy.

Then several of Glock's students salvaged this sociological proposition by noting that rich and poor tend to express their religion in different ways or along different dimensions (Demerath, 1965; Stark, 1964, 1972). Thus, for example, lower-class people are more likely than upper-class people to pray in private, to believe in the doctrines of their faith, and to have intense religious experiences. But the upper classes display greater religious commitment when it comes to church membership, church attendance, and all other aspects of the ritual dimension (Stark, 1972).

Although Glock's initial five dimensions made it easy to spot these contrary tendencies, his scheme did not lend itself very well to isolating and explaining them. The data strongly hint that different social classes get different things from religion. But how can these be identified?

Part of the answer can be found in our discussion of compensators earlier in this chapter. We noted that religion offers compensators for scarce rewards — those for which some people experience relative deprivation. Religion also offers compensators for rewards that seem not to exist at all in this world. In terms of these rewards, all humans, rich and poor alike, are potentially deprived. But religious organizations provide more than compensators. Any organization that provides a stage for human action and interaction will provide numerous direct rewards. As we explore in length in Chapter 14, religious movements deal not only in compensators, in intangibles, but also in very tangible, direct rewards. Thus, people can gain a variety of rewards from religious commitment. They can earn a living from religion. Religions offer human companionship, status as an upright person of good character (Weber, 1946: 303–305), leisure and recreational activity, opportunities for marriage, courtship, and business contacts — a whole host of things people value.

While analyzing what people can get out of religion, we must realize that this can be influenced greatly by their *power*. We use this term rather broadly to mean a superior ability to win rewards in social exchanges based on all the talents and resources that allow some people to profit more than others in social interactions (cf. Blau, 1964). Because power means the ability to gain rewards, it is especially critical in the case of scarce rewards. It follows that the powerful will tend to monopolize the rewards available from religion, just as they tend to monopolize those from all other sources. Our theory leads to the deduction that people will prefer rewards over compensators and that they will seek the former whenever possible. This means that the more privileged people will have less need and desire for those compensators religion offers for rewards that are only scarce. Privileged people will succeed in getting the scarce rewards themselves. Persons who lack the means to get the rewards must content themselves with compensators for these rewards. Such compensators will have their greatest utility among the poor and powerless. But we also can see that power is irrelevant in the case of rewards that seem not to exist at all. Neither rich nor poor can gain eternal life in this world. All have equal need of compensators for this desire.

These ideas are captured in three propositions we are able to deduce from our formal theory of religion. Each concerns the relationship between power and religious commitment:

1. The power of an individual or a group will be *positively* associated with control of religious organizations and with gaining the rewards available from religious organizations.

2. The power of an individual or group will be *negatively* associated with accepting religious compensators when the desired reward exists.

3. Regardless of power, persons and groups will tend to accept religious compensators when desired rewards do not exist.

These three propositions are consistent with the empirical literature and help make the many conflicting findings coherent. The data consistently show that the powerful dominate religious rewards (excel in membership and attendance) and the powerless dominate religious compensators for scarcity (excel in prayer and belief). But powerful and powerless are equally likely to believe in life after death — a compensator for unavailable rewards (Stark and Bainbridge, 1980).

A New Approach

We may now translate these theoretical propositions into a tidy conceptual scheme for identifying dimensions of religious commitment. The second proposition captures the long intellectual tradition asserting that religion serves to comfort the poor for their relative deprivations — for their deficits in scarce rewards. We can name this the *other-worldly dimension* of religious commitment to identify the way compensators can assuage worldly suffering by emphasizing the better life to come. As we see in following chapters, this dimension of religious commitment is dominant in sects.

However, the first proposition lets us see that religion is not wholly a response to deprivation. Rather, this proposition reflects the religious expression of privilege. We can name this the *worldly dimension* of religious commitment to identify the importance of the tangible rewards of which it consists. This mode of commitment tends to be dominant in churches.

These two dimensions are really opposite sides of the same coin — expressions of relative deprivation and its antithesis. But religious commitment is too complex to be captured adequately by these two dimensions alone. Indeed, one well may wonder why the powerful bother with religion at all. Surely they could gain as many, perhaps even more, rewards by participating in purely secular organizations and pursuits.

The third proposition explains this phenomenon. In terms of the most intense human desires, everyone is potentially deprived. Here we isolate what we can call the *universal dimension* of religious commitment, religious compensators capable of binding powerful and powerless alike to religious organizations.

These three dimensions consolidate Glock's important recognition that religious commitment is not a unidimensional phenomenon. They also have affinity with Gordon W. Allport's (1960: 33) distinction between *extrinsic* and *intrinsic* types of religious faith. Allport characterized extrinsic faith as "utilitarian, self-serving, conferring safety, status, comfort and talismanic favors upon the believer. . . . People who are religious in this sense make use of God. . . . [They are] dependent and basically infantile."

In his view, the intrinsic type of religion "can steer one's existence without enslaving him to his limited concepts and egocentric needs. . . . It is the polar opposite of the utilitarian, self-centered, extrinsic view."

Ignoring Allport's contempt for those who accept the invitation of religion to "take it to the Lord in prayer" and his attempt to define liberal Protestantism as indicative of better mental health, we may glimpse affinities between the extrinsic type and our otherworldly dimension. The intrinsic type is more heavily weighted on the universal and the worldly dimensions.

Both Glock and Allport arrived at their dimensions of religious commitment inductively, as summaries of empirical data. This approach is valid if one's scientific purpose is the systematic description of how a particular culture conceptualizes religious experience, that is, if one is working as an ethnographer. Today a number of statistical tools, such as factor analysis, are used to reduce the opinions of numerous respondents to a single cognitive structure (cf. King, 1967). But when such studies are replicated on different populations, they tend to give different results. In so doing, they may accurately chart cultural differences in the nature of religion and in how it is conceptualized. Done properly, this line of research permits sensitive intercultural comparisons, thus adding to the tools available for systematic ethnology.

We derived our conceptual scheme from a formal theory rather than through distillation of the folk ideas of any single culture. Thus, it is designed as an objective analytic tool for understanding all varieties of religion. The trouble with inductive conceptual schemes is that an infinite number of alternatives can be found, and there is no way to choose among them. Unlike hypotheses (statements that assert a relationship linking two or more concepts), mere definitions can be neither true nor false. Each notes a distinction someone has made and simply gives it a name. But if we want to develop scientific explanations, the test of the concepts is their utility for effective theorizing. Concepts that are not incorporated into theories may or may not be useful for theorizing; there is no way to tell. Because our conceptualization derives from a theory of religion, it is fruitful to the extent that the theory is successful.

In later chapters, we show that these three dimensions of religious commitment serve as an essential starting point for a theory of church and sect movements. They tell use to expect an "internal contradiction" within all religious organizations — the presence of groups with a conflict of interest over whom the organization is to serve and how. Some will want emphasis on the otherworldly dimension. Some will want major emphasis on the worldly dimension. These two dimensions tend to be incompatible and one can be emphasized only at the cost of deemphasizing the other. Thus, the seeds of internal conflict and for the transformation of religious organizations are inherent in the composition of religious organizations. Our dimensions efficiently identify this conflict; we see the correspondence between our definition of religion and our analysis of individual religious commitment.

AN ASIDE ON FAITH

Readers must not let our use of the term *compensator* in our definition of religion cause them to assume we therefore imply that religion is false. As will be clear in many subsequent chapters, it is impossible to demonstrate that the most general compensators are false. Science is completely helpless in the face of claims made on behalf of a being, world, or force beyond the natural world (cf. Dodd, 1961). We may send cameras through the far reaches of space to photograph the rings of Saturn and the moons of Jupiter, but they cannot be sent to reveal the face of God or the topography of heaven. Religion, in its purest forms, lies beyond the reach of all science and surely is not vulnerable to the definitions of two social scientists. It is not our intent to suggest anything about the truth of religion. We seek only to discover its visible aspects — the social forms it takes in the world we all can see. We leave its invisible aspects to others to comprehend or dispute. That we must discuss in Chapter 8 that some people who found religions are rascals gives us no ability to pass upon the authenticity of the private religious visions of other religious founders. The thrust of this book is that religion will prosper and endure no matter what social scientists, or any others, have to say about faith.

PLAN OF THE BOOK

The next chapter continues the definitional task already begun. In it, we distinguish two primary forms of deviant religious movements: *sects* and *cults*. First, we see how these can be distinguished from religious institutions or churches. Then we see why it is vital to distinguish one form of deviant religious group from another. Finally, we distinguish between cults that are fully developed religious movements and other cult groups and activities that represent magic, not religion. In the remainder of the book, we use these distinctions, and we show that they are very sensitive to empirical nuances. They often permit us to make sense of what otherwise might appear to be only odd blips and glitches in the data.

In order to understand religious movements, we must examine the interplay between them and their environments. For example, one cannot discuss religious deviance without knowledge of the conventional standards against which this deviance is judged. One cannot fully understand religious deviance unless one knows the extent to which the coercive powers of the state are used against religious nonconformity. Is the state repressive or permissive of novel religions? But even where religious freedom is greatest, new religions must find a niche in the religious economy in order to survive. Thus, Part I examines the religious economy of the United States and Canada. In Chapter 3, we examine the diversity of faiths making up the religious spectrum and demonstrate the utility of the notion of tension with the environment to order the huge array of competing faiths. Chapter 4 is devoted to important regional variations in conventional religion and serves as a preface to later chapters that examine where and when sects and cults thrive.

In Part II, we take up sects. Chapter 5 explains why religious organizations tend to move into low tension with their environments. We then see how low tension religious groups are unable to provide as efficacious compensators for scarcity as high tension groups readily offer. This permits us to see the conditions under which religious schisms develop — sects are schismatic groups that leave a lower tension group in order to form one in higher tension. We examine where sect leaders come from and why. The chapter also considers the relatively rare circumstances in which church movements break off from sects. In the latter part of the chapter, we consider the chronic threat sect movements pose to monopoly churches. We then specifically examine the medieval church and the many ways it devised to rechannel sect movements and to serve everyone's religious needs. We shall see that the Reformation was not a sudden breakdown in the universality of the Catholic church.

The church was never able to monopolize religious activities and was unable either to provide adequate magic or to eliminate magical competitors, all of which culminated in the Inquisition.

Chapter 6 moves up to the present and examines the first large, quantified set of data on American-born sect movements. How many are there? Where are they? How big are they? How many are growing? What are the most common varieties? Chapter 7 introduces and tests a fragment of our theory of religious movements. What mechanisms account for the transformation of sects into churches? The chapter identifies the forces that cause the social class composition of sects to rise over time and shows how this reduces their tension with the outside world.

Part III is devoted to cults. Chapter 8 is conceptual and theoretical. In it, we identify three models of cult formation — how new religions are created. First, we examine the process by which people believe they have received a new religious insight and how they are able to share their conviction with others. Then we examine how people create new religions in much the same way as they might start any commercial venture. Finally, we examine the dynamic processes by which certain small groups of people evolve a new religious doctrine and come to believe in it. We show that these three models summarize a huge, but disorganized, literature on religious innovation and that they differ from one another only in their emphasis on common elements.

Chapter 9 does for cults what Chapter 6 does for sects. Based on 501 contemporary cult movements, it establishes basic facts. Where do cults flourish? What kinds of cults are forming now as compared with the past? Is cult formation becoming more frequent? Chapter 10 poses similar questions, but about groups that are not (or are not yet) fully developed cult movements — groups we identify as client and audience cults. In Chapter 11, we examine cult membership in the 1920s. Here we chart in detail the rise of some of the most successful American cult movements and demonstrate that there is nothing new about the formation of new religions.

In chapters 12 and 13, we analyze two highly successful and very recent cult movements. Chapter 12 shows how Scientology is able to get thousands of members to agree that they have achieved "clear" status despite their inability to perform the superhuman mental feats claimed to be easy for clears. In Chapter 13, we chart the extraordinary rise and the precipitous fall of Transcendental Meditation, a cult movement that in the mid-1970s was initiating tens of thousands of Americans a month. We explain why the flow of new members suddenly dried up and how this radically changed the movement.

Part IV is concerned with recruitment to sects and cults. How do deviant movements attract new members? Chapter 14 sums up current knowledge on this subject and considers data on several religious movements, showing the importance of interpersonal bonds for the recruitment process. Chapter 15 carries this network approach to recruitment farther and explores the salience of religious and occult beliefs for pairs of close friends. In Chapter 16, we consider the impact of the arithmetic of conversion for the career of cults and cult leaders. We discover that, unless they achieve truly phenomenal rates of growth, cult founders and their initial circle of followers are likely to lose heart after 20 or 30 years of effort. We see that cults are more easily started in larger societies but are more likely to succeed in small ones.

Chapter 17 shows that the recent rise of occult beliefs and movements does not stem from the rise of new kinds of "consciousness," but from weakness in the conventional religions. It provides further support for our claim that no secular meaning system can provide such general explanations about life that it replaces religion. Chapter 18 examines the best currently available information on who joins cults, concluding that, under present conditions, cults can have great success recruiting persons who are fully normal.

Part V brings all these themes together. In the chapters making up this section, we explain how secularization—the weakening of many major church organizations—prompts religious innovation. We argue that the future is not to be a time of no religion, but that it may be a time of new religions. That is, sects and cults arise in the vacuums created by weak churches. Chapter 19 examines how this process works, first using data on contemporary cults, sects, and churches and then data from the 1920s. Chapter 20 shifts to Canada and again discovers that cults flourish where the churches are weak, even in a very different religious economy from that of the United States. Chapter 21 places our theory at risk in a social environment where many social scientists would predict it would fail. But once again, in Europe, our propositions are fully supported.

In Chapter 22, we return to issues raised in this chapter—the inability of naturalistic faiths to supplant supernatural faiths. In Chapter 22, our focus is not upon weak, secularized churches or upon ephemeral alleged consciousness reformations, but upon powerful political movements and officially atheistic states. We demonstrate why political radicals are so susceptible to joining cults and sects and why political movements frequently are transformed into fully developed religious movements. Finally, we examine officially atheistic totalitarian states to discover why they fail in their efforts to root out religion. Put another way, we explore the meaning of the aphorism that trying to drive out religion is like driving in a nail—the harder you hit, the deeper in it goes.

This book is unified by a consistent, social scientific theory based on concepts outlined in this chapter and developed in the following pages. Alongside the empirical and traditional theoretical work represented by this book, we have been refining a formal, systematic, deductive theory of religion. We wrote the first technical paper sketching the rudiments of such a theory five years ago (Stark and Bainbridge, 1980), and we have recently returned to that more abstract work with renewed clarity after confronting the vast troves of data we describe and interpret here. The result of our efforts to build a general theory of religion requires book length treatment in its own right. All our work shows religion to be the direct expression of universal human needs, and thus the future is bright for both religion and the social scientific study of it.

2 Of Churches, Sects, and Cults

Many new religious bodies are created by schisms — they break off from other religious organizations. Such new religions commonly are called sects. Many other new religious bodies do not arise through schisms; they represent religious innovation. Someone has a novel religious insight and recruits others to the faith. These new religions are also often called sects, but a theory that explains why schismatic religious groups occur may have nothing to say about religious innovation. Is it then only a partial theory of sect formation? Or shall we distinguish among religious groups on the basis of their origins? If so, what names should we employ for this distinction? And what of the many "quasi religions," such as astrology, yoga, and the like? Are they religious movements? How shall we identify them? These questions are not merely academic; they must be settled before coherent discussion, let alone research, is possible.

Un-Ideal Types

The conceptual literature on churches and sects is dominated by typologies. Indeed, the literature refers not to churches and sects, but to the "church-sect typology." Sad to say, the *kind* of types sociologists usually

A briefer and somewhat different version of this chapter was published as Rodney Stark and William Sims Bainbridge, "Of Churches, Sects, and Cults," *Journal for the Scientific Study of Religion*, 1979, 18:2, pp. 117–133.

develop are of no use in theory construction. They serve as tautological substitutes for real theories and tend to prevent theorizing.

The trouble started with Weber, who introduced both the church-sect typology and a misunderstanding of the ideal type. In his classical work on methods, Weber (1949:91, 97) advocated the construction of ideal types

> ... by the one-sided accentuation of one or more points of view and by the synthesis of a great many diffuse, discrete, more or less present and occasionally absent *concrete individual* phenomena, which are arranged according to these one-sidedly emphasized viewpoints into a unified *analytical* construct. In its conceptual purity, this mental construct cannot be found anywhere in reality.... They are used as conceptual instruments for *comparison* with the *measurement* of reality.

Generations of sociologists have regarded Weber's ideal type as similar to concepts commonly found in the physical sciences. Physics, for example, abounds with "ideal gases" and "frictionless states." It is understood that such do not exist, but are the absolute base points on a measuring continuum against which degrees of friction or the expansion of gases can be calibrated. But there is an immense and fatal difference between these ideal types and those Weber proposed and compounded. The ideal types of physics anchor a single continuum along which it is possible to rank all empirical or hypothetical cases. Comparisons with the ideal are direct and unambiguous and thus permit measurement. But Weber's types prevent comparison and measurement, despite his claim that they are indispensable for this purpose.

Following Weber, sociologists often use *correlates* in their definitions of concepts. But it is *attributes*, not correlates, that belong in a definition. Consider the most minimal use of a definition: to permit clear identification of cases as belonging or not belonging to the defined class. Because correlates are not always present and often may not be present, their use as defining features often leads to misclassification. Worse yet, when many correlates are involved (as Weber advised they should be), the result is a jumble of mixed types that cannot be ordered and thus cannot yield measurement. The usual outcome is a proliferation of new subconcepts or types, and sometimes it seems that each new empirical case must become a unique type — which is to classify nothing.

When attributes are the basis of definition (because they are always present in the phenomena to be classified) and when enough attributes have been utilized to limit the class in the desired fashion, no ambiguity results, for then the concept forms an underlying unidimensional axis of variation. This kind of ideal type does provide a zero point for comparison and ranking.

CHURCHES AND SECTS

Although Weber introduced the notions of church and sect, his student, Ernst Troeltsch (1931), first made them important. Troeltsch used an ideal type of church and an ideal type of sect to categorize roughly what he regarded as the two main varieties of religious bodies in pre-19th-century Christian Europe. Each type was identified by a host of characteristics that were, at best, weak correlates of one another and of the phenomena to be classified. Subsequent attempts to utilize Troeltsch's types in other times and places caused frustration. The empirical cases just would not fit well; so new users created new church-sect typologies, some of them extremely ornate with many subcategories. Indeed, it would be close to the truth to claim that *each* new user, or at least each new user with new cases to classify, created a new typology based on different correlated features of the phenomena to be classified. Each new typology suffered the same defects as those it replaced: It would not organize the data.

Many social scientists have pointed to the serious inadequacies in church-sect conceptualizations (Eister, 1967; Goode, 1967; Gustafson, 1967; Dittes, 1971; Knudsen et al., 1978), and many of the best sociologists of religion have labored long and hard to perfect the distinction. Thomas O'Dea (1966:68) summarized some of the definitions proposed by Troeltsch and later scholars, suggesting that church and sect had the following "attributes":

CHURCH:
    1. Membership in fact upon the basis of birth
    2. Administration of the formalized means of grace and their sociological and theological concomitants — hierarchy and dogma
    3. Inclusiveness of social structure, often coinciding with geographical or ethnic boundaries
    4. Orientation toward the conversion of all
    5. The tendency to adjust to and compromise with the existing society and its values and institutions

SECT:
    1. Separatism from the general society and withdrawal from or defiance of the world and its institutions and values
    2. Exclusiveness both in attitude and in social structure
    3. Emphasis upon a conversion experience prior to membership
    4. Voluntary joining
    5. A spirit of regeneration
    6. An attitude of ethical austerity, often of an ascetic nature

These definitions have a certain intuitive rightness to them, but they also are imprecise and ambiguous. One can easily name a church with all five attributes of church (the Catholic church in Spain). And religious groups that seem to fit the definition of sect may come to mind fairly easily. But one can also name many religious organizations that scramble the 11 defining points in many different ways. The 6 points defining sect may tend to go together—they correlate to some extent with each other—but many of the religious groups commonly called sects fail to have some of the properties listed. In fact, the attributes O'Dea lists are not really attributes at all, but correlates, properties that may tend to go together but often do not. In the American and Canadian context, it is hard to find any religious group that fits the definition of church; so we commonly use the term *denomination* to refer to religious groups possessing several churchlike qualities, but not all of them. If denominations are watered-down churches, then adding this third category to the typology only renders fluid and uncertain an intellectual scheme that was supposed to be a solid basis for analysis. What about a group like the Hutterites (Eaton and Weil, 1955; Peters, 1965; Hostetler, 1974), separated from the general society and stressing austerity, yet gaining members through birth rather than conversion and having no greater emphasis upon voluntary joining than any large denomination? Is it a sect or a church? Clearly, the church-sect typology cannot be applied to religious groups in our own society without letting most cases be exceptions to the rule. But what good are categories if we cannot place cases in them with confidence and without ambiguity?

No typology so constructed will ever create the organization needed for theorizing. This problem is easy to illustrate. Suppose five correlates are used to define the ideal church, with negative values on these same five defining the ideal sect. Then suppose we treat these criteria as dichotomies. The result is 32 logically possible types (because the defining criteria can vary independently), of which 30 are mixed types. These mixed types cannot be ordered fully. Which is more churchlike, a group possessing characteristics A and B but lacking C, D, and E or one with D and E but not A, B, or C? In the empirical world, mixed types have been the rule.

Underlying most sociologists' interest in churches and sects is a theory about religious movements. In 1929, H. Richard Niebuhr argued that the sect is an unstable type of religious organization that, through time, tends to be transformed into a church. But, he argued, following this transformation, many members' needs that had been satisfied by the sect go unmet by the church. In time, this leads to discontent, which prompts schism and the splitting off of a new sect, which is then transformed slowly into a church, thus to spawn a new sect: an endless cycle of birth, transformation, schism, and rebirth of religious movements. This theory has long captivated sociologists of religion. Unfortunately, a typological conception of churches and sects prevents all theorizing. How can one theorize about the movement from sect to church when one cannot rank groups as more or less churchlike? It would humble physicists to try to theorize under such handicaps.

Thus it was an event of considerable magnitude when Benton Johnson (1963:542; cf. 1957, 1971) discarded dozens of correlates from the various definitions of church and sect and settled on a single attribute to classify religious groups: "*A church is a religious group that accepts the social environment in which it exists. A sect is a religious group that rejects the social environment in which it exists.*"

Johnson postulated a continuum representing the degree to which a religious group is in a *state of tension* with its surrounding sociocultural environment. The ideal sect falls at one pole, where the surrounding tension is so great that sect members are hunted fugitives. The ideal church anchors the other end of the continuum and virtually *is* the sociocultural environment — the two are so merged that it is impossible to postulate a basis for tension. Johnson's ideal types, unlike Weber's, are ideal in precisely the same way that ideal gases and frictionless states are ideal. They identify a clear axis of variation and its end points.

Johnson's reconceptualization also permits clear definition of two other important concepts: religious *movement* and religious *institution*. When we look at the low tension end of his axis, we find not only churches but also religious institutions. That is, we find a stable sector of the social structure, a cluster of roles, norms, values, and activities associated with the performance of key social functions.

Social institutions are not social movements if we define social movements as *organized groups* whose primary goal is to *cause* or *prevent* social change. Institutions adapt to change. Social movements seek to alter or become institutions. Thus, if religious institutions are one pole of the tension axis, as we move along the axis in the direction of greater tension, we discover religious movements. That is, *religious movements are social movements that wish to cause or prevent change in a system of beliefs, values, symbols, and practices concerned with providing supernaturally based general compensators.* Religious movements are organized groups wishing to become religious institutions. Such groups would like to become the dominant faith in their society, although they may make little effort to achieve this end if they are convinced that their chances are too remote.

Johnson's axis also permits us to characterize the direction taken by religious movements. When they move toward less tension with their sociocultural environment, they are *church movements* (although a group may remain a sect during a long period of movement in this churchlike direction). When groups move toward the high tension pole, they are *sect movements*. In Chapter 3, we show that the degree of tension experienced by a religious group can be measured easily and unambiguously and explain that tension with the sociocultural environment is equivalent to subcultural deviance in which the relationship between the high tension group and the surrounding society is marked by difference, antagonism, and separation — three integrated but conceptually distinguishable aspects of deviance. Tension so defined can be measured; so numerous empirical studies testing any hypothesis or theory in which tension plays a part can now be performed.

Using Johnson's reconceptualization of church and sect, we may see at a glance that the Catholic church in the United States is more sectlike than is the Catholic church in Ireland. In most prior typologies, this could not be seen. Because the axis of variation is clear, variation cries out for explanation. It becomes obvious how to proceed toward theories to rectify and extend Niebuhr's work. Indeed, many important variables long thought to influence the eruption of sects or their transformation into churches can now be examined. In the past, these variables have been utilized in typologizing and thus were locked in tautology. Now we can ask, for example, if the arrival of a generation of members socialized into the sect as children, rather than converted into it as adults, plays a major role in pushing sects down the road to churchliness (chapters 6 and 7). In the past, this variable was lost in the creation of (1) sects with converted members, (2) sects with socialized members, (3) churches with converted members, and (4) churches with socialized members. These four boxes tell us nothing. A proposition that relates socialization to the transformation of sects into churches could tell us much.

SECTS AND CULTS

There are at least two kinds of religious movements in a high state of tension with their surrounding sociocultural environment, and it demonstrably inhibits efficient theorizing to regard both kinds as sects and ignore differences between them. Therefore, we must now add some complexity to Johnson's elegant parsimony.

Niebuhr's theory exclusively concerns schismatic religious movements, which he identifies as sects. He was not speaking of all small, deviant religious movements, but only of those whose existence began as an internal faction of another religious body. This is, of course, a very common kind of religious movement. However, it is not the only kind of religious movement in a high state of tension with the surrounding sociocultural environment. Many such movements have no history of prior organizational attachment to a "parent" religion; thus, they are not schismatic. Indeed, they lack a close cultural continuity with (or similarity to) other religious groups in a society.

These nonschismatic, deviant religious groups are themselves of two types. One type represents cultural *innovation*. That is, along with the many familiar components of religious culture appearing in the beliefs, values, symbols, and practices of the group, there is something distinctive and new about them as well. The second type exhibits cultural *importation*. Such groups represent (or claim to represent) a religious body well established in another society. Examples are various Asian faiths in the United States or Christianity in Asia. In common parlance, these deviant but nonschismatic bodies are often referred to as *cults* (Eister, 1972).

Both cults and sects are deviant religious bodies — that is, they are in a state of relatively high tension with their surrounding sociocultural environment. However, sects have a prior tie with another religious organization. To be a sect, a religious movement must have been founded by persons who left another religious body for the purpose of founding the sect. The term *sect*, therefore, applies only to schismatic movements. It is not required in this definition that a sect break off from a church, as Niebuhr argued. To do so would land us back in the wilderness of typologies, for sects sometimes break off from other sects. Indeed, it has happened that churches have broken off from sects (Steinberg, 1965). Furthermore, we plan to apply elements of church-sect theory to the career of cults. Therefore, these are matters to theorize about, not to lock into definitions.

Because sects are schismatic groups, they present themselves to the world as something old. They left the parent body not to form a new faith but to reestablish the old one, from which the parent body had "drifted" (usually by becoming more churchlike). Sects claim to be the authentic, purged, refurbished version of the faith from which they split. Luther, for example, did not claim to be leading a new church, but the true church, free of worldly encrustations.

Cults, with the exception to be noted, do not have a prior tie with another established religious body in the society in question. The cult may represent an alien (external) religion, or it may have originated in the host society, but through innovation, not fission.

Whether domestic or imported, the cult is something new vis-à-vis the other religious bodies of the society in question. If domestic — regardless of how much of the common religious culture it retains — the cult adds to that culture a new revelation or insight justifying the claim that it is different, new, "more advanced." Imported cults often have little common culture with existing faiths; they may be old in some other society, but they are new and different in the importing society.

Cults, then, represent a deviant religious tradition in a society. In time, they may become the dominant tradition, in which case there is no longer much tension between them and the environment, and they become the church or churches of that society. Long before cults become churches, they too are prone to internal schisms. Thus, within the context of cult movements, schismatic movements can form. A theory to explain sect formation can then be applied to cults to explain their schismatic tendencies. But a theory of sect formation simply will not serve as a theory of cult formation. The geneses of the two are very different.

To sum up, sects are breeds of a common species. That is, sects are deviant religious movements that remain within a nondeviant religious tradition. Cults are a different species and occur by mutation or migration. That is, cults are deviant religious movements within a deviant religious tradition. Sects, being schismatic movements, begin life as religious organizations and thus their status as religious movements is clear. However, many cults do not develop into full-blown religious movements. Therefore, it is necessary to survey more closely the range of cults to identify various forms, only some of which fall within the scope of a theory of religious movements.

Cults

Three degrees of organization (or lack of organization) characterize cults. The most diffuse and least organized kind is an *audience cult.* Sometimes some members of this audience actually may gather to hear a lecture. But there are virtually no aspects of formal organization to these activities, and membership remains at most a consumer activity. Indeed, cult audiences often do not gather physically but consume cult doctrines entirely through magazines, books, newspapers, radio, and television.

More organized than audience cults are what can be characterized as *client cults.* Here the relationship between those promulgating cult doctrine and those partaking of it most closely resembles the relationship between therapist and patient or between consultant and client. Considerable organization may be found among those offering the cult service, but clients remain little organized. Furthermore, no successful effort is made to weld the clients into a social movement. Indeed, client involvement is so partial that clients often retain an active commitment to another religious movement or institution.

Cult movements can be distinguished from other religious movements only in terms of the distinctions between cults and sects previously developed. We address only cult movements in our subsequent theory, but the less organized types currently are more common and need to be described so they will not be confused with the full-fledged cult movement.

Audience Cults

In 1960, Rodney Stark and John Lofland (Lofland and Stark, 1965) went in search of a cult movement to study. William Bainbridge began a similar search in 1970 (Bainbridge, 1978c). Our initial discovery was that the bulk of cult activity is not connected to cult movements, but, to the degree it involves face-to-face interaction at all (as opposed to reliance on mass communications media), it most closely resembles a very loose lecture circuit. Persons with a cult doctrine to offer rely on ads, publicity, and direct mail to assemble an audience to hear their lectures. Efforts almost invariably are made at these lectures to sell ancillary materials — books, magazines, souvenirs, and the like — but no significant efforts are made to organize the audience. Furthermore, these public gatherings often are most unsystematic. A description of a typical spacecraft convention held during the early sixties illustrates this point.

About 500 persons registered for the annual spacecraft convention held in Oakland, California. The alleged focus of interest was flying saucers (UFOs). Approximately 20 speakers were scheduled over each two day convention, and many others with a cult message set up booths.

Some of these speakers devoted their time to describing their trips to outer space on flying saucers piloted by persons from other planets. Some even showed (and sold) photographs of the saucer they had gone on and of outer space creatures who had taken them for the ride. What seemed astounding in context, because tales of those contacted by spacemen (contactees) seemed to be accepted uncritically, was the fact that other speakers spent their time trying merely to demonstrate that some kind of UFOs must *exist*, but without claiming that they necessarily came from outer space. People who had given nodding support to tales of space travelers also gave full attention to those who merely suggested that saucers might exist. Moreover, many speakers (and the majority of those working out of booths) had little connection with the saucer question at all. Instead, they pushed standard varieties of pseudoscience and cult doctrines on the ground that these flourish on the more enlightened worlds from which UFOs come. Astrologers, medical quacks, inventors of perpetual motion machines (seeking investors), food faddists, spiritualists, and the like were all present and busy.

Conversations with many in attendance at space craft conventions revealed that these people are not the stuff of which social movements can be made. They accept everything, more or less, and in effect accept nothing. They are "interested" in all new ideas in the general area of the eccentric and the mystical. Their sheer openmindedness makes it impossible for them to develop a strong commitment to any complete system of thought; they are constitutional nibblers. Many speakers at the conventions want to found cult movements, but efforts to create organization meet no significant success. Later observation within several cult movements taught us that such movements soon learn to avoid the cult audiences in their search for converts. It is easy to get a hearing from such persons, but serious commitment is almost never forthcoming.

Nevertheless, persons who attend events like the spacecraft convention are among the most committed and active members of cult audiences. Perhaps the majority of persons who presently give credence to ideas that are defined as cult doctrines in American society do so entirely through impersonal communications. They read astrology columns and books and swell the circulation of the *National Enquirer* and other publications that give play to psychics, biorhythms, spiritualism, UFOs, and similar pseudoscientific, mystical meaning systems. Although many people who end up in cult movements seem to have once been part of this audience, few members of the audience are ever recruited into a cult movement.

Client Cults

Some cults manage to become service and therapy occupations. In the past, the primary services sold were medical miracles, forecasts of the future, or contact with the dead. Since Freud, however, cults increasingly have specialized in personal adjustment. Thus, today one can "get it" at *est*, get "cleared" through Scientology, store up orgone and seek the monumental orgasm through the Reich Foundation, get rolfed, actualized, sensitized, or psychoanalyzed.

Although cults of this type more fully mobilize participants than do audience cults, their mobilization is *partial*, rather than all-embracing. Most participants remain clients, not members. Some of them participate in two or more cults simultaneously, although with greater involvement than is usual in cult audiences. And quite often clients of these cults retain their participation in an organized religious group. In our travels through the cult world, we found that many people who frequent spiritualist groups go regularly to a conventional church come Sunday morning. (It is significant that they usually go to churches, not sects. As we show in Part IV, sects are much more hostile than are churches to anything with religious implications that is external to the sect.) Indeed, it is not uncommon to find clergy from conventional churches at various client cults, particularly those of the personal adjustment variety, apparently feeling little stress from their dual involvements.

Cult Movements

When the spiritualist medium is able to get his or her clients to attend sessions regularly on Sunday morning, and thus, in a Christian context, to sever their ties with other religious organizations, we observe the birth of a *cult movement*. Cult movements are full-fledged religious organizations that attempt to satisfy all the religious needs of converts. Dual membership with another faith is out. Attempts to cause social change, by converting others, become central to the group agenda.

Nevertheless, cult movements differ considerably in the degree to which they attempt to mobilize their members and to usher in the "New Age." Many cult movements are very weak organizations. They are essentially study groups that gather regularly to hear discussions of the new revelations or latest spirit messages gained by the leader. Little more than modest financial support, attendance at group functions, and assent to the truth of the cult doctrines is asked of members. Frequently, the group observes no moral prohibitions more restrictive than those of the general society. Unless an outsider gets into a religious discussion with members, no indication of their religious deviance is likely to be evident.

Many other cult movements function much like conventional sects. Levels of member commitment are quite intense; tension with the outside world is high (moral prohibitions exceed those of the general society); but participation is only partial. That is, most members continue to lead regular secular lives—they work, marry, rear children, have hobbies, take vacations, and have contact in the ordinary way with noncult members such as family and friends.

But some cult movements demand much more. They are a total way of life. They require members to dispense with their secular lives and devote themselves entirely to cult activities. Such members become, in Philip Selznick's (1960) felicitous expression, "deployable agents." Their lives are circumscribed wholly by the demands of the cult. Usually they live in. If they hold jobs, it will be only where and when they are directed to do so, often in enterprises the cult owns and operates. Today it is common for cult members to support themselves and their movements by working the streets, sometimes begging, sometimes selling books, pamphlets, charms, or even candy and flowers for a "donation" (Bromley and Shupe, 1980). When not hustling money, these deployable agents seek converts or devote themselves to group chores or worship activities. Most people would be very surprised at how much money a small number of deployable agents can raise by street hustling these days, and perhaps this is one reason why cults seem so liable to adopt this strategy at this time. But the requirement that members become deployable agents probably has drawbacks. It may limit the growth of the group (Chapter 14), and, as we discuss later in this chapter, it increases tension with the outside world.

If we did no more than catalogue variations among cults, we would be guilty of the same empty typologizing we criticized at the start of this chapter. However, these variations can be organized efficiently by concepts introduced in Chapter 1. Thus, our three varieties of cults can be distinguished on the basis of the *quality* and *generality* of the compensators they offer. Audience cults offer compensators of modest value at a correspondingly modest cost — that is, audience cults deal in vague and weak compensators often amounting to no more than a mild vicarious thrill or social entertainment rather than a credible promise that a reward of significant value will eventually be obtained. Client cults offer valuable, but relatively *specific* compensators. Psychoanalysis and Dianetics claim to cure neurosis, but they do not promise everlasting life. Astrologers offer specific advice, but they do not reveal the meaning of the universe. Witches sell love potions, but not the secret of eternal youth. Only cult movements offer the most *general* compensators, the kind we have defined as available from religions. Thus, only cult movements are fully developed religious movements.

MAGIC AND RELIGION

In Chapter 1, we severely criticized Emile Durkheim's definition of religion. But here we acknowledge that he, much more adequately than other writers who dealt with the issue, found the key to distinguish magic from religion, which led him to conclude, quite correctly, that magic does not concern itself with the meaning of the universe, but only with the manipulation of the universe for specific goals. Although religion addresses the most general questions and the most general human desires, Durkheim (1915:42) pointed out that magic is "more elementary, undoubtedly because, seeking technical and utilitarian ends, it does not waste its time in pure speculation."

Put into our conceptual language, magic deals in relatively specific compensators, and religion always includes the most general compensators. This characteristic of magic has two extremely important implications for understanding religious movements and makes it possible to distinguish cult movements from other cult phenomena.

First, because magic deals in specific compensators, it often becomes subject to empirical verification. This means that magic is chronically vulnerable to disproof. Claims that a particular spell will cure warts or repel bullets can be falsified by direct tests. This makes magic a risky exchange commodity and accounts for the rapid turnover among popular magicians.

In Part V, we suggest that the inclusion of magic in the traditional teachings of the major world religions made them extremely vulnerable to attacks by science over the past several centuries and that this has resulted in considerable secularization of these faiths. But we also pay considerable attention in those chapters to the fact that it is only magic, not religion, that is vulnerable to scientific test. The most general compensators, based on supernatural assumptions, are forever secure from scientific assessment. It is this feature of religion that leads us to conclude in chapters 19 through 22 that, although particular religions, perhaps those of greatest prominence, may go into eclipse, religion will continue.

The empirical vulnerability of magic also helps us identify the line between magic and science. Here we fully agree with Max Weber (1963:2), who distinguished magic from science on the basis of the results of empirical testing: "Only we, judging from the standpoint of our modern views of nature, can distinguish objectively in such behavior those attributes of causality which are 'correct' from those which are 'fallacious,' and then designate the fallacious attributions of causation as irrational, and the corresponding acts as 'magic.'" Magic flourishes when humans lack effective and economical means for such testing. Indeed, it can be said that we developed science by learning how to evaluate specific explanations offered by magic. That is, science is an efficient procedure for evaluating explanations.

We have not identified magic with supernaturally based compensators. Often magic does invoke supernatural assumptions, as when ritual magicians attempt to call up devils to do their bidding. However, the supernatural is often not clearly implicated in magic. Thus, magicians may attempt to overcome natural law — in effect, to perform miracles — without relying on supernatural agents or clear supernatural assumptions to accomplish such wonders. Indeed, magical properties often are thought to inhere in a particular substance — love potions or Laetrile "work" because of their inherent magical qualities. Some people believe they can cause pain by sticking pins in a Voodoo doll, and, as Richard Kieckhefer (1976:6) notes:

> For most processes that they employ, people have some vague (and perhaps incorrect) notion of the mechanism involved, or else they assume that they

could ascertain this mechanism if they so endeavored, or they take it on faith that someone understands the link between cause and effect. But the man who mutilates his enemy's representation cannot make any of these claims. He may believe that the magical act works, but he cannot explain how.

Similarly, people often will believe in their own or others' magical powers without necessarily explaining these powers by reference to supernatural agents. Psychics, fortune-tellers, water dowsers (water witches), and even astrologers often claim inexplicable gifts, but many do not attribute these to supernatural sources. By excluding clear supernatural assumptions from our definition of magic and focusing instead on claims to circumvent natural laws, we leave room in our definition of magic for many folk practices and "superstitions" as well as for present-day pseudosciences, which also often lack clearly supernatural assumptions. This is important later in the book because it permits us to see the conditions under which such "secular" magics do turn toward supernatural assumptions or even evolve into fully developed religions. It also makes it possible to see that religious organizations may impute supernatural assumptions to magical practices that, in fact, do not clearly make such assumptions. For example, as we see in Chapter 5, Christianity often has interpreted folk magic as performed by the devil, even though its practitioners did not believe this. Whether or not they assume the supernatural, these magics can be identified as compensators (and thus as magic) in the manner suggested by Weber and by Kieckhefer, that is, by empirical falsification of their claims. They constitute magic rather than incorrect efforts at science because they are offered without regard for their demonstrable falsity. Thus, we reserve the term *magic* for compensators that are offered as correct explanations without regard for empirical evaluations and that, when evaluated, are found wanting.

The second important implication of the fact that magic deals only in specific compensators is that magic lacks the exchange characteristics needed to sustain organizations (cf. Fortune, 1932; Evans-Pritchard, 1937). The most general compensators often require individuals to engage in a lifelong commitment in order to maintain the value of these compensators, but specific compensators can sustain only short-term commitments. In our formal theory, we are able to deduce these differences between magic and religion as follows:

1. Magicians cannot require others to engage in long-term stable patterns of exchange.
2. In the absence of long-term, stable patterns of exchange, an or-

ganization composed of magicians and a committed laity cannot be sustained.

3. Magicians will serve individual clients, not lead an organization.

In the case of religions, however, all these "cannots" become "cans." Religious leaders can create stable organizations because the most general compensators do require long-term, stable patterns of exchange. The Christian, Jew, Moslem, Buddhist, Mormon, or Moonie who lapses from his or her religious obligations risks losing those vast rewards promised by the general compensators of his or her faith.

To summarize this discussion, we quote the most insightful passage in Emile Durkheim's *The Elementary Forms of the Religious Life* (1915:44–45):

> . . . whenever we observe the religious life, we find it has a definite group as its foundation. . . . It is quite another matter with magic. To be sure, the belief in magic is always more or less general; it is frequently diffused in large masses of the population, and there are even peoples where it has as many adherents as the real religion. But it does not result in binding together those who adhere to it, nor uniting them into a group leading a common life. *There is no Church of magic.* Between the magician and the individuals who consult him, as between these individuals themselves, there are no lasting bonds which make them members of the same moral community, comparable to that formed by believers in the same god. . . . The magician has a clientele and not a Church, and it is very possible that his clients have no other relations between each other, or even do not know each other; even the relations they have with him are generally accidental and transient, they are just like those of a sick man with his physician. It is true that in certain cases, magicians form societies among themselves. . . . But what is especially important is that when these societies of magic are formed, they do not include all the adherents to magic, but only the magicians; the laymen . . . are excluded. . . . A Church is not a fraternity of priests; it is a moral community formed by all the believers in a single faith, laymen as well as priests. But Magic lacks any such community.

MAGICAL AND RELIGIOUS CULTS

We have given so much attention to the distinction between religion and magic because it plays a vital role, not only in many later chapters, but in helping us here to distinguish among our three varieties of cults. Briefly put, some cults deal only in magic, although only cult movements deal in religion.

Audience cults are preoccupied with simple mythology and with only very weak forms of magic. To attend a film such as *In Search of Ancient Astronauts*, which presents the theories of Erich von Däniken, is to confront magical claims about the history of civilization (Bainbridge, 1978a). But the film provides no grand explanation of the meaning of life and does not offer compensators for even the most limited rewards. Similarly, Uri Geller may convince people that he has bent a key with psychic energy, but he offers to provide no more useful services with his magic (Randi, 1975).

Client cults deal in serious magic. They exchange specific compensators for rewards of substantial value. Astrologers do not offer access to heaven, but they claim to be able to give us valuable advice by reading the heavens. If astrologers really could improve our life chances by telling us the right day to make investments, get married, or stay away from the office, those would indeed be valuable rewards. To the extent that astrologers' clients believe in them, their compensators also have value.

Whether or not they also offer magic, cult movements provide religion. Reverend Sun Myung Moon's Unification Church does explain the meaning of the universe and instructs us how to gain everlasting life. The same is true of the Divine Light Mission of Guru Maharaj Ji.

That only some cults are full-fledged religions helps us understand why disputes so often arise over the religious status of many deviant groups. Scientology and Synanon are both embroiled in a series of court cases in which they seek to be considered religions; Transcendental Meditation recently lost a court case in which it tried to resist classification as a religion (see Chapter 13). Part of this dispute concerns the fact that many cult groups are not (or not yet) religions and this makes it confusing to determine which ones are. A second reason is that, because cults are not merely deviant religions, but new religions (at least new to the society in question), the conventional definitions of religion do not automatically apply to them. When a sect breaks away from a church, it takes with it the label "religion." But cults are not born with the religious label attached. To identify which cults are religious requires examination to determine whether they offer general or only specific compensators.

It must not be supposed, however, that what is only a client cult today will necessarily be one tomorrow. Just as sects are sometimes transformed into churches, so magical cults are often transformed into religions. In later chapters, we inquire more deeply into why this occurs. Here two examples suffice to demonstrate the point: Scientology (Wallis, 1976) and The Process (Bainbridge, 1978c). Both groups began as limited psychotherapy services. Because they were culturally novel and were not based on any body of verified scientific research, they were magical client cults rather than technical medical services. As the years passed, both began offering compensators that were more and more general and for which no equivalent rewards existed. Their ideologies ramified into complex systems of ultimate meaning. Both became highly developed cult movements.

Within our conceptual framework, we can also apply to cults many of the ideas originally developed in understanding sects and churches. For example, we can discuss the degree of tension that a cult experiences with the surrounding society. It would appear that cults can enjoy relatively low tension with their environment as long as they do not organize into religious movements. Participating in cult audiences seems to be a very low risk activity. A 1976 Gallup poll suggests that 22 percent of Americans believe in astrology, and astrology columns and publications flourish. But very little flak is directed toward astrology. In general, the clergy of American churches seem to ignore the astrology cult. At most, persons who participate in audience cults may risk censure from those immediately around them.

Client cults, too, do not provoke great hostility in the surrounding sociocultural environment. As long as they do not run afoul of fraud statutes (by selling building lots on a fictitious planet, for example) or licensing statutes governing medical practice, they are not subject to much harassment. Client cults usually do not serve a low status market, if for no other reason than they charge for their services. Consequently, client cults also seem to be somewhat protected by the high status of their clientele. For example, the spiritualists primarily have drawn on a middle-class and upper-class clientele, as do most of today's personal adjustment cults. This clientele seems to have lent them considerable protection from opposition.

It is when cults become religious movements that their environment heats up. For example, as Scientology evolved from a client cult to a movement seeking major commitment from members, its legal troubles grew. In similar fashion, Transcendental Meditation took little heat so long as it concentrated on teaching clients to meditate during a few training sessions. With its transformation into an intense religious movement — amid claims that advanced members could fly (levitate) — public reaction has grown. It is cult movements, not client cults or audiences, that today face opposition from irate parents who hire deprogrammers to kidnap their children from the bosom of the cult.

Among cult movements, the more a cult mobilizes its membership, the greater the opposition it engenders. Cults whose members remain in the society to pursue normal lives and occupations engender much less opposition than do cults whose members drop everything and become full-time converts. In part, this is probably because cults that function as total institutions rupture converts' ties to conventional institutions, which generates personal grievances against the movement. It is one thing to think your son or daughter, for example, attends a weird church and has odd beliefs, but it is something else to lose contact with a child who takes up full-time participation in an alien faith. Indeed, Catholic parents often find it painful to lose a child to a convent or monastery, even though the question of deviant faith is not at issue. Thus, the rule seems to be, the more total the movement, the more total the opposition to it.

CONCLUSION

Concepts must not only facilitate theorizing; they ought to inspire it. Concepts should identify a phenomenon that arouses our interest and should present a clear enough picture of the phenomenon's variation that we are prompted to explain it. We believe the conceptual scheme we have developed encourages such theory construction. Some basic questions are thrown into relief by these particular formulations and they must be answered by any adequate theory of religious movements.

The most obvious task is to seek a set of premises from which a theory of religious schism can be deduced. Why and under what conditions do factions form in a religious group? Why and when do these result in the splitting off of a sect movement or church movement? Under what conditions do schismatic forces produce secular rather than religious movements? This last question reminds us that we must theorize not merely about the internal workings of religious bodies, but also about their external environment. Thus, for example, we need to know not only how sects form within a parent body, but the social conditions under which religious schisms are more and less likely.

In posing these questions, we are permitted, by our concepts, to avoid the assumption that sects split off from churches. We are directed, instead, to the problem of faction and exodus in any kind of religious body. This is important because the historical record makes it clear that sect formation is probably more common within bodies that are themselves sects rather than churches. It also permits analysis of schismatic movements originating in cults, just as it lets us deal with church movements that have split off from sects or cults. Instead of converting these alternatives into un-ideal types, our conceptual scheme makes it possible to construct propositions to account for these variations.

Our concepts make it clear that a theory of religious schism pertains to only some religious movements. Cults are not the result of schism (although, once founded, cults become subject to schism). Therefore, a theory of cult formation may have very few propositions in common with a theory of religious schism (a term to be preferred to sect formation because it is more inclusive). We must explain when the sociocultural environment is conducive to cult formation and why. We must also specify the process by which people actually form a cult, and we must explain the contingencies governing importation of cults.

The next requirement is for a theory of development and transformation. Once a sect or cult is formed, what contingencies govern whether it will grow, stall, or fail? What factors operate to push it in a churchlike direction, toward lower tension? What factors push toward higher tension?

Finally, we must close the circle by showing how and to what extent the factors involved in the formation of religious groups influence their development and transformation and how these in turn are involved in the onset of schism and of cult formation and importation.

This is, of course, a formidable list. But, given clear concepts, it is at least possible to see where to begin. In later chapters, we attempt at least partial answers to many of these questions.

The Religious Economy

3 *The Spectrum of Faiths*

The most singular fact about religion in the United States and Canada is diversity. Perhaps no other advanced industrial nations have such an amazing variety of religious groups. In his *Encyclopedia of American Religions* published in 1978, J. Gordon Melton listed more than 1,200 different religious groups active in the United States. Since then, he has located nearly 100 more, and he assures us that there are many more he has yet to find. A recent check of the Yellow Pages for all Canadian metropolitan areas revealed that most larger groups active in the United States are also established across the border (Chapter 20). Despite this incredible array of faiths — from Adventism to Zen — in recent years the general perception of religious differences in our society has progressively narrowed.

In the 18th and 19th centuries, most Americans were painfully aware of religious diversity. For many, the cacophony of scores of competing faiths, all claiming they alone had the true faith, was vexing. In fact, some of the most religious individuals of those times dropped out of organized religion in reaction against the endless sectarian bickering. Religious conflict prompted repeated efforts, such as the Holiness Movement and later the Fundamentalist Movement, that attempted to unify Protestantism. But these movements produced none of the hoped

The second half of this chapter, dealing with tension and its measurement, is a revision of an article that was published as William Sims Bainbridge and Rodney Stark, "Sectarian Tension," *Review of Religious Research*, 1980, 2, pp. 105–124.

for denominational mergers. Ironically, each of these movements actually increased religious diversity as more sects split from the large denominations in response to the calls for unity.

But, by the middle of the 20th century, perceptions of diversity had narrowed to the threefold division of Protestant-Catholic-Jew (Herberg, 1955). Soon afterwards, prompted by court suits against school prayers, "none" was added as the fourth significant religious category. Then, for the sake of completeness, sociologists began adding a fifth category: "other."

MISPERCEPTIONS OF RELIGIOUS UNITY

This fivefold conception of our religious culture was based on very serious misperceptions by leading religious intellectuals and by the press, the most important of which was that theological differences had all but vanished within Protestantism, that theological differences were to be found only in the small sects on the periphery of the great Protestant mainstream. This perception was encouraged by several major denominational mergers during the 1950s and led to a period of extreme ecumenical optimism. It was regarded as so certain that soon all the major Protestant bodies would merge that books were even written to explain in advance why this could occur, why the old points of doctrinal dispute had lost their force (cf. Lee, 1960). Indeed, other clergy were prompted to write in despair at this crumbling of doctrinal barriers to unity (cf. Marty, 1959). Before these misperceptions began to recede, they even sustained optimism over the possibility of uniting Catholicism and Protestantism and of achieving close organizational ties between Christianity and Judaism. But it was not to be, for the great homogenization of doctrine that seemed so real from the confines of the headquarters of the National Council of Churches or from the campuses of the famous liberal seminaries had not occurred at all.

Protestant

It was at the height of this ecumenical optimism in early 1961 that Stark began survey studies of the members of many American churches. From the start, he considered those who wrote of the demise of religious differences out of touch with reality, at least the reality of the people who sat in the pews on Sunday morning. Indeed, he found the writing about the new "common core" Protestantism curiously without religious content. It struck him that church intellectuals were reporting mainly their discovery that they now believed alike, regardless of their denominational backgrounds, because they had come to believe so little. It was all well and good for a Baptist professor like Harvey Cox (1965) to celebrate the secularization of theology from his secure haven in a liberal seminary, but it seemed foolish to mistake Cox's views for those of most other Baptists.

When the huge surveys of American religion were complete, it was certain that there was no common core Protestantism and that dreams of continuing mergers were without substance. The results were first published in an essay titled "The New Denominationalism" to call attention to the great gulfs of faith that sunder the map of Protestantism (Stark and Glock, 1965).

Table 3.1 reprints a few of the key findings from this survey. It would be hard to find a greater amount of theological diversity. In some of the denominations on the left of the table, only a small minority of members express faith in major doctrines of the Christian tradition (indeed, a majority of members of the United Church of Christ expressed reservations about the existence of God). But as we move to the right side of the table, we find that overwhelming majorities in these denominations retain unwavering faith in the divinity of Jesus, in the Virgin Birth, in the Second Coming, and in the reality of the devil.

Historically, disputes among Christians were not over the beliefs shown in Table 3.1, but over subtle points of doctrine and over proper ritual practice. These may well have lost their divisive power, but they have been replaced by even more potent grounds of dispute. Arguments over how to worship God properly have been replaced by disagreement about the existence of God. Debates over whether the bread and wine of communion are only symbolic or become actual flesh and blood have given way to questions about the divinity of Jesus. There is no Protestant unity in sight.

As predicted from these data, the church merger dream soon burst. No more important mergers did occur, and those denominations that seemed most interested in merger have instead become preoccupied with severe internal problems as their liberal clergy have faced determined opposition from the rank and file (Hadden, 1969; Longino and Hadden, 1976). Indeed, rather than merging with other liberal Protestant groups, as once was confidently expected, the Episcopalian church has lost a substantial sect movement as priests and laity, incensed over abandonment of the traditional creed, have chosen to abandon the denomination.

A period of decay, conflict, and decline has set in for all the Protestant denominations on the left side of Table 3.1. Progressively, they fail to sustain member commitment. Compared with the denominations toward the right side of the table, their members now attend church less regularly, give much less money to their church (despite substantially

TABLE 3.1   *The Spectrum of Belief — Percent Giving the Indicated Response*

	U.C.C. (151)	Meth. (415)	Epis. (416)	D. of Christ (50)	Pres. (495)	Am. Luth. (208)	Am. Bapt. (141)	Mo. Luth. (116)	S. Bapt. (79)	Sects (255)	Total Prot. (2326)	Total Cath. (545)
"I know God really exists and I have no doubts about it."	41	60	63	76	75	73	78	81	99	96	71	81
"Jesus is the Divine Son of God and I have no doubts about it."	40	54	59	74	72	74	76	93	99	97	69	86
It is completely true that "Jesus was born of a virgin."	21	34	39	62	57	66	69	92	99	96	57	81
Definitely, "Jesus will actually return to the earth some day."	13	21	24	36	43	54	57	75	94	89	44	47
It is "completely true" that "the Devil actually exists."	6	13	17	18	31	49	49	77	92	90	38	66

Note: The Protestant churches represented are United Church of Christ (Congregationalists), Methodists, Episcopalians, Disciples of Christ, United Presbyterian Church, Lutheran Church in America and American Lutheran Church, American Baptist Church, Missouri Synod of Lutherans, and Southern Baptist Church.

higher average incomes), and place less importance on their church membership. The liberal denominations have begun to lose members, although the more traditional denominations remain healthy (Stark and Glock, 1968; Kelley, 1972).

Bibby (1979b) finds the same patterns in Canada. Great gulfs in belief concerning basic elements of Christian faith separate the Protestant denominations. And, in Canada, too, the liberal denominations are in decline and disarray, although the more traditional denominations prosper (Bibby, 1979a).

The slumping morale of the liberal Protestant denominations is not limited to the rank and file. Data on clergy in these denominations show the majority of the younger, more liberal ministers admit that, if they had the choice to make over again, they might very well not enter the ministry (Stark et al., 1971). So much, then, for the high hopes among these denominations that their "new breed" of young clergy was the vanguard of a reunified and reinvigorated Protestantism.

In all the discussions of a common core Protestantism, participants simply ignored hundreds of Protestant groups for whom it was obvious that theological differences still mattered greatly. These groups prized their doctrinal positions so highly that they scorned all invitations to join the National Council of Churches, which they condemned as a blatantly "godless," "unbiblical," "antireligious" movement. Indeed, some of these groups originated as protesting sect movements out of denominations that did join the council. Viewed from the towering New York council headquarters, from the famous East Coast divinity schools, or from the editorial offices of the *Christian Century*, this host of sects may have seemed unimportant and unworthy of mention. Yet these Protestant bodies enroll many millions of members and continue to grow rapidly while the major Protestant bodies decline. Members of these traditional groups have recently preempted the term *Christian* to mean only persons like themselves who are "born again."

In Chapter 6, we examine data on 417 of these Protestant sects, limiting ourselves to those that split off from another religious group in the United States and ignoring the many sects that arrived here by immigration. In chapters 5 and 7, we examine the forces that cause sects to lose their fervor, to progressively reduce their tension with the outside world. The major liberal Protestant churches that today are so conventional and so at ease with the world usually began as militant sects. The United Church of Christ once was called the Congregational church and was founded by the Pilgrims, who were so at odds with their sociocultural environment that they fled to the New World. However, it is not only the deep divisions among Protestants that demonstrate that the fivefold conception of American religious diversity is much too narrow. The other four categories — Catholic, Jew, none, and other — are equally misleading.

Catholic

As Protestant is not a meaningful category, so in many ways Catholic is not either. For one thing, there are more than 30 separate Catholic denominations in the United States. But even if we restrict the term *Catholic* to the Roman church, we have not identified a group of like-minded believers. Half the Catholic church members surveyed along with the Protestants (Stark and Glock, 1965) believe in the Second Coming, but half do not. One-fourth are certain a person must be Catholic in order to be saved and a fourth are equally certain that is not true. About half believe the pope is infallible; about half do not. A substantial number of American Catholics support the church's ban on contraception; yet the majority of Catholic couples in their childbearing years practices contraception (Westoff and Jones, 1977; Westoff, 1979).

Disunity among rank-and-file Catholics reflects conflicts among the clergy. Thus, although some famous Catholic theologians express doubts about the Virgin Birth, others pronounce the Shroud of Turin to be authentic. And fierce battles have rocked the church over the fate of the Latin Mass.

In the early sixties, while Protestants hailed the imminent reunification of the major denominations, many Catholics expected the changes set in motion by Vatican Council II to wipe out the theological barriers separating Catholics and Protestants. They, too, saw theological liberalism as the grounds for a new unity. But they, too, misread the opinions of intellectuals for the opinions of the rank and file. Lay reactions against abandonment of historic teachings and practices have been swift and severe. The rapid growth of the Catholic charismatic movement is but one obvious sign of the grass-roots demand for a more intense religion. Indeed, Pope John Paul II has halted the Catholic swing to the theological left. However, clear signs of weakness continue to mark the church. High rates of defection still exist among priests and nuns; seminary enrollments have continued to decline. The Roman Catholic Church is not as vigorous a force in the religious economy as it was even a few decades ago.

Jew

The category Jew is equally misleading and useless. In a study closely modeled on the survey of the Christians, Lazerwitz and Harrison interviewed a large national sample of American Jews. They reported that "the lines of ideological division and the denominational structure closely resemble those found in Protestantism. Among both Jews and Protestants, there are clear divisions between an inactive sector, liberals, moderates, and conservatives" (1979:664). And, as with Protestants, serious signs of organizational decline and member disaffection afflict the more liberal Jewish congregations. For example, although 51 percent of the members of the Orthodox synagogues reported frequent attendance of services, only 24 percent of members of Conservative and 13 percent of members of Reform synagogues reported frequent attendance. Of those Jews without a denominational preference, only 1 percent were frequent attenders. These signs of religious disaffection coincide with data on actual defection. Several studies have found Jews to be overrepresented in recent cult movements, a fact we document in Chapter 18.

Lazerwitz and Harrison reported that Americanization was the primary factor determining Jewish denominational preferences. The Orthodox synagogues appear to have a hard time holding members past the third generation of American residence. But the more liberal Jewish groups also seem to fail to meet the needs of their potential constituency, and those with Reform affiliation appear much more likely to marry out of the Jewish faith than do those with Conservative affiliation (Cavan, 1971). When religious organizations engender little commitment from their nominal members and when substantial numbers turn elsewhere in search of faith, such organizations are no longer very effective forces in the religious economy.

None

It is generally believed that people who report they have no religious affiliation have rejected belief in the supernatural. Even if this were true, it might seem unwise to consider organized atheists, militant Marxists, and people who simply have no interest in religion as similar. But, in fact, the premise that "nones" are irreligious is itself false (Vernon, 1968). As we demonstrate in chapters 15 and 17, the majority of people who say they have no religious affiliation express considerable belief in the mystical and supernatural. Indeed, these people are the group *most* taken with several occult beliefs and are, perhaps, the most easily available for conversion to a cult movement. Their claim of no religion applies only to their lack of membership in a conventional religious organization.

Perhaps even more interesting is that "none" is the least stable of all religious backgrounds. Survey studies show that the great majority of Americans raised in a particular denomination remain members after they become adults. But of persons who report that the religious affiliation of their parents was "none," less than 40 percent remained without a religious affiliation when they grew up. Thus, the majority of the offspring of "nones" converts to some religion (Kluegel, 1980).

The bottom line appears to be that liberalism has failed to provide the rallying point for a new religious unity. Diversity, not unity, remains the single most potent feature of the American and Canadian religious spectrum. Indeed, there may be more religious diversity in these nations today than at any previous time. Even if we restrict our examination to the largest, most respectable, and conventional religious bodies, we must use a very wide angle lens.

Other

To grasp the full spectrum of religious diversity, we must look far beyond the conventional religious bodies to the most misleading and useless of all religious categories, the one sociologists of religion usually deal with as "other."

The "others" are Mormons, Christian Scientists, Theosophists, Spiritualists, Zen Buddhists, Moonies, Hare Krishnas, Scientologists, Moslems, Satanists, Witches, Pagans, Rosicrucians, Lemurians, Druids, Sufis, Vedantists, Swedenborgians, Flying Saucerians, Baha'ists, Divine Scientists, and followers of hundreds of other religious movements. In Chapter 9, we analyze data based on 501 cult movements active in the United States today. In Chapter 20, we see that cults similarly abound in Canada. Thus, what sociologists, church intellectuals, and the media lump into the residual category of "other" are the novel religious movements of central importance in this volume.

It is the "others" who have caused so much public consternation, fear, and hostility in the wake of the Jonestown tragedy. It is because of "others" that state legislatures consider anticult laws. It is because of "others" that professional deprogrammers solicit business from parents who want their children reclaimed from the cults. And all of this is because "others" are religious deviants.

CLARIFYING THE CONCEPT OF TENSION

In Chapter 2, we adopted Benton Johnson's concept of tension between a religious group and its environment as a basis for distinguishing sects and cults from churches. In his classic paper, Johnson (1963:544) actually used the term *tension* only once: "A sect tends to be in a state of tension with its surroundings." In his primary definitions, he speaks instead of sects rejecting their social environments. We chose to utilize the concept of tension rather than rejection because the latter term blurs a relationship that is a two-way street. Sects (and cults) not only reject society; they, in turn, are rejected by society. This interaction is best captured by the concept of tension, as Johnson says once and implies often. In recent conversations, Johnson has accepted our interpretation of his important contribution.

Johnson (1963:543) suggested that a church-sect scale developed by Russell Dynes (1955) might serve as an appropriate measure of tension. Dynes (1955:555) had, in fact, come rather close to defining the church-sect dimension in terms of tension with the sociocultural environment: "The construct of the Church has generally signified a type of religious organization which accepts the social order and integrates existing cultural definitions into its religious ideology. The Sect, as a contrasting type, rejects integration with the social order and develops a separate subculture, stressing rather rigid behavioral requirements for its members."

However, Dynes's scale is not adequate. He did not follow his own definitions when he constructed it, but instead fell back on a list of putative correlates of the sect proposed by Liston Pope (1942). Thus, Dynes created a scale rooted in the same tradition of typologies we seek to avoid. His scale is extremely culture bound. For example, one item considers as sectarian the view that "a congregation should encourage the minister during his sermon by saying *amen*" (Dynes, 1955:556). The agree-disagree battery seeks to determine individuals' commitment to some sects, primarily those of the rural South. Such a measure will not do what we need. Indeed, our concern is not to identify the religious preference of individuals, but to find a way to characterize groups in terms of their degree of tension.

As groups, Dynes recognized, sects are subcultures. In the previous chapter, we gave greater specificity to the concept of tension by pointing out its equivalence to another standard sociological concept: *subcultural deviance*. This refers to groups who develop or maintain a culture at variance with the dominant culture of a society. Three elements mark subcultural deviance or tension: *difference, antagonism,* and *separation.*

The sect (or cult) and the surrounding society disagree over proper beliefs, norms, and behavior. They judge each other harshly, each asserting its superiority over the other. The dispute is reflected in the social relations of sect and cult members. Rejected by and rejecting the larger society, sects and cults draw together in relatively closed and cohesive groups. In the case of extreme tension, sects and cults will be socially encapsulated, and the members will have relatively little intimate contact with nonmembers (cf. Wallis, 1975).

It might be objected that defining subcultural deviance in terms of difference, antagonism, and separation introduces yet another un-ideal collection of disparate variables that defies unambiguous measurement and confident use. But this triad of terms really describes a single concept, and the three are worth distinguishing primarily because they allow us to arrange the indicators of subcultural deviance in a meaningful pattern, thereby rendering them more intelligible and easier to survey. Traditional definitions of deviant behavior describe it not only as different from the standard set by dominant groups in the society, but also as punishable, drawing disapproval and negative sanctions of at least some level of severity.

A deviant subculture provides a competing standard, setting deviant norms and thus asserting antagonism toward those of the larger society. Social relations across the border of a deviant subculture are strained, and therefore there is a strong tendency for a social cleavage to form, as people avoid painful disputes, separating the subculture from the surrounding community. Seen the other way around, without some degree of social separation, the subculture will find it difficult to sustain deviant norms and counteract the pressures to conform communicated through social relations with outsiders. *Deviant subculture* is a unitary concept, although we find it convenient to group its indicators under three headings.

MEASURING TENSION

In our exploration of empirical means to assess each aspect of tension, we restrict ourselves to comparisons between churches and sects within Protestantism, although we use data on Roman Catholics for comparison, because no cults were included in the sample of religious bodies in which useful measures of tension can be found. The data we use are from the same sample on which Table 3.1 is based. At the end of the chapter, we consider some Gallup poll data that suggest that measures of tension apply equally well to cults as to sects.

There are two standards against which we can measure tension or deviance. First, we can follow a purely statistical approach, defining deviance as any significant departure from the average for the population as a whole. Second, we can emphasize the importance of power and influence, defining deviance as any behavior or characteristic that is scorned and punished by powerful elites in society. The problem with the first approach is that it may define an elite itself as deviant, even when the elite has the power to enforce its standards on others. To a great extent, elites represent the society with which sects and cults are in tension. For our purposes, the proper standard is a combination of the two approaches, an informed analysis that is interested in both the population average and in the norms set by elites.

In many of the tables that appear in this chapter, the low and medium tension denominations are in fact very close to the average for Protestants as a whole. In other cases, the low tension group is somewhat far from the average, although the high tension groups tend to be further from the average in the opposite direction. Perhaps both ends of the distribution represent tension with the social environment? But this conclusion, following the purely statistical model of deviance, is unwarranted. Ours is a relatively secular society in which the otherworldliness of high tension sects and cults does not harmonize with the assumptions built into economic, political, and nonreligious cultural institutions.

Many studies have shown that the denominations we label "low tension" are in fact most favorably placed in the class structure. This is true for the respondents in our study, as several analyses showed. For example, only 13 percent of members of the low tension denominations identified themselves as working class, but 40 percent of the sect members applied this label to themselves. Forty percent in the low tension group had completed college, compared with 17 percent of sect members. Fifty-five percent of those in the low tension denominations held high status jobs: professional, technical, and similar workers or proprietors, managers, and officials. Half this proportion of sect members, 27 percent, said they held such high status jobs. The low tension end of the spectrum is anchored closest to the centers of societal power. This fact allows us to identify these denominations conclusively as the low tension groups, even when they depart somewhat from the average for the population as a whole. In a theocratic society, low tension might mean intense involvement in religion (of a certain kind), but, in our secularized nations, low tension means low levels of commitment to traditional religion.

Difference

Johnson (1963:544) drew the connection between tension and deviance, saying "religions enforcing norms on their adherents that are sharply distinct from norms common in secular quarters should be classed as relatively sectarian." At the other extreme, "bodies permitting their members to participate freely in all phases of secular life should probably . . . be classified as churches." We cannot specify a priori precisely which norms will be subjects of disagreement between high tension groups and the rest of society because sects will reflect the culture and the history of the particular societies in which they emerge. But, in general, we would expect that issues of personal morality will be the most common areas of dispute. If we wanted to identify sects in a society of which we had no previous knowledge, we would have to do a preliminary survey to identify norms concerning personal behavior that were foci of heated debate in religious circles. After that, we could survey different religious groups to see which professed extreme minority views on these matters.

The survey data in hand primarily concern behavior permitted by secular society but forbidden by some religious groups. However, we know that some kinds of behavior are prohibited by the larger society but encouraged by these groups. For example, several high tension sects encourage speaking in tongues, although such behavior would be considered psychopathological in many secular settings. Norms of mental health do differ significantly from one religious group to another, with fundamentalist groups showing the greatest disagreement with psychiatrists' standards (Larson, 1964, 1968). A few sects encourage ritual poison drinking and serpent handling, despite laws against these practices (La Barre, 1969). Several cults use hallucinogenic drugs, despite their secular prohibition, including the Native American Church and Rastafarians (Furst, 1972) and the Love Family, which initiated members through drug-induced revelations. In Canada, repeated political and economic disputes have focused on the differences between the majority and such deviant religious communities as the Hutterites and Doukhobors. We have data on some relatively mild forms of religious behavior required by the sects, but the clearest starting point is to look at behavior the sects prohibit.

The data shown in Table 3.2 are from the same source as those shown in Table 3.1, but there is an important difference: As presented in Table 3.1 and in all other original publications based on these data (Glock and Stark, 1965, 1966; Stark and Glock, 1965, 1968), the Protestant groups were intuitively ranked from left to right, from the most churchlike to the most sectlike. But a number of small Protestant bodies were lumped together to make up a single category identified as "sects." These include the Church of God, the Church of Christ, Nazarenes, Assemblies of God, Seventh-Day Adventists, the Gospel Lighthouse, and the Foursquare Gospel Church. Here, the sects are of major interest, so we will consider them separately. However, two of them, the Gospel Lighthouse and the Foursquare Gospel Church, do not have enough cases for stable statistical results; we have therefore excluded them, except for computations based on the total "sects" category or on the "total Protestants" category.

To save space, we also have collapsed some Protestant denominations into "low tension" and "medium tension" groups. Those in the low tension group are the United Church of Christ, Methodists, Episcopalians,

TABLE 3.2 *Deviant Norms — Percent Giving the Indicated Response*

	Denominations		Sectlike		Sects					Total Prot. (2326)	Total Cath. (545)
	Low Tension (1032)	Medium Tension (844)	Mo. Luth. (116)	S. Bapt. (79)	C. of God (44)	C. of Christ (37)	Naza-rene (75)	Assem. of God (44)	7th-Day Ad. (35)		
The respondent feels that morals in this country "are pretty bad and getting worse."	41	47	53	71	66	73	71	84	83	48	43
The respondent disapproves of dancing.	1	9	28	77	77	95	96	91	100	18	1
The respondent disapproves of gambling.	62	67	81	96	89	100	92	98	97	69	27
The respondent approves of censorship of movies and books.	31	36	49	65	57	57	73	82	66	39	72
The respondent disapproves "highly" of someone who drinks moderately.	4	6	2	38	43	57	57	57	60	11	1
The respondent feels that drinking liquor would definitely prevent salvation.	3	3	1	15	30	38	39	30	46	7	2
The respondent is "rather concerned with trying to live as sinless a life as possible."	55	67	76	90	86	92	91	91	94	65	76
The respondent believes what we do in this life will determine our fate in the hereafter.	31	45	53	89	82	84	95	93	94	46	71

and the Disciples of Christ. The medium tension category includes Presbyterians, American Lutherans, and American Baptists. Because Missouri Lutherans and Southern Baptists stand at the borderline of the sect domain, we report data for these two "sectlike" denominations separately. The collapsing was done after careful examination of the data, which revealed little variation among groups in a given category. Hence, economy is gained and no pertinent information is lost.

Table 3.2 shows that members of sects and higher tension denominations do disagree with the majority on a number of moral issues. Members of sects are more likely than others to feel that morals in this country "are pretty bad and getting worse." The most extreme differences in this table are in attitudes toward dancing and the moderate use of alcohol. The overwhelming majority of members of low tension denominations tolerates such behavior, but the majority of sect members rejects it. These huge differences demonstrate strikingly that the sects do reject normative standards that the society at large accepts, although churches accept these standards. But differences need not be this large before they are significant. Obviously, a number of factors other than religious concerns may influence individual opinions. For example, gambling may be opposed on purely practical and economic grounds. The majority in every Protestant group disapproves of gambling, but the proportion is 20 to 30 percentage points higher in the sects than in the total Protestant population. As groups, the sects reject gambling more strongly than do the low tension denominations, even if a majority in all Protestant groups opposes this behavior.

Table 3.3 shows that high tension groups hold a number of deviant beliefs, opinions that are distinctly different from secular standards, even if more than half our sample of respondents accepts two of these opinions. Low tension denominations do not reject Darwin's theory, nor are they convinced by stories about the devil, biblical miracles, or the Second Coming. Medium tension denominations tend to accept the historical reality of biblical miracles, including the story that Jesus walked on water, but these two beliefs describe a distant past that need not have much relevance for participation in contemporary secular society. Beyond their utility as indicators of disagreement, the five beliefs listed in Table 3.3 also represent tension because they indicate dissatisfaction with the world as it can be perceived by the human senses, studied by science, and analyzed by reason. Taken together, they indicate rejection of the world as it seems, or at least the feeling that the material world is not rich enough unless supplemented by the supernatural. All people probably desire more than life can actually give them, but, in Table 3.3, we see that this dissatisfaction is probably much greater for the sects than for the low tension denominations.

TABLE 3.3   *Deviant Beliefs — Percent Giving the Indicated Response*

	Denominations		Sectlike				Sects				
	Low Tension (1032)	Medium Tension (842)	Mo. Luth. (116)	S. Bapt. (79)	C. of God (44)	C. of Christ (37)	Naza-rene (75)	Assem. of God (44)	7th-Day Ad. (35)	Total Prot. (2326)	Total Cath. (545)
Darwin's theory of evolution could not possibly be true.	11	29	64	72	57	78	80	91	94	30	28
It is completely true that the Devil actually exists.	14	38	77	92	73	87	91	96	97	37	66
Biblical miracles actually happened just as the Bible says they did.	39	61	89	92	84	97	88	96	91	57	74
It is completely true that Jesus walked on water.	28	55	83	99	84	97	93	96	100	50	71
Definitely, Jesus will actually return to the earth some day.	22	48	75	94	73	78	93	100	100	44	47

One of the disadvantages of survey research is that we must usually accept at face value whatever our respondents tell us. Sometimes attitudes and opinions are very poor reflections of social reality and fail to predict behavior (Schuman and Johnson, 1976). Even self-report behavioral items may provide more direct evidence. Table 3.4 lists five such measures and has very much the same pattern of results as seen in previous tables. Of course, the first one, frequent prayer, is not inherently deviant. Over two-thirds of our church member respondents pray often or daily. But the sects are 25 percentage points above the low tension denominations. High tension groups have a somewhat higher norm for prayer but much higher norms for saying grace, reading the Bible at home regularly, listening to religious programs, and spending evenings in church. Thus, high tension denominations not only reject some important secular norms and hold deviant opinions, but also set unusual standards for positive religious behavior.

Antagonism

High tension means not only difference from secular society, but also antagonism toward it. Table 3.5 lists four items that bear on *particularism*, "the belief that only one's own religion is legitimate" (Glock and Stark, 1966:20). Particularistic beliefs and attitudes serve as a compensator for relatively low honor and status in the larger society. As James Coleman (1956:53) has commented, "Each religious sect is, in a sense, a mutual admiration society." By defining themselves as especially righteous, members of high tension groups gain a basis for this mutual (and self) admiration. But to do this, they must disvalue nonmembers' attributes. The first two items in Table 3.5 give special honor to Christians, saying that heaven and salvation are reserved for true believers in Jesus Christ. High tension groups within the Christian tradition are especially likely to agree with these two items. The pattern of responses to the statement that Hindu religion would prevent salvation is not the simple reflection of the two previous items, as logic would require it to be. It may be that rejection of Hindu religion by sect members is not stronger because Hindus are not part of the surrounding American sociocultural environment.

Table 3.6 describes the social struggle that goes on at the border of high tension groups. Members of the sects frequently attempt to convert others to their faith and at the same time are concerned about defending their religious group against outside influences. In part, conversion attempts may be public dramatizations of particularistic pride, but they are also based in hostility toward outsiders. Unless outsiders can be converted to the sect, sect members will have difficulty carrying on close relationships with them. Conversion appeals typically claim that the

TABLE 3.4   Deviant Behavior — Percent Giving the Indicated Response

| | Denominations | | Sectlike | | Sects | | | | | Total Prot. (2326) | Total Cath. (545) |
	Low Ten-sion (1032)	Mediu n Ten-sion (844)	Mo. Luth. (116)	S. Bapt. (79)	C. of God (44)	C. of Christ (37)	Naza-rene (75)	Assem. of God (44)	7th-Day Ad. (35)		
The respondent prays "quite often" or "regularly once a day or more."	63	71	80	87	89	92	85	91	91	70	76
Grace is said at all meals in the respondent's home.	16	25	41	53	66	65	69	80	77	28	22
The respondent reads the Bible at home regularly.	12	24	21	63	48	49	59	57	69	23	5
The respondent regularly listens to or watches religious services on radio or television.	7	10	13	28	18	22	33	34	40	12	6
In an average week, the respondent spends two or more evenings in church.	6	10	8	52	61	70	56	70	23	15	5

TABLE 3.5   Particularism — Percent Giving the Indicated Response

	Denominations		Sectlike		Sects					Total Prot. (2326)	Total Cath. (545)
	Low Tension (1032)	Medium Tension (844)	Mo. Luth. (116)	S. Bapt. (79)	C. of God (44)	C. of Christ (37)	Naza- rene (75)	Assem. of God (44)	7th- Day Ad. (35)		
Only those who believe in Jesus Christ can go to heaven.	13	39	80	92	59	89	81	89	77	36	12
Belief in Jesus Christ as Savior is absolutely necessary for salvation.	47	71	97	97	96	97	93	100	94	65	51
Being of the Hindu religion would definitely prevent salvation.	4	15	40	32	32	60	35	41	17	14	2
Tithing is absolutely necessary for salvation.	8	12	7	18	52	43	45	39	69	14	10

TABLE 3.6 Conversion and Defense — Percent Giving the Indicated Response

	Denominations		Sectlike		Sects					Total Prot. (2326)	Total Cath. (545)
	Low Tension (1032)	Medium Tension (844)	Mo. Luth. (116)	S. Bapt. (79)	C. of God (44)	C. of Christ (37)	Naza-rene (75)	Assem. of God (44)	7th-Day Ad. (35)		
Once or more the respondent has tried to convert someone to his or her religious faith.	38	50	63	89	86	84	83	86	83	50	40
Often the respondent has tried to convert someone to his or her religious faith.	5	8	10	32	32	32	27	36	34	10	5
The respondent sometimes prays to ask God to bring someone else to Christian faith and belief.	26	38	48	87	84	95	85	86	89	40	37
The respondent is "very interested" in knowing the religious affiliation of people he or she meets.	12	16	19	44	34	49	32	39	34	18	9
The respondent feels "we should not allow missionaries from non-Christian religions to spread their teachings in a Christian community."	17	27	35	41	36	41	41	55	23	25	23
The respondent says, "I tend to distrust a person who does not believe in Jesus."	19	27	34	53	46	51	47	55	33	27	22

converting group is better than any other and that the secular world is quite bad. Members of high tension groups are most likely to distrust nonbelievers and to feel their community needs to be defended against non-Christian missionaries. For these people, the perimeter of their sect is a battlefront; the conversion struggle is a fight for acceptance from other persons, yet rejection of society as a whole. Interestingly, the Seventh-Day Adventist respondents are not especially worried about Hindus (Table 3.5) or about other non-Christians (Table 3.6). This unusual tolerance in a sect is probably the result of this group's experience of persecution in overseas missionary work.

Separation

High tension with the societal environment is not merely a matter of strong opinions and deviant behavior; it is also manifested in patterns of social relations. In extreme cases, high tension groups separate completely from the social life of the larger society and retreat into geographical isolation. Such extreme separation is not just an antique phenomenon affecting Hutterites, Amish, and Mormons. Even in the 20th century, some high tension groups have fled their societies of origin, wandered in the wilderness, and sought completely new sociocultural environments (Zablocki, 1971; Bainbridge, 1978c). Table 3.7 shows six indicators of less complete separation.

The first two items show that sects are most likely to disapprove of marriages with members of other religious groups. In tension with the social environment, their relations with outsiders are strained. Conversely, relations with other insiders are favored. Members of sects are more than twice as likely to say they fit in very well with their church congregation than are members of low tension denominations. The sect member's friends are much more likely to be fellow members of the same group. Social separation from outsiders and closer relations with other insiders are implied by each other. Together, they constitute *encapsulation* of the sect, isolation of each high tension subculture as a distinct, closed social world (cf. Dynes, 1957).

In a sociometric study of Protestant ministers, Balswick and Falkner (1970:310) found that sectarian ministers were bound together in a "fairly tightly knit clique" in comparison to ministers of low tension denominations, who had "the most loosely structured relationships." This finding suggests that not only the members, but also the clergy of high tension religious groups tend to be socially encapsulated.

Further evidence for this observation is reported in a recent survey study of 1,559 Protestant clergymen by Harold E. Quinley (1974). Unfortunately, the sample did not include ministers of small, radical sects, but there were 131 Missouri Lutherans and 167 Southern Baptists, and

TABLE 3.7 *Social Encapsulation — Percent Giving the Indicated Response*

	Denominations		Sectlike		Sects					Total Prot. (2326)	Total Cath. (545)
	Low Ten-sion (1092)	Medium Ten-sion (844)	Mo. Luth. (116)	S. Bapt. (79)	C. of God (44)	C. of Christ (37)	Naza-rene (75)	Assem. of God (44)	7th-Day Ad. (35)		
Respondent disapproves of religious mixed marriages.	31	39	70	80	55	68	85	86	94	43	65
Respondent feels marrying a non-Christian would "possibly" or "definitely" prevent salvation.	9	16	22	20	46	51	68	73	57	18	27
Respondent says, "I fit in very well with my church congregation."	22	23	25	42	48	47	53	66	54	27	23
Half or more of the people the respondent associates with are members of his or her congregation.	29	37	36	51	77	59	72	75	69	38	47
Three or more of the respondent's five closest friends are members of his or her congregation.	22	25	26	49	61	65	65	66	83	29	36

42 percent of the total described themselves as fundamentalist or conservative. Quinley combined responses to several questionnaire items to produce a five-point index of religious orientation, from "most modernist" to "most traditionist." The 320 most traditionist clergymen expressed views that place them at the high tension end of the distribution. For example, they believed that Jesus walked on water and that the devil actually exists. The questionnaire also asked how frequently they visited informally with other ministers, either of their own denomination or of other denominations. Visits with fellow ministers of their own denomination did not vary significantly by religious orientation. Such visits were made less than once a month by 22 percent of the most modernist clergy and by 21 percent of the most traditionist. But there was a great difference in visits with clergy of other denominations. Only 28 percent of the most modernist clergy made such visits less than once a month, but 52 percent of the high tension ministers made interdenominational visits this seldom (Quinley, 1974:249).

SOCIAL REJECTION OF SECTS AND CULTS

We have shown that tension can be measured as antagonism toward the sociocultural environment by religious groups that have deviant norms and that are somewhat socially encapsulated. The other side of tension, rejection by the larger society, can also be measured and gives the same general results. Our church member survey included a few social distance items that allow us to compare public acceptance of seven religious groups. A recent Gallup poll also included social distance measures that bear on this point.

Table 3.8 summarizes social distance data from the church members. The original question actually listed 27 different categories of person, including such varied stimuli as German, alcoholic, conservative, liberal, and teetotaler. The respondent was asked if he or she "would feel friendly and at ease" with each stimulus person. The most important data are the two columns for total Protestant and total Catholic. These figures suggest how much each stimulus group is accepted or rejected by church members as a whole. The majority of all respondents say they would probably feel friendly and at ease with a Methodist, an Episcopalian, a Roman Catholic, or a Jew. That is, these church members find little problem with established conventional faiths, even if this means a non-Christian faith. However, the Jehovah's Witnesses, the only sect among the stimuli, receive a much lower level of acceptance. Except for two fellow sects that show some warmth toward the Jehovah's Witnesses, there is rejection across the board. Atheists and Spiritualists receive

TABLE 3.8 *Social Distance — Percent Giving the Indicated Response*

	Denominations		Sectlike				Sects			Total Prot. (2326)	Total Cath. (545)
	Low Tension (1032)	Medium Tension (844)	Mo. Luth. (116)	S. Bapt. (79)	C. of God (44)	C. of Christ (37)	Naza-rene (75)	Assem. of God (44)	7th-Day Ad. (35)		
Would feel friendly and at ease with a Methodist.	82	86	83	82	87	70	80	82	86	84	57
Would feel friendly and at ease with an Episcopalian.	84	80	82	62	80	60	60	71	77	80	65
Would feel friendly and at ease with a Roman Catholic.	73	72	78	58	68	49	48	52	71	70	78
Would feel friendly and at ease with a Jew.	72	69	75	49	71	70	52	68	77	69	63
Would feel friendly and at ease with a Jehovah's Witness.	29	32	26	27	25	49	13	18	46	29	27
Would feel friendly and at ease with an atheist.	29	23	19	16	23	30	7	16	11	24	23
Would feel friendly and at ease with a Spiritualist.	26	22	22	18	16	43	9	5	3	23	25

even greater rejection, primarily because the higher tension denominations are less likely to accept them than is the low tension group. Spiritualists are the only cult members included in the questionnaire.

Comparable data were collected by a 1977 Gallup poll of a national sample of about 1,500 adults. Respondents were asked to indicate on a ten-point scale how much they liked or disliked each of 15 religious groups and three religious leaders. Because the respondents included people who were not church members and because many may have felt inhibited from expressing a negative judgment of other citizens, we do not expect the levels of rejection to be very high. The number who failed to express any opinion at all varied from stimulus to stimulus; so we have removed them from our reanalysis, calculating the percentage of those holding a definite opinion who disliked the given group or leader. Only 6 percent disliked Protestants, and the main Protestant denominations (Methodists, Lutherans, Presbyterians, Baptists, and Episcopalians) received low rejection scores, ranging from 4 to 8 percent.

Higher scores indicate some measure of rejection by the dominant groups in society. Catholics were disliked by 11 percent of the respondents, and between 12 and 15 percent rejected the following higher tension groups: Southern Baptists, Eastern Orthodox, Evangelicals, Jews, and Quakers. Unitarians are disliked by 21 percent, Mormons by 25 percent, and Seventh-Day Adventists by 27 percent. The Mormons and Seventh-Day Adventists are distinguished by the sectarian intensity of their religion, and the Unitarians are probably regarded as deviant in terms of irreligiousness. Unitarians do not belong to the National Council of Churches because the full name of that organization is National Council of Churches of Christ, thus excluding Unitarians for rejecting the divinity of Jesus. Thus, a low tension religious identity in America today is not be irreligious — to reject supernatural beliefs — but to claim membership in a traditional denomination that is well accommodated to the world.

It is interesting that Pope Paul VI received the same score, 11 percent, as did Catholics, the religious group he led. Billy Graham got an intermediate score of 15 percent, about the same as Evangelicals at 14 percent. But cult leader Sun Myung Moon, the founder of the Unification Church, got an extremely unfavorable rating — 93 percent of those familiar with him dislike him. This shows that his cult is in extremely high tension with the sociocultural environment.

The Gallup data also permitted us to look at how several of the groups judged themselves. Between 47 and 60 percent of members in major Protestant denominations and the Catholic church gave their own group a most highly favorable rating. Among the Mormons, relatively rejected by other respondents, 91 percent gave their own group the top score. As Gordon W. Russell (1975) has reported, Mormon respondents tend to see themselves as the Chosen People. This reflects the pattern we have already found: High tension groups are rejected by outsiders but evaluate themselves highly.

Another Gallup poll, carried out in December 1981, asked a national sample of American adults to examine a list of groups and indicate any they "would *not* like to have as neighbors." Thirty percent of Americans did not want "cults and sects" as neighbors, making them the most unpopular of groups evaluated. In contrast, only 11 percent did not want "religious fundamentalists" as neighbors, 2 percent rejected Jews, and only 1 percent indicated a dislike of Protestants or of Catholics as neighbors. In the wake of the deportation of thousands of prison and mental hospital inmates from Cuba to the United States, only "Cuban refugees," at 25 percent, approached the level of rejection earned by cults and sects. Clearly, a substantial number of Americans will openly admit their desire for physical separation from high tension religious groups.

Although the main focus of our analysis has been comparison of low tension and high tension Protestant groups, attention should also be called to differences between the total Protestant and Catholic groups. Johnson (1963:545–546; cf. Boling, 1973) suggests that "it is wise to classify Catholicism (in America) as somewhat more sectarian than most of the major Protestant bodies." When it was a weak religious minority in a predominantly Protestant country, as was the case decades ago, Catholicism experienced palpable tension with the sociocultural environment. For a variety of reasons, that tension has diminished over the years, but discrimination against members of the Catholic faith still exists in some sectors of important societal institutions (Greeley, 1977a, 1977b).

The picture given by our tables is much simpler for the Protestant sects than for the Catholics. Often, the Catholic average is almost identical with the Protestant average. At other times, the Catholics are in the same direction from that average as are the Protestant sects, and occasionally the Catholics are on the side away from the sects. This pattern is not consistent with a simple description of Catholicism as a high tension group. Rather, it reminds us that Protestantism and Catholicism are distinctly different traditions of religious culture. The best measure of Catholic tension in our data set is found in tables 3.7 and 3.8, where we see evidence of some social encapsulation and social distance separating Catholics and Protestants. Other tables were designed primarily to measure the tension of sects within the Protestant tradition. We do not have the data to distinguish higher and lower tension groups within the

Catholic tradition to complete a definitive analysis of the relationship between Catholicism and the sociocultural environment.

CONCLUSION

The false idea that North American religion is a unity may be attractive on two grounds. First, it offers a simple picture, and the alternative might seem a confusion of faiths far too complex to comprehend. Second, by minimizing differences, it ignores conflict and thus may comfort those who would find cause for alarm in the deep disputes that divide citizens into rival churches, sects, and cults. But this chapter shows that our theory provides a coherent way of understanding most religious diversity in terms of a single dimension of variation — degree of tension with the sociocultural environment. And however disquieting social and religious conflicts may be, they in fact exist and provide much of the dynamism in the religious marketplace, giving rise to revival and innovation.

If awareness of diversity focuses attention on the most lively religious movements, it also highlights the declines that we find in many major denominations. In later chapters, we explore how new religious groups successfully move into these gaps left by low tension churches and how religious organizations often change in tension, moving along the dimension as they mature and evolve. At the high tension extreme, the myth of religious unity dissolves in a discord of religious subcultures. However inharmonious this babble of faiths may be, it is consistent with our underlying concept: sociologically, sectarian tension is subcultural deviance.

As a first step in drawing together the many social indicators of tension, we have found it useful to collect them under three headings: *difference* from the standards set by the majority or by powerful members of society, *antagonism* between the sect and society manifested in mutual rejection, and *separation* in social relations leading to the relative encapsulation of the sect. These are not to be considered as three different axes of tension or as three dimensions of sectarianism. Although they can be distinguished conceptually, in our theory each is directly implied by the other two. One might think of these as the three moving parts by which tension is created and sustained. Like a set of moving parts, they may be considered separately for purposes of measurement, but it would be folly to disassemble the set.

The data we have examined justify use of tension as the ordering principle of the church-sect axis. Groups we intuitively regard as more churchlike or more sectlike displayed marked quantitative differences on the many items we examined and did so in a very consistent way.

Nevertheless, this chapter is best regarded as no more than a successful reconnaissance. We have made do with items written for other purposes. Clearly, it would be possible to construct much more sensitive and appropriate measures of tension and thereby gain much greater precision in ranking various religious groups. Indeed, it would be desirable to consider measures based on policies, procedures, and structures of religious organizations as such, in addition to measures created by aggregating individual level data. Some promising work along those lines has already been accomplished by Michael Welch (1977).

Whatever improvements in measurement can be achieved, our results establish the important point. Theoretical use of the concept of tension is warranted: *Tension can be measured.* This is extremely important, for no significant theories concerning the origins and transformations of religious movements can be tested unless it is possible to rank order religious groups in an unambiguous way. For example, it is impossible to test the hypothesis that the arrival of an adult generation of socialized members tends to transform sects if we cannot be sure that particular religious groups are (or are not) less sectlike at time two than at time one (see Chapter 6). This is a very old hypothesis. That it has waited so long to be tested is indicative of the impediment created by the multidimensional typological schemes that produced primarily unorderable mixed types. Tension opens the door to testing this and all the other things we think we know about the church-sect process, and it is time we got on with the job. Fifty years have now passed since H. Richard Niebuhr first made it evident that a church-sect theory was desirable and likely to be possible.

4 *Religious Regionalism*

The previous chapter examined the spectrum of faiths to be found in North America. However, few citizens of the United States or Canada actually have such a diverse religious menu to choose from locally, for each nation has a pronounced religious geography. Quebec is Catholic, as is Massachusetts, and Protestantism dominates the rural Great Plains of both nations. Jews are concentrated in the large cities of the East, as Mormons are concentrated in the American West.

There are even more remarkable, if little known, aspects to religious regionalism, aspects that have great impact on what kinds of new religious movements are likely to succeed where. For purposes of economy, we defer extensive examination of Canada's religious regionalism until Chapter 20. In this chapter, we are concerned with religion in general in the United States. Where is conventional religion strong; where is it weak? Thus, we examine geographic patterns in rates of church membership, church attendance, conventional religious belief, prayer, and religious experiences. In later chapters, we explore the geography of sects and cult movements and client and audience cults.

Two significant facts about America's religious regionalism will be obvious as we map the data:

1. There is supposedly a "Bible Belt" — a bastion of intense evangelical Protestantism — stretching across the American South. The South is very Protestant, but in fact, we find virtually no trace of the famous Bible Belt. We suggest some reasons why the myth of a southern Bible Belt arose.

2. The most marked feature of American religion has gone virtually unnoticed. A very prominent "Unchurched Belt" runs along the shores of the Pacific, from the Mexican border through Alaska, including Canada's most western province, British Columbia, and the Yukon territory. In this chapter, we suggest why this belt exists, and we consider its implications for cult formation in Part V.

CHURCH MEMBERSHIP

We are able to study church membership in the United States today only because of a private census of the nation's religious denominations (Johnson et al., 1974). However, two serious omissions of this study had to be rectified before we could use it to produce accurate results. First, millions of members of the Black denominations were omitted from the count. But because Blacks were not omitted from the population denominators used in the study, state and local church membership rates were distorted in proportion to the size of their Black populations. The larger the Black population, the more the church membership rate was driven down. We developed means to estimate local church membership among Blacks and thus to correct the rates (Stark, 1980). Jews also were omitted from the membership counts. However, good data on local Jewish membership were available and we used them to correct the rates (Newman and Halvorson, 1979).

The initial studies based on these religious census data were limited to characterizing the denominational makeup of various locales. These may be of considerable intrinsic interest, but our research on the impact of religion on delinquency, crime, and suicide suggests that it is not important what kinds of religious organizations people belong to, but whether they belong to any at all (Stark, Doyle, and Kent, 1980; Bainbridge and Stark, 1981; Stark, Kent, and Doyle, 1982; Stark, Doyle, and Rushing, 1983). The same principle applies to religious deviance: People who are committed to any religion do not shop for another.

We have transformed the data on church membership into rates, expressed as the number of persons per 1,000 who belong to a church. Variations in this church membership rate are huge from one place to another in the United States. This fact is often overlooked because of the consistent results of public opinion polls, which find that about 95 percent of the population will name a denomination when asked "What is your religious affiliation?" But many respondents who name a denomination are at best "cultural" members. Their names do not, in fact, appear on the membership list of any specific congregation or parish. Indeed, in questionnaires we have gathered among university students on which Protestants had to write in their denomination, we frequently have found the denomination students claim as their own to be wildly misspelled (Piscable and Luthern, for example). Such people are unchurched. This does not mean they are irreligious (Vernon, 1968). Indeed, as we shall see, religious belief everywhere runs much higher than does church membership. But nonmembership does mean a lack of systematic support for belief and a lack of organized social expression of faith.

Metropolitan Areas

We computed church membership rates for 215 metropolitan areas (SMSAs) defined by the U.S. Census. Some New England states are formed by very large townships rather than by counties. In constructing SMSAs for this region, the Census Bureau breaks up these units, often assigning different parts of a single township to different SMSAs. Unfortunately, we are unable to do this with the published church member census; thus, some New England SMSAs, among them Boston, are not included in our study. A metropolitan area is a major city and its surrounding suburbs, although sometimes several close together cities are combined to make one metropolitan area (for example, Minneapolis and St. Paul, Minnesota).

Table 4.1 shows the church membership rates for a number of metropolitan areas: the top and bottom 25 and a number of the larger cities. The number one church membership city in America is Provo, Utah, with 966 church members per 1,000 population (or 96.6 percent). Close behind is La Crosse, Wisconsin, with 903, then Waco, Texas, 891, then three Louisiana cities. There is great variety among the top 25 metropolitan areas. Provo is overwhelmingly Mormon, but La Crosse and Waco are predominantly Protestant, and Louisiana is Catholic. There is a tendency for metropolitan areas at the top of the list to be located in rural states, but there are no very marked geographic biases, and the South is, if anything, underrepresented.

However, when one examines the bottom 25 cities, a very striking geographic bias appears. All but four of these metropolitan areas are in the Far West. Eugene, Oregon, is the most unchurched metropolitan area in the United States. Eugene is primarily a college town (home of the University of Oregon), but so is Provo, Utah (home of Brigham Young University). It is region, not institutions of higher learning, that the bottom 25 cities have in common. Santa Rosa, California; Tacoma, Washington; Salinas, California; and Seattle, Washington make up the rest of the bottom five.

Looking at the other major urban centers shown in the table makes it clear that church membership is rather evenly spread across the nation,

TABLE 4.1   *Church Membership of American Metropolitan Areas —*
the Top 25, the Bottom 25, and Selected Others

	Rank on Church Membership	Area	Church Members per 1,000 Population
Top 25:	1	Provo-Orem, Utah	966
	2	La Crosse, Wisconsin	903
	3	Waco, Texas	891
	4	Lake Charles, Louisiana	858
	5	New Orleans, Louisiana	835
	6	Lafayette, Louisiana	834
	7	Dubuque, Iowa	829
	8	Brownsville-Harlingen-San Benito, Texas	827
	9	Ogden, Utah	820
	10	Salt Lake City, Utah	808
	11	Green Bay, Wisconsin	804
	12	Jackson, Mississippi	803
	13	Owensboro, Kentucky	781
	14	Beaumont-Port Arthur-Orange, Texas	780
	15	Johnstown, Pennsylvania	775
	16	Sioux Falls, South Dakota	767
	17	Appleton-Oshkosh, Wisconsin	760
	18	Wilkes-Barre–Hazelton, Pennsylvania	753
	19	Tyler, Texas	731
	20	Laredo, Texas	723
	21	Scranton, Pennsylvania	718
	22	Shreveport, Louisiana	715
	23	Fargo-Moorhead, North Dakota-Minnesota	712
	24	Pittsburgh, Pennsylvania	711
	25	Monroe, Louisiana	709
Bottom 25:	215	Eugene-Springfield, Oregon	262
	214	Santa Rosa, California	281
	213	Tacoma, Washington	282
	212	Salinas-Seaside-Monterey, California	287
	211	Seattle-Everett, Washington	288
	210	Reno, Nevada	303
	209	Las Vegas, Nevada	308
	208	Fayetteville, North Carolina	320
	207	San Jose, California	320
	206	Vallejo-Fairfield-Napa, California	324
	205	Muncie, Indiana	325
	204	Portland, Oregon	329
	203	Jackson, Michigan	331

(continued)

TABLE 4.1   (continued)

Rank on Church Membership	Area	Church Members per 1,000 Population
202	Sacramento, California	331
201	Honolulu, Hawaii	332
200	Santa Barbara-Santa Maria-Lompoc, California	332
199	Terre Haute, Indiana	332
198	Modesto, California	336
197	Boise, Idaho	336
196	Los Angeles-Long Beach, California	343
195	Salem, Oregon	345
194	Anaheim-Santa Ana-Garden Grove, California	346
193	San Diego, California	347
192	Riverside-San Bernardino-Ontario, California	355
191	San Francisco-Oakland, California	361

Other Selected Metropolitan Areas

31	San Antonio, Texas	685
32	Chicago, Illinois	679
40	Milwaukee, Wisconsin	656
54	Philadelphia, Pennsylvania	623
58	Newark, New Jersey	616
61	Memphis, Tennessee	614
62	Albuquerque, New Mexico	614
67	New York City	610
71	Birmingham, Alabama	606
75	Louisville, Kentucky	602
76	Cleveland, Ohio	601
78	Columbia, South Carolina	600
87	Charleston, South Carolina	590
88	St. Louis, Missouri	589
93	Minneapolis-St. Paul, Minnesota	587
104	Detroit, Michigan	570
106	Houston, Texas	568
113	Cincinnati, Ohio	560
114	Atlanta, Georgia	560
115	Baltimore, Maryland	556
116	Oklahoma City, Oklahoma	552
123	Dallas, Texas	538
127	Wheeling, West Virginia	528
128	Omaha, Nebraska	526
130	Miami, Florida	523

(continued)

TABLE 4.1   (continued)

Rank on Church Membership	Area	Church Members per 1,000 Population
135	Nashville, Tennessee	508
136	Des Moines, Iowa	507
137	Wichita, Kansas	507
139	Kansas City, Missouri	504
154	Billings, Montana	468
171	Indianapolis, Indiana	423
174	Denver, Colorado	407
175	Phoenix, Arizona	404
179	Columbus, Ohio	396
184	Spokane, Washington	388

except for the West Coast. And there is no evidence of a Bible Belt — at least not in terms of church membership — when cities such as Chicago, Philadelphia, Newark, and New York City have considerably higher church membership rates than do such major southern centers as Atlanta and Nashville.

States
The absence of a southern Bible Belt, at least in terms of unusually high church membership rates, and the existence of a West Coast Unchurched Belt are even more obvious in Table 4.2, where state church membership rates are shown.

Utah is number one with a rate of 836. Louisiana is second with 814. But Louisiana is a Catholic state and therefore lends no credence to a Protestant Bible Belt. Rhode Island, also a Catholic state, is in third place; North Dakota is fourth; and Mississippi, in fifth place, is the highest of the states in the Deep South.

Regional solidarity appears only at the bottom of the table, where we find the Unchurched Belt in Washington (331), Oregon (332), California (364), Alaska (376), Hawaii (380), and Nevada (394). There is a saying from frontier times that "There's no law west of Dodge City, and no God west of Laramie. Frisco's west of both of them." Something about the Far West is clearly inhospitable to churches, and this is not a new phenomenon. When we examine reliable data on church membership rates collected by the U.S. Census near the turn of the century, we find things then like they are now (See Chapter 11).

Regions
These patterns come into bold relief as mapped in Figure 4.1. The West Coast sits apart from the rest of the nation, a kind of continental

TABLE 4.2 *Church Membership by State*

Rank	State	Church Members per 1,000 Population
1	Utah	836
2	Louisiana	814
3	Rhode Island	768
4	North Dakota	766
5	Mississippi	762
6	South Carolina	719
7	South Dakota	692
8	Wisconsin	689
9	Minnesota	667
10	Massachusetts	666
11	Pennsylvania	656
12	New Mexico	640
13	Connecticut	638
14	Illinois	634
15	North Carolina	631
16	Texas	630
17	Iowa	629
18	Alabama	623
19	Nebraska	617
20	Georgia	598
21	New Jersey	590
22	Oklahoma	584
23	Kentucky	583
24	Tennessee	581
25	New York	577
26	Missouri	562
27	Kansas	550
28	Idaho	537
29	Maryland	529
30	Vermont	521
31	Virginia	518
32	Ohio	515
33	Michigan	508
34	Arkansas	505
35	New Hampshire	503
36	Florida	500
37	Delaware	493
38	Arizona	481
39	Wyoming	477
40	Indiana	475
41	Montana	466
42	Maine	448
43	Colorado	424
44	West Virginia	418

(continued)

TABLE 4.2   (continued)

Rank	State	Church Members per 1,000 Population
45	Nevada	394
46	Hawaii	380
47	Alaska	376
48	California	364
49	Oregon	332
50	Washington	331
National		557

shelf in which conventional churches seem unable to put down healthy roots. The Mountain region also is somewhat low in church membership, especially if Utah, with its huge and well-churched Mormon population, is excluded. Yet even the Mountain region more closely resembles the rest of the nation than it does the West Coast. Variations across the other major regions are quite small. The West South Central is highest, closely followed by Catholic New England. The South Atlantic is tied with the East North Central for the lowest regional rate outside the West.

This underscores the fact that the South is no different from most of the rest of the nation in terms of church membership. Later we examine the possibility that southern religion is more traditional or fundamentalist than is religion elsewhere in America. But that southerners are as unchurched as anyone else (except for westerners) chips away at the stereotype of the Sunday-go-to-meeting South.

CHURCH ATTENDANCE

In the remainder of this chapter, we use the results of national opinion surveys to map American religion. We especially rely on a study conducted by the National Opinion Research Center in November 1972. Complete details of design and sampling can be found in McCready and Greeley (1976) and Greeley (1975). Because of the limited size of the samples, it is not possible to characterize individual states, let alone metropolitan areas. Fortunately, regions have turned out to be objects of greatest interest, and there are sufficient cases to characterize each.

One important defect in the regional portraits must be understood, however. Through a quirk in NORC's national sample design, the religious portrait of the Mountain region is distorted in most of the findings we report. NORC conducted interviews in only three states in this region: Colorado, Arizona, and Montana. Omitted were Utah, Idaho, Wyoming,

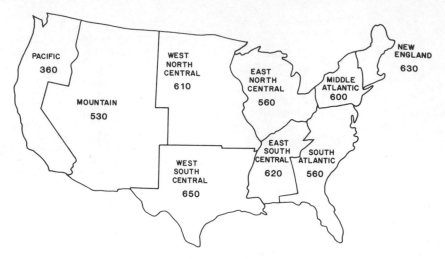

FIGURE 4.1   *Church Membership Rates per 1,000 Population*
(National rate = 560 per thousand)

Nevada, and New Mexico. Table 4.2 shows that the omitted states tend to be very much higher in church membership rates than the included states. Moreover, the two highest church membership states (Utah in 1st place and New Mexico in 12th) in the region are also two of the largest states, and both are omitted. This means that levels of religious participation and belief will be underestimated for the Mountain region.

Figure 4.2 charts regional patterns in the proportions of the population who report they attend church at least twice a month. We used this cutting point in order to minimize Catholic-Protestant differences. Catholics lay greater stress on attending every week than do Protestants, but Catholics are no less likely than Protestants to be infrequent attenders (Stark and Glock, 1968). Looking at the map, we see that regional patterns of church attendance are similar to patterns of church membership. The Unchurched Belt along the West Coast reappears: Not only do people on the West Coast fail to join churches, they also do not attend church very often. The Mountain region, as noted, is underestimated—the real rate of attendance is substantially higher than shown, but still probably lower than in more easterly regions. New England and the Middle Atlantic regions are slightly lower than the other easterly regions (the Middle Atlantic rate is depressed by the very low attendance among Jews). The South does not differ noticeably from the North.

Figure 4.3 permits a maximum test of religious nonparticipation. Here we see the proportion of people who say they never attend church.

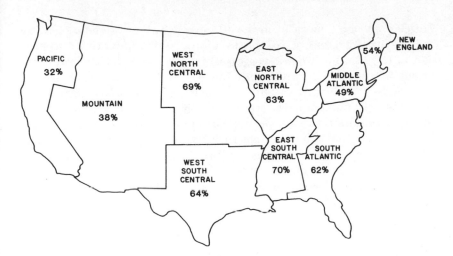

FIGURE 4.2   *Percent Attending Church More Often Than Once a Month*
(National rate = 54 percent)

Note: Mountain region includes only Colorado, Arizona, and Montana.

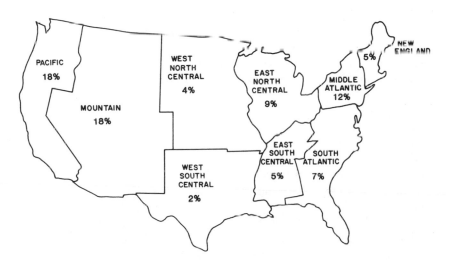

FIGURE 4.3   *Percent Never Attending Church*
(National rate = 9 percent)

Note: Mountain region includes only Colorado, Arizona, and Montana.

Fewer than one American in ten (9 percent) never attends. Here too there is little variation across most regions. Nonattendance is only average in the Middle Atlantic region when Jews are excluded from the calculation, and the relatively high rate for the Mountain region is exaggerated by sampling flaws. Only the Pacific region stands out from the rest; there 18 percent never attend church. Even so, the overwhelming majority of Americans in the Pacific region have not severed all ties with the churches. They are not official members and they do not go as often as once a month, but they still find their way to church once in awhile. That the Unchurched Belt is not an irreligious belt will be even more evident as we examine religious beliefs.

RELIGIOUS BELIEF

Thus far we have examined the strength of conventional religious organizations. But many people manage to remain religious even though they are not affiliated with any specific religious body. Some find their religious needs wholly met by the "electronic church" — the many religious ministries conducted over radio and television (Hadden and Swann, 1981). Many others are satisfied by their personal religious beliefs and by private prayer. As we already have pointed out, however, religious people adrift from organized religion are especially vulnerable to recruitment to new religious movements: Religion is most powerful when it has a fully social expression. In what follows, we begin to glimpse the many open sectors in the American religious economy that exist because faith is so much more widespread than is church membership, especially in the Unchurched Belt along the West Coast.

God

We have placed belief in the supernatural at the center of our definition of religion. Thus, the most basic way to assess the extent of religion is through belief in the existence of the supernatural. In American culture, the focus of supernatural belief is the existence of God. Figure 4.4 shows that Americans overwhelmingly express belief in God. Eighty-four percent agreed with the statement "I believe in the existence of God as I define Him." This phrasing certainly makes specific allowance for many different conceptions of divinity. For some Americans, the God in whom they express belief may be a very vague and inactive entity — a kind of goodness in the universe. Indeed, such highly abstracted and secularized versions of God are typical of the most liberal clergy and of many Unitarians and Universalists. Yet most Americans are not expressing belief in a

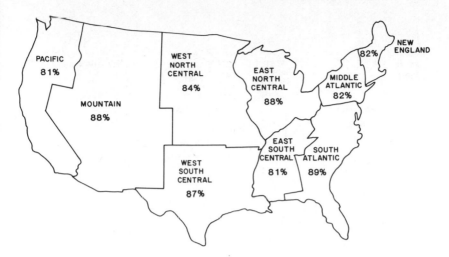

FIGURE 4.4   *Percent That "Believe in the existence of God as I define Him"*
(National rate = 84 percent)

Note: Mountain region includes only Colorado, Arizona, and Montana.

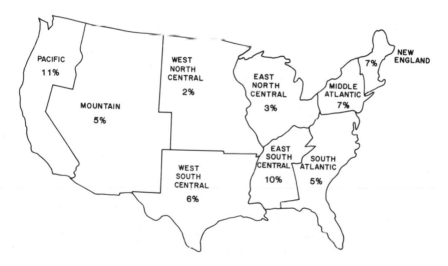

FIGURE 4.5   *Percent Rejecting the Existence of God*
(National rate = 6 percent)

Note: Mountain region includes only Colorado, Arizona, and Montana.

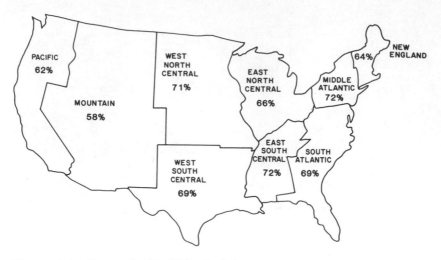

FIGURE 4.6   *Percent Saying That "God's love is behind everything that happens"*
(National rate = 67 percent)

Note: Mountain region includes only Colorado, Arizona, and Montana.

remote and inactive God, but in a supernatural being who hears prayers, notes the fall of the sparrow, and acts in history.

The most striking thing about Figure 4.4 is the *lack* of regional variation. Westerners are not especially apt to doubt the existence of God, and southerners are not unusually apt to believe. All regions are very close to the national average. Regionalism comes into no clearer focus in Figure 4.5, which maps steadfast atheism. Nationally, 6 percent of Americans wholly reject the existence of God. This rises to 11 percent in the Pacific region, but runs at 10 percent in the East South Central region in the Deep South. The Unchurched Belt is not Godless.

Let us examine more closely the kind of God Americans have in mind when they express their faith. Seventy-four percent strongly agreed that "God's goodness and love are greater than we can possibly imagine." We have not included a regional map of these responses, but they did not reveal important geographic variations. Figure 4.6 maps the proportion who said yes to the statement "God's love is behind everything that happens." This is a vast claim — God's love is behind catastrophe as well as good fortune. Still, two-thirds of Americans said yes, and again, regional variations are small.

Figure 4.7 is a very strong test of commitment to the supernatural. Respondents were asked "How close do you feel to God most of the time?" and to place themselves on a six-point scale where one stood for very close and six stood for not at all close. Nearly half the American

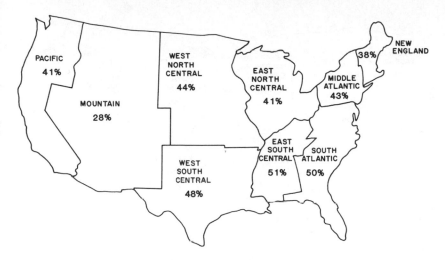

FIGURE 4.7   *Percent Feeling "Very close to God most of the time"*
(National rate = 44 percent)

Note: Mountain region includes only Colorado, Arizona, and Montana.

population (44 percent) placed themselves at one. Another 17 percent placed themselves at two and another 21 percent at three. Thus, 82 percent feel somewhat close to God. To give maximum opportunity for regional differences to appear, Figure 4.7 shows the proportions who placed themselves at one on the closeness scale. Aside from the obviously faulty low rate for the Mountain region, once again there is little difference across the regions.

We think these findings justify our assertion that the vague God of liberal theologians is not the God of the American people. Such a God is not behind everything that happens; one could hardly feel very close to so remote a God.

The fact that belief in God does not fluctuate much by region, and everywhere is very high, suggests that low church membership and attendance rates in the Pacific region are a sign of weak church organizations, not a symptom of the rise of secular humanism. This will be very important to our analyses in Part V, where we see how cults flourish where substantial numbers of people are unchurched but not irreligious, which is a very good description of the Pacific region.

Afterlife

One of the most recurrent themes in religious doctrines is life beyond death. The burial practices of the Neanderthal demonstrate that this belief was well developed at least 100,000 years ago, and it would not be

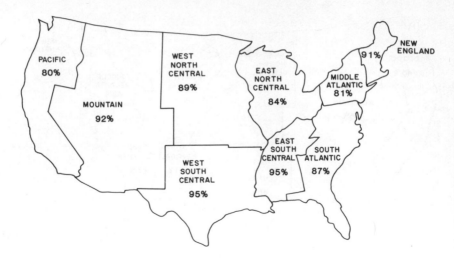

FIGURE 4.8   *Percent Sure That "There is life beyond death"*
(National rate = 86 percent)

Note: Mountain region includes only Montana, Arizona, and Utah.

surprising to find it among even earlier ancestors of our species. Belief in an afterlife is a religious compensator of extraordinary power and flexibility. It comforts those who feel shortchanged in their earthly existence, for they will benefit thereby in the world to come. Moreover, it offers immense comfort for the universal human predicament — that life is short. Rich and poor alike are promised triumph over their mortality.

To assess Americans' belief in life after death, we found it necessary to draw upon a national sample other than the one used to examine belief in God. That study also attempted to assess belief in an afterlife, but the two items devoted to this matter were seriously defective. The data we show in Figure 4.8 also were collected by NORC, as part of a massive study of anti-Semitism conducted by the Survey Research Center, University of California, Berkeley (Glock and Stark, 1966). Details of the sample design can be found in Selznick and Steinberg (1969). Unfortunately, once again many states in the Mountain region were omitted. However, in this sample, Utah replaced Colorado; thus, the Mountain region is based on respondents from Montana, Arizona, and Utah. Because Colorado, with very low church membership (424), was replaced with the number one church membership state of Utah (836), the data are probably somewhat more representative of the region as a whole, thus bringing it into closer alignment with other regions. These data were collected in 1964, making them nearly ten years older than the other survey used in this chapter. But this should not matter because examinations of poll data show impressive stability in religious belief over time; levels of belief have remained high and have varied little since the 1930s, when national polling first began.

Figure 4.8 shows that Americans overwhelmingly do believe that there is life beyond death; nationally, 86 percent are sure. Two of the three southern regions are slightly above the national average, but so are New England and the Mountain region. The Pacific region is just slightly below the national average (80 percent). The best description of these findings is a lack of regional variation. They do not sustain the existence of a Bible Belt or suggest that the West Coast is truly irreligious. The great majority of westerners believe in God and in life beyond death.

PRAYER

If belief in God is the central American religious belief, prayer is the primary mode of religious action. Prayer is the accepted means for communicating with God. Survey findings on prayer fully reinforce the conclusion that belief in God is nearly universal. Six percent of Americans reject the existence of God, but only 4 percent do not pray (the variation between the two percentages is within the normal estimation errors of samples of this size). Moreover, 75 percent of Americans report that they pray once a week or oftener. Prayer is part of the normal way of life in this country.

Given that nearly all Americans (96 percent) pray sometimes, there is little likelihood of regional variation, and no significant variations were found. In order to provide sufficient latitude for potential regional differences to appear, we selected a very stringent standard of prayer activity: the proportion who report that they pray at least once a day. Even using this criterion, America is very prayer oriented — 54 percent pray once a day or oftener.

Figure 4.9 maps the regional rates of daily prayer. With the exception of the known to be defective data on the Mountain region, only one region departs from the national average, the East South Central region (Mississippi, Alabama, Kentucky, and Tennessee). Is this our first strong hint of a Bible Belt? We think not. The rate for this region is based on a relatively small number of cases (73), and thus one can expect some random instability in the data. That means that, purely because of random fluctuations, this region will occasionally yield results far from the actual state of affairs. Because this sharp departure from the national average and from the rates for other parts of the South is the first we have observed for this region, we judge it to be random error. Even if this were

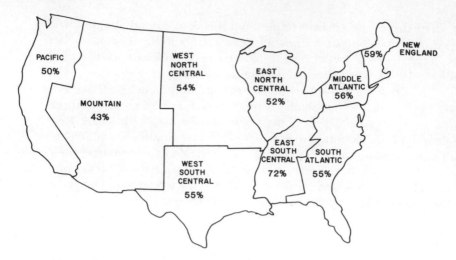

FIGURE 4.9   *Percent Praying at Least Once a Day*
(National rate = 54 percent)
Note: Mountain region includes only Colorado, Arizona, and Montana.

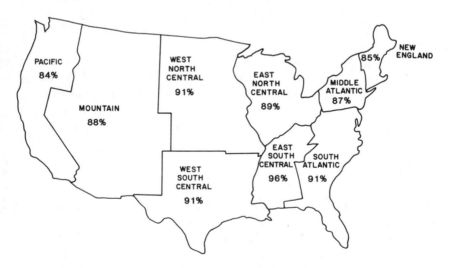

FIGURE 4.10   *Percent Saying "My prayers are heard"*
(National rate = 88 percent)
Note: Mountain region includes only Colorado, Arizona, and Montana.

not random error, we would have to diminish the size of the alleged Bible Belt because the rest of the South prays at the national average.

The most notable aspect of Figure 4.9 is that the Pacific region is not significantly below the national average. Westerners are unchurched, but they are as likely as are other Americans to pray. Even on the West Coast, 91 percent pray from time to time. One might minimize the retention of belief in God in the Unchurched Belt as a last lingering vestige of "premodern" thought. But it is hard to believe that the West Coast is the vanguard of a developing postreligious culture and a rising tide of scientific rationalism and secularity when one finds that half still pray daily and two-thirds pray at least once a week. Westerners may not be too likely to do their praying in church, but they continue to pray nonetheless.

It is not likely that West Coast prayers are nothing but empty ritual, such as saying a traditional table prayer before a festive meal. Like most Americans, people in the Pacific region believe their prayers are heard. Nationally, 88 percent gave an unqualified yes when asked if their prayers were heard. As seen in Figure 4.10, regional variations on this measure are trivial.

Once again we have failed to find the Bible Belt. Perhaps more important, we have seen that the Unchurched Belt is the proper designation for the Far West. It should not be called the secularized belt; it is not populated by a brave band of enlightened rationalists who have learned to overcome the temptations of religious compensators. Instead, the religious impulse retains its power in the West. Something is wrong with the churches in the West, not with the wellsprings of faith. In our judgment, that is to be expected. Throughout this book, we argue that religion is rooted in the inescapable and universal human predicament. People in the Pacific region may enjoy an unusually attractive and pleasant environment — beaches, mountains, immense tracts of forest and wilderness, and a soothing climate — but they have not gained the Garden of Eden. Tragedy, pain, and mortality remain life's constants. The desire to know what it all means is not to be satisfied by sunsets over Santa Catalina Island unless such a moment of natural beauty invokes special awareness of a person's religious beliefs or of the existence of the supernatural.

RELIGIOUS EXPERIENCES

In the early days of the social scientific study of religion, a great deal of attention was paid to what William James (1902) called religious experiences. These are occasions when people believe they have achieved a sense of special contact with the supernatural. But after a very active start, little attention was paid to this aspect of religion for many years.

Rodney Stark's (1965c) essay outlining a conceptual scheme for classifying the many varieties of religious experiences was the first attempt in
decades to pay serious attention to this aspect of religious commitment.
Further impetus was given to reopening such inquiry by Stark's (1965a)
second paper, which reported that, rather than being a rarity confined
to high tension sects and cults, religious experiences were common —
that the majority of members of even the most liberal and staid denominations reported having such experiences.

Since then, there has been a flood of studies of religious experiences
(cf. Back and Bourque, 1970; Greeley, 1975; Wuthnow, 1976a). Moreover, the new visibility of evangelical Protestantism, with its emphasis on
the born again experience, and the rapid growth of the charismatic
movement among Roman Catholics, with its emphasis on speaking in
tongues, have rewakened interest in religious experience even in the
mass media. Unfortunately, an important distinction has been lost in
much of the new research and writing. All manner of incidents involving drug-induced states of altered consciousness and oddments of parapsychology have been mixed in with events given religious significance.
Thus, people are asked about episodes of alleged precognition, déjà vu,
or even contact with ghosts along with experiences to which people give
religious interpretations. The results are a great jumble of disconnected
elements. We do not deny the worth of examining the prevalence of
these other mental and emotional phenomena; we simply think it important not to mistake magic and odd mental states for religion. We
therefore choose to restrict our treatment of religious experiences to
episodes people define as "an encounter between themselves and some
supernatural consciousness" (Stark, 1965c). Moreover, we continue to
think that the efficient axis for organizing such encounters is the degree
of intimacy between the two "persons" involved (Stark, 1965c).

Unfortunately, the widespread new interest in religious experiences
has not led to the collection of much useful data on the subject from
nationwide studies. Stark's initial study was limited to church members
in four Northern California counties. Most subsequent studies have
been based on students at one college or even in one course in college.
We could find only two questions about religious experience in national
polls, and one of these is of only limited use.

Confirming Experiences

The least intimate form of contact between humans and the gods is
the confirming experience. It amounts to little more than a *"specific
awareness of the presence of divinity,* akin to what James (1902) called the
'something there' experience" (Stark, 1965c:100). At issue here is not

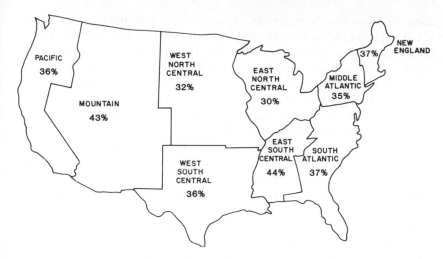

FIGURE 4.11   *Percent Ever Having "Felt as though you were very close to a*
powerful spiritual force that seemed to lift you out of yourself"
(National rate = 36 percent)

Note: Mountain region includes only Colorado, Arizona, and Montana.

simply a generalized sense of the holy or that God is everywhere, but an
episode of intense conviction that the divine is specifically and powerfully present. In a study based on church members in the San Francisco
Bay Area, more than 70 percent reported an occasion during which
they had the feeling that they were in the presence of God.

National data are available for a question written by Andrew Greeley
(1975) to measure confirming experiences. People were asked if they
had ever "Felt as though you were very close to a powerful, spiritual
force that seemed to lift you out of yourself?" The very general wording
of the question avoids the special vocabulary of particular religions; it
does not even mention God, let alone Jesus or the Holy Spirit. Thus, we
judge it a good measure of the prevalence of confirming experiences
nationally.

Figure 4.11 shows that 36 percent of Americans say they have had
such an experience. Regional variations are trivial.

Salvational Experiences

During confirming experiences, the individual feels the special presence of the divine. But in many encounters with the divine, some degree
of interaction occurs — the divine indicates awareness of the individual
and may communicate feelings, instructions, or wisdom. Among the
more common and less intimate of such interactions are *salvational expe-*

riences — episodes during which the individual feels the divine has signaled a special blessing and conferred special status on the individual. In the Christian tradition, this has been highly routinized as the "born again" experience during which individuals feel that Christ has come into their lives. Many evangelical Protestant bodies hold special services meant to produce such an experience (Stark, 1965a).

In 1975, the Gallup poll asked a national sample of Americans "Would you say that you have been 'born again' or have had a 'born again' experience — that is, a turning point in your life when you committed yourself to Christ?" There was considerable astonishment in the mass media when it was reported that 34 percent of Americans answered yes. Note, however, that, unlike the item measuring confirming experiences, this question uses the very distinctive vocabulary of evangelical Protestantism. Not surprisingly, there were sharp Catholic-Protestant differences in the proportions who answered yes — 48 percent among Protestants and only 18 percent among Catholics.

In an earlier study based on church members in the San Francisco Bay Area, even a very modest shift away from so Protestant a vocabulary greatly minimized Catholic resistance: 60 percent of Protestants and 49 percent of Catholics said that they had experienced "a sense of being saved in Christ" (Stark, 1965a). Moreover, on confirming experiences, there are no significant Catholic-Protestant differences. Thus, the Gallup item is of very limited use. It is a much better measure of how Protestant an area is than of how widespread is religious experience. Nevertheless, we can learn something from the geography of these responses.

Gallup divides the nation into four huge regions in his published reports. On this item, the South stands out: 55 percent of southerners say they are born again, but only 23 percent of easterners, 34 percent of midwesterners, and 20 percent of westerners say likewise. Does this indicate there really is a Bible Belt? The answer depends upon what one means by the term. The South stands out on this item because the item has such markedly Protestant content and because the South is so overwhelmingly Protestant. According to public opinion surveys, more than 80 percent of the population of the South Atlantic region and more than 90 percent of the population of the East South Central region are Protestants. In contrast, Protestants make up only 40 percent of the populations of the New England and the Middle Atlantic regions and about 60 percent of the populations of the other regions. If the South had only half as many Protestants as it has, its born again rate would be about the same as that of the East. Or, if the East's Protestant population were doubled, to equal that of the South, its born again rate would about equal the South's.

If we are willing to call a place a Bible Belt because its population is Protestant rather than Catholic, then the South is a Bible Belt. But if we use that term to mean fervent religious commitment, then the South is not different. Southerners are more likely to have been born again, but they are no more prone to report religious experiences when these are not defined in special Protestant terminology.

THE BIBLE BELT: MYTH AND REALITY

Thus far in this chapter, we have been unable to discover the existence of a Bible Belt in the American South. The South is notable only for its very high proportion of Protestants; it is not notable for its levels of church membership, church attendance, conventional religious belief, prayer, or religious experience. Why, then, is the South so widely and confidently perceived as a Bible Belt? We suggest two reasons. The first is sheer misperception and misrepresentation of the South by northerners, especially by liberal intellectuals and the news media. The second is more basic. We suggest there is a reality behind the Bible Belt image — a reality rooted in southern legal codes.

Northern Bias

The South has long been the target of northern scorn. This scorn began in conflicts between the urban, industrial Northeast and the rural, agricultural South, but it grew intense during the long dispute over southern racial policies and attitudes. The bitterness of the Civil War was sustained long afterwards by the obvious injustices imposed on Blacks in the South. In consequence, the South was a safe target for critics in the North, and many religious skeptics found an ideal outlet for irreverence in ridicule of southern fundamentalism. Indeed, it was inviting to dismiss all southerners as red-neck, racist Holy Rollers.

That some degree of liberal antagonism toward all religion lurked within these characterizations of the South seems evident to us in the embarrassment with which northern liberals dealt with the overwhelming religious elements in the southern civil rights movements. For example, northern liberals greatly underplayed the manifest religious content of Martin Luther King's great speeches, treating his appeals to God as mere symbols embellishing his demands for social justice. But these same journalists and intellectuals were quick to note every religious element invoked on behalf of segregation. The Bible Belt imagery was a convenient way to dismiss southerners as ignorant, superstitious bumpkins whose opinions on all matters could be rejected out of hand.

Indeed, as the South has emerged from its stigmatized past, many ex-southerners have written of the intense prejudice they have faced among northern liberals.

Despite northern distortions of southern reality, it would be incorrect to dismiss the Bible Belt as only a myth rooted in prejudice. We believe we have isolated a reality behind the myth. Three intertwined elements are involved: the extreme lack of religious diversity in the South; the extreme rural domination of state legislatures; and, growing out of these elements, a climate of intolerance for religious deviance and the enactment of this intolerance into laws.

Lack of Religious Diversity

The South is overwhelmingly Protestant, and southern Protestantism is so overwhelmingly Baptist and Methodist that southerners have had little need to accommodate even many major Protestant denominations, let alone Catholics or Jews. Thus, anti-Semitism and anti-Catholicism are relatively common in the South, as they are in very Protestant areas outside the South (Glock and Stark, 1966). It is not that Protestantism causes religious intolerance; religious intolerance is central to the entire Judeo-Christian tradition. It is not difficult to understand why religions holding that they alone possess the true faith are intolerant of "false" faiths.

The more interesting questions are about how such religions become tolerant of other faiths. Although many factors are probably involved, a key element seems to be social necessity — religions accommodate themselves to one another when they must coexist. For example, Roman Catholicism did not evolve its doctrine of the "unconscious Catholic," which opened the possibility of salvation for all persons sincere in their particular religion, so long as the church enjoyed majority status. It was as a minority faith in the United States and Great Britain that this accommodation took place. Similarly, many Protestant groups would have welcomed being named the established church of the new American nation, but each lacked the power to dominate and thus all were denied establishment. Religious tolerance came hard wherever it has been achieved and has always been in response to religious diversity. Lacking such diversity, the South has not faced the necessity or the opportunity to develop a social climate hospitable to religious differences.

Rural Domination of Legislatures

Until well into the 1960s, when the Supreme Court intervened, many state governments were disproportionately influenced by rural districts. This was especially true for states in the South. Rural districts with sparse populations often had as much or even more representation in state legislatures as did a large city. This often was described as giving more votes to cows than to people, but, in fact, cows were not represented in government. It was rural people who had the most say in enacting laws. If there is a Bible Belt, it is to be found in the rural areas of America.

The consequence of rural domination of legislatures in the South, in combination with a lack of religious diversity, was the enactment of sectarian religious positions into law. Indeed, if one examines the media depiction of the South as a Bible Belt, it is clear that the coverage usually has been prompted by legal disputes rooted in religious doctrine. Among the earliest of these to attract northern scorn were prohibition (both before and after the national experiment with prohibiting the sale of alcoholic beverages) and obscenity statutes. But the high point of media characterization of the South as a benighted Bible Belt was the famous Scopes monkey trial in 1925. At issue was a Tennessee statute that prohibited teaching the theory of evolution in public schools. A high school teacher in the small town of Dayton intentionally violated the statute in order to bring a test case before the courts. The famous monkey trial became a national sensation in the press and has since inspired movie and Broadway reenactments. Scopes was convicted and fined $100, and anti-evolution laws long remained in force in many southern states.

Religiously inspired legislation has sustained the view of the South as a Bible Belt, for the passage of such laws appears to indicate that the majority of southerners supports them. How could religion be enacted into statutes if most people opposed such laws? But that may well have been the case. The excessive rural domination of legislatures across the South made it entirely possible that a fundamentalist minority could pass such statutes.

We first became interested in legislation as the basis of the perception of the South as a Bible Belt when we discovered that the South was unusual in having so few cult movements and that those to be found there are all so new (see chapters 9 and 10). This could not be attributed to unusually high church membership rates. Trying to explain these findings, we discovered that, until very recently, most cults were illegal in the South. For example, until recently, most southern states prohibited fortune-telling. Broadly interpreted, this statute not only prohibited astrologers and palm readers, but Spiritualists and Theosophists whose claims to communicate with the spirit world involve foretelling the future. We have many occasions in this book to note the inability of even the most repressive government to eliminate religious deviance, but legal sanctions will deter such activity considerably and will prompt many people to go elsewhere to pursue their religious or magical commitments in a more hospitable environment. Having found that southern laws accounted for the lack of southern cults, we were led to examine the role of rural domination of legislatures in enacting the laws that earned the South its mythical status as a Bible Belt.

Intolerance of Religious Diversity

Laws carry a legitimacy of their own. People who might have tolerated an act had it not been illegal often will judge this same act to be bad because it is prohibited by law. This is not simply to say that people do not care to risk legal penalties, but that they will tend to be influenced in their perceptions of the moral status of an act by knowing that it has been deemed unlawful. Thus, many southerners probably took a more negative view of fortune-telling, for example, because it was outlawed than did people in states where it was legal. We suspect that the South will display noticeably high levels of intolerance for religious deviance not just from lack of experience with religious diversity, but because of the many legal sanctions directed against religious deviance. Put another way, if our analysis of the reality behind the Bible Belt myth is correct, if it rests on religious homogeneity and the enactment of religious conformity into law, then southerners ought to reflect higher levels of intolerance for religious deviance.

Figures 4.12 and 4.13 examine this hypothesis. Using the same survey as we did to examine belief in life after death, we are able to examine tolerance for atheists. Each respondent was asked, "Suppose a man admitted in public that he did not believe in God." Figure 4.12 shows the proportion who said no when asked, "Do you think he should be allowed to teach in a public high school?" Nationally, nearly two-thirds (61 percent) of Americans did not believe an acknowledged atheist ought to be permitted to teach. But here, as we suspected, the South does stand out sharply. A majority takes this position everywhere except in the Pacific region (47 percent), but the southern majorities are overwhelming.

Figure 4.13 shows the proportions who think an acknowledged atheist's book ought to be removed from a public library. Only about a third of Americans (35 percent) nationally took this position, and in most regions outside the South, the proportions are below 30 percent. In the southern regions, however, 48 to 50 percent would remove an atheist's book from the library.

Thus, we have mapped the underlying reality behind the myth of the Bible Belt. It is not southern religiousness, but southern laws and southern attitudes toward religious dissent and deviance, that have sustained the imagery of the South as a backwater bastion of fulminating fundamentalist passions.

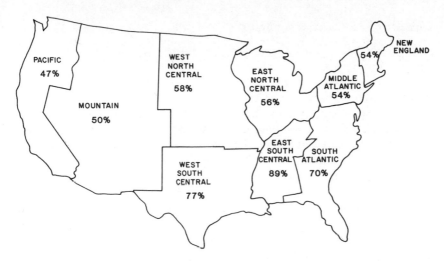

FIGURE 4.12   *Percent Thinking an Acknowledged Atheist Should Not Teach in a Public High School*
(National rate = 61 percent)

Note: Mountain region includes only Montana, Arizona, and Utah.

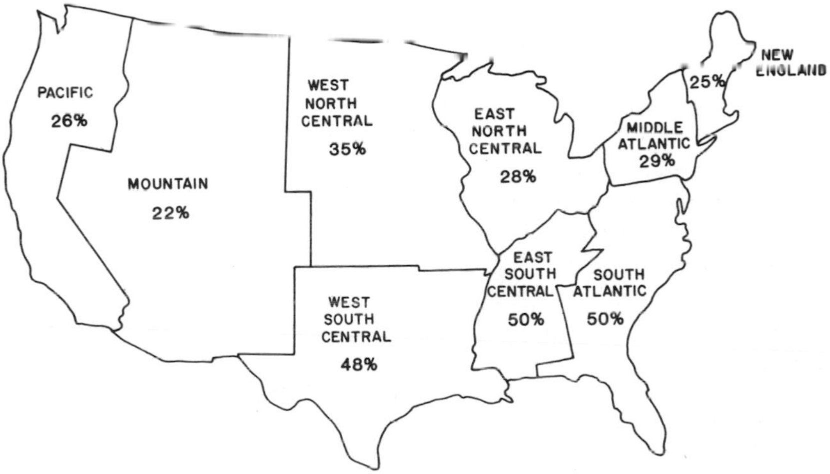

FIGURE 4.13   *Percent Thinking an Acknowledged Atheist's Book Ought to be Removed from a Public Library*
(National rate = 35 percent)

Note: Mountain region includes only Montana, Arizona, and Utah.

SOURCES OF THE UNCHURCHED BELT

If the Bible Belt is substantially mythical, the Unchurched Belt is not. And it is not new. We have examined data for 1906 that show that then, as now, church membership rates were far lower along the shores of the Pacific than anywhere else in the nation (Bainbridge and Stark, 1981). In this chapter, we have seen that it is not for lack of religious belief or reliance upon prayer that people on the West Coast are unchurched. The "irreligiousness" of the region is limited to a lack of affiliation with religious organizations.

What makes the churches so weak in the West? At present, we have only just begun research on the sources of the Unchurched Belt. In time, we hope to offer a relatively complete explanation. But already we have discovered a major part of the answer: *population instability*.

The Old West was socially disorganized. It was difficult to establish order in brand-new towns filled with newcomers, drifters, and strangers. Churches and schools had yet to be built. Often there was not even a sheriff or a marshal, let alone a court or a jail. This was the essence of the Wild West. Today there are no gunfights in the streets of the West; the saloons must observe licensing laws; the courts are busy; and the jails are full. Yet, in the most fundamental sense, frontier conditions persist. Western cities are still filled with newcomers and strangers, for western populations have remained extremely mobile. Large numbers of newcomers move into western cities each year; large numbers move out; and large numbers shift their residence from one neighborhood to another. For example, 55 percent of the people in San Diego, California, moved during the 1960–1970 decade. Such massive rates of movement erode all forms of voluntary organizations, including churches.

People who move to a new city, or from one suburb to another, must reaffiliate with a church, a fraternal lodge, a service club, and other such organizations. People who move often must reaffiliate often or let their memberships lapse. At the very least, there will be a natural lag time in reaffiliation, and some people will move again before this normal lag time is up, thus continuing to be unaffiliated. These effects of movement undoubtedly are greatly amplified in communities where large proportions of the population move often. In more stable communities, newcomers are easily reconnected to a church or to other organizations by neighbors and fellow workers who are members. But to the degree that one's neighbors and fellow workers are themselves unaffiliated newcomers, the reconnecting process is impeded.

Wuthnow and Christiano (1979) have found that people who have recently moved are less likely than nonmovers to attend church. We have found that cities with high rates of population turnover have low church membership rates. Thus, for example, we found a correlation of −.39 between population growth for the decade 1960–1970 and the church membership rate for American metropolitan areas. When we restricted the analysis to the 60 largest metropolitan areas (for which complete data on in-migration and intracity migration were available) we found an even stronger correlation (−.65) between population turnover and church membership. We explore these matters more fully in Chapter 14.

Thus, the transience of western living appears to be the primary force undercutting membership in religious organizations. This is not the whole story, of course. We also suspect that people who move West are less inclined to belong to churches and that the mainline churches have failed to adapt to western conditions, to learn to go out and find their members among the mobile masses of strangers.

CONCLUSION

The regional patterns of religion we have examined in this chapter make it clear that the United States does not have a religious economy; rather, it has several religious economies. Although religious belief and prayer are high everywhere, organized religion is very weak in the West. There, in an unbroken belt beginning at the Mexican border and continuing through Canada and Alaska, church membership rates are very low — only about a third or less of residents actually belong to a religious organization. These people are unchurched, but not irreligious. Hence, a major market exists in the Unchurched Belt for new religious organizations.

In later chapters, we explore the numerous efforts of new religious movements to fill this unmet need. We show that cults abound in the West precisely because the conventional churches are so weak and that the South is notable for having so few cult movements and members. But, as we have seen in this chapter, this feature of the South is not a reflection of the unusual strength of conventional religions there. The Bible Belt is mainly myth. Church membership and attendance are not unusually high in the South, nor is religious belief. Instead, the reality behind the mythical Bible Belt is to be found in an unusual tendency to enact sectarian Protestant norms and values into law. In part, this is a reflection of the South's lack of religious diversity. In part, it was produced by an unusual degree of rural domination of state legislatures. We have seen that the South does differ from other regions in its opposition to religious deviance. Thus, both the West and the South demonstrate the importance of the surrounding sociocultural environment in the rise of new religious movements.

▌▌ *Sect Movements*

5 *The Eternal Exodus:*
Causes of Religious Dissent and Schism

Among the most common events in the history of religions is schism — a group of disgruntled members breaks away from a religious organization in order to found a new organization. When such groups leave, they rarely do so quietly or amicably. Instead, they justify their departure in severe denunciations of their parent body. "The church has betrayed its holy mission on earth." "It has become worldly and sinful." Indeed, the departing sect claims that it, not the parent body, embodies continuity with the original faith. The sect is not a *new* church, but the restored original. The parent body is the "new" religion — a sinful perversion of the original legacy.

In this chapter, we describe how sects are born. But to do so, we must describe how sects are transformed, how they lose their original fervor, their high tension stance toward the world. Sects erupt from established religious bodies because those bodies have changed; behind the excessive rhetorical denunciations sects direct over their shoulders as they exit the church is a basic truth. Successful sects do tend to be transformed into churches and, in so doing, compromise with the world. Thus, the causes of sect formation are to be found in the process by which successful sects tend to become worldly.

NIEBUHR'S THEORY

It was by recognizing the link between sect transformation and the formation of new sects that H. Richard Niebuhr made his great contribution to the sociology of religion. Niebuhr wanted to account for the existence of the crowded religious economy of Christian nations, especially the existence of the vast number of competing Protestant denominations and the continuing emergence of new ones. In his classic book, *The Social Sources of Denominationalism* (1929), he found a cycle in the history of Protestant groups. New groups nearly always began in protest against the "loss of faith" of the body out of which they came. That is, the great, respectable denominations — the churches — all began as sects. They arose precisely because the parent body, having made peace with the world, no longer served the needs of a substantial minority of members, namely, the disinherited, those who need the most intense otherworldly comforts to compensate them for the deprivations they experience in this life. As Niebuhr (1929:19) put it: "In Protestant history the sect has ever been the child of an outcast minority, taking its rise in the religious revolts of the poor, of those who were without effective representation in church or state."

But, in Niebuhr's opinion, sects are unable to maintain their high tension with the world. As we see in Chapter 7, he was unclear about why sects tended to be transformed into churches (and, as we shall see, many are not). But he was clear that, if sects prospered, if they attracted a large following of the disinherited, over time they lost their fervor. That is, sects that arise as effective vehicles for religious protest, and that therefore provide for the intensely otherworldly needs of their founders, over time make peace with the world and therefore abandon the religious needs of the deprived people they originally were formed to serve.

Because the really successful sects are transformed into churches, the conditions are reestablished that previously produced these sects. Within churches, religious frustrations build up among the deprived until they burst forth once more in a new sect movement. Then this movement, too, is transformed into a church, and once again a new sect bursts forth. The many denominations are the result of many cycles in this process. Because the process is dynamic, it provides for the endless formation of new sects and for them successively to be tamed by the world.

Niebuhr's original theory has the attraction of being very general and therefore very widely applicable. It had the shortcoming of being vague or silent about the mechanisms that specifically operate to transform sects into churches. He merely asserted that the coming of a second generation dooms the sect's resistance to the world:

> By its very nature the sectarian type of organization is valid for only one generation. The children born to the voluntary members of the first generation begin to make the sect a church long before they have arrived at the years of discretion. . . . Rarely does a second generation hold the convictions

it has inherited with a fervor equal to that of its fathers, who fashioned these convictions in the heat of conflict and at the risk of martyrdom. As generation succeeds generation, the isolation of the [sect] from the world becomes more difficult. (Niebuhr, 1929:19–20)

In Chapter 7, we spell out why the second generation may have this impact on sects.

Niebuhr also is uninformative about the processes by which schisms actually form within religious organizations, where sect leadership comes from, and why people prefer to reestablish their old faith (form a sect) rather than to embrace a wholly new faith (a cult movement). Finally, he does not really explain why a religious body cannot both make peace with the world and continue to provide adequate compensators for scarce rewards. He takes it for granted that worldly churches lack powerful otherworldly resources, but he does not clearly explain the fundamental contradiction between these two dimensions of religious commitment.

THE BASIS OF SCHISM

By the term *schism,* we mean the splitting of an organization into two or more groups. We conceive of all organizations as consisting of *social networks,* which consist of the interpersonal relationships among members of the organization. To belong to an organization, an individual must enjoy relatively close and enduring ties to at least one other group member. Groups differ in the degree to which their members are attached to one another; they can be characterized according to the density and intensity of interpersonal relations among members. Individuals within a group may differ not only in their number of attachments to others, but in the distribution of their ties to others. That is, if we map the complete set of attachments within a group, we may find *cleavages* — lines of weak attachments between cliques (subnetworks that are internally strongly interconnected) — persons being attached mainly to members of the same clique.

Schisms in organizations or groups are most likely to occur along lines of cleavage. That is, when internal conflicts break out in a religious organization, they usually do so between subnetworks that existed prior to the outbreak of dispute. Thus, Harrison White and his associates (White and Breiger, 1975; White et al., 1976) showed that the eruption of conflict in a monastery — culminating in the resignation and expulsion of many members — arose precisely at a long-standing line of cleavage. Long before the fighting began, the monks had constituted two distinct subnetworks within which relationships among individuals

were dense and intense, but with few and only weak relationships existing among individuals of different subnetworks.

All forces that act to produce or enhance cleavages in an organization's social network will greatly facilitate the outbreak of conflict and
thus the danger of schism — the exodus of one subnetwork to form a
new organization. Many factors can produce cleavage. In the next chapter, we suggest that Amish and Mennonite groups split so often because
they tend to form new communities distant from the main group, and
over time the isolation of these communities produces cleavage. Cleavages can also be caused by geographic barriers, political boundaries,
cultural or language barriers — by everything that limits the formation
or maintenance of close ties within a network. However, sect movements
often are not produced by distance, language barriers, or political
boundaries. They frequently erupt in a single, small congregation made
up of people who have known one another their entire lives. What
causes cleavages in such a group?

Sources of Cleavage

We propose in Chapter 1 that there are three dimensions of religious
commitment and that these are differentially related to power. There
are the *worldly* rewards available through religious organizations. These
tend to be dominated by the powerful and, indeed, the powerful will
prefer religious organizations to yield high levels of rewards. There are
the *otherworldly* compensators offered by religious organizations for
scarce rewards. These will be of greatest salience to the less powerful,
for they, not the powerful, most experience such scarcity. There are also
universal compensators of religion, which serve the needs of powerful
and powerless alike for those intensely desired rewards that seem not to
exist in the natural world.

The universal dimension of religious commitment gives humans
common cause to sustain religious organizations. It inspires the view
that rich and poor alike are in the hands of God. But the worldly and
otherworldly dimensions of religion reflect the fact that members of a
religious organization do not have identical concerns. Indeed, these
propositions rest on the more general principle that all religious organizations encompass members who differ in their degree of power and
privilege, that the reality of social stratification penetrates into all religious organizations. Some members are leading more successful lives
and gaining a greater share of earthly rewards than others. We are able
to deduce in our theory that, where stratification exists, there will be
cleavage in a social network.

We propose that people who lack a substantial share of some scarce reward will tend not to enjoy close relationships with those who possess this reward in abundance. Misery may love company, but it does not love company that heightens the sense of misery. Moreover, when people have very unequal levels of rewards, relationships between them are awkward and often embarrassing. The privileged fear envy. The disadvantaged risk a blow to self-esteem by close contact with the privileged. Where there is substantial inequality in a network, subnetworks will tend to separate as people pursue relationships with others who are similarly situated. The conception of who is and who is not "our kind of people" is endemic in highly stratified groups.

Sources of Conflict

Stratification does more within religious organizations than merely produce lines of cleavage. It also constitutes an inevitable basis for dispute over whom the religious group is to serve and how. To the extent that a religious group emphasizes the otherworldly dimension of commitment (stresses effective compensators for scarce rewards), it must deemphasize the worldly dimension. Religious movements can supply really efficacious otherworldly compensators only if they are in a relatively high state of tension with the surrounding society. But such tension is contrary to the interests of more powerful members.

It is very difficult for a religious organization to offer credible and effective compensators to some members for scarce rewards if it is at the same time exhibiting, in the lives of its most influential members, the legitimacy and availability of the rewards in question. For example, the most credible form of religious compensators for unfulfilled worldly desires is to reject worldly values. For people who are poor, the most effective compensators define material goods as of little value in comparison to heavenly bliss: self-denial on earth buys riches in the world to come. That this is the most credible form for such compensators to take is demonstrated by their competitive advantage in the religious marketplace. They are so commonly in use because they tend to drive out other varieties.

But what happens if a religious body offering such compensators also contains many members who are not rejecting earthly rewards, but are piling them up? Suppose, too, that these people need not hide their "sinful love of worldly things," but in fact openly display their success while basking in the approval of the church — that, indeed, they control the church. Such people erode the credibility of the compensators. Moreover, the privileged will dislike continued emphasis of these particular compensators, for they are a slur against their own moral standing. Their own religiousness is based not upon compensators for scarce rewards, but upon the need for compensators for unavailable rewards (such as eternal life). High tension is not needed to provide universal compensators because no one can be observed to achieve these rewards directly and thus make mockery of the promises of faith.

It is not simply the case that religious organizations will contain two constituencies, one committed to higher tension, the other to lower. Rather, as Niebuhr recognized, over time, the privileged faction will tend to get its way. It will use its control of the religious organization to reduce tension with the surrounding society, for such tension will tend to hamper the privileged. That is, to the degree that the religious group is in tension with the external society, it will limit powerful members' ability to realize their full potential for success in secular life and it will reduce the supply and value of the direct rewards the religious group supplies to members. Thus, to the extent that a religious group contains or comes to contain a number of relatively privileged members and to the extent that they can influence group policies, tension with the external world will be reduced. In Chapter 7, we examine several mechanisms by which sects will tend to develop a privileged membership and show how these members will cause a transformation of sects into churches.

The opposite side of this coin is that, to the extent a religious group reduces its tension with society, there will be a growing demand among its less powerful members for more efficacious compensators for scarcity. These less privileged members' concerns will have clear focus, for they will recognize that their grievance was caused by change. They will believe that their religious group has deserted them, as it has deserted its historic theology. They will not need to cast about for a more suitable faith. Rather, they will demand restoration of the tried and therefore true religious solution to their needs. Put another way, as religious movements reduce their tension and thus better serve the needs of their dominant members, support in favor of a sect movement grows. All that is needed then is leaders, people capable of mobilizing the discontented and organizing them into a counterforce.

Sources of Sect Leadership

The rank and file do not produce social movements; they merely support them. All movements need leaders — persons with the capacity to focus discontent and direct organized actions. The notion that "the times" produce the needed leadership is an empty slogan. The times produce opportunities, not leaders. Indeed, when one looks at leaders of any social movement — be it sect, cult, or political rebellion — one finds leaders with considerable preparation for their roles. They are not thrust up from the rank and file; they have past experience relevant to leading the movement and the resources to dominate it. In the case at hand, sect leaders usually have previous leadership experience — and thus some significant status — in the parent body. They have usually been clergy or at least prominent lay leaders.

Why will some people sacrifice their standing in a parent religious body in order to lead a schismatic sect movement? Often they sincerely believe their actions are motivated wholly by theology. Although they are not among the least privileged themselves, they will have been so situated in the network of the parent group that they will have had their primary social relations with the subnetwork in need of more efficacious compensators for scarcity. That they will interpret these needs as justification for the historic high tension theology of the religious group is to be expected.

But there is more here than theological conviction, and certainly more than altruism. For some experienced leaders, the opportunities inherent in leading a new sect will much more than offset their potential losses from giving up their standing in the parent body. For example, it obviously is more rewarding to be bishop of a large, reputable denomination than to be bishop of a small, deviant sect; but it may be more rewarding to be bishop of a sect than to be assistant pastor of a rural congregation of a large, reputable denomination. We propose that, when some potential sect leaders can expect to increase their rewards by leading a sect movement, they will do so. Those leaders who already have the closest contact with a potential sect constituency will have the most to gain by defection from the parent organization. Thus are sects born.

External Forces

When people calculate the costs and benefits of launching sect movements, they do not do so in a vacuum. In proposing to move into a higher state of tension with the environment, people must consider how that environment is likely to respond, for religious deviance sometimes engenders coercive reactions from society. Thus, sect formation will be most frequent when the environment is most tolerant of religious diversity. To the extent that the environment punishes religious deviance, sect formation is curtailed. As we see later in this chapter and many times throughout this book, no environment, no matter how hostile toward religious deviance, is able wholly to curtail sect (or cult) formation. Repression will inhibit such actions, but only the actual formation of deviant religious movements is curtailed by repression, not the impulses to form them or the real needs behind these impulses. To the degree that sect formation is suppressed, the religious impulse for higher tension faith may take on exotic and extremely militant forms.

The environment also influences levels of deprivation — the number of people experiencing relative deprivation and the degree of their deprivation. Thus, for example, an economic depression can greatly increase both the proportion of persons in a religious organization who desire a higher tension faith and the depth of their need. Thus, sect formation ought to increase at such a time. An uneven economic boom can have a similar effect by greatly increasing the gap between the least privileged and everyone else.

Not only people on the very bottom of the stratification system produce sects (cf. Pinard, 1967; Curtis and Zurcher, 1971). Relative, not absolute, deprivation is the basis of sect formation. Sects can be produced by people who are not on the bottom, but whose standard of comparison is with those better off than themselves (cf. Simon and Gagnon, 1976). Moreover, such people may be at the bottom of the social scale within a given religious organization. Thus, middle-class people may launch a sect to break away from a church dominated by an aristocracy, a common pattern in Europe that can be seen in the case of the recent sect movement that erupted from the Episcopalian church in the United States.

An excellent example that has been the subject of good quantitative research is the schism that divided Pennsylvania Quakerism in 1827 (Doherty, 1967). The dominant clique within the Quakers was rapidly moving this former sect churchward because its leading members had achieved high status in secular society and wished to accommodate their religion to the world that was rewarding them so greatly. Compared with other Quakers, this clique had also developed many deep social relationships with non-Quakers and thus had an interest in reducing the cultural gap with these valuable associates. But Quakers who participated less in the benefits of this secularization process provided a constituency for a sect movement that was organized under the leadership of a fiery but aged ideologue, Elias Hicks.

The Quakers split into two parts of comparable size, an Orthodox faction and a Hicksite faction. The Orthodox group consisted of the previously dominant clique, which was now able to reduce still further its tension with the surrounding sociocultural environment. The Hicksites sought to reverse this secularization by reemphasizing the old sectarian traditions, and they went into higher tension with the sociocultural environment than Quakerism as a whole had experienced before the split.

Copious quantitative data culled from old records by Robert W. Doherty demonstrate that the Orthodox faction enjoyed greater wealth and social position than the Hicksites, just as our theory of sect formation predicts. However, the Quakers had been so successful in farming and commerce that even the Hicksites were generally better off than the average non-Quaker. In Philadelphia, only 15 percent of the non-Quakers who were sampled owned real estate worth more than $3,000 (Doherty, 1967:43, 107). But 34 percent of the Hicksites and 46 percent of the Orthodox faction were this prosperous. In agricultural Chester County, the same pattern is revealed in a variety of data. Only 9 percent of non-Quakers owned six or more grown cattle, compared with 18 percent of the Hicksites and 29 percent of the Orthodox. Just 41 percent of the non-Quakers owned more than 100 acres, but 51 percent of the Hicksites and 64 percent of the Orthodox had this much land (Doherty, 1967:57, 60, 108).

Whatever the objective wealth of a religious group, relative differences between members tend to produce a worldly faction wishing lower tension with the sociocultural environment and an otherworldly faction wishing efficacious, specific compensators for the rewards possessed by their more prosperous coreligionists. If the differences are great enough and if sufficiently deep social cleavages exist, relative deprivation will produce a sect movement seeking higher tension, as was the case for the Hicksite schism of 1827.

A religion can become so worldly that it is unable to offer efficacious compensators of the universal form. If a religion's conception of the supernatural becomes too vague, distant, inactive, that religion's ability to explain the meaning of life and to offer life beyond death may suffer. In Part V, we argue that this is what has so weakened many mainline Protestant denominations in recent times. In such cases, even the most powerful members may defect in search of more adequate religion.

Implications

All religious organizations contain an internal contradiction that creates cleavage and can ignite conflict. To the degree that members differ in power and privilege, they will tend to form subnetworks, each having distinctive and conflicting religious needs. The more powerful will want to reduce tension; the less powerful will want to raise it or keep it high. No religious organization can simultaneously be in both low and high tension with its environment. Therefore, to serve one constituency is to fail to serve the other.

In the next two chapters, we note that many sect movements never reduce their tension with the world, but this consigns them to obscurity — they fail to grow. Sects that thrive soon develop and attract a substantial number of successful members. In consequence, it is the truly successful sects, those most able to provide effective compensators for scarcity and those that perform that function for substantial numbers of the least powerful, that, over time, abandon their otherworldly function. Lutherans, Presbyterians, Methodists, Congregationalists, Disciples of Christ, and Quakers were great sect movements in times past. Today they do not dwell upon the passages of the Bible that condemn the pleasures of the world, for each of these sects was transformed into a church, and each in turn spawned many new sects.

An analysis of the sources of sect formation leads to the conclusion that no single religious organization can offer the full range of religious services for which there is substantial market demand. No one church can minister to the needs of everyone. This means that the natural state of the religious economy is pluralism. To the extent that religious freedom exists, there will be many organized faiths, each specializing in certain segments of the market. Moreover, this market will be dynamic, with a constant influx of new organizations and the frequent demise of others.

Can such a conclusion be squared with history? Have there not been societies dominated by a single, universal religious organization? With the possible exception of tiny, primitive societies, we know of no society in which one religious organization—even though backed by the full coercive force of the state—was able to come even close to serving the full religious market. To justify this statement, we examine what must be seen as the most plausible exception to our claim—the medieval Catholic church.

In historical impression, the Catholic church towers above feudal Europe, an imposing, international monolith, jealous of its claims to be the One True Church, bloody in its response to challenge, ever alert to the slightest breath of heresy or schism. But this historical impression is illusion. The Catholic church may well have been the noblest attempt ever made to serve the whole range of the religious market through one organization, but it never succeeded, despite the wisdom and administrative skill of the clergy and some real strokes of organizational genius in adapting the church to the contradictory demands placed upon it. Henry VIII and Martin Luther did not sunder the religious unity of Europe. It never was.

However, before we examine the religious situation of medieval Europe and the inability of a single church to serve the major segments of that religious economy, it is necessary to consider a second cruel dichotomy that confronts religious organizations. This concerns whether the religious organization will also be a purveyor of magic.

PRIESTS AND MAGICIANS: THE UNEASY BALANCE

In Chapter 2, we distinguish between religion and magic on the basis of the generality of the compensators each provides. Religions always deal in the most general compensators, some so huge they require a supernatural source, but magic involves only rather specific compensators, which sometimes do not require any specific supernatural assumptions. But most magic, in most of human history, has, like religion, invoked the supernatural.

In discussing magic, we approvingly invoke Durkheim's famous dictum that there can be no church of magic. This follows from the fact that magicians deal only in short-term exchanges and lack the long-term compensators needed to bind people into durable organizations. This proposition, of course, applies only to pure magicians, those who deal only in magic. Clearly, the obverse does not hold. There can indeed be churches that, in addition to religion, also supply a great deal of magic. In Western civilization, especially since the rise of Christianity, churches have typically supplied a considerable amount of magic. But this is not typical of the other great world religions. Throughout Asia, for example, there long has been a very clear separation between priest and magician, between churches and client cults.

To better grasp the terrible dilemmas faced by the Catholic church during the era when it tried in vain to be the universal Church, we must first see why there is good reason for religions to eliminate magic from the services they supply. To do so, of course, they must let magicians take over that function. Thus arises the typical Asian symbiosis in which religion condones or at least ignores the existence of magicians and the public is free to seek magic from magicians and religion from the priests.

The Risks of Magic

The great compensators on which religions are based are beyond empirical disproof. It is impossible to show that God did not create the universe. It is impossible to prove that humans do not have souls or that these souls do not rise to heaven at the moment of death. It is impossible to prove that Jesus will not come again. Science is helpless to disprove reincarnation or to show that eating pork is not a sin. In contrast, magic often is very vulnerable to disproof. Magic deals in specific compensators that promise fulfillment in the empirical world. When a shaman casts spells to heal a sick child, the child is supposed to recover. A love potion is supposed to cause infatuation. Such promises can fail and be shown to have failed. The child may die. The object of affection may scorn an advance. Compared with religious compensators, magic is very risky goods.

That the most central compensators of religion are immune to disconfirmation, while the compensators of magic often are disconfirmed, has a profound sociological implication. It leads to the conclusion that there will be a marked tendency for religion and magic to become differentiated, for religious organizations not to deal in magic, and for specialists dealing only in magic to appear in societies. That is, as full-time religious elites appear in human societies and create powerful religious organizations, these elites will tend to pursue their own best interests by getting out of the magic business. Although the primitive, part-time priest will deal in both, as societies become more complex, the priesthood will move away from providing magical services, for to provide magic is to risk not only the failure of these services but the implication that, if their magic is false, perhaps their theology is too. Churches do not really need magic, even though a substantial demand for magic persists. Let others with less to lose run the risks of dealing in magic.

That serious risks are entailed in the practice of magic is clear from rapid fluctuations in magicians' reputations. Magicians may even be killed when they disappoint a client too greatly. Examination of the record of European witchcraft trials reveals that those tried had often practiced magical healing for a considerable time before they were denounced. Denunciations typically were prompted by a run of bad luck in treatments — often a number of children would die of a childhood epidemic despite the ministrations of the "witch" (Kieckhefer, 1976). Priests need not run such risks; so they usually withdraw from them.

The Eastern Symbiosis

Steeped as we are in the cultural patterns of the West, we are perhaps not comfortable with the notion that churches will condone magicians' activities. But that usually is the case. The hostility of Western churches to magic is a legacy of the medieval church's efforts to dominate all aspects of supernaturalism and thus to monopolize magic as well as religion. Great grief came to the Catholic church (and subsequently to many Protestant churches as well) because it tried to remain in the magic business. Elsewhere in the world, religions have tended to live in a harmonious and symbiotic relationship with magic. The major Eastern religions recognize the usefulness of magicians. People are expected to seek the most general compensators through religion but to turn to magicians to satisfy specific, immediate needs. As David Mandelbaum (1966) put it in his classic paper on this topic, a Brahmin priest will not (or only very rarely) attempt to cure an immediate and specific ailment. For this, people must consult a magician.

Surveying many Asian nations and faiths, Mandelbaum found a sharp differentiation between priests and magicians. Indeed, the two roles are recruited from very different social strata. Priests tend to come from high status families; magicians are from low status backgrounds. There usually is little or no rivalry between them; they are not competitors. The magicians lack the means to establish a church (except as they augment their magic with a fully developed religious system, an evolution we examine in Chapter 8). They spare the priests from pressures to deal in risky magical compensators — pressures that priests often find inescapable when magicians are not readily available, for the human predicament is such that we frequently confront troubles beyond direct solution for which only appeals to the supernatural seem a plausible option. If the churches will not help people seek aid, the churches must permit others to help them. Because such aid often fails to be forthcoming, churches are best advised to not deal in so "mundane" an activity.

THE ILLUSION OF A UNIVERSAL CHURCH

Our formulation of church-sect theory leads to the conclusion that no single religious organization can serve adequately the whole spectrum of needs and desires found in the religious marketplace. No society can survive with a wholly otherworldly church, for we must exist in this world and hence some people must be free of religious fetters to pursue worldly aims. Moreover, those most inclined to worldliness will have the power to create (or transform) religious organizations to suit their needs. But many other people deeply desire otherworldly comforts for their earthly dissatisfactions. This creates a social chasm no one organization can straddle successfully. But the Roman Catholic church tried to do just that. It is instructive, therefore, to examine how it tried to resolve this inherently contradictory mission and how it failed. In so doing, we shall be able to illustrate more fully the fundamental dynamics of sect formation.

What follows is not the familiar and too often distorted tale of how the Catholic church grew corrupt and worldly and thus provoked the Reformation. Subsequent Protestant attempts to create a universal Church were even less successful and, given their slimmer resources, Protestants were as vindictive in their efforts to crush religious deviance and dissent. Our primary focus is not on the Catholic church, but on the throngs who never fully accepted the church and on the countless thousands of religious movements that popped up throughout Christendom even during the height of the temporal power of the church. It is the existence of these masses of religious deviants and their unceasing organizational efforts that demonstrates the illusory nature of the universal Church.

The Persistent Pagans

In the Edict of Milan, issued in 313 A.D., the Roman Emperor Constantine revoked all anti-Christian decrees, thus legalizing the practice of this rapidly growing new religion. Imperial recognition came only after the Christian movement had become a potent social force whose support was valuable to the state. But legalization of the church did not immediately elevate Christianity into the One True Church any more than it actually signaled Constantine's authentic conversion to Christianity. Despite the later claims by Christian writers that the emperor converted upon receiving a sign from heaven before the battle of Milvian Bridge, Constantine continued, in characteristic Roman fashion, to adhere to a great variety of faiths, including the then popular sun religion as well as the Mithraic faith that flourished among the officers of the army. Constantine placed the sun, not the cross, on all his coins and declared Sunday a day of rest — in honor of the sun. Even as the Christian bishops had to ignore their emperor's mingling of Christianity with an exotic variety of other faiths and superstitions (and even his pretensions to be the thirteenth apostle), so too had they to contend with a still flourishing array of pagan competitors.

Slowly the church consolidated its power. As the empire weakened, the church filled the gap, building itself along the old imperial structure — bishops replacing imperial officials. The assault upon paganism began at the local level — wherever the church had sufficient local power to loose its monks to tear down pagan temples, topple statues of the gods, smash the shrines, and harry and drive away the priests and priestesses of the "false gods." There were periodic efforts to restore paganism (Julian attempted it in the 360s) and to protect pagan freedom, but the public manifestations of paganism were slowly smashed.

In addition to a direct assault on paganism, Christianity had, from very early days, tried to erase it by overlaying it or absorbing it. Thus, Christmas was set on December 25, the traditional day of the sun's birth (now the Son's birth) — the winter solstice. Many pagan gods and godlings became thinly disguised Christian saints.

Paganism also freely borrowed from early Christianity: "the followers of Isis adored a madonna nursing her holy child; the cult of Attis and Cybele celebrated a day of blood and fasting, followed by the Hilaria resurrection-feasts; the elitist Mithraics . . . ate a sacred meal . . . [and the sun cult] referred to Christ 'driving his chariot across the sky'" (Johnson, 1979:67). Christianity was further aided in overlaying paganism by borrowing back these pagan borrowings. Similar tactics were employed as the church moved out of the Mediterranean area into Britain, Ireland, and northern Europe. Local "pagan" faiths were attacked from the front by repression and from the flanks by overlay and absorption.

Yet the church never wholly eradicated paganism; pagan elements continued to recur in many of the deviant religious movements we consider later, and there are many historical clues to suggest that isolated groups and secret societies continued to sustain a variety of the old pagan faiths into modern times. Indeed, elements of paganism are clear in many of the practices that brought tens of thousands before ecclesiastical courts charged with "superstition" or "witchcraft" from the 14th century on into the 17th.

The Constancy of Sect Movements

From its earliest days, Christianity was afflicted with conflict and schism. It arose as a Jewish sect that Paul transformed into a cult, which in turn produced deep conflict with the Jerusalem branch of the faith. Slowly the formative conflicts were overcome and an orthodox theology was developed. Yet unity did not result. Pockets of dissent were widespread. As the church overcame its extreme tension with surrounding society, as it came to be the dominant faith, its increased worldliness prompted the inevitable reaction: Sect movements began to break away. Near the end of the second century the Montanists sprang up, condemning church compromises and reemphasizing the imminence of the Second Coming. The Montanist demand for a return to a high tension faith and its embodiment in schismatic organizations was repeated unceasingly down through the centuries.

The Manichaeans were an early and very successful sect movement; St. Augustine himself was a member of this group for nine years before reconverting to the Roman church. The Manichaean commitments to absolute chastity and stringent asceticism are reflected in Augustine's views on monastic life. Other sect movements that achieved widespread followings include the Waldensians and the Albigensians. As Paul Johnson put it in his lucid *A History of Christianity* (1979:250):

> We mistakenly think of medieval institutional Christianity as an immensely solid and stable structure . . . [but it] disorganized with comparative ease; an accidental conjunction of two or more of a huge number of forces could bring about de-Christianization over quite a large area very suddenly. Thus St. Bernard of Clairvaux on a preaching tour of southern France in 1145 reported

that a number of heresies were common and that in large areas Catholicism, as he understood it, had disappeared.

The defections from Catholicism always constituted an effort to gain a higher tension faith—to call the church back to its early days of intense otherworldliness. When the poor of Lyons, France, rallied to the call of Waldo in the late 12th century to return to apostolic poverty, they quickly sent representatives to Rome to urge the church fathers to restore high tension Christianity. Upon seeing these Waldensians in Rome in 1179, Walter Map wrote: "They go about two by two, barefoot, clad in woolen garments, owning nothing, holding all things in common like the Apostles . . . if we admit them, we shall be driven out" (Johnson, 1976: 251).

Three years later, the Waldensians were excommunicated. But even though the church moved with fire and sword against its sect challengers, it could not prevent chronic organized dissent. In Chapter 22, we review the constant outbreak of messianic sect rebellions in the medieval cities of northern Europe. But it would take an enormous volume to report even the barest outline of the thousands of sects that challenged the medieval church. When Martin Luther thundered against the worldliness of the church, he said nothing new. He merely repeated what had been said by countless previous sect leaders ever since the church began to come to terms with external society. Our theoretical results show that no one religious institution can serve the whole religious economy, that no institution can be both church and sect. That the Catholic church was thus attempting the impossible explains why it failed to be the universal Church.

Religious Orders as Official Sect Movements

If the church failed, it was not for lack of brilliant efforts to solve its dilemma between this-worldliness and otherworldliness. The most impressive of these was the creation of monastic orders. Organized asceticism has always had a place in Christianity. Indeed, it was a highly developed element in Judaism and may have been a major element in the emergence of Christianity. Many biblical scholars now suspect that Jesus himself spent a period of his life as a member of an ascetic Jewish order. From its earliest days, Christianity harbored monastic communities that withdrew from the world to pursue an extraordinarily high tension version of the faith. The early monks are famous for extremes of self-imposed suffering—for mortifying their flesh to demonstrate their contempt for this world. They exposed themselves to the elements, ate little, and abused their bodies. Simon Stylites lived for 37 years atop a stone column on a platform two yards square and prostrated himself 1,244 times a day.

Such monks were recruited from among the desperately poor (Johnson, 1979) and lived mainly by charity. In time, however, monastic communities that supported themselves by agriculture began to form. Although they too were intensely otherworldly and often endured severe restrictions on their behavior (never combing or cutting their hair, for example), they were solidly organized communities capable of performing many valuable activities for the church (such as preaching in the villages).

The monasteries provided an alternative to many for whom the conventional church could not offer a sufficiently high tension faith. In the early 13th century, Pope Innocent III recognized the potential of monastic orders to serve as official sects, thus attempting to ease the constant eruption of rebellious sect movements. He founded two great orders, the Franciscans and the Dominicans. Innocent thought that these orders could accomplish two aims that would finally consolidate Catholicism as the universal Church. First, they could meet the sect movements on their own terms. The monks could match the standards of asceticism—of poverty and otherworldliness—that animated the sect movements. Thus, they could demonstrate to the public a facet of the church that was uncompromised. Moreover, the monastic orders could recruit those most prone to launch sectarian challenges to the church— the most energetic, religious, and potentially most dangerous of the poor and deprived. Thus could the sectarian impulse be rechanneled into safe directions. Second, the orders could serve as active agents against unauthorized sects. The orders could preach the orthodox faith to the deprived classes with an authentic voice via monks recruited from the ranks of the deprived. The monks could be deployed to keep close surveillance upon local affairs and thus to spot potential sect eruptions before they got a good start.

The fact that monks were celibate meant that the orders would not tend to "go soft" because of the arrival of second-generation members who lacked the fervor of the founding generation. Rather, membership was replaced by recruiting the most fervent and potentially disruptive persons in each generation. It was a brilliant organizational strategy and undoubtedly it succeeded to some extent—many potential sect movements probably were avoided because of the monastic alternative. Yet the orders did not stem the tide of religious dissent, and they produced new threats to the church.

As closed, intensely integrated social networks, the monastic orders themselves posed constant threats to become schismatic movements.

That is, they frequently evolved novel theological views and issued challenges to papal authority. They often aroused mass religious movements through their preaching that then posed a serious challenge to the church. Many historians interpret the Crusades as efforts to defuse sect movements stirred up by monastic preachers by literally getting them out of Christendom (Johnson, 1979).

Despite the recruitment of monks, the orders continually lapsed from asceticism and became worldly, thus ceasing to function as official sects. Because the orders were more efficiently organized than the feudal manors, they rapidly became rich and capable of offering considerable luxury. Thus, they always posed a grave dilemma to church authorities. If the church imposed strict asceticism on the orders and encouraged their fervor, they became a threat to the church—they tended to get out of control and stir up mass followings. If their fervor was controlled too tightly, the orders rapidly became too worldly to serve as an alternative to unauthorized sects. Finally, the formation of unofficial sect movements continued despite the most intense efforts of the monastic orders. The orders were a brilliant idea, but one that failed (Johnson, 1979).

The Unceasing Demand for Magic

In Chapter 22, we examine in detail Malinowski's theory of magic. He argued that magic is a substitute for science, an attempt to give humans control over important phenomena that they lack direct methods to deal with. Thus, for example, farmers do not try to use magic to get the weeds out of their fields; they know how to pull weeds. They do often try to use magic to make it rain, for they have no scientific means to control the weather. To understand the ceaseless demands for magic that faced the medieval church, one must understand the conditions of life people faced during that period.

Perhaps the two most crucial differences between modern and premodern societies are in expected levels of health and mortality. In medieval Europe, most people died before the age of 35, and as many as half died before age 12 (Wrigley, 1969:131). The majority of those still living suffered serious health problems—chronic health conditions that caused them pain and disability. In addition, epidemics periodically ravaged the population; perhaps half of Europe's population died during the outbreak of plague in the 14th century. Worse yet, there was virtually no reliable medical knowledge or dependable treatment for even the most common illnesses. Indeed, most of what even the best trained physicians believed about anatomy, physiology, and disease was elaborate nonsense. It is widely agreed today, and was recognized by many people then, that most persons suffering from most illnesses were better off if they did not go to a physician.

Little wonder, then, that people turned to all manner of healers, nostrum sellers, and conscious quacks in their search for relief. Because most of what even the most reputable physicians offered patients was magic, not science, an uncontrollable market of medical magic flourished. Some of this magic specifically invoked the supernatural in order to achieve cures; some of it did not.

Thus, as Catholicism moved to become the One True Church, it encountered a world filled with magical practitioners. Every village had its "wise ones," many of whom mixed magical treatment with folk medicines and commonsense treatments that often actually were beneficial. People also sought many other magical applications: weather magic, love magic, protection from enemies, and the like.

Magic is risky, and religious organizations typically withdraw from the magic business, leaving it in the hands of magical specialists. If the other great world faiths followed this strategy, living in secure symbiosis with magic, why did Christianity not follow suit? The answer lies in the ambition to be the universal Church, in the effort to monopolize religion and prevent heresy and dissent.

In order to monopolize religion, a church must monopolize all access to the supernatural. If outsiders are permitted to deal directly with the supernatural, they retain the potential to compete with the church, indeed, to claim new revelations that discredit the church. But if the church is to deny others access to the supernatural, it must remain in the magic business. The demand for magic is too great to be ignored. It is hopeless to prohibit nonchurch magic unless a churchly supply of magic is provided. Thus, the Catholic church remained deeply involved in dispensing magic. Immense numbers of magical rites and procedures were developed to serve parishioners. Saints and shrines that performed specialized miracles proliferated, and new procedures for seeking saintly intercession abounded. Many forms of illness, especially mental illness, were defined as cases of possession, and legions of official exorcists appeared to treat them.

We have mentioned that magic often does not invoke supernatural assumptions, but this is not true of church magic. Although a peasant may be content to invoke magical methods without understanding why they are supposed to work — without examining their theoretical underpinnings — this will not satisfy a theologian. Hence, church intellectuals required theological explanations of church magic. And, of course, answers were easy to discover. The church could perform miracles because it could enlist the aid of the divine — God, Jesus, Mary, the Holy Ghost, and the Communion of Saints would, under certain conditions and when the proper rituals were observed, act within the natural world on behalf of supplicants.

This theory of church magic gave intellectual satisfaction to the clergy, but it had dire implications for nonchurch magicians, for it followed that their magic too must work through supernatural means, regardless of whether they understood the true basis of their magic's power. Had church magic been able simply to supplant nonchurch magic, had the church been able to monopolize magical practice, this implication would have been irrelevant. But magical monopolies are impossible.

Magical monopolies are impossible because magic often fails and often is recognized to have failed. Moreover, any magic sometimes will seem to succeed and be recognized to have succeeded. Church magic, therefore, could not drive out other magics on the basis of its reliability or on the basis of the poorer efficacy of nonchurch magic. Faced with dying children, pain-wracked bodies, festering wounds, and similar woes, people would try anything. Sometimes church magic seemed to work. Sometimes it failed. Sometimes nonchurch magic would appear more effective. In such circumstances, it was impossible to prohibit nonchurch magic successfully.

Despite increasingly harsh efforts to impose prohibitions, the medieval church could not get its clergy to reject nonchurch magic. The clergy themselves constantly performed prohibited magic and even referred parishioners to illicit nonchurch magicians when church magic failed. That this occurred frequently is demonstrated by the large numbers of prosecutions brought against members of the clergy, and especially against exorcists, by the church for engaging in "superstition" — practicing or condoning nonchurch magic. Several such cases from the archives of church trials in Modena during the 16th century illustrate how the clergy were unable to resist resorting to prohibited magic in the face of dire need and the demands of the populace. These cases have been translated and analyzed by Mary O'Neil (1981).

One of the many cases in which clergy were charged with complicity in nonchurch magic was that of Fra Girolamo Azzolini, a Franciscan Tertiary who was a professional exorcist. The specific instance involved a child brought before him with an illness he diagnosed as caused by bewitchment but that he felt incapable of dealing with. He told the child's mother to take her to a local witch (*strega*) and to "tell her on my behalf that she should cure this child of yours, and she will do it" (O'Neil, 1981:19).

Why did Fra Azzolini make such a referral, knowing that it was prohibited by the church? During his trial, he admitted that he had suffered from an illness similar to that of the child's and churchly forms of treatment had failed to cure him. In desperation, Fra Azzolini's relatives had sent for the *strega*. When she arrived, she refused to treat him because, she said, "her confessor no longer wanted to absolve her when she did such things." Fra Azzolini told her that, because she had performed her remedy before and had been absolved, he could assure her that she would be absolved again. The *strega* accepted this reassurance and performed her procedure, whereupon Fra Azzolini recovered. In consequence, he faced future cases with the conviction that, if church magic failed, he knew of a treatment that actually worked. Thus, not only the laity, but the clergy faced a constant dilemma concerning nonchurch magic. As O'Neil (1981:20) put it: "under the duress of illness, such a recourse [to nonchurch magic] remained a culturally valid option, even when the Church's prohibitions were fully understood."

Ecclesiastical authorities were especially offended by clergy who supported or practiced nonchurch magic. For Fra Azzolini, a specialist in "ecclesiastical medicine," as exorcists were known, to have referred clients to a local *strega* was public admission of "the relative deficiency of his own powers, constituted propaganda in favor of the opposition," and was proof that he was unfit to hold his position of responsibility. He was suspended from the practice of exorcism and exiled from the city of Modena for his offenses.

The effects of social pressure on the clergy, especially when requests were made by their social superiors, is revealed in the case of Don Gian Battista, a priest at the cathedral church in Modena, who was tried in 1585. A noblewoman approached him and asked that he baptize a piece of magnet so she could use it as a love charm to keep her husband from consorting with promiscuous women. At first the priest refused, knowing this was defined as a sacrilegious abuse of a sacrament. He explained to the court: "Although I had refused her more than ten times, in the end I was obliged by the many importunities of the Signora, and I promised to serve her in the matter" (O'Neil, 1981:11).

The priest attempted to protect himself by performing the baptism incorrectly. He used ordinary water rather than holy water and common oil rather than holy oil. And he did not wear his surplice. He explained: "I never intended to serve the Signora Costanza in this matter by baptizing the magnet perfectly. . . . I only did it to get her off my back because she entreated and harassed me so" (O'Neil, 1981:11). But the court was more concerned with the fact that the priest had cooperated in prohibited magic than in technical loopholes. Indeed, these intentional errors were seen as further abuse of a church sacrament.

For centuries, and with increasing effort, the church sought to monopolize magic and to prohibit unorthodox practices and practitioners. Nonchurch magic was defined as "superstition," and, by the 15th century, the church was determined to root it out once and for all. It used three tactics against nonchurch magic. First, the church ramified and publicized its own magic: shrines, pilgrimages, miracles, the assignment of specialized services to various saints, and the use of sacraments to effect cures (Thomas, 1971; Cohn, 1975; Kieckhefer, 1976; O'Neil, 1981). The ranks of exorcists grew large. The second tactic was to condemn nonchurch magic regularly from every pulpit and to press against it during confession. The third was to punish those who violated the prohibition, eventually giving jurisdiction for such offenses to the highest church court, the Roman Inquisition. From the late 16th century on, cases involving prohibited magic made up the bulk of trials conducted by regional courts of the Inquisition.

But the strategy failed. As O'Neil (1981:3) has pointed out, to have any hope of success required cooperation of the local clergy:

> The elimination of superstition . . . required that the clergy themselves be of certified orthodoxy, so that in the most remote village there would be at least one person qualified to tell a legitimate prayer from a superstitious charm, or a natural remedy from a magical cure. The numerous accusations of and trials against clerics and exorcists on charges of superstition . . . indicate . . . a flaw in the model.

The church could not bring the clergy into conformity for the same reason it could not gain conformity from the masses — church magic too often failed and prohibited magic too often seemed to work. Given the immense demand for efficacious remedies, people could not be prevented from exhausting all possible options.

The Witchcraft Craze

For a long time, the church was remarkably mild in the punishments given persons, both lay and clerical, convicted for using nonchurch magic. In the many Modena trials O'Neil studied, the harshest sentence was banishment from the city, and usually the punishment was limited to a series of rites of penance. None of the convicted clergy was expelled from holy orders.

However, as the church grew increasingly threatened from rebellious sect movements and as the Reformation erupted, it sought to suppress all signs of religious dissent and resorted to increasingly harsh means. In this it was joined by the many emerging Protestant groups, which also feared religious competition and were especially prone to interpret all magic as Catholic and hence as anathema. As attempts to suppress nonchurch magic escalated, so did doctrinal interpretations of the fundamental mechanisms of such magic.

We have already mentioned that church intellectuals explained the efficacy of church magic on the basis of active intervention by the supernatural. But they also had to explain why prohibited magic worked, for they did not doubt that it did! They concluded that this magic, too, must work because of supernatural influences. But which ones?

For a long time, the church did not pursue an answer to this question with any vigor. Trials for superstition sometimes held that people had erred by attempting to coerce the saints into giving them aid or had abused a sacrament by incorrect application. But as the number of trials grew and as both Catholic and Protestant churches grew increasingly anxious about the persistence of nonchurch magic, the theoreticians went to work.

Because God is on the side of the church, He could not be the agent that animated nonchurch magic. Therefore, nonchurch magic must be animated by evil supernatural beings — Satan and his daemons. Because God requires certain things of humans in order that they receive divine aid, it followed that the devil too must ask something of humans in order to aid them. Thus, the logical deduction was that devil worship and diabolic sacrifices must be entailed in nonchurch magic. Otherwise how could it be effective?

Modern historians of witchcraft agree that the idea of diabolism was imputed to nonchurch magic by church intellectuals in the deductive fashion we just outlined. Richard Kieckhefer (1976:36) flatly asserts that diabolism "played little or no role in popular belief" about sorcery. Rather, "the idea of diabolism . . . was evidently the product of speculation by theologians and jurists, who could make no sense of sorcery except by postulating a diabolical link between the witch and her victim."

Norman Cohn (1975:169) reports that "nowhere" in the surviving medieval books of magic "is there a hint of Satanism." Indeed, multitudes of those brought to trial for witchcraft freely admitted their magical activities, but they steadfastly denied charges of Satanic rites and the conjuring up of daemons until they had endured several sessions of torture, during which the details of Satanism were taught to them through accusations and then wrung back from them.

For most of this century, it has been fashionable to dismiss the religious nature of the great witchcraft "craze" that swept Europe during the 15th and 16th centuries and to explain this phenomenon in wholly secular terms. Indeed, the question has been posed as how to account for the imputation of witchcraft. Sociologists have interpreted this primarily as a political phenomenon (making obligatory comparisons with modern McCarthyism). In turn, the causes of this "political persecution" are sought in class conflict, anomie, industrialization, the rise of the centralized state, urbanization, shifting sex roles, and the like (cf. Smelser, 1962; Currie, 1968; Trevor-Roper, 1969; Lewis, 1971; Nelson, 1975; Schoeneman, 1977; Ben-Yehuda, 1980).

One need not argue that all these factors were irrelevant to see that all explanations that fail to grasp the fundamentally religious character of the mass of witchcraft trials cannot address the central phenomenon. The modern mind correctly grasps that these unfortunate victims were not flying off on brooms to witches' sabbaths or actually conjuring up real daemons. But to dismiss these charges as fantasy must not cause us to fail to ask: What, in fact, were these people really doing and why did it cause learned, and often sincerely humane, clergy to think they were active Satanists?

Recently, the fashionable, secular interpretations of European witchcraft have collapsed under the findings of scholars who have gone back to the original sources: all agree that those tried for witchcraft were not innocent targets of political persecution, but were guilty of practicing nonchurch magic, mainly healing (Thomas, 1971; Midelfort, 1972; Cohn, 1975; Kieckhefer, 1976). The high proportions of females and members of subordinate social classes among the victims of the witchcraft trials are not proof that these trials were political, but merely reflect the facts that women traditionally were responsible for folk medicine and that few healers, indeed, few people, were members of the elite. And it was usually failed magic that provoked indictments for witchcraft.

Because magic is inherently risky, it cannot be monopolized, even by so powerful an organization as the medieval church. As many as 500,000 people may have been executed for witchcraft, but the church could not stamp out its competitors because church magic also failed so often. Only because it aspired to monopolize the religious economy did the Catholic church fail to follow the usual rule for low tension religion and withdraw from the magic business.

So much, then, for the illusion of the universal Church. Despite extraordinary efforts to repress dissent and schism, the medieval church failed. It was fighting the legendary Hydra; for each dissenting head it cut off, two more sprang from the severed neck.

CHURCH MOVEMENTS

Not all schisms within religious bodies produce sects. Sometimes, under special conditions, a group exits a religious body to form a new group in a lower state of tension with society. These are called *church movements.* Church movements are relatively rare because those who most strongly desire to reduce the tension between a religious organization and its environment usually have sufficient power to cause such a reduction. Sometimes, however, they do not because there may be a great discrepancy between persons' status and power in the external world and their status and power within a sect.

What we are describing is a classic application of the concept of *marginality* (Stonequist, 1937). The initial condition is that some members of a high tension, relatively isolated religious group begin to acquire status in the surrounding society. To do so, they often must bend the norms of the sect. In any event, their loyalty and commitment are suspect within the sect because of their "worldliness." Their continuing association with a deviant religious organization impedes their rise in the surrounding society, because outsiders see them as deviant. Such people are caught in two worlds, with a stake in each. Their membership in each world makes them marginal members of the other.

Often people solve this status dilemma by cutting their ties to one of these worlds, for example, by defecting from the deviant religious group and assimilating into the mainstream religious culture. In contemporary America, large numbers of sect members do precisely that (Stark and Glock, 1968). But for some people the problem is not so easily solved. If sect membership also entails a very distinctive ethnic or racial marker, defection becomes more difficult. For one thing, the surrounding society will still tend to code the defector as a member of the deviant religious group. Thus, for example, European Jews who accepted Christian baptism still tended to be regarded as Jews. Secondly, a double bond of loyalty links such people to their religious community — not merely religious traditions but racial and ethnic loyalties.

In such circumstances, there is a powerful motive for upwardly mobile members of a deviant religious group to seek to lower their group's tension. But if these members are too marginal to the group, if they are not in fact its most powerful members, they may be unable to cause a reduction in tension. In such a predicament, these persons may form a new religious organization that is in lower tension with the world than is the parent body.

A well-documented case of a church movement is Reform Judaism (Steinberg, 1965). For centuries, Jews were a highly isolated, deviant religious body within European society. Then, in the 19th century, came emancipation. Jews were granted citizenship, and rules against their employment in high status positions and occupations were withdrawn. Some Jews emerged from the ghettos to seize these opportunities. But they found it impossible fully to observe the law as defined by

Orthodox Jewry and succeed outside the ghetto. Traditional Jewish dress and tonsorial customs not only proclaimed the identity of a Jew, but deviated from gentiles' standards. Then there was the question of kosher food, which was unavailable except in the ghetto.

Jews rising in the gentile world desired to remain Jews, but to do so at less cost—to reduce the tension between Judaism and its surroundings. However, having left the ghetto, initially in small numbers, they had lost status among other Jews; sometimes they had even been formally excommunicated. They lacked the influence to transform Judaism into a state of lower tension. The result was the Reform movement, which discarded the bulk of Jewish traditions as "superstition and antiquated custom" (Steinberg, 1965:125). Little emphasis was given compensators, but rewards were increased substantially. Tension between Reform Judaism and its surroundings was very low. In consequence, especially in the second generation (who did not wholly inherit their parents' power-giving attributes), a constituency in need of stronger compensators developed within Reform Judaism. Soon the new church movement gave birth to a new sect movement, Conservative Judaism.

CONCLUSION

By its very nature, religion is a dynamic force, forever changing and renewing itself. Hope for supernatural aid arises in those unmet needs that plague human beings, and humans differ greatly in their needs. Therefore, a free religious marketplace will be a tumult of competing faiths differing in their tension with the dominant secular institutions and in the degree to which they offer magic. The clergy and leading lay members of low tension denominations are unsympathetic to what they see as an unholy bedlam, but their efforts to create a single universal Church, whether through political domination or gentle ecumenism, are doomed to failure.

Religious schisms are inevitable. Because inequality is fundamental to organized human life, there always exist strong demands for both worldly and otherworldly faiths. No religious group can be both church and sect, congratulating powerful members for obtaining scarce rewards while promulgating compensators that substitute for them. The most successful otherworldly organizations will always tend to be transformed into more worldly faiths, thus abandoning their historical constituency. Relatively deprived persons will defect in schism, reestablishing a less worldly faith more able to provide efficacious specific compensators.

Churches are ill advised to offer significant amounts of magic to their followers, even though a great demand always exists for specific compensators that promise attainment of the desired reward here and now. Magicians can pack up their bottles of snake oil and leave town when their magic fails, but priests cannot easily abandon their cathedrals. Christianity violated these principles when it sought to establish a universal Church, prohibiting independent magicians as it did independent sects, struggling to monopolize access to the supernatural. The result was costly partial successes, marked by periodic purges and autos-da-fé, inevitably followed by the reemergence of independent magicians and sectarians.

Christianity's historic failure to create a universal Church is the best evidence of the power of church-sect theory. The social processes it identifies continue despite the most monumental efforts to bring them to a halt. Sect formation is an inevitable feature of organized religion, a never-ending cycle of schism, secularization, and schism.

6 *American-Born Sect Movements*

The abundance of sects in the United States, and especially their continual formation, has made these schismatic religious groups of particular interest throughout the existence of American sociology (cf. Noyes, 1870; Nordhoff, 1875). Given such sustained interest and the vast literature it has produced, one would suppose that a great deal is known about sects and that they have been the object of much comparative study. But one would be wrong.

Sects have not even been counted with any precision, let alone compared in any significant numbers or in systematic or quantitative fashion. The bulk of the writing on sects is purely conceptual, consisting primarily of efforts to construct typologies. The overwhelming proportion of the extant empirical work consists of historical or ethnographic accounts of a particular sect, descriptions of several sects in order to illustrate cells in a typology, or qualitative comparisons of several sects. There have been very few studies involving quantified comparisons, and these have been limited to only a few cases (cf. Kanter, 1972; Welch, 1977).

The reason for the vast gap between the interest shown in sects and the quality of research devoted to them is not entirely a matter of collective sloth or aversion to quantification. The whole typological approach to sects was doomed from the beginning, but the typological approach

This chapter is a revision of an article that originally was published as Rodney Stark and William Sims Bainbridge, "American-Born Sects: Initial Findings," *Journal for the Scientific Study of Religion*, 1981, 20:2, pp. 130–149.

was not the main impediment to progress. The chief problem has been that no effective efforts have been devoted to data collection. Lacking any large number of sects that have been adequately documented on comparable features, there has been nothing to compare, nothing to quantify.

In consequence, a great deal that has been taken for granted about sects is no more than oft-repeated opinions based on impressions, intuitions, or whatever. Indeed, it is not even clear that the United States *is* unusually prolific of sects. If we do not know how many sects there are in this nation or in other nations, how can we be sure that any comparative statements of this sort are accurate? Recently, somewhat primitive but unprecedented data on U.S. sects have become available, and they permit quantification of some fundamental features of sects and thus make it possible for the first time to begin to assemble some elementary findings.

Our ultimate interest in these data is to test propositions about religious movements, a task we take up in later chapters. Here we present and discuss the distribution of certain primary features of American-born sect movements. Viewed in terms of the sophisticated analysis typical in current quantitative social science, this chapter is primitive. Yet we think it will be clear to readers how important even a few elementary facts about some important social phenomenon can be when prior knowledge was all "by guess and by gosh." This chapter deals only with initial findings. In later chapters, we begin to test hypotheses about why sects grow or stagnate and why they do or do not undergo transformation into churches. Although we frequently comment on these theoretical matters as we examine findings, this chapter aims only to establish some elementary, if important, facts and to demonstrate the utility of quantified, comparative analysis of a large number of sects.

IDENTIFYING SECTS

Our findings are based on a preliminary coding of an attempted census of American-born sects. Our primary source was the *Encyclopedia of American Religions* by J. Gordon Melton (1978). We supplemented this with additional data from other published sources, notably the extraordinary and almost wholly neglected national census studies of religious bodies produced by the U.S. Census for 1890, 1906, 1916, 1926, and 1936. These volumes provide membership statistics for hundreds of religious groups, broken down to the level of cities and counties as well as states and regions. The census volumes include a wealth of historical and doctrinal detail for each group, as well as such quantitative details as sex ratio, finances, and date of founding of congregations. In this chapter, we use these historic data to gauge trends in growth or decline for this period, contrasting these with contemporary data. For other useful data, we consulted various denominational annual reports and in some instances contacted denominational officials to seek missing data.

A number of important restrictions define the data set. First, the data are limited to sect movements. We define sects as high tension, schismatic religious movements within a conventional religious tradition, as stated in Chapter 2 and elaborated in Chapter 3. That is, sects are groups that break off from other religious bodies and remain within a religious tradition that is regarded as normal (nondeviant) within the society in which the sect arises. Groups within deviant religious traditions, whether they occur by innovation or by schism, are identified as cults. In consequence, with two exceptions, we have counted only groups within the Christian tradition as sects in the United States. Thus, although a particular group, such as a snake-handling Pentecostal group, might be extremely deviant—that is, in a very high state of tension with its surrounding environment—it is not a cult because it remains within a nondeviant religious tradition: Christianity. Conversely, a Spiritualist group might experience comparatively lower tension with its environment, but it is still a cult because it constitutes a deviant tradition.

In addition to Christian groups, we coded groups in two other traditions as sects. Considerable research indicates that the American public regards Judaism as a legitimate and respectable faith. We therefore coded schismatic Jewish groups as sects rather than as cults. We also coded Utah-born Mormon schismatic groups as sects on the grounds that they arose in a cultural setting where Mormonism is the dominant and most legitimate religious tradition. That is, schismatic Mormon groups in Utah are no more deviant than are schismatic Baptist groups in Texas. As it turned out, only two Jewish sects were coded because of a second restriction: that groups originate in the United States.

A very substantial number of sects to be found in America are not native born; they were the result of religious schisms somewhere else (usually Europe) and they came to America because large numbers of sect members—sometimes even the entire body—emigrated. Because our main interest is in sect formation, such migrant sects are of little use. We are not in a position to enumerate the other sects that formed where and when they did or to depict the sociocultural environment within which they arose. Hence, we have excluded such groups from our data set. However, after arrival in the United States, many of these immigrant sects gave birth to additional sects. These sects, and the ethnic communities in which they occurred, are part of our data.

All major Protestant bodies began as sects; so the most churchlike groups in the nation once were sects. But very few of the mainline Protestant denominations formed as sects here. Thus, their foreign origins excluded them from this data set. However, some of the groups included in our set probably are not sects today. Instead, they have been transformed into lower tension denominations. Despite their current lower tension, all such groups are included in our basic data set because the process by which such transformations in tension occur is central to our theoretical interests. For the same reason, we excluded from consideration at least 31 schismatic American religious groups that are church movements, not sects, born at unusually low tension.

We also excluded splits that were wholly due to the Civil War because these were externally imposed on some denominations. Most of these groups have long since reunited, so the problem is academic as we have coded only sects that currently exist. Hence, many colorful groups do not appear in our data because they are now defunct, whether totally extinct or nearly so, like the Shakers, who have been reduced to only nine members. It would be preferable to have full data on all sects that ever came into existence in the United States, but that is impossible. To code some defunct groups, while missing scores of others, would give a false picture of completeness. We have settled for attempting to code every sect in operation today, thus providing an initial benchmark for creation of an adequate historical data set.

Trying to find all the existing sects is not the same as finding them. Because of Melton's enormous industry and skill, we can be sure that we have included all groups of any consequence, as well as a great many that seem to be closing out utterly insignificant careers. But some unknown number of very small groups undoubtedly has gone all but undetected, even in their local environments. Groups most likely to have escaped us are the tiny family sects that often develop in remote rural areas, although they may also arise in large cities. These are initiated by a dominant family figure and often include no one beyond the close kinship network other than in-laws. If such sects have taken a specific name and installed a church telephone, we are likely to have found them. But they often meet only in homes and bear a name no more specific than "my mother's church" or "our church." We would like to have data on every such group. However, growing and successful sects today seem not to have had any significant period of such obscurity. From the first, they took their message public. Indeed, among the primordial organizational acts of ambitious sect movements is to begin publishing tracts and periodicals, often before they even have a church building.

Finally, we have eliminated several groups Melton listed because they are exclusively ministerial organizations and incorporate no lay members or congregations. Several such organizations exist to license and make legitimate fundamentalist ministers who serve nondenominational congregations, run rescue missions, are itinerant evangelists, hold chaplaincy positions, or claim the status of "minister" while earning their livings at secular work. We exclude them because a sect is not simply a leader with a special doctrine, but a social movement, and thus must include followers.

BASIC CHARACTERISTICS

Number and Size

Applying our criteria, we found and coded 417 different native-born sects operating in the United States today. Of these, two are Jewish groups and five grew out of Mormonism in Utah; the remainder are Christian. This is a substantially smaller number than the 501 cult movements we examine in Chapter 9. One reason is that the sects, but not the cults, were limited to those born in the United States. But in comparing the number of sects with the number of cults, we must keep in mind that more Americans even today are prepared to join sects than cults. Therefore, we might expect there to be far more sects than cults. But sects typically are much larger than cults. Given a finite pool of potential recruits, the larger the average sect, the fewer that can secure a following. Similarly, the smaller the average cult, the more that can secure a following.

Table 6.1 makes it clear that sects do tend to be much larger than cults. Fourteen sects (3 percent) have more than 500,000 members and thus are far larger than any current cults except the Mormons and, perhaps, Christian Scientists. Although we lack precise membership statistics on all but a few cults, we know that most have only a few hundred members and only rarely do they have even 2,000 members. In contrast, 44 percent of sects (183 of 417) have more than 2,000 members. Despite being larger than cults, sects do tend to be small. Twenty-eight percent of them have fewer than 500 members, and many of these probably have only a few dozen members. An additional 29 percent of these sects have between 500 and 2,000 members.

Age

Sects also are older than cults. Table 6.2 compares the founding dates of sects and cults. Nineteen percent of existing sects were founded prior to 1900, but only 7 percent of cults go back that far. Less than 20 percent of sects have been founded since 1960, but over 60 percent of cults are of such recent origins.

There are several reasons sects tend to be older than cults. First, both

TABLE 6.1 *Size Distribution of American Sects*

Size	Number	Percent
Less than 500	114	27
500 to 1,999	120	29
2,000 to 9,999	80	19
10,000 to 24,999	26	6
25,000 to 99,999	47	11
100,000 to 500,000	16	4
Larger than 500,000	14	3
	417	99[a]

[a]Rounding error.

TABLE 6.2 *When American Sects and Cults Formed*
— Percent Formed in the Indicated Period

Historical Period	Sects (405)[a]	Cults (484)[a]
1899 and before	19	7
1900–1929	22	8
1930–1949	23	10
1950–1959	16	14
1960–1969	14	38
1970–1977	3	23
	100	100

[a]No date of founding known for 12 sects and for 17 cults.

the sects and the cults we have data on are those that still survive. Sects are of older vintage partly because of a better survival rate. Because they are less deviant, sects have had an easier time attracting and holding members over the years, which is reflected in their considerably greater average size. Although cults often seem to depend upon their founder's influence for their survival and often disappear upon his or her death, sects have been more solid organizationally.

There is good reason to suppose that sects had a much easier time surviving in the 18th and 19th centuries than did cults. There are abundant signs that secularization has made it easier in recent times for cults to form and to survive. For example, there has been a massive shift away from the tendency of cults to adopt Christian-sounding names since the turn of the century (see Chapter 9). When non-Christian cults utilize Christian-sounding names, it suggests much about the pressures against religious deviance present in their environment. For them to dispense with such tactics in the 20th century suggests a major decline in such pressure, which suggests a second reason why cults tend to be younger than sects: Proportionately more cults have probably formed in recent times than in the 18th and 19th centuries. Finally, the survival of many older sects reduces the available recruits for newer sects and thus tends to limit current sect formation.

Racial and Ethnic Bases

Race has played a major role in sect formation because of the extreme segregation of religious life. Historically, the mainline denominations that played an active role in mission work among Black slaves and free Blacks tended to form their converts into Black congregations. This tendency was greatly increased following Reconstruction, when much stricter laws and norms of segregation came into effect. In consequence, sect movements breaking away from the major denominations tended either to be Black or White. Subsequent fragmenting has thus occurred within groups that already were virtually all White or all Black.

Table 6.3 shows that the proportion of sects having a primarily Black membership (10 percent) is very close to the proportion of the population that is Black. This suggests that, despite greater relative deprivation, the Black population has not produced more sects than the White population. However, rough calculations of the membership of the Black and White sects suggests that Blacks are more likely than Whites to belong to a higher tension (more sectlike) group. The "other" category shown in Table 6.3 is primarily Asian and also shows a proportion of sects quite close to Asian representation in the total population.

TABLE 6.3   *Racial and Ethnic Bases of American-Born Sects*

	Number	Percent
Predominant Racial Composition		
White	365	88
Black	43	10
Other	9	2
	417	100
Of Non-Black Sects:		
Founded primarily by a distinctive ethnic group	56	15
Founded in part by a distinctive ethnic group	8	2
Not founded on a distinctive ethnic base	310	83
	374	100

The table also indicates that ethnicity has played some role in the formation of American sects. In 56 cases, the founding members of a sect were overwhelmingly members of a distinctive ethnic group. Often this has represented further schisms in the United States of a sect that arrived here through immigration, as in the case of the Amish and Mennonite sects. In other cases, particularly within the Lutheran and Eastern Orthodox traditions, American sects have emerged from churches having primarily a distinctive ethnic base. In 8 additional cases, a distinctive ethnic group played the primary, but not the sole, role in the formation of a new sect.

Three-quarters of all American-born sects (74 percent) are not the product of racial or ethnic minorities. They were rooted in the religious and social discontents of White, assimilated Americans.

Growth

The central thesis of church-sect theory is that, as sects grow, they begin to accommodate themselves to their environment. But here we see that, whatever else they may do, most sects do not continue to grow indefinitely. Table 6.4 shows the current growth tendency of these sects. Although our assessment of current growth was somewhat impressionistic, we nonetheless coded only 6 percent of them as currently growing rapidly (we have attempted to eliminate growth through fertility alone).

TABLE 6.4   *Career Growth Curves of American Sects — Percent Making Indicated Change*

Declining 51 percent	
1. Slow decline since formation	20
2. Fast decline since formation	1
3. Slow growth, followed by slow decline	17
4. Fast growth, followed by slow decline	8
5. Slow growth, followed by fast decline	2
6. Fast growth, followed by fast decline	3
Stable 18 percent	
7. Little or no change since formation	11
8. Slow growth, then no growth	3
9. Fast growth, then no growth	4
Growing 31 percent	
10. Slow growth since formation	20
11. Fast growth since formation	6
12. Fast growth, then slow growth	5
	100
	(417)

An additional 25 percent seemed to be growing slowly, and 18 percent seemed to be static. Forty-five percent of the sects were slowly declining in membership, and 6 percent were declining rapidly.

In addition to current growth, we attempted to characterize and code the career growth pattern of these sects. In the beginning, sects need not experience any growth. They can fail to grow or even decline from their moment of founding because sects occur by schism; they do not depend upon a leader who slowly collects some followers and founds a movement. Sects can start large — a very sizeable chunk of a religious organization may defect to start a new sect. In our judgment, nearly a third of all sects (32 percent) reached their high-water mark on the day they began. Twenty-one percent of these sects began to decline in membership from their first day. Another 11 percent have not grown since formation.

Sects typically do not have a period of fast growth (only 26 percent have). However, they rarely have a period of fast decline (only 6 percent). The four most common career patterns for sects are (1) a slow decline since formation; (2) slow growth, followed by slow decline; (3) little or no change since formation; (4) slow growth since formation.

Later we examine connections between career growth patterns and other aspects of sects, particularly changes in their tension with their environment, but these curves are based on crude data. Thus, although we treat them here in a quantitative way, they rest on our relatively qualitative judgments. One day we hope to possess good quantitative data on the growth curves of a large number of sects (and cults). But for now we are making do with crude estimates.

TENSION

The fundamental proposition of church-sect theory is that many groups that begin in a state of high tension with their environment are subsequently transformed into a state of lower tension. Such a decline in tension is likely to occur when (1) the initial level of tension was not so high that group membership was so stigmatizing to individuals as to prevent their upward mobility and (2) the group was not so socially encapsulated that members were physically prevented from participating in the outside society (see Chapter 7).

All the groups we have coded as sects began in a state of relatively high tension with their environments, but some have already made considerable progress toward being transformed into churches — to a low state of tension with their environments. That is, many of these groups are less sectlike than they used to be, and some have achieved so low a level of tension that they ought no longer to be considered sects. The tension measure we used is a simple six-point scale. To clarify each point on the scale, it is useful to consider several representative Protestant bodies for each.

1. Low: Groups scored here are very accommodated to their environment and have been fully transformed into churches. The Protestant Episcopal Church and the United Church of Christ are representative.

2. Moderate: Greater tension exists here than in groups scored one, but there is still very little tension. The American Lutheran Church and the American Baptist Church are typical.

3. Somewhat High: Here we come close to the tension range that might be identified with sects, but perhaps not quite. Tension with the environment is quite noticeable, but the groups in question enjoy "respectability." Examples are the Southern Baptist Convention and the Lutheran Church–Missouri Synod.

4. High: Bodies in this level of tension are definitely sects, although many have lowered their original level of tension. They frequently will already have given birth to new sect movements as a result of a reduction in their level of tension. A typical example is the Church of the Nazarene, which, in 1956, after decades of prohibiting movie attendance, voted to permit members to watch television. Two dissident sects immediately left the church, followed by a third in 1967. A second example is the Seventh-Day Adventist Church.

5. Very High: Groups at this level of tension are regarded as quite deviant and experience considerable friction with society. Few of these groups have yet lowered their initial level of tension. The many Pentecostal groups, which emphasize speaking in tongues at their services and whose ministers and evangelists often claim divine gifts of healing, are representative of this level on the scale.

6. Extreme: Here we locate the groups that engender both ridicule and serious antagonism, even to the point of chronic legal intervention in their affairs. Many of these groups are highly physically encapsulated and many wear distinctive dress (for example, the Amish and the Mennonites). Here we place the snake-handling groups, polygamous Mormon communes, all groups that are urgently millenarian (for example, Jehovah's Witnesses), and the like.

Table 6.5 assesses the current tension levels of American sects. None of the American-born sects we coded has yet achieved a low tension level. (Keep in mind the distinction between church movements and sects.) All such bodies found in the United States today formed as sects long ago in Europe and have always been relatively low tension bodies here.

TABLE 6.5   *Current Tension Levels of American-Born Sects*

Tension Level	Number	Percent
1. Low	0	0
2. Moderate	8	2
3. Somewhat High	33	8
4. High	122	29
5. Very High	122	29
6. Extreme	132	32
	417	100

Only eight sects, or 2 percent, are currently coded at level two. Many of these are of the Old Catholic family, which we describe later in this chapter. Another 8 percent of the sects are at tension level three, about equivalent to the Southern Baptists or the Missouri Lutherans. Twenty-nine percent were coded as high, 29 percent as very high, and 32 percent as extreme.

This clearly suggests the likelihood that many sects fail to grow (and are never transformed into churches) because their initial level of tension is so high as to cause their early social encapsulation. Once encapsulated, a sect may persist for centuries, depending on group fertility and the ability to minimize defection, but it will rarely be able to recruit an outsider. For such recruitment to occur, there must be contact between members and nonmembers of sufficient quality and duration to permit the formation of close interpersonal bonds, as we explain in Chapter 14.

That nearly a third of current sects score six on tension reflects the prevalence of encapsulated groups that are fundamentally living footnotes to our religious history but are unlikely to have a significant future. Indeed, many of the groups scored six are isolated rural groups, such as the many schismatic Amish. Encapsulation seems to play a role in causing a sect to continue to fragment, for it severely limits communication between one component of the group and another. For example, growth through fertility has frequently caused the Amish to form a new colony some distance from the old (Hostetler, 1968). In time, the lack of contact between the groups, combined with intense interaction within each group, leads to schism. Indeed, anything that causes a line of cleavage in the social network that constitutes a group is highly conducive to schism.

These data raise a second issue. Although all these groups originated as sects, some are no longer far out on the tension axis. We must emphasize that tension is a continuum and our tension codes are simply relative positions on this continuum, not sharply defined categories. Hence, there is no sharp dividing line between churches and sects. Nonetheless, for purposes of simple description, groups whose present tension level was coded as two probably ought to be excluded in a count of current sects. Excluding them would reduce the total from 417 to 409. Groups scored three raise more ambiguity. If one is inclined to regard the Southern Baptists and the Missouri Lutherans as at present more sect-like than churchlike, then groups scored three belong in the sect total. If one sees the balance as slightly more on the church than the sect side, they should not be included in the total. We do not regard this as an urgent matter. Our main interest is in ranking groups, not in assigning them a name.

We attempted to code not only the current level of tension between a group and its environment, but also whether this level had changed over time. This will, of course, be of considerable interest for attempts to test church-sect theory because it captures the fundamental process on which that theory rests. Only as sect movements are slowly transformed into a state of reduced tension are conditions for the emergence of new sect movements reestablished. Our data show that the overwhelming majority (84 percent) of American-born sects have not changed their initial level of tension. Indeed, only 17 groups (4 percent) have substantially reduced their level of tension, and another 10 percent have undergone a modest reduction in tension. However, groups virtually never increase their tension level following formation; only six were coded as having done so.

One reason so many sects may not have changed their tension level is that they are relatively new organizations. In the next chapter, we argue that no major change in tension is likely until there has been a significant rise in the class composition of the group, which usually cannot occur until the second generation has matured and taken over positions of influence in the movement. Many of these sects have not had time for that process to occur.

However, lack of time does not account for why most sects have not reduced their tension. Indeed, we doubt that most of them ever will change. However, the failure of most American-born sects to be transformed from higher to lower tension does not challenge the basic premise on which church-sect theory rests. It is not that most sects that manage to form must eventually be transformed that is at issue. Most sects are, in fact, dead ends. They start small, remain small, and slowly wither away. What is important to church-sect theory is what happens to sect movements that amount to something. What happens to movements that successfully attract a growing and significant following? That is, what happens in groups that, in their initial period, are serving the religious needs for high tension compensators of a substantial segment of deprived people? When these groups begin to make peace with this world, substantial numbers of people begin to feel the need for a more otherworldly faith.

SECT FAMILIES

Sects form families. Sects are born when they break off from other religious bodies, and many in turn foster additional sects. Because sects attempt to restore aspects of practice and doctrine from which the parent body was alleged to have drifted, sect families bear rather close resemblances in terms of theology and worship forms. Thus, Baptist sects, for example, have a family likeness in terms of adult baptism by immersion as well as many common doctrinal features.

One of Melton's major achievements in presenting his massive material on sects is in tracing the specific organizational origins of nearly all groups — from whom did they separate and why — in addition to specifying similarities and differences in doctrine and practice. In general, we have used Melton's family divisions in coding these sects, departing on several occasions only by ignoring minute subdivisions within some of these family trees. Table 6.6 shows the family makeup of America's sects.

By far the largest family, with 26.4 percent of the total, is the Pentecostal group. The primary characteristic that distinguishes Pentecostal sects from other Protestant groups is the central emphasis given to speaking in tongues during church services. Glossolalia played a role in the earliest days of Christianity. It reemerged in Christianity in the late 17th century among French Huguenots during their period of intense persecution by French Catholics. Since then, it has reappeared a number of times, among the Quakers during the 18th century, in the United States during the 19th century, and among Roman Catholics in Europe and the United States in very recent years. The American family of Pentecostals began in Iowa in 1895, spread to Topeka, Kansas, then to Los Angeles, and then back to Arkansas and Tennessee. The largest contemporary group is the Assemblies of God, with well over one million members. Another large Pentecostal group is the Church of God (Cleveland, Tennessee) with well over 300,000 members.

A second distinctive aspect of American Pentecostal groups is their practice of faith healing. Most Christian bodies accept the possibility of healing through divine intervention, but few other than Pentecostal groups hold special healing services and advertise the power to heal. During his years as America's most famous faith healer, Reverend Oral Roberts was a Pentecostal. However, subsequent to reaffiliating with the Methodist church some years ago, Roberts has shifted to more tradi-

TABLE 6.6   *Family Origins of American-Born Sects*

Family	Number	Percent
1. Pentecostal	110	26.4
2. Holiness	61	14.6
3. Baptist	41	9.8
4. Adventist	27	6.5
5. Methodist	25	6.0
6. Old Catholic (Roman)	23	5.5
7. Fundamentalist	20	4.8
8. Mennonites and Amish	17	4.1
9. Eastern Orthodox	15	3.6
10. Lutheran	12	2.9
11. Disciples of Christ	12	2.9
12. Presbyterian	9	2.2
13. Quakers	7	1.7
14. Anglican (Episcopalian)	7	1.7
15. Russellites	6	1.4
16. Other Adventists	5	1.2
17. Mormons (Utah)	5	1.2
18. Pietist	4	1.0
19. Reformed	3	.7
20. Communes	3	.7
21. Congregational	3	.7
22. Jewish	2	.5
	417	100

tional evangelism and does not emphasize specific healing powers.

The second largest sect family is the Holiness group. The Holiness Movement that swept American Protestantism in the 19th century had its roots in Methodism. Emphasis was placed on a personal salvation experience in which the individual is "born again" in Christ and undergoes sanctification — the individual becomes personally holy and strives for perfection. As with many revival movements of the 19th century, the Holiness Movement represented the discomfort of many Americans with the constant bickering among the multitude of Christian bodies, all claiming to be the one true church. The Holiness Movement aimed at a general reconciliation across denominational lines. In time, this led to conflicts between the Holiness activists and the various denominational leaders, particularly the bishops of the Methodist church. Thus, what began as a unification drive soon led to new religious bodies as internal schisms began to rend the Holiness Movement. Today we can identify 61 different religious bodies within the Holiness family. The largest of these is the Church of the Nazarene, one of the more successful of recent sect movements, with a membership of 441,000 and 4,733 congregations in 1975. Another sizeable sect of the Holiness family is the Church of God (Anderson, Indiana), with more than 160,000 members.

The Baptists constitute the third most numerous sect family in contemporary America, with 41 different sects, or about 10 percent. Church historians have long disputed the origins of the Baptists. We favor those who reject direct linkage between the Baptist family of England and the United States, on the one hand, and the Anabaptists who flourished in Europe, on the other. The Anabaptists remain committed to very high tension positions and practices never found among the Baptists, such as refusing to swear oaths, hold public office, or serve under arms. Such practices persist among the clear descendents of European Anabaptists, such as the Amish and the Mennonites. But they have not existed among Baptists. The two have been linked, in our opinion, because of superficial resemblances in name and in the practice of adult baptism.

Modern Baptism seems to have arisen among English Puritans, perhaps during a sojourn in Holland. The first Baptist group known in America was founded in Rhode Island in 1639 by Roger Williams. The movement grew rapidly by mission work in the middle colonies, where there were no established churches to impede them.

The northern and southern branches of the Baptist movement split in 1844 over the issues of slavery and organizational centralization. The two halves, the American Baptist Churches in the U.S.A., with more than 1.6 million members, and the Southern Baptist Convention, with more than 12.7 million, have never reunited. Each has, in turn, produced a variety of sects, although the Southern Baptists have produced more.

The Southern Baptists produced a major sect within months of their separation from northern Baptists. This group proposed that non-Baptists could not be considered Christians; thus, no relations with them could be maintained. Today this sect, known as the American Baptist Association, has more than a million members. Baptist sects tend to be larger than those in other sect families. The Baptist Bible Fellowship counts more than a million members, and the Baptist Missionary Association of America and the General Association of Regular Baptist Churches each has more than a quarter of a million.

The fourth most prominent sect family is in the Adventist tradition, with 27 sect groups (6.5 percent). Adventists can be distinguished by their emphasis on the imminence of the Second Advent — when Christ will return to receive the saved into everlasting glory. The American Adventist movement began with one of the most influential prophets in our religious history, William Miller, a layman who believed he had discovered that the date for the Second Coming was between March 21,

1843, and March 21, 1844. Miller aroused tens of thousands of followers. As the end of the year Miller specified approached, thousands sold their property and gathered to be taken into heaven. The end failed to come.

By May 1844, Miller humbly admitted his error. However, his followers did not. Samuel S. Snow readjusted Miller's computations and everyone enthusiastically awaited the millennium set for October 22, 1844. This date is referred to as the "Great Disappointment" among Adventists, but still the movement did not disband. A modern study suggests they could not because they had placed all their eggs in the Adventist basket and had to protect themselves from the immense dissonance of so futile an act (Festinger et al., 1956). In any event, a great many very significant American sect movements originated out of the Great Disappointment. Most of these groups still await an imminent Advent, but strict rules are enforced against setting any specific dates. The largest of the sects in this family is the Seventh-Day Adventist Church, with about 500,000 members, founded by Mother Ellen G. White in the aftermath of the Millerite disappointment. This family also eventually gave rise to another sect family, the Russelites, whom we discuss later in this chapter.

It should be no surprise that 25 sects fall within the Methodist family, for Methodists are second only to Baptists in terms of the denominational affiliation reported by American Protestants. Methodism arose in England under the leadership of John Wesley in 1739. The movement came to the United States with English immigrants shortly before the Revolutionary War and spread rapidly. Today the United Methodist Church, with about ten million members, is the direct heir to the English Wesleyan movement.

Methodist sects have been especially common among Black Americans. The African Methodist Episcopal Church, with over two million members, and the African Methodist Episcopal Zion Church, with more than a million, are leading examples. In fact, a third of Methodist sects are Black organizations.

The Old Catholic family has also been productive of many American sects. Probably because of the historic dominance of Protestantism, the continuing emergence of sects from Roman Catholicism in the United States has gone almost wholly unremarked by social scientists. The most important impetus for the formation of Roman Catholic sects in the United States was the First Vatican Council during the 1870s. That council declared that the pope was infallible in matters of faith and morals, a profound change. In reaction, many small Catholic groups, usually led by parish priests, broke with Rome. These groups rejected Vatican I and based their teachings on the doctrines agreed to by earlier church councils. These schisms were often facilitated by underlying ethnic conflicts.

By far the largest of current Old Catholic sects is the Polish National Catholic Church of America, with around 200,000 members. This group not only objected to the First Vatican Council, but to the nearly universal practice of assigning non-Polish priests (usually Irish) to Polish parishes. Interestingly enough, Blacks have played leading roles in the Old Catholic movement, and at present the Bishop of the Old Roman Catholic Church (Marchenna), headquartered in New York, is a Black.

Seventh in terms of number of sects is the Fundamentalist family. This name is the source of great confusion among observers of American religion, for often all religious groups that embrace traditional doctrines are collectively referred to as fundamentalist. There is obvious utility in having such a shorthand term; so such general usage will persist. Yet there is a much more precise historical meaning to the term, and only a few American religious groups are best described by it. The Fundamentalist Movement arose at the turn of the century with one essential goal — to reassert and defend the absolute truth of a literal interpretation of the Bible. In 1890, a group of ministers, primarily from the major Baptist and Presbyterian denominations, who had for several years been holding annual meetings at Niagara, Ontario, adopted a 14-point statement of creed. This step soon led to major disputes within these denominations because the points of fundamentalism were not followed by the majority of clergy in these bodies. By the 1920s, sects began to break away to adhere to the Niagara Creed. The largest of these is the Independent Fundamental Churches of America, founded in Iowa in 1922, which today claims nearly 90,000 members. Other sects in this family are very small.

The Mennonite and Amish family has many different sects, but has depended almost entirely on its original immigrant base and fertility to sustain membership. As mentioned earlier, splits seem to be the result of the extreme encapsulation of these groups and the consequent poor communications between centers.

Eastern Orthodox schisms have produced 15 current sects, also within ethnic communities. Often these splits have centered on relations with a state church in the nation of origins that has accommodated itself to a Communist regime.

The large Lutheran denominations have primarily produced small, rural sect movements, usually sustained by a single ethnic group. However, one very large sect broke off from Lutheranism in the 19th century. This sect is the Lutheran Church–Missouri Synod, which has nearly three million members. A second large Lutheran sect, the Wisconsin Synod, also developed as a response to the evangelical impulses of the 19th century. It counts about 400,000 members.

The Disciples of Christ family includes 12 current sects, the largest being the North American Christian Convention, with more than one million members.

The Presbyterian, Quaker, and Anglican (Episcopalian) traditions each provide a few current sects.

The Russellite family is the source of only six current sects, but one of them, the Jehovah's Witnesses, is among the most extreme of the larger American-born sects and is perhaps the best known. Charles Taze Russell picked up where the Adventist Millerites left off. He reworked the Millerite doctrines and date calculations and began to preach powerfully that the end was close at hand. In 1879, Russell and his followers began to publish *Watch Tower*, which is still sold door-to-door every week by Jehovah's Witnesses.

As time passed, Russell became increasingly specific about the date of the millennium. He set the "dawn period" as 1874–1914. During this time, the Jews would return to Palestine (which they already were doing when the prophesy was made), and there would be a gradual overthrow of the secular leadership of Gentile nations. The climax would come in 1914, when the saints would receive glorification and God would begin direct rule over the earth. The outbreak of World War I in 1914 was not seen as the failure of Russell's prophesy, but as dramatic evidence of its truth. The war was interpreted as the apocalypse and as the certain signal that God had indeed taken direct control of human events. The end would come in 1918. Russell died in 1916; so he did not face any problems with the 1918 date when the war ended, but the Advent did not come. However, his followers reinterpreted the scheme to mean that Christ began a period of "invisible rule" in 1914, which soon will end — "Many now living will never die." There is still firm belief that only those who witness for Christ before the end will live in glory, while the meek (those unconverted) will only inherit the earth.

Russell's followers have splintered a number of times, but the main body of Witnesses claims more than 500,000 followers in the United States and another million abroad.

The Reformed family is rooted in the religious traditions of early Dutch settlers. Several radical rural Protestant communes, prominent in the 19th century, still survive. Jewish and Mormon sect families are small and have been discussed earlier in this chapter.

SECT REGIONALISM

In Chapter 4, we examine the geographic patterns of conventional religion and find the most remarkable feature to be an Unchurched Belt along the West Coast. In Chapters 9, 10, and 11, we see that the geography of cult movements, as well as that of client cults, is a mirror image of the geography of church membership. Cults thrive in the Unchurched Belt.

Popular wisdom would have it that sects are very much a southern phenomenon. Others would suggest that sects will cluster in the same fashion as cults — that all forms of religious deviance will prosper where the mainline churches are weakest. Our data belie both conclusions.

Admittedly, our data on the locations of sects are not all that one would desire. Only one state gets credit for a sect, the state in which the headquarters of the group is located. Thus, for the largest sects, some states get no credit, despite having a substantial number of members of the sect within their borders. Yet most sects are so small that they really are significant in only one state. Nevertheless, our data undoubtedly underestimate sect activity nationally, especially the sect activity of small states. We also worried that sects might tend to put their headquarters in the nearest major regional center and thus cause us to inflate the rates for states with such centers. But when we looked through the data, we found many sects headquartered in small communities, despite their being very close to a major city. For example, the bulk of Tennessee's 23 sects are not based in Nashville or Memphis, but in small towns — four are headquartered in the small community of Cleveland, Tennessee. Table 6.7 shows the number of sects headquartered in each state and the number of sects per million state residents.

Tennessee seems to deserve its reputation as an active sect state; it leads the nation with 5.48 sects per million residents. Utah and Indiana have the next highest rates, and Pennsylvania (which has the largest number of sects) places fourth. Sects, unlike cults, are not abundant in the western states. Although California is home for 167 cults (a rate of 7.9 per million), it has only 29 sects, for a rate of 1.37 per million. Nevada and New Mexico are the top two states for cult rates, but neither has a single sect headquarters.

Perhaps even more surprising, the list of high sect states is not dominated by southern states. This is consistent with our findings that the South is not exceptional in terms of church membership, church attendance, or religious belief. Here we see that it is not unusually hospitable to sects.

These geographic trends come into sharp relief in Figure 6.1. Here sect rates have been computed for the nine census regions. The East

TABLE 6.7 *State Rates of Sects per Million Population*

State	Number of Sects	Sects Per Million Population
1. Tennessee	23	5.48
2. Utah	5	4.17
3. Indiana	20	3.77
4. Pennsylvania	39	3.72
5. Arizona	8	3.64
6. North Carolina	19	3.45
7. North Dakota	2	3.33
8. Missouri	16	3.33
9. Oklahoma	9	3.33
10. South Carolina	9	3.20
11. Mississippi	7	3.04
12. West Virginia	5	2.78
13. Montana	2	2.86
14. South Dakota	2	2.86
15. Minnesota	11	2.80
16. Georgia	13	2.65
17. Kansas	6	2.60
18. Idaho	2	2.50
19. Colorado	6	2.40
20. Arkansas	5	2.38
21. Illinois	26	2.36
22. Michigan	19	2.07
23. Kentucky	7	2.06
24. New York	35	1.94
25. Oregon	4	1.74
26. Alabama	6	1.67
27. Maryland	6	1.46
28. Washington	5	1.43
29. California	29	1.37
30. Nebraska	2	1.33
31. Wisconsin	6	1.30
32. Ohio	14	1.30
33. Texas	15	1.23
34. Virginia	6	1.20
35. Hawaii	2	1.11
36. Rhode Island	1	1.11
37. New Jersey	8	1.10
38. Maine	1	.91
39. Florida	7	.83
40. Iowa	2	.69
41. Delaware	1	.60
42. Louisiana	1	.26
43. Massachusetts	1	.17
Washington, D.C.	3	4.29
National	116[a]	1.96

Note: Alaska, Connecticut, Nevada, New Hampshire, New Mexico, Vermont, and Wyoming had no sect headquarters.
[a]One sect omitted because of ambiguity as to location.

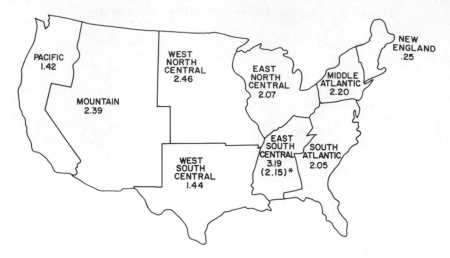

FIGURE 6.1   *Regional Sect Rates per Million Population*
(National rate = 1.96)

*Tennessee omitted from East South Central region.

South Central region does have the highest rate (3.19), but that is heavily influenced by Tennessee's extremely high rate. With Tennessee removed, the rate for this region drops to 2.15 per million, similar to most other regions. The map also shows that the Pacific region falls below the national average for sects, which suggests that sects and cults do not cluster together and do not represent functionally alternative kinds of religious deviance. In Chapter 19, we explain why this is so.

The most striking feature of the map of American sects is the astonishingly low rate of 0.25 sects per million for the New England region. What accounts for this? Here we can only offer plausible hunches. The New England region is an area of very early settlement. Once this was a hotbed of sect formation. Some of these sects died out long ago; many others migrated with the waves of westbound settlers that this region produced in the late 18th and early 19th centuries. The people who left were most likely to have been members of sects or to have helped form new ones—people who had the least social and economic stake in staying put. Then, when new sects might have formed to replace those that died out or moved, new waves of immigrants made the region predominantly Roman Catholic. American Catholicism has produced some sects, but they are few and small. Generally speaking, American Catholics have not been prone to create sects or to join them. We suspect that migration took away New England's sects and immigration prevented their replacement.

CONCLUSION

The map of American sectarianism is a patchwork of amazing variety, but one important lesson to be learned from these data is that the United States is not unusually prolific in sects. Nationally, there are just 1.96 sects per million population. Our work preparing Chapter 21, on Europe's cults and sects, suggests that the sect rate for many parts of Europe is about the same. In contrast, counting only Christian sects gives Africa a rate of 12.5 sects per million (Barrett, 1968). If adequate data were available so that the large number of Muslim sects as well as those that have emerged out of indigenous faiths could be added, Africa's sect rate would be astonishingly high.

This does not surprise us. Anything that produces a line of cleavage in the social relations of an organization (thus creating distinct social networks) will promote a schism within that organization. Among such factors are linguistic differences, geographical barriers, and political boundaries. Africa far surpasses the United States on such factors and therefore ought to far surpass it in sect formation. Let there be an end to the notion that America is the land of the sect.

Many other parts of the world are, or will be, favorable ground for sect emergence and invasion. Latin America is united by language, Spanish and Portugese being dominant over more than a continent, but it is cut by many geographical, economic, and social cleavages. The Roman Catholic Church is painfully aware that it faces many almost insurmountable problems in Latin America today, not the least of them being a severe shortage of clergy. The pressures toward schism are most dramatically illustrated by the large proportion of priests who feel drawn into the political struggles of the region on the side of the relatively deprived. Today, many schisms are partially contained by the great skill and experience the Catholic church possesses for limiting open breaks in its community of faith. But we would have to predict that the future map of Latin American sectarianism will exceed in complexity that of the United States, falling short only of that of Africa.

An important implication of our data on American-born sects is that most sects do not grow and do not reduce their initial high level of tension because their initial tension level was so high that they could not successfully recruit new members. The connections among successful growth, initial tension level, and changes in tension level are complex and reciprocal; but these connections hold the key to all versions of church-sect theory. To explore these connections successfully, we must stop dealing with sects only in terms of case studies and begin dealing with them in case lots.

Research on what happened in a particular case, the Nazarenes, for example, can suggest and illustrate many elements of a comprehensive theory of the transformation of sects into churches. Throughout this book, we use case studies to sharpen our thinking, and two chapters specifically focus on single religious organizations. But debates over small numbers of apparently contradictory cases often generate more heat than light. Does the case of the Amish refute the hypothesis that sects are transformed into churches, and, if it does not, which features of the Amish and Nazarenes account for their different evolutions?

To study how particular factors impede or prompt transformation, we must examine correlations, statistical regularities that pertain to a number of cases. We need to know probabilities and to discard the simpleminded "yes-no" binary logic inherent in case studies. Moreover, quantitative comparative analysis can identify important deviant cases that warrant closer inspection. Such inspection, in turn, will lead us to seek and to test crucial intervening variables rather than to proliferate ad hoc exception rules for individual cases.

Although religion springs into being to serve the needs of individual humans, its life is rooted in social exchanges. Thus, many of the most important scientific questions concerning religion can be studied best through systematic research in which the unit of analysis is the congregation or denomination. Religion is created, sustained, defended, and transmitted by organizations. And societies' dominant religious organizations and traditions are not threatened primarily by individual apathy or disenchantment, but by competing religious organizations. This chapter shows that we can quantitatively study sect movements, not just sectarian attitudes, and that the data that document the tremendous diversity of American religion also permit systematic research on its sources.

7 Sect Transformation and Upward Mobility: The Missing Mechanisms

When H. Richard Niebuhr (1929) first formulated a church-sect theory by applying elements of Marxism to explain the proliferation of Christian denominations, he did not argue that *all* sects are transformed into churches. He merely observed that *many* are transformed, especially those that enjoy considerable early success. Many sects are short lived and never reduce their initial high level of tension. As Chapter 6 shows, many others live on without lowering their tension with the world, but usually they cease to grow after the initial wave of enthusiasm that gave them birth. At the conclusion of this chapter, we remark further about factors that prevent some sects from becoming churches, but our interest here is with the fact that a dynamic process by which sects are transformed into churches appears to offer a satisfactory explanation of the rise of new churches and the emergence of new sect movements, as outlined in Chapter 5.

Our use of the term *sect* is restrictive, referring to a schismatic, high tension movement within a dominant religious tradition. It does not include new religious movements that constitute a deviant religious tradition. Such groups are *cults*, not sects. Hence we do not challenge the importance placed on the lower classes in sect formation by pointing out the centrality of upper-class and middle-class persons in the formation of cults such as Spiritualism, Theosophy, or Christian Science. Cult formation involves religious innovation, not mere schisms within conventional religious organizations, and thus demands separate consideration. The next chapter addresses the formation of cults; here our goal is to clarify and expand church-sect theory.

Two related propositions have been advanced to explain why sects tend to be transformed into churches. The first of these is that an upward shift in the class composition of sects tends to take place over time. The second proposes that such a change in class composition will lead to a reconciliation between the religious movement and its environment. Such a reconciliation is expected when control of a sect movement passes from the lower class, whose religious needs are best served by rejection of a society in which they have little stake, into the hands of the middle and upper classes, who have a considerable stake in the external society (cf. Doherty, 1967).

Although a rise in the class composition of sects is thought to serve as the crucial dynamic in the theory, no satisfactory mechanism has been suggested to account for this process. Niebuhr (1929) never even attempted such an explanation in his classic statement of church-sect theory. He merely asserted that, when sect movements prove to be vigorous and popular, middle-class and upper-class persons rush to join and then co-opt the sect. At some point, successful sects do begin to attract converts from among the more privileged, but this "attraction" argument begs the essential question. An influx of upper status converts can only occur *after* a sect has been considerably transformed — after a considerable reduction in its initial level of tension. To think otherwise is to suppose that significant numbers of persons of power and privilege will rush to join a highly deviant, stigmatizing religious movement that is hostile to their fundamental interests. If such a supposition is implausible, then Niebuhr left it a mystery why the class composition of sects tends to rise before there is an influx of higher status converts.

One solution sometimes proposed to solve this problem (cf. Wilson, 1966) is to apply Weberian conclusions about the positive economic impact of certain religious values and norms. It is argued that the values and norms found in high tension, otherworldly religious groups have the latent consequence of fostering upward mobility. However, Weber specifically denied that this was true of all sects and limited the Protestant ethic to certain Puritan sects within Christianity. Possibly the theology of these groups did prompt thrift, industry, and honesty and result in upward mobility, but it seems unwise to rely on an uncanonical extension of Weber to supply the missing mechanism that generally transforms sects. For one thing, modern empirical studies have not sustained the hypothesis that members of Protestant sects pursue wealth more intensely or successfully than others (cf. Bouma, 1973). More important, a great many sect movements, especially non-Christian sects, clearly do not possess the indicated theology; yet they seem to display the same trend toward upward mobility, with a resultant transformation of the sect from higher to lower tension. Indeed, some Buddhist sects, such as Myochikai in Japan, promise that membership alone will result in economic success and thus tend to discourage individual initiative (Moroto, 1976). To push the argument to the point of claiming that upward mobility among sect members must stem from their theology, regardless of "superficial" appearances, is to embrace tautology.

Another possible solution to the mystery of sect mobility lies in moral regeneration, an application of control theory that can be traced at least back to Durkheim. Travis Hirschi (1969:3) has stated the control theory explanation for deviant behavior: "According to *control* or bond theories, a person is free to commit delinquent acts because his ties to the conventional order have somehow been broken." Generally, satisfaction and success demand a good measure of conformity to the conventional social order; so persons lacking effective social bonds will deviate to their own disadvantage.

Moral regeneration names the process of reaffiliation with the social order leading to successful conforming behavior under the influence of new, strong social bonds (Homans, 1950, 1961; Burgess and Akers, 1966; Scott, 1971; Akers, 1977). The argument is that persons adrift in society, lacking ties to the moral order, are strongly reattached to society by virtue of their recruitment into an intensely integrated moral community — a sect. It even can be argued that the very deprivations that cause people to join sects are abated by sect membership, thus enabling people to improve their circumstances. Indeed, the story of personal moral regeneration and a rise in fortune is a central focus of conversion and commitment in many sects — "For years I was a wino. Then I found the Lord, and now I have a good job." There seems ample evidence that persons unable to hold jobs or otherwise cope with life often are enabled to do so once they are integrated into the community of the sect. The whole range of ways that religions provide efficacious solutions to human problems merits careful study.

Our own research on the power of religion to prevent the commission of crimes and suicide indicates that membership in a religious organization does promote conformity to others' wishes and a measure of stability in the pattern of an individual's life (Stark, Doyle, and Kent, 1980; Bainbridge and Stark, 1981; Stark, Kent, and Doyle, 1982; Stark, Doyle, and Rushing, 1983). Our research on suicide, especially, suggests that religious *doctrine* is not the key element, but rather the social bond to members of the congregation and the comforting power of religious compensators. Thus, our research supports the moral regeneration argument, but it does not support explanations based purely on the values and norms promulgated by religious doctrines.

However, social science does not proceed merely through the comparative testing of classic ideas. It also demands contemporary imagination. Therefore, we propose a third explanation, based not on beliefs or on social bonds, but on the operation of chance within stable statistical distributions. Hints of this alternate explanation can be found lurking just outside the sociology of religion, and we believe it deserves serious consideration within the field as a way of understanding several aspects of religious commitment as well as the evolution of religious organizations.

We have nothing against the moral regeneration perspective. Indeed, as just indicated, our own research has convinced us that it has a major role to play in explaining sect transformation. Nevertheless, we suspect that the moral regeneration thesis alone is not sufficient to explain the initial upward shift in the class composition of sects. One important shortcoming is that the moral regeneration may pertain primarily to *intra*generational mobility, but the focus of the massive literature on sect transformation is on *inter*generational mobility. A model that explains mobility both in the first generation and across the generations would be particularly attractive.

Many individual sects have been subjected to detailed historical study. It has been remarked again and again how the arrival of the second generation — of persons socialized rather than converted to sect membership — undercuts the intense rejection of the world the first generation established. Many arguments about why the second generation transforms sects are virtual tautologies. Having defined sects as having a converted membership, some analysts take the fact that the second generation requires mechanisms for raising people in the faith as prima facie evidence that the sect has compromised with the world and become less sectlike. Others stress that "there is certainly a difference between those who are converted to a revolutionist sect, and those who accept adventist teachings at their mother's knee" (Wilson, 1966:207), but see this largely in terms of personality.

There is no reason to suppose that as fervent a rejectionist faith cannot be learned at mother's knee as from a revivalist if the two individuals' life circumstances turn out to be the same. Second generation sectarians ought to be as prone to high tension as first generation members if they have an equal need for a faith that rejects this world and offers compensation in the next. The observation that the second generation tends to change a sect stems from the fact that the second generation tends to contain many members who do not desire so rejectionist a faith and who are more prone to seek reconciliation with the external world. It is this variation that must be explained in order to have a more clearly specified theory.

If the softening caused by a second generation is the result of mobility, then we need to account for intergenerational mobility. Indeed, because the second generation is thought to produce such great change in sects, what is needed is a theoretical mechanism that produces a substantial amount of upward mobility between the first and second generations. Our current efforts to construct a deductive theory of religious movements led us to identify such a mechanism.

Sect Mobility

The technical theory on which this book is based (Stark and Bainbridge, 1980) produced several simple propositions that underlie our thinking on the transformation of sects from high tension to markedly lower tension. The first of these is that the higher the state of tension between a religious organization and its environment (or the more sectlike it is), the more efficacious are the religious comforts it can provide for persons frustrated in their pursuit of earthly rewards. The greater the degree of tension between a religious group and its environment, the greater the extent to which it will be composed of relatively powerless persons and the greater their degree of powerlessness. That is, high tension groups (sects) will be most attractive to the least powerful and least attractive to the most powerful. Many additional factors may contribute to belonging to sects, but sects are greatly overrecruited from among the relatively deprived sectors of society.

We define power as the ability to control one's exchange ratio — the net of rewards over costs in social exchanges. Rewards and costs are not limited to the purely economic or material, but consist of all things, including affection and contempt, that humans seek or shun. In practice, power is a somewhat elusive concept for direct analysis. Hence, attention turns to those attributes of persons and groups that produce power, that contribute to control over one's exchange ratio.

There are many power-giving attributes. Some, such as height and strength, are physical. Some, such as education, are achieved. Still others, such as caste, are ascribed. Whatever their source, our theory predicts that sects are overrecruited from among persons lacking power-giving attributes, and the more sectlike the group, the greater its proportion of deprived members.

Few power-giving attributes of persons and groups are wholly hereditary. It is mainly ascriptive characteristics that, at least over the short run,
can have a wholly hereditary transmission from parents to children.
Thus, in highly developed caste systems, caste membership remains constant from parents to their children. But very few power-giving attributes
are hereditary in this constant parent-to-child fashion. Indeed, virtually
none of the physical attributes that influence power are transmitted in
such a one-to-one fashion. Thus, although the children of lower caste
parents inevitably are lower caste, the children of short parents are not
invariably short, and the children of low IQ parents are not invariably of
low IQ (Jencks, 1972; McCall, 1977). Rather, there is a great deal of variation in such traits from parents to children. The same seems to be the case
for personality traits, even though these are not known to be genetic to
any substantial degree. Children of neurotic parents are not always neurotic; children of shy parents are not always shy, and so on (Pollin et al.,
1969; Kay, 1978).

The variability in the transmission of most nonascriptive traits con-
forms to a well-known statistical phenomenon identified as regression
toward the mean. Two assumptions must be met for regression toward
the mean to occur. First, the trait or traits of interest must tend to cluster
around the population mean. Second, there must be variability in the
trait or traits either over time or from one generation to the next. Given
these assumptions, statisticians have demonstrated that there will be a
tendency for cases lying above or below the mean to move (or regress)
toward the mean — either over time or through intergenerational transmission (Brownsberger, 1965; cf. Singer and Spilerman, 1976).

The tendency of cases to regress toward the mean is of critical concern whenever attention is focused on cases initially lying far from the
mean. For example, if a group of parents is selected on the basis of their
very high mean IQ, their children will have a noticeably lower mean IQ.
Conversely, children of extremely low IQ parents will have a noticeably
higher mean IQ than their parents. In both instances, the children's
mean IQ will regress toward the population mean — in effect, they will
be more average than their parents. If the response characteristics measured by IQ tests confer social power and an increased likelihood that
exchanges with conventional societal institutions will be rewarding, the
children may be less deviant in other respects as well (Hirschi and Hindelang, 1977).

Suppose we were to pick a group of parents who are extreme low
scorers on a variety of traits that tend to give power. Assume that these
are not wholly ascriptive characteristics and thus vary intergenera-
tionally. It is entirely predictable that their children will have a higher

mean score on these traits. Because these are power-giving traits, one would also predict a substantial amount of upward mobility between the first and second generations.

If it is true, as much evidence suggests, that sects are greatly overre-cruited initially from among extreme low scorers on many power-giving attributes, then it follows that the arrival and maturation of the second generation will result in a great deal of upward mobility by sect members. That is, if the sect is able to retain the second generation within the faith, there will be great change in the class composition of sects simply through regression toward the mean.

INDIVIDUAL UPWARD MOBILITY

Although our emphasis in this chapter is on intergenerational mobility, the process of regression can explain some intragenerational mobility as well and contributes to individual religious commitment. There are ups and downs in life. We can never know all the causes of good and bad fortune; so social scientists attribute much of the variation to "chance" and are prepared to analyze the phenomena in statistical terms. People generally seek help when they are experiencing bad fortune and are content with their circumstances when experiencing good fortune. Thus, those who turn to any source of special help — including high tension religious groups — tend to be at abnormally low points in their lives. The operation of many obscure factors (call them "chance") gives most of these people better times over the years following their search for help.

This pattern has two consequences for sects that recruit people suffering temporary deprivation. First, the average level of satisfaction of new recruits will tend to rise over time, apart from any real help the religion offers them. Second, new recruits will tend to attribute the improvement to the religion and gain a strong level of commitment. Others, seeing their improvement, may also gain in faith. A third factor operating simultaneously may also aid the sect. The minority of deprived individuals who continue to experience deprivation, or whose deprivation returns after a short remission, will not come to value the sect and will defect in search of a better solution to their problems. Their departure, too, increases the average level of satisfaction of the recruit cohort and may contribute to net upward mobility for the group as a whole.

These processes have been observed in the realm of psychotherapy, a field that we and many other writers consider adjacent to religion (Lederer, 1959; Frank, 1961; Rogler and Hollingshead, 1961; Kiev, 1964, 1972; Kennedy, 1967; Berkower, 1969; Breggin, 1971; Torrey, 1972; Finkel, 1976). The various brands of psychotherapy promise specific benefits, as do sects, and, to the extent that the claims of psychotherapy remain without firm scientific support, they might be described as client cults offering specific compensators. Although psychotherapists and many patients report great benefit from the treatment, controlled experiments often fail to show the effectiveness these people believe they see with their own eyes (Rachman, 1971). Eysenck (1965) and Brownsberger (1965) suggest that regression may provide a false impression of therapy-caused improvement (cf. McConaghy and Lovibond, 1967; May, 1971; McCleary et al., 1979). A group in treatment improves, but so does a control group not in treatment. Because therapists and patients do not have a control group against which to compare their own experience, they are unaware that the improvement does not stem from the treatment, but from obscure factors unrelated to treatment that obey our regression model.

Thus, chance produces faith. As Eysenck (1965:136) put it, "If the majority of neurotics tend to improve under moderately favorable external circumstances anyway, those who are under therapy while improving will be talking about their current actions and feelings in the sessions, and client and therapist will naturally attribute any changes to the therapy."

One reason for mentioning the literature on psychotherapy is that we have found very little in the sociology of religion itself that bears on these hypotheses. One relevant study was a survey of 83 members of Myochikai Kyodon, carried out by Aiko Moroto (1976). This group is one of the new religions of Japan, created by schism in 1950. Because the membership has grown to an estimated 130,000, this must be counted among the more successful sects of recent years, a group to which our propositions should apply. Moroto divided her respondents into three categories in terms of how much they participated in the group. Seventeen of her respondents were counted as "active," 20 as "moderate" in their activity, and 46 as "dormant," showing a much lower level of participation. Almost all had joined during the first five years of the sect, when it was recruiting from the extremely deprived populations that abounded in postwar Japan. But time had brought improvement for many people.

We would predict that those persons who had experienced upward social mobility would tend to attribute their good fortune to Myochikai Kyodon and display their increased commitment through greater activity. Indeed, Moroto's results can be interpreted to support this hypothesis. Of the active members, 88 percent had experienced upward social mobility since joining, compared with 50 percent of the "moderate" group and 41 percent of the "dormant" group (Moroto, 1976:35).

Prosperity is only imperfectly inherited, of course, and this individual upward mobility may explain only part of the group upward mobility that leads to tension reduction in successful sects. But the second generation may start from a more advantageous situation than their parents experienced when they joined, and further regression toward the mean may bring them entirely out of the deprived category.

MOBILITY AND TENSION REDUCTION

There are two important ways in which high tension collides with the interests of the privileged. First, rejection of the world and its delights denies the worth of the rewards that the privileged are successfully pursuing and gaining. Indeed, sect members who are succeeding in the external world often are targets of suspicion and even of abuse within the sect—they are sinners who covet the very rewards the sect exists to devalue. Second, the greater the degree of tension between the sect and its environment, the more that sect membership is a burden on the more successful. As we establish in Chapter 3, the degree of tension is equivalent to the degree of subcultural deviance. Such deviance always engenders impediments in dealing with outsiders. Thus, tension tends to impede the ease with which the more powerful sect members can increase their position in the external society. It follows that those with the greatest stake in the surrounding society (high status sect members) will desire to reduce these impediments by altering the sect in ways to make it more socially acceptable and thereby more socially accepting. If this is so, then, if the class composition of sects rises, they ought to move from greater to lesser tension.

These remarks represent a very condensed version of a complex chain of deductions. However, because these conclusions conform to a long intellectual tradition, it is unnecessary to elaborate them further here. Instead, our primary concern in this chapter is empirical. In what follows, we test two fundamental hypotheses. The first focuses on regression toward the mean as a major mechanism in the rising class composition of sects. Ideally, we would want longitudinal, intergenerational data on a number of sects and thus be able to demonstrate regressions toward the mean on a number of traits and show how this results in considerable upward mobility. No such data are likely to be available anytime soon. We must, therefore, settle for a weaker hypothesis that we can test on cross-sectional data: *Persons who join sects as adults will be of lower mean SES than persons who were born into the sect.*

The assumption made by this hypothesis is that persons recruited to a sect will reflect the overselection of persons low on various power-giving attributes. Persons born into sect membership will represent the offspring of such persons and, by their higher SES, will indicate the occurrence of regression toward the mean. We are fully aware that, in cross-sectional data, the born sectarians are not the offspring of the adult converts, for they are from the same birth cohorts. We must assume that current converts serve as an adequate proxy for data on converts of the prior generation. To the extent that a sect already has substantially reduced its initial state of tension, current converts may not be as deprived as the founding generation; thus, the comparisons available to us may greatly minimize the differences that actually existed between first and second generation members. Because this bias works against our hypothesis, it cannot be blamed for positive findings.

Given that mobility can be demonstrated as predicted by the first hypothesis, the question remains whether this is a major mechanism transforming sects from higher to lower tension. Once again, longitudinal data are desirable, but not available. However, the following cross-sectional hypothesis can yield a strong basis for inference: *Among members of sects, SES will be positively related to religious beliefs and practices that constitute lower tension with the surrounding society.* Put another way, higher SES sect members will be less different religiously from outsiders than are lower SES members.

The Data

Only one available data set contained the necessary variables and a large enough number of cases of sect members. These data are based on a random sample of church members in four urban counties in Northern California (Glock and Stark, 1965; Stark and Glock, 1968), the same set of data we used to such good effect in Chapter 3. The fact that the data are now nearly 20 years old is irrelevant to the task at hand. Our hypotheses are not bounded by time or culture, and 300-year-old data collected in China would be entirely suitable (and much more dramatic). Furthermore, the passage of time has allowed many early findings from these data to be replicated, thus lending confidence to the entire set.

Because our hypotheses are applicable to sect members alone, the analysis is limited to respondents selected from the membership rolls of seven religious groups that we demonstrated in Chapter 3 to be clearly identifiable as sects: Church of God, Churches of Christ, Nazarene, Assemblies of God, Seventh-Day Adventist, Gospel Lighthouse, and Foursquare Gospel.

The Regression Hypothesis

To test the hypothesis that sect converts are of lower SES than are socialized members of sects, we first separated sect members into those who had been raised in the sect and those who had joined as adults. We then compared the two groups on four SES measures. We found a modest difference in favor of the socialized members on each. However, when we introduced a series of control variables to test for spuriousness, a very dramatic interaction appeared. SES differences among males became very small, but, among females, the differences increased substantially. We quickly discovered the cause of this interaction.

In the United States today, people often switch religious affiliation, and more than half of sect members in this sample were adult converts. Furthermore, a good deal of church switching does not reflect religious concerns. A very common form of switching occurs because of mixed-denominational marriages (Greeley, 1981). When a mixed-denominational couple settles on a joint religious affiliation, it is more often the wife's church that they select. In consequence, our sample of adult converts to sects included a number of persons who can be classified as marital rather than religious converts, and these marital converts were disproportionately (61 percent) men. In contrast, only 30 percent of nonmarital converts were males and only 38 percent of all sect members were male (this sexual composition is similar to that of all Protestant churches). The result of this was the interaction when sex controls were introduced. The presence of a very disproportionate number of marital converts among the males greatly attenuated the SES differences between male converts and socialized members, but had little impact on female sect members. Having been alerted to this problem, we removed marital converts of both sexes from the analysis.

Table 7.1 shows four tests of the regression hypothesis. In every comparison, adult converts are of lower SES than are socialized members of sects. The majority of socialized members had attended college; the majority of converts had not. Socialized members were twice as likely as sect converts to earn more than $12,000 (a substantial income in 1963) and only about half as likely to earn less than $4,000. Subjective class is not an excellent SES measure; yet it, too, produces a modest difference in the predicted direction. The predicted relationship also appears when a four-level measure of occupational prestige is used to measure SES. Of these four tests of the hypothesis, only the one based on occupational prestige falls short of statistical significance. When significance is based on the probability of getting four such predicted relationships out of four tries, the likelihood that the results are due to chance is not worth serious consideration.

TABLE 7.1 *Socioeconomic Comparisons of Converted and Socialized Sect Members — Percent in Indicated Category*

	Adult Converts	Socialized Members
Education		
Some College	39	57
High School	35	35
8th Grade or less	26	8
	100	100
	(110)	(110)
Income		
$12,000 or more	5	12
$8,000–$11,000	31	33
$5,000–$7,000	32	37
$4,000 or less	32	18
	100	100
	(98)	(106)
Subjective Class[a]		
Middle	54	63
Working	46	37
	100	100
	(103)	(110)
Occupational Prestige		
Upper White Collar	28	34
Lower White Collar	17	18
Upper Blue Collar	37	39
Lower Blue Collar	18	9
	100	100
	(91)	(106)

Note: Converts via marriage are excluded.
[a]The item gave respondents a choice of working, upper, lower, and middle classes. None of these respondents chose either upper or lower.

The question of spuriousness always remains in nonexperimental studies. Because the sample is of Whites only and from a small area of California, race and region controls are not pertinent, but age and sex presented plausible counterexplanations. However, controls for these variables did not reduce these or other relationships reported in this chapter.

By 1963, when these data were collected, each of these bodies classified as a sect had been in existence for several generations. An examination of their histories reveals that each had undergone significant reduction in its tension with the external society during that time. Therefore, there is every reason to suppose that living converts were not as deprived as the founding generation had been. Yet, despite this obvious bias against our hypothesis, the data fail to reject it. We take this as a crucial test of our theoretical mechanism that simple regression toward the mean will result in a marked rise in the class composition of sects as the founding generation is replaced by its offspring. It can also be seen in the data that, even in a society marked by massive church switching, sects are able to *retain* enough of their higher status offspring to produce a rise in class composition. That is, the upwardly mobile sons and daughters of sect members do not simply defect to lower tension, less deviant faiths, but many remain members and thus could constitute an influential and growing constituency for change.

The Transformation Hypothesis

The second postulated mechanism in the transformation of sects into churches is based on the premise that middle-class and upper-class persons will have little need for a high tension faith and, indeed, will find such a faith somewhat incompatible with their needs. If this is so, then the principal of regression toward the mean would explain the transformation of religious groups in the direction of reduced tension with their environments. Do class divisions within sects create distinctive constituencies for higher or lower tension?

In Chapter 3, we supplied greater conceptual rigor to the concept of tension and demonstrated empirical means for measuring it. Because we define tension as equivalent to subcultural deviance, it is composed of three elements: difference, antagonism, and separation. When we examined tension in Chapter 3, we selected a number of empirical measures of each of these dimensions of tension and demonstrated how they markedly and interchangeably identified certain religious groups as sects—the same groups whose members served as the sample in this chapter. We may now draw upon these measures of tension to test our second hypothesis that the higher the SES of the sect member, the less his or her personal religious outlook will conform to a high tension pattern. That is, upper SES sect members should be less different from members of low tension religious groups in terms of their religious beliefs. Similarly, they should express less antagonism toward other religious groups. However, as we consider in detail below, they should not be less separated from nonsect members. Table 7.2 permits ten tests of these conclusions.

TABLE 7.2 *Socioeconomic Status and Sectarian Tension — Percent Holding Indicated Views*

	Sect Members SES:			Sect Total (193)	Low Tension Prots. (1,032)	All Prots[b] (2,326)	Roman Caths. (545)
N[a] =	Lower (81)	Middle (80)	Upper (32)				
Religious Difference							
1. Express literal belief in biblical miracles	96	91	78	91	39	57	74
2. Say the theory of evolution could not possibly be true	92	86	56	84	11	30	28
3. Believe drinking will prevent salvation	39	26	19	30	3	7	2
Religious Antagonism							
4. Say belief in Jesus is absolutely necessary for salvation	100	96	88	96	41	65	51
5. Say membership in their particular faith required for salvation	26	19	13	21	5	11	28
6. Would tend to distrust someone who does not believe in Jesus	55	42	29	45	19	27	22
7. Think non-Christian missionaries should not be allowed to spread their teachings among Christians	41	45	19	40	17	25	23
8. Have often tried to convert others to their own religion	30	33	23	30	5	10	5
Separation							
9. Have half or more of their associates from within their congregation	70	70	85	73	29	38	47
10. Have 3 or more of their 5 best friends from their congregation	63	66	72	65	22	29	36

[a]Ns vary by several cases across these tables due to missing data.
[b]Includes sect members.

The table shows that SES does greatly influence the degree of religious difference between sect members and their environment. Although virtually all lower SES sect members claim literal belief in biblical miracles, only about three-fourths of higher SES sect members hold this position. A central matter that sets sects off from churches in contemporary America is a rejection of the theory of evolution in favor of the biblical account of creation. Only 30 percent of all Protestants deny the possibility that Darwin's theory could be true (28 percent of Roman Catholics), and only 11 percent of members of the lowest tension Protestant bodies express this view. In contrast, the huge majority of sect members rejects evolution as impossible — a rejection that finds constant expression in conflicts over school textbooks. However, within the sects, a near majority of the upper SES members is "soft" on evolution — only 56 percent hold evolution as not possibly true, compared with 92 percent of lower SES members.

Drinking liquor is a historic norm dispute between Protestant sects and the larger society. Sects reject it; society permits it. The item shown in Table 7.2 greatly minimizes the opposition to alcohol among all respondents, for it links it to the possibility of gaining salvation. A Christian can be unalterably opposed to drinking and still think such behavior has little or no bearing on salvation because of faith in the forgiveness of sins. Nevertheless, sects differ markedly from lower tension groups on this item. The upper SES sect members are much more like other Protestants on the subject of drinking than they are like the lower SES members of their groups.

Similar patterns are revealed when we examine measures of religious antagonism — the higher a sect member's SES, the less likely that he or she will reject the religious legitimacy of other faiths. The majority of these Christian respondents believes that only those who accept Jesus can be saved, but 100 percent of the lower SES sect members hold this view. Only a small minority of Christians believes that a person must be a member of their particular faith in order to be saved, but lower SES sect members are twice as likely as upper SES sect members to hold this view. Most Christians would not "tend to distrust a person who does not believe in Jesus," but a majority of lower SES sect members would. Although 41 percent of lower SES sect members would prevent non-Christian missionaries from proselytizing among Christians, only 19 percent of their upper SES coreligionists would do so. The question of trying to convert others to one's faith is not prima facie a measure of antagonism toward outsiders. Yet it does indicate belief in the superior status of one's own religion and often is the occasion for conflict among religious groups. Sect members are much more likely than other Christians to have often tried to lead someone into their own faith. However, upper SES sectarians are noticeably less likely to have done so.

Eight tests of the SES-tension relationship have confirmed the transformation hypothesis. Upper SES sect members are less religiously different from the external society and less antagonistic toward it. Given a rise in the proportion of higher SES members in a sect, one would expect the sect increasingly to reflect these lower tension views — as the SES of a sect rises, it will begin the process of transformation that leads to accommodation with the world. Thus, class does seem to be the mechanism that propels the church-sect cycle by transforming sects into churches and thus creating the conditions for the splintering off of new sects.

The two "separation" items in Table 7.2 further indicate how upper SES members transform sects. We did not predict that upper SES sect members would be less socially immersed within the sect because church-sect theory requires that upper SES sect members transform a sect, not defect from it. We have already seen that upper SES sect members are somewhat deviant within the sect in terms of their theology. If such persons also shifted the weight of their interpersonal relations outside the sect, it is likely that they would soon simply shift their religious affiliation to that of their outside friends. To the extent that this occurs, sects are not transformed. Defection prevents the growth of an influential constituency for reduced tension.

For transformation to occur, a growing proportion of upper SES members must not only remain within a sect, they must gain decisive influence within the group. Marginal members, deviant in theological terms and in the density of their social ties to the outer society, do not possess the influence to transform a group. Therefore, if sects are to be transformed, upper SES members must be at the center of the network of social relations that identifies the sect.

Items nine and ten in Table 7.2 show that this is in fact the case. Sects differ greatly from lower tension religious bodies in their degree of separation. Although only few members of lower tension groups limit their associations and friendships to their religious congregation, most sect members limit their social relations in this fashion. Moreover, upper SES sect members are more likely to report a high degree of social separation than are lower SES members. Eighty-five percent of upper SES sect members have half or more of their associates within their congregation, compared with only 70 percent of lower SES sectarians. Similarly, 72 percent of upper SES sect members report that three or more of their five best friends are from their congregation, but 63 percent of the lower SES members restrict their friendships in this fashion.

The limited data available to us have not permitted the most decisive tests of the regression hypothesis, but we were able to show that the hypothesis predicts just the results to be found in the only available relevant data set. The moral regeneration hypothesis is also in line with the findings. In particular, the two separation items from Table 7.2 measure the extent to which the respondent has strong social ties to the congregation, and stronger ties are associated with higher status. However, these measures have the disadvantage of not taking into account that some people have a larger number of strong associations than others. Control theory would be very interested in how many (if any) close friends a person had and would not assume they did have five, as implied by the final question in the table. Therefore, our data are more relevant to the regression hypothesis, although they do not give us grounds for rejecting a moral regeneration hypothesis based in control theory. One could argue the relative merits of regression versus regeneration at great length on purely theoretical grounds, but we think it is best to conclude that both are very live hypotheses that can be distinguished conclusively only on the basis of future research looking directly at the processes that produce upward mobility among sect members.

The Weberian hypothesis that religious doctrines communicate success-giving norms and values does not fare well in Table 7.2. The respondents who have succeeded in secular affairs are less likely than their unsuccessful brethren to hold the beliefs that are normative in the sectarian subculture. Other hypotheses that assume that sects rise by converting high status people to elevate a low status native membership fail in the light of Table 7.1.

CONCLUSION

The picture that emerges from these data gives a highly plausible and parsimonious account of how sects are tranformed into churches. First, socialized sect members differ from converted members in the way predicted by our regression-toward-the-mean mechanism. Socialized members are of higher SES than are adult converts, which means that nothing more than a succession of generations is required to raise the class composition of sects. Indeed, the class composition of the socialized members of these Protestant sects already is quite similar to that of many lower tension denominations, such as the Lutherans. Upward mobility by the offspring of sect members would not raise the class composition of sects if these persons mainly defected to lower tension faiths, but, even in so free-floating a religious marketplace as the United States today, a large enough proportion of upwardly mobile sect members is retained so that the class composition of the sect is raised.

Given that these upper SES members are retained, the data also show that they do adopt a lower tension religious outlook than that of the sect's founders and than that held by lower SES members.

The last step in the transformation process lies in the fact that upper SES sect members are not socially marginal, but establish themselves in the center of the social network of the sect. In this fashion, they are able to influence group policies and decisions. In effect, over time, they are able to adapt the sect to better suit their personal needs and desires for greater accommodation with the world.

History supplies the final, and telling, datum. The sects we have examined here, and within which we have found the elements necessary for their transformation, are primarily sects that are undergoing transformation from higher to lower tension. If we exclude the single congregation sect (the Gospel Lighthouse) and the apparently declining Church of the Foursquare Gospel (founded by the famous Aimee Semple McPherson), which together provide only 9 percent of our sect respondents, we are left with five thriving sect movements, each of which has clearly moved toward lower tension since its founding. One very obvious sign of this transformation is the fact that each of these sect movements has in turn already given birth to several new sect movements. The Church of the Nazarene, for example, has produced at least three new sects since 1956. The precipitating factor producing these three schismatic movements was undoubtedly a reduction in tension, a continuing process of "lowering standards of holiness and a regression from spirituality" (Melton, 1978:237). In similar fashion, the other four "successful" sects have sloughed off higher tension sect movements. The Church of God has produced at least five.

Thus, not only are there elements present in these sects that ought to be transforming them; these sects are in fact being transformed. But not all sects undergo transformation. As we showed in the previous chapter, many do not. The critical factor is the degree of initial tension the sect adopts. If it is too high, the sect risks becoming so totally isolated, and membership in and of itself becoming so totally stigmatizing, that mere membership in the sect relegates persons to very limited chances for mobility. For example, a sect that isolates its members in a rural retreat makes it impossible for them to pursue most occupations (or to do so without first defecting). Similarly, a sect that does not permit members to complete more than the legally required amount of schooling has effectively prevented upward mobility (cf. Keim, 1975). If the sect is labeled as sufficiently deviant, its members will be denied the possibility for status achievement in the outer world. Suppose a sect fully embraced mortification of the flesh (as has occurred in Christian history), including that members never wash their bodies or clothing and change clothing only when wear raises risks of immodesty. In contemporary society, members of such a sect would find their prospects for upward mobility virtually nil.

When the degree of tension between a sect and its environment serves as a sufficient barrier to member mobility, the series of mechanisms of transformation outlined and tested in this chapter will not occur. Sect founders wholly devoted to establishing a permanently high tension faith ought, therefore, to cross the tension threshold beyond which mobility is excluded. Yet, if they do so, they also sacrifice all prospects for substantial growth. Groups that are too isolated cannot gain converts, for conversion requires that group members have access to outsiders. Thus, the desire to construct a successful and growing movement often keeps sect founders from maximizing tension with the environment. In consequence, their movements often do grow rapidly. But, in thus succeeding, they also cease to be sects, and therein lies the dynamic of the church-sect process Niebuhr saw so clearly 50 years ago.

▮▮ *Cults*

8 Three Models of Cult Formation

The origins of the great world faiths are shrouded by time, but cult formation remains available for close inspection. If we would understand how religions begin, it is the obscure and exotic world of cults that demands our attention. This chapter synthesizes the mass of ethnographic materials available on cult formation as the necessary preliminary for a comprehensive theory. Although it represents an important step in our continuing work to formulate a general theory of religion, this chapter is primarily designed to consolidate and clarify what is already known about this subject.

The published literature on cults is at present as chaotic as was the material on which cultural anthropology was founded a century ago: an unsystematic collection of traveler's tales, mostly journalistic, often inacurate, and nearly devoid of theory. For all the deficiencies of this mass of writing, three fundamental models of how novel religious ideas are generated and made social can be seen dimly. In this chapter we develop and compare these models. Although we find it convenient to discuss them separately, each is but a different combination of the same theoretical elements.

The three models of cult formation, or religious innovation, are (1) *the psychopathology model*, (2) *the entrepreneur model*, and (3) *the subculture-evolution model*. Other social scientists have presented the first in some

This chapter was originally published as William Sims Bainbridge and Rodney Stark, "Cult Formation: Three Compatible Models," *Sociological Analysis,* 1979, 40:4, pp. 283–295.

detail, but the second and third have not previously been delineated as formal models.

Cult formation is a two-step process of innovation. First, new religious ideas must be *invented*. Second, they must be *socially accepted* by at least a small group of people. Therefore, we must first explain how and why individuals invent or discover new religious ideas. Many (perhaps most) persons who hit upon new religious ideas do not found new religions. So long as only one person holds a religious idea, no real religion exists. Therefore, we also need to understand the process by which religious inventors are able to make their views social — to convince other persons to share their convictions. We conceptualize successful cult innovation as a social process in which innovators both invent new religious ideas and transmit them to other persons in exchange for rewards.

RELIGIONS AS EXCHANGE SYSTEMS

To understand how cults are formed, a brief reprise of our general theory of religion is in order. We have noted that human action is governed by the pursuit of rewards and the avoidance of costs (Stark and Bainbridge, 1980). Rewards, those things humans will expend costs to obtain, often can be gained only from other humans; so people are forced into exchange relations. However, many rewards are very scarce and can be possessed by only some, not all. Other rewards appear to be so scarce that they cannot be shown to exist at all. Having learned to seek rewards through exchanges with other persons, in their desperation humans turn to each other for these highly desired scarce and nonexistent rewards. And from each other humans often receive compensators for the rewards they seek.

When rewards are very scarce, or not available at all, humans create and exchange compensators — sets of beliefs and prescriptions for action that substitute for the immediate achievement of the desired reward. Religions are social enterprises whose primary purpose is to create, maintain, and exchange supernaturally based general compensators. But how do new compensators and new systems of compensators get invented? Modest rates of compensator production may take place in any social organization, but, to see mass production and radical innovation, we must look to cults.

Cults are social enterprises primarily engaged in the production and exchange of novel or exotic compensators. Thus, not all cults are religions. Some offer only magic — for example, psychic healing of specific diseases — and do not offer such general compensators as eternal life. Magical cults frequently evolve toward progressively more general compensators and become full-fledged religions. Then they become true *cult movements:* social enterprises primarily engaged in the production and exchange of novel and exotic general compensators, based on supernatural assumptions.

Often, a cult is exotic and offers compensators that are unfamiliar to most people who encounter it because it migrated from another, alien society. In this chapter, we are not interested in these imported cults, but in those novel cult movements that are innovative alternatives to the traditional systems of religious compensators that are normal in the environment in which the cult originated.

Two points should be kept in mind about the three models of cult formation. First, they are *compatible*. Any pair, or even all three, could combine validly to explain the processes of innovation that produced a given cult. Second, the processes described can take place at a reduced rate in any religious organization — or even in secular organizations. Only if the compensators produced are very general and based on supernatural assumptions shall we speak of *religion*. Only when the degree of innovation is extreme shall we speak of a *cult*. But all the dimensions we describe are matters of degree, and the models could be applied in attenuated from to even very slight episodes of compensator innovation.

The first model appears to be the most extreme, although it also is the most familiar. It locates the creative spark of religion in human experiences of ultimate despair and confusion; yet there is no reason why diluted variants of the same processes could not also occur.

THE PSYCHOPATHOLOGY MODEL OF CULT INNOVATION

The *psychopathology model* has been used by many anthropologists and ethnopsychiatrists, and it is related closely to deprivation theories of revolutions and social movements (Smelser, 1962; Gurr, 1970). A similar approach has been used to explain involvement in radical politics (Lasswell, 1930; Smith et al., 1956; Langer, 1972). The model describes cult innovation as the result of individual psychopathology that finds successful social expression. Because of its popularity among social scientists, this model exists in many variants, but the main ideas are the following:

1. Cults are novel cultural responses to personal and societal crisis.
2. New cults are invented by individuals suffering from certain forms of mental illness.
3. These individuals typically achieve their novel visions during psychotic episodes.

4. During such an episode, the individual invents a new package of compensators to meet his own needs.

5. The individual's illness commits him to his new vision, either because his hallucinations appear to demonstrate its truth or because compelling needs demand immediate satisfaction.

6. After the episode, the individual will be most likely to succeed in forming a cult around his vision if the society contains many other persons suffering from problems similar to those originally faced by the cult founder, to whose solution, therefore, they are likely to respond.

7. Therefore, such cults most often succeed during times of societal crisis, when large numbers of persons suffer from similar unresolved problems.

8. If the cult does succeed in attracting many followers, the individual founder may achieve at least a partial cure of his illness because the self-generated compensators are legitimated by other persons and because the founder now receives true rewards from his followers.

The psychopathology model is supported by the traditional psychoanalytic view that all magic and religion are mere projections of neurotic wish fulfillment or psychotic delusions (Freud, 1927, 1930; Devereux, 1953; Roheim, 1955; La Barre, 1969, 1972). However, the model does not assume that cultic ideas are necessarily wrong or insane. Rather, it addresses the question of how individuals can invent deviant perspectives and then have conviction in them, despite the lack of objective, confirmatory evidence.

All societies provide traditional compensator systems that are familiar to all their members and that have considerable plausibility both because their assumptions are familiar and because of the numbers of people already committed to them. Then why should some persons reject the conventional religious tradition, concoct apparently arbitrary substitutes, and put their trust in these novel formulations? The psychopathology model notes that highly neurotic or psychotic persons typically do just this, whether in a religious framework or not. By definition, the mentally ill are mentally deviant. Furthermore, especially in the case of psychotics, they mistake the products of their own minds for external realities. Thus, their pathology provides them not only with abnormal ideas, but with subjective evidence for the correctness of their ideas, whether in the form of hallucinations or of pressing needs that cannot be denied.

A number of authors have identified occult behavior with specific psychiatric syndromes. Hysteria frequently has been blamed. Cult founders often do suffer from apparent physical illness, find a spiritual "cure" for their own ailment, then dramatize that cure as the basis of the cult performance (Messing, 1958; Lévi-Strauss, 1963; Lewis, 1971). A well-known American example is Mary Baker Eddy, whose invention of Christian Science apparently was a successful personal response to a classic case of hysteria (Zweig, 1932).

In other cases, a manic-depressive pattern is found. John Humphrey Noyes, founder of the Oneida community, had an obsessive need to be "perfect." In his more elevated periods, he was able to convince a few dozen people that he had achieved perfection and could help them attain this happy state as well. But the times of elation were followed by "eternal spins," depressive states in which Noyes was immobilized by self-hatred (Carden, 1969).

Classical paranoia and paranoid schizophrenia also have been blamed for producing cults. A person who founds a cult asserts the arrogant claim that he or she (above all others) has achieved a miraculous cultural breakthrough, a claim that outsiders may perceive as a delusion of grandeur. For example, L. Ron Hubbard (1950b: 9) announced his invention of Dianetics (later to become Scientology) by saying, "The creation of dianetics is a milestone for Man comparable to his discovery of fire and superior to his inventions of the wheel and arch."

Martin Gardner has shown that the position of the cultist or pseudoscientist in the social environment is nearly identical to that of the clinical paranoid. Neither is accorded the high social status he or she demands from conventional authorities, and each is contemptuously ignored or harshly persecuted by societal leaders. Gardner (1957: 12) notes that paranoia actually may be an advantage under these circumstances because, without it, the individual "would lack the stamina to fight a vigorous, single-handed battle against such overwhelming odds."

Many biographies of cult founders contain information that would support any of these diagnoses, and often the syndrome appears to be a life pattern that antedated founding the cult by a number of years. However, the symptoms of these disorders are so close to the features that define cult activity that simplistic psychopathology explanations approach tautology. Lemert (1967) has argued that social exclusion and conflict over social status can produce the symptoms of paranoia. It may be that some cult founders display symptoms of mental illness as a result of societal rejection of their cults. Another problem faced by the psychopathology model is the fact that the vast majority of mental patients has not founded cults.

The simplest version of the model states that the founder's psychopathology had a physiological cause. Religious visions may appear during psychotic episodes induced by injuries, drugs, and high fevers. If an episode takes place outside any medical setting, the individual may find a supernatural explanation of the experience most satisfactory (Sargant, 1959). Innumerable examples exist. Love Israel, founder of a cult called the Love Family, told us that his religious vision was triggered by hallucinogenic drugs that enabled him to experience a state of fusion with another man, who subsequently became a prominent follower. The stories of some persons who claim to have been contacted by flying saucers sound very much like brief episodes of brain disorder to which the individual has retrospectively given a more favorable interpretation (Greenberg, 1979).

More subtle variants of the psychopathology model present psychodynamic explanations and place the process of cult formation in a social context. Julian Silverman (1967) outlined a five-step model describing the early career of a shaman (sorcerer, witch doctor, magical healer) or cult founder. In the first stage, the individual is beset by a serious personal and social problem, typically severely damaged self-esteem, that defies practical solution. In the second stage, the individual becomes preoccupied with this problem and withdraws from active social life. Some cultures have even formalized rituals of withdrawal in which the individual may leave the settlement and dwell temporarily in the wilderness. The Bible abounds in examples of withdrawal to the wilderness to prepare for a career as a prophet.

Withdrawal immediately leads to the third stage, in which the individual experiences "self-initiated sensory deprivation," which can produce very extreme psychotic symptoms even in previously normal persons. Thus begins the fourth stage, in which the future cult founder receives a supernatural vision. "What follows then is the eruption into the field of attention of a flood of archaic imagery and attendant lower-order referential processes such as occur in dreams or reverie. . . . Ideas surge through with peculiar vividness as though from an outside source" (Silverman, 1967: 28).

In the fifth stage, which Silverman calls *cognitive reorganization*, the individual attempts to share this vision with other people. Failure drives the person into chronic mental illness. Success in finding social support for these supernatural claims transforms the person into a mentally stable shaman or cult leader. If the followers reward the leader sufficiently with honor, the originally damaged self-esteem that provoked the entire sequence will be repaired completely, and the cult founder may even become one of the best adapted members of the social group (cf. Boas, 1940).

The theory of *revitalization movements* proposed by Anthony F. C. Wallace (1956) is similar to Silverman's model but adds the important ingredient of social crisis. Wallace (1956: 269) suggests that a variety of threats to a society can produce greatly increased stress on members: "climatic, floral and faunal change; military defeat; political subordination; extreme pressure toward acculturation resulting in internal cultural conflict; economic distress; epidemics; and so on." Under stress, some individuals begin to go through the process Silverman outlined and, under favorable circumstances, achieve valuable cultural reformulations that they can use as the basis of social action to revitalize their society. Although Wallace (1956: 273) advocates a pure form of the psychopathology model, he concludes "that the religious vision experience per se is not psychopathological but rather the reverse, being a synthesizing and often therapeutic process performed under extreme stress by individuals already sick."

Wallace's suggestions that many historically influential social movements, and perhaps all major religions, originated according to its principles underscores the importance of the psychopathology model. This view is held by Weston La Barre (1972), who says that every religion originated as a *crisis cult*, using this term for cults that emerge according to the pattern Wallace described. He specifically describes Christianity as a typical crisis cult. Writing in an orthodox Freudian tradition, La Barre identifies the source of a cult founder's vision: "A god is only a shaman's dream about his father" (La Barre, 1972: 19, cf. Freud, 1916). He says the shaman is an immature man who desperately needs compensation for his inadequacies, including sexual incapacity. In finding personal magical compensations the shaman generates compensators for use by more normal persons as well (La Barre, 1972: 138).

Claude Lévi-Strauss, an exchange theorist as well as a structuralist, emphasizes that the shaman participates in an economy of meaning. Normal persons want many kinds of rewards they cannot obtain and can be convinced to accept compensators generated by fellow citizens less tied to reality than they. "In a universe which it strives to understand but whose dynamics it cannot fully control, normal thought continually seeks the meaning of things which refuse to reveal their significance. So-called pathological thought, on the other hand, overflows with emotional interpretations and overtones, in order to supplement an otherwise deficient reality" (Lévi-Strauss, 1963: 175). In shamanism, the neurotic producer of compensators and the suffering normal consumer come together in an exchange beneficial to both, participating in the exchange of compensators for tangible rewards that is the basis of all cults.

THE ENTREPRENEUR MODEL OF CULT INNOVATION

The *entrepreneur model* of cult innovation has not received as much attention from social scientists as has the psychopathology model. We have known for decades that the psychopathology model could not explain adequately all cultic phenomena (Ackerknecht, 1943), but attempts to construct alternate models have been desultory. It is difficult to prove that any given cult founder was psychologically normal, but, in many cases, even rather lengthy biographies fail to reveal significant evidence of pathology. Although the psychopathology model focuses on cult founders who invent new compensator systems initially for their own use, the entrepreneur model notes that cult founders often may consciously develop new compensator systems in order to exchange them for great rewards. Innovation pays off in many other areas of culture, such as technological invention and artistic creativity. If social circumstances provide opportunities for profit in the field of cults, then many perfectly normal individuals will be attracted to the challenge.

Models of entrepreneurship have been proposed to explain many other kinds of human activity, but we have not found adequate social scientific models specifically designed to explain cult innovation. Journalists have documented that such a model would apply well to many cases, as our own observations in several cults amply confirm. Therefore, we sketch the beginnings of an entrepreneur model, with the understanding that much future work will be required before this analytic approach is fully developed. The chief ideas of such a model might be the following:

1. Cults are businesses which provide a product for their customers and receive payment in return.

2. Cults are mainly in the business of selling novel compensators, or at least freshly packaged compensators that appear new.

3. Therefore, a supply of novel compensators must be manufactured.

4. Both manufacture and sales are accomplished by entrepreneurs.

5. These entrepreneurs, like those in other businesses, are motivated by the desire for profit, which they can gain by exchanging compensators for rewards.

6. Motivation to enter the cult business is stimulated by the perception that such business can be profitable, an impression likely to be acquired through prior involvement with a successful cult.

7. Successful entrepreneurs require skills and experience, which are most easily gained through a prior career as the employee of an earlier successful cult.

8. The manufacture of salable new compensators (or compensator packages) is most easily accomplished by assembling components of pre-existing compensator systems into new configurations or by further developing successful compensator-systems.

9. Therefore, cults tend to cluster in lineages. They are linked by individual entrepreneurs who begin their careers in one cult and then leave to found their own. They bear strong "family resemblances" because they share many cultural features.

10. Ideas for completely new compensators can come from any cultural source or personal experience whatsoever, but the skillful entrepreneur experiments carefully in the development of new products and incorporates them permanently in his cult only if the market response is favorable.

Cults can, in fact, be very successful businesses. The secrecy that surrounds many of these organizations prevents us from reporting current financial statistics, but a few figures have been revealed in various investigations. Arthur L. Bell's cult, Mankind United, received contributions totaling $4 million in the ten years preceeding 1944 (Dohrman, 1958:41). Between 1956 and 1959, the Washington, D.C., branch of Scientology took in $758,982 and gave its founder, L. Ron Hubbard, $100,000 plus the use of a home and car (Cooper, 1971:109). Today, Scientology has many flourishing branches, and Hubbard lives on his own 320-foot ship. In 1979, an English expatriate cult, The Process, was grossing $100,000 a month, $4,000 of this going directly to the husband and wife team who ran the operation from their comfortable Westchester County estate (Bainbridge, 1978c:168). In addition to obvious material benefits, sucessful cult founders also receive intangible but valuable rewards, including praise, power, and amusement. Many cult leaders have enjoyed almost unlimited sexual access to their followers (Orrmont, 1961; Carden, 1969).

The simplest variant of the entrepreneur model, and the one preferred by journalists, holds that cult innovators are outright frauds who have no faith in their own product and sell it through trickery to fools and desperate persons. Certainly, we have many examples of cults that were pure confidence games, and we cite examples of fraud in three kinds of cult we defined in Chapter 2: audience cults, client cults, and cult movements.

In 1973, Uri Geller barnstormed the United States, presenting himself as a psychic who could read minds and bend spoons by sheer force of will. As James Randi (1975) has shown, Geller's feats were achieved through trickery; yet untold thousands of people were fascinated by the possibility that Geller might have real psychic powers. The whole affair was a grand but short-lived audience cult.

Medical client cults based on intentional fraud are quite common. A number of con artists have discovered not only that they can use the religious label to appeal to certain kinds of gullible marks, but also that the label provides a measure of protection against legal prosecution (MacDougall, 1958; Glick and Newsom, 1974). In many of these cases, it may be impossible to prove whether the cult founder was sincere or not, and we can only assume that many undetected frauds lurk behind a variety of client cults.

In some cases, the trickery is so blatant that we can have little doubt. Among the most recent examples are the Philippine psychic surgeons, Terte and Agpaoa, and their Brazilian colleague, Arigo. These men perform fake surgery with their bare hands or brandishing crude jack-knives. In some cases, they may actually pierce the patient's skin, but often they merely pretend to do so and then spread animal gore about to simulate the results of deep cutting. Through a skillful performance, they convince their patients not only that dangerous tumors have been removed from their bodies, but also that the surgeon's psychic powers have instantaneously healed the wound. But their failure actually to perform real operations in this manner must be clear to the psychic surgeons themselves (Flammonde, 1975).

Arthur L. Bell's cult movement was a fraud based on the traditional Rosicrucian idea that a vast benevolent conspiracy prepares to rule the world and invites a few ordinary people to join its elite ranks. Bell claimed only to be the superintendant of the Pacific Coast Division, in constant communication with his superiors in the (fictitious) organizational hierarchy. In this way, he was able to convince his followers that they were members of an immensely powerful secret society, despite the fact that the portion of it they could see was modest in size. Like several similar fraudulent movements, Bell's cult did not originally claim religious status, but became a "church" only after encountering legal difficulty (Dohrman, 1958).

In order to grow, a cult movement must serve real religious functions for its committed followers, regardless of the founder's private intentions. Many older cults probably were frauds in origin but have been transformed into genuine religious organizations by followers who deeply believed the founder's deceptions.

But fraud need not be involved in entrepreneurial cult innovation. Many ordinary businesspeople are convinced of the value of their products by the fact that customers want to buy them, and cult entrepreneurs may likewise accept their market as the ultimate standard of value.

Many cult founders do appear to be convinced that their compensator packages are valuable by testimonials from satisfied customers. This was probably the case with Franz Anton Mesmer, who saw astonishing transformations in his clients, apparently the beneficial results of his techniques, and found in them ample evidence of the truth of his theories (Zweig, 1932; Darnton, 1970). Practitioners of all client cults frequently see similar evidence in favor of their own ideas, no matter how illogical, because all such cults provide compensators of at least some strength (Frank, 1961). We describe mechanisms that would encourage them in Chapter 7.

Another source of confidence for cult innovators is their experience with other cults. Early in their careers, innovators typically join one or more successful cults and honestly may value the cults' products themselves. However, they may be dissatisfied with various aspects of the older cults and come to the sincere opinion that they can create a more satisfactory product. Despite their often intense competition, cult leaders frequently express respect and admiration for other cults, including the ones with which they themselves were previously associated. L. Ron Hubbard of Scientology has praised Alfred Korzybski's General Semantics; Jack Horner of Dianology has praised Hubbard's Scientology; other examples abound.

Once we realize that cult formation often involves entrepreneurial action to establish a profitable new organization based on novel culture, we can see that concepts developed to understand technological innovation should apply here as well. For example, a study of entrepreneurship and technology by Edward B. Roberts (1969) examined the cultural impact of the Massachusetts Institute of Technology, the preeminent center of new technological culture. Over 200 new high technology companies had been founded by former M.I.T. employees who concluded they could achieve greater personal rewards by establishing their own businesses based on what they had learned at M.I.T. The current cult equivalent of M.I.T. is Scientology, which Bainbridge studied in 1970. Cultic entrepreneurs have left Scientology to found countless other cults based on modified Scientology ideas, including Jack Horner's Dianology, H. Charles Berner's Abilitism, Harold Thompson's Amprinistics, and the flying saucer cult described in the ethnography *When Prophecy Fails* (Festinger et al., 1956). Scientology, like M.I.T., is a vast storehouse of exotic culture derived from many sources. Social scientists studying patterns of cultural development should be aware that an occasional key organization can be an influential nexus of innovation and diffusion.

Future research can determine the most common processes through which entrepreneurial cult founders actually invent their novel ideas. We suspect that the main techniques involve the cultural equivalent of recombinant DNA genetic engineering. Essentially, the innovator takes the cultural configuration of an existing cult, removes some components, and replaces them with other components taken from other sources. The innovator may simply splice pieces of two earlier cults together. In some cases, the innovator preserves the supporting skeleton of practices and basic assumptions of a cult he or she admires and merely grafts on new symbolic flesh. Rosicrucianism affords a sequence of many connected examples (Hall, 1928; King, 1970; McIntosh, 1972). In creating the AMORC Rosicrucian order, H. Spencer Lewis took European Rosicrucian principles of the turn of the century, including the hierarchical social structure of an initiatory secret society, and grafted on a veneer of symbolism taken from Ancient Egypt, thus capitalizing on public enthusiasm for Egyptian civilization that was current at the time. His headquarters, in San Jose, California, is a city block of simulated Egyptian buildings. Later, Rose Dawn imitated Lewis in creating her rival Order of the Ancient Mayans. In great measure, she simply replaced AMORC's symbols with equivalent symbols. Instead of Lewis's green biweekly mail-order lessons emblazoned with Egyptian architecture and Egyptian hieroglyphics, she sold red biweekly mail-order lessons decorated with Mayan architecture and Mayan hieroglyphics.

The highly successful *est* cult is derived partly from Scientology and well illustrates the commercialism of many such organizations in contemporary America. Werner Erhard, founder of *est*, had some experience with Scientology in 1969. Later, he worked for a while in Mind Dynamics, itself an offshoot of Jose Silva's Mind Control. After Erhard started his own cult in 1971, he decided to emulate Scientology's tremendous success and hired two Scientologists to adapt its practices for his own use. Conventional businesses, such as auto companies and television networks, often imitate each other in pursuit of profit. Erhard's research and development efforts were rewarded, and, by the beginning of 1976, an estimated 70,000 persons had completed his $250 initial seminar (Kornbluth, 1976).

We suggest that cult entrepreneurs will imitate those features of other successful cults that seem to them most responsible for success. They will innovate either in nonessential areas or in areas where they believe they can increase the salability of the product. In establishing their own cult businesses, they must innovate at least superficially. They cannot seize a significant part of the market unless they achieve product differentiation. Otherwise, they will be at a great disadvantage in direct competition with the older, more prosperous cult on which theirs is patterned (cf. Hostetler, 1968; Cooper and Jones, 1969). The apparent novelty of a cult's compensator package often may be a sales advantage because the public has not yet discovered the limitations of the rewards that members actually will receive in the new cult, although older compensator packages may have been discredited to some extent. Much research and theory building remains to be done, but the insight that cults often are examples of skillful free enterprise immediately explains many of the features of the competitive world of cults.

The Subculture-Evolution Model of Cult Innovation

Although the psychopathology and entrepreneur models stress the role of the individual innovator, the *subculture-evolution model* emphasizes group interaction processes. It suggests that cults can emerge without authoritative leaders, and it points out that even radical developments can be achieved through many small steps. Although much social psychological literature would be useful in developing this model, we are not aware of a comprehensive statement on cult innovation through subcultural evolution; so again we attempt to outline the model ourselves.

1. Cults are the expression of novel social systems, usually small in size but composed of at least a few intimately interacting individuals.

2. These cultic social systems are most likely to emerge in populations already deeply involved in the occult milieu, but cult evolution may also begin in entirely secular settings.

3. Cults are the result of sidetracked or failed collective attempts to obtain scarce or nonexistent rewards.

4. The evolution begins when a group of persons commits itself to the attainment of certain rewards.

5. In working together to obtain these rewards, members begin exchanging other rewards as well, such as affect.

6. As they progressively come to experience failure in achieving their original goals, they will gradually generate and exchange compensators as well.

7. If the intragroup exchange of rewards and compensators becomes sufficiently intense, the group will become relatively encapsulated, in the extreme case undergoing complete social implosion.

8. Once separated to some degree from external control, the evolving cult develops and consolidates a novel culture, energized by the need to facilitate the exchange of rewards and compensators, and inspired by essentially accidental factors.

9. The end point of successful cult evolution is a novel religious cul-

ture embodied in a distinct social group which must now cope with the problem of extracting resources (including new members) from the surrounding environment.

In writing about juvenile delinquency, Albert K. Cohen (1955) described the process of *mutual conversion,* through which interacting individuals could gradually create a deviant normative structure (cf. Thrasher, 1927). This process may result in criminal behavior, but it may also result in the stimulation of unrealizable hopes and of faith in the promise of impossible rewards. Thus, mutual conversion can describe the social process through which people progressively commit each other to a package of compensators that they simultaneously assemble. It begins when people with similar needs and desires meet and begin communicating about their mutual problems. It takes place in tiny, even imperceptible, exploratory steps, as one individual expresses a hope or a plan and receives positive feedback in the form of similar hopes and plans from fellow members.

> The final product . . . is likely to be a compromise formation of all the participants to what we may call a cultural process, a formation perhaps unanticipated by any of them. Each actor may contribute something directly to the growing product, but he may also contribute indirectly by encouraging others to advance, inducing them to retreat, and suggesting new avenues to be explored. The product cannot be ascribed to any one of the participants; it is a real "emergent" on a group level. (Cohen, 1955:60)

Cohen (1955:50) says that all human action "is an ongoing series of efforts to solve problems." All human beings face the problem of coping with frustration because some highly desired rewards, such as everlasting life, do not exist in this world. Through mutual conversion, individuals band together to solve one or more shared problems, and the outcome presumably depends on a number of factors, including the nature of the problems and the group's initial conceptualization of them. We suspect that a cultic solution is most likely if the people begin by attempting to improve themselves (as in psychotherapy) or to improve their relationship to the natural world and then fail in their efforts. Criminal or political outcomes are more likely if people believe that other persons or social conditions are responsible for their problems.

The quest for unavailable rewards is not reserved for poor and downtrodden folk. Many elite social movements have been dedicated to the attainment of goals that ultimately proved unattainable. One well-documented example is the Committee for the Future, an institutionally detached little organization that formed within the network of technological social movements oriented toward spaceflight. Founded in

1970 by a wealthy couple, the CFF was dedicated to the immediate colonization of the moon and planets and to beginning a new age in which the field of human activity would be the entire universe. The biggest effort of the CFF, Project Harvest Moon, was intended to establish the first demonstration colony on the moon, planted using a surplus Saturn V launch vehicle. Ultimately, high cost and questionable feasibility prevented any practical accomplishments.

In struggling to arouse public support, the CFF held a series of open conventions at which participants collectively developed grand schemes for a better world. Blocked from any success in this direction, the CFF evolved toward cultism. The convention seminars became encounter groups. Mysticism and parapsychology replaced spaceflight as the topic of conversation. Rituals of psychic fusion were enacted to religious music, and the previously friendly aerospace companies and agencies broke with the committee. Denied success in its original purposes and unfettered by strong ties to conventional institutions, the CFF turned ever more strongly toward compensators and toward the supernatural (Bainbridge, 1976).

Cults are particularly likely to emerge wherever numbers of people seek help for intractable personal problems. The broad fields of psychotherapy, rehabilitation, and personal development have been especially fertile for cults. A number of psychotherapy services have evolved into cult movements, including those created by some of Freud's immediate followers (Rieff, 1968; cf. Brown, 1967; Jung, 1909). Other independent human service organizations may also be susceptible to cultic evolution. The best known residential program designed to treat drug addiction, Synanon, has recently evolved into an authoritarian cult movement that recruits persons who never suffered from drug problems.

Two important factors render cultic evolution more likely. First, the process will progress most easily if there are no binding external constraints. For example, psychiatrists and psychologists who work in institutional settings (such as hospitals or universities) may be prevented by their conventional commitments from participating in the evolution of a cult, but independent practitioners are more free. Second, the process will be facilitated if the therapist receives compensators as well as gives them and thus will participate fully in the inflation and proliferation of compensators.

A good example is The Process, founded in London in 1963, which began as an independent psychotherapy service designed to help normal individuals achieve supernormal levels of functioning (Rowley, 1971; Cohen, 1975; Bainbridge, 1978c). The therapy was based on Alfred Adler's theory that each human being is impelled by subconscious goals, and it attempted to bring these goals to consciousness so the person could pursue them more effectively and escape inner conflict (Adler, 1927, 1929). The founders of The Process received the therapy as well as gave it, and frequent group sessions brought all participants together to serve each other's emotional needs. The Process recruited clients through the founders' preexisting friendship network, and the therapy sessions greatly intensified the strength and intimacy of their social bonds.

As bonds strengthened, the social network became more thoroughly interconnected as previously distant persons were brought together. The rudiments of a group culture evolved, and many individuals contributed ideas about how the therapy might be improved and expanded. Participants came to feel that only other participants understood them completely and found communication with outsiders progressively more difficult. A social implosion took place.

In a social implosion, part of an extended social network collapses as social ties within it strengthen and, reciprocally, those to persons outside it weaken. It is a step-by-step process that may be set off by more than one circumstance. In the case of The Process, the implosion was initiated by the introduction of a new element of culture, a "therapy" technique that increased the intimacy of relations around a point in the network. Correlated with the implosion was a mutual conversion as members encouraged each other to express their deepest fantasies and to believe they could be fulfilled. The Adlerian analysis of subconscious goals was ideally designed to arouse longings and hopes for all the unobtained and unobtainable rewards the participants had ever privately wished to receive. The powerful affect and social involvement produced by the implosion were tangible rewards that convinced participants that the other rewards soon would be achieved.

Concomitant estrangement from outside attachments led The Process to escape London to the isolation of a ruined seaside Yucatán plantation. Remote from the restraining influence of conventional society, The Process completed its evolution from psychotherapy to religion by inventing supernatural doctrines to explain how its impossible, absolute goals might ultimately be achieved. When the new cult returned to civilization in 1967, it became legally incorporated as a church (Bainbridge, 1978c).

Nonreligious groups can evolve into religious cults; so it is not surprising that cults also can arise from religious sects — extreme religious groups that accept the standard religious tradition of the society, unlike cults that are revolutionary breaks with the culture of past churches. An infamous example is the Peoples Temple of Jim Jones, which destroyed itself in the jungles of Guyana. This group began as an emotionally extreme but culturally traditional Christian sect, then evolved into a cult as Jones progressively became a prophet with an ever more radical vision. Either the psychopathology or entrepreneur models may apply in this case, but the committed members of the sect probably contributed to the transformation by encouraging Jones step by step and by demanding that he accomplish impossible goals. Even when a single individual dominates a group, the subculture-evolution model will apply to the extent that the followers also participate in pushing the group toward cultism. In this case, the needs of the followers and their social relationships with the leader may have served as a psychopathology amplifier, reflecting back to Jones his own narcissism multiplied by the strength of their unreasonable hopes.

CONCLUSION

Each of the three models identifies a system of production and exchange of compensators. In the psychopathology model, a cult founder creates compensators initially for his or her own use, then gives them to followers in return for rewards. In the entrepreneur model, the cult founder sets out to gain rewards by manufacturing compensators intended for sale to followers. The subculture-evolution model describes the interplay of many individual actions in which various persons at different times play the roles of producer and consumer of novel compensators.

Although the models may appear to compete, in fact, they complement each other and can be combined to explain the emergence of particular cults. After cult founders have escaped a period of psychopathology, they may act as entrepreneurs in promoting or improving their cult. Entrepreneurs threatened with loss of their cult may be driven into an episode of psychopathology that provides new visions that contribute to a new success. The subculture-evolution model may include many little episodes of psychopathology and entrepreneurial enterprise participated in by various members, woven together by a complex network of social exchanges.

Taken together, the psychopathology, entrepreneur, and subculture-evolution models foreshadow a general theory of cult innovation that can be constructed using their elements connected logically within the framework of exchange theory. Although the technical derivation of a theory to accomplish this cannot be given here (cf. Stark and Bainbridge, 1980), several later chapters of this volume contribute detail to the three models and suggest how they might fit together. But even at the level of competing models, the three offer numerous explanatory hypotheses that could be tested using the store of historical information found in any large library or new data collected in future field research. The models provide a checklist of important questions to guide the ethnographer in studying a cult. Until now, the social science of cult innovation has lacked a clear body of theory and a research program. The three models developed in this chapter provide a solid basis for studying the emergence of new religions, and they have already begun to influence the teaching of the sociology of religion (Chalfant et al., 1981:260–263).

9 Cult Movements in America: A Reconnaissance

WITH DANIEL P. DOYLE

Since the Puritans first set foot on this continent, America has been a fertile ground for new religions. Literally hundreds of new faiths have appeared here, and some of them, such as Christian Science and Mormonism, have achieved lasting success.

In Chapter 6, we explored American-born sect movements. In this chapter, we explore cult movements, novel religious movements in a deviant religious tradition. Here we do not limit ourselves to native-born cults; we also examine the many imported cult movements if they are based primarily on converts recruited here, rather than on an immigrant ethnic population. For example, we include a variant of Zen Buddhism if its members primarily are Americans of European stock but we eliminate such a group if its members primarily are Japanese-Americans for whom it is their traditional ethnic faith brought with them from Japan. The latter seem best regarded as ethnic churches, much like the Greek Orthodox church, although we admit this was a borderline decision. As it happens, many imported cults do not even have branches in the countries from which their founders came, but exist only as American organizations.

Hundreds of cult movements are found across the nation, and a pri-

This chapter is a much revised version of Rodney Stark, William Sims Bainbridge, and Daniel P. Doyle, "Cults of America: A Reconnaissance in Space and Time," *Sociological Analysis*, 1979, 40:4, pp. 347–359. Regional data were recalculated so that this chapter would correspond with others in its geographical division of the nation.

mary interest in this chapter is to locate them in space and time. Where do cult movements of various kinds find the most hospitable social environment in the United States? Have these patterns changed over time? In Part V, we use these findings to test a theory about the relationship between secularization and cult formation. Here we devote our attention to description.

LOCATION

Cults are not randomly distributed across the map. Some parts of the country are especially hostile to religious deviance; so cults are discouraged from settling in these places. Other parts of the country may be especially conducive to the social processes that create cults, as described in the previous chapter. Melton's great volumes list the addresses of the headquarters of the many cults he found; so we can tabulate them by state and region, thus performing a reconnaissance in space (Melton, 1978).

For most cults, the national headquarters is located in the state where the group originated. Typically, this is also the state in which most, if not all, of its current members reside. Many cults consist of a single group or congregation and others consist of only two or three groups, but some large cults, such as Scientology, have many groups from coast to coast. Therefore, our count of cult national headquarters tends to minimize the picture of cult activity across the nation.

A glance in the classified telephone directory of any large city proves that branch offices of large cults may abound, even in places without a single national headquarters. For example, Melton found no cults headquartered in Delaware; yet, in 1980, Wilmington had branches of eight groups that might be called cults: Baha'i, Christian Science, Eckankar, Latter-day Saints (Mormons), Reorganized Latter Day Saints, Spiritualists, Swedenborgians, and the Unification Church (Moonies). Alaska has no national headquarters; yet Fairbanks has two Baha'i groups, a Scientology center, and branches of Christian Science and the Mormons. Montana abounds in Latter Day Saints groups and has at least nine Christian Science churches. There are Baha'i groups in Helena, Billings, Miles City, Missoula, and Great Falls. Unity groups are also to be found in Billings, Missoula, and Great Falls, and Missoula may boast branches of Eckankar and the Unification Church as well. Yet Montana does not have a single national headquarters.

But we think the data in Melton's encyclopedia offer a good measure of the level of cult activity, so long as we understand that it represents cult activity, rather than being a full census of all functioning congregations.

Because almost all cults are small, a state that does not harbor a home-grown cult group is less fertile soil for religious novelty than are states that produce such groups. The state of Washington has ten national cult headquarters; yet the central Seattle classified telephone directory lists 61 cult centers, and one cult with its headquarters in the very middle of the city is not even listed because it does not believe in telephones. Indeed, it is our impression that the large cults have their major outposts in places where there are also many other active cult groups.

An additional problem is that cults sometimes move. An extreme instance is Scientology, whose effective world headquarters for a number of years has been at sea — aboard a 320-foot ship. Where cults move *to* is perhaps even more diagnostic of the character of environments than is where they originate. Jim Jones did not move his Peoples Temple from Indiana to California in pursuit of milder winters; he went to gain greater freedom to develop the cult in more radical directions. That he later fled to the jungles of Guyana shows that even California places some limit on religious deviance.

One might prefer to have a census of each branch office of all cults. A massive study of the nation's telephone directories might produce a decent roster, but such a project would require heavy funding and must therefore remain a dream for the future. We also would love to see an accurate census of cult membership across the nation, but such a huge and politically sensitive trove of data seems even further out of reach at present. In the chapters that follow, we introduce partial but good data on the distributions of cult branches and the membership of several specific groups. We begin here by examining cult headquarters because their geography shows where cults often arise and where they take their public stands against an often unfriendly world. The pattern uncovered here emerges again and again in other measures of cult activity.

Table 9.1 shows that states differ greatly in terms of cults. California leads in the absolute number of cults. One of every three American cult groups has its headquarters in the Golden State. Next highest is New York, with 12 percent of the nation's cult headquarters, followed by Illinois with 7 and Florida with 4. Cults are located in 41 of the 50 states and in the District of Columbia. Seven states claim only one cult headquarters.

Population differences play an important role in where cults flourish. Presumably, the more people in an area, the greater the number of groups that can gain a founding nucleus. This is a major proposition in Claude Fischer's (1975) theory of subcultural diversity within cities. Therefore, we took population differences into account by dividing a state's population by the number of cults located in it and expressing the

TABLE 9.1 *American Cults by State*

State	Number of Cults	Cults per Million Residents	State	Number of Cults	Cults per Million Residents
1. Nevada	6	10.0	23. Michigan	10	1.1
2. New Mexico	10	9.1	24. Rhode Island	1	1.0
3. California	167	7.9	25. Iowa	3	1.0
4. Colorado	15	6.0	26. Arkansas	2	1.0
5. Arizona	13	5.9	27. Tennessee	4	1.0
6. Oregon	11	4.8	28. Minnesota	4	1.0
7. Hawaii	4	4.4	29. Indiana	5	0.9
8. New York	59	3.3	30. Ohio	9	0.8
9. Missouri	15	3.1	31. Wisconsin	3	0.7
10. Illinois	34	3.0	32. New Jersey	5	0.7
11. Washington	10	2.9	33. Oklahoma	2	0.7
12. Wyoming	1	2.5	34. Alabama	2	0.6
13. New Hampshire	2	2.5	35. North Carolina	3	0.6
14. Florida	20	2.4	36. Maryland	2	0.5
15. Nebraska	3	2.0	37. Kansas	1	0.4
16. Massachusetts	11	1.9	38. Georgia	2	0.4
17. Utah	2[a]	1.7	39. South Carolina	1	0.4
18. Virginia	8	1.6	40. Kentucky	1	0.3
19. Connecticut	5	1.6	41. Louisiana	1	0.3
20. Pennsylvania	18	1.5			
21. Idaho	1	1.3	Washington, D.C.	11	15.7
22. Texas	14	1.2			

Note: Alaska, Delaware, Maine, Mississippi, Montana, North Dakota, South Dakota, Vermont, and West Virginia had none.
[a]Utah Mormon Groups omitted.

result as the number of cults per million residents. The rates for many states are based on a very small number of cases. Had we located one fewer cult for Nevada, for example, its rate would have dropped from 10.0 to 8.3. A loss of a cult or two in California, however, would make no difference in the rate. For this reason, the regional rates are probably somewhat more trustworthy. Yet it is interesting to note the high similarity of rates among the states making up given regions, which suggests that the rates for individual states are relatively accurate. They have been included in Table 9.1.

With population taken into account, California falls to third place as a cult locale. Two states that lack a reputation for cult activity rise to the top: Nevada, with a rate of 10 cults per million, and New Mexico, with a rate of 9.1. California is third, with a rate of 7.9, followed by Colorado (6.0) and Arizona (5.9) to make up the top five cult states in the Union.

The table also shows that the District of Columbia has a higher rate of cult headquarters per million than does any state (15.7). When we first saw this result, we thought it probably was caused by a tendency for large cult groups to establish a national headquarters in the nation's capital, but this was not the case. The cults of D.C. seem indigenous. Indeed, they closely coincide with population patterns of the district and with impressions about whom various cult groups primarily appeal to. The two most notable features of the population of Washington, D.C., are an unusually high proportion of older, single females and a very high proportion of Blacks. The older, single females primarily are government clerks (married civil servants live mainly in suburbs outside the district). They are relatively well educated, and it has long been thought that women of this kind were the backbone of membership for cults of the New Thought, Theosophical, Spiritualist, and psychic varieties. Such cults constitute 54 percent of those found in the capital. All the remaining cults are adaptations of Asian faiths — mainly varieties of Muslims. These are cults that flourish in the Black community. Given the district's unusual population distribution, its very high cult rate makes intuitive sense.

An important qualification must be noted about how we scored Utah. Utah has a rather high rate of cults (5.8) if schismatic Mormon groups are counted. The much lower rate shown in Table 9.1 for Utah (1.7) occurs because we did not classify Mormon groups as cults if they were located in Utah. Relative to the religious climate of the nation as a whole, Mormon groups are cults. Too much novel culture has been added to the Christian-Judaic tradition for Mormonism simply to be another Christian sect. However, in the state of Utah, Mormonism is the dominant religious tradition. To be a Mormon in Utah is to be normal, not deviant. In consequence, it seemed wise to classify schismatic Mormon groups in Utah as sects, not cults: They remain part of the religious mainstream of Utah in precisely the same fashion as do small Baptist sects in Georgia. But we did code Mormon groups outside Utah as cults. Where they are located, Mormonism is a deviant faith. It is the presence of a number of small Mormon groups that raises Missouri to ninth place on the list. Many of these Missouri groups have survived from the days of the great schism that beset Mormonism following the assassination of Joseph Smith in Carthage, Illinois. They remained behind and drifted back to Missouri while Brigham Young led the majority of Mormons west.

Table 9.1 shows a huge regional bias in cult geography. The top seven states, in terms of cults per million residents, are all located in the West. However, these regional differences are even more dramatically evident in Figure 9.1, which shows that the leading region is the Pacific, which consists of Alaska, Hawaii, Washington, Oregon, and California. The Pacific region has 2.9 times the national rate of cults per million residents and 1.4 times the rate for the second-ranking region, the Mountain. Taken together, the Pacific and Mountain regions comprise the western part of the nation. Third place is held by the Middle Atlantic region, with a rate only a third that of the Pacific, even slightly lower than the national rate. Lowest of all are the West South Central and East South Central regions, with less than one cult headquarters per million residents. Although the South Atlantic region has a rate just below that

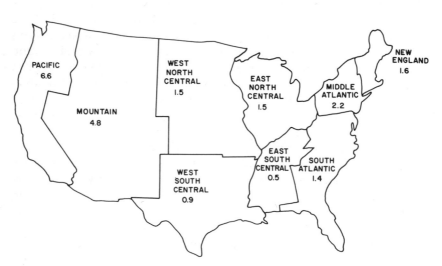

FIGURE 9.1   *Regional Cult Rates per Million Population*
(National rate = 2.3 per million)

shared by the two North Central regions, a glance back at Table 9.1 reveals that the leading state in the region is Florida and the second greatest contributor to the region's rate is the nation's capital. Southern Florida, where most of its cults are headquartered, is the area that least resembles the South culturally; so we can observe that a vast cult-free belt covers the South, missing only a few border areas.

If we want to find cults, we must look to the West. Thirty-eight percent of the cults are headquartered in the Pacific region alone, and 48 percent are in the combined Pacific and Mountain regions. In Chapter 4, we show that the West also is unusual in its low rates of church membership, and in Chapter 19, we bring these two facts together to explain the distribution of American cults. But one observation that shines forth again and again in these pages is that the far West is especially hospitable to novel and exotic religions.

V INTAGE

Our data include only cults currently in existence. Some of these, like the Mormons, are old; others were founded within the past several years. In Chapter 6, we draw on information in Melton's (1978) encyclopedia to compare the dates of founding of American-born sects and of the cults described in this chapter. Table 6.2 demonstrates that the average cult is much younger than the average sect. Here we use the same data to chart more precisely the vintages of the cults.

For the nation as a whole, only 15 percent of existing cults were founded prior to 1930. This suggests that most cults are short-lived. Perhaps many of them depend so heavily on their founder's efforts and effectiveness that they fold up quickly when the leader dies. Whatever the reason, almost two-thirds of American cults (61 percent) are less than 20 years old.

However, the age of cults is very strongly related to geography, as can be seen in Table 9.2. Some of the regions contain few cult headquarters; so we might want to combine them into larger geographic units for the most reliable comparison. In the combined New England and Middle Atlantic regions, 25 percent of the cults were founded before 1930. The proportion is 20 percent in the two North Central regions, 13 percent in the three regions of the South, and only 9 percent in the combined Mountain and Pacific regions.

The youthfulness of cults in the more westerly regions probably reflects population changes. Prior to 1930, the population in these areas was much smaller than today, even relative to the rest of the nation. Therefore, relatively fewer cults should have been forming there in that

TABLE 9.2   *Proportion of Cults in Each Region Founded Before 1930*

Region	Percent of Cults Founded Before 1930
New England	21
Middle Atlantic	26
East North Central	18
West North Central	24
South Atlantic	11
East South Central	0
West South Central	22
Mountain	4
Pacific	10
National	15

period. However, population shifts do not account for the youth of southern cults. Our hunch is that both the current low rate of cults in the South and the absence of older cults reflect the greater hostility of the South to religious deviance, a phenomenon we document in Chapter 4. Indeed, it seems historically likely that a few decades ago the South was so hostile toward cults (compared with the rest of the nation) that cult formation was impeded, cult survival was diminished, and cult migration to more hospitable regions was stimulated.

VARIETY

Cults form a number of distinctive religious traditions of their own. They are subject to schism, just as are churches. That is, the church-sect process operates within any religious tradition, not just in dominant traditions. Thus, a number of American cults formed by fission. However, having broken off from the parent body, if they remain within a novel tradition, they also remain cults.

Cults tend to form lineages even when they do not originate via schism. Many cult founders engage in wholesale borrowing from other cults and have often served an apprenticeship in an established cult group before leaving to start a new group with a slightly modified version of the established cult's teachings and ceremonies. The result of such modes of cult formation is that cults form distinctive families or similarity clusters.

One of the most valuable and original features of Melton's (1978) massive cataloguing of religious movements is the care with which he traced family groups on the basis of schism and similarities in doctrines. Our analysis follows Melton's division of cults into families. In Table 9.3, we have collapsed his more detailed divisions into 13 categories, which we consider the fundamental divisions among cult groups. Some of the 13 categories also are related to each other, forming whole tribes of cults, but our divisions permit useful analysis of geographic differences and trends. Table 9.3 shows that different cult families are more represented in some regions than in others. Later chapters, especially Chapter 11, give further historical information about particular organizations, but here we can comment briefly on the characters of the families and their geographic distributions.

Mormon groups make up an unusually large proportion of the cults located in the West Central region, primarily because of the number located in Missouri.

Cult communes are pretty well scattered, except for their absence from the two West Central regions.

New Thought groups stem from Phineas Parkhurst Quimby (1802–1866) of Belfast, Maine, who was a student of Mesmerism and animal magnetism. His most famous student, Mary Baker Eddy, founded Christian Science, the most successful New Thought group in America. However, many other similar groups also exist. New Thought groups are overrepresented in New England and in the two South Central regions where cults of other kinds are rare.

Theosophy and *Spiritualism* are closely intertwined traditions. Spiritualism is the older tradition, being based on the teachings of two controversial figures of the 18th century: Emmanuel Swedenborg and Franz Anton Mesmer. American Spiritualists trace their movement back to the Fox sisters, who became nationally famous mediums in the mid-19th century. Theosophy, like Spiritualism, embraces the principle of direct contact with the spirit world. It was founded by Helena Petrovna Blavatsky, a Russian of aristocratic origins who gained great popularity in Europe and the United States during the latter part of the 19th century. Theosophical and Spiritualist groups constitute the largest of American cult families — one out of every four.

The most popular of the *occult orders* is the Ancient and Mystical Order of the Rosae Crucis (Rosy Cross), one of the groups commonly referred to as Rosicrucians and whose prominent ads can be found in many popular magazines. These occult groups are modeled after the Freemasons — secret societies with many levels of membership to be achieved by study and initiation ceremonies. There are a number of such occult orders besides the AMORC in the United States.

Flying saucer cults are based on the hope of contacts with spiritually advanced races from outer space. Some prominent cult leaders in this tradition claim actually to have gone on trips to other planets and to

TABLE 9.3 *Cult Composition of Regions of the United States — Percent in Each Region of a Given Type*

Kind of Cult	Pacific	Mountain	West South Central	East South Central	South Atlantic	West North Central	East North Central	Middle Atlantic	New England	National
1. Mormon[a]	0	10	0	0	0	24	3	2	0	3
2. Cult Communes	5	2	0	14	2	0	3	1	5	3
3. New Thought	5	4	21	43	4	8	3	6	21	7
4. Theosophy and Spiritualism	26	29	16	14	34	4	23	22	21	25
5. Occult Orders	5	2	5	0	0	0	3	2	0	3
6. Flying Saucer	6	2	5	0	6	4	3	1	0	4
7. Psychedelic	2	4	0	0	2	0	0	0	0	1
8. Psychic	12	18	11	14	15	20	0	7	16	11
9. Magick, Witches, Satanists	8	8	16	14	17	20	16	11	16	12
10. Pagans	7	0	5	0	0	4	8	1	0	4
11. Asian Faiths	19	18	16	0	19	0	23	38	21	21
12. Jesus People	4	0	0	0	0	4	7	0	0	2
13. Miscellaneous	2	2	5	0	0	12	7	7	0	4
Total	100	100	100	100	100	100	100	100	100	100

[a]Utah Mormon groups omitted. Because of rounding, some columns may not total exactly 100 percent.

have gained great mystical wisdom in the company of 'brothers' from outer space. Flying saucer cults had their peak during the 1950s and early 1960s but today make up only 4 percent of the total.

Psychedelic cults employ drugs to stimulate religious visions. These groups were more popular during the days of widespread experimentation with LSD and other hallucinogens in the 1960s. Today they are heavily overconcentrated in the West.

Psychic groups believe the mind has incredible powers that can be developed only through proper training. Scientology is the leading psychic cult of the moment, and many groups have broken off from it. Many other psychic groups base their teachings on older mental power traditions.

We come now to a family of cults that, although it has received a great deal of publicity in recent times, is not taken seriously by many people, including scholars: groups committed to ancient traditions of *magick*, *witchcraft*, and *Satanism*, often attempting to rekindle pre-Christian faiths and ceremonies. These cults are seriously involved in what they call "magick" — real spells distinguished from trick prestidigitation by deviant spelling of the word. Many who read of covens of witches who gather under the full moon, naked, to form the "magick circle" (usually made up of 13 persons) or of Satanists who celebrate black masses and ornate sexual rituals think the people involved are simply thrill seekers. Although some groups may play-act at witchcraft as an excuse for kinky sex, there exist many such groups that are in deadly earnest about their faith, and some of them have become increasingly militant. A Witches Anti-Defamation League exists. In June 1979, we inspected and photographed a Seventh-Day Adventist church in Seattle, Washington, that had been spray painted with slogans such as "The Blood of Witches is on Christians' Hands" and "Off Jesus, back to the Mother" by a self-proclaimed lesbian witches' coven. Oddly enough, the Pacific region is noticeably low in the proportion of its cults that fall into this family.

Pagans are often close cousins of the magick and witchcraft family. They are groups who have attempted to reinstate the ancient, pre-Christian faiths of Greece, Rome, Egypt, and Great Britain. Among these are the Neo-Dianic Faith and the Reformed Druids of North America.

The *Jesus people*, or Jesus freaks, sufficiently novel to be called cults rather than sects, flourished during the late 1960s and very early 1970s. They are headquartered only in the Pacific and North Central regions.

Only 4 percent of cults can be placed in a residual miscellaneous category.

Table 9.4 shows the cult family composition of the top ten cult states, in terms of cults per million residents, plus number 15 (Florida) and the

TABLE 9.4   *Cult Composition of High Ranking States — Percent in Each Category*

Rank: Number of Cults:	1 Nev. 6	2 N.M. 10	3 Calif. 167	4 Colo. 15	5 Ariz. 13	6 Ore. 11	7 Haw. 4	8 N.Y. 59	9 Mo. 15	10 Ill. 34	15 Fla. 20	D.C. 11	National Total 501
Kinds of Cult													
1. Mormon Groups	0	10	1	0	15	0	0	0	47	0	0	0	3
2. Cult Communes	0	10	4	0	0	18	0	0	0	6	5	0	3
3. New Thought	0	0	6	13	0	0	0	8	13	0	5	9	7
4. Theosophy and Spiritualism	33	30	27	13	46	0	25	22	7	18	50	18	25
5. Occult Orders	0	0	5	7	0	0	0	2	0	3	0	0	3
6. Flying Saucer Cults	0	0	3	0	0	55	0	2	0	3	10	0	4
7. Psychedelic	0	20	2	0	0	0	0	0	0	0	0	0	1
8. Psychic	33	30	12	13	15	9	0	10	13	0	5	27	11
9. Magick, Witches, Satanists	0	0	9	13	8	0	0	12	0	15	20	0	12
10. Pagans	0	0	6	0	0	18	0	0	7	12	0	0	4
11. Asian Faiths	33	0	21	40	8	0	50	37	0	31	5	46	21
12. Jesus People	0	0	3	0	0	0	25	0	0	6	0	0	2
13. Miscellaneous	0	0	1	0	8	0	0	7	13	6	0	0	4
	100	100	100	100	100	100	100	100	100	100	100	100	100

Note: Because of rounding, some columns may not total exactly 100 percent.

District of Columbia. These states show quite different mixes of cults. California closely approximates the national distribution. (It has so many cults, it almost *is* the national distribution.) New Mexico and Nevada have an unusually large proportion of psychic groups, and New Mexico also has an extremely high proportion of psychedelic groups making up its total. Colorado and New York are special havens for Asian faiths, and Arizona and Florida have very disproportionate numbers of Theosophical and Spiritualist groups. These groups are believed to appeal especially to the elderly because the focus is on communication with the dead and with the world beyond. Because both Florida and Arizona attract very large retirement populations, this finding would seem to make sense.

Anyone who wondered where the flying saucer cults have gone can now see that many of them went to Oregon. Although such groups make up 4 percent of the national total, they are 55 percent of the cults in Oregon. As we noted earlier, Missouri is high in Mormon cults. Florida is above the norm in the magick, witches, and Satanist family.

Finally, as we have already pointed out, the District of Columbia's cults are concentrated in the Asian and the psychic families, with the remainder in the traditions of New Thought and Theosophy and Spiritualism.

CULT NAMES

As we coded the data on cults, we were struck by the fact that the name a cult group adopts reveals much about its stance toward society at large. We encountered many cults, if one went by their names alone, that one would assume did not belong in the cult category. For example, among groups we counted were Society of Christ, Universal Christ Church, and the Liberal Catholic Church. It would surely seem that these groups fall within the dominant Christian tradition of American society, but they do not. The first two are Spiritualist and the third is Theosophical. Then there are many groups that, although they do not include an explicit Christian referent in their name, strongly suggest that they are Christian: St. Timothy's Abbey Church or the Congregational Church of Practical Theology. Again, the first is a Spiritualist body; the second belongs to the psychic family.

Other cults, however, bear names that proclaim their departure from conventional religion: "Ruby Focus" of Magnificent Consummation, Universal Faithists of Kosmon, Enchanted Moon Coven, Church of Satanic Brotherhood, or the Self-Revelation Church of Absolute Monism.

Differences such as these suggest something about the climate surrounding various cults. Presumably, the more hostile the environment is toward cults, the more pressure there is on a group to adopt a facade of respectability. Hence, a person who tells outsiders that he or she belongs to the Universal Christ Church will not be so easily labeled as weird or wicked as will a person whose affiliation is with "Ruby Focus" of Magnificent Consummation, to say nothing of a person affiliated with an overtly Satanist or witchcraft group.

We coded each cult according to the degree that its name would pass as conventional. We anticipated that groups in the Pacific region might be more inclined to adopt cultish-sounding names, and such a difference does exist. However, this turns out to be a function of the fact that cults in western regions tend to be younger. The major factor in what kind of a name a cult has is when it was founded, not where.

As can be seen in Table 9.5, nearly half the cults founded before 1910 have an explicit Christian referent in their name. An additional 14 percent do not have an explicit Christian referent, but nonetheless have names that sound like conventional religion. Hence, nearly two-thirds of the surviving cults from the pre-1910 period chose to "pass" — to reduce friction with the surrounding society by taking on the coloration of the dominant religious tradition. This probably helped them recruit members. Many of the middle-class recruits to Spiritualism or Theosophy, the groups that most flourished during that era, undoubtedly were reassured by the Christian trappings, including a "normal-sounding" name.

In the 20-year period 1910 through 1929, however, there was a decline in passing. The major shift was away from explicit Christian references in group names. Only 29 percent of those groups founded during this period included such references, and just under half employed names that would pass as ordinary. Following 1930, passing fell dramatically again. Since then, only one cult in ten has put a Christian referent in its name, and only a third have ordinary-sounding names.

This changing pattern suggests that the decline in power of conven-

TABLE 9.5   *Trend Away from Christian-Sounding or Conventional-Sounding Names*

Period	Percent with Christian-Sounding Names	Percent with Christian-Sounding or Conventional-Sounding Names
1909 and before	47	61
1910–1929	29	49
1930–1949	9	37
1950–1977	10	33

tional religion during the 20th century has made life easier for cult groups. There are fewer costs associated with religious deviance and hence less reason for cult groups to hide behind a Christian facade. Moreover, there is probably an advantage for cult groups not to pose as Christian in today's environment. As we report in several later chapters, studies of the process of recruitment to cult groups indicate that converts have broken their ties to conventional religious bodies (but have maintained belief in the supernatural) prior to encountering a cult group. Such persons seem little interested in resuming a Christian commitment; thus, a group that explicitly, and at first glance, is not within the Christian tradition may have recruitment advantages over groups whose names imply Christianity.

TIME AND KIND

Not only have the names of cults changed over time, the variety of cults also has changed. Some cult lineages are much older than others. Table 9.6 shows the distribution of each of the major kinds of cults across the decades — the proportion of groups making up a cult variety that was founded in various time periods. These data apply only to cults that currently exist; therefore, they are influenced not only by when cults of certain kinds were *forming*, but also by what kinds of cults founded during earlier periods have *survived*. As we have mentioned, it appears that most cults fail to last more than about 20 years. Hence, differential survival rates can and do influence the data shown in the table. As we examine specific findings, we will point out how closely these data conform to well-known historical facts. Changes in proportions over time shown here are quite plausible, both as indicators of the age of some cult traditions and as indicators of the difficulty some cult lineages faced in surviving during early times, when they evoked greater hostility from the external world.

A third of *Mormon* groups were founded in the 19th century. Much more surprising may be the fact that 55 percent of them have been founded since 1930 and a quarter since 1950.

The data on *communal* cults is consistent with historical knowledge. Such groups flourished in the 19th century, but most of them ultimately failed (cf. Kanter, 1972). A resurgence of experimental cult communes occurred as part of the counterculture of the 1960s (Houriet, 1972; Gardner, 1978), and 88 percent of existing cult communes date from the 1960s or later.

New Thought groups flowered in the 19th century and again during the Depression, in conformity with the data shown in Table 9.6 (cf. Bu-

TABLE 9.6   *When Various Kinds of Cults Formed — Percent in Each Period*

| | Historical Periods | | | | | | | |
Kind of Cult	Before 1900	1900– 1929	1930– 1949	1950– 1959	1960– 1969	1970– 1977	Total %	(N)
1. Mormon Groups[a]	35	10	30	20	5	0	100	20
2. Cult Communes	12	0	0	0	69	19	100	16
3. New Thought	15	16	32	6	28	3	100	32
4. Theosophy and Spiritualism	7	12	16	22	34	9	100	114
5. Occult Orders	13	27	27	13	13	7	100	15
6. Flying Saucers	0	0	0	48	48	4	100	21
7. Psychedelic	0	0	0	0	83	17	100	6
8. Psychic	0	7	11	11	49	22	100	55
9. Magick, Witches, Satanists	0	0	0	2	38	60	100	58
10. Pagans	0	0	0	0	52	48	100	21
11. Asian Faiths	2	9	4	16	40	29	100	97
12. Jesus People	0	0	0	8	42	50	100	12
13. Miscellaneous	5	6	30	6	18	35	100	17
Total	7	8	10	14	38	23	100	484[b]

[a]Utah Mormon groups omitted.
[b]Seventeen groups omitted for lack of data on when they were founded.

reau of the Census, 1941). The 1960s also was a peak time for the formation of New Thought groups.

Theosophical and Spiritualist groups also were a major cult tradition in the late 19th and early 20th centuries (cf. Bureau of the Census, 1930). Here the data appear to suggest that such groups have a poor survival rate. Sixty-five percent of the cults in this lineage postdate 1950. However, this is a misleading conclusion. Seventy-five percent of *all* cults postdate 1950. The Theosophical and Spiritualist group is the largest American cult lineage (24 percent), and this group makes up 25 percent of cults remaining from the 19th century and 35 percent of those from the 1900–1929 period. However, such groups form only 9 percent of the cults begun in the 1970s. Hence this group may be losing ground, at least in terms of the formation of new groups, but appears to have a quite robust survival rate. Perhaps few new cults of this type are forming at present *because* of the existence of long-established competitors.

Occult orders follow the pattern of the Theosophical and Spiritualist lineage. They flourished in the 19th and early part of the 20th centuries, but have had a relatively low rate of formation in recent decades.

Flying saucer cults are known to be very new, and the data are in agreement. All existing groups formed since 1950. However, unless movies such as *Close Encounters of the Third Kind* rekindle saucer mania, they appear to be waning. Few new groups have formed since 1970.

Like flying saucer cults, the *psychedelic* family is very new and already appears to be on the wane. Eighty-three percent of these groups formed in the 1960s, and only one new group has appeared since then.

The general *psychic* family of cults is also quite old, but has gained its greatest vigor recently. Forty-nine percent of current groups were founded in the 1960s.

The *magick, witchcraft, and Satanist* family is an old lineage, even if we ignore all claims of current groups to descent from a centuries-old tradition. The historical record indicates that groups of this kind did form in the late 19th and early 20th centuries, but no current groups survive from that period. All existing groups in this lineage postdate 1950, and almost two-thirds have appeared since 1970, confirming previous evidence examined in this chapter concerning a change in the environment surrounding cults. This cult family has long provoked the most vigorous opposition from Christianity (one need not burn witches to make things too hot for them). The fact that this family accounts for a third of all cults founded since 1970 suggests that secularization has lowered the social costs of forming and joining these kinds of cults and thus has permitted them to burst forth. The fact that there are no old groups of this type still around suggests that not too long ago such groups were much less tolerated.

Pagan faiths display a similar lack of old groups and a sudden flowering since 1960. We suspect this also reflects a reduction in the tensions between cults and the society at large.

Asian faiths have a long tradition in the United States, including those considered here that are not merely ethnic Asian congregations. We suggest that their current prominence, shown forcefully in Table 9.6, may be due in part to a change in immigration regulations during the mid-1960s. Prior to that time, Hindu gurus and Buddhist priests rarely were able to become permanent U. S. residents, except when they were members of relatively limited ethnic communities. Cult formation and the spread of religious movements may be greatly affected by such practical matters as immigration policies and even the technologies of transportation and communication. Research in this area is indicated and might provide valuable insights.

The *Jesus people*, of course, are a product of the counterculture, and cults of this family are all of recent origin.

CONCLUSION

Late one night when everybody was asleep, a parable says, God picked up America, using Maine as a handle, and shook it. Everything loose tumbled to Southern California. Our data support this story only in part. Although California deserves its reputation as the land of cults, in terms of cults per million inhabitants, Nevada, the gambling capital of the nation, is also the cult capital. Cults flourish throughout the West but are rare in the Old South. Apparently God used both hands when He shook America, one holding Maine and the other, Florida.

The parable is a good one because it suggests that people tumbling loose through life, lacking stable bonds to conventional churches, may be especially apt to lodge in novel cults. In other chapters, we examine a number of the factors that encourage creation of novel religious groups and recruitment to them. But here we must emphasize the simple fact that regions of the country differ enormously in the extent to which cults are part of the familiar cultural environment. Where cults are common, they may breed more cults, and the stigma attached to experimenting with them may be slight. Because the range of variation is so great, quantitative studies of the correlates of cultism are entirely feasible.

There is considerable variation also in the kinds of cults found in different parts of the country, some of it interpretable as the result of demographic or other nonreligious factors. For example, the strength of Theosophy and Spiritualism in Arizona and Florida probably reflects the large retirement populations of those states. The histories and beliefs of various families of cults undoubtedly affect their distribution. For example, believers explain the concentration of flying saucer cults in Oregon as the result of the Oregon "energy vortex," which attracts visitors from outer space (Melton, 1978:2:210). We merely note that some cultists believe the area between Mount Rainier and Mount Shasta is filled with psychic powers, and they are drawn there by this belief.

The fact that we were able to make sense of the trend in the names of new cults suggests that much research could profitably focus on shifts in cultic symbolism over the years. At the turn of the century, cults tended to cloak their deviance in Christian-sounding names, but today they are very unlikely to do so. Time-series analysis of data on such beliefs and practices as healing procedures, images of science, and styles of formal organization should reveal similar shifts both in the cults' defensive camouflage and in the cultural features that make them appeal to recruits. Trends in the types of existing cults founded in various periods reflect rates of birth and death of categories of religious movements. Cult mortality and growing public acceptance of cults combine to make the average cult relatively young, 75 percent of the list having been founded after 1950.

As we commented at the beginning of the previous chapter, the sociology of religion has suffered to the extent that it has paid little attention to cults. There has been a tendency to dismiss them as ephemeral, silly, and bad imitations of "real" religions. It is true that most of them do not succeed, but it is equally true that some tiny, deviant, odd cults have changed the world and have given sociology of religion its subject matter. Jesus never preached in a cathedral, and Mohammed did not start out in a mosque. It is hundreds of years too late to study Christianity and Islam as newly formed cults. If we want to understand how religions begin and what determines whether they survive, we shall have to study contemporary cults.

10 *Client and Audience Cults in America*

It has been a long time since the Middle Ages. The Christian church may dream of universality, but it no longer executes witches and magicians. The modern world abounds in unproven treatments designed to improve clients' health, prosperity, or love life. Although these varieties of magic do not qualify as real religions, they may tell us much about the origins of religion, the receptivity of the sociocultural environment to deviant supernatural beliefs, and the routes people take on the way to joining cult movements. Fortunately for humanity, if not for present scientific purposes, we cannot analyze contemporary statistics on conviction for witchcraft or burnings at the stake per million population. But we have found a surprising wealth of other data on the distribution of cults and cult interests.

Our theory of religion predicts that there will be regular, intelligible geographical variations in the popularity of cults because cults exist in varying tension with the surrounding sociocultural environment. The degree of tension is a product of how alien the cult is and how intolerant the environment. When we compare the map of cult movements with maps of many other cult measures, we should see an underlying pattern

A slightly briefer version of this chapter was published as William Sims Bainbridge and Rodney Stark, "Client and Audience Cults in America," *Sociological Analysis*, 1980, 41:3, pp. 199–214. Our thanks go to Daniel H. Jackson for the TM data, to Curtis G. Fuller for the *Fate* subscription statistics, and to Charlie Millington for great help in collecting the data on astrologers.

representing variations in communities' receptivity to cults and occultism. But there should also be differences in the maps, reflecting the degrees of deviance of three levels of cults: cult movements, client cults, and audience cults.

THE DIMENSIONS OF CULTISM

In Chapter 2, we develop the concept of cult to identify novel, deviant faiths. But many cults do not constitute fully developed religions. Many cults do not offer a sufficiently complete theology to qualify as religions, but instead are limited to providing magical services or to propagating myth and amusement.

Cults limited to providing magical services are *client cults*. They offer specific compensators but do not provide the very general compensators that mark true religion. Often competing directly with medical and psychiatric services, client cults frequently offer cures for specific physical and emotional problems. Others promise to improve an individual's economic situation or social competence, but they do not offer complete answers to the existential problems of human life. Because client cults provide compensators pretending to solve very specific, limited problems, they cannot involve the client in long-term membership in a large, stable organization. As Durkheim (1915) recognized long ago, unlike the situation for religious clergy, the relationship between magician and customer is limited to the consultant/client or therapist/patient model, short-term exchanges with relatively specific aims.

Audience cults are even less close to being religions. Usually, they display little or no formal organization. Most who take part in audience cults do so entirely through the mass media: books, magazines, newspapers, TV, astrology columns, and the like. Somewhat greater, but still minimal, organization exists among those who attend occult lectures, frequent occult bookstores, or take part in informal discussion groups on occult topics.

Sometimes audience cults make rather grand claims about the nature of the world and of the human species. Books on biorhythms tell us that three inflexible sine waves determine our physical, emotional, and intellectual state from day to day (Bainbridge, 1978a; Cole, 1980). In books, movies, and television programs, Erich von Däniken entertains his audience with the idea that all human culture derives from ancient contact with extraterrestrial astronauts (Bainbridge, 1978b). Notions such as these — including belief in ESP, astrology, pyramid power, and the intelligence of plant life — have great implications for our view of the world. Thus, they may encroach upon the territory reserved for the most general compensators, but this fact does not make audience cults into true religions. There is no organized group committed to a particular dogma.

One of the hallmarks of audience cults is that the typical audience is interested in several of them simultaneously and does not have a secure faith in any one of them. When an audience of 121 college students was shown a movie about von Däniken's theory and then given a questionnaire asking their opinions of other audience cults, those who tended to believe the movie also accepted the reality of flying saucers, the existence of ESP, and the truth of astrology. Another audience of 114 students revealed that those who accept von Däniken also tend to accept biorhythms (Bainbridge, 1978b). But these occult and pseudoscientific notions are not parts of one religious creed; they float freely and independently through the occult milieu.

One very general but vague compensator is communicated through all audience cults: *diffuse hope*. If extraordinary things are possible, then one may hope for anything and everything. Audience cults proclaim the existence of cracks in the structure of the mundane world through which any imaginable marvel might suddenly appear. Although each audience cult makes a relatively specific fantastic claim, thus providing a specific compensator, collectively, the entire range of audience cults implies the very general compensator that all things are possible. If each audience cult projects a narrow ray of hope, then, together, audience cults project a broad if dim spectrum of hopes combining to form a vague impression of heaven. Thus, although each audience cult is far from being a religion, collectively, they communicate a pale reflection of the religious.

Psychiatrists often interpret neurosis as a state of free-floating anxiety—the constant presence of fears that have no particular object. We might say that audience cults are connected to a state of free-floating optimism—something less than true belief in the notions of the cults—the diffuse feeling that all things are possible but that nothing is certain to be true. Although sociologists imagine that such a state would mean dangerous and unpleasant levels of anomie, for many people it may instead produce a feeling of freedom and hope. Rather than thrusting people into a storm-tossed sea of confusion without anchor or life raft, it may compensate for an all too rigid, mundane life. Rather than demanding belief, audience cults may require only the "willing suspension of disbelief for the moment, which constitutes poetic faith," in the familiar words of Coleridge. This interpretation may explain why audience cults seldom solidify into cult movements. To the extent that any one of them solidifies into a formal organization, it begins to demand true belief and can no longer function as an antidote to order, regulation, rigidity, and the demands of consistency that may inspire people to seek modest solace in audience cults.

If Coleridge's words are apt, and audience cults provide the same kinds of compensators found in poetry, then perhaps all the arts offer the same dilute balms against the irritations of life. A study of public reactions to two audience-cult television shows indicates that the tie between audience cults and fantasy fiction may be a close one. A group of 379 knowledgeable respondents were asked to rate two occult and pseudoscientific TV documentaries, "In Search Of" and "Project UFO," along with several fantasy shows and three factual science and nature documentaries. Statistical analysis of the preference patterns demonstrated that respondents did not classify the audience-cult programs with the factual documentaries or even with relatively adult fiction, but with fantastic programs offering the most extreme wish fullfilment. Rather than being placed in a class by themselves, the two audience cult shows were as closely tied to such pure dream compensator shows as "Fantasy Island" as they were to each other (Bainbridge, 1979).

If this analysis of audience cults is correct, then sociologists may often suffer complete frustration when they seek to explain acceptance of a particular cultic notion. Whether one finds comfort in astrology, poetry, music, spectator sports, or any one of a thousand other inexpensive, vicarious pleasures may depend only upon pure accidents of personal history. When an audience cult is new, only people plugged into the right information network have the opportunity to hear about it and then to accept it, and when the sociocultural environment either punishes or rewards people for accepting an audience cult, then certain categories in the population will be more or less apt to adopt it. But without such potentiating factors, no general independent variables — other than accidents of personal history — may explain individual acceptance.

Although social scientists should not ignore audience cults altogether, they may have more luck studying client cults and cult movements. Only cult movements are full-fledged religions. They can be distinguished from churches on the basis of their relatively high tension with their surrounding sociocultural environment. They can be distinguished from sects in that they constitute or remain within a deviant religious tradition, while sects are schismatic movements within a conventional religious tradition.

Cult movements command our interest because they represent new religions. As we argue in Chapter 8, if we would know how religious innovation occurs and the conditions governing whether new religions prosper or fail, we must examine cult movements.

Client cults command our interest because they often evolve into cult movements, following the subculture-evolution model outlined in Chapter 8. Recent examples of magical therapy cults that evolved into fully developed religions are Scientology (Wallis, 1976) and The Process (Bainbridge, 1978c). And, as chapters 12 and 13 demonstrate, movement along the dimension from client cult to cult movement will have sociologically interesting causes and consequences.

However, the role of audience cults in generating religious innovation or in providing a potential pool of recruits for new cult movements is still somewhat unclear, as chapters 14 and 15 explain. Most who are part of the mass audience for occultism never join cult movements; some combine their interests in the occult with a firm commitment to a wholly conventional religious body. Yet many who do join cults seem to have had prior exposure to audience cults (Balch and Taylor, 1977; Lynch, 1977, 1979).

We have proposed that cults vary in how general or valuable are the compensators they offer, and the degree of followers' involvement varies in parallel fashion. As cults range from fully developed religions down to mere promulgators of vague mythology, involvement varies from full-time participation to mild interest in occult ideas as a source of diversion and entertainment. If this is so, we can expect to observe several things:

1. The proportion of the population involved in cults ought to increase as we move from the most intense levels of involvement down to the more transient and ephemeral.

2. Public hostility toward cults ought to decline in similar fashion from the more to the less intense levels of involvement. Thus, for example, people ought to be strongly sanctioned for becoming full-time members of a cult movement, but they should be sanctioned only very weakly for believing in astrology.

3. Regional concentration of cult involvement ought to decline as we shift from examining participation in cult movements to examining interest in audience cults.

In the concluding chapters of this book, we explain at length why cults ought to flourish in some places and times rather than in others. We argue that cults thrive where conventional faiths are weak, but where many people still believe in the supernatural and desire effective answers to questions of ultimate meaning. Hence, cults will flourish in such places as the Pacific region of the United States today: There the average person is unchurched, but retains belief in the supernatural.

In the previous chapter, we examine the temporal and spatial distribution of cult movements in the United States. The social climate seems everywhere in the nation to have become more tolerant of cults. Yet we also find dramatic regional differences of the kind anticipated. Cult movements are concentrated along the shores of the Pacific, precisely where church membership rates are the lowest in the nation. However, to the extent that cults are not recognized as competing religions, their popularity ought to be less influenced by the strength of conventional faiths. Thus, audience cults should be less concentrated in the West than cult movements are.

In this chapter, we assess these hypotheses as we examine the distribution of client and audience cults in the United States. If the data do not conform to these expected patterns, then the utility of our conceptualization of levels of cults must seriously be doubted. In examining these data, we also add to the remarkably small number of solid facts available about cults. Indeed, one of our purposes in this chapter is to demonstrate how much useful data on cults is readily available at the cost of only a few weeks of effort.

CLIENT CULT DIRECTORIES

Among the most comprehensive sources of geographic data about cults is the *Spiritual Community Guide,* published by an ecumenical cult movement in San Rafael, California (Singh, 1974, 1978). Its editor describes his group's aims in bringing out the guide: "*Spiritual Community* is the new-clear family. We are a group of communicators dedicated to the planetarization of consciousness and the coming of the New Age. Although we follow different paths we are united in our love and our work" (Singh, 1974:5). The guide is an extremely professional, large directory, edited with a computerized system, based on information from an apparently very well developed national network. The editor says, "The spiritual energy in North America is accelerating so rapidly that virtually every community in every state has its own blend of satsangs and services" (Singh, 1974:5).

The guide seems to emphasize imported oriental cults and native organizations with a similar perspective. The 1974 edition contains short essays by many spiritual leaders, including Swami Satchidananda (of the Integral Yoga Institute), Alan Watts, Meher Baba, Ram Dass (formerly Richard Alpert), Bubba Free John (formerly Franklin Jones), Swami Kriyananda (of the Ananda Cooperative Village), Werner Erhard (of the *est* cult), Yogi Bhajan (of the 3HO or Healthy Happy Holy cult), Elizabeth Clare Prophet (of the St. Germain cult called Summit Lighthouse), and several others. The coverage of nonoriental cults is a bit spotty; for example, the many Scientology centers are not listed. There is some possibility of a West Coast bias, but, in conjunction with other measures of cult activity, the *Spiritual Community Guide* provides a wealth of useful data.

The 1974 edition contains a classified "Community Directory" listing the names and addresses of 2,470 establishments around the United States that offer New Age services. Figure 10.1 is a U.S. map showing the distribution of these listings across nine geographical regions, expressed in the rate of listings per million population. When computing rates for this chapter, we always used census estimates for the appropriate year or the nearest available statistics, if necessary interpolating or extrapolating from the best available figures. For the case of directories, we decided the best year was the year prior to publication of the directory, assuming that compilation took several months.

Figure 10.1 shows that the Pacific region towers over the others, as it did in our study of cult movements reported in the previous chapter. California contains 784 listings, nearly a third of the total, which works out to a rate of 37.9 per million residents. But other Pacific states have high rates as well. Alaska, with only 14 listings, achieves a rate of 42.0 because of its small population. Oregon has a rate of 37.4 per million; Hawaii has 30.8; and Washington has 16.8 per million.

Because the guide is a classified directory, we can analyze the distributions of types of listings. Many of these are the local offices of cult movements, such as Baha'i and 3HO, and the ashrams of various small cults. But because each one offers a service to the interested general public, it qualifies to a greater or lesser degree as a client cult outlet, whatever the sponsoring organization. Of the 2,470 listings, 51.5 percent are centers, "devoted to the spiritual path, raising one's consciousness, transmitting higher knowledge or promoting universal love and unity" (Singh, 1974:110). A further 3.4 percent are communities, residential centers that welcome friendly guests. These two categories, representing more than half the total, are close to cult movements in many respects, but frequently offer the limited, temporary exchanges with outsiders that mark client cults. In many cases, they are the front organizations of cult movements and function to recruit new members. Therefore, we would expect the geographical distribution of centers and communities to be similar to that of cult movements reported in the previous chapter.

Three other classified categories provide services that are much more impersonal and seem less closely tied to the milieu of cult move-

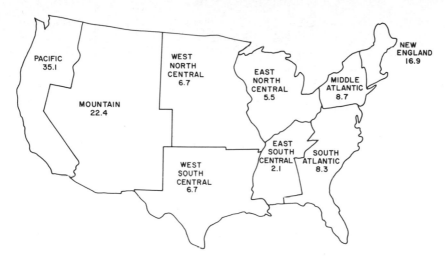

FIGURE 10.1   *Rates per Million for Listings in the 1974* Spiritual
Community Guide
(National rate = 11.8)

ments: bookstores, foodstores, and restaurants. Of the total 2,470 listings, 10.2 percent are of bookstores, "specializing or providing metaphysical, spiritual, esoteric, devotional, natural life style books." A
larger category, comprising 25.7 percent of the total, is foodstores, specializing in natural foods. The restaurants, 5.5 percent, specialize in
vegetarian or macrobiotic meals. One might ask why we should include
these businesses in a study of cults. For one thing, the guide itself considers these enterprises integral parts of the new consciousness movement. But the main reason is that these businesses do offer something
more than just books and food — they offer unconventional hopes for
spiritual, emotional, and physiological benefit. They offer magic, the
prime commodity of client cults. It is hard to predict exactly what geographic distribution these semimagical services should display. If they
really are integrated into a New Age subculture, perhaps relying on cult
movement members for customers, they might show the same distribution as cult movements. The distribution will depend partly on where
Americans draw the line between deviant religious or magical practices
and conventional activities. If the stores and restaurants are not dependent upon a New Age subculture and are not generally considered to be
as deviant as cult movements, they may show a more even distribution
across the nation.

Table 10.1 compares rates per million in nine geographic regions of

TABLE 10.1   Cult Movements and Client Cults — Rates per Million

Region	Cult Movements	Spiritual Community Guide			Organic Traveler	Psychic Register	Who's Who in the Psychic World
		1974 Centers	1974 Stores	1978 Total			
New England	1.6	6.7	9.3	4.9	3.1	2.1	1.3
Middle Atlantic	2.2	5.3	3.3	2.9	1.8	3.0	1.5
East North Central	1.5	3.0	2.4	2.1	1.4	3.5	1.5
West North Central	1.5	3.3	3.3	3.0	1.2	1.4	1.7
South Atlantic	1.4	5.1	2.9	3.1	2.0	1.6	1.6
East South Central	.5	1.4	.8	1.1	1.2	.2	.8
West South Central	.9	3.9	2.6	2.3	1.6	1.1	1.9
Mountain	4.8	11.7	9.8	9.6	4.0	5.3	4.6
Pacific	6.6	19.1	14.1	12.8	5.1	9.3	6.1
National	2.3	6.5	4.9	4.4	2.2	3.3	2.2
Total	501	1355	1023	943	475	705	444

cult movements (from Chapter 9), *Spiritual Community Guide* listings, and listings from three other supportive directories. We have combined centers and communities from the 1974 guide in one column and bookstores, foodstores, and restaurants in another. We omitted 92 entries in a miscellaneous "other" category, a classification that was especially strong in the Pacific region, where 50 (54 percent) of the cases were concentrated.

The fourth column in Table 10.1 gives the distribution of all classified listings from the 1978 edition of the guide, a total of 943. From edition to edition, the format of the guide has changed; so it may be inappropriate to read a real decline in client cults in the drop in classified guide listings from 1974 to 1978. Unlike the 1974 edition, the 1978 guide introduces the classified by announcing, "Following is a directory of New Consciousness businesses, organizations and individuals. All have paid for their listings" (Singh, 1978:194).

Concerned that the *Spiritual Community Guide* might have a Pacific bias because of its California origins, we sought other directories published in other regions. *The Organic Traveler* (Davis and Tetrault, 1975) is a guide to organic, vegetarian, and health food restaurants published in Syracuse, New York. Although its authors received some help from the *Spiritual Community Guide*, they say, "Some eight months were spent sifting through phone books, perusing existing lists, talking to friends and traveling acquaintances, and sending out questionnaires" (Davis and Tetrault, 1975:viii). Therefore, although the book is somewhat more amateur than the guide and may have its own local bias, we felt it was a good source of data comparable to the stores and restaurant listings in the guide.

A source of more explicitly magical listings is the 1979 edition of *The International Psychic Register* (McQuaid, 1979), published in Erie, Pennsylvania. This directory of psychic and metaphysical practitioners contains 705 entries from the United States, 33 from Canada, and 161 from Great Britain. These numbers translate to rates of 3.3 per million in the United States, 1.4 in Canada, and 2.9 in Great Britain. Of course, the register may be less complete in enumerating foreign psychics. One of the cross-listings is a subject index, and the following services were offered by ten or more practitioners: aura reading, dowsing, dream interpretation, hypnosis, parapsychology, readings of past lives, regression to past lives, research of psychic phenomena, psychic art, psychic development, psychic investigations, psychometry, tarot reading, and teaching of metaphysics.

Who's Who in the Psychic World (Finch and Finch, 1971) is an early and rather amateur directory published in Phoenix, Arizona. Although any of the directories may have local biases, the bias seems excessively great in this case. Fifty-two of the total 496 listings are in Arizona, giving the directory's home state a rate of 29 per million, 12 times the national rate and over 4 times the rate for California. Therefore, in our calculations, we have dropped the Arizona cases, figuring the Mountain region on the basis of the seven states remaining.

The rates in Table 10.1 are useful for understanding the extent of cult activity in any region and for comparing within each column of figures. However, they are awkward if one wants to compare one column with another. Therefore, in Table 10.2, we have recalculated, dividing the regional rates in each column by the appropriate national rate. For example, the New England rate of cult movements is 1.55 per million, which, divided by the national rate of 2.32, gives a ratio of 0.67. This means that New England has 0.67 times the national rate.

A glance across Table 10.2 shows a pattern that is very consistent — except for one notable variation. In each case, the Pacific region is highest, followed by the adjacent Mountain region. The East South Central region is always lowest. Although the figures are not exactly constant, scanning from left to right, the variation usually stays in a narrow range. The interesting exception, and a departure from the cult movement distribution, is the above average figures for New England in the *Spiritual Community Guide* and *Organic Traveler* data. This preliminary study cannot attempt to explain such local phenomena, but a suggestion can be made. Perhaps New England is more open to client cult services that are not explicitly occult or supernatural in nature, but the region is not especially tolerant of obviously deviant cult movements or professional psychics. With this exception, Table 10.2 shows that the pattern for cult movements is followed very closely by the patterns of six other sets of data concerning client cult services.

These findings suggest one or both of two compatible conclusions. First, client cults may be so closely tied to the milieu of cult movements that they show the same geographical distribution. Second, Americans may consider client cults to be just as deviant as cult movements, and therefore they show the same distribution as cult movements because both are indicators of public tolerance for religious and magical deviance. Further insights about these possibilities can come from examination of the weakest and least social form of cult activity: audience cults. Our best data come from a popular magazine.

FATE MAGAZINE

Since its first issue at the beginning of 1948, *Fate* magazine has been a prime medium of communication and entertainment for persons interested in parapsychology, the occult, and related matters. Although it

TABLE 10.2 Cult Movements and Client Cults—Regional Rate÷Divided by National Rate

Region	Cult Movements	Spiritual Community Guide			Organic Traveler	Psychic Register	Who's Who in the Psychic World
		1974 Centers	1974 Stores	1978 Total			
New England	.67	1.03	1.91	1.12	1.39	.65	.57
Middle Atlantic	.96	.82	.67	.66	.80	.90	.67
East North Central	.64	.47	.49	.47	.62	1.07	.67
West North Central	.66	.51	.67	.69	.53	.43	.78
South Atlantic	.59	.79	.60	.72	.87	.49	.71
East South Central	.22	.21	.15	.25	.53	.07	.35
West South Central	.38	.60	.53	.52	.69	.34	.87
Mountain	2.07	1.82	2.01	2.20	1.79	1.61	2.08
Pacific	2.84	2.96	2.90	2.93	2.27	2.83	2.77
National	1.00	1.00	1.00	1.00	1.00	1.00	1.00
U.S. Rate	2.32	6.46	4.87	4.36	2.25	3.28	2.20
Total	501	1355	1023	943	475	705	444

Note: The calculations for this table were made before rounding off results for Table 10.1

does not sell as many copies as the leading mass circulation magazines, *Fate* has a national audience and serves a specialty interest group of many thousand persons. In 1960, when popular magazines were first required to publish sale figures, *Fate* sold an average of 58,725 copies each month. By 1965, the figure had risen to 92,762 total paid circulation, 59 percent through mail subscriptions. In 1970, the average issue sold 111,052 copies, again 59 percent by mail. By 1975, *Fate* had achieved 148,091 copies of each issue, now 72 percent by mail.

Fate is a perfect audience cult medium. Unlike cult movements, it demands no commitment. Unlike most client cults, it is inexpensive. *Fate* can be brought anonymously and enjoyed privately. Articles and other features cover a wide range of occult and marginal topics, providing weak compensators through stories of supernatural events and miracle cures. A remarkable source of information and ideas for scholars of religion, *Fate* unfortunately is not in many major libraries. Our own collection came from the back-number department of the publisher and from used magazine stores. Further information, including subscription figures, was kindly provided by Curtis G. Fuller, *Fate*'s publisher.

In its first year, *Fate* began a feature called "True Mystic Experiences." For a modest reward (originally $5, currently $10), readers submit brief stories about their encounters with the paranormal. In 1954, a second monthly feature began; "My Proof of Survival" consists of reader reports of apparitions, messages from the beyond, and near-death experiences. Published reader stories almost invariably include the author's name and home town, and many are illustrated with photographs of their authors.

Although *Fate* is an audience cult phenomenon, mystic experiences and proofs of survival enter the territory of client cults and the occult milieu populated by cult movements. By submitting stories, readers initiate a public exchange with *Fate*. Not only are they exchanging testimonials for cash, but they are taking public stands on behalf of often very deviant supernatural beliefs. Indeed, one would suspect that public fame within the occult milieu is the major reward sought, because the amount of cash is so small. These considerations lead us to hypothesize that the geographic distribution of writers of mystic experiences and proofs of survival will reflect that of cult movements and miscellaneous client cults more strongly than will the distribution of subscriptions to *Fate*.

Table 10.3 shows regional and national rates for several sets of *Fate* data. We were able to obtain copies of 79 issues published in the 1950s, and the first column is based on the 748 reader stories of both types found in them. Columns two through six analyze distributions of 2,086 mystic experiences and proofs of survival found in all 237 issues published from January 1960 through September 1979. In calculating the rates, we used mid-decade population estimates for each of the decades and 1970 estimates for the 1960–1979 period. The last column in the table is based on a tabulation of all subscribers to the magazine as of November 1979. Subscription figures fluctuate up and down somewhat, mainly reflecting occasional campaigns by the publisher that achieve temporary increases in circulation. The issue for which we have data appears to be about average in this respect, mailed to 82,812 persons, 79,907 of whom lived in one of the 50 states or the District of Columbia.

Table 10.4 standardizes the columns from Table 10.3 by dividing each regional rate by the appropriate national rate. Published in Highland Park, Illinois, the magazine should not have a western bias such as might distort data from a California source. Each of the columns tabulating reader stories clearly reflects the pattern shown by cult movements. The Pacific region is generally highest — more than twice the national rate. The Mountain region is second, also considerably above the rest of the nation, and the East South Central region is very low. However, as hypothesized, the subscription figures show the pattern much more weakly.

Table 10.4 also shows a trend over time, interesting in itself, that might be the cause of the relatively flat 1979 subscriber distribution. Changes from decade to decade are complex, partly reflecting the unstable, small numbers of stories from some regions. The Pacific region, rich in both stories and inhabitants, shows a steady decline in its rate compared with the national rate. In the 1950s, the Pacific rate was about 3.2 times that of the nation. For both kinds of story, it dropped to 2.7 times in the 1960s and 2.1 times in the 1970s. A simple, linear extrapolation of the decline predicts that the reader stories' Pacific rate would be about 1.9 times the national rate in 1979. This is still 0.4 above the actual ratio for subscribers, 1.5. Therefore, we conclude that the relatively flat subscriber distribution represents both a general equalizing trend for *Fate* statistics and a real difference in social meaning between private subscriptions and public testimonials. The decline in Pacific dominance suggests that standards have changed in other populous areas of the country, rendering *Fate* less deviant and therefore less dependent on exceptional levels of tolerance. This trend probably reflects the increasing national tolerance of cults documented in the previous chapter. We examine *Fate* data again, in Chapter 18, in a section about sex ratio in recruitment, and in Chapter 20, where we discuss the Canadian situation.

TABLE 10.3 *Fate Magazine Data—Rates per Million*

Region	Reader Stories 1950s	Mystic Experiences		Proofs of Survival		Total Stories 1960–1979	November 1979 Subscribers
		1960s	1970s	1960s	1970s		
New England	2.7	1.5	2.4	1.5	2.1	7.5	297
Middle Atlantic	2.4	1.6	2.2	1.5	1.8	7.0	308
East North Central	3.8	2.2	2.3	1.5	2.2	8.0	393
West North Central	3.0	2.3	2.8	2.0	2.5	9.5	351
South Atlantic	3.3	1.8	2.0	1.6	1.8	7.3	307
East South Central	1.9	1.4	0.8	1.0	0.6	3.8	218
West South Central	3.4	2.0	2.5	1.7	2.0	8.4	295
Mountain	9.6	7.6	4.5	4.4	4.4	21.4	555
Pacific	14.4	7.6	5.7	6.0	5.3	24.1	565
National	4.5	2.8	2.8	2.2	2.5	10.2	366
Total	748	546	586	430	524	2086	79,907

TABLE 10.4 Fate *Magazine Data—Regional Rates Divided By National Rate*

Region	Reader Stories 1950s	Mystic Experiences		Proofs of Survival		Total Stories 1960–1979	November 1979 Subscribers
		1960s	1970s	1960s	1970s		
New England	.59	.53	.87	.68	.87	.73	.81
Middle Atlantic	.54	.56	.81	.67	.72	.68	.84
East North Central	.83	.77	.83	.67	.89	.79	1.07
West North Central	.67	.81	1.02	.88	1.02	.93	.96
South Atlantic	.73	.63	.72	.74	.72	.71	.84
East South Central	.42	.48	.50	.46	.24	.37	.59
West South Central	.75	.72	.92	.77	.80	.82	.81
Mountain	2.12	2.75	1.62	1.98	1.77	2.10	1.52
Pacific	3.18	2.71	2.06	2.68	2.14	2.36	1.54
National	1.00	1.00	1.00	1.00	1.00	1.00	1.00
U.S. Rate	4.53	2.82	2.75	2.22	2.46	10.24	366

Note: The calculations for this table were made before rounding off results for Table 10.3.

TRANSCENDENTAL MEDITATION

One of the most successful client cults of recent years was Transcendental Meditation, a simplified Indian meditation technique adapted for the Western market by Maharishi Mahesh Yogi. In Chapter 13, we document and explain the rise and decline of TM; so here we merely mention a few observations rendering the statistics meaningful. In 1977, Transcendental Meditation became a moderately deviant cult movement and accepted public labeling as a religion. Prior to that time, the organization was in the business of training persons to do a streamlined form of meditation said to be of great value for physical and mental health. Originally, despite its ultimately religious origins, there was little hint that TM was based on supernatural assumptions, and numerous apparently scientific articles were published to substantiate TM's claims to be a practical technique for achieving worldly benefits (Wallace, 1970; Anonymous, 1975).

Daniel H. Jackson was able to obtain for us a remarkable set of data giving essentially complete figures on Americans initiated into Transcendental Meditation from 1967 through 1977. The data analyzed here come from one data tape prepared by the TM organization that lists the number of persons initiated each year whose homes were in 5,629 urban areas, a total of 735,280 people. The cult keeps very good records, primarily to make sure that local chapters pay their mandated percentages of initiation fees to the central organization. The particular data tape was laboriously prepared by TM statisticians not only to monitor progress in towns and cities, but also to test (or illustrate) a theory about the cult's impact on society. The TM organization hypothesized that, when the proportion of meditators reached 1 percent of any community, there would be a significant improvement in social conditions, including such measurable changes as a drop in the crime rate.

The years 1967 to 1969, when the cult was still getting started, are combined in the data set. Nearly half (47 percent) of the 34,046 urban initiates gained in these three years lived in the Pacific region, 42 percent of the total in California alone. The first separate year for which we have detailed information is 1970, when 16,066 were initiated. The peak year in initiation was 1975, when 232,306 took training, and TM boasted of 375 centers across the nation. Because this data set excluded rural initiates, we used census figures and estimates for the urban populations of the states in computing regional rates. Table 10.5 shows regional rates for 1970 and 1975, along with other data to be described shortly.

Although the Pacific region had the greatest number of initiates in 1970 (5,165), the highest rate was achieved by New England, which had

TABLE 10.5 Urban Initiation to Transcendental Meditation and SMSA Professional Astrologers

Region	Rate: Number/Million Population				Ratio: Regional Rate/National Rate			
	1970 Urban TM Initiates	1975 Urban TM Initiates	1972 Urban TM Initiators	1978–1979 SMSA Astrologers	1970 Urban TM Initiates	1975 Urban TM Initiates	1972 Urban TM Initiators	1978–1979 SMSA Astrologers
New England	254	2,551	18.0	3.7	2.36	1.79	1.41	.95
Middle Atlantic	57	1,287	7.4	4.6	.53	.90	.58	1.18
East North Central	84	1,243	6.7	3.2	.78	.87	.53	.82
West North Central	78	1,256	7.8	2.2	.73	.88	.61	.56
South Atlantic	54	1,230	5.6	2.4	.51	.87	.44	.61
East South Central	24	610	2.5	1.3	.23	.43	.17	.32
West South Central	73	729	4.9	2.9	.68	.51	.38	.75
Mountain	206	1,970	28.3	6.9	1.91	1.39	2.25	1.77
Pacific	227	2,126	37.4	6.9	2.11	1.50	2.93	1.76
Total U.S.	108	1,422	12.3	3.9	1.00	1.00	1.00	1.00
Number of Cases	16,066	232,306	1,977	517				

only 2,298 initiates. It is not our job here to explain specific details in TM history, because such an analysis would require a lengthy social history of this cult. There are several reasons any one cult, of whatever type, may have a geographical distribution noticeably different from others like it. Any organization may be strongest near its headquarters or in the place where it began operations. Client cults, especially, may appeal to segments of the population that are themselves unevenly distributed. Furthermore, policy set by cult leaders may direct special attention to a particular region, resulting in more recruits. Whatever the reason in this case, the elevation in TM's New England rate is not unique. We already saw above average New England rates for the *Spiritual Community Guide* and *The Organic Traveler*.

The rest of the 1970 TM distribution is very familiar. The Pacific region is quite high; the Mountain region is only slightly lower; and the East South Central region is extremely low. In 1970, TM was new and may have seemed fairly deviant to most people who encountered it, but it probably did not seem like an extension of the occult milieu, and the ratio of Pacific rate over national rate (2.11) is lower than for any of the variables in Table 10.2. By 1975, there had been extensive favorable mass media coverage and a much increased likelihood that any individual had respected friends who were already meditators (cf. Granovetter, 1973, 1978). By the end of 1974, over 360,000 urban Americans had received TM training, still a small minority but much more substantial than the minuscule subcultures possessed by most cult movements. We would expect TM to be less deviant in 1975 than 1970, and consequently that the geographic variations would be less pronounced. Table 10.5 shows that this is the case. With a single exception (West South Central), regional rates have moved significantly closer to the national rate.

A TM training manual printed in October 1972 lists 1,977 trained initiators working at 135 centers across the country in 43 states and the District of Columbia. Being an initiator is more like being a member of a cult movement; simply learning to meditate is a one-week process in the role of client. Therefore, regional receptivity to cult movements should show more strongly in the distribution of initiators than in that of those they initiate. The figures show just this. Not only are the Mountain and Pacific regions much higher for initiators, and the East South Central much lower, but the New England region is lower as well. Even within one data set, Transcendental Meditation, New England is more favorable toward apparently nonsupernatural client cult activity than toward membership in a cult movement. Comparison with the 1970 initiate figures is good because initiators were created over several years previous to 1972. But if one wants to compare with 1972 initiation rates, in that year, the Pacific rate was only 1.39 times the national rate, the Mountain, 1.58 times, and New England, 1.91 times. The East South Central region was 0.54 times the national rate. Clearly, clients are more evenly distributed than movement members.

In 1977, the Gallup poll gave a national sample of 1,500 respondents a list of "experiential religions" and asked, "Which, if any, of these are you involved in or do you practice?" Although only about 0.5 percent of American adults had been initiated by that time, a total of 4 percent claimed to practice Transcendental Meditation (Gallup, 1977). Therefore, this question must be tapping willingness to express positive sentiments about TM rather than actual involvement. Table 10.6 shows the geographic distribution of responses to this and two other Gallup questions, along with a few of our own data for comparison. Gallup's West region is simply our Pacific plus Mountain, and Gallup's Midwest is our two North Central regions. The other two gross regions meet along Virginia's northern border. Of course, Gallup has found only about 60 people who claimed to practice TM, rather too small for stable rates. But the geographic distribution of 1975 initiates is very close to that of Gallup's percentages. We rely upon Gallup in examining another, less well organized cult — astrology.

ASTROLOGY

Interest in the possibility that the planets and stars influence human fate can be found all across the spectrum of cults, but astrology is most commonly a limited client or audience phenomenon. One cult movement that uses astrological principles is the Rosicrucian Fellowship (Oceanside, California), and lists of astrology organizations include the Abundant Life Church, the Church of the Light, Church of the Cosmic Harmony, and the First Temple of Astrology (Weingarten, 1977). More important are the thousands of amateur and professional astrologers who cast detailed horoscopes for friends and paying customers. Still larger audiences are reached through astrological newspaper columns and magazines. Personalized horoscopes cast for specific clients represent pure client cult activity; impersonal, mass media horoscopes are pure audience cult communications.

Although some regional listings of astrologers have been assembled (Marks, 1978), we do not have a good source of national data. We created our own national list using classified telephone directories. It was not practical to obtain copies of phone books for all the little towns and rural counties, but we discovered that a modest effort would allow reliable mapping of astrologers if we confined ourselves to telephone list-

TABLE 10.6 *Measures of Client and Audience Cult Activity, Gallup Regions*

Measure	West Region	Midwest Region	South Region	East Region	Nation
1975 TM Initiates per Million	2094	1246	930	1530	1422
Regional 1975 TM Rates Divided by the National Rate	1.47	.88	.65	1.08	1.00
Gallup: Percent Practicing TM	6	3	3	5	4
Gallup: Regional Percents Practicing Divided by the National Percent	1.50	.75	.75	1.25	1.00
SMSA Astrologers per Million	6.89	2.96	2.54	3.85	3.91
Regional Astrologer Rates Divided by the National Rate	1.76	.76	.65	.98	1.00
Astrologer Groups per Million	.99	.55	.38	.90	.67
Regional Group Rates Divided by the National Rate	1.47	.82	.57	1.34	1.00
Gallup: Percent Who Believe in Astrology	25	19	22	23	22
Gallup: Regional Percents Believing Divided by the National Percent	1.14	.86	1.00	1.05	1.00
Gallup: Percent Who Read an Astrology Column Regularly	24	22	23	24	23
Gallup: Regional Percents Reading Divided by the National Percent	1.04	.96	1.00	1.04	1.00

ings for standard metropolitan statistical areas (SMSAs). We were able to count the astrologers advertised in all classified telephone directories for all 277 SMSAs, a total of 571 astrologers. Many SMSAs have but a single phone book. The boundaries of metropolitan areas are fairly easy to determine by telephone exchanges, at least when one is counting a relatively small list of numbers. Table 10.5 gives rates of astrologers per million metropolitan population for the nine regions.

In tabulating the data, we found an anomaly — not a single astrologer was listed in Pennsylvania books. We checked with an astrological research organization in Pittsburgh and discovered that an old state law against fortune-telling prevents astrologers from advertising. Public policy in Pennsylvania has invalidated phone listings as good measures of astrological activity in the state's 12 SMSAs; so we were forced to eliminate them from further analysis. We know of several horoscope services in Pennsylvania that would have been listed had they been permitted. The Middle Atlantic region has 100 astrologers listed for New York and New Jersey SMSAs, and, of course, none for Pennsylvania. The region's rate, leaving Pennsylvania in, is 3.1 per million; with this state out, the rate jumps to 4.6 per million. Removing Pennsylvania causes the national rate to rise from 3.64 to 3.91.

The geographical pattern for astrologers is reminiscent of that for Transcendental Meditation. The familiar cult movement distribution appears in attenuated form, but one of the northeastern regions is unusually high, in this case, the Middle Atlantic. As usual, the Pacific and Mountain regions are highest and the East South Central is lowest. Evidence that astrology is a relatively limited client cult, not necessarily embedded in and discredited by the occult milieu, is found in comparing the Pacific and national rates. Although the Pacific region has more than its share of astrologers, its rate is only 1.76 times the national rate. This contrasts, for example, with the ratios for cult movements (2.84), listings in the *Spiritual Community Guide* (2.90 to 2.96), and even *Fate* magazine readers' stories from 1960 to 1979 (2.36). It is almost as low as the latest TM and *Fate* subscribers ratios (1.50 and 1.54). Were involvement with an astrologer a publicly deviant act drawing powerful negative sanctions and requiring strong subcultural support, we might expect a Pacific rate approaching three times the national rate.

Because the base for our astrologer rates was standard metropolitan statistical areas, we were able to examine the relationship between city size and astrologers per million. The populations of SMSAs ranged from Meriden, Connecticut, with 57,300 people, up to New York City, with 9,508,600, a factor of 166. We could predict that the rate of astrologers in small cities should be very low. Nationally, there are about 256,000 metropolitan residents for every listed astrologer. Cities with many fewer than 256,000 people may not provide a big enough market for a full-time caster of horoscopes.

We divided SMSAs into three groups by size. The 112 metropolitan areas under 200,000 population had only 24 astrologers among them, a rate of 1.64 per million. The 120 middle-sized cities, from 200,000 to 1 million, showed a rate of 3.02. The 33 large metropolitan areas, above a million in population, shared 390 astrologers for a rate of 4.76. The greatest number of astrologers, 54, was listed in New York City phone books and constituted more than half the total number of astrologers in the Middle Atlantic region. Thus, the strong relationship with size may have helped elevate the Middle Atlantic rate. Removing New York City from this region drops the region just below the national rate, to 3.8. The three large metropolitan areas with highest rates are in the Pacific region: San Francisco (13.6), Seattle-Everett (13.4), and Portland, Oregon (11.9). The rate for New York City is only 5.7, despite the size effect.

Evidence to confirm that our phone book count does represent the real distribution of professional astrologers comes from *The NASO International Astrological Directory* (Weingarten, 1977), which lists 146 astrological societies in the United States. Some of these seem to be stargazer clubs; others are like astrology clinic businesses, but all aspire to the status of serious professional organization. Because the total number is small, we cannot calculate reliable rates for nine geographic regions; so rates and ratio comparisons for Gallup's four regions in Table 10.6 are as far as we want to go with this limited data set. The NASO pattern is very similar to that in our count of SMSA astrologers — the West is highest, but the East stands out as well.

In 1976, the Gallup poll asked a national sample of 1,500 people two questions tapping their attitudes toward astrology. Nationally, 22 percent answered yes when asked "Do you believe in astrology, or not?" Twenty-three percent said they read a newspaper or magazine astrology column regularly. However, there was far from a perfect correlation between responses to these questions, and even 17 percent of those who do not believe claimed to read a column regularly.

We suggest that actual *belief* in astrology refers to a measure of faith in astrologers' ability to give their clients real benefits, such as good advice based on a horoscope reading. But mere interest in published, mass media horoscopes may often be no more than taste for a particular kind of entertainment. Thus, belief in astrology relates to the client cult aspect of astrology and interest in horoscope columns is an audience cult attitude. Therefore, we would expect belief to mirror the cult movement geographic pattern slightly more than does reading a horoscope column. Table 10.6 shows exactly this, although both distributions are nearly flat, much flatter than either professional astrologer distribution. This final fact supports our general interpretation of geographic differences. Private beliefs and attitudes show much weaker regional differences than do public cult activities, such as visiting an astrologer or actually being one.

CONCLUSION

Our client cult measures all reflect the geographic distribution of cult movements, but the pattern weakens as we move along the spectrum away from cult movements toward pure audience cults. Our method, comparing regional rates, is a valid approach, but an obvious alternative is to look at statistical correlations based on rates for smaller geographic units, such as states. Table 10.7 is a correlation matrix for nine variables, the cult movement headquarters rates and eight of our best other measures. With only 51 cases (the states plus Washington, D.C.), our coefficients are rough estimates, but most of them achieve the 0.001 level of significance. The correlations are not entirely fair because many low population states may easily outweigh a few populous ones. For example, the TM figures may be distorted slightly by the fact that the six New England states outweigh the five states in the Pacific region, even though the latter have two and a half times the urban population.

Table 10.7 reveals very high correlations linking most of the nine variables, but there are a few low and insignificant figures. The first column, listing associations between the cult movements rate and the others, identifies the main axis of variation among the measures. The centers and communities listed in the *Spiritual Community Guide* are outlets of actual cult movements or are client cult services that fall just short of being movements. The bookstores, foodstores, and restaurants in the same guide are much less saturated with explicit occultism and require less public commitment from customers. Centers correlate strongly with cult movements (.57). Stores do so only weakly (.16). Psychic practitioners, each of whom might be qualified to found a cult movement, show a high correlation with cult movements (.58). *Fate* reader stories, public testimonials on behalf of the paranormal, correlate more strongly than mere subscriptions to the magazine (.51 versus .38). In 1970 and 1975, Transcendental Meditation did not want to be known as a religious cult and offered very limited, apparently secular services to short-time clients. Although there is a strong association with *Spiritual Community Guide* centers (and still higher with stores), TM is not significantly correlated with cult movements. Although today it *is* a cult movement, for a few years, it was able to appear to be at the opposite end of the spectrum. Finally, like both TM measures, SMSA astrologers correlate less strongly with cult movements than with any other measure, indicating the highly limited nature of astrological services.

In earlier tables, we showed that several measures of cult activity agree with the distribution of cult movement headquarters, indicating

TABLE 10.7 *Correlations (r) Linking Nine Cult Activity Measures*

	Cult Movements	1974 Spiritual Community Guide		Psychic Register	Fate Magazine		TM Initiates	
		Centers	Stores		1960–79 Stories	Sub-scribers	1970	1975
Cult Movements	1							
S.C.G. Centers	.57	1						
S.C.G. Stores	.16	.57	1					
Psychic Register	.58	.48	.24	1				
Fate Stories	.51	.53	.35	.60	1			
Fate Subscribers	.38	.63	.35	.58	.80	1		
1970 TM Initiates	.05	.58	.79	.14	.47	.52	1	
1975 TM Initiates	.18	.48	.73	.41	.38	.54	.74	1
SMSA Astrologers	.29	.34	.49	.44	.60	.46	.41	.34

Note: Coefficients above 0.34 achieve the 0.01 level of significance, and those above 0.41 achieve the 0.001 level. N = 51 (rates for 50 states and Washington, D.C., except for SMSA astrologers, for which three states could not be coded).

that cult activity is extremely high in the Pacific region, all the way from Alaska to Mexico. The Mountain region also has much cult activity, while the East South Central region has a very low rate. Departures from this simple pattern can be explained and have theoretical interest in their own right.

First, the geographic distribution is flatter for cult activities that are more private, less based on deviant supernatural assumptions, or both. Cult movements, by definition, involve long-term commitments to explicitly supernatural beliefs and deviant practices. The less a cult has these qualities, the flatter the distribution because regions of the country differ greatly in their tolerance of religious deviance and perhaps in the proportions of their populations whose religious urges are not satisfied by conventional religion.

Second, there is a consistent but as yet unexplained tendency for New England to achieve high rates for measures of client cults that are not saturated with supernatural assumptions. In Chapter 6, we noted that New England was especially weak in sect headquarters and hypothesized that the history of migration from and into the region produced this anomaly. To the extent that the market for deviant religion is incompletely satisfied, magic may fill the vacuum.

Third, the strong city size effect with SMSA astrologers reminds us that client cults are competitive businesses. When the proportion of potential cult customers is low in the general population, only large cities may provide a sufficient number of customers (cf. Fischer, 1975).

Our final task was to assess whether adequate measures of cult activity exist and can be used in future studies testing sociological theories. Clearly, we have found a number of quite varied measures. We have shown that a fairly consistent geographic pattern is expressed through them and that departures from it are intelligible. These measures will be adequate for future research, so long as one is clear that cult activities show at least one dimension of variation. Many good measures beyond those reported here undoubtedly languish unappreciated in libraries. While developing our measures, we were astonished to discover what rich troves of data exist and are publicly available. Indeed, we came to wonder why the sociological literature is so poor in quantitative studies of cults when so much good information can be had by anyone who seeks it.

11 *Cult Membership in the Roaring Twenties*

WITH LORI KENT

This chapter adds a historical dimension to the quantitative study of cults. The two previous chapters developed means to study many aspects of cult strength and activity in the contemporary United States. These data revealed marked geographic differences in receptivity to cults. In the 1970s, the heaviest concentration of cults and occult activity was along the West Coast, the area where the conventional churches are weakest.

The fact that many different measures produced similar results lent confidence to our conclusions. However, as is often the case in social science, the results were very circumscribed in time and space. Our work is constantly guided by deductions from a general theory of religion that predicts that cults will always be stronger where conventional religion is weaker, other things being equal. In the concluding chapters of this book, we provide a careful test of this conclusion, but so general a theory demands testing in many times and places, not just in contemporary America. In consequence, we have sought means to pursue our studies of religious movements in other societies and other times. Chapter 20 draws on Canadian data; Chapter 21 considers Europe; and here we develop and assess measures of cult strength and activity in the United States in 1926.

The original version of this chapter was published as Rodney Stark, William Sims Bainbridge, and Lori Kent, "Cult Membership in the Roaring Twenties: Assessing Local Receptivity," *Sociological Analysis,* 1981, 42:2, pp. 137–162.

Of course, our theory does not naively predict that cult geography is a static phenomenon. Although today the conventional churches are weak and cults are numerous on the Pacific, conceivably, in earlier years, it was New England where religious innovation filled the gap left by secularization. Thus, it will be interesting for purely historical reasons, as well as to provide data for theory testing, to see where cults were strong in 1926.

Although we developed several kinds of measures in the two previous chapters, none were actual counts of the members of cult movements. This chapter is based primarily on information about cult membership. Although actual membership statistics might seem the ideal measure of cult activity, this is not necessarily so because of idiosyncracies in the historical development of some cult movements. We consider a variety of data in this chapter, but we demonstrate that only some of these data are useful as measures of local receptivity to cults. In evaluating the 1926 data, we also contrast cults of the twenties with cults of the seventies, thus assessing the stability of basic patterns.

Only in Chapter 19 do we use these data in attempts to replicate tests of our theory. Here we wish to demonstrate the validity of some measures of cult activity in the 1920s and to contribute to historical understanding of certain significant cult movements. A major purpose of this chapter is to bring to the attention of social scientists the existence of an extraordinary wealth of good data on religion—data that have languished relatively unused for many decades in university libraries (cf. Azzi and Ehrenberg, 1975; Meyer et al., 1979).

REDISCOVERING THE RELIGIOUS CENSUS

After attempting less complete surveys in the 19th century, beginning in 1906 the U.S. Bureau of the Census conducted an elaborate census of religious bodies every decade through 1936. Painstaking efforts and systematic procedures produced data of very high quality and great completeness. These data make it possible to compute church membership rates for every city over 25,000, for every county, and for every state in the nation. The denominational composition of these units is reported in exquisite detail, and such information as the number and size of congregations, when congregations were founded, the number of ministers, annual expenditures, missionary activity, sex ratios of congregations, and a host of other interesting data are also available. For each religious body included, the census also provides a first-rate summary of its history, doctrine, and rituals.

Even more important, the Census Bureau took an unusually broad view of what constitutes a religion. Hence, they not only gathered data on a host of small Christian sects, they also included many cults. Membership statistics on these cults are the basic source of data for this chapter.

Each of these four voluminous census reports warrants extensive analysis, but 1926 is the best of the four. There was modest improvement in the scope and completeness of each of the reports through 1926. Then the social dislocations caused by the Dust Bowl and the Great Depression were reflected in the 1936 census. For example, the number of Northern Baptist churches and church members increased slightly between 1926 and 1936, but the number of Southern Baptist congregations declined by 40 percent between the two reports, and the number of Southern Baptists fell by nearly a million. This probably reflected the massive uprooting of rural America, especially in the Dust Bowl region. These missing Baptists were simply gone from the farms and small towns where they had been in 1926 and had not yet showed up on the rolls of Baptist churches elsewhere. How frustrating that the census ceased its studies of religion at that point!

For our purposes, it seems best to use data for a relatively more settled and "normal" time. Thus, we have coded data from the 1926 census to create a variety of rates. As we examine the data, it will be obvious that it was not possible simply to lump all the cult membership statistics together to create a single measure. Groups differ so greatly in size that to do so would be simply to ignore data on most groups. Moreover, we must keep a close eye on the history of specific groups if we are to interpret their membership statistics correctly.

Even in 1926, the census failed to locate or to include a substantial number of cults in existence at the time. Our data set of 501 cults active in the United States today includes 60 that were founded prior to the 1926 census. Surely many others must have existed then that failed to survive until now; yet the 1926 census included only 15 groups that we classify as cults. This is a serious shortcoming if the aim is to count cults. It is of minor importance if the aim is to count cult members. The omitted groups were extremely tiny and did not grow later. Most would have consisted of but a single congregation in 1926 with probably fewer than 100 members. Indeed, the census did include Vedanta, with only 3 congregations and 200 members nationwide, and the General Church of the New Jerusalem (a Swedenborgian group), with 13 congregations and 996 members. Moreover, the census reported a number of congregations with as few as 2 members.

Looked at this way, although many cult groups were missed, few cult members failed to be counted. We would be surprised if the uncounted cultists amounted to more than 5 percent of those counted. Because the purpose of this chapter is to take advantage of a rare opportunity to base cult rates on actual membership, we can ignore the omission of some tiny cult groups.

Table 11.1 lists all 15 cult movements we identified in the 1926 census. We discuss our justification for including a given movement in the cult category later in this chapter, but this array of data serves as a useful introduction to the material to be discussed and offers some basic generalizations relevant to research on cults. Generally speaking, cults are small and extremely urban, and their members primarily are adult females. The main exceptions to these generalizations are the Church of Jesus Christ of Latter-day Saints (the Utah-based Mormons) and the Reorganized Church of Jesus Christ of Latter Day Saints. Later we examine how different these two groups are from most other cults. These groups aside, however, the generalization that cults are urban is forcefully sustained — most report more than 90 percent of their members residing in urban areas. This high percentage is congruent with Claude Fischer's (1975) argument that deviance is more likely to occur in urban places, where it is easier to gather the absolute number of like-minded persons needed to sustain a deviant subculture. For this reason, in future chapters, we often give primary attention to cities rather than to states in studying cult membership — for the smaller cults lack members in the more rural states. But in this chapter, state and region are the most useful descriptive units.

Table 11.1 also shows that cults are very disproportionately made up of females. In 1926, three of four Christian Scientists were female. In considering this fact, however, we must keep in mind that the majority of members of most mainline denominations also are female. For 1926, 55.7 percent of all church members were female, and females made up 57.0 percent of all church members over the age of 12. Finally, cults report very few members under age 13, but 18.4 percent of all church members counted by the census were preteen children.

For purposes of analysis, some of these 15 cults are too small to be of any use. Nothing can be learned, in terms of the spatial distribution of cults, from groups with fewer than 1,000 members nationwide. We thus eliminated the Christian Science Parent Church and the Vedanta Society from further study, combined the two Swedenborgian "New Jerusalem" groups, and added the Theosophical Society of New York to the national Theosophical organization. As mentioned, not all the groups

TABLE 11.1   *Cult Groups in America, from the 1926 Census of Religious Bodies*

| Cult | Groups | Number | *Membership* | | |
			Percent Urban	Percent Female	Percent Under 13
American Theosophical Society[a]	223	6,780	97.9	65.1	0.0
Baha'i	44	1,247	95.1	?	?
Christian Science Parent Church	29	582	98.6	75.3	0.7
Church of Christ, Scientist[b]	1,913	140,081	94.0	75.5	0.0
Church of Jesus Christ of Latter-day Saints (Mormons)	1,275	542,194	51.7	49.9	23.1
Divine Science Church	22	3,466	100.0	71.1	1.2
General Church of the New Jerusalem	13	996	42.6	58.2	1.5
General Convention of the New Jerusalem in the U.S.A.	85	5,442	91.2	60.6	1.9
Liberal Catholic Church	39	1,799	100.0	61.3	14.8
National Spiritual Alliance of the U.S.A.	59	2,015	87.9	62.6	2.0
National Spiritualist Association	543	41,233(?)	91.4	61.8	1.5
Progressive Spiritual Church	9	7,383	100.0	59.4	0.0
Reorganized Church of Jesus Christ of Latter Day Saints	592	64,367	61.9	57.8	7.3
Theosophical Society of New York	1	55	100.0	45.5	0.0
Vedanta Society	3	200	100.0	62.5	0.0

[a]The American Theosophical Society also claims 668 national members, not affiliated with any local group.
[b]The Church of Christ, Scientist also claims 62,017 members of the Mother Church, not affiliated with any local group.

serve to indicate local receptivity to cult movements. Yet each offers insights into how cults developed in the United States, insights that often seem to have far wider application.

BEST MEASURES OF THE CULTURAL CLIMATE

Christian Science

Christian Science offers the best basis for gauging local receptivity to cult movements in the 1926 data. Unlike some other cults, it originated in America and is well suited to this cultural setting. Unlike some other groups, such as the Mormons, it appeared in particular places through local recruitment, not primarily via migration. Finally, by 1926, the group was large enough and old enough to have "smoothed out" any idiosyncratic effects, such as the impact of one skilled missionary who went to one particular locale — a problem that does influence rates for small or young groups.

Christian Science was founded in 1879 in Boston by Mary Baker G. Eddy. The facts that the group was founded by a woman and that women predominated in leadership positions undoubtedly had some impact on recruitment — Christian Science membership in 1926 was unusually disproportionately female.

Christian Science is classified as a cult, not a sect, because of the amount of novel culture it added to traditional Christian doctrine. Mrs. Eddy was a student of Phineas P. Quimby, the founder of New Thought, and drew on his work to produce Christian Science. Mrs. Eddy's sharpest break with traditional Christian teaching was in denying the reality of matter. The mind is the only reality. Disease, evil, and sin are the result of erroneous thinking. The mind, misguided by faulty metaphysical ideas, creates a harmful material reality. If we can convince ourselves of the truth, reality will thereby be changed in beneficial ways.

The 1926 census located 1,913 Christian Science congregations with 140,081 members, plus another 62,017 members affiliated not with a local group but directly with the Mother Church in Boston. Our analysis is based on members affiliated with a local congregation, for the others cannot be located geographically.

Figure 11.1 maps Christian Science membership for the nine regions of the United States. The cult receptivity of the Pacific region stands out; its rate of Christian Scientists far surpasses that of any other area. The Mountain region is second. These geographic patterns are very similar to those found in our research on contemporary cults. Today cults are highly concentrated along the shores of the Pacific, with the

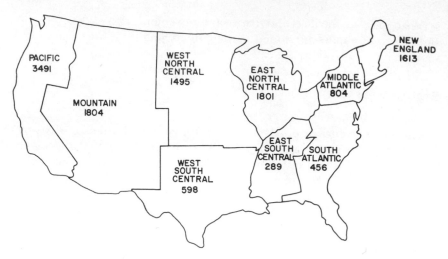

FIGURE 11.1   *Christian Scientists per Million Population, 1926*

Mountain region following. A major factor in the contemporary high cult rates for the Pacific region is that many new cults form in that area. This underscores the importance of the Christian Science data, for Christian Science began across the continent from the Pacific states. Yet, with the passage of 50 years, any geographic bias based on the location of the Mother Church in Boston had disappeared.

As can be read in Table 11.2, California, Oregon, and Washington are by far the highest states in terms of Christian Science membership rates. The New England region, birthplace of Christian Science, runs a poor fourth and Massachusetts is only seventh among states, being surpassed by the three Pacific states as well as by Nevada, Colorado, and Illinois. Figure 11.1 also shows that the South displays little hospitality for cult movements, with the East South Central region (Kentucky, Alabama, Tennessee, and Mississippi) having the lowest rate. This, too, is in close accord with contemporary findings reported in chapters 9 and 10.

A final point in favor of Christian Science membership statistics as a good measure of local receptivity to cults is that this is a successful cult movement. Many of the other cults we examine in this chapter were relative failures that have gone downhill since 1926. Indeed, the vast majority of cults are short-lived failures; thus, the bulk of data on cults at any given moment is heavily influenced by groups that have gotten something important wrong, be it doctrine or organizational tactics. Cults that get things right give us the best insights into where cult growth is possible.

TABLE 11.2   *Cult Membership Rates per Million Population by States and Regions*

Location	Christian Science	Theosophy	Liberal Catholic	Divine Science	Baha'i
New England	1,613	27	4	0	14
Maine	1,163	0	0	0	32
New Hampshire	1,545	0	0	0	0
Vermont	871	0	0	0	0
Massachusetts	2,107	45	8	0	17
Rhode Island	898	0	0	0	0
Connecticut	1,016	16	0	0	10
Middle Atlantic	804	43	9	31	15
New York	1,004	62	18	53	21
New Jersey	886	41	0	0	15
Pennsylvania	521	21	2	16	7
East North Central	1,801	70	26	22	15
Ohio	1,528	62	10	38	10
Indiana	1,788	9	0	0	0
Illinois	2,375	122	54	24	25
Michigan	1,489	51	29	0	16
Wisconsin	1,449	52	11	43	13
West North Central	1,495	65	18	79	1
Minnesota	1,790	135	59	0	6
Iowa	1,301	37	1	14	0
Missouri	1,700	72	12	280	0
North Dakota	619	32	0	0	0
South Dakota	794	15	0	0	0
Nebraska	1,559	95	28	0	0
Kansas	1,490	0	0	0	0
South Atlantic[a]	456	35	5	2	9
Delaware	425	30	0	0	0
Maryland	579	32	0	0	10
Virginia	260	22	0	0	0
West Virginia	299	21	0	0	0
North Carolina	172	12	0	0	0
South Carolina	72	4	0	0	0
Georgia	279	23	13	0	0
Florida	1,661	133	0	0	34
East South Central	289	22	0	0	10
Kentucky	336	18	0	0	0
Tennessee	430	15	2	0	0
Alabama	217	36	0	0	0
Mississippi	138	15	0	0	0

(continued)

TABLE 11.2   (continued)

Location	Christian Science	Theosophy	Liberal Catholic	Divine Science	Baha'i
West South Central	598	40	3	3	0
Arkansas	281	0	0	0	0
Louisiana	404	54	6	0	0
Oklahoma	957	38	5	15	0
Texas	628	51	3	0	0
Mountain	1,804	82	17	111	3
Montana	1,705	201	28	0	0
Idaho	1,758	25	0	0	0
Wyoming	1,710	190	0	0	0
Colorado	2,985	87	45	396	10
New Mexico	583	0	0	0	0
Arizona	870	0	0	0	0
Utah	1,256	56	0	0	0
Nevada	2,137	166	0	0	0
Pacific	3,491	239	78	104	39
Washington	3,269	266	65	284	21
Oregon	3,331	124	0	85	35
California	3,593	252	98	50	45

[a]Washington, D.C., included.

Theosophy

The Theosophical Society failed to live up to its early promise. After a period of rapid growth in America, Europe, and India in the 1880s, Theosophy was rocked by scandals concerning the use of fakery during seances by its founder, Helena Petrovna Blavatsky. Although this setback greatly harmed the cult movement, it did no lasting harm to Blavatsky's reputation among occultists. Her writing is still widely read and admired, despite her many outlandish claims. (For example, after several marriages and an illegitimate child, she maintained she was still a virgin.) Blavatsky was replaced as the leader of Theosophy in the 1890s by Annie Besant, a prominent English radical and feminist. During Besant's early years in office, the society resumed its growth. Then schisms developed and Besant ceased her public activities. Since then, Theosophy has shown no signs of significant growth. It has given rise to a number of schismatic groups, but none has attracted a significant following. In the 1926 census, 223 congregations of the American Theosophical Society were located, with 6,780 members, an average of 30 members per congregation.

Despite being small and relatively unsuccessful, Theosophy is useful as a gauge of local receptivity to cults. First, the group is easily recognized as a cult — it is obviously not a Christian sect. Blavatsky not only claimed to communicate with the spirit world, but she included a great deal of Eastern mysticism in Theosophical doctrines. Therefore, to be a Theosophist, one will encounter whatever degree of stigma and sanction is imposed on religious deviants in a given community. Second, like Christian Science (and unlike Mormonism), Theosophy recruited its members locally and did not prompt any substantial amount of migration. That is, Theosophical membership rates for a given community reflect local conversion, not in-migration of Theosophists.

Table 11.2 shows that Theosophy's geographic distribution closely approximates that of Christian Science. It, too, began on the East Coast (New York), and it, too, after the passage of nearly 50 years, had found its most fertile recruitment grounds along the Pacific shores. The Pacific region again far surpasses all other regions in its membership rate, and again the Mountain region is in second place. Washington is the state with the highest rate (266 per million residents) and California is a close second. As usual, the East South Central region is noticeably low, one reason being its high proportion of rural population, and another that many typical cult practices were long against the law in this part of the South. Statutes against fortune-telling, for example, outlawed the seance activities of Theosophy.

Liberal Catholics

Among the offshoots of Theosophy are the Liberal Catholics. By the turn of the century, Theosophy had attracted many English clergymen, especially Anglicans and Old Catholics. The inclusion of Theosophical mysticism in Christian services drew disapproval from Anglican and Old Catholic bishops. As a result, a number of clergymen formed a new cult movement combining Blavatsky's doctrines with traditional Christian rites, such as High Mass. They took the name Liberal Catholic Church. In 1917, Liberal Catholicism was brought to the United States by Bishop James Wedgwood, who traveled the nation and ordained a number of priests.

The Liberal Catholic Church met strong opposition from the Theosophical Society, but, in 1926, only nine years after the group began here, the census enumerated 39 Liberal Catholic congregations with 1,799 members. However, these are limited statistics. Many states lack any Liberal Catholics; no state has a large number. Despite these limits, the geographic distribution of Liberal Catholics shows the familiar western tilt. California and Washington are the top two states in Liberal Catholic membership rates and the Pacific region is much the highest. Again the Mountain region is second, and southern areas are markedly low.

Divine Science

Divine Science is a New Thought cult that emphasizes healing. It began as two independent movements, one in Denver, the other in San Francisco, in the late 1880s. In 1889, they merged and based their headquarters in Denver.

The group has never been very successful. In 1926, it had only 22 congregations and 3,466 members nationwide. As can be seen in Table 11.2, Divine Science was most successful in its home territory — Colorado has the highest rate of members. Yet even these data display the cult affinity of West Coast culture. Washington has the second highest rate of Divine Science members and the Pacific region stands out from the rest.

Baha'i

Baha'i is a Persian cult that sprang up among the Sufis in the middle of the 19th century. Its doctrine combines the teachings of all major Eastern faiths and thus claims universality. In 1893, a world parliament of religion held in Chicago drew Baha'i representatives, and this led to the formation of an American branch in Chicago. Indeed, many Eastern cults made their appearance in the United States via this 1893 Chicago assembly.

The 1926 census located 44 Baha'i congregations in the United States, with a total of 1,247 members. Although the small size of the membership makes the statistics of limited use, once again a cult has been influenced by the cultural geography of the nation. The group was founded in Chicago; so it is no surprise to find Illinois among the states with higher rates. Nevertheless, California is the highest state, with Oregon in second place. The Pacific region is much higher in Baha'i membership than any other region.

The fact that Maine is the fourth highest state merely alerts us to idiosyncracies that can influence the size and distribution of any specific small cult group. For example, the decision of one relatively effective missionary to go to a particular place can have decisive implications. In the case of such a small cult, the rates are very sensitive to individual action, and the rate for Maine represents only 25 members. We must always remember that social movements are composed of *individuals*. Cults do not make decisions — individuals do. Among the important decisions that cult leaders must make is where to expend their limited resources in pursuit of new converts. This probably accounts for the extreme urbanism of most cults, because cities offer the cult founder or missionary greater prospects for rapid growth than could be achieved in smaller communities. This also may partly account for the West Coast strength in cults. New cults tend to be founded by people who had experience in former cults, as we explain in Chapter 8; so any excess of Pacific cults would tend to increase as they reproduced themselves, and such an excess would attract other founders and missionaries because it would seem to indicate especially fertile cultic ground. Although the degree of receptivity of the environment sets a limit for the success of cults, a favorable cultural climate is not sufficient for growth. There also must be effective cult leaders who hunt for new members, and membership statistics are a record of their successes.

INVALID MEASURES OF THE CULTURAL CLIMATE

Mormons

The Church of Jesus Christ of Latter-day Saints presents problems of classification. Clearly it is not just another Protestant sect. Especially following the revelations in Nauvoo, Illinois, the Mormon church has added so much novel doctrine to the Christian-Judaic tradition that it represents a new religious tradition in its own right, and there can be no doubt that this tradition is deviant. The destruction of Nauvoo and the murder of Joseph Smith by an angry mob testify to great tension with the environment. Clearly, Mormonism fits our definition of a cult. However, because the Mormons succeeded in building their Zion in the empty deserts of the West, most Mormons do not experience life as members of a religious minority. In Utah, Mormonism is the dominant religious tradition, and this feeling sustains Mormons in nearby states as well. For this reason, in Chapter 9, we classified schismatic Mormon groups in Utah as sects, coding such groups as cults only if they developed outside of Utah.

However, in dealing with the 1926 data, we have included the Mormons among the cults. When necessary, we simply exclude Utah from some of our calculations — for example, in calculating a Mormon rate for the Mountain region.

In many ways, Mormons ought to provide an exceptional measure of cult receptivity — the church is both old and very large. However, for many states, Mormon membership rates do not reflect conversion nearly so much as migration. Thus, the Mormons do not dominate Utah because they recruited its population; Utah had no appreciable population until the Mormons migrated there. Similarly, the large Mormon populations of Idaho, Nevada, Wyoming, and Arizona are primarily the results of migration from Utah.

We are able to establish the importance of migration for Mormon membership not just by reference to historical impressions, but empirically. For large and middle-sized American cities, we coded the number of people born in Utah as a proportion of those native citizens born out of state — that is, the relative importance of Utah as a source of in-migration compared with other states. For the 181 cities (excluding those in Utah) for which data were available, the correlation with the proportion of Mormons in the population was astronomical, $r = .82$. In contrast, when we did the same thing for Christian Science, correlating the proportion of native citizen in-migrants from Massachusetts with the proportion of Christian Scientists in the population, we got an insignificant $-.12$ for 167 cities, excluding those in Massachusetts itself. These findings demonstrate again the utility of Christian Science membership as a measure of the local religious climate, but they also reveal why Mormon rates are of very limited use for that purpose. Still, Mormon membership patterns for 1926 are of considerable intrinsic interest and reveal one suggestive surprise.

The impact of migration on Mormon membership shows in bold relief in Figure 11.2. With Utah left in, the Mountain region has 132,411 Mormons per million. Even with Utah omitted from the computation, the Mountain region towers above all others, having 42,350 Mormons per million population. After Utah, Idaho is the top state, with about 20 percent of its population being Mormon in 1926. However, excluding the Mountain region, the Pacific far surpasses the rest of the nation, with 4,970 Mormons per million. No doubt much of this is due to westward Mormon migration from the Mountain region.

Proximity to Utah and westward migration play no role in the surprising strength of Mormonism in the East South Central and South Atlantic regions. On all contemporary measures of cult activity and on all others we examine in this chapter, the states of the Southeast tend to have among the very lowest rates. Sometimes Florida, Virginia, or Maryland rise above the other states in this area, but the regions as a whole show very low receptivity to cults. Why are Mormons an exception to this pattern? We think the answer is that Mormonism often acts more like a sect than a cult and that it appeals to a very different population segment than do most other novel religious movements. Deviant aspects of Mormon history and doctrine are not emphasized in its recruitment appeals, but tend to be submerged under a much more general and traditionally Christian orientation when the church confronts potential converts. Furthermore, Mormons are in sharp contrast to most other cults in that half their 1926 membership was rural. Also unlike the other cults, half the Mormons were males and nearly a fourth were children under age 13.

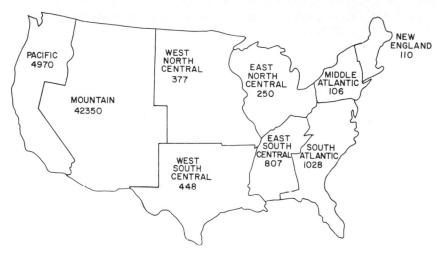

F IGURE 11.2   *Mormons per Million Population, 1926*
Note: Mountain region excludes Utah.

These differences testify to a point we support with evidence in Chapter 14 — that Mormons tend to convert whole families, not isolated individuals. Moreover, Mormonism is a very strong religious organization in the sense that it deeply immerses members in a dense and active subculture of believers. In these ways, Mormonism more closely resembles militant Protestant sects than most cults, which often are very loose and diffuse organizations. Thus, Mormonism may do better in areas where sects also do better because they draw upon the same sorts of people and provide similar organizational features. In Chapter 6, we note that the East South Central region is first in terms of Protestant sects, which is consistent with this interpretation of the area's high rate of Mormonism. Moreover, that the West South Central and the West North Central regions, rural areas abundant in sects, also stand higher on Mormonism encourages this suggestion. Finally, Mormonism is very weak in northeastern regions, despite having originated in New York State.

Reorganized Church of Jesus Christ of Latter Day Saints

Although members of the Utah-based Latter-day Saints readily accept the name Mormon, members of the Reorganized LDS headquartered in Missouri refuse to be called Mormons. The Reorganized LDS formed around the family of Joseph Smith following his murder in Illinois and was made up of those who rejected Brigham Young's authority and who did not trek west. At serious issue were the revelations Smith promulgated during the Nauvoo period, including the practice of po-

TABLE 11.3 *Cult Membership Rates per Million Population by States and Regions*

Location	Mormons	Reorganized Latter Day Saints	Sweden-borgians	Spiritualists[a]
New England	110	301	203	1,636
Maine	0	1,450	137	38
New Hampshire	0	0	324	207
Vermont	414	0	0	117
Massachusetts	126	191	294	2,938
Rhode Island	58	494	181	198
Connecticut	103	77	11	230
Middle Atlantic	106	88	74	422
New York	127	52	38	566
New Jersey	39	0	40	118
Pennsylvania	107	168	133	363
East North Central	250	744	58	755
Ohio	119	552	95	498
Indiana	344	194	24	438
Illinois	344	599	76	1,434
Michigan	537	1,880	35	488
Wisconsin	232	302	3	324
West North Central	377	2,171	36	213
Minnesota	248	210	39	242
Iowa	229	3,406	14	289
Missouri	535	3,815	46	237
North Dakota	298	574	0	0
South Dakota	198	285	0	0
Nebraska	574	1,282	0	98
Kansas	392	1,985	95	270
South Atlantic[b]	1,028	71	42	35
Delaware	0	0	281	152
Maryland	420	85	206	74
Virginia	749	0	8	0
West Virginia	868	416	0	87
North Carolina	696	0	0	0
South Carolina	1,818	0	0	0
Georgia	1,150	0	10	0
Florida	2,043	200	33	74
East South Central	807	221	4	17
Kentucky	826	150	0	34
Tennessee	893	69	11	0
Alabama	727	513	2	29
Mississippi	794	132	5	0

(continued)

TABLE 11.3   (continued)

Location	Mormons	Reorganized Latter Day Saints	Sweden-borgians	Spiritualists[a]
West South Central	448	334	4	233
Arkansas	216	215	0	10
Louisiana	578	59	15	49
Oklahoma	291	990	0	400
Texas	545	203	3	309
Mountain	42,350[c]	797	18	151
Montana	4,750	661	0	0
Idaho	194,307	1,295	0	0
Wyoming	55,286	400	0	167
Colorado	5,987	1,415	63	465
New Mexico	3,939	0	0	118
Arizona	44,450	539	0	0
Utah	702,500	450	0	0
Nevada	61,113	0	0	0
Pacific	4,970	694	65	499
Washington	3,487	743	11	733
Oregon	6,932	516	106	271
California	5,102	715	74	467

[a]As explained in the text, the statistics for Spiritualists are not reliable.
[b]Washington, D.C., included.
[c]Utah excluded.

lygamy, which had begun among Mormon leaders in Nauvoo. The reorganized church rejected the Nauvoo revelations and polygamy and, led by Smith's widow and sons, headquartered first in Plano, Illinois, then moved to Lamoni, Iowa, and finally, in 1930, to Independence, Missouri, the location of a pre-Nauvoo LDS settlement in Smith's day.

This background raises serious questions about the status of the reorganized branch of LDS as a cult. The Book of Mormon does not contain much in the way of a novel theology. Most of the novel culture that qualifies Utah Mormons as a cult is subsequent to the Book of Mormon and occurred during the Nauvoo period. In turning away from all the theological developments of the Nauvoo period, the reorganized LDS may, in fact, have regained the conventional religious tradition of Christianity, which may make reorganized members so concerned about being confused with Utah Mormonism.

Our inclination is to classify the Reorganized LDS as a Christian sect on the basis of theology, although we think that outsiders, including potential converts, often have regarded them as a cult. Our reconceptualization of the concepts church, sect, and cult does not define these three as wholly separate "ideal types." Rather, the terms mark extremes on two axes of variation. Cults and sects differ from churches in that they are significantly more deviant. Cults differ from sects in that their culture (beliefs and practices) is significantly more novel or exotic. These differences are matters of degree. Both LDS groups, and Christian Science as well, are mixtures of novelty and standard Christian traditions. Over their history, the LDS groups have moved along the sect-cult spectrum and, by 1926, were near or in the grey area where they might be called either sects or cults.

If the identification of a group as sect or cult is a matter of degree, is it not also a matter of opinion? And who is to decide, if it is a matter of opinion? Sociologists may be able to measure the differences between groups with some precision, by examining beliefs and practices and analyzing them both qualitatively and quantitatively. But the effective judge in deciding where to draw the line between sect and cult is the surrounding society. At origin, both LDS groups experimented with cultural novelty and thus met our definitions of cult. By 1926, they had changed sufficiently that many Americans were treating them mainly as sects. Indeed, the quantitative findings reported in this chapter may be taken as good evidence that the American public, including potential recruits, primarily identified LDS groups as sects and continued to see Christian Science as a cult. The LDS groups are important cases for sociological research on cults because they show how religious movements can evolve along the sect-cult dimension. But by 1926, they were probably no longer good measures of regional receptivity to cults.

Given that the reorganized church was long headquartered in Iowa and then shifted to Missouri, it is not surprising that these two states have by far the highest rate of membership in this religious group and that the West North Central region, which includes both states, is the highest in the regional comparisons shown in Table 11.3. Nor does the relatively high rate for the neighboring East North Central region seem remarkable. What seems surprising, perhaps, is the strength of the reorganized group in the Mountain region, the second highest of the regions. The reorganized church has been able to attract followers in the heart of Utah-based Mormonism, especially in Colorado and Idaho. It also has succeeded in attracting followers in the Pacific region, although some of this could reflect nothing more than the general westward migration of population, especially from the rural Midwest.

But westward migration could hardly be the reason for the rather astonishingly high rate for Maine. Indeed, Maine is so high that it greatly distorts the rate for the New England region. This shows the danger in trying to infer too much about general trends from data on a single group because Maine's high rate reflects nothing more dramatic than the presence of 1,131 members of the reorganized church. This easily could have been the result of historic accident. It is not unthinkable that a single missionary of special talent could have achieved this result over a period of years. That he happened to choose Maine for his territory rather than New Hampshire or Florida may have been wholly idiosyncratic.

As with the Utah Mormons, the effects of migration are so pronounced as to mask regional differences in receptivity. Receptivity to cults is best measured by the success of groups that recruit their members in each locale. It is much less clearly measured by the movement of cultists into a locale, even though to some extent this movement may be in search of an environment less hostile to religious deviance. Thus, although the data on both varieties of LDS suggest the cult receptivity of the Far West, they are of very limited value because of the immense role played by migration in determining geographic rates.

Spiritualists

The Spiritualist movement originated in the United States, although it owed intellectual debts to Swedenborgianism. It all began with the Fox sisters of Hydesville, New York, who convinced large numbers of people, including some of the leading literary figures of the time, that they had the ability to communicate with the spirits of the dead through a code of knocking sounds (later the girls confessed the noises were made by cracking their toe joints). Spirit communication rapidly became a nationwide fad during the 1850s, and soon mediums practiced variations on the Fox sisters' seances in nearly every city and town in the nation.

In the beginning, the Spiritualist fad was not a religious movement, for it presented no new theology, only communication with the souls of the departed. Indeed, it was widely discussed primarily as a new scientific invention on the order of the telegraph — its most important journal was called the *Spiritual Telegraph*. But, as time passed, the movement generated considerable opposition from conventional Christian denominations and it began to develop a novel theology. By the 1880s, Spiritualism had become a fully developed cult movement, and, in 1893, the oldest and largest Spiritualist group, the National Spiritualist Association, was formed in Chicago.

The Spiritualists are a clear example of our thesis that secularization is a self-limiting process that in the long run generates religious innovation (see Chapter 19). One might suppose that Spiritualism attracted its following from among the deprived elements of society—the uneducated, the poor, the immigrants. On the contrary, the movement caught on among the educated and the privileged who were religious skeptics. Some of the nation's leading literary figures, including Harriet Beecher Stowe, William Dean Howells, and Walt Whitman, became deeply involved in the movement, and popular magazines such as *Harper's* carried frequent claims by prominent converts to Spiritualism that it had saved them "from atheism" (Kerr, 1972). Spiritualism gained an unusually high proportion of its converts from the ranks of political radicalism, as ardent socialists exchanged their faith in an earthly utopia for a "scientifically demonstrated" perfect society beyond this vale of tears. Robert Owen and Victoria Woodhull were among the prominent radicals involved, and Spiritualism flourished in many of the leading utopian communes of the 19th century (Noyes, 1870; Bassett, 1952; Kerr, 1972).

Even more important to our secularization thesis is the leading role played by religious radicals drawn from the Universalists and the Unitarians in developing a Spiritualist theology, thus making it into a cult movement, and in furnishing the bulk of members as the movement became a formal organization. These two denominations were the first of the highly secularized Protestant denominations, anticipating by more than a century the "demythologized" theology of today's liberal bodies. They had rejected the divinity of Jesus and had eliminated virtually all traces of supernaturalism from traditional Christianity. Their conception of God was extremely remote and inactive. Our theory suggests that such a theology is unable to serve basic needs that usually sustain religious commitment. This is congruent with the fact that the novel and extremely active supernatural doctrines of Spiritualism found such avid response among Unitarians and Universalists.

This response can be illustrated in several ways. First, Universalist clergy played the leading role in developing a theology for Spiritualism (Podmore, 1902; Kerr, 1972). Second, the founders of the National Spiritualist Association were Harrison D. Barret and James M. Peebles, both former Unitarian clergymen who lead many members of that denomination into the new cult movement (Melton, 1978). Third, we have discovered empirical evidence of the strong link between Spiritualism, Unitarianism, and Universalism. These data are based on the 1906 religious census—the best available data closest in time to the rise of Spiritualism as an organized cult movement. Combining Unitarian and Universalist membership statistics to produce state rates, we found a correlation of .67 between these rates and rates of Spiritualist membership. Spiritualism was strongest in the states where Unitarianism and Universalism were strongest.

When Spiritualism was imported into England, it was even more successful than in the United States, and it displayed the same pattern of appeal (Nelson, 1969). Former atheists such as Alfred Wallace (who with Charles Darwin developed the theory of evolution) and Arthur Conan Doyle (the creator of Sherlock Holmes), as well as masses of socialists, flocked to the new faith (Barrow, 1980). And Spiritualism attracted a large number of adherents from middle-class and upper-class Anglican church members and clergy (Nelson, 1969).

Because Spiritualism's rise depended so much on defectors from more conventional religious bodies, its pattern of growth differs from that of most new cult movements — cults tend to recruit from among the unchurched. Moreover, the cult status of early Spiritualism is somewhat cloudy. Many Spiritualists continued to think of themselves as Christians. Indeed, even today it is common to find Spiritualist groups that do not hold their services on Sunday morning because so many followers retain membership in conventional denominations. Still, we are satisfied that Spiritualism was and is a cult movement.

Oddities in the initial formation of Spiritualism are not the only problems in using Spiritualist membership data. The early, impressive growth of the movement was braked late in the 19th century by revelations of fraud. The Fox sisters were detected using simple stage magic to produce spirit contacts during seances, and they made public confessions that all their seances were faked. Later one of them recanted her confession and was welcomed back by the organization. Ever since that time, fraud has remained a severe problem afflicting Spiritualism (Nelson, 1969). Every few years a new exposé has discredited leading spiritualists. In 1960, for example, the *Psychic Observer* published infrared photos taken during seances at Camp Chesterfield (a major Spiritualist center) showing how leading mediums' accomplices faked materialized spirits. In 1979, Elizabeth Kubler-Ross and her associates were detected in fake materializations.

The importance of such episodes of fraud goes beyond implications for the growth of Spiritualism. In our judgment, fraud invalidates the 1926 membership statistics for the group. There is both quantitative and qualitative evidence that, by the turn of the century, Spiritualism was in decline. Between the 1906 and the 1916 religious census reports, membership in the National Spiritualist Association declined by 34 percent. But the 1926 census reported an astonishing increase of 78 percent from 1916's figures.

It is possible that such growth truly occurred — that 18,000 more members were gained than were lost during a ten-year period. But our suspicions are aroused by several additional facts. First, once a cult begins to decline in membership, it virtually never recovers. We know of no other cases where a rapid decline has turned into a rapid rise. Second, the 1936 religious census reported massive losses over the next decade — a 73 percent decrease in members between 1926 and 1936. To believe the statistics for the full three decades is to assume a roller-coaster pattern of decline, rise, decline. A third major reason we do not find the data credible is that more than half of the 1916–1926 growth is located in one state: Massachusetts. If the figures are accurate, we must suppose that Spiritualists in Massachusetts declined from 3,885 in 1906 to 1,510 in 1916, then roared up to 11,805 in 1926, only to plummet to 665 members in 1936. The remainder of the 1926 spurt was accounted for by New York and Illinois — most other states only held steady or declined in membership between 1916 and 1926.

It is possible that trends in these three states were simply very different from trends elsewhere in the nation. But, in other work, we have found that cult membership tends to wax and wane in a highly coordinated way across the states. For example, curves for initiation rates in Transcendental Meditation over the 1970s show extreme similarity year by year for all states, as reported in Chapter 13. Study of trend data by states for other cults reported in this chapter do not show marked interstate variations or any rapid downward-to-upward shifts.

A final basis to suspect the 1926 data for Spiritualism is that the new converts had no reported gender. The census enumeration asked religious bodies to break their membership statistics into males and females. In earlier reports, the National Spiritualist Association complied with this request, and, in 1936, they reported the gender of all but 188 members. But, in 1926, they failed to report the gender of 14,495 members. For all these reasons, we regard the 1926 Spiritualist membership increases as "materializations." As such, they lack utility for researchers deficient in psychic gifts.

Data on the other two Spiritualist bodies included in the 1926 census also prove not to be useful. The Progressive Spiritualist Church had members in only five states, 82 percent of them in Illinois. The National Spiritualist Alliance had members in only 17 states, and that included four states with fewer than 15 members and four with fewer than 61. Thus, we cannot rely upon the 1926 Spiritualist statistics.

Swedenborgians

The Churches of the New Jerusalem follow the doctrines of the Swedish medium and mystic Emanuel Swedenborg (1688–1774). Swedenborg claimed to be able to communicate with the spirits of many famous historical figures and to travel in the spirit world via "astral projection." During his lifetime, Swedenborg's work attracted its greatest response in England, particularly among Anglican clergy. Migration from England brought the new cult to Baltimore in 1792, and soon other congregations formed along the eastern seaboard.

The largest of the American Swedenborgian groups is the General Convention, formed in 1817 and headquartered in Newton, Massachusetts. The General Church is the result of an 1840 schism. By the time of the 1926 census study, the Swedenborgians long had been in decline. The group never was particularly large and, in the latter 19th century, lost some members to Spiritualism and to Theosophy. The 1906 religion census reported a 35 percent drop in congregations of the General Convention since 1890. The next decade brought a 9 percent drop in congregations and the next, another 21 percent drop. Meanwhile, the number of members declined by 23 percent between 1890 and 1926. The 1936 religion census did not include either Swedenborgian group. However, data for 1970 (Melton, 1978) show there were only 60 percent as many Swedenborgians then as in 1926.

What we have here is a group that, even in 1926, was far past its time of growth and hope, a group slowly going out of existence. We would need data from early in the 19th century to catch Swedenborgianism in its prime and thus to use it as a good gauge of cult receptivity. What we see in Table 11.3 is where an early 19th-century cult was still clinging to existence. Thus, Swedenborgians were strongest in the oldest parts of the nation: New England, the Middle Atlantic, and Ohio, Illinois, and Kansas, the longest settled of the midwestern states. The group is missing from most states west of the Mississippi because it was in decline before there was appreciable settlement of most of these states. That Swedenborgians were stronger in the Pacific region than in other western regions is no doubt a symptom of the unusual receptivity of those states to any novel religion, even one in decline. Nonetheless, the data on Swedenborgians seem of little relevance for studying cult receptivity of communities in 1926.

VALIDITY OF CULT MEASURES

How good are all these measures of cult activity in the Roaring Twenties? Thus far we have suggested that data on five cult movements in 1926 seem useful as indicators of local receptivity to cult movements. These groups did not spread by migration, but by local recruitment, and they were relatively young and vigorous groups, not ones that long had been declining. Table 11.4 shows the correlations among all the membership rates discussed thus far. The rates for five groups are highly and consistently intercorrelated. Of these, Christian Science seems the best of the measures in that it correlates better with the others. Theosophy seems the next most consistent measure. Our criticisms of Swedenborgian membership rates seem confirmed because of the inconsistent pattern of its correlations with other cult membership rates. The likelihood that the Spiritualist data are badly fudged is further supported by the poor and inconsistent correlations of these rates with the others. Mormonism does not tell us as much about recruitment to cults as about the effects of migration. Mormon membership is not correlated with membership rates for other cults. The same is substantially true for the Reorganized Latter Day Saints.

For purposes of further research, such as carried out in Chapter 19, a multitude of independent measures of cult receptivity is not needed. Having as many as five historical measures is satisfactory (perhaps even excessive). Thus, the results of Table 11.4 provide adequate grounds for our subsequent studies.

CLIENT CULTS

In Chapter 2, we noted that not all cults are fully developed religions. Client cults deal primarily in magic, not religion. Although such cults often evolve into religions, they rely on relatively short term and specific exchanges until they do so. In the previous chapter, we found that contemporary client cults tend to thrive in the same environments that are receptive to cult movements. Was the same true in the 1920s?

There were no data on client cults in the 1926 religious census for the reasons Durkheim spelled out long ago — there can be no church of magic. Client cults do not deal in the kind of compensators that can bind members into long-term exchanges. Thus, such organizations were not there to be found by the census enumerators.

Nonetheless, the regular U.S. Census of 1930 did collect data on client cult activities that we can draw on in this chapter because some of the occupational categories the census used isolate client cult practitioners. One such category is chiropractors. Some will find this a controversial designation, but then some also object when we classify water dowsers and astrologers as client cult practitioners. Chiropractors, especially back in the 1920s, rejected the fundamental scientific discoveries on which modern medicine is based. They specifically rejected the germ theory of disease. In its place, they proclaimed the doctrine that pressure on the nerves, especially misadjustments of the spine, caused most, if not all, disease.

Chiropractic was founded by Daniel D. Palmer, a grocer in Daven-

TABLE 11.4 *Correlations (r) Among 1926 Cult Measures (N = 48 States)*

	Christian Science	Theosophy	Baha'i	Liberal Catholic	Divine Science	Sweden- borgians	Spirit- ualists	Mormons	Reorg. Latter Day Saints
Good Measures									
Christian Science	1								
Theosophy	.75	1							
Baha'i	.47	.51	1						
Liberal Catholic	.68	.75	.53						
Divine Science	.53	.36	.13	.43	1				
Poor Measures									
Swedenborgians	.25	.06	.51	.15	.02	1			
Spiritualists	.40	.10	.16	.29	.15	.38	1		
Mormons	.04	.00	-.08	-.11	-.07	-.13	-.12	1	
Reorg. Latter Day Saints	.27	.04	-.08	-.11	.41	-.10	.05	.01	1

port, Iowa, who in 1895 claimed to have discovered the ability to cure people through "animal magnetism." Ten years later he claimed to have discovered that subluxations of the back caused disease when he cured Harvey Lillard of deafness by adjusting his back. Palmer founded a school in Davenport and he, and his son B. J. Palmer after him, began training chiropractors in such things as the doctrine that diphtheria is not caused by germs, but by the subluxation of the sixth dorsal vertebra (Gardner, 1957).

The 1930 U.S. Census counted 11,916 chiropractors in the United States (Bureau of the Census, 1933). Table 11.5 shows the rate of chiropractors for each state as the number per 100,000 employed persons. Colorado has the highest rate, closely followed by California and Oregon. The Pacific region has the highest rate, followed by the Mountain region, with the West North Central region close behind. The high rate of the latter reflects the location of the center of the chiropractic movement in Iowa (the fourth highest state) and the spread of the movement into the states closest to Iowa. After all, by 1930, chiropractic had been in operation for only about 30 years. Despite this, the hospitable climate of the Far West for magical services had managed to overcome the initial geographic origins of the chiropractic movement.

A second client cult occupation listed in the 1930 census is healer. Physicians, dentists, nurses, osteopaths, and chiropractors were enumerated separately. Healer is a residual category made up of 17,640 naturopaths, homeopaths, faith healers, and others who rejected medical science and offered magical medical services instead. As is shown in Table 11.5, New Mexico topped the nation in healers in 1930, while Arizona was number three. This reflects the large numbers of people who, in those days, flocked to these states to seek cures for lung ailments in the dry desert air. Not only physicians ran such clinics in New Mexico and Arizona, but a host of quacks did, too. That California is close behind New Mexico, in second place, while Oregon and Washington are fourth and fifth, says more about the cultural than the physical climate of the West Coast. The Pacific region had much the highest rate of healers. Each of these measures of client cults displays a slight regional anomaly that makes good historic sense. But neither anomaly obscures the basic patterning of client cults in a way fully consistent with our best cult membership rates.

Many modern client cult practitioners are pseudoscientists. That is, they present their magic as science. Thus, chiropractors do not claim mystical powers to cure, but a superior science. We can distinguish chiropractic from incorrect science, however, by the disregard for scien-

TABLE 11.5   *Rates of Client Cult Practitioners per 100,000*
Employed Persons

Location	Chiropractors	Healers	Inventors
New England	10	45	8
Maine	19	32	4
New Hampshire	27	22	4
Vermont	23	23	0
Massachusetts	5	60	11
Rhode Island	17	34	9
Connecticut	12	28	8
Middle Atlantic	19	39	5
New York	18	50	7
New Jersey	17	32	5
Pennsylvania	21	25	2
East North Central	23	38	5
Ohio	24	29	5
Indiana	38	34	3
Illinois	16	52	7
Michigan	21	31	5
Wisconsin	30	32	4
West North Central	41	28	3
Minnesota	29	37	4
Iowa	60	23	3
Missouri	34	32	3
North Dakota	24	18	1
South Dakota	42	22	0
Nebraska	40	29	2
Kansas	55	21	3
South Atlantic[a]	10	16	2
Delaware	15	25	4
Maryland	12	18	3
Virginia	8	11	2
West Virginia	10	10	1
North Carolina	8	6	1
South Carolina	5	3	0
Georgia	6	9	1
Florida	21	43	6
East South Central	12	8	1
Kentucky	17	11	1
Tennessee	9	11	1
Alabama	10	6	0
Mississippi	11	5	0

(continued)

TABLE 11.5 (continued)

Location	Chiropractors	Healers	Inventors
West South Central	17	20	2
Arkansas	11	18	1
Louisiana	1	11	1
Oklahoma	41	21	3
Texas	31	17	3
Mountain	46	58	4
Montana	31	29	1
Idaho	33	22	2
Wyoming	47	19	2
Colorado	75	69	7
New Mexico	30	123	0
Arizona	36	102	3
Utah	30	31	6
Nevada	58	42	5
Pacific	62	105	12
Washington	38	74	7
Oregon	61	89	7
California	69	116	15

[a]Washington, D.C., included.

tific verification. It is this, not an incorrect theory, that makes chiropractors magicians.

As one moves across the occult milieu, the line between magic and science is sometimes hazy. One has no trouble classifying works on talking to plants, pyramid power, the Bermuda Triangle, and tales of prehistoric visitors from outer space as occultism and pseudoscience. One can make this judgment after examining the specific works in question. But when one cannot examine the specific work, it is hard to know whether a person is doing science or pseudoscience. However, a strong indicator of pseudoscience is isolation. For all that we treasure the notion of the lonely, untaught genius inventing wonderful new things, the fact is that this occurs very rarely. The lonely, untaught genius at work in his or her barn, attic, garage, or basement usually does not make inventions and discoveries of real worth (Gilfillan, 1970). Usually, such people produce crank machines and implausible theories. Those who do something they call science in isolation from scientific subcultures have a very high proportion of pseudoscientists among them (Gardner, 1957).

On these grounds, we took interest in an occupational category the census called inventors. These were 2,300 people who had not been classified as engineers, scientists, chemists, and other such conventional scientific occupational titles. When asked their occupation, they said they were inventors. Admittedly, some of these people were busy making a better mousetrap, a better gun sight, or some other practical device, but we suspect that this is a measure of pseudoscientists and thus stands on the borderline of cult activity. This interpretation is encouraged by the distribution of inventors across states shown in Table 11.5. California is number one, followed by Massachusetts, and the Pacific region is the highest area.

The validity of these three measures of client cults is strengthened by the high correlations among them. Healer and chiropractor rates correlate .49, healers and inventors, .59, and chiropractors and inventors, .31. Even more persuasive evidence can be seen in Table 11.6, where we observe the very high correlations between these three client cult measures and our two best sets of cult membership rates. All three measures of client cults are very highly correlated with Christian Science membership rates and only slightly less strongly with Theosophy membership rates.

CONCLUSION

Throughout this chapter, we have mentioned the great stability between the 1926 data and our contemporary findings. Table 11.7 shows the correlations between five cult movement and client cult rates for 1926 and 1930 and four contemporary measures of cult strength. The first of these contemporary measures is based on the location of 501 cult movements described in Chapter 9, and it is strongly and highly significantly correlated with each of the five historic measures. State subscription rates for *Fate* magazine, based on 79,907 cases, are an even more sensitive measure, as mentioned in Chapter 10. Once again we find very strong correlations. The third measure of contemporary cult activity is based on the state of residence of people who sent *Fate* a total of 2,086 letters describing their personal mystical experiences over the past three decades. The final measure consists of 2,470 cult movements and client cult centers listed in the *Spiritual Community Guide* (Singh, 1974). All four of these rates correlate well with those from the 1920s.

The stability of these patterns over so long a time does not surprise us. In later chapters, we show that cults do best where conventional religion is weakest. If this is so, we should expect great stability in the pattern of cult rates in this nation since the 1920s because there has been very great stability in church membership patterns. Church membership rates for states in 1926 correlate .75 with those for 1971. Our the-

TABLE 11.6   *Correlations (r) Among Cult Movement and Client Rates (N = 48 States)*

Client Cult Practioners 1930	Cult Membership Rates 1926	
	Christian Science	Theosophy
Healers	.65	.45
Chiropractors	.69	.45
Inventors	.72	.54

Note: All correlations significant beyond .001.

TABLE 11.7   *Correlations (r) Between Cult Rates for the 1920s and 1970s (N = 48 States)*

	Christian Science Membership 1926	Theosophy 1926	Healers 1930	Chiro- practors 1930	Inventors 1930
Cult Movement Rate, 1978	.54	.52	.73	.43	.51
Fate Subscribers, 1979	.68	.58	.53	.72	.30
Fate Letter Writers, 1960–1979	.62	.52	.61	.65	.32
Spiritual Community Guide Cult Centers, 1974	.48	.36	.47	.52	.37

ory of secularization is much happier with this stability than some competing theories might be because we do not postulate that religion faces a precipitous decline, but merely a gradual transformation.

Our aims in this chapter are modest; other chapters develop our theory of the historical role of cults. We have shown that satisfactory data can be found in the 1926 Census of Religious Bodies to permit analysis of cult membership in the United States. Although some groups were too affected by migration, too small, too feeble, or too untruthful to serve these purposes, data for five movements offer valid, reliable measures of cult receptivity. We have also demonstrated the quality of three client cult measures taken from the occupational data reported for the 1930 census. The fact that we found both popular cults and familiar patterns of cult receptivity in data over 50 years old proves that cults are not merely ephemeral residues of the radical 1960s. They are a vital aspect of American religion, and their distribution offers a sensitive indicator of the sacred in a supposedly secular age.

12 *Scientology: To Be Perfectly Clear*

Magic is risky merchandise. Sometimes it will seem to work. At other times, it will clearly fail. The more specific and serious the aims of the magic, the more often it will be seen to fail. For example, magic meant to improve our spirits will succeed more often than magic meant to cause passionate response in a specific object of our affections. Magic intended to bring rain soon will more often seem to succeed than magic intended to bring rain tomorrow. Yet even unspecific magic can fail. Personal misfortunes can follow a ritual meant to cheer us up, and it might not rain again for a year.

In previous chapters, we have emphasized that religion *as such* is not vulnerable to empirical disconfirmation and that, for this reason, religions tend to discard the practice of magic. For similar reasons, magical client cults often are prompted to evolve into fully developed religions. In this chapter, we examine these matters closely through a case study of the Church of Scientology. This case is of special interest for a number of reasons. First, Scientology is not just another obscure cult movement, but an international organization of considerable magnitude (see Chapter 21). Second, Scientology has been the training ground for a host of other cult founders and has served as an inspiration for many

An early version of this chapter was given at the 1979 annual meeting of the Association for the Sociology of Religion and published as William Sims Bainbridge and Rodney Stark, "Scientology: To Be Perfectly Clear," *Sociological Analysis*, 1980, 41:2, pp. 128–136.

new cult movements (Bainbridge, 1984). Third, its history has been extremely well documented, not only by journalists, scholars, and even government commissions and courts, but in exquisite detail through its own prolix publications. Finally, Scientology is of exceptional interest because it has not yet been able to escape its primary basis in extremely specific and serious magical claims.

This chapter examines the heroic attempt of Scientology to preserve its high tension magic — indeed, to convince clients it has delivered on its impossible promises — and the extreme lengths to which it went to protect its magic from disconfirmation. But this struggle is doomed to failure. Early in its history, Scientology switched from a pure client cult to one that presented two faces to the world. Many a recruit was told the group's specific claims were based on science and that the most marvelous real benefits would be received almost immediately. But, at the same time, the group claimed the official protection of religious status. That this double game was a very difficult one for the cult to win will be evident as we see the extreme tactics required to defend Scientology's magic.

Although this chapter is primarily theoretical, it rests on an empirical base. Bainbridge (1970) carried out six months of intensive ethnographic research inside the Boston branch of this group. Subsequently, we obtained a large library of Scientology publications, reports by outsiders and former members, and literature from groups related to this important innovative religion. Ten years ago, the Founding Church of Scientology in Washington, D.C., was kind enough to provide tape recordings of many lectures by the founder. More recently, the Seattle church provided the quantitative data that we have incorporated in Chapter 18. The ethnographic research on Scientology was supplemented by more extensive investigations of The Process (Bainbridge, 1978c), a derivative cult, and of the science fiction subculture from which Scientology sprang (Bainbridge, 1976, forthcoming). Finally, we are guided by Roy Wallis's (1976) fine sociological study.

In our view, Scientology has great difficulty protecting its magic from empirical disconfirmation, a view that may not be held by all of our colleagues or (at least officially) by many practicing Scientologists. Yet there is much public evidence that the defense of its magic is a tough job for the cult. For one thing, Scientology has taken several authors and publishers to court, seeking to stop publication of debunking reports. Among the popular books involved were *Scientology, The Now Religion* by George Malko, *The Scandal of Scientology* by Paulette Cooper (Wallis, 1976:22, 218), and, more recently, *Snapping* by Florence Conway and James Siegelman.

It seems to us that expensive legal action to block publication of these books would not be necessary were Scientology in a position to refute the debunking of its system carried out by the authors. As an experiment, in 1970, Bainbridge, while engaged in participant observation as a trainee in a Scientology course, quietly raised the question of whether Malko's book might be accurate. He was immediately isolated from contact with other students, given various therapy routines designed to make him feel better about the problem, but was provided no objective evidence of any kind to dispel Malko's criticisms.

Certainly, Scientology has good reason to resent the attacks made upon it by the secular institutions of society over the years, which are, typically, aggressive rejections of the cult's claims. One of the more dramatic moments in this continuing struggle came in 1963 when agents of the U.S. Food and Drug Administration raided the Founding Church of Scientology in Washington, D.C., confiscating "E-Meter" electronic equipment allegedly used in improper attempts to cure diseases, action finally reversed by the U.S. Court of Appeals six years later. For a time, both the Australian and British governments seemed bent on banning Scientology, and disputes with the American government have continued unabated, marked by such extreme indicators of tension with the sociocultural environment as another government raid in 1977, this time on the Los Angeles branch.

Although Scientology has frequently succeeded in getting unfavorable court decisions overturned on appeal, often relying on the protection of its status as a religious organization, it has suffered from many attacks by dissatisfied customers of its magic. In 1979, an Oregon court awarded just over $2 million in damages to Julie Titchbourne, supporting her claim that Scientology had defrauded her in its promises to improve her life. Following a preparatory judgment by the state supreme court, the jury had been instructed that Scientology did not enjoy religious immunity for any promises that were not religious in nature (Lang, 1979).

From our perspective, many of Scientology's claims promise specific benefits, capable of empirical test but offered without public evidence of their truth. Thus, Scientology provides the specific compensators of magic, perhaps overshadowing the general compensators that mark religion. In effect, the Oregon courts decided that many of Scientology's claims were indeed magical, not religious, and thus susceptible to empirical refutation and legal attack. The following analysis demonstrates this point, with particular focus on the chief benefit originally promised by the cult.

Clear Status

Scientology, the vast psychotherapy cult founded by science fiction writer L. Ron Hubbard, offers members an alleged state of high mental development known as *clear*. A recent advertisement urged: "Go Clear—For the first time in your life you will be truly yourself. On the Clearing Course you will smoothly achieve the stable State of Clear with: Good Memory, Raised I.Q., Strong Will Power, Magnetic Personality, Amazing Vitality, Creative Imagination." For years, going clear has been the prime goal for Scientologists and for members of Hubbard's earlier Dianetics movement. Outsiders may doubt that Scientology actually can create *clears*, as clear persons are called, but *Clear News*, a Scientology newspaper, reported that a total of 16,849 people had reached this marvelous state by the middle of 1979.

Perhaps Scientology's claims are true, and these legions really have attained a supernormal level of mental functioning and emotional health. But there are good reasons for doubting the testimonials of even 16,849 Scientologists. First, other techniques based on tested principles of behavioral science cannot produce a state like clear. Second, controlled, scientific studies verifying the characteristics claimed for clears have not flooded the standard journals. Third, although Scientologists have created a vigorous religious movement, they have not taken charge of major secular institutions as true supermen and superwomen could. Fourth, reports by independent observers (including one of us) who have interacted with clears do not convey the impression that clears are markedly superior people. Of course, alternate explanations exist for each of these four points, but they render plausible the view that the claims for clear are false and raise the question of how thousands of individuals could be seriously mistaken about their own abilities.

This chapter offers an analysis explaining how people might agree they had indeed gone clear without a significant real change in their objective abilities or even in their subjective state. Although inspired by six months' participant observation inside the cult and by a large body of literature by and about Hubbard's movement, this chapter is theoretical rather than ethnographic. Our central thesis is that clear is not a state of personal development at all, but a *social status* conferring honor within the cult's status system and demanding certain kinds of behavior from the person labeled clear. Such externally demonstrable qualities as good memory and high IQ may have nothing to do with it. Although our theory of clear is designed to explain acceptance of this status within Scientology, it might be adapted to explain a variety of similar statuses of alleged personal perfection, such as salvation in fundamentalist Christianity and satori in Zen.

Hubbard first described clear in an article in the May 1950 issue of *Astounding Science Fiction*. He began by discussing "the optimum brain," modeled on "the optimum computing machine." Hinting that his readers might personally acquire an optimum brain, he said, "modified by viewpoint and educational data, it should be *always* right, its answers *never* wrong" (Hubbard, 1950a:46). A calculator can give wrong answers if, for example, a constant five is added to every computation because of false programming. To restore the calculator's mathematical perfection, we need only *clear* the five. To restore perfect functioning to any intact human brain, we need only clear false programming acquired in the owner's past experiences. The task of Dianetics, as Hubbard called his early techniques, was to develop the right procedures for successful clearing. In the bible of his cult, *Dianetics, the Modern Science of Mental Health*, Hubbard's (1950b:30) claims for clear were extremely optimistic.

> A *clear* can be tested for any and all psychoses, neuroses, compulsions and repressions (all aberrations) and can be examined for any autogenic (self-generated) diseases referred to as psycho-somatic ills. These tests confirm the *clear* to be entirely without such ills or aberrations. Additional tests of his intelligence indicate to [sic] it to be high above the current norm. Observation of his activity demonstrates that he pursues existence with vigor and satisfaction.

The sense perceptions of a clear are said to be more vivid and precise than those of a *preclear*, a neophyte still working to go clear. The clear is unrepressed.

> A clear does not have any "mental voices"! He does not think vocally. He thinks without articulation of his thoughts and his thoughts are not in voice terms. . . . Clears do not get colds. . . . A clear . . . has complete recall of everything which has ever happened to him or anything he has ever studied. He does mental computations, such as those of chess, for example, which a normal would do in half an hour, in ten or fifteen seconds. . . . The dianetic *clear* is to a current normal individual as the current normal is to the severely insane. (Hubbard, 1950b: 38, 101, 107, 179, 15)

In 1950, Hubbard thought that clears might be produced in short order; yet the movement now says that the first member did not go clear until early 1966 (Hubbard, 1968b:111). Apparently, it took this long for Hubbard to develop the social mechanisms to establish and defend clear status. He developed innumerable rules, procedures, and doctrines over these years; but our theory conceptualizes them in terms of four main interdependent strategies: (1) prohibition of independent creation and evaluation of clears, (2) development of a hierarchy of statuses below clear, (3) isolation of the preclear at the crucial stage in upward progress, (4) development of a hierarchy of statuses above clear. Running throughout these is the theme of costs and rewards — for the committed Scientologist, failing to achieve clear is extremely costly, but the apparently ever-increasing rewards to be gained rising through the ranks cannot be obtained outside the Scientology organization. We will examine the strategies, in turn, as Scientology employed them in the 1970s.

Prohibition of Independent Evaluation

Hubbard's first Dianetics publications urged readers to try the technique, becoming *auditors* (therapists) either by simply following the instructions in the first book or by joining in the formal Dianetics movement. A strong impression was conveyed that clears had already been produced and that a skilled auditor could duplicate Hubbard's successes. Dr. J. A. Winter, who collaborated with Hubbard in setting up the movement, says Hubbard claimed "that a 'clear' had been obtained in as few as twenty hours of therapy." But Winter himself never saw a single convincing clear during his association with Hubbard. "I have not reached that state myself, nor have I been able to produce that state in any of my patients. I have seen some individuals who are supposed to have been 'clear,' but their behavior does not conform to the definition of the state. Moreover, an individual supposed to have been 'clear' has undergone a relapse into conduct which suggests an incipient psychosis" (Winter, 1951:34; cf. Wallis, 1976:85).

Martin Gardner reports that, in 1950, Hubbard presented a young woman to a Los Angeles public meeting, saying she was a clear with a perfect memory. "In the demonstration which followed, however, she failed to remember a single formula in physics (the subject in which she was majoring), or the color of Hubbard's tie when his back was turned. At this point, a large part of the audience got up and left" (Gardner, 1957:270). The second Dianetics book (Hubbard, 1951) continued to claim that the great benefits of treatment could be measured objectively and listed a number of diseases it could cure. These strong claims may have attracted sufferers seeking real solutions for specific problems, but they left the entire Dianetics movement open to being discredited in public. The safer course was to prevent outside evaluation, especially of clears, insulating individual followers from knowledgeable independent assaults on their hopes.

Not only was failure a threat, so was the alleged success of rivals. Sociologist Roy Wallis (1976:84) reports, "A severe challenge to Hubbard's standing in the movement came when independent auditors began to proclaim that they had produced 'clears.' Such auditors were eagerly sought for guidance, training and auditing, and rapidly moved into positions of leadership in the Dianetics community." Dianetics had been presented as a *science*, a public process of discovery, open to all who would experiment with the new techniques. This meant not only that some, like Winter, would be disappointed at the empirical results, but also that more sanguine auditors could claim to equal or surpass Hubbard's achievements. This, presumably, was one of the main reasons Hubbard recast his science as a religion, establishing the authority of a prophet with the incorporation of the Founding Church of Scientology in 1955 (Hubbard, 1959; Malko, 1970; Wallis, 1976).

Today, clear status can be conferred only by high ranking ministers of the church, and clears are not presented for examination by outsiders. Clears are discouraged from demonstrating paranormal abilities even for lower ranking insiders. Persons taking the clearing course are enjoined from communicating about it to anyone other than those directly in charge of it (Hubbard, 1968b:112). Attainment of new status, however, is marked by triumphant ceremony, especially in the case of clear. Each new clear is given a unique international clear number, engraved on a silver bracelet, awarded a "beautiful Permanent certificate," and "joyously announced" in a Scientology newspaper. Clears have higher status than the many preclears below them, whether or not their individual abilities have increased.

Scientology does not recognize claims to status of members of rival groups, such as Jack Horner's schismatic Dianology movement, which also attempts to produce clears (Horner, 1970). Thus, clear has become a status within the social system of Scientology, rather than an objective state of being. Aside from the social power it confers within the cult, it is a compensator. Within the limits of the cult, it is not vulnerable to challengers from outsiders.

A Hierarchy of Lower Statuses

The years from 1950 to 1966 may have been frustrating for persons who had long followed Hubbard in the quest for clear, but, during this period, the movement developed a complex structure of other statuses to distribute among members. One kind of status was professional, which designated various levels of skill and training in performing the therapy. By 1954, these went as high as a doctor of Scientology, or D.Scn. degree (Hubbard, 1968a:12). Since then, the number of levels of auditor has steadily increased, each empowered to perform therapy on preclears and clears of different statuses. Of course, these auditors have a stake in maintaining conviction in their own successes. Their training is time-consuming and expensive. The honor they receive is partly dependent on their clients' satisfaction.

Another kind of status invented was that of *release.* When Hubbard had to confront the fact that his first clears were not very clear, he redefined their status as Dianetics release, a condition of superior improvement, but not yet clear. Hubbard developed literally hundreds of mental exercises and therapy routines, each supposed to deal with a problem of the human mind identified by the ever-growing ideology of the cult. As the years passed, levels of release proliferated, until, in 1970, there were five basic release statuses, listed here from the lowest (grade 0) to highest (grade IV): communications release, problems release, relief release, freedom release, and ability release (a sixth release grade is awarded in the midst of the clearing process). Below these levels is the mass of newcomers, active in various introductory classes, the main effect of which is to create social bonds linking the neophytes and incorporating them in the social structure of preclears, who stand in the release hierarchy (see Chapter 14).

Many of the lower level therapeutic procedures seem well designed to train the preclear in compliance to the role demands of clear. Perhaps the most important attribute acquired is a confident acceptance of impossible ideas with a consequent willingness to make statements that outsiders would find incredible. At the very beginning, in the so-called Alice Games of the Communication Course, preclears are made to recite wild sentences from *Alice in Wonderland* as if they were their own confident statements about reality. Later, in Dianetics and Scientology auditing, they will come to "recall" traumatic experiences in the womb, as their mother tried to abort them, and to relive the adventures of previous incarnations centuries ago (Hubbard, 1950b, 1958). On the one hand, preclears are trained to express their emotions through the radical ideology of the cult, and, on the other, numerous exercises reward them for inhibiting spontaneous expressions of feeling. In one of the most basic, TR-0, they must sit immobile and unresponding for up to two hours, regardless of what stimuli are bombarding them.

After as much as a year or more of work at the lower levels, a preclear is probably heavily committed, having invested time, money, and emotion in the clearing process. To abandon the quest at grade IV release, when clear is supposedly within reach, would be to lose a great investment that could be preserved at little apparent extra cost. Although they originally may have been invented to mollify impatient preclears while they awaited Hubbard's discovery of real clears, the release grades now serve to commit Scientologists to extreme exertions to achieve clear and give them psychological momentum in its direction.

Isolation of the Preclear

Preclears will have received their release grades and other preliminary treatment and training at their local Church of Scientology or at the mission branch of a church. But when it comes time to go clear, they must travel to one of the advanced organizations or to Flag Land Base. Since the late 1960s, there have been three "advanced orgs" — in the United States (Los Angeles), Britain (East Grinstead, Sussex), and Denmark (Copenhagen). In 1976, an extensive Flag Land Base was established near Tampa, Florida, offering a full range of advanced processing, including many courses and levels not available even at advanced orgs.

Preclears must pilgrimage to these four centers from as far away as churches in Australia and South Africa. Each center is organizationally and physically separate, even from its local Scientology church. At the org or at Flag, preclears are removed from the social supports for their old status in the cult, isolated from the audience for which they will later play the clear role, and subjected to an unfamiliar situation among strangers, fraught with psychological challenges.

To this point, preclears have always been relatively passive recipients of auditors' treatments, but now they must complete a solo auditor's course and take responsibility for raising themselves up to clear. Several of the earlier processes involved the use of a simple lie detector, the E-Meter. The preclear would sit on one side of a desk or table, clutching tin-can electrodes, one in each hand, while the auditor would sit on the other side, asking penetrating questions and giving commands while privately watching the dial that gave an approximate reading on the preclear's emotional responses. As part of our empirical research on Scientology and related cults, we obtained an E-Meter, received training in its use, and experimented extensively with it. In addition to giving a "scientific" flavor to the therapy sessions, the E-Meter really does guide the auditor to some extent and increases his or her authority with the preclear.

After months or even years of passively receiving authoritative auditing, in preparation to go clear, the preclears must learn to play both roles simultaneously, holding the two cans (separated) in one hand while operating the E-Meter with the other. All alone, they will process themselves up the last few steps to clear. Thus, at the last moment, Scientology transfers responsibility for achieving clear status to the preclears. If anything goes wrong, the fault is theirs. Isolated from fellow preclears, they are prevented from launching a serious challenge to the validity of the process.

There remains the possibility that the person will seek help, either before or after being labeled clear. Help is available, but at extra cost. Unlike other religions, Scientology charges precise amounts for its services. In mid-1979, the Los Angeles org was charging $3,692.87 for the solo audit course, $1,777.84 for the grade VI release that followed it, and $2,844.54 for the clearing course. Solo assists, if done separately from the solo audit course, cost $923.22 for those individuals who sought this help. Among the most expensive special aids, New Era Dianetics, offered to clears, was sold at about $250 an hour. How many hours an individual needs depends on how long it takes him or her to decide to play the assigned role and stop asking for help. The org offers package deals, and, in mid-1979, 50 hours of New Era Dianetics suitable for clears was available for a straight price of $12,603.61. Over the years, Hubbard devised many "case remedies" and other special processes. The alternatives to acceptance of the clear role can be expensive.

Of course, when the new clears return home, they are likely to defend their valuable status in the group by making a public show of *being clear*. They may give inflated testimonials, whether formal statements of how wonderful they feel or more subtle hints about their new-found confidence and ability. Given the social isolation of the clearing process, the new clear probably operates in a condition that social scientists call *pluralistic ignorance*: each person thinks that his or her experience is unique, but in fact it is identical to that of many others. In this case, clears may feel that their state is not as good as those of their fellows, but be reluctant to admit it. They may privately wonder how they can become as successful a clear as their fellows, misled by their inflated testimonials and ignorant of the fact that each of them has similar private reservations (cf. Schanck, 1932).

Our field research in other cults suggests that pluralistic ignorance is a widespread mechanism by which faith is maintained, or at least insulated from overt expressions of doubt. For example, Stark spent a considerable period in the early 1960s with the flying saucer cults that flourished at that time, observing "contactees" — persons who claimed to have had direct personal contact with creatures from outer space and even to have taken interplanetary trips with them. A great number of separate clues strongly encouraged the conclusion that most contactees were aware that they were making it all up. Some of them, among the most successful, were not bothered by this knowledge because they were con artists of long standing who were merely exploiting the latest sting. But the majority of contactees appeared to believe the claims of the *other* contactees and to think they were the only ones who were shamming.

We have also found evidence that some quite successful contemporary cult leaders are conscious frauds, aware that they have no psychic or mystical powers, but still think some other people are genuine psychics and mystics. Thus, we have the odd spectacle of cult leaders who have thoroughly convinced a group of adherents that they alone possess access to the divine mysteries yet who continue to seek their own religious answers by dabbling incognito in other cult movements, unbeknownst to their followers.

In these examples, pluralistic ignorance was sustained without benefit of an organization designed to promote and preserve such misperceptions. In Scientology, such a design is highly developed and perfected. Individuals confer the title of clear upon themselves. If they privately think they are not as clear as they hoped to be, they are at fault. But to admit their shortcomings will only cost them their coveted status in the group and a great deal of money for the additional therapy needed to become more adequate. Indeed, one could usefully think of Scientology as an elaborate and most effective behavior modification program in which potent reinforcement schedules are employed to cause individuals to learn how to act like clears and to keep their doubts and problems to themselves (cf. Bandura, 1969). Scientology may or may not help anyone solve psychological problems. But it most certainly makes it extremely expensive for people to admit their therapy has been less than a resounding success. It is a therapy in which patients rapidly are taught to keep silent about their dissatisfactions and to perceive satisfaction in the silence of other members.

It is vital for the movement that clears not communicate dissatisfaction to preclears. One aid to this is that the clears are finished with the basic processing offered by their local church and will come around the place only for group meetings at which they are one of a parade of celebrities, socially rewarded for playing the clear role well. If they are members of the church staff, they will have regular contact with preclears, but thorough training and constant reinforcement will guide them to play a convincing clear. Of course, expressions of dissatisfaction may begin to leak to Scientology friends and relatives. Hubbard developed a final strategy to sustain the clear's optimism: minimizing the significance of the clear state and creating several levels of status above clear.

A Hierarchy of Higher Statuses

Although the first Dianetics book remains required reading for all Scientologists, its descriptions of clear are no longer definitive. The *Scientology Abridged Dictionary* (Hubbard, 1965) defines the word as follows: "CLEAR: (noun) A thetan who can be at cause knowingly and at will over mental matter, energy, space and time as regards the First Dynamic (survival for self). The state of Clear is above the Release Grades (all of which are requisite to Clearing) and is attained by completion of the Clearing Course at an Advanced Organization."

The second sentence is quite intelligible and summarizes information we have already given about how the status of clear fits into the Scientology hierarchy. The first sentence is utterly unintelligible to persons untrained in cult doctrine and therefore does not represent a claim that is disconfirmable by outsiders. The word *thetan* might be translated as "soul of a human being" and to be "at cause ... over mental matter, energy, space and time" means "good mental and emotional health."

Cult advertisements and informal comments vary, but, in general, it is no longer boldly asserted that clears are geniuses or that they never get colds. Clear status has been mystified and subtly deflated. Even the most doctrinally learned Scientologists may be unsure exactly what palpable qualities a clear is supposed to manifest, other than confidence and loyalty to the cult. Therefore, new clears may not feel justified in criticizing the quality of the clear experience, but they still may want more than they have received. The original promise of clear, and much more, is offered by a still growing series of levels above clear, the operating thetan or "OT" statuses. The "first dynamic" overcome by clears is only one of eight dynamics, each representing a sphere of human motivation — the first is the drive for personal survival; the second is the urge toward sexual reproduction. Mastery of dynamics beyond the first, and ultimately full control over the physical as well as mental universe, are among the goals for OTs.

For OT processing, the Scientologist must return to the advanced org, and a common pattern is periods of normal life and money raising at home punctuated by trips to gain one or two more levels. A February 1980 price list from the Los Angeles org offers a package deal for basic processing from OT I through OT VIII, costing $15,760.03, not counting special treatments. OT processing continues the exchange of wealth for status that began when the individual entered Scientology and is the chief way a member may remain an active Scientologist after going clear. The cult does not worship a deity, and, except for lectures and occasional celebrations, a clear who had not become a professional auditor would have little cause to come to the church. Outside Scientology, clear status has no meaning; so the status can be maintained, let alone increased, only by further expenditure for further therapy.

Progress up the Scientology status pyramid remains slow, and only just over a thousand persons had achieved OT VII at the Los Angeles org by mid-1979. A high proportion of these probably consists of professional auditors committed by all aspects of their lives to the cult. Therefore, the value of the top OT levels has not been disconfirmed within the cult, and they may be followed by yet other levels in future years. Essential to preservation of their value are two conditions: (1) maintaining secrecy and isolation of these statuses and (2) keeping the numbers of people at the top of the Scientology pyramid relatively small. If everyone were at the top, and everyone could see that even OTs are not superhuman, the entire structure might be threatened. But, for the time being, the OT levels serve to defend clear and other lower statuses by offering continued hope that ultimately all the promised benefits will be provided.

From Magic to Religion

Clear is not a state of being, but a status in a hierarchical social structure. It demands that its incumbents play the role of superior person and surrounds them with strategic mechanisms that prevent departure from prescribed behavior. Many people come to Scientology with specific complaints about chronic unhappiness or inability to perform at the level they demand of themselves. We suspect that Scientology cures the complaints by ending the person's freedom to complain, not by solving the underlying problem.

Of course, for some people suffering low self-esteem or anomie, the status of clear may be an efficacious compensator for the problem, even though it is only a status and does not transform the person's basic nature. Our analysis is meant to explain the successful creation and maintenance of clear status without assuming that anyone necessarily benefits objectively from Scientology. If clear were a true reward rather than a compensator, it would not be so closely guarded from evaluation.

After we completed the analysis presented in the foregoing pages, we received a new piece of evidence supporting our interpretations. In 1978, Hubbard once again redefined clear, reducing the importance and thus the vulnerability of this status. Scientology is always changing, and the fluidity of its claims and practices shows how precarious is its definition of reality. As the cult becomes larger, better established, and more familiar to outsiders, its effort to convince members that they have achieved the impossible gets progressively more difficult. Calling 1978 "the year of lightning fast tech" (*tech* means auditing technology), Hubbard (1979:6) announced, "We are making Clears these days in many cases so fast that Clearing Course bracelet numbers are jumping up by the thousands per month. We are also finding that some old Dianetic pcs [preclears] had gone clear and the auditors didn't even notice."

Thus, there came to be two routes to clear, the newer one designed to facilitate advancing those Scientologists who previously could not meet the role requirements of clear and the higher release grades. It seems that the significance of clear—and of any single plateau—is being dissolved into a long staircase of statuses leading upward into the stratosphere of OT. If the importance of clear has been diminished somewhat in the past few years, our theory is not made less relevant. Rather, the analysis of this chapter now extends more broadly to explain how all the higher statuses are maintained. And the progressive deflation of clear demonstrates our main point that magic is difficult, if not impossible, to sustain within a stable organization.

In the 1980 journal article on which this chapter is based, we suggested that clear would continue to lose significance as the cult evolved, and new evidence continues to support our prediction. Scientology publications issued in 1982 indicate that New Era Dianetics has become the standard route to clear. Release grades V and VI, and the solo audit course, are required only if the person "did not go clear on NED." Apparently, clear has become sufficiently deflated that the solo audit strategy is now necessary only in especially difficult cases. The progressive deflation of clear has implied a continuing proliferation of OT levels, and, by 1982, there were 11 of these higher statuses. Eventually, clear may be submerged completely as but one of the steps in Scientology's stairway to heaven. Or perhaps it will become a step of special ritual significance, similar to adult baptism or confirmation rituals experienced by Protestants who had been practicing members of their church for some time previously.

In 1950, Dianetics offered just two statuses: preclear and clear. By 1954, the reorganized Scientology movement offered six statuses to members: general member, Scientology group leader, Hubbard certified auditor, bachelor of Scientology, doctor of Scientology, and the still unattained status of clear. About 1965, according to the first "Classification, Gradation and Awareness Chart," there were eight classification grades, labeled "0" to "VII." Grade IV was simply "release," later to become a series of release grades, VI was "clear," and VII was "OT" or "operating thetan." In 1970, after clear had been achieved, there were 41 distinct, named statuses, not to mention graduation certificates for various special courses.

Most recently, the 1982 booklet, "From Clear to Eternity," lists 64 named statuses. The effective number of statuses is even greater than this because there are a further 30 steps in the processing regimes that do not confer a degree. The system *always* includes statuses that no member has yet attained. Clear used to be the most advanced unreached goal; now OT VIII is just being offered, and OT IX, OT X, and OT XI are not yet "released" and thus play the roles of rather general, superhuman compensators formerly played by clear.

In addition to the processing levels, there are innumerable bureaucratic statuses in the Scientology organization, many of which are called "hats." On September 25, 1970, the organizational chart of the Boston org identified 27 departments under nine divisions, following a plan designed by Hubbard, in addition to the chief executive roles of "director" and "guardian." The fact that staff actually numbered only 13 while 46 of these organizational positions were filled meant that each person, on average, held 3.5 positions. And levels of processing and training interacted in complex ways with these organizational statuses, the ranks in the bureaucracy and in the processing correlating highly, but not perfectly. For example, there were 30 Boston area clears, but only 4 of the 13 Boston staff were clear, and 3 of the top 5 executive positions were held by clears. Until Scientology lowers its tension with the surrounding sociocultural environment and becomes a respected church, none of these statuses will have much significance outside the closed system of the cult.

THE PRECARIOUS DEFENSE OF MAGIC

Although our analysis was designed to fit a single, special phenomenon, maintenance of clear status in Scientology, it really explains something of more general interest: how people can sustain their faith in magic despite day-to-day experience of its failure. The Scientology processes to create clear are indeed examples of modern magic: mental and symbolic exercises undertaken to accomplish the impossible. The four strategies of Scientology show that faith in magic can be sustained:

1. By separating performance of the magic from the world of ordinary experience;
2. By committing participants to magical success through requiring great investment and membership in a cohesive, influential social group;
3. By maneuvering each participant into accepting personal responsibility for success of the magic;
4. By providing supplementary hopes for ultimate future success to compensate participants for any private dissatisfaction they may continue to feel.

Together these factors protect Scientology's claims and insulate its magic against disconfirmation. However, the system is not wholly effective, nor is it, in principle, beyond empirical disconfirmation. That it is not wholly effective can be seen in the constant tinkering with the system that seems designed to add stronger inducements to members to continue their quest for supernormal powers. Even so, the system remains subject to potential disconfirmation because it primarily is dealing in magic, not religion. The difference is critical.

Magic offers to provide specific results that are subject to empirical verification. Although Scientology has fairly effectively prevented neutral tests of the results it claims, it does promise to provide members with tangible benefits that *they*, at least, are positioned to assess. Indeed, so long as the original claims about clear status were maintained, no clears could be created (and were not), for the fact is that, even within the persuasive structure of the cult, it was not possible to convince people that they had supernormal powers of such potency and specificity when they did not. Only by deferring these results to the new OT levels was it possible to create clears. But this is only postponement. Thousands of Scientologists still hope to gain the magical powers promised to them.

In contrast, religion offers its results in an inherently unverifiable context. Christianity, for example, does not promise eternal life in this world, but only after physical death and in another, nonempirical realm. Nor does Hinduism promise that a better life will come to the holy during their present incarnation — but only that they will be reborn in a more exalted status. Such promises are beyond all possible empirical evaluation. Christianity is not haunted with people who have gone on to heaven but who still come around to Sunday services and who might suggest that heaven is highly overrated. But this is precisely Scientology's current situation.

For 30 years, Scientology has sought public status as a religion while privately claiming to be a science as well. For a time, auditors sometimes appeared in public wearing crosses, and a book comparing passages from the Bible with utterances by Hubbard seemed to claim Christian connections for the cult (Briggs et al., 1967). But today the church suggests that it is closer to the Eastern traditions. A label on our E-Meter says, "This Hubbard Electrometer is a Religious Artifact, Used in the Church Confessional, and is not Intended, Effective, or Ever to be Used for Attempted Diagnosis, Treatment, or Prevention of any Disease." And the costs of various courses and processing given on price lists are called "donations." Flag Land Base is said to be "a religious retreat maintained by the Church of Scientology for its parishioners." "Sunday Services" are held at Flag Land Base and many other centers, and, in many cities, Scientology branches have sought membership in local councils of churches.

Recently, new leaders, in the central organization as well as in the many regional orgs, seem to be moving Scientology further in the direction of pure religion and of lower tension with the sociocultural environment. But shifts like this have happened before, only to be reversed later on. Thus, we resist the powerful urge to predict that Scientology will soon abandon its magic to seek more comfortable status as a new member in the family of conventional churches.

The history of a cult is shaped by the decisions of individual leaders, by accident, and by general sociological principles. Our theory can explain and predict general processes of evolution much better than it can prophesy the fortunes of any particular religious organization. But this, of course, is a limitation faced by all social science. Such examples as Scientology can demonstrate the extreme precariousness of such bold magical claims as clear, and we can see in Scientology both the potential to abandon magic for religion and social forces moving in that direction. But there can be counterforces as well, and the future success of Scientology may depend upon the outcomes of struggles between different constituencies within the cult and different segments of the leadership.

Abandonment of the most precarious magic and evolution into a purely religious organization may be more in the interests of local Scientology churches than in the interest of Flag Land Base and the advanced orgs. Local leaders increase their own importance to the extent that they can build congregations content to hold the status of laity and enthusiastic about accepting the ministrations and rituals offered at the local church. But the advanced orgs and Flag need a constant flow of ambitious clients willing to leave the local org and invest great sums and much time in processing to climb the ladder of higher statuses. And it is the magical claims that provide a basis for that extensive hierarchy of processes.

Furthermore, the current magic is extremely labor intensive, and a switch to the pattern of more conventional religion would put many staff members out of work (and out of status) unless there were a sudden explosion in recruitment of new members, a trick Scientology seems unable to turn at the moment. Scientology is labor intensive because so many of the most important processing routines require an auditor to work for several hours a week with a single preclear, as is also the case for Psychoanalysis. When there were 13 staff members in Boston and an additional 4 at the Cambridge branch of the org, the total number of active Scientologists in the area was hardly 200. Thus, there were on the order of 10 lay members for each person who might be called clergy. At the same time, there were about 440 church members to each paid religious worker in the United States as a whole. Thus, Scientology was overclergied to a factor of about 44.

A religion might assign its staff extensive recruiting work to justify a high ratio of clergy to laity, but Scientology already does this and can hardly expand its recruiting efforts to fill slack time released by the abandonment of magical practices. Lower echelon staff members are now kept busy in such tasks as writing hundreds of letters to inactive members or immersed in labor intensive recruiting campaigns. For example, one week the Cambridge branch of the Boston org sent letters to a thousand schoolteachers in the area, and during another week it attempted to contact the 400 persons who had signed its guest book. From January through May 1970, this tiny branch distributed approximately 590,000 tickets on the streets, inviting people to attend the introductory lecture that recruited to the inexpensive HTHP-I communication course, which itself was the main recruiting ground for Dianetics auditing. This is long, hard work. Yet, over these five months, only 62 people signed up for the course, most of them only to drop out soon after.

If the cult evolved fully into a real religion, and abandoned most of its magical work, there would be fewer organizational statuses to go around even in the local orgs. As earlier chapters have told us, such conflict between the interests of different constituencies can lead to schism. Thus, if Scientology were to move in the direction of a real religion, and lower its tension significantly, some leaders might try to lead unemployed auditors from the local orgs in a sect movement, thereby reestablishing an emphasis on the old magical traditions.

To reduce tension significantly, Scientology need not abandon *all* magic, only what is most difficult to sustain in the face of likely empirical disconfirmation. Many intangible benefits promised by auditing are difficult to evaluate systematically. Both privately to their friends and publicly in formal testimonials, Scientologists habitually report moments of ecstasy achieved in the treatments, often coupled with a highly personal sense of new insights. Who but the persons experiencing these grand moments can judge their authenticity?

If it stops making refutable promises to achieve the impossible, Scientology may become even more effective in its use of a therapeutic model as the basis of recruitment and as a primary focus of member activity. That is, by becoming less specific and ambitious, Scientology will become a more "effective" therapy. As we pointed out in Chapter 7, all therapies seem to work because of regression toward the mean and the random ebbs and flows of life. People who seek a therapy at a "bad" time in their lives (which is when they have a motivation to seek it) are likely to find that their lives soon improve—just as most people will recover from many kinds of illness whether they receive medical treatment or not. Thus it is that magic always has gained and regained its plausibility. Magic often "succeeds." If the shaman, the medieval witch, the psychoanalyst, and the water dowser must endure frequent failure, they also profit from frequent success. In similar fashion, many who begin Scientology courses find their expectations for increased happiness and self-confidence fulfilled, thus giving them "proof" that Scientology is valid and a reason for increased commitment.

Moreover, these therapeutic successes involve more than chance, regression to the mean, or placebo effects. In Chapter 14, we examine in detail the fact that human relations lie at the core of the conversion process. People convert to new faiths because their friends believe. In the encounter between an individual and a religious movement, a central feature is the formation of new and strong bonds of affection with members. Indeed, converts often markedly increase their self-esteem and social competence from being treated as personally valuable by other members. Affection is a truly powerful therapy and a specific cure for those suffering loneliness and isolation. Whatever else Scientology may offer, it is well designed to provide a rich supply of individual attention and affect to newcomers. The close-knit, mutually gratifying group of friends thus created needs only a religious creed to become a congregation.

Scientology already promulgates a belief that could be used to shift the cult away from its present reliance on magic to adopt a more religious solution to member needs: the doctrine of reincarnation. The superhuman capacities once associated with clear status, and now ascended to the levels of OT, may eventually move out of the empirical realm altogether. That is, people may no longer expect to develop genius-level IQ, perfect health, and a magnetic personality in this incarnation. But they may be promised such achievements in their next life, if they scrupulously follow Scientology's procedures. The failure of our world to be flooded by superhuman Scientologists returned from the grave will be explained by the cult's doctrine that reincarnation typically transfers one to a new planet. When Scientology truly becomes a church, dealing in supernatural general compensators, it will have escaped the pitfalls that beset all organizations based primarily on magic. And to be perfectly clear will be a posthumous award.

CONCLUSION

For Scientology, reduction of magic means reduction of tension with the surrounding sociocultural environment. It also means reduction in the capacity to offer specific compensators for scarce rewards. Many longtime members and new recruits will still want efficacious specific compensators, however. In Chapter 5, we note that a likely result is schism, especially if the religious group is cut by deep social cleavages. Such is the case for Scientology, which consists of dozens of relatively independent local orgs and branches, often in uneasy competition with the advanced orgs.

In some cases, the local orgs are in direct competition with each other. Not long ago, a Scientologist canvassing the neighborhood came to Bainbridge's door in Cambridge, Massachusetts, thus conveniently, if inadvertently, making a home delivery of sociological data. The revealing fact was that he came not from the Cambridge org, but from the rival Boston org, which is closely allied with the central organization of the church and appears much stronger than the one in Cambridge. The *New York Times* (Lindsey, 1983) reported that disputes over authority have recently caused several orgs to split away, although the decentralized corporate structure of the church can blur the degree of association so that only the most overt conflicts are visible.

There have been other periods in which the threat of schism for Scientology has been high, and always before unity was reestablished in a short time. But now the situation is rendered more tense by apparently premature claims that Hubbard has died. Even if he survives for many years and actively guides his church through the rough waters ahead, this death scare underscores the fact that Hubbard has held in check the schismatic tendencies fueled by competing interests of different constituencies in both the leadership and the ordinary membership.

Aside from any guidance he gives the church, Hubbard is vital to its unity for two reasons. First, he is a figurehead and rallying point whom only one group may claim as its own so long as he lives. Many competing churches may claim the patronage of Jesus Christ because each has him only in spirit, not in the flesh. Clergy of one Christian denomination do not have to explain to their congregations why Jesus attends services at the church down the road rather than at theirs. Until Hubbard becomes a spirit, he will remain the property of the central organization.

Second, Hubbard is the only source of new auditing techniques and new levels of OT. Over the years, there has been an intense battle between Scientology and competing organizations, such as The Process, founded by ex-Scientologists seeking their own independent routes to spiritual advancement. Indeed, the surest sign that a schism or leadership defection was brewing was unauthorized experimentation with new processes. So long as Hubbard lives and produces the higher levels above clear so useful in protecting the magic from disconfirmation, the central organization will hold a very strong hand in its dealings with the local orgs, with him as their trump card. But once his time on earth has come to an end, the forces pressing for schism will be fully unleashed.

Among the wisest steps Hubbard has taken to preserve his movement as a whole, but one injurious in the long run to the central organization, is to make the new, streamlined version of clear available at the larger local orgs. Recent interviews at the Boston org indicate that members are of two minds over which kind of clear is actually superior. The traditional, more psychologically demanding, and more expensive Scientology clear offered only at the advanced orgs has a certain majesty and implies the person has gone through some very special experiences. But it also implies the person may have been incapable of going clear by the shorter, local Dianetics route and thus was someone initially inferior to those who could go clear at home. We note that one of the three officers named on the Boston org's letterhead achieved clear locally, one indication that it is a highly respectable route to status.

These developments are good for the movement in the long run not only because they strengthen the local churches, which, after all, are the organizations that recruit new members and through which the movement must spread. But perhaps more important, the movement will enter the period after Hubbard's stewardship with a number of centers of authority, each of which can innovate somewhat independently, giving the movement as a whole more chances of coming up with the right combination of beliefs and practices to achieve enduring growth.

This chapter describes a series of tactics designed to promote and protect Scientology's magic that Hubbard developed over nearly 20 years of experimentation. After his departure, Scientologists must experiment further to create a religious denomination of moderate tension attracting congregations interested in a faith designed for the modern world of science. Other Scientologists will undoubtedly find ways to keep the magic high, whether in small, high tension sects of Scientology or through independent therapy services. Then Scientology will fully illustrate the religious dynamic that is the theme of this book.

Reduction of magic and tension constitutes the secularization process. In Scientology, as in the larger world of religion, this process is self-limiting, calling forth schisms in the form of sect movements and innovations in the form of cult movements. Thus, if Scientology is really successful, it will not merely evolve into a single, solid, liberal denomination. Rather, it will give birth to a whole range of groups at different levels of tension and degrees of organization, a space-age copy of what Protestantism has become.

13 *The Rise and Decline of Transcendental Meditation*

WITH DANIEL H. JACKSON

Transcendental Meditation is a simple spiritual exercise practiced at one time or another by a million Americans. Purveyed through
an organized social movement headed by an Indian guru, Maharishi
Mahesh Yogi, TM was said to be a scientifically validated means for improving personal satisfaction and effectiveness. Although TM was derived from Hindu religious tradition, it allegedly was not a religious
practice. However, the inner core of the movement took on a distinct
religious quality, and, in 1977, a New Jersey court ruled that TM was
religious and therefore could not be taught in the public schools.

Like the previous chapter, this brief examination of Transcendental
Meditation is based on extensive empirical field research, as well as on
the literature and statistics we cite. And, like our discussion of Scientology, our analysis of TM emphasizes the distinction between religion and
magic, between superempirical general compensators and empirically
vulnerable specific compensators. This chapter documents again how
actual or potential disconfirmation of specific compensators can drive
an organization toward the safer general compensators, and thus toward religion. And, as in the previous chapter, we see how strong desires
for rewards, both tangible and intangible, can lead people to the social
exchange of compensators for those rewards. The distinctive strength

This chapter was originally published as William Sims Bainbridge and Daniel H. Jackson, "The Rise and Decline of Transcendental Meditation," in Bryan Wilson (ed.), *The Social
Impact of New Religious Movements*. New York: Rose of Sharon Press, 1981, pp. 135–158.

284

of this chapter is the wealth of quantitative data on trends in TM membership over a period in which great changes in the balance between religion and magic took place in the cult.

A Secular Magic

In the years of its greatest success, TM was a client cult, and, like many in modern society, it claimed to be a form of science rather than a form of supernatural magic. Yet much of what TM claimed was unsupported by rational deduction or empirical evidence. Thus, it can be said to have offered *secular magic*. But the meditation technique was not mere magic, but a composite of reward and compensator.

Perhaps few people in modern society feel free to rest during the day. American culture sets a rapid pace of activity and accomplishment, with no mandated afternoon tea or siesta. TM gave meditators authority to stop and rest because the practice was supposed to accomplish important social benefits rather than being sheer self-indulgence. Thus, the reward gained through TM (rest) was facilitated by the assertion that the technique was something more than a means to that reward. The compensators associated with TM ranged from the claim that the practice would increase the meditator's mental clarity and energy to the grand hope that widespread meditation would utterly transform human society.

In the definitions we have offered, magic can be distinguished from religion by the narrower scope of compensators it offers. TM's more modest claims are not religious in nature. They promise specific benefits, capable of empirical test, and enter the realm of magic. The more grandiose claims—some shared by core members of the movement from the beginning, others publicly announced only recently—fully qualify TM for the status of religion. They promise the most general and astonishing benefits.

TM's greatest public relations success was not the movement's endorsement by the Beatles musical group or other celebrities, but the large number of articles published in scientific journals, apparently proving TM's claims or at least giving them scientific status. "Physiological Effects of Transcendental Meditation," by the TM leader Robert Keith Wallace, appeared in the March 27, 1970, issue of *Science*. Writing with another TM enthusiast, Wallace published "The Physiology of Meditation" in the February 1972 issue of *Scientific American*. These articles proclaimed to a wide scientific audience that TM produced a new state of consciousness, distinguishable from the waking state, sleep, or the hypnotic state. Although the very concept of "state of consciousness" remains of dubious scientific value, at the end of the 1960s, many scholars accepted it and lay people assumed it was a valid part of respectable psychology (cf. Forem, 1973; Bloomfield et al., 1975; Denniston et al., 1975).

By early 1973, a TM booklet listed 88 more or less scientific publications apparently supporting the Maharishi's assertions that TM provides an entirely new experience for the mind capable of curing drug addiction, improving work efficiency, facilitating education, increasing life satisfaction, raising athletic performance, and awakening creative abilities. Some of these items were private TM documents, but others were articles published in respectable scientific journals. The movement used to good propaganda effect this apparent endorsement by the scientific community, distributing reprints of the most favorable articles and citing them at every opportunity. Only after TM had achieved its greatest expansion did a number of debunking articles appear in magazines and journals, suggesting that the original findings had been false or exaggerated (Pagano et al., 1976; White, 1976a, 1976b; Allen, 1979).

Further capitalizing on its putative scientific status, the movement staged many well-publicized conferences, often sponsored by respectable institutions, such as universities or business groups. TM received many kind words from state and local governments — recognition that was very useful in the cult's publicity. One TM handout listed 76 government proclamations supporting the value of the Transcendental Meditation program, mainly dating from 1973 and 1974. Statements from the offices of 8 governors and 47 mayors were included. The cult also distributed copies of a resolution adopted by the Illinois House of Representatives in 1972. This effusive document urged state agencies to look into TM's potential as a tool in solving a variety of problems and listed as facts a number of the cult's claims.

The growth of TM in the United States was based to a great extent on its appeal to students, and its ability to seem an intellectually respectable but novel technique of personal development undoubtedly was especially important with this group. Although the Maharishi had visited the United States briefly in 1959, the real organizational beginning came in 1965, when a favorable response from students at UCLA prompted the formation of the Students' International Meditation Society (SIMS), the aegis for much of the later recruitment. In 1967, the first year in which new American initiations could be counted in the thousands, the Maharishi spoke at UCLA, Berkeley, Yale, and Harvard. In 1970, the movement distributed a book of testimonials from 128 meditators who had practiced the technique for an average of 14.5 months. Their average age was 23.3 years, which implied that they began meditating at an average age of 22. Fifty-three percent gave their current occupation as student.

The United States was the most fertile ground for TM. In mid-1971, the German magazine *Der Spiegel* reported that 70,000 Americans and nearly 20,000 West Germans had learned TM. *Time* magazine, in 1975, estimated that the U.S. total had risen to 600,000, augmented by half that number elsewhere, including 90,000 in Canada and 54,000 in West Germany.

ENTERING TRANSCENDENTAL MEDITATION

First, the newcomer attends two free lectures to hear the conceptual basis of TM and claims of its value. Then the student is invited to enroll for meditation instruction, paying the fee, which, in 1977, ranged from $65 for a junior high school student to $165 for a nonstudent single adult. The actual instruction is carried out in private between the newcomer and teacher. A TM "Information Packet for Researchers" describes the session:

> The teacher first performs a brief, traditional ceremony of gratitude to the tradition of knowledge from which the TM technique comes. The student witnesses but does not take part in the ceremony; however, he does provide fruit, flowers, and a handkerchief, which are some of the traditional ingredients. Then the new student learns the technique and practices it, first with the instructor and then by himself. He discusses his experience with his teacher, and is given further instruction based on those experiences.

The instructor undertakes the ceremony while the student merely observes. The ritual is the possession of the core members of the movement — not of the mass of meditators. The ritual is supposed to remind initiators of the tradition they transmit and to ensure that they do the job precisely as required, but it appears to contain religious elements as well. Many teachers saw these as essentially philosophical concepts merely expressed through the esoteric language of Hinduism, but the sacred and supernatural qualities of the metaphors were always ready to assert themselves. The official teacher bulletin, "Explanations of the Invocation," states:

> The Lord of Creation has to maintain all levels of creation — both gross and subtle. Therefore he cannot be limited to any level of time or space, for the Lord is omnipresent — the omnipresent level of life is his abode. The recital of the words helps us to gain Transcendental Consciousness and establish the eternal truth of gaining purity in the inner and outer fields of individual life. . . .

The truth of Brahma, the Creator, born of the lotus, rooted in the eternal Being, is conventionally and traditionally depicted by a picture where Lord Narayana, lying in a restful pose, has the stem of a lotus emerging from his navel, and Brahma, the Creator, is seated on that lotus. So the wisdom of Transcendental Meditation, or the philosophy of the Absolute knowledge of integrated life came to the lotus-born Brahma from Lord Narayana.

After teachers complete the ceremony, they give the initiate a personal *mantra*, a word that is the "mental vehicle" permitting the person to do Transcendental Meditation by focusing on its sound for each 20-minute session. Meditators were told to keep their mantras secret even from their closest friends. Supposedly, each mantra was carefully selected to harmonize with the individual's nervous system and would not be suitable for other persons. In fact, the mantras were assigned purely on the basis of the new meditator's age and were taken from a list of just sixteen Sanskrit words.

The day after initiation, new meditators attend the first of three "checking" meetings, where they share their experiences and have their meditating fine-tuned. Over the months and years that follow, meditators may occasionally visit the local TM center for free, individual checking. But after initiation, most meditators go their private ways, perhaps continuing to meditate but no longer in contact with the movement. Thus, for the majority, TM was a simple technique learned in a few trips to the local center. They had to become more fully involved to experience Transcendental Meditation as a religion.

The next step for someone drawn all the way into the movement might be to attend one of the many residence courses given all across the country. These weekend retreats were said to produce gains equaling those of months of twice-daily meditation. They included videotape lectures, group discussions, and yoga exercises. An enthusiastic meditator might attend several such meetings. From October 2, 1975, through May 9, 1976, a total of 80 residence courses were scheduled in the Pacific region alone. According to official TM statistics, meditators had spent a total of 110,000 days at residence courses in the United States by the end of 1972.

Although the introductory lectures leading to instruction in meditation were designed to appear secular and scientific, higher levels of indoctrination contained explicitly religious elements. Advanced lectures were based on the Bhagavad-Gita and sought to apply principles from this holy book to problems of modern life. In 1972, the Maharishi videotaped what was said to be the first complete recitation of the Rig Veda in the West, and he also completed an English translation of the Brahma Sutras.

The movement's involvement in formal intellectual education culminated in the establishment of Maharishi International University, an institution of higher indoctrination for TM teachers, first conducted in 1972 in rented facilities at Santa Barbara, California. Later, MIU purchased the campus of defunct Parsons College in Fairfield, Iowa.

The MIU program did not merely provide TM training alongside ordinary academic courses, but sought to produce a new version of each basic college subject, reinterpreted in terms of the movement's ideology, the "Science of Creative Intelligence." Already by its second year at Santa Barbara, MIU offered 24 "interdisciplinary" courses, including world literature and the Science of Creative Intelligence, art and SCI, technology and SCI, music and SCI, psychology and SCI, biological sciences and SCI, and physics and SCI.

The Science of Creative Intelligence was presented to students through a basic SCI course consisting of color videocassette lessons based in great measure on the Bhagavad-Gita. The content was an elaboration of claims for Transcendental Meditation, laced with parables and metaphysical postulates, rather than anything that can be recognized as conventional science. Like Scientology and Christian Science before it, SCI used the name of science in a scientific age to express its boundless pride. An MIU report explained, "The TM technique enables students to experience directly the pure field of creative intelligence within their own minds, thereby providing a personal basis for the verification of the intellectual concepts presented by the study of SCI." Further study, ascending to ever higher levels of enlightenment on the basis of meditation, supposedly allows the person to see beyond petty political and intellectual disputes to achieve a unification of human knowledge and to turn all energies to the good.

A good example of MIU courses is "Western Philosophy and the Science of Creative Intelligence: From Plato's *Republic* to Maharishi's World Plan." Students read a number of excerpts from standard works of famous philosophers, such as Plato, Aristotle, Locke, Hume, Marx, Kant, Sartre, Descartes, Leibniz, and Russell. The instructor's lectures attempt to show that all these men's ideas flow into and are fulfilled by the Science of Creative Intelligence. At the outset, students are told that the three main branches of philosophy are ontology, epistemology, and ethics, which are said to correspond with the "three fields of life" identified by the Maharishi: existence, thought, and action.

SCI seeks to *transcend* philosophical disputes, as the following example shows. One study question attached to the first Western philosophy lesson asks, "How does SCI unify Rationalism and Empiricism?" The mimeographed course packet provides the approved answer: "Empiricism emphasizes experience, and Rationalism emphasizes the presumably unexperienceable foundations of experience. By expanding the realm of experience to include the transcendental pure field of creative experience, SCI provides a unifying meeting ground for Rationalism and Empiricism." Put another way, in lesson six, the course asserts "SCI offers the ultimate paradigm for scientific research by providing scientific knowledge of the foundation of all science, namely, intelligence itself." Of course, SCI does not really offer answers to the great questions of Western philosophy. Rather, it offers a compensator, packaged in quasi-philosophical theology. Through its superempirical interpretation of the meditation experience, it pretends to give an actual transcendence of all disputes and problems.

THE MOVEMENT

Only a minority of meditators took the extra steps toward full movement membership and became teachers, but even 1 or 2 percent of a million is a large number. There were only 17 American TM teachers at the end of 1966, but, by the end of 1972, a total of 2,555 people had taken the teachers' course. *Time* magazine estimated there were about 6,000 teachers by the middle of 1975, and a movement report claimed "over 10,000 teachers had been trained" by January 1977.

The entrepreneur model from Chapter 8 might well be applied to TM, and the growth of the cult was in great part the spread of small businesses across the landscape. One or more trained teachers would establish a center, perhaps by renting office space or more cheaply by offering introductory lectures and meditation training in schools or homes. After 1972, initiation fees were supposed to be paid to the national center, with half the amount being returned to the teacher responsible for each new meditator, less personal income tax withheld.

In 1972, the standard fee was $35 for a high school student, $45 for a college student, $75 for a nonstudent adult, and $125 for a nonstudent married couple. Thus, the amount returned to a teacher for each initiation might be as little as $17.50 (less income tax) or as much as $37.50. Out of the returns, initiators were supposed to pay their share of maintaining the local center, including even the cost of publicity materials and TM's own data forms. It is clear that an initiator needed to handle a very large number of initiations to make a living at this work, but at least there existed a prospect of financial success.

Even in times of peak growth, after the very beginning, there was hardly enough initiating work to go around. In 1973, when 132,634 Americans were initiated, on average only one new client was available each week per trained teacher. Many centers intentionally distributed the work among their several teachers, rather than let one or two dominate while others went without the gratifications (including status in the movement) of being a professional initiator. Teachers, and those in training to be teachers, performed many kinds of unpaid work around the centers. They put up posters, arranged for lecture rooms, gave promotional speeches, maintained the center, and gave checking sessions. To the extent that they were unpaid volunteers, all these people were members of a social movement rather than merely a profit-making spiritual service corporation.

In many respects, Transcendental Meditation is a *millenarian* movement, promising the radical transformation of society. This message was proclaimed in the booklet "To Create an Ideal Society":

> The quality of life in society is determined by the quality of life of individual citizens. If citizens are enjoying enrichment of body, mind, and behavior then the whole community will be characterized by peace, harmony and progress. The Transcendental Meditation program of His Holiness Maharishi Mahesh Yogi provides the technology to develop the full potential of the individual thereby improving the quality of life and creating an ideal society. . . .
>
> Thus, the Transcendental Meditation program is a scientifically validated program to create an ideal society and to usher in and perpetuate the Age of Enlightenment. The ideal society will be a reality sooner as more individuals the world over begin to practice the Transcendental Meditation technique.

In 1972, this millenarian spirit was expressed in the world plan, a program to bring TM to all the world's people. Members bought world plan bonds and contributed to a world plan fund. The central organization planned a system of 3,575 future centers around the world, including 203 for the United States, 241 for the Soviet Union, 543 for India, and 745 for China—a center for every million people throughout the world. Few of the projected world plan centers materialized, but this grand scheme expressed TM's intention to expand until it encompassed all humanity.

GROWTH STATISTICS

In 1965, the TM organization began keeping fairly careful, ultimately computerized records of initiations in the United States. Data made available to us report the cumulative total of persons initiated, month by month, from January 1967 through December 1977, a total of 918,281 meditators. Table 19.1 summarizes these numbers by year. Other sources indicate that nearly 1,000 Americans had been initiated before

TABLE 13.1   *Annual Growth in TM Initiations in the United States*

Year	Cumulative Total at the End of Each Year	Increase in the Year	
		Number	Percent
1966	about 1,000	—	—
1967	5,500	4,459	450
1968	15,300	9,847	180
1969	24,800	9,474	62
1970	45,200	20,444	83
1971	96,400	51,192	113
1972	182,700	86,332	90
1973	315,400	132,634	73
1974	436,800	121,420	38
1975	729,300	292,517	67
1976	869,600	140,273	19
1977	919,300	49,689	6

1967, about three-quarters of them in 1966. The growth curve is not smooth. We see initiation declines in 1969, 1974, 1976, and 1977. The peak came in 1975, when nearly 300,000 learned TM. In percentage terms, 1967 was the boom year, with a 450 percent growth; most later years fell far short of 100 percent. Understandably, the greatest percentage growth occurred early, because an influx of relatively few neophytes produces rapid percentage growth if the base number of members is low. But these observations ignore the question of *how* persons are drawn to the movement.

Chapters 14 and 15 show that recruitment tends to occur through personal relationships — through social bonds. TM leaders believed that social bonds were more important than mass media appeals. One set of instructions for public lectures told the recruiter, "Be friendly. Remember, most people start TM due to the advice of 'friends.'" Another bulletin, distributed in 1972, said, "Experience has shown that about 80% of the new meditators start TM because they hear about it from their friends who are strong meditators and are getting good results." If new recruits are brought in by old recruits, then one might postulate that constant percentage growth is possible. If each meditator brings in just one new meditator each year, the total will grow by more than 100 percent annually.

This simple model ignores four facts. First, it fails to subtract the number of people who stop meditating or otherwise drop out of the movement — former meditators who may even spread negative sentiments toward TM. Second, it assumes that people make friends at random across the entire population; in fact, many latecomers to the movement are prevented from recruiting anyone because all their friends are already meditators. Third, this model assumes an infinite pool of potential recruits; in fact, meditators may come from certain limited subgroups in the population, perhaps individuals with very special backgrounds and needs. Fourth, it neglects the competition faced by TM: other movements recruiting in the same market, including audience cults, client cults, and health fads, gained prominence after TM's rise.

A more detailed picture of the rise and decline of TM recruitment is shown in Figure 13.1, a chart of initiations per month for the 11 years 1967–1977. The curve rises fairly steadily to a peak at the beginning of 1974, when February saw 19,121 initiations. Then followed nearly a year of slow decline, until the figures leapt upward again early in 1975. In May of that year, 31,443 were initiated, and the all-time high was 39,535 in

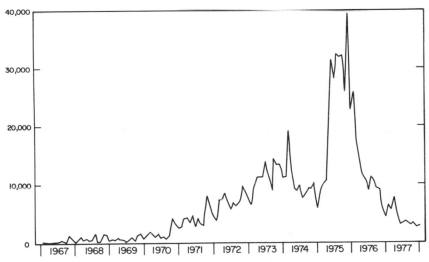

TRANSCENDENTAL MEDITATION INITIATIONS PER MONTH

FIGURE 13.1   *The Rise and Decline of Transcendental Meditation in the United States*

November. The curve then plummets, with only brief halts, to a low of 2,735 in November 1977, only 7 percent of the figure two years earlier. Not only was 1977 the lowest total year since 1970, as Table 13.1 reports, but November 1977 was lower than any month since December 1970. We have been told informally that, since 1977, initiations have dipped below 1,000 a month.

We cannot attempt here to explain the shape of TM's growth curve, and Chapter 16 explores rigorously the mathematics of religious recruitment, but we can make a few comments. We might simply describe TM as a fad with no inherent staying power. First, the rumor went out that TM was valuable. Many people tried it, and specific compensators are susceptible to empirical test and refutation. Then, perhaps from disgruntled former meditators, the rumor went out that TM was not valuable. When the second rumor caught up with the first, the fad stopped.

The time of catastrophic decline corresponds roughly with a rise in the fee for initiations and a rise in competing fads. For example, in a popular book, William Glasser (1976) said that running is a better way of achieving the same goals sought by TM, and the less organized and cheaper jogging fad may have gained recruits at the expense of TM. Like TM, jogging provides a pleasurable physical experience — the reward of emotional relaxation — packaged in the compensator claim that the procedure is a virtuous means for self-improvement. But TM is more than a past fad, because it produced a lasting religious movement with committed members willing to endure but forced to react to a period of decline in recruitment.

GEOGRAPHIC DISTRIBUTION

Several earlier chapters showed that we can learn much through the geographic analysis of cult activity. In general, we found that cults are most successful in the western parts of the United States, exactly where conventional churches are weaker. As Chapter 10 reveals, different types of cults show greater or lesser regional variation, dependent upon the degree of the cult's *deviance*. We already discussed TM along with other measures from that area of the cult spectrum between cult movements and audience cults where client cults of varying degrees of deviance are found. But it is worth reviewing our findings, examining the TM data a little more closely in the light of our historical and ethnographic information on this cult.

Transcendental Meditation confronted the world as a mixture of client cult and cult movement. For most meditators, it provided only a brief educational experience. For teachers and other committed members, TM became an all-encompassing cult movement.

Figure 13.2 is a pair of maps of the United States showing rates of TM activity per million urban inhabitants in each of the nine geographic regions. The first map reports again (from Table 10.5) data from a TM training manual printed in October 1972, which lists 1,977 teachers working in 135 centers across the country, in 43 states and the District of Columbia. The geographic distribution is almost identical to the patterns previously found for other cult movements. The Pacific region has the highest rate; the Mountain region comes second; and the East South Central region is lowest. The chief departure, as mentioned in Chapter 10, is the somewhat elevated New England rate. These figures show the cultural receptivity to religious deviance in different parts of the nation.

The second map shows rates of initiations per million urban inhabitants, data derived from the very complete membership files made available to us by the TM organization. We tabulated the number of persons initiated from 1967 through 1977 whose homes were in 5,629 urban areas, a total of 735,280 meditators. Although the distribution of meditators reflects that of teachers, there are some differences. Now the Mountain region achieves the same rate as the Pacific, and the New England rate is highest. Bainbridge studied the TM movement briefly in the Boston area in 1970, and it was clear that the central organization was promoting a very big push to expand in this region. It seemed that the many fine universities here were an especially attractive recruitment target. A special receptivity to client cults that do not appear religiously deviant has already been noted for the New England region, and apparently TM was especially able to exploit this market from its strong base at Yale, Harvard, and other universities in this region.

That TM was a socially acceptable client cult for meditators but a deviant cult movement for teachers is seen not only in the gross pattern of the two maps, but also in comparison of the intensity of variation between them. In 1972, 15.6 percent of the nation's urban population lived in Alaska, Washington, Oregon, California, and Hawaii, the states of the Pacific region. But 24.3 percent of the meditators and 45.7 percent of the teachers lived in this region. Thus, the Pacific region had somewhat more than its share of meditators, who participated only as *clients*, and much more than its share of teachers, who were full *members* of the movement. New England, more receptive to client cults than to cult movements, had 6.0 percent of the urban residents, 10.7 percent of the meditators, but just 8.4 percent of the teachers. For meditators, the highest region had 4.0 times the rate of the lowest region, but for teachers, the ratio of highest over lowest was 17.0.

TEACHERS PER MILLION, 1972

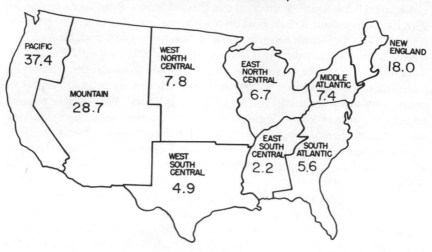

INITIATES PER MILLION, 1967-1977

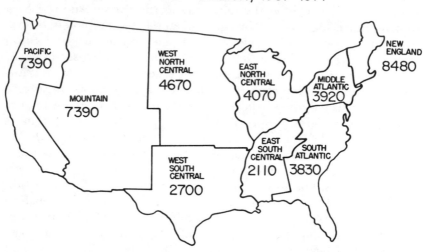

FIGURE 13.2   *Geographic Distribution of the TM Movement*

Examination of the growth of TM in the nine regions, year by year, reveals that national trends predominate. In each region, the number of initiations rises from 1970 to 1971, 1971 to 1972, and 1972 to 1973, then drops very slightly from 1973 to 1974, before leaping up to the peak year of 1975. The figures drop by half across the board for 1976 and plummet still further for 1977, the lowest year since 1970. Although there are great regional differences in rates each year, the trends are remarkably synchronized. This suggests that regional differences are not simply a matter of geographic backwaters that are out of communication with cultural centers. Rather, standards of judgment vary across the nation, and new trends are communicated rapidly but received differentially.

Table 13.2 examines the geographic distribution of urban initiates through measures of the variation across states and the correlations across states for pairs of years. The first column reports the coefficient of variation for each of the years. High coefficients of variation mean big differences in the initiation rates in various states. Low coefficients of variation mean smaller differences from state to state.

The coefficient of variation drops steadily from 1970, when it is 1.14, to 1974, when it is 0.59. This shows the broadening acceptance of TM as a relatively nondeviant client cult (cf. Granovetter, 1978). Despite the fact that the total figure more than doubles from 1974 to 1975 and drops by more than half to 1976, the coefficient of variation is nearly constant for these three years: 0.59, 0.58, and 0.57. This establishes a limit to the evenness of distribution that TM was able to achieve when most popular and least deviant. In the final year, the coefficient rises again to 0.78, a fact we return to later.

The second and third columns in Table 13.2 give the correlations (Pearson's r) linking state rates for 1970 and 1977 with the rates for other years. Of course, there is a tendency for the rates in any one year to correlate most highly with rates for adjacent years. The year 1970 correlates most highly with 1971; 1977, most highly with 1976. Each has the weakest association with 1975, the peak year in initiations. But the most striking feature of the correlations in Table 13.2 is that all the rest

TABLE 13.2 *Rates of TM Initiation (50 States and the District of Columbia)*

Year	Coefficient of Variation	Correlation (r) with	
		1970	1977
1970	1.14	1.00	.86
1971	0.95	.89	.83
1972	0.85	.85	.86
1973	0.77	.88	.87
1974	0.59	.81	.87
1975	0.58	.74	.81
1976	0.57	.85	.93
1977	0.78	.86	1.00

of them are almost identical, falling in the narrow range from 0.81 to 0.87. The correlation between the extreme years, 1970 and 1977, is one of the highest, 0.86. This means that the pattern of rates remained about the same over the eight years, even while the rates and their spread moved over wide ranges. Again, we see evidence that TM's reception from state to state was a function of differential regional responses to religious deviance rather than a result of slow communication of the TM fad into cultural backwaters.

DECLINE AND TRANSFORMATION INTO A PURE CULT MOVEMENT

Our general theory of magic and religion predicts that, when people are denied access to desired rewards, they are apt to accept compensators instead. This is facilitated if the people involved already exchange compensators of some level of generality and need only increase the emphasis on compensators as rewards become unavailable. Applied to the case of Transcendental Meditation, a movement that always had a religious aspect for inner members, the theory predicts an intensification of the supernatural element as a response to the decline in initiations.

We have seen that the decline in initiations was extreme, a drop of 93 percent from November 1975 to November 1977. By the beginning of 1977, 10,000 people had been trained to perform initiations, but only 49,689 meditators were added to the movement in 1977. Thus, on average, the teachers could have initiated only *five* new meditators each in the entire year! Of course, many teachers had already quit the movement. But others, losing their main source of material and status rewards within TM, must have been open to the offer of new and more powerful compensators.

One reward that many teachers lost in 1977 was quite tangible — credits toward advanced training and refresher (ATR) course tuitions and expenses. According to the system in effect at the end of 1973, teachers earned credits for each new meditator they taught. Each initiation was worth 1 percent of the $535 fee for the six-week course in Switzerland, plus 1 percent of the transportation costs up to a total of $250. A letter to all initiators from the World Plan Executive Council, dated July 21, 1977, wiped out all such credits, citing the decrease in initiations as its justification. Not only did members lose a promised return on investment, but they had good reason to feel cheated by the central organization that now failed to meet its obligation to them. By offering what appeared to be greater rewards, TM might restore members' dedication.

Millenarian movements never succeed in recruiting all potential members, and they have developed various tactics for convincing their adherents to keep up their hopes. One is the idea that success, rather than requiring the recruitment of the whole population, can be achieved by a small but critical number of members. An article published in 1973, in a TM handout directed at the military, quoted the Maharishi as saying, "If only one-tenth of the adult population of the world were regularly to meditate for short periods every day . . . war would be impossible for centuries to come." After recruitment dropped precipitously, and that one-tenth seemed out of reach, TM claimed that society would be improved radically if only one-hundredth of people were meditators. A 1977 flier for Maharishi International University claimed that crime and other social problems diminished greatly when this more modest level of meditation was reached. The 1977 MIU catalog went even further, asserting that world peace could be achieved when only one-thousandth of humanity meditated.

A decisive change in the TM movement came with the announcement of "a new breakthrough in human potential," the *siddhis*. MIU's 1977 catalog says, "The siddhis are performances of higher states of consciousness described in the yoga system of Patanjali, one of the six systems of Indian philosophy which elaborate the knowledge of the Vedas." Among the attendant qualities are "the ability to know the past and future, knowledge of other minds, the ability to become invisible, passage through the sky. . . ." An addendum pasted into the catalog described siddhis as "supernormal powers" and announced, "Students entering MIU in the fall of 1977 will be among the first to qualify for these historic new courses and raise their capabilities to the level of the siddha (superman): command over material nature by mere intention of the mind." A handout advertising a public lecture on this breakthrough listed among the new results of TM: "levitation, invisibility, mastery over nature, fulfillment of all desires and aspirations, creation of an ideal society in the Age of Enlightenment."

Some of the siddhi qualities could be construed as subjective feelings of peace or rapture that were given exaggerated or poetic names because they were unusually splendid. "Levitation" might be a metaphor for a sensation of intense relaxation; "invisibility" might mean a freedom from social anxiety. Whatever the Maharishi meant by those terms, the movement took them literally. In so doing, TM took the final step from client cult to cult movement and entered the realm of supernatural religion.

Supernatural claims were published alongside more modest brain-wave studies in the booklet *Enlightenment and the Siddhis,* issued by Maharishi European Research University in Switzerland. One testimonial reported an experience of clairvoyance; another described levitation:

> A friend has lost a pen. He said it was in the hotel kitchen that he had lost it and when I did the technique I saw it in my mind under some boards by the stove. When I went to look for it later, I found it exactly where I had seen it while practicing the technique.

> I was sitting on a couch meditating at the time. I felt a tremendous amount of energy go through me and simultaneously I had a vision of my spine and my chest being just white light and a form in the air some place and then my body moved up and down on the couch about three times. I thought, 'Oh, what is that?' and the next experience I had was of hearing my body touch the floor. I say 'hearing' because I didn't feel it until after I heard it. It touched down, very, very softly. There was very little feeling of contact. I moved about a six foot distance at that time.

Not only was such levitation supposed to be the subjective sensation of floating through the air, but physical suspension and movement as well. The siddhi booklet was accompanied by a photo labeled, "Canadian Christiana Quarton flies while sister-in-law Gail and her baby look on." It shows a woman apparently floating cross-legged in midair. The levitator seems to be six to ten inches above a large mattress upon which another woman sits, holding a small child. There can be no question; the picture purports to show real, physical levitation.

Separately, clairvoyance and levitation are feats of magic. But the siddhi program promised so many extreme magical benefits that it was a full package of supernatural claims comprising the general compensator of real religion.

Public announcement of the siddhi program was made in April 1977. By mid-May, lecture teams were giving public talks that disappointed many by failing to demonstrate levitation while asserting that it had been achieved. The national television network news programs derisively reported TM's astounding new claims and suggested that gymnastic meditators might have learned to hop aloft for an instant using their knees or a sudden thrust of their backs. Indeed, the photo of Christiana Quarton could be attributed to just such an athletic accomplishment. She appears to be lightly built. The mattress might provide some trampoline bounce. Her face and flying scarf are blurred as if by rapid movement, although her legs and her hands, which are held between them, are in sharp focus. Perhaps she had launched herself upward by muscle power and was caught in the middle of a short bounce by the camera.

Unflattering public attention continued to be directed at TM's levitation for several months. *Newsweek* commented in its June 13 issue that the Maharishi had forbidden public demonstrations. In its August 8 issue, *Time* suggested a hypothesis to explain the new turn in TM's career: "What is a maharishi to do when sales start to grow sluggish? One answer: announce a shiny new product."

The most active month of 1977, in terms of initiations, was March, when 7,963 newcomers learned to meditate. This figure was far below that of the peak month of November 1975, when there were 39,535 initiations. The introduction of siddhis certainly did not help the recruiting trend. April, when news of levitation began to leak out, saw only 4,437 initiations, a drop of 44 percent from the previous month. May was down 62 percent from March, at 3,025 initiations. The average for the last seven months of 1977 was 3,169. We cannot be sure that bad publicity about levitation reduced the influx of initiates because the trend had been downward for more than a year already, but the conclusion is not unreasonable.

Simultaneously with its experiments in levitation and its public evolution from client cult to cult movement, TM struggled to avoid the legal label of religion. Although TM was based in a religious tradition, for a long time, its more religious teachings and practices were revealed only to the inner core of members while ordinary meditators were offered an apparently nonreligious, practical technique. Even so, some observers had accused TM of being a religious cult expediently masquerading behind a false scientific mask (LaMore, 1975).

In March 1976, a group of parents, clergy, and other interested persons took TM to court in New Jersey, seeking to stop TM programs in the public schools. The plaintiffs charged that TM was religious in nature and had assumed secular camouflage in 1967 or 1968 in order to reach a wider audience. Late in 1977 (after TM launched levitators but unaffected by this development), a judge of the Federal District Court in Newark halted the TM school programs and announced that he had found that both the courses and the initiation ceremony were of religious character.

The movement's World Plan Executive Council informed the American centers that it would not appeal the New Jersey court decision, quoting the Maharishi as saying, "If the law of the country will demand from us that we teach in the name of religion, then fine, we will abide by the law and feel nearer to God." In our view, a successful appeal would have required not only much money for legal fees, but also a transformation of TM's ideology and practices to make them seem more secular. After some indecision, TM did appeal the case, without first reasserting secular status. Early in 1979, the United States Court of Appeals in Philadelphia supported the lower court's ruling that TM was religious in nature.

CONCLUSION

Transcendental Meditation's emergence as a religious cult movement is related to the fall in initiations documented earlier. Two alternate hypotheses might try to explain the connection: first, that transformation into a religious cult movement caused the drop in recruitment because the general public rejects deviant cults and, second, that the drop in recruitment caused an intensification of the religious element.

The first hypothesis is entirely reasonable but does not fit the facts. The decline in recruitment began more than a year before levitation and nearly two years before the adverse court decision. Perhaps the changes of 1977 prevented a recovery in recruitment or forced the figures below what they might otherwise have been. But they could not have caused the decline throughout 1976.

The second hypothesis fits well. After recruitment had fallen off, the supply of material and social rewards available for movement members was severely restricted. Furthermore, the decline discredited some TM compensators, notably those that hinted at growing status and other rewards that were to follow as TM became an established cultural force and influential institution in the United States. Loss of expectation of these rewards might be compensated by an increase in more extreme postulations of future rewards. That is what happened. No longer able to promise the material and social resources of many new recruits, the movement promised instead magical benefits symbolized by the defiance of physical nature through levitation. Taken together, the promises added up to an almost boundless promise, the general compensator of religion.

The court decision was based on the religious aspects of TM that had always been shared by inner members, not on changes after 1975, but a successful appeal against its ruling might have been achieved through modification of the program for training meditators. The references to Hindu religious texts could have been dropped from the Science of Creative Intelligence courses, and the initiation ritual could have been purged of devotional elements. But a dramatic shift toward greater secularism would have undercut the shift toward greater and more general compensators for inner members. The needs of dedicated TM teachers pressed toward more religion, not less.

Once TM was publicly branded as a radical cult, public reaction to religious deviance may indeed have reduced recruitment still further.

Table 13.2 shows a significant rise in the coefficient of variation for recruitment rates across states, from 0.57 in 1976 to 0.78 in 1977. This measure had achieved a stable level in 1974 and remained steady for a significant rise and then for a drop in recruitment; so this increase for 1977 is probably meaningful. It most likely indicates that increased deviance in TM's status was reflected in more varied reaction in different states. We conclude that at least part of TM's 1977 loss was due to an increase in the movement's cultic deviance.

Transcendental Meditation did not die in 1977. The decline left a solidly organized religious cult movement, undoubtedly one of the largest new religions in America. Recruitment continues, if at a greatly reduced rate. Now that highly supernatural magic and general compensators have become the cult's main business, we cannot expect another period of rapid growth. But if it establishes a firm social base in the community of current members, TM may achieve less explosive but more lasting conversions. In its short and brilliant history, Transcendental Meditation shows how the failure of rewards and modest compensators may lead to intensification of the supernatural and to an evolution from client cult to cult movement.

IV *Recruitment*

14 Networks of Faith: Interpersonal Bonds and Recruitment to Cults and Sects

For decades, social scientists have paid modest but steady attention to how persons are recruited into exotic and unusual religious groups — those commonly designated as sects or cults. The result is a cumulative body of theory that has been subjected to a significant amount of empirical testing. The sharp conceptual distinction we drew previously between cults and sects is vital when attention is given to how unusual or deviant religious groups *form*. However, once sects and cults are going operations, there do not appear to be significant differences in how they gain membership. Therefore, although this chapter speaks mainly about cults, the principles we identify apply equally well to sects.

Key Elements in Recruitment

Deprivation and Ideological Appeal

The long-established point of view on why people join cults and sects combines assessment of the particular appeals offered by a group's ideology with an analysis of the kinds of deprivations people suffer to which this ideology offers relief (Clark, 1937; Linton, 1943; Hobsbawm, 1959; Wilson, 1959; Cohn, 1961; Smelser, 1962; Glock and Stark, 1965).

A condensed version of this chapter was read at the 1979 annual meeting of the Pacific Sociological Association. An intermediate version was published as Rodney Stark and William Sims Bainbridge, "Networks of Faith: Interpersonal Bonds and Recruitment to Cults and Sects," *American Journal of Sociology,* 1980, 85:6, pp. 1376–1395. The authors wish to thank Jane Allyn Piliavin (formerly Hardyck) and Armand Mauss for data and advice.

Cults and sects, like other deviant social movements, tend to recruit people with a grievance, people who suffer from some variety of deprivation. To understand whom a particular group recruits, it is necessary to see to whom its ideology offers the most. Although it explains much, this line of analysis can be carried to extremes. And, by the start of the 1960s, in combination with the then popular mass society theories, it was carried too far.

Mass society theories postulated that modern urban life was inimical to human relations (Wirth, 1938, 1940; Kornhauser, 1959). People in earlier times lived in intimate relations that firmly bound them to the moral order, but in modern urban societies, people are adrift in a Durkheimian sea of anomie. Lacking restraints, and seeking to belong, mass society residents are prone to respond impulsively to propaganda blitzes by social movements such as Nazism, Communism, or extremist religious movements that offer a false sense of community (Brown, 1943; Almond, 1954; Arendt, 1958; Kornhauser, 1959; Allen, 1965).

Later, of course, it was recognized that this view of urban life was faulty. Closer examinations of urban life found that many, and perhaps most, people remain deeply embedded in primary relationships (Whyte, 1943; Young and Willmott, 1957; Gans, 1962a, 1962b; Lewis, 1965). Studies of the effects of the mass media discovered that their messages are typically mediated greatly by social networks through a "two-step flow of communications" (Katz and Lazarsfeld, 1955).

As credibility ebbed for the notion that social movements arouse a following by direct ideological appeals to atomized masses of people, it became obvious that the deprivation and ideological appeal explanation of cult and sect recruitment was incomplete. Granted that some people will find a particular ideology more appealing than others, but what determines why only *some* of these ideologically suited people actually join a specific group?

Interpersonal Bonds

In the early 1960s, John Lofland and Rodney Stark conducted a participant observation study of the first group of American members of the Korean-based cult of the Reverend Sun Myung Moon — popularly known today as the Moonies (Lofland and Stark, 1965; Lofland, 1966). A close watch on recruitment as it occurred revealed the essential role played by interpersonal bonds between cult members and the potential recruit. When such bonds did not exist and failed to develop, newcomers failed to join. When such bonds did exist or develop (and when they were stronger than bonds to others who opposed the individual's recruitment), people did join. Indeed, persons were sometimes drawn by their attachment to group members to move into the Moonie commune while still openly expressing rejection of the Moon ideology. Acceptance of the ideology, and the decision to become full-time cultists, often came only *after* a long period of day-to-day interaction with cult members. Rather than being drawn to the group because of the appeal of its ideology, people were drawn to the ideology because of their ties to the group — "final conversion was coming to accept the opinions of one's friends" (Lofland and Stark, 1965:871).

This field study also revealed that recruitment often moved through preexisting social networks. The great majority of cult members at that time had been mutually linked by long-standing relationships prior to any contact with Moon's movement. In fact, once Moon's missionary had made her first American convert, all subsequent members were drawn from this first recruit's immediate social network until the group uprooted from Eugene, Oregon, and moved to San Francisco. In San Francisco, the group was unable to grow for a considerable time because they were strangers lacking social ties to potential new recruits. Indeed, some new recruits continued to come out of the old, original Eugene network. Only when the cult found ways to connect with other newcomers to San Francisco and develop serious relations with them did recruitment resume. But in relying on befriending lonely newcomers, the Moonies were unable to grow rapidly. New members did not open new social networks through which the cult could then spread. Later in this chapter, we see how much more effective is the Mormon approach to recruitment, which produces recruits who lead to others.

Following the publication of these findings, others began to report similar observations. When Bainbridge studied the nominally Satanic cult, The Process, from 1970 to 1976, he not only found that interpersonal bonds played the critical role in recruitment assigned them in the Lofland and Stark study, but that they had been essential to initial cult formation. We describe the birth of this cult in Chapter 8, showing that it was a good example of the subculture-evolution model, an explanatory scheme that stresses exchanges linking a number of individuals. The Process originated with two defectors from Scientology who set up shop as psychotherapists in London during 1963. To develop a clientele, the male member of the couple solicited through his upper-middle-class friendship network. Individual therapy sessions soon gave way to group encounters. Participants' relations with one another began to take on a depth and uniqueness far beyond their relations with others outside the therapy group. Soon they were spending almost all of their time in marathon sessions. This, of course, greatly weakened their ties outside the group. The result was a social implosion. As ties within the group strengthened, external ties weakened until the group socially collapsed inward to engage exclusively in intragroup relations. It was in this imploded network that the first religious ideas began to grow. Soon the group left for a remote and unpopulated stretch of beach in Mexico where, in total isolation, they evolved their novel and exotic cult doctrines. From Mexico, the group reentered society, seeking to recruit others. And, like the Moonies, they succeeded only with those with whom they first developed strong personal ties (Bainbridge, 1978c).

From 1967 to 1971, The Process wandered over Europe and North America, not staying long enough in most places to establish firm connections to established friendship networks. The people recruited were almost without exception social isolates, people whose prime deprivation was precisely a lack of social ties (cf. Phillips, 1967). Many of these people apparently suffered from no other serious problems and were isolated social atoms merely because they were geographically mobile. Several were students in universities or professional schools who had recently left home and had not yet established a new set of social relationships. Others were recruited while on extended world tours or while attempting to set up residence in a new land — Americans in France, for example. Some recruits were teenage offspring of upper-class "jet-set" families who alternated between two or more residences, often in different countries, and were therefore low in social attachments to peers. Bainbridge noted that the crucial step in joining was the development of strong social ties with members and argued that deprivations and personal problems were facilitating factors, neither sufficient in themselves nor always necessary. Their contribution to the recruitment process was contingent upon a variety of conditions in the social environment and upon cult recruitment strategies.

Other research also has found that interpersonal bonds play an important role in cult membership. Lynch (1977, 1979) found that social ties played an important role in providing converts for the Church of the Sun, a new cult movement in Southern California. Indeed, he discovered that members had virtually no social life apart from cult activities, even though this was not a communal group and members did not give up their regular jobs.

Several studies have suggested that interpersonal bonds also play an important role in conversion to sects. Richardson and Stewart (1977) found that social networks were a critical factor in the Jesus movement. Gaede (1976) reported supportive quantitative findings in a study of Mennonites that showed that interpersonal ties to other Mennonites strongly influence retention of the orthodox tenets of that sect.

In 1966, Bryan R. Roberts (1968) studied two small Protestant groups in Guatemala City. At that time, less than 5 percent of the Guatemalan population was Protestant, and the groups' neighbors treated them as strange, annoying intrusions in this overwhelmingly Catholic country. Prior to joining, the members had been especially weak in stable social ties compared to their neighbors who remained Catholic. Roberts reported that the act of joining a Protestant group provided gratifying relationships, and, through them, the members acquired and maintained deviant beliefs.

Convergence of the Theories

Acceptance of the thesis that social relations play an essential role in cult and sect recruitment does not imply that the deprivation and ideological appeal thesis is wrong. Recent research has rejuvenated interest in and support for this thesis (Anthony et al., 1977; Balch and Taylor, 1977; Lynch, 1977, 1979; Richardson and Stewart, 1977). Moreover, when Lofland and Stark first introduced the interpersonal bond component in recruitment theories, they not only retained deprivation and ideological appeal components, they gave them considerable scope. Close observations of people who both did and did not convert after a period of exposure to the Moonies made it evident that people do not join the cult unless something is bothering them. Lofland and Stark hypothesized that people must experience enduring and acutely felt tensions before they will join a cult. People for whom life is going well continue to do as they have done and are unlikely to join.

Not everyone is ideologically suited to join a cult or a sect. Some minimal kind of ideological preparation or predisposition is needed. Hence, Lofland and Stark postulated that people will not join deviant religious groups unless they accept the plausibility of an active supernatural. Indeed, Moon's missionary was so aware of this lack in some potential candidates for recruitment that she sent them to Spiritualist meetings in hopes that there they would find irrefutable proof of the existence of an active spirit world. She explained that, once people could see for themselves the existence of "lower spirits," they would need a doctrine that can explain this.

Many people who accept the supernatural do not join cults or sects because they possess a satisfactory framework for these beliefs in an established religion. No matter what else may be required to produce a cult member, the process is greatly facilitated if the person has a problem, believes in the possibility of supernatural interpretations of that problem, and is essentially unchurched (see also De Santis, 1927; Catton, 1957; Dohrman, 1958).

Elsewhere (Bainbridge, 1978c), we have argued that the importance of deprivation is *variable,* a point we take up again in Chapter 18. That is, deprivation will be of greater significance in the recruitment process to the extent that the society in question is hostile toward deviant religious groups and thus makes it costly to join one. In the days of classical paganism, cults and sects were not regarded as especially deviant and it was not costly, in terms of social sanctions, to join one. At other times — medieval Europe, for example — it was extremely costly to engage in cult or sect activities. We suggest that the more costly it is to be religiously deviant, the greater the countervailing pressures (or deprivations) required to motivate joining. However, in periods when established faiths are organizationally weak and when little disapproval is directed toward novel religious movements, many people lacking any noticeably acute deprivations may well be attracted to cults and sects. Indeed, one might argue that, in some sections of the United States today (for example, the West Coast), the social environment of radical religious groups is nearly as benign as in pagan Rome.

There is nothing contradictory between the deprivation and ideological appeal line of analysis and the analysis that stresses the importance of social networks. Both seem obvious requirements of any adequate theory. If deprivation alone explained recruitment to cults, then millions more people would become members than actually do. Recruits must not only suffer relevant deprivations and be open to a radical group's ideological appeal; they must also be placed in a situation where they will develop social bonds with existing members of the group (cf. Granovetter, 1973).

RECRUITMENT THROUGH NETWORKS

Until now, the available evidence on the role of interpersonal bonds has been qualitative and insufficient to demonstrate their importance in determining which potential members will, in fact, join. To make good this deficiency, we present quantitative data on four varied religious movements.

Transcendental Meditation

In the previous chapter, we reported the belief of Transcendental Meditation leaders that most new meditators tried the technique on the advice of friends. In 1973, Mary Florence Fagerstrom was able to quantify this impression in a survey of 61 new meditators at the Seattle TM center. Other parts of the Lofland-Stark model were also supported. For example, many of the TM beginners had a strong orientation toward self-improvement activities of a more or less cultic sort and thus were ideologically prepared to accept TM. Twenty-one of the 61 respondents had previously tried yoga. Eleven had been in sensitivity groups, eight in individual therapy, and eight had even practiced other forms of meditation.

When asked what life situations led them to begin TM, several respondents mentioned problems and deprivations. Twenty-six had health concerns. Eight said they were unhappy or tense. Three cited a bad drug experience. One deprivation also bears on the network thesis—eight said they tried TM after a broken relationship. Loss of extracult social bonds not only leaves persons free to experiment with novel activities, but also impels them to seek new attachments. And many cults offer quick and easy social life for persons in need of friends. But the life situation mentioned most often by Fagerstrom's respondents was the influence of friends, 31 out of the 61 citing this as a main reason they began TM.

Because TM was a relatively cheap, short-term service, requiring no deep commitment and generally causing little social rejection by unsympathetic outsiders, we might expect many people to become involved out of personal whim inspired by mass media reports. By 1973, Transcendental Meditation had carried out several vast media campaigns and received a great amount of free publicity, but Fagerstrom discovered that social relationships were the main channel through which her respondents had received information about TM and therefore essential to their considering it as a solution to any problem they might have or as an interesting recreational possibility. Table 14.1 is a tabulation of how the 61 respondents learned about the Transcendental Meditation program prior to trying it.

Seven of the respondents mentioned three different sources, and 15 more mentioned two; so the number of responses in Table 14.1 is

TABLE 14.1   *Sources of Meditation Information for 61 TM Meditators*

Source of Information	Number of Respondents Mentioning This Source	Percent of 61
Friends and Relatives	43	70
Advertisements	16	26
Literature	16	26
Lectures	7	11
Other	6	10
Church	1	2
Teachers	1	2

Source: Mary Florence Fagerstrom, "A Descriptive Study of Beginning Transcendental Meditation," unpublished master's thesis, University of Washington, 1973, p. 59.

greater than 61. Over two-thirds of the group cited friends and relatives as a prime source of information, and the four lesser information channels at the bottom of the table may have rested upon social bonds as well. Although TM initiation does not involve any interaction whatsoever between neophytes, 77 percent of Fagerstrom's respondents said they knew other meditators.

In Chapter 13, we explain that TM exists on two levels, acting as a mild client cult for those hundreds of thousands who merely learn to meditate and functioning as a rather powerful cult movement for the much smaller group who become teachers. By 1977, approximately a million Americans had learned TM; yet only about 10,000 had gone further to become teachers. Of course, the organization had trouble finding enough work for even these 10,000. But the fact that only about 1 percent of those who invested in the meditation training subsequently became full members of the cult suggests that TM might have been wise to find roles for a larger percentage of the meditators to play within the organization. The fact that newcomers tended to have ties to other meditators indicates that TM could have built a larger movement through their networks, but only if it had been prepared to offer bond-strengthening activities such as those of Scientology and The Process. The fact that only 1 percent of the clients became members of the movement testifies to the lack of such means for producing strong bonds between the individual meditator and his or her local TM center.

A Doomsday Group

In the early 1960s, Hardyck and Braden (1962) studied a radical religious group that retreated into underground shelters to survive a prophesied atomic Armageddon. As time passed, a trickle of defections began, but most group members stuck to the end. Finally, they received a new revelation that they should come out. God had been testing them, and they had passed the test with flying colors.

Hardyck and Braden did not attempt to explain recruitment or defection because these topics were beyond the scope of the original study. However, during a conversation with Stark, Professor Hardyck (now Piliavin) once remarked that the group was essentially a large, extended family. She consulted her field notes and identified each of the 60 adult members in terms of kinship ties to the group's leader and her two lieutenants. She computed that 45 out of 60 adults who went underground were members of an extended kinship structure linking them to the three leaders. That is, 75 percent of the group formed a single and obvious social network based on kinship, and nearly all the other members were longtime friends of those in the kinship network. Clearly, this group formed by spreading along well-established interpersonal bonds.

In addition to furnishing us with this kinship count, Professor Hardyck also gave us Table 14.2, which offers dramatic quantitative data on the power of interpersonal bonds to shape religious faith. The obverse of recruitment is defection. If social ties pull people into cults and sects, it follows that such ties also should influence who leaves. In this case, a very unambiguous measure of defection was available: those who quit awaiting the holocaust and went above ground. All told, 18 of the 60 adult members defected in this fashion. Table 14.2 shows the proportions of defectors by three degrees of relationship to the group's leaders.

Among members who were direct kin of the leaders, only 13 percent quit. Of those who were related to kin of the leaders, but not directly to the leaders (for example, in-laws), 25 percent defected. But of those who had no relatives in the group, two-thirds left prematurely. For those who had to abandon their families as well as their faith, defection was rare, but, for those without familial ties to the group, defection was the *rule*. This does not suggest that theology played no role in the recruitment and maintenance of this group. But it surely does suggest that blood is thicker than attitudes.

Ananda: A Mystical Commune

Ananda is a rural commune near Nevada City, California, that Ted A. Nordquist (1978) studied. It was founded in 1967 by Swami Kriyananda, an American who had been baptized in the Episcopalian faith as James Donald Walters. While living in Los Angeles, Walters became a follower of Swami Paramahansa Yogananda, an Indian who attracted a following in California during the 1940s and 1950s. Having adopted an Indian name, Kriyananda specialized in self-realization teaching and gained sufficient backing to open a commune, Ananda Cooperative Village.

Nordquist (1978) administered a questionnaire to 28 Ananda members. A number of the items were meant to disclose their social situations prior to coming to the village. Overwhelmingly, they were characterized by "social withdrawal or introversion" prior to joining Ananda (Nordquist, 1978:87). For example, 82 percent reported they never or hardly ever attended parties, social gatherings, and the like.

These findings speak to several points about recruitment. First, these people did not have social bonds that could have restrained them

TABLE 14.2 *Kinship Bonds and Defection from a Doomsday Cult*

Degree of Kinship	Percent That Defected	
Related to cult leaders	13	(29)
Related to others, but not to leaders	25	(16)
Not related to another group member	67	(15)

Table 14.3   *Top Seven Choices on Rokeach's List of 18 Instrumental Values*

Michigan State Students		Ananda Cultists	
1. Honest	(2)[a]	1. Loving	(5)[b]
2. Responsible	(8)	2. Honest	(1)
3. Broadminded	(7)	3. Forgiving	(11)
4. Ambitious	(13)	4. Helpful	(13)
5. Loving	(1)	5. Cheerful	(14)
6. Independent	(10)	6. Self-controlled	(8)
7. Courageous	(9)	7. Broadminded	(3)

Source: Adapted from Nordquist (1978).
[a]Ranking among Ananda cultists.
[b]Ranking among Michigan State students.

from joining a cult. Second, such people were very open to forming social bonds within the Ananda group. Presumably, social isolation was one of the deprivations that caused these people to seek a religious answer. Indeed, when asked by Nordquist what was the most important single factor keeping them in Ananda, 61 percent chose "fellowship with other devotees" and an additional 25 percent chose their relationship with Swami Kriyananda as the reason they remained. In expressing interpersonal bonds as the prime factor keeping them in the cult, these members noticeably ignored the special qualities of the life-style, the religious exercises, or ideology. Nordquist (1978:87) noted: "Undoubtedly, joining Ananda provided the individual with companionship unavailable in the larger society."

These concerns with interpersonal bonds also show up clearly in Table 14.3. Ananda members were given a list of 18 "instrumental values" developed by Rokeach (1973) and were asked to rank them in terms of personal preferences. The table shows the top seven values in the rankings by Ananda members. For comparison, the top seven values in ratings made by undergraduates at Michigan State University are shown on the left of the table. The differences are clear and easily characterized. The Michigan State students gave the highest ratings to values related to personal competency; the Anandans gave the highest ratings to values pertinent to stable interpersonal relations. Over time, many persons who were prepared to accept mysticism drifted through the Ananda village. Those who were retained were those who formed interpersonal ties.

The Mormons

In Chapter 11, we discussed the fact that the Church of Jesus Christ of Latter-day Saints could be considered either a cult or a sect. One of

TABLE 14.4   *Mormon Church Growth, 1900–1978*

Year	Total Membership	Number of Full-Time Missionaries
1900	268,331	796
1925	613,653	2,500
1947	1,016,170	4,132
1957	1,488,314	6,616
1967	2,614,340	13,147
1978	4,180,000	27,399

Source: *Church News 49* (January 6, 1979), p. 5.

the oldest and most successful of novel religious movements, it began as a highly deviant cult. With the passing of the years, the Mormons have accommodated significantly to the sociocultural environment and have won a measure of respect from the more traditional denominations. Indeed, in the state of Utah, Mormonism is the dominant religious tradition and cannot properly be called either cult or sect. However, despite growth and success, the church remains intensely conversionist and each year sends out thousands of young men on two-year missionary forays around the world. The spectacular rise of this group and the continuing missionary activity are documented in Table 14.4. But where these missionaries work, and where the bulk of recruits join, Mormonism remains a significantly deviant religious movement. Because cults and sects recruit new members through the same means, placing equal emphasis on the development of social bonds, it does not matter which we call the Mormon movement. Group belief and practices remain strange and unusual to most outsiders.

Mormon missionaries seek recruits through a variety of means. The church has long recognized the immense importance of social networks in recruitment. Therefore, they work through such networks whenever possible. However, to fill the time of the many available missionaries, approaches are often made, aided little, if at all, by network supports. Table 14.5 breaks down contacts between Mormon missionaries and potential recruits according to the degree to which contact was mediated or facilitated by a Mormon friend or relative. The results offer dramatic testimony for the role of interpersonal bonds. When Mormon missionaries merely go door to door without the aid of social bonds, the success rate is only 0.1 percent. But, at the other extreme, if a Mormon friend or relative provides his or her home as the place where the contact occurs, the odds of success reach 50 percent.

Another way of looking at these findings is that missionaries do not

TABLE 14.5   *Interpersonal Bonds and Conversion to Mormonism*

Degree to which a Mormon friend or relative took part in the recruitment process	Percent of all missionary contacts that resulted in successful recruitment
None (door-to-door canvass by missionaries)	0.1
Covert referral (name of Mormon who suggested contact is not used)	7
Overt referral (name of Mormon who suggested contact is used)	8
Set up an appointment with missionaries	34
Contact with missionaries took place in the home of Mormon friend or relative	50

Note: Entirely by coincidence, the figures in this table add up to approximately 100%. That is not the correct way to read them. Each figure reports the percentage of recruitment attempts in each category that succeeded.

serve as the primary instrument of recruitment to the Mormon faith. Rather, recruitment primarily is accomplished by the rank and file of the church as they construct intimate interpersonal ties with non-Mormons and thus link them into a Mormon social network.

Mormon leaders are acutely aware that this is the case. In consequence, they give considerable attention to developing an explicit network strategy among rank-and-file members. All social scientists interested in religious recruitment could learn much from a detailed, 13-step set of instructions published in June 1974 in *The Ensign,* an official church magazine widely circulated among members. Written by Ernest Eberhard, president of the Oregon mission, the article constitutes a practical guide to enable church members to bring their faith to their neighbors and acquaintances in order to fulfill the goal that each member should help bring one new person into the church each year.

The important thing about the instructions is that they are directed toward building close personal ties and at many points admonish Mormons to avoid or downplay discussion of religion. Although proselytizers of many denominations imagine they should stress theology in their initial appeals, social scientific observational studies show that interpersonal bonds must come first. From experience, Mormons ratify this point.

The 13-step plan advises Mormons to select a target family whose members express concerns about raising their children in a modern urban environment or a family that has just moved into the neighborhood and lacks friendship ties. Mormons are urged to include non-Mormons in their friendship network and are given a strategy of politeness and helpfulness to cement such ties. The instructions include effective ways to invite the target family into the Mormon home and to find ways of going out together socially.

Only in step five does religion enter the picture, and then to defuse rather than ignite the subject. The Mormon family is shown how to let it drop casually that they are Mormons, perhaps by mentioning in passing their involvement in some church activity. They are discouraged from mentioning intense personal spiritual experiences or anything else that might trigger religious disagreement. With great discretion, in step six, the target family might be given a low-key church publication, perhaps one on a topic they would find personally interesting, but nothing controversial.

The first chance to participate in a Mormon activity does not come until step seven, when the neighbor family is invited to the living room of their new Mormon friends for a family home evening. Once a week, ordinarily on Monday, each practicing Mormon family gathers at home to study a church lesson and to consider any family problems according to procedures instituted by the church. For the neighbors, the Mormon family sets up a special evening focused almost wholly on family problem solving; religion is downplayed and social relations are emphasized.

Care is taken against premature exposure to too much religion, and the emphasis is on the development of friendship and on showing how Mormonism can provide happy family life. The potential recruits are invited to Mormon groups, but not to religious services, in steps eight and nine. Only in step ten may they attend a Sunday service. Because the unique and more sacred ritual aspects of Mormonism occur only in a regional temple, Sunday services are quite informal and would not strike persons with a Christian background as particularly unusual.

Only after these experiences with the social life of the church does the potential recruit hear a profession of faith from Mormon friends, and even then restraint is the rule. Step 12 raises the possibility that the person ought to investigate Mormonism more deeply. If the first attempt does not produce a sufficiently interested response, the Mormon is advised to keep the friendship alive and try again later. When interest is shown, the final step has been reached. It is now time to arrange for missionaries to teach the new recruits in the home of their Mormon friends. The data in Table 14.5 show that, if this step is achieved, successful recruitment is the result half the time.

If we can assume the Mormons know what they are doing, and the fact that they are the most rapidly growing large religious movement in the United States suggests they surely do, then there seems compelling reason for sociologists to accept that interpersonal bonds are the fundamental support for recruitment.

NETWORKS

We have seen a considerably expanded empirical basis for claiming that interpersonal bonds play a vital role in recruitment of cults and sects. We now seek the boundaries of this phenomenon. Is it that recruitment must be sustained by social relations only in order to shield the individual from sanctions against deviant behavior, but no such shield is necessary for commitment to conventional faiths? Or is the role of interpersonal influence much more general than this — is all religion sustained by social networks?

Conventional Faiths

A variety of evidence suggests that all faiths rest on network influences. Welch (1981) assessed the role of interpersonal bonds in sustaining commitment to orthodox beliefs among members of mainline Christian denominations in the United States. He found strong positive correlations between various measures of orthodoxy and the proportion of one's best friends who are members of one's own religious congregation or parish. He also found that, the greater the number of memberships in nonchurch organizations and clubs, the lower the orthodoxy. These relationships remained strong despite controls for education, occupation, denomination, and age. It would appear that, even in such low tension faiths as Episcopalianism or Methodism, belief is firmest among those whose social network and whose religious affiliation are coextensive.

Similarly, Stark's (1965a) study of the effects of social contexts upon religious experience (moments when the individual believes he or she has had a personal encounter with the supernatural) found that, in Christian groups ranging from the lowest tension denominations to the highest tension sects, such experiences were highly concentrated among those who chose their closest friends from among their coreligionists.

Several studies of the spread of the charismatic movement among American Roman Catholics also have found that interpersonal bonds play a significant role. Harrison (1974) found this among a sample of students at two Catholic universities, as did Heirich (1977) among students and other adults in the Ann Arbor area. Heirich's study is especially interesting because he carefully assessed the relative significance of deprivation, prior socialization, and social influence in determining recruitment. Although Heirich feels that other factors not identified by any of these approaches may also be important, his detailed analysis shows that social ties had a powerful effect. "It is clear that members of the movement, when recruiting, turn to previous friends and to persons they meet at daily Mass. It is also clear that introduction to Catholic Pentecostalism by a trusted person, together with positive inputs from others while exploring its claims produces fairly positive outcomes" (Heirich, 1977:667).

In our discussion of defection from the doomsday cult, we said that defection was the mirror image of recruitment. People with weak social bonds to a group are most likely to leave it. This applies to conventional religious denominations as much as to deviant cults. Anything that tears an individual away from the other people in a church leads to defection from the formal organization as well. Effective membership in a denomination means membership in the social group that constitutes a particular congregation of it. Loss of social bonds to a denomination entails loss of effective membership in it. Cast adrift from an old affiliation, the person is liable to be recruited by a vigorous religious movement or to drift indefinitely in an unchurched state.

Powerful evidence on this point can be found in several studies of geographic migration and church membership. When individuals move to a new town, in modern societies, they are not automatically inducted into a church congregation. The ties they lost to the church in their former home are not replaced by strong ties to a church in their new home. Perhaps the newcomers will acquire a few friends in the new town, and they will invite them to their church and make them feel welcome in it. But, in religiously plural societies, there is a good chance that the first several people migrants meet will belong to different faiths — and they may well be migrants like themselves, without a local religious affiliation to offer. Therefore, we would expect a high proportion of the population to be unchurched in communities with high rates of geographic mobility.

Research consistently shows that residential migration does in fact tend to reduce church membership and attendance (Wuthnow and Christiano, 1979; Welch, 1983). The data on which several chapters of this book are based show the same thing. For example, the 1926 church membership rate for 78 large American cities shows a strong negative correlation with the percentage of the population born in a different state ($r = -.63$) and with the rate of population growth ($r = -.47$), two indicators of instability. Data for 60 of the largest metropolitan areas in 1971 show a very powerful negative correlation between the proportion that has moved in the past five years and the proportion that belongs to a church ($r = -.65$). Thus, migration severs the bonds that hold many people to a religious organization, producing a kind of religious vacuum. We note this fact at the end of Chapter 4; in Chapter 19, we see how cults may arise in response.

The Occult Milieu

Recently, there has been a considerable resurgence in the popularity of occult and pseudoscience beliefs in the United States. In 1977, Gallup reported that 27 percent of Americans believe in astrology. Millions of others daily consult their biorhythm charts in the daily press. Others meditate or attend lectures by a whole host of traveling mystics. This constellation of mildly deviant supernatural beliefs and activities has been identified as the *occult milieu,* and specific interest groups within it constitute what we have called audience cults (see chapters 2 and 10). Some students of cult recruitment suspect that participation in the occult milieu plays a vital preparatory role leading to membership in organized cult movements (Wuthnow, 1976a, 1978; Balch and Taylor, 1977; Lynch, 1977). Because these beliefs are mildly deviant, experimentation with them may help disconnect people from conventional religious affiliations while preparing them to consider novel religious doctrines.

Although considerable research has been conducted on how people are recruited into cults, little or nothing is known about how they enter the occult milieu. However, persons may take up occult interests as a result of membership in a social network where such interests prevail. If so, then the occult can be characterized as a true subculture — a distinctive set of cultural elements that flourish as the property of a distinctive social group. Or occult interests may reflect a much more superficial phenomenon. Participation in such interests could be more like being a member of a theater audience — a transitory and relatively private amusement that is not supported by significant social relations. If the former is the case, then entry into the occult milieu is quite plausibly interpreted as a significant symptom of potential recruitment to a deviant religious group. If the latter, then consumption of occult teachings may be little more than a minor exercise of idiosyncratic taste having little meaning for future religious actions. We examine this question empirically in the following chapter.

CONCLUSION

Social networks play an essential role in recruitment to cults, sects, and conventional denominations. The most important influences bringing people to try Transcendental Meditation are friends and relatives. TM's inability to create and sustain social bonds with many new meditators prevented more than about 1 percent from becoming lasting members. Kinship was central to the structure of a doomsday cult and discouraged defection. Members of the Ananda commune showed greater concern for interpersonal ties than for ideology. In Mormon recruitment, lay members build bonds of friendship and trust with non-Mormons, and the power of social bonds has given this church its great successes in gaining new adherents.

Despite the importance of interpersonal bonds for religious recruitment, we cannot reject the complementary deprivation and ideological appeal position. Any complete theory of recruitment to cults and sects must include both these elements. However, deprivation and ideological compatibility seem unable to serve as more than very general contributory conditions in any satisfactory theory of recruitment. Although they do limit the pool of persons available for recruitment, they do not limit it very much in comparison to the very small numbers of such persons who actually join. Many people are deprived and are ideologically predisposed to accept a cult's message. But in explaining why so few of them actually do join, it is necessary to examine a number of situational variables.

Many people simply fail to encounter missionaries from a deviant cult. Furthermore, a group's effectiveness in gaining recruits depends greatly on the extent to which its members have, or can enter, social networks outside the group. Thus, groups with procedures that tend to recruit social isolates will have a very slow growth rate. The new members do not provide the group with entree to new social networks through which the group may then spread. Religious groups that tend to recruit entire nuclear families (as is often the case in Mormon recruitment) may grow rapidly as they spread on through friends and relatives of the new members.

The deprivation theory focuses on population segments that lack rewards enjoyed by others and are open to an ideology compensating them for their deprivation. The network theory makes no assumptions about the relative deprivation or prosperity of recruits. The deprivation theory is strengthened greatly, and is best integrated with evidence on interpersonal attachments, if a major missing element is included — the significant *direct rewards* available to members of religious movements.

Previous discussions of the importance of deprivations in creating recruits for cults and sects have focused on how such group's ideologies function to make deprivations more bearable. Thus, for example, a doctrine that the poor will stand first in heaven offers balm against present poverty, but it does not reduce poverty. However, as ongoing social organizations, sects and cults generate and exchange a great array of rewards that can serve directly to reduce various kinds of deprivations. While observing the Moonies, Stark noted remarkable improvements in some members' ability to manage interpersonal relations. They came to the group suffering greatly from low self-esteem and lack of confidence that disrupted their interactions with others. For example, one man routinely whispered and looked only at his toes when he talked with others. Forging strong affective ties to other group members noticeably raised new recruits' self-esteem. Indeed, the man just described "recovered" to the extent that was able to preach in the streets after a period with the group.

Direct rewards available to cult and sect members are not limited to affection. Groups such as the Hare Krishnas and the Moonies offer specific material inducement. They clothe, feed, and shelter adherents. Indeed, they offer them a career that, at least within the group, enjoys considerable prestige. Having joined such a group, members no longer must wonder what to do in life or explain why they were not doing very well. Furthermore, there is considerable scope for ambition within cults and sects. Some members can rise to positions of status and power. In our discussion of the entrepreneur model of cult formation in Chapter 8, we note the wide range of valuable rewards, including great wealth, that cult leaders can receive.

The 13-step Mormon program for gaining new recruits reveals the priority given to showering tangible rewards upon potential new members. The notion of showing people how rewarding it is to be a Mormon is not meant metaphorically or only in a theological sense. Today, many middle-class and upper-class families are threatened by divorce and a wide range of other problems that money cannot cure. Therefore, people with the advantages of wealth, education, and power may be deprived of the most intimate and important social rewards and join a sect or cult for benefits many such groups can in fact deliver.

Religious movements do not rely solely upon otherworldly solutions to human problems. Whatever else they may be, religious organizations also are worldly organizations and have at their disposal resources to reward many members. Indeed, the affective bonds that constitute social networks, which we feature in this chapter, are direct rewards. Humans desire interpersonal bonds, and they will try to protect them from rupture, even if they must accept a new religious faith in the process.

15 *Friendship, Religion, and the Occult*

In several chapters of this book and in other publications, we attempt to demonstrate that religion is a social rather than an individual phenomenon. Individual religiousness does not prevent criminal behavior, for example, except for persons situated within a relatively religious social climate (Stark, Doyle, and Kent, 1980; Stark, Kent, and Doyle, 1982). In the previous chapter, we explained that people do not join new religious movements on the basis of theological reflection, but only as they are linked to such movements by interpersonal bonds with group members (see also Lofland and Stark, 1965; Bainbridge, 1978c). In Chapter 17, we show that ideologies, whether religious or secular, seem to lack coherence and potency unless they are developed and promulgated by vigorous formal organizations and social movements.

These observations do not contradict the fact that the main function of religion is to provide compensators to individuals who strongly desire scarce and nonexistent rewards. If most of the needs served by religion are individual, the sources of faith are social. In Chapter 8, we note how difficult it is for individuals to invent their own compensators and then believe in them. All three models of religious innovation depended upon social exchanges to generate faith in compensators. The previous

A shorter version of this chapter was published as William Sims Bainbridge and Rodney Stark, "Friendship, Religion and the Occult: A Network Study," *Review of Religious Research*, 1981, 22:4, pp. 313–327.

325

chapter shows that people gain faith from strong social relationships, not from personal deprivation alone.

In this chapter, we examine how religious beliefs and practices become salient for dyadic personal friendships and find that here, too, the key factor is whether religion is anchored in a vigorous formal organization or social movement.

Like the rest of this book, this chapter is based on our efforts to formulate a deductive theory of religion (Stark and Bainbridge, 1980). Here we test three simple propositions derived from our theory and germane to our other empirical studies:

1. Objectively important ideological positions and questions of social policy are not *in themselves* salient for personal relationships.

2. Objectively trivial individual habits and matters of taste often are extremely salient for personal relationships.

3. Religious attitudes and supernatural beliefs are salient for personal relationships only when they are promoted by social movements and vigorous formal organizations.

One may find exceptional individuals who violate one or more of these propositions, but the three are meant to hold for the majority of human beings.

The first proposition leaves open the possibility that external factors can render ideology important for personal relationships, for example, the influence of a church or active political movement to which a significant number of people belong. A few ideological positions, such as approval of sexual freedom, may directly concern interpersonal behavior; but, even in these cases, words and deeds may diverge unless brought into line by social forces (Miller and Simon, 1974; cf. Zellman, 1975; Schuman and Johnson, 1976).

The second proposition approaches tautology. Personal habits and passions certainly ought to be salient for personal relations. But the reason for stating this proposition is to remind us that the objectively trivial matters of everyday life are frequently more important for individuals than great matters of philosophical depth. The meaning of life may be less salient, most of the time, than objectively petty questions of whether one likes to drink beer, diet soda, or milk. Taken together, these two propositions imply that religious beliefs and attitudes may not be salient for personal relationships unless something makes them salient.

The third proposition affirms the crucial importance of social structure in promoting religion and rendering it salient for personal relationships. But there is something more — the religion must be *vigorous,* flowing from active social organizations, perhaps religious social movements that seek to transform or transcend society. To the extent that a religious body accepts its sociocultural environment, it may be powerless to influence behavior. In our pluralist society, some of the more liberal churches seem merely to add their weak assent to the words of secular leaders. It is when religion significantly dissents that it may have an independent effect on human attitudes and actions. Sects and supernatural social movements may have the greatest salience for personal relationships, not only because they marshal considerable social energies to bear on members, but also because they urge discernible alternatives. Some highly institutionalized religious bodies, even polar opposites of the typical sect, may retain some of the vigor of social movements to the extent that they seriously promote ideologies dissonant in important respects with the secular consensus or government policy. To be specific, the most liberal denominations may not provide a kind of religion that is salient for personal relationships, but very powerful influences may come from sects (and such movements as the current born again phenomenon) and from the still incompletely assimilated Catholic church.

In this chapter we use a wealth of data from a large network survey of college students at the University of Washington in Seattle to evaluate the salience of religious beliefs and attitudes for personal relationships and to determine whether the influences of vigorous formal organizations and social movements are indeed required to give religion the power to shape friendships. Before considering these questions in the light of the results from this large survey, we describe briefly the pilot project that proved our methods for acquiring a network sample would work and provided interesting results of its own.

THE PILOT STUDY

Attempts to study the interaction between personal relationships and individual attitudes have posed serious methodological difficulties for survey research. The best strategy has always been to collect data from each research subject directly (Duncan et al., 1968). But cost has often required that information on the beliefs and opinions of a respondent's friends or relatives be based on the respondent's own report. Unfortunately, in some cases where studies have actually interviewed all the relevant parties, considerable discrepancies have been found in comparison with studies based on indirect reports from convenient respondents about their peers' or parents' feelings. For example, studies of drug use have found a considerable similarity between parental behavior and that of their children when children were the source of information on the parents. But little correlation on drug use has been found when the behavior of parents and children was assessed independently (Kandel, 1974; Kandel et al., 1976). Therefore, it is preferable in a study such as ours to survey both parties to a friendship about their own personal attitudes, rather than to ask one to answer on behalf of both. Simple ignorance, as well as a tendency for persons to overestimate the degree to which others agree with them, might intrude on secondhand reports.

We managed to devise a research design that was adequate to deal with this problem without being prohibitively expensive, a design we think could profitably be adopted for many research questions. We began in the customary way, by enlisting student volunteers from a large introductory sociology class at our university. But, instead of asking each student only to fill out a questionnaire, we asked each also to distribute three additional, identical questionnaires in the following way:

1. To a close friend: a member of the university student body who was not enrolled in the class

2. To an acquaintance: "someone you know by name but are not close friends with" who was a member of the university student body but not enrolled in the class

3. To a parent: either of the student's parents

Each of the three additional questionnaires (which, with the student's own questionnaire, made a set of four) was distributed in an envelope that could be sealed for return to us — the parent's questionnaire having two envelopes to permit mailing out and back. Each questionnaire had a code number so we could reassemble each set of four for analysis. This technique yielded a total of 571 respondents: 161 student volunteers from the class, 139 of their close friends, 129 acquaintances, and 142 parents.

Had our primary concern been descriptive, we should have begun with a random sample of the student body. But we believed we could not establish sufficient rapport outside the classroom to get a random sample of students not only to complete a questionnaire but also to distribute three others. Perhaps it would be worth a small pilot study to see if our technique would work with a random sample. In any event, our primary concern was with relationships, and therefore we were willing to trade off descriptive certainty for more adequate assessment of the opinions of parents and peers of the initial respondents. Moreover, our design offers means for checking potential descriptive biases. If the students enrolled in the class are importantly atypical, their response patterns ought to differ from those produced by their acquaintances, if not from those of their close friends. As it turned out, the three groups of students produced virtually identical distributions on each questionnaire item. However, there was considerable difference between students and the parent group on many of the items. These facts suggest that our data are of good descriptive quality for the student body as a whole.

The survey consisted of a list of statements, and the respondents were asked to check one of five boxes to register their reactions to each one: strongly agree, agree, not sure, disagree, strongly disagree. We wanted to know whether student volunteers tended to hold the same opinions and attitudes as their friends, acquaintances, and parents; so we cross-tabulated responses to the same item from student and friend, student and acquaintance, and student and parent. Table 15.1 shows *concordances* on five interesting questionnaire items — measures of similarity between the opinions of the class member who distributed the set and each of the other categories of respondent.

Consider the first row of coefficients, concordances measured by tau, showing whether the student volunteers and the other respondents in each set are of the same mind about the existence of God. We see a weak but statistically significant concordance (tau = .17) with the close friend, an only slightly smaller but insignificant concordance (tau = .16) with the acquaintance, and a much stronger concordance (tau = .26) with the parent. Of course, the essentially identical concordances for friend and acquaintance are weak — they are not convincing evidence that belief in God is hugely salient for college friendships. The concordance with par-

TABLE 15.1   *Opinion Concordances from the Pilot Study*

Statement	Correlations (tau) Between the Opinions of the Students and the Opinions of		
	139 Close Friends	129 Acquaintances	142 Parents
I definitely believe in God.	.17*	.16	.26**
Miracles actually happened just as the Bible says they did.	.30**	.16	.19*
Darwin's theory of evolution is probably false.	.27**	.01	.24**
Extra-sensory perception (E.S.P.) probably does not exist.	.13	−.07	.27**
There is much truth in Astrology — the theory that the stars, the planets, and our birthdays have a lot to do with our destiny in life.	.25**	.03	−.02

*Significant at the .01 level.
**Significant at the .001 level.

ent means that the student volunteers do tend to agree with their parents on the existence of God. Believers tend to have believers for parents; non-believers tend to have nonbelievers for parents.

The second item in Table 15.1, "Miracles actually happened just as the Bible says they did," is a measure of fundamentalist sentiments and shows a strong concordance between the student volunteer and the close friend. Because this attitude may be spread through vigorous religious movements, it is gratifying to see a stronger concordance than on simple belief in God, and we will find the same difference in the main study, but we must not leap to conclusions about our main hypotheses on the basis of the purely exploratory pilot study. The next statement in the table probably is a good indicator of traditional religious faith, although it does not state a religious belief directly. Those who feel "Darwin's theory of evolution is probably false" will include many who believe in a literal interpretation of the Genesis story. On this item, there are strong concordances with close friend and parent, but not with acquaintance.

These three items plausibly measure traditional religious faith and are, in fact, connected by strong correlations for each separate category of respondents. For the 161 student volunteers, belief in God is linked to belief in miracles (gamma = .76) and to rejection of Darwin (gamma = .50); belief in miracles and rejection of Darwin also are linked (gamma = .54). Thus, the concordances do show that young people tend to share the religious views of their parents and close friends, although perhaps not of their mere acquaintances.

The fourth and fifth items in Table 15.1 attempt to measure occult opinions. As it turned out, belief in astrology is not rampant at the University of Washington, and only about 11 percent of the students and 13 percent of the parents think their destiny is shaped by the stars. However, only about 8 percent in each group was willing to reject completely the possibility of ESP. These skewed distributions for our only two occult items, coupled with the small number of respondents, render these items less effective than we might wish, but there was a decent amount of variation within the majority opinions over whether they were held "strongly" or not. Furthermore, these two items were connected in respondents' minds, accepting astrology and rejecting ESP showing a strong negative correlation (gamma = −.42) among the 161 student volunteers. But, as we see in Table 15.1, the two items show opposite concordance patterns, students sharing opinions on ESP with their parents and opinions on astrology with their close friends.

Because this was a pilot study, we did not expect to gain conclusive findings, but the results in Table 15.1 were encouraging and gave promise that the main study would succeed. First, we demonstrated that opinion items such as these are capable of generating concordances strong enough that they could be measured adequately even with only a few more than a hundred cases (pairs of respondents). Second, the overall pattern was quite reasonable because the concordances with mere acquaintances were always insignificant, and statistically significant similarity was often found with the close friend or parent. Certainly, we would expect people who share a close social bond to influence each other and to share some opinions. Third, the three religion items showed a rather consistent pattern of concordance worthy of further investigation. If religion had showed no concordance, it would have been futile to explore other conditions that might explain similarities in religious faith. Although the two occult items do not show a uniform pattern, the possibility that the irregularities might result from spuriousness can be investigated in the main study.

Perhaps, for example, female students are more apt to accept the possibility that there is some truth in astrology. If students naturally choose close college friends of their own sex, then a real concordance on sex could produce an apparent but spurious concordance on astrology. Because students have parents of both sexes, there would not be even an apparent astrology concordance with the parents. Many such interpretations come to mind. Of course, the pilot study was so modest in its aims that we could not test our main hypotheses on its findings. Not only did it lack a wide range of survey items, but the number of respondents was so low we could not explore the concordances statistically to see if other variables might explain some of them. But, in addition to encouraging us to proceed with the main study — and acting as a useful introduction to the research approach for the reader—the pilot study shows that future research probing the religious heritage young people receive from their parents could be carried out successfully using these methods.

THE MAIN STUDY

After evaluating the pilot study, we designed and pretested a much longer questionnaire and prepared for a more ambitious data collection program. To maximize the number of similar pairs of respondents who could be surveyed with our limited resources, we reluctantly decided not to survey parents this time, but to concentrate on pairs of close friends. We distributed the questionnaire in sets of four to the largest sociology class of 1979, asking students to complete one copy themselves and to distribute the other three to members of the student body (outside the class) as follows:

1. To a close friend
2. To a second close friend
3. To an acquaintance

A total of 1,439 questionnaires were completed, 554 by students in the class, 612 by close friends, and 273 by acquaintances. Of course, many students in the class may not have known suitable other students outside the class. We wanted to be sure relationships were categorized correctly. The first question answered by friends and acquaintances was, "How close a friend is the person who gave you this questionnaire?" A seven-point scale was provided for the answer, from zero (not at all close) to six (very close). Respondents sealed their questionnaires in envelopes to protect confidentiality; so we have every reason to believe they responded honestly to this key question. In our analysis, we often focus on 424 close friend pairs, defined as those in which the friend rated the friendship a five or six on the closeness scale.

Again, our research design offers means for checking potential descriptive biases in the sample of respondents. If the students enrolled in the class are importantly atypical, their response patterns ought to differ from those produced by their acquaintances, if not from those of their close friends. Again, as it turned out, the three groups of students produced virtually identical distributions on each item in the questionnaire. Several variables, such as preference for the social rather than the physical sciences, that ought to have revealed an important bias if there was one, not only were constant across the groups of student respondents, but also failed to correlate with variables of greatest interest for this book. We have added confidence in the respondents because results closely replicated findings from a San Francisco survey of a random sample of young people (see Chapter 17).

Table 15.2 shows concordances on 13 questionnaire items, measuring agreement between the opinions and preferences of the class member who distributed the set and a close friend. If the student and close friend tend to be similar with respect to an item, this concordance in attitude or characteristic will be revealed by a strong positive coefficient. The first two items, sex of respondent and year in school, are not opinions, of course, but objective characteristics of the student. We see a strong tendency (gamma = .79) for our college respondents to choose friends of the same sex and same year in school. There are significant concordances also for seven personal behavior variables.

TABLE 15.2   *Selected Personal Behavior and Ideology Statements*

	Concordance (gamma) in		Association (gamma, N=1439) with	
	424 Close Friend Pairs	219 Neither Born Again Pairs	Church Atten-dance	Importance of Religious Beliefs
1. Sex of respondent (male = +)	.79	.82	−.14	−.13
2. Year in school	.59	.62	−.02	−.02
Personal Behavior				
3. "It is all right for an unmarried couple to have sexual relations."	.57	.44	−.57	−.59
4. How often respondent has been "high" on drugs	.48	.40	−.31	−.30
5. Respondent's preference rating of marijuana	.45	.41	−.30	−.32
6. Respondent's preference rating of beer	.32	.33	−.17	−.21
7. Respondent's preference rating of tobacco cigarettes	.50	.44	−.14	−.16
8. Respondent's preference rating of diet soda	.27	.28	.08	.05
9. Respondent's preference rating of rock music	.25	.22	−.14	−.18
Secular Ideologies				
10. Respondent's preference rating of the physical sciences	.01	.00	.01	.04
11. Respondent's preference rating of the social sciences	.04	−.02	.01	.03
12. Respondent's politics on NORC liberal-conservative 7-point scale (liberal = +)	.12	.02	−.22	−.19
13. "The potential dangers of nuclear energy are outweighed by its potential benefits."	.06	.05	.01	.03

Three of these items reflect formal procedures of the university, to some extent, as well as students' personal preferences. Many students apply individually to live in dormitories and are assigned strangers as roommates. They may then grow to consider their roommates as their best friends at college, at least until they have been at school long enough to have acquired other friends. Of course, the university assigns rooms only to same-sex pairs of strangers, and most of them will be in the same year of school. Furthermore, students are asked their preferences for smoking or nonsmoking roommates, but they are not asked whether they prefer roommates who drink diet soda or who use illegal drugs. The fact that formal university procedures contribute to three of the concordances does not invalidate these measures for comparison with religion variables. If religion were highly salient for friendships, and students demanded same-faith roommates, the university would institute a formal procedure supporting this personal preference.

The salience for college friendships of attitudes toward sex and drugs is revealed by very strong correlations. Several of the concordances illustrate our point that objectively trivial individual characteristics and habits are often extremely salient for the development of personal relationships. The four items that conclude Table 15.2 are opinions about secular ideologies that ought to be of great objective significance. One would think that the physical and social sciences provide powerful and distinctive ways of understanding human existence — world views that should influence an individual's whole style of behavior. But we see no concordance. There is a minuscule concordance (gamma = .12) on general political orientation, as measured by the seven-point, liberal-conservative scale used in the annual General Social Survey conducted by the National Opinion Research Center. Apparently, political ideology is not salient for most of these college friendships. The last item, attitude toward nuclear power, concerns one of the most crucial policy issues facing our society, one whose salience ought to have been strengthened by the great publicity given a serious accident at the Three Mile Island atomic power plant just weeks before we administered the questionnaire. But attitude toward atomic power is not salient for friendships, as a concordance very close to zero proves.

In evaluating concordances, we must keep in mind the possibility that respondents' background characteristics or other powerful variables create spurious apparent concordances for any variables with which they happen to correlate. For example, perhaps the concordances on personal behavior items really reflect the influence of religion. Students may choose friendships on the basis of religion or may be influenced by the religion of friends they choose for other reasons, and religion may dictate attitudes toward such things as premarital sex, drug use, and rock music. The second, third, and fourth columns of gammas in Table 15.2 both show the influence of religion and control for it.

The most effective single religion item in our questionnaire was a question taken from the Gallup poll: "Would you say that you have been 'born again' or have had a 'born again' experience — that is, a turning point in your life when you committed yourself to Christ?" In Gallup's survey, 34 percent of respondents said they were born again. Despite the secularizing effect of college and the low church membership rates on the West Coast, reported in earlier chapters, 368 (25.6 percent) of our college students checked the "yes" box. In the second column of Table 15.2, we use the born again question as a control variable, removing from consideration all respondents who said they were born again and looking only at the 219 close friend pairs in which neither claimed to have had this religious experience. All the personal behavior items show highly significant concordances after this control, indicating that they are salient for friendships, independent of religion. We see slight declines in concordances on premarital sex and on drug items, but the coefficients remain quite high. Interestingly, the small concordance on political opinion vanishes.

The concluding columns in Table 15.2 show that religion does have an influence, reporting associations linking frequency of church attendance and professed importance of the respondent's religious beliefs with the other items. There are especially strong negative associations between the religion variables and both premarital sex and drugs, as one would expect. We cannot say, on the basis of present data, what the causal direction is. Perhaps religion urges people to reject premarital sex and illicit drugs, or perhaps involvement in a free life-style produces a rejection of religion. This study is concerned with the salience of supernatural beliefs and practices for close friendships, salience that is socially meaningful whichever the causal direction. We were interested to see that such objectively trivial pleasures as tobacco cigarettes, diet soda, and rock music are salient for friendships, that religion does not greatly explain concordances on sexuality and drug use, and that impersonal secular ideologies are not salient.

Religious Behavior, Belief, and Affiliation

Table 15.3 examines the salience for friendships of 13 religion variables. All of them seem to matter. As the first coefficient (gamma = .34) shows, students who attend church often tend to have friends who do likewise. Students who say their religious beliefs are important to them tend to have friends who say the same. The five following opinion items show significant concordances, and even two personal preference items, on "religious books and articles" and "hymns and spirituals," do as well. But these concordances are really not huge, as comparison with Table 15.2 demonstrates. They fall in the same range as preferences for beer and diet soda and below tobacco cigarettes.

We have said that religious beliefs and attitudes should become salient if they are promulgated by vigorous formal religious organizations and social movements. One question in our survey asked respondents' religious affiliations, and 323 said they were Catholics; 545 were Protestants; and 257 claimed no religious affiliation. The largest Protestant denominations were the Lutherans, with 135 members, and the Presbyterians, with 132. There also were 80 Methodists, 73 Episcopalians, and 51 Baptists. The 45 Jews and 213 "others" are excluded from this part of our analysis because the groups to which they belong are too small for reliable statistics.

Concordances in Table 15.3 do show a clear tendency for Catholic students to choose Catholic friends, Protestants to choose Protestants, and those with no religion to choose others with the same lack of affiliation. The born again question is especially significant for our hypothe-

TABLE 15.3   *Concordances on Religion Variables*

	Concordance (gamma) in	
	424 Close Friend Pairs	219 Neither Born Again Pairs
1. Frequency of church attendance	.34	.14
2. "How important to you are your religious beliefs?"	.28	.01
3. "I definitely believe in God."	.22	.07
4. "God or some other supernatural force has a very strong influence on my life."	.29	.05
5. "Suffering often comes about because people don't obey God."	.25	.12
6. "Man evolved from lower animals."	.29	.10
7. "Miracles actually happened just as the Bible says they did."	.34	.18
8. Likes religious books and articles	.25	.03
9. Likes hymns and spirituals	.22	.07
10. Respondent is Catholic	.30	—
11. Respondent is Protestant	.35	—
12. Respondent has no religion	.37	—
13. Respondent is born again	.59	—

sis because it taps involvement in the most powerful religious movement active in the cultural environment. We predicted that being born again would prove quite salient for friendships. And, indeed, the high concordance (gamma = .59) shows that it is.

Several earlier studies have shown that members of sects and other high tension religious movements tend to be socially encapsulated, choosing a high proportion of friends from among fellow members. We saw evidence of this in Chapter 3, and now it emerges in our student data as well. Born agains constituted 26 percent of the respondents from the introductory sociology class. Those in the class who were not born again chose friends who included 24 percent born again, essentially the same proportion. But the born agains in the class chose close friends 55 percent of whom also were born again, showing a very powerful tendency to select friends who shared their involvement in this intense religious movement.

The importance of the born again movement can be demonstrated by using this question as a control variable, as we do in the second column of Table 15.3. Controlling in this way drives all the coefficients way down, most of them to the vanishing point. Of course, removing the born agains takes a good deal of the variation out of some of the religion variables. Although 49 percent of all the born agains attend church once a week or more, only 9 percent of those not born again do so. If we take both the born agains and the Catholics out of the total sample of 1,439, only 4 percent of those remaining attend religious services this often, and 62 percent say they "hardly ever" or "never" attend religious services. Church attendance cannot be very salient if it is so rare.

The question, "How important to you are your religious beliefs?" is especially interesting. Removal of the born agains still leaves 181 (18 percent) who say their religious beliefs are "very important" to them and 339 (34 percent) who say they are "fairly important." Perhaps religious beliefs are privately important to many who are not born again, but they certainly are not salient for friendships, as the essentially zero concordance (gamma = .01) shows.

We believe that Table 15.3 has provided ample support for our hypothesis that religious attitudes can become salient for personal relationships when they are supported by a vigorous social movement, in this case, the born again phenomenon. We shall now look at variations in religious attitudes across denominations, to see the impact of formal organizations. The collapse of the concordances in Table 15.3 after we removed the born agains brings into doubt the significance of mere attitudes and of denominational affiliations that do not have strong support from a vigorous social movement.

Denominational Affiliation

Table 15.4 shows the distribution of responses across major denominations and denominational groupings. We are fortunate to have a large number of respondents who claim no religious affiliation to provide a baseline above which to measure true religiousness. Construction of the Protestant categories requires comment. Respondents who checked boxes indicating that their religious affiliation was "Protestant" or "other" were asked to specify which denomination they belonged to. Based on previous work, such as that described in Chapter 3, we identified Episcopalians, Methodists, United Church of Christ (Congregationalists), and Unitarians as "liberal." We put members of the Disciples of Christ, most Lutherans, and Presbyterians in the "moderate" group. "Conservatives" included Baptists, Missouri Lutherans, and members of a couple of similar groups. Although we could identify only 35 respondents as members of extreme Protestant "sects," the consistency of results warrants reporting this small category.

The Protestant groups are ordered along the dimension of *tension* with the sociocultural environment. The "liberal" churches are at the low tension end of the scale, and the "sects" are at the high tension extreme. To the extent that a religious group is in relatively high tension with the sociocultural environment, it represents a religious social movement, at odds with prevailing norms, values, and beliefs and potentially dedicated to radical transformation of society and culture. Table 15.4 provides further support for the concept of tension because the pattern of responses shows a very consistent and great rise from the liberal low tension groups to the high tension sects.

Once more, the born again question deserves consideration. Of course, it is no surprise that only 6 percent of those with no religious affiliation claim to have had the born again experience, and the 20 percent figure for Catholics seems reasonable. As one might expect, the percentage rises as one scans from low to high tension across the Protestant groups, to the maximum percentage, 80 percent for the sect members. Born agains are strewn across Table 15.4, not limited to the sects and conservative denominations. The born again movement cuts across the boundaries that separate formal religious organizations. It is a popular movement touching many in each denomination who wish intense religion, high tension individuals who might choose a sect or conservative denomination if they were to decide affiliation afresh.

A glance at the table strongly suggests that the born agains are creating much of the variation from left to right in the other variables. The final column in Table 15.4 shows how strongly each of the other religion variables is associated with being born again in a series of nine ex-

TABLE 15.4 *Religious Attitudes and Religious Affiliation — Percent Giving Indicated Response*

	257 with no Affiliation	323 Catholics	Protestants				Association (gamma) with Born Again
			180 Liberal	269 Moderate	57 Conservative	35 Sect Members	
1. Attend church once a week or more often	0	33	8	20	34	74	.67
2. Their religious beliefs are "very important" to them	8	38	27	34	52	80	.76
3. Respondent is born again	6	20	25	34	52	80	—
4. Strongly agrees "I definitely believe in God."	9	60	48	58	67	89	.79
5. Strongly agrees: "God or some other supernatural force has a very strong influence on my life."	4	30	23	31	51	66	.80
6. Agrees: "Suffering often comes about because people don't obey God."	6	22	22	32	49	67	.68
7. Disagrees: "Man evolved from lower animals."	9	34	28	42	53	89	.68
8. Strongly agrees: "Miracles actually happened just as the Bible says they did."	3	24	23	34	44	66	.77
9. Likes religious books and articles.	5	20	24	32	44	68	.72
10. Likes hymns and spirituals	12	18	31	36	44	68	.64

tremely powerful coefficients. We have already seen that being born again or Catholic (or both) is almost a requirement for students who attend church frequently. Indeed, 91 percent of those who attend religious services once a week or more are born again or Catholic, and less than 5 percent of the Protestants who are not born again attend church this often.

Whatever their "opinions" and "beliefs" may be, it is hard to say that Protestant students who are not born again have any real religion at all. They seldom attend church; so they cannot be said to be members of congregations. Their religious beliefs, however precious, seem irrelevant to their friendships. Some Catholics appear to derive similar meaning from their church as do born agains from their movement, and, of course, the Catholic church is the most influential formal religious organization in the world. Apart from these powerful social influences, religion does not appear salient for our students' friendships. We have shown that traditional Christian religion takes on importance for personal relations to the extent that it is embodied in vigorous formal organizations (which the liberal Protestant denominations do not seem to be for our students) or in active social movements, such as the born again phenomenon.

The Occult

Our hypothesis about cults is the same as our hypothesis about Christian religion: Occult beliefs and attitudes become salient for personal relationships only if they are associated with social movements or vigorous formal organizations. In earlier chapters, we distinguished three levels of cultic involvement — audience cults, client cults, and cult movements — and found they have different patterns of geographic distribution. Audience cults show little if any social organization, no membership lists or formal requirements for participation, and represent little more than consumer activity. Widely shared superstitions, such as belief in ESP, and individual, low cost consumer products, such as occult literature, are examples. Somewhat more organized are client cults, which provide occult services for individual customers, for example, the casting of horoscopes by professional astrologers. Cult movements are well-organized, fully religious bodies, novel or exotic supernaturally oriented groups ordinarily called cults. We found that cult movement rates show the greatest geographic variation.

In general, cult movements are higher in tension with the sociocultural environment because they present more total challenges to conventional beliefs and practices than client cults (which focus on narrow areas of human concern) and audience cults (which tend merely to offer vague, vicarious satisfactions and entertainment). Although few of our student respondents may be deeply involved in cults themselves, their attitudes toward cults of different types ought to reflect perceptions of how intensely each challenges conventional culture. Positive attitudes toward cult movements ought to reflect strong, socially relevant characteristics of respondents; therefore, they ought to be salient for personal relationships. At the other extreme, individual attraction to pale audience cults should not be salient for personal relationships. In this, cult movements are similar to the born again movement, and audience cults are like widely held religious beliefs detached from institutional support. Client cults should fall between the extremes, potentially salient for personal relationships, but not as strongly salient as cult movements. They probably display complex patterns of salience, along the lines of the subgroups in the population that use the services particular client cults provide.

Table 15.5 lists six questionnaire items concerning cults and the occult, with concordances between friendship pairs. They are arranged roughly in terms of the degree of tension and social organization behind them. Eastern practices, such as yoga, Zen, or Transcendental Meditation, are true cult movements. Of course, there are several yoga groups and various ways one can become involved in Zen, but these represent something like sects and denominations within these exotic traditions. Transcendental Meditation is the product of a specific social movement, embodied in a formal organization. As the strong concordance (gamma = 42) indicates, the cult movements are tied to factors extremely salient for college friendships. At the other extreme, private enjoyment of occult literature and that free-floating, uninstitutionalized, audience cult superstition, ESP, show no concordance.

Three items fall between these extremes, two about astrology and one about a variety of occult practices — tarot reading, seances, and psychic healing. Respondents have some freedom whether they are going to perceive these as client cults or as audience cults. Professional astrologers cast horoscopes for their clients, performing a client cult service. Similarly, persons may buy tarot readings, seances, and psychic healing from professionals. Newspapers and magazines spread impersonal horoscopes to millions of anonymous people in their audiences, and anyone can buy tarot cards. Students generally do not have contact with occult practitioners and mediums and may therefore place most occult practices in the category of entertaining fiction, acting like an audience rather than prospective clients. Whether they are aware of the many professional organizations, such as the local astrologers' guild (Weingarten, 1977), or know that the extension division of the university sponsors eight or ten astrology courses every quarter, they probably know that professional astrologers exist. In any case, the three putative

TABLE 15.5   *Concordances on Occult Belief*

	424 Close Friend Pairs	Controlling for Born Again and Sex			
		219 Neither Born Again Pairs	167 Female Pairs	105 Mixed Pairs	144 Male Pairs
1. "Some Eastern practices, such as Yoga, Zen, or Transcendental Meditation, are probably of great value."	.42	.32			
2. "There is much truth in Astrology — the theory that the stars, the planets, and our birthdays have a lot to do with our destiny in life."	.30	.18	.44	.25	.17
3. How much the respondent likes "your horoscope."	.27	.20	.29	.15	.11
4. "Some occult practices, such as Tarot reading, seances, or psychic healing, are probably of great value."	.19	.04			
5. How much the respondent likes occult literature.	.07				
6. Respondent's opinion on whether "E.S.P. (extra-sensory perception) exists, or not."	.00				

Note: Lack of a significant correlation renders controlling superfluous in empty cells.

client cult items show the expected concordances, falling between the cult movement and audience cult extremes.

One source of concordance for occult opinions is the opposition to cults exhibited by conservative Christian religion. Both cult movements and sect movements are high in tension with respect to the sociocultural environment, as we said in Chapter 2, but, rather than sympathizing with each other's status, they tend to condemn each other. Most notably, the sects vehemently assert that theirs is the only proper religious tradition, as we demonstrated in Chapter 3, and, in their constant status war with the liberal denominations, they assert superiority through claiming to fulfill the one true heritage. Thus, they reject cults, representatives of alternative traditions, as threats to their sense of special value and righteousness (Lewis, 1966). For example, there is a strong negative relationship (gamma = −.47) between being born again and feeling that yoga, Zen, and Transcendental Meditation are probably of great value. In the second column of Table 15.5, we have removed the born agains from the analysis once more to see how much of the concordances on occult beliefs and attitudes were due to rejection by members of the high tension born again movement.

The two audience variables, occult literature and ESP, did not require controlling for born again, but the concordance on three occult practices is driven from .19 down to an invisible .04. The Eastern practices and two astrology items are depressed somewhat, but retain significant concordances. Thus, we see once more the power of the born again movement in affecting salience of supernatural belief for personal relationships, but we also see that the cult movement item and astrology are salient in their own rights.

We might be content to end the analysis there, but the two astrology items present interesting relationships with other variables that deserve examination. Female respondents are more likely than males to say they believe in astrology and to say they like their horoscopes. Twenty-one percent of the women, but only 15 percent of the men, agree with the statement about the truth of astrology. Thirty-eight percent of the men, but only 26 percent of the women, strongly disagree with the statement. Thirty-two percent of the women, but only 16 percent of the men, give "your horoscope" a preference rating of four or more on a seven-point scale from zero (do not like) to six (like very much). The correlation between sex and astrology demands that we control for sex in Table 15.5. Of the 424 close friend pairs, 167 are known to be composed of two women, 144 of two men, and 105 are mixed male-female pairs. When we examine concordances on the astrology items in the three types of pair, as reported in the third through fifth columns of Table 15.5, we find that the concordances rise for female pairs and drop for mixed and male pairs. The concordances for male pairs would essentially vanish if we further controlled for born again. It seems that astrology is salient for women's friendships, but not for men's. Earlier we suggested that client cults may be salient for personal relationships of those subgroups that are the most likely customers, and here we see evidence in support of this proposition. Women are more favorably disposed toward astrology, and it, in turn, is more salient for their friendships.

CONCLUSION

Living religion is a social enterprise, and religious beliefs take on significance for human affairs only as they are tied to social exchanges. Lone individuals, and even pairs of exchange partners, are seldom able to sustain strong supernatural orientations without powerful outside assistance, as we noted in chapters 8 and 12. Therefore, vigorous, formal religious organizations and social movements can give beliefs and attitudes considerable salience for personal relationships; in the absence of such mass social support, beliefs and attitudes are not generally salient.

Our research used a network sample of 1,439 college students to explore these propositions. We found that matters of individual taste, such as cigarette smoking, tend to be quite salient for personal relationships, and objectively important ideological positions may not be, unless rendered salient (like religion) through influential social structures. Several religious beliefs and attitudes proved salient, but the concordances tended to collapse when members of the born again social movement were removed from the analysis. Membership in the born again movement, and attitude toward a triad of Eastern cult movements, showed great salience for friendships, further illustrating the pivotal importance of vigorous social movements for energizing attitudes toward the supernatural and rendering them salient for human relations in the mundane world.

Our research incidentally discovered profound weakness in the more liberal Protestant denominations. Indeed, many Protestants who were not born again seemed to act more like an audience than a congregation, treating their religious beliefs as attractive but unimportant notions, just like the vague fantasies of audience cults. In many respects, the Catholics and Protestants who are not born again often respond very much like those with no religion, even on matters for which religion ought to be relevant, as we see again in Chapter 17. It has long been suggested that Americans of different religious origins are converging on a single, American brand of religion (Herberg, 1955; Bellah, 1970a). In the university's student body, the point of convergence seems to be one of no religion at all, but a significant minority of students seems bound in the opposite direction, toward renewed, traditional, intense religious involvement.

The cultural environment in which our study was done, Washington state, has the lowest church membership rate in the nation, and the entire West Coast, from Alaska through British Columbia, Washington, and Oregon to Southern California, is weak in conventional religion and especially open to radical supernatural alternatives such as cult movements. This means not only that similar studies done outside the West might find lower rates of respondents with no religious affiliation and less acceptance of cults, but also that religious beliefs and attitudes might show broader salience. In more religious environments, religion might retain its salience even when born agains, or other high tension respondents, are removed from the analysis. Such findings would not disconfirm our results, but rather support and extend them. In other parts of the country, a greater portion of the population is probably bound into social structures that render religion salient, whether these structures are formal organizations or community-based social movements. Our sample of respondents was especially good for present research purposes because it included balanced groups of persons all across the religious spectrum, from those with no affiliation to born agains. But whatever the mix of religious affiliations, belief and attitude will be salient for personal relationships to the extent that they are promoted by vigorous organizations and social movements.

16 *The Arithmetic of Social Movements: Theoretical Implications*

WITH LYNNE ROBERTS

Knowledge of the rise of mass movements is oddly misshapen. A great deal of attention has been paid to why and how individuals join such movements, especially religious movements. Somewhat less attention has been paid to the tactics movements use to gain followers (cf. Lofland, 1966; Balch and Taylor, 1977; Bainbridge, 1978c; Bromley and Shupe, 1979). But virtually no attention has been paid to the implications of growth for the structure and fate of social movements per se. It is recognized, of course, that movements must grow in order to succeed. But, beyond this truism, growth is not examined from the point of view of movements rather than from the point of view of individual recruits and recruiters.

Here we depart from this restricted view. In this chapter, we pay little attention to why people join social movements. Instead, we postulate a small, new religious cult movement and consider the implications of growth for this movement per se. What growth rates are needed for this group to be successful under a variety of conditions? What factors govern what growth rates can be achieved? What are the consequences of various growth rates for the morale of the movement's founders and for maintaining the movement's original ideology?

In pursuit of these matters, we sometimes draw upon data for partic-

This chapter is a revision of a paper published as Rodney Stark and Lynne Roberts, "The Arithmetic of Social Movements: Theoretical Implications," *Sociological Analysis*, 1982, 43, pp. 53–68.

ular cult movements. But, for the most part, we rely on "thought experiments." Given certain likely assumptions, what are the arithmetic possibilities, and what are the likely implications of various outcomes? Some readers undoubtedly will object that such an approach is merely hypothetical. We respond that pursuit of the hypothetical can establish clear limits on the possible. Moreover, we hope to show that a lack of awareness of the arithmetic of growth rates often has obscured the vision not only of social scientists studying social movements, but, more important, of movement founders and their first generation of followers.

Although we focus our discussion on a cult movement, our conclusions apply to any social movement that begins with but a few members and seeks to establish a permanent and highly committed mass following. Keep in mind that cults always start small. Successful sects often result from schisms within organizations so large that they begin life with a large number of members. But innovative cults that offer new conceptions of the supernatural and unfamiliar compensators inevitably begin in a very small social group. As described in Chapter 8, an individual may invent or discover a new religion, or one may emerge within an intensely interacting small group. Only then can recruitment begin. Our concern in this chapter is with what happens to groups after the initial founding nucleus has formed and the effort to spread the faith has commenced.

By combining a series of arithmetic projections with theoretically grounded assumptions, we hope to demonstrate the following conclusions:

1. In large societies, cults must grow at extremely high annual rates in order to become numerically significant within a generation or two.

2. Despite relatively high rates of annual growth, the small absolute number of recruits gained during the first generation is a plausible reason why cult founders so typically lose hope and turn movements inward.

3. Given certain restrictions on who is available for recruitment, cult members must form implausibly high numbers of strong bonds with outsiders in order to sustain "adequate" growth rates.

4. Simple calculations about the formation of cult nuclei sustain widely held impressions about the "charisma" of cult founders.

5. The arithmetic of expanding social networks suggests that an initial high rate of cult growth often is braked because the founder is "smothered" by internal relationships, thus preventing the formation of relations with new potential members.

6. Rates of growth that doom cults in large societies can produce

success for cults in small societies or in a small population segment, such as a political elite.

7. Cults can grow more rapidly when they spread through preexisting networks than when they recruit from among social isolates.

8. Cults probably are easier to start in large, loosely integrated societies.

9. Cults probably are more likely to succeed in smaller, more tightly integrated societies.

10. Even quite modest growth rates will result in the majority of cult members being converts rather than socialized members at all points in time.

11. Growing cults will tend to retain their doctrinal intensity indefinitely.

GROWTH RATES

We begin with a hypothetical cult that consists of 20 members. We need not be concerned with details of their doctrine, but only with what growth rates they need in order to amount to something over a reasonable interval of time. For now, we shall assume that this cult is operating within a large society — one with, say, a population of 50 million or more.

Suppose that over the first year of observation our cult attracts two new members. This is a growth rate of 10 percent for the year. Let us assume this rate is maintained for the indefinite future. Let us also suppose that no one ever quits the group and that the group is demographically stable — births equal deaths so there is no growth through fertility and no decline through mortality. With a 10 percent annual growth rate, will this group become large over a reasonable time span? In part, that depends upon what one means by "large" and how long is a "reasonable" time span. But, as is shown in Table 16.1, at a 10 percent annual growth rate, in 10 years, this group will have 52 members. In 20 years, it will number only 135. In 40 years, it will number only 905. Even after 100 years it will number only 275,000.

If our group grows at twice this rate, at 20 percent per year, it still grows very slowly, having only 124 members after a decade and 767 after 20 years of recruitment efforts. Indeed, a group that maintains an annual growth rate of 20 percent for 40 years will still number only slightly more than 29,000 — and that is a small absolute size if the surrounding society is large. Of course, the table shows that, should a group keep up a 20 percent annual growth rate for 100 years, it would be triumphant even in the largest society, for, at that rate, it would have gained 1.6 billion members.

TABLE 16.1 *Consequences of Various Annual Growth Rates for Cult Membership*

Annual Growth Rate — Percent	Absolute Number of Members				
	After 10 Years	After 20 Years	After 40 Years	After 100 Years
10	52	135	905	275,612
20	124	767	29,395	1.6 billion
30	276	3800	722,377	4.9 billion
40	578	16,733	14 million	8.2 billion
50	1153	66,505	221 million	81 billion

Note: Assumptions here include an initial nucleus of 20 members, no defections, and a balance of births and deaths.

The table shows that, even when a 30 percent annual growth rate is assumed, growth in absolute numbers is slow over the first two decades: After 10 years, the group would have only 276 members, and, after 20, it would have 3,800. Indeed, to become numerically strong during one generation, a cult must grow at a truly phenomenal rate.

Consider the case of the Unification Church, popularly known as the Moonies. When first observed in late 1962 (Lofland and Stark, 1965), they had but 20 members in the United States — the same total as our hypothetical cult. There were about 6,000 Moonies in the United States in 1980. In the context of American society, 6,000 people mean little numerically. Yet, in order to achieve this rate of growth in about 17 years, the Moonies must have maintained a 40 percent annual growth rate. This is an extraordinary performance. If they could keep this up for another 13 years, there would be 500,000 American Moonies.

GROWTH AND HOPE

Even for our hypothetical group, it seems reasonable to suppose that its members are mortal and that they experience hope and disappointment. When we consider the small absolute size of our group after 20 years of active recruitment, even with high annual rates of increase, it ought not surprise us that cults so often lose heart and turn inward.

You have discovered the true religion. You have set out to bring it to the world, or at least to a significant portion of your society. You have worked hard at this task for 20 years. Even though you have grown at a rate of 30 percent a year, there are still fewer than 4,000 persons who have responded to the word. True enough, if you could keep this up for *another* 20 years, you would have more than 700,000 members. But this, too, would be a very small religious group in a large society. Moreover, the prospects of even this level of success must seem dim to people who already have given their all and have not yet been rewarded by a really impressive increase in absolute numbers of converts.

Let us assume that our cult founder began his or her efforts to start a new religious movement at age 35. The first several years were spent gathering the original founding nucleus of 20. Let us assume that converts are about the same age as the founder. Twenty years later, they remain the most influential followers of the movement. Like the founder, they are not so young anymore — they are in their middle to late fifties. Even if they accepted our arithmetic projections about growth over the next 20 years, they would not expect to live to see the movement become large, let alone dominant. Moreover, people are not adept at interpreting their affairs in terms of compound rates. They tend, instead, to project the past into the future in terms of absolute rather than geometric increases — to think that 4,000 in 20 years projects as 8,000 in 40 years.

One reason a rapidly growing cult might not seem successful is that success may be measured not by a high rate of increase in members but by the low rate of decrease of nonmembers. Consider a cult such as the Moonies, which rapidly grew in only 17 years to 6,000 members. In a society of a constant 50 million population, this would mean that the proportion of nonmembers decreased over the 17 years only from 100 percent to 99.988 percent. A given cult member, encountering other citizens entirely at random, would accidentally meet a fellow member only about once in every 10,000 encounters. In an 18th year of 40 percent annual growth, when 2,400 members would be added, the number of nonmembers would decrease by only .005 percent. If the point of recruiting is to "convert" or "save" humanity, then even a cult as successful as this might feel a failure after 17 years because it had made no perceptible dent in the ranks of the unconverted.

The ethnographic and historical literature on cults abounds with examples of movements that, after a decade or two of growth, turned inward and ceased to seek converts (Dohrman, 1958; Whitworth, 1975; Bainbridge, 1978c, 1982). As we note in Chapter 13, doctrines once directed toward saving the world often shift to conceptions of an elect or a saving remnant of believers. We think our simple arithmetic computations help illuminate this common phenomenon. It takes truly astounding percentage rates of growth to produce a large absolute number of members over the course of one generation. In the absence of such response, it seems understandable that the first generation often loses heart and transforms the movement in ways that assuage its own waning hopes.

Of course, we have set no limits on potential growth rates. If a group of 20 grew by 100 percent per year, in 20 years, it would number 20 million members. But, because cults seem not to grow at such high rates, it seems time to impose some further assumptions on our calculations.

LIMITS ON RECRUITMENT

Not all members of a population can be recruited into a cult movement. Although the proportion of potential converts will vary from time to time and from one society to another (we explore some of these variations later in this chapter), several categories of people are very unlikely to be converted. For example, studies find that people who do not accept the existence of an active supernatural do not join cult movements.

This is more than tautology. One supposes that people who do not believe in the supernatural could be convinced of its existence during the recruitment process. But the very deviant nature of cult religion typically means that the visitor to the cult is bombarded with supernatural images. Apparently, like high tension sects, many cults need to assert their difference from the world and express their antagonism to it through constant brandishment of their novel compensators. Lofland and Stark (1965) and Barker (1984) found that such cults could recruit only persons who already possessed supernatural belief, that such an orientation was a necessary precondition (or background factor). In contemporary America, this factor would reduce the pool of cult recruits by perhaps 10 percent and by considerably more in some contemporary European nations.

There are exceptions, to be sure, cults that do not broadcast supernatural demands at newcomers. But consider the three we have discussed already at length in this book: Scientology, Transcendental Meditation, and the Mormons. In chapters 12 and 13, we explain how difficult it is for a cult to offer desirable compensators that do not appear religious—that an emphasis on apparently scientific claims for magical compensators rather than on superempirical, supernatural compensators is a very precarious strategy that is bound to fail in the long run. We suspect that, although "secular magic" may draw upon a pool of recruits, some of whom lack supernatural beliefs, and thus have a higher recruitment rate, the defection rate also will be high because people will discover for themselves the empirical shortcomings of the compensators. Although we report in Chapter 14 that the Mormons deemphasize their religious doctrines and practices until late in the recruitment process, this fact does not present us with a counterexample. Because of their exceptional success, the Mormons have long outgrown the stages in development covered by this chapter. Indeed, they are realistically confident enough in their religion that they do not need to defend it through loud proclamations of faith that might repel persons not already imbued with religious attitudes.

A second category of persons unlikely to be potential recruits are those firmly committed to another religious organization or cult movement. People whose religious needs are being met adequately do not take up an alternative faith. At present, about 56 percent of Americans are official members of a particular religious congregation. Not all of them are active or well-satisfied members, of course. Many others who are not official members continue to hold conventional religious beliefs, to pray, and to claim a cultural affiliation with a particular denomination. Thus, roughly three-quarters of the U.S. population probably are not available for conversion to a non-Christian cult movement.

Depending on the way the surrounding sociocultural environment responds to cults, the pool may be limited still further. For example, if cult participation is treated as extremely deviant and consistently punished, persons who have a stake in the conventional society, and thus have something to lose, will be unlikely to join. However, if cults are permitted but have not yet penetrated the culture, then only persons well connected to channels of communication may be sufficiently aware of their novel assumptions to be likely recruits. Although we are not prepared to assert any firm estimates of the pool of potential recruits for cult movements, it is clear that this pool is very limited in many societies.

More than one cult will be dipping into this pool. Recall that Chapter 9 is based on a tabulation of 501 different cults in America, each competing with the others for recruits. There were 2.3 cults per million population, or, to turn that ratio over, one cult for every 435,000 people. A quarter of these will be children 16 years old or younger, not yet able to adopt a new religious affiliation. And, as we suggested, more than three-quarters of the adults will be prevented by church membership or resolute irreligiousness from joining. Thus, each cult's potential recruit pool would be well under 100,000 persons. Of course, some cults take a disproportionate share of the recruits, and others lose out in the competition. Many cults respond to the competition by focusing their efforts on a particular, small segment of the population, seeking safe growth by responding especially to its needs. But each of the many cults has only a tiny minority of the population as its effective pool of recruits, and, before it can convert them to membership, it must *find* them.

By now it is well established that recruitment to cult movements flows through networks of social relations. Whatever else enters into recruitment, it seems necessary that a person must possess or develop a strong interpersonal attachment to a member of the group. But if not just anyone can be recruited to a cult movement, then not all such bonds will result in recruitment. A most important finding from Eileen Barker's major study of recruitment to the Moonies in Great Britain helps illuminate this point. Barker (1979, 1981, 1984) collected data from all persons attending two-day weekend workshops run by the Moonies in London during 1971 as a first step in seeking recruits.

Table 16.2 shows the attrition of these potential recruits as they moved from the start of the two-day workshop through progressively longer ones. During the first weekend, 13 percent dropped out before it was over. Fifty-five percent dropped out before undertaking a seven-

TABLE 16.2   *Attrition of Persons Being Recruited by the Unification Church in London During 1971*

Percent That Began a Two-Day Unification Workshop Who:	
Stayed to the End	87
Returned to Begin a Seven-Day Workshop	45
Completed the Seven-Day Workshop	33
Returned for a Three-Week Workshop	22
Completed the Three-Week Workshop	11
Were Unification Members One Year Later	4.6

Source: Barker (1984).

day workshop, and only 33 percent actually stayed through this week. Twenty-two percent continued into the three-week workshop, and only 11 percent completed it. Of those who began the whole workshop process, only 4.6 percent were members of the church a year later.

All these people had *some* prior contact with the Moonies — enough to get them to the first weekend. Some who filled out Barker's questionnaire during the first two-day workshop indicated they did not believe in God. None of them returned for a seven-day workshop. Others found the weekend boring or incompatible with their conventional religious commitment. In addition, many newcomers probably failed to develop (and did not already possess) close interpersonal relations with Moonie members during the first weekend — hence the very high dropout rate. However, it seems reasonable to assume that those who came back for a whole week of immersion in Unification teachings had more significant ties to the group. Still, substantial attrition continued. Moreover, of those who stayed through the whole sequence, completing the three-week session, more than half did not become Moonies or did so only briefly.

These data suggest that there are severe restrictions on the pool of potential recruits to the Unification Church in England. Presumably, those who attend an initial workshop are not a random cross-section of the English public, but already have been screened considerably. If so, then the English pool must be substantially less than 5 percent. These data are in agreement with observations of the first American cell of the Unification church during its operations in San Francisco during 1962 and 1963. Only about 1 person in 20 who attended meetings of the group eventually joined. Of course, the potential pool of Moonies in Britain and the United States could be smaller or larger than that for many other cult movements (compare TM in Chapter 13). But these data do encourage the assumption that very significant limits face all such movements. Therefore, let us make some assumptions about pool limits and explore their implications.

Assume that, in order for a recruitment to occur, a cult member must form a close interpersonal bond or activate a preexisting bond with an outsider. If each member could do this once a year, and if nothing else influenced recruitment, then the group would double in membership annually. But other things do influence recruitment. To the extent that outsiders are unavailable for recruitment, many bonds cult members form or already possess to outsiders will not produce a recruit.

In Table 16.3, we explore various estimates of potential recruitment pools and see what this implies for the number of interpersonal bonds an average cult member must form or activate annually in order to achieve various rates of growth. If we assume that only 1 percent of the population are potential recruits, then, in order to achieve even the very low growth rate of 10 percent per year, each cult member must form or activate 10 interpersonal bonds. To grow at a 40 percent rate, as the American Moonies have done, requires 40 such bonds each year. In our judgment, these figures are implausible. Humans simply cannot form so many relationships so quickly. Moreover, as we see in a later section, many cult members are likely to be quite deficient in social skills. If so, then the more skilled members would have to produce staggering numbers of intense interpersonal bonds a year to achieve even modest growth rates.

However, if 5 percent of the population consists of potential recruits, the picture becomes more credible. The average Moonie would need to

TABLE 16.3 *Growth Determined by Population Pools and Interpersonal Bonds*

Average Number of Bonds Needed Per Member Per Year if	To Achieve Annual Growth of				
	10%	20%	30%	40%	50%
Only 1 Percent of Population is Recruitable	10	20	30	40	50
Only 5 Percent of Population is Recruitable	2	4	6	8	10
Only 10 Percent of Population is Recruitable	1	2	3	4	5
Only 20 Percent of Population is Recruitable	.5	1	1.5	2	2.5

Note: Assumptions here include an initial nucleus of 20 members, no defections, and a balance of births and deaths.

create or activate only eight bonds a year to produce a 40 percent growth rate. And, as the potential pool becomes even larger, a correspondingly higher proportion of bonds will produce recruits and a correspondingly smaller number of such bonds per member is needed. Thus, if 20 percent of the population is potential Moonies, then each member needs only two bonds a year to produce a 40 percent growth rate.

The major implication of this hypothetical arithmetic is that most cults probably remain so small because their pool of potential recruits is such a small percentage of the population that most member contacts are unproductive. Clearly, the size of the potential pool differs both among cult movements and societies. But unless the pool is substantial, it will remain largely untapped. Cult members will dissipate their efforts on the unconvertible. This is exacerbated because, as most cult members will testify, it is difficult a priori to distinguish potential recruits from others — at least not until after a very substantial investment of time and affect has been made. Thus, for example, many with a very positive initial reaction to cult doctrine do not join, and many with quite negative initial reactions do join.

CHARISMA

Sociologists often decry journalistic use of the term *charisma* to mean merely an unusual capacity to influence others, to inspire intense liking and respect from others, as a woeful corruption of Weber. Yet we think this might be the most useful definition of charisma if it is to be used at all to describe cult founders. Indeed, we suspect that this is exactly why sociologists so often apply the term *charisma* to the special qualities of cult founders. For cults to get started requires a founder able to attract others, to convince them to accept a new truth. Converts often will report how strongly attracted they were to the leader and hence to the movement. Indeed, given the centrality of close interpersonal bonds in the conversion process, cult leaders can succeed only if they have unusual social skills.

Let us reconsider our hypothetical cult. Recall that we assumed it already had 20 members. Now let us examine how these 20 people were drawn into the movement. If we start with a lone cult founder without followers and suppose even a very high 50 percent annual growth rate, in five years, the group would have grown to only 7.5 persons. That is far short of our initial group of 20. Indeed, for a founder to recruit a group of 20 in the first five years of effort requires an annual growth rate of nearly 90 percent. We know that is unrealistically high for most cults once they have gotten going. But it seems *typical* for the first five years of almost any cult that has ever come to scholarly notice —cult leaders usually are able to attract 20 or more followers over the first five years of the movement. This suggests that they are uncommonly skilled at recruiting. Indeed, unless such recruiting skill were uncommon, cults would continue to grow at much higher rates than they do. Thus, simple arithmetic reveals that the vast majority of cult founders must have been extremely skilled at building strong interpersonal ties with others. In this sense, then, they deserve to be called charismatic.

Smothering the Leader

That cults must grow at extraordinary rates if they are to gain a founding nucleus, after which they usually grow at a much slower rate, suggests an important trend in the career of cults. As the group gets larger, the leader's contribution to the growth rate must decline.

We have seen that cult formation is possible because leaders are gifted recruiters. Suppose nothing interferes with this gift and each year the leader is able to convert the same number of new recruits as before. Even so, these new recruits will constitute a declining growth rate if the leader is the only effective recruiter. A constant number is a declining percentage of a growing number. Thus, to the extent that cult growth rests on the recruiting skills of a single leader or of a small group of founders, growth will be progressively slower. This must be quite common because so many cults do reach a size of 50 to 100 and then stall. Moreover, it seems unlikely that a cult leader could continue indefinitely even to produce the same number of converts each year.

Cult leaders will tend to become swamped in internal social relations as the group gets larger. Because people join cults on the basis of close interpersonal bonds, to the extent that the leaders play the major role in early recruitment, they will tend to be the foci of the group's social network. This, in turn, will limit their capacity to continue to form new bonds with outsiders. As this develops, leaders will bring in a declining number of new recruits.

Declining Social Skills

To the extent that cults depend upon the formation of bonds between members and outsiders for recruitment (as opposed to spreading through preexisting bonds), recruits will be overselected for lack of interpersonal skills. Studies of recruitment report that converts were very deficient in social bonds prior to recruitment (cf. Lofland and Stark, 1965; Bainbridge, 1978c; Lynch, 1979; cf. Chapter 14). Such people are most accessible to forming intense social bonds with cult members and are little restricted from recruitment by their bonds with outsiders.

Some recruits lack social bonds because of circumstances. For example, they may be newly arrived strangers in the city where they encountered the cult movement. But, for many others, their lack of bonds reflects limited ability to form such bonds. They were very approachable because of their unfulfilled desire for social relations, but not very good at approaching, and for that reason lacking in relations. People with excellent social skills and many firm attachments to others are not high probability recruits. For such people, there is no special premium in finding a warm reception from cult members. But for the wallflowers of life, to be treated as very socially valuable is a heady experience.

From this it follows that those most readily recruited by cult movements will tend to be below average in social skills or interpersonal attractiveness. Yet, if the cult is to continue to grow, these recruits must become effective recruiters. Sometimes a period of immersion in warm relations inside the group enables recruits to develop effective social skills. But often they remain of limited capacity to win friends and influence people. As the proportion of such persons rises in a cult movement, the growth rate will decline. This, too, must inform the common observation that cult movements often stall after an early period of growth and that they frequently fall apart upon the death or withdrawal of the founder.

SIZE AND STRUCTURE OF SOCIETY

Thus far we have been considering the arithmetic of growth in the context of a large society — 50 million or more. We have seen that, even with quite optimistic assumptions about annual recruitment rates, groups grow very slowly during the first generation. Such growth rates are independent of the size of the target population so long as that population is large enough to provide the additional needed recruits. This being the case, growth rates that frustrate hope among the founding generation in large societies are adequate to spell success in small societies.

Small Groups
Consider a small tribe of several hundred. Even a very modest rate of growth, say 10 percent, would lead to the conversion of the majority within a 20-year span. Even in relatively larger pastoral or agrarian societies, the small absolute numbers recruited over the first 20 years would be relatively large.

Thus, it may be much harder for cults to succeed in modern societies simply because such societies are so large. In the context of large populations, even high percentage rates of growth yield relatively small numbers of members over the first generation. This seems a paradox; large societies seem to offer so many more *potential* members. But the arithmetic of growth shows that, the larger the society, the larger the apparently unfulfilled potential growth, at least in the critical early period.

It may well be harder for cults to get their initial nucleus together in small, stable, traditional societies. But, if they do, it is much easier for them to find hope and power in the same set of absolute numbers that can crush hope in large societies. Indeed, our impression of the historic record is that cults have more often triumphed in small societies. Exactly the same number of recruits that made, for example, the Ghost Shirt Dancers a major historical phenomenon among the Plains Indians would have constituted but another small, curious cult in the context of any 19th-century industrialized nation.

Small societies are not, of course, the only small groups relevant to cult formation. Elites are often small groups, especially in societies with highly centralized power. And here, too, small absolute numbers can take on great relative importance. Thus, to get a cult started among members of the Roman imperial court or the Party elite in the Soviet Union and to acquire a few thousand members in 20 years would promise great success for the movement. The conversion of a society has often occurred in precisely this fashion. The Vikings were not Christianized because monks went from farm to farm, leading the peasants to Christ. Instead, the monks converted the nobility, and the peasants did what they were told. By the same token, Lysenko did not spread his magical claims of acquired genetic characteristics among collectivized farmers, but among the ruling Soviet elite (Medvedev, 1971). The arithmetic of growth rates is inexorable, but its relative meaning depends upon context.

Pools and Networks

Clearly, societies differ in the proportions of their populations that are potential recruits for a new religious movement—indeed, a society may vary in this respect quite dramatically over time. At least two factors influence recruitment pools: (1) the degree of social integration of the society and (2) the strength of a society's conventional religious organizations.

If we think of societies as relatively closed networks of social relations, their degree of social integration is the proportion of members having strong ties within this network. Conversely, to the extent that societies contain persons who are only weakly connected to others, such societies are poorly integrated (cf. Durkheim, 1897). Given what we know about the cult recruitment process, it must follow that poorly integrated societies will contain larger proportions of potential recruits (other things being equal). Joining a cult is not simply a function of forming a bond with a member, but also of having relatively weak bonds to nonmembers. The more numerous and strong the bonds an individual has to noncult members, (1) the more such bonds will restrain entry into a deviant group and (2) the less likely that a person will form strong bonds with cult members, for the less such a person is open to new relationships and the less important such relationships are in the person's overall interpersonal economy.

From these considerations, it follows that the more socially unattached members a society contains, the easier it will be to start a cult, as there is a greater probability that a given cult founder will meet and form bonds with enough people to get a movement going. Other things being equal, then, it will be easier to *found* cults in modern industrial societies than in more stable agrarian societies. But it may be in the more stable societies that cults, if started, have the best probability of real success.

People do not turn to new religions if their old religion serves them adequately. The abundance of cults in modern times stems not only from poor social integration, but from the progressive weakening of the long-dominant religious organizations. The loss of commitment to an active supernatural by leading Christian denominations, for example, has left these bodies with but tepid means for dealing with fundamental human concerns. As such changes take place in societies, the proportions who are open to new, more satisfying religion grow. In chapters 19, 20, and 21, we test this theoretical proposition rigorously through quantitative analysis of good empirical data. The secularization of conventional faiths periodically creates market openings for new religions.

However, such market opportunities can occur suddenly as well. Natural disasters, economic collapse, war, contact with more advanced societies, and other causes of social disorganization can overwhelm the conventional religious system. In such circumstances, new religions often spring up. Some scholars claim that *all* successful new religions originate during social crises (cf. Wallace, 1956). In such crises, one need not look to social isolates to recruit cult members, for cults can form and prosper among those well integrated into the society.

Crises need not envelop a whole society for new religions to prosper. If an integrated subgroup within a society is particularly deprived and available faiths fail to suffice, a major market opportunity is created for a new faith. We may note the frequency with which new religions have sprung up among dissatisfied peasants and the frequency of millenarian cult outbursts in medieval cities straining under feudalism.

We may pull many of these themes together by postulating two societies. Society A, like modern industrial societies, is not highly integrated. Perhaps as many as a third of its members have but few or weak ties to others. Society B is preindustrial, and no more than 5 percent of its members are poorly attached to others.

Other things being equal, it will be much easier to found a cult in society A. It will be relatively easier to locate social "atoms," people lacking ties that would restrain them from joining and for whom the opportunity for close ties with members will facilitate joining. Moreover, both experience and selection will amplify a tendency to recruit social isolates. In societies having many unintegrated people, cult members will learn from experience that such people are more easily recruited and may shape their recruitment tactics, and even their doctrines, to maximize appeal to the unattached. For example, the Moonies in California developed various singles parties and activities in order to attract the unattached and then concentrated on "love bombing" such newcomers in order to construct intense bonds (Bromley and Shupe, 1979). In addition, there will be a selection bias in favor of groups that concentrate on the unattached, for they will more easily build a sufficient nucleus to amount to something. As mentioned, of course, such groups will thereby tend to overrecruit persons deficient in social skills. Such groups will also maximize the need to depend upon new social bonds in order to grow. That is, by overselecting members lacking in social bonds, they will not gain access to a preexisting network of relationships along which the group can grow by converting new members. Finally, when a cult movement is based on the unattached, it will exhaust the potential pool of recruits without converting the majority of members of society A, for, even in poorly integrated, modern societies, most people are not unattached social atoms, but enjoy dense and intense relations to others.

In society B, few are unattached. In such a society, we doubt that cults will focus on the unattached, for it will be clear from the start that their numbers are too few. Here success rests on making headway among the well-attached. Obviously, this is a much greater initial challenge. One cannot just appeal to marginal people, but must find means to attract the main body of society. That often will be difficult or even impossible, which is probably why cults are more numerous in poorly integrated societies. However, as we have already sketched, there are times when it is possible for a new religion to supplant an old one right at the center of the most integrated social network. Cult founders have no control over these conditions; they either come along at a favorable time or they remain in obscurity. But, if they do come with the right alternative at the right moment, they may achieve true success, for, when a cult movement gets going inside a well-integrated social network, amazing growth comes rapidly (cf. Granovetter, 1973). When a new religion penetrates a preexisting social network, the following occurs:

1. There will be no tendency to overrecruit persons deficient in social skills. Instead, recruits will possess the normal range of social skills.

2. Members need not possess unusual social skills in order for the movement to grow, for they will not need to form new bonds, but merely influence others with whom they long have had close relations.

3. Given even very modest assumptions about the social relations of the average new recruit, the movement will grow very rapidly.

Table 16.4 examines growth under these conditions. If a cult movement penetrates a well-integrated social network, we can assume that its appeal is not aimed at a marginal minority of the unattached, but will suit the majority. Hence, the potential pool is very large and most bonds will not be with the unrecruitable. Furthermore, the average recruit will have a number of such bonds prior to recruitment. If a religion has strong appeal for a given individual, it ought to appeal to that person's intimates. Hence, a new recruit ought to be able to recruit many of his or her friends and relatives.

Let us see how such preexisting bonds can cause rapid growth of a movement. Suppose that each new recruit has one preexisting bond that can be activated within two years after conversion to produce one additional recruit. Again assuming a nucleus of 20, we can see in the first column of Table 16.4 that only very slow growth would result—after 20

TABLE 16.4   *Impact of Prebonded (Network) Conversion on the Growth of a Group*

Years Since Group was Founded	Total Membership if Each Convert Quickly Brings In			
	1 New Member	2 New Members	3 New Members	4 New Members
0	20	20	20	20
2	40	60	80	100
4	60	140	260	420
6	80	300	800	1,700
8	100	620	2,420	6,820
10	120	1,260	7,280	27,300
12	140	2,540	21,830	109,220
14	160	5,100	65,570	436,900
16	180	10,220	196,790	1,747,620
18	200	20,460	590,450	6,990,500
20	220	40,940	1,771,430	27,962,020

years there would be only 220 members in the cult movement. But suppose that the average recruit has two preexisting bonds that can be activated for recruitment. Then after 20 years, the cult would have more than 40,000 members. If the average recruit possessed three preexisting bonds that could be activated within the first two years following conversion, the group would have nearly 1.8 million members in 20 years. If the average convert had four unique and recruitable preexisting bonds, the group would number almost 28 million members in 20 years.

In our judgment, we do not strain plausibility by supposing that an average recruit might produce four new members. If a group begins to recruit followers who are socially integrated members of a stable society, such growth seems quite plausible. Most such people would have many more than four close bonds to draw upon. In fact, we think columns three and four approximate what often has happened in history when a new religion has swept through a society or geographic area. The rise of new religions often does not take generations. Rather, like Islam, Christianity, and Buddhism, they have arisen with great rapidity. Indeed, we suspect that cult movements either get big fast or they are likely always to be small.

GROWTH AND ORTHODOXY

It is a commonplace that, once new religions have swept to a dominant position in a society, they tend to compromise their original stance toward the world. Once dominated by those with a substantial stake in this world, religious organizations tend to deemphasize their pristine otherworldliness. This is, of course, the well-known process by which sects are transformed into churches and by which churches are secularized until they no longer function adequately as religions. We have discussed this process at length in other chapters. Here we introduce an important consideration about *when* the secularization process is likely to make headway. How long can a successful new religious movement maintain its original orthodoxy? We believe a cult movement will remain very orthodox as long as it is growing at even a modest rate via recruitment.

We begin with the truism that "converts are more Catholic than the pope." Here is captured the recognition that people who take up a new faith because of the way in which it satisfies their religious needs are unlikely to favor changing that religion. More specifically, people who join a religious movement because of the potency of its "otherworldly" compensators will not want to weaken those compensators, for this would reduce the benefits they gain. Religions tend to be transformed from emphasis on the otherworldly to greater accommodation of this world when they are supported primarily by socialized, rather than converted, members and when many of their members have been upwardly mobile. As long as most members are converts, this process is likely to be greatly retarded.

Even with a very modest rate of annual growth via recruitment, a group will always contain a majority of converts among adult members, unless it also has a very high fertility rate. Even if a group's fertility is high, it will always contain a majority of converts if recruitment continues at any substantial rate.

It appears that successful cult movements gain relatively young recruits. We therefore assume that the average recruit will spend as many adult years in the group as will the average socialized member. That is, recruits will enter at the same age as socialized members become effective adults. Suppose that a group is growing via recruitment at a rate of 10 percent a year—a very slow growth rate. If we assume that the average member (whether recruited or socialized) spends 40 years as an adult member of the group, then for each adult, 0.1 new recruits will be added to the group annually, or 4 over their lifetimes. If we set fertility at replacement level—one offspring per adult member—then .025 new socialized members per adult will be added each year, or one over their lifetimes. Hence, recruits will outnumber socialized members by four to one indefinitely.

If we increase fertility so that the group doubles its members each generation, recruits will still outnumber socialized members by two to one indefinitely, even with only a 10 percent recruitment rate. For socialized members to overtake converts in numbers when a group recruits at a 10 percent annual rate, we must assume an even sex distribution and an average fertility of eight per female.

These calculations suggest that secularization of a religious movement will be impeded until significant growth by recruitment ceases. Growing movements retain their otherworldliness as a simple function of having a substantial majority of converted members. Hence, the Mormons' ability to withstand secularization probably rests upon their continuing rapid growth via recruitment. The ease with which converts rise to influential positions in Mormonism is probably due to the fact that they are not a small minority of newcomers, but a very sizeable proportion of the membership. The more rapidly a religious movement exhausts its recruitment potential, the more rapidly it will come to be dominated by socialized members. Thus, growth not only influences a religious movement's morale and its sense of destiny, but its fundamental store of zealous members.

CONCLUSION

Although hundreds of new religious movements form in modern societies, they rarely amount to much because modern societies are so large. Thus, social movements must grow at astonishing rates in order to reach significant size in a generation or two. Such rapid growth seems impossible unless it occurs within a well-integrated social network, for when recruitment depends upon the formation of bonds between members and outsiders, the arithmetic of rapid growth becomes implausible. Because most cults gather their initial nucleus from among those lacking in social bonds, the average recruit will be somewhat deficient in interpersonal skills, thus further limiting the prospects for rapid growth. Rapid early growth will decline as the founders become smothered in internal relationships.

To achieve the needed growth, new religions must appeal to mainstream members of a society, not only to marginal members. Rapid growth must travel along preexisting social relations — thus, the group must gain access to well-integrated members of a society. This seems to have been precisely how the truly successful historical religious movements did achieve their success. Jesus first recruited his immediate family, as did Mohammed. The case of Mormonism in the early 19th century is well documented. Joseph Smith's first followers were his family, a teacher who boarded in his home, and the closest neighbor family. Early Mormon growth flowed along a network of close kinship, spreading out from this initial nucleus as converts brought in their brothers, sisters, parents, aunts, and uncles. Under these conditions, Mormon growth boomed, and the rapid growth rate of modern Mormonism is based on the ability to appeal to well-integrated people, not just social isolates, and therefore to gain entry to new networks.

The bottom line seems to be that new religions must grow rapidly or fail. To grow rapidly, they must not be deluged with recruits who are social isolates. They must appeal primarily to the social mainstream. In this sense, prophets do not control their own destinies. They must not only discover the right religious message, but they must also appear in the right place at the right time, for only when dominant religions are failing to serve most people is there a real opportunity for a new faith to flourish in the heart of a society. Such moments may occur only rarely. Thus, although new religions constantly form, most are fated to oblivion. However, the constancy of religious innovation guarantees that, whenever conditions are right, there will be no anxious wait for the new messiah to appear. Salvation is always at hand.

17 *The "Consciousness Reformation" Reconsidered*

There is a powerful tradition among sociologists of religion to regard human beings as theologians or philosophers. It is assumed that people almost universally possess a relatively coherent, overarching, and articulated "Weltanschauung," "world view," "perspective," "frame of reference," "value orientation," or "meaning system" (Glock and Stark, 1965: 3–17). This assumption encourages purely cultural explanations. That is, with religion defined as a meaning system, variations in such a system are considered explained when they have been traced to internal, logical imperatives of the system itself or to ideological conflict and competition with other meaning systems. Hence, religious doctrines may change, it is thought, because of growing tension between major premises (faith and works, for example) or because of inroads made by a competing meaning system that possesses appealing elements absent from the religion in question (a clear promise of eternal life, for example).

This perspective was the main tradition within the sociology of religion until quite recently, and we have used it in our earliest work. Consider the opening paragraph of an essay about recruitment to cults (Lofland and Stark, 1965:862):

A much shorter version of this chapter was published as William Sims Bainbridge and Rodney Stark, "The 'Consciousness Reformation' Reconsidered," *Journal for the Scientific Study of Religion*, 1981, 20:1, pp. 1–16.

All men and all human groups have ultimate values, a world view, or a perspective furnishing them a more or less orderly and comprehensible picture of the world. Clyde Kluckhohn [1962:409] remarked that no matter how primitive and crude it may be, there is a "philosophy behind the way of life of every individual and of every relatively homogeneous group at any given point in their histories." When a person gives up one such perspective or ordered view of the world for another we refer to this process as *conversion.*

We can no longer endorse these words. However, we are not prepared to jettison the concept of *ultimate values* or *world view*, only the assumption that all humans and all societies swear allegiance to particular, coherent systems of meaning. Subsequent research has shown that many people do follow coherent systems of meaning — and that these people are those who possess traditional religious faith. Societies and individuals who are not fundamentally religious may lack ultimate values or a coherent set of beliefs about the nature of existence. But religion can provide them, for "at the core of all religions is a set of beliefs about the nature, meaning, and purpose of reality" (Glock and Stark, 1966:3).

Yet even within religion, this faith is a variable. As previous chapters would lead us to expect, the higher tension religious groups are better able than low tension churches to give their members a secure sense of meaning. One question included in the survey of Northern California church members reported in Chapter 3 was "How sure are you that you have found the answers to the meaning and purpose of life?" Sixty-eight percent of the Catholic respondents and 56 percent of the Protestants were certain they had found these answers. Less than half were certain in four of the lower tension Protestant denominations: United Church of Christ (39 percent), Methodists (42 percent), Episcopalians (45 percent), and American Lutherans (48 percent). Despite the fact that all respondents were church members, 10 percent felt, "I don't really believe there are answers to these questions."

Thus, we have come to doubt the tradition that assumes all human beings and groups possess coherent systems of values and beliefs. This issue has taken on great importance for our work because the newer emphasis on social relationships as the essence of commitment and conversion seems in direct competition with the older tradition. Either we must find ways of combining the two, as we do to some extent in Chapter 14, or we must abandon one in favor of the other. But evaluation of the older tradition has been very difficult because it was never asserted in the form of clear propositions that could be readily operationalized and tested. The empirical evidence was mainly qualitative and suggestive, rather than quantitative and conclusive. This situation has changed recently, since Robert Wuthnow performed the crucial service of operationalizing and apparently testing the older tradition, working as a highly articulate proponent of it, providing us the opportunity to build on his important work and progress toward a resolution of these great issues.

Wuthnow (1976a) has given what superficially appears to be extremely strong support for the older tradition through quantitative analysis of one of the largest and richest bodies of survey data on religion collected in the 1970s. In his book, *The Consciousness Reformation*, he analyzes part of the great trove of data he and his associates gathered from a random sample of San Francisco area residents in 1973, seeming to explain much of the variation in personal experimentation with new life-styles, including liberal sexual practices, political attitudes, drug use, and even experimentation with new religious alternatives. He attributes these cultural developments to the rise of several new meaning systems.

A close reading of Wuthnow's work caused us some unease, partly because we doubted the face validity of some of his key survey items. Our primary reaction was dissatisfaction with any explanation that is limited to interrelating elements of meaning systems. Meaning systems exist only as they have *social* meaning. All culture must be created, sustained, and transmitted. Hence, if there has been a "consciousness reformation," we want to know how it occurred in terms of concrete human activities. Given our efforts to trace meaning systems, especially religion, to social networks and social organizations, we were stimulated by Wuthnow's work to take it as a point of departure. Hence, we designed and conducted a study to explore the network basis of the competing meaning systems Wuthnow apparently had uncovered.

This chapter reports our results. Its fundamental focus is on the unfortunate fact that Wuthnow's seemingly solid base of empirical findings gave way beneath us. Through no methodological contortions — not even by basing our analysis on Wuthnow's original data — could we restore any semblance of his conclusions. What we report is the apparent nonexistence of the *new* meaning systems Wuthnow reported, or at least their nonexistence as he measured them. Thus, they could not be the source of the cultural experimentation he thought he had explained. Instead, we found that the effects Wuthnow reported are produced by the *old* meaning system — religion — and then only as it is embedded in religious organizations, not just in cognitive states. The actual relations are much more compatible with other work, and with a broader theoretical view, than were Wuthnow's wholly cultural interpretations.

Wuthnow is an important and conscientious colleague. We would hardly have set out to replicate and extend trivial work. Any scholar who tries to say important things is bound to be wrong quite often. It is as the champion of an army of social theorists that Wuthnow takes the field — for this he deserves much honor—and it is with that army that we wish to do battle.

MEANING SYSTEMS

Wuthnow's analysis begins with the major assumption we noted, shared by many social scientists but doubted by others: "Societies are organized with reference to systems of ultimate meaning" (Wuthnow, 1976a:vii). He further declares, "We also accept as given the assumption that people adopt relatively comprehensive or transcendent, but nonetheless identifiable, understandings of life which inform their attitudes and actions under a wide variety of conditions" (Wuthnow, 1976a:2). He calls these understandings *meaning systems* and defines them as "overarching symbolic frames of reference . . . by which people come to grips with the broader meaning and purpose of their lives" (Wuthnow, 1976a:2–3).

We believe these propositions should be treated as hypotheses, not as assumptions. Our view, elaborated throughout this book and elsewhere (Stark and Bainbridge, 1980), is that persons want general explanations about the meaning of life and about how they can obtain rewards and avoid costs. Perhaps all humans would like comprehensive understandings of life that unite many lesser conceptualizations of aspects of life under single, general principles. But, we suggest, such meaning systems are very difficult for the individual to construct and to defend both against other meaning systems and against empirical disconfirmation. Indeed, societies may or may not be organized with reference to systems of ultimate meaning. Societies are relatively closed systems of social exchange. Under some conditions, but not others, social exchange of symbols and explanations may lead to the establishment of a fairly coherent, shared culture unified by some small number of postulates. But a society's culture is often an incoherent aggregation of diverse symbols and explanations having only the most accidental relations to each other.

Within a society, cultural specialists, such as priests, will tend to band together in formal organizations that gradually assemble what we call *cultural systems*. A true cultural system is a structure of explanations about some aspect of life that are connected by overarching general explanations that give the system its coherence. The medical profession has not yet achieved full coherence of its explanations of disease, but it does follow some systems of explanation that represent modest cultural systems. For example, many specific diagnoses and treatments are united by the general explanation that disease is often the result of infection by microorganisms. In Christianity, Judaism, and Islam, very complex theological structures are held together by the assumption that the world was created and is ruled by a single deity. As the years pass, cultural specialists try to increase both the coherence and the scope of their systems. Cultural systems of great scope that provide general explanations answering the major questions of life qualify as meaning systems in the sense used by Wuthnow (cf. Bainbridge, 1984).

Such meaning systems are difficult to construct and sustain. Only very powerful and well-organized social organizations can generally succeed in this task, and individuals will have the benefit of a meaning system only if they are connected to the organization through influential social relationships. In the sphere of religion, where the most general explanations (such as the existence of one God) are beyond empirical test, it is probably most feasible to create and sustain a really general meaning system. Although Wuthnow looks for several alternative meaning systems and hopes to explain many important cultural trends in terms of their interplay, we would expect to find meaning systems in one area only: religion.

Wuthnow (1976a:9) sets out to measure the impact of meaning systems said to be influential in American culture and says a main purpose of his study is "to determine whether or not highly general meaning systems can even be tapped with standard survey techniques." He believes that he achieved accurate measurement of four distinct meaning systems and that he demonstrated their great influence in causing or preventing many kinds of social experimentation. Each of the four "supplies a distinct understanding of the meaning and purpose of life." They can be "distinguished from one another by what they identify as the primary force governing life" (Wuthnow, 1976a:3). Wuthnow names and defines the four meaning systems as follows:

1. *Theism:* God is the agent who governs life.
2. *Individualism:* The individual is in charge of his or her own life.
3. *Social Science:* Life is governed chiefly by social forces.
4. *Mysticism:* The meaning of life and the forces that govern life cannot be understood by the human intellect.

Although Wuthnow agrees that these ideal types are not mutually exclusive and identified many questionnaire respondents who seem to combine two or more meaning systems, he does postulate that each of the four is a distinct and philosophically comparable ideology for understanding life. He focuses on large groups of respondents who appear to hold to one meaning system more than to the others and suggests that each system can serve a basic human need for psychological coherence: "In sum, transcendent systems of meaning, viewed from the standpoint of the individual, are the components of consciousness which both overarch the compartmentalized spheres of everyday reality and include other realities that lie beyond its boundaries as well. Theoretically, their function is to integrate the discrete realms of personal life and to provide a larger frame of reference in relation to which personal meaning can be perceived" (Wuthnow, 1976a:76–77).

In his analysis, Wuthnow provided what seems to be powerful evidence in support of his assumptions by showing that many different opinions and attitudes toward social experimentation vary markedly with allegiance to different meaning systems. Our research was originally intended simply to replicate Wuthnow's empirical research outside the special ideological climate of the San Francisco area and then extend his findings by examining the implications of the meaning systems for social relationships. As defined by Wuthnow, each of the four meaning systems seems to govern individual understandings of social exchange and to provide a framework for interacting with other human beings. We decided to explore the distribution of the meaning systems in a social network and examine mutual influences, mediated by interpersonal relationships, between the meaning systems and social experimentation.

Therefore, we included a number of items from Wuthnow's work in our survey of Seattle college students (see Chapter 15). As a simple replication, our study permits retesting Wuthnow's hypotheses on a significantly different, large body of respondents. But, beyond this, we have been able to return to Wuthnow's original data set and test our conclusions on it as well. Robert Wuthnow and Charles Y. Glock kindly provided us data from the original 1973 survey. The clarity of our findings, essentially the same in both data sets, gives us much confidence in them, despite the unorthodox means by which we acquired our 1,439 student respondents.

The 1973 survey administered a large questionnaire to 1,000 residents of the San Francisco area (Wuthnow, 1976a:7–9). Youth were intentionally oversampled; so to avoid methodological problems in reconverting this quota sample and to make the most direct comparisons with our own data, here we use the 1973 youth sample, consisting of 565 respondents aged 16 through 30. In the course of our research, we performed numerous calculations based on Wuthnow's entire sample, often using his age-weighting procedure, which included responses from 435 persons older than 30. The results of interest here came out substantially the same either way (as comparing tables 17.3 and 17.8 shows), and we very much prefer tabulations based on the actual number of respondents to those based on weighted estimates.

Wuthnow had used 12 items in the 1973 survey, 3 at a time, as indicators of his four meaning systems. Although some can be criticized in terms of face validity, we decided to use all 12 in our questionnaire. They had appeared in a number of very different formats, strewn throughout the 1973 questionnaire, and we felt that replication demanded not only a different set of respondents, but a slightly different research approach. Therefore, we adapted his 12 items, expressing them uniformly as statements embedded in a series of agree-disagree opinion items. Respondents were asked to check one of four boxes indicating how much each of the statements expressed their own feelings. Did they agree strongly, agree, disagree, or disagree strongly?

Testing the Meaning Systems
Table 17.1 lists the 12 items as they appeared in our questionnaire, arranged according to the meaning systems they are supposed to indicate. This table shows the strength of agreement shared by students in the class with their close friends, what we call *concordances* of opinion, measured by gammas expressing the degree of association in responses to a given item by pairs of respondents. For this table, we chose pairs consisting of students and those friends who gave their relationships to the student a five or six rating on the closeness scale. If close friends tend to agree about a given statement, there will be a significant positive gamma. Positive concordances may reflect social influence. One friend has a strong opinion and, through interaction, causes the other to adopt the same views. But concordances may also simply reflect the old dictum, "Birds of a feather flock together." People may form friendships on the basis of underlying characteristics (such as sex or ethnicity) that produce the opinions measured, or even on the basis of these specific attitudes. For example, highly religious persons may tend to choose other religious persons as friends. In any case, concordances represent agreement on matters that are salient to social relations, agreement that emerges in social exchanges or upon which social relationships are predicated.

As we look down Table 17.1, we see great variety in the strength of concordances for the different statements. Following the logic of Chapter 15, we would expect concordances for any good set of indicators of real meaning systems. But Table 17.1 shows a very irregular pattern. By this test, theism does act like a meaning system because its indicators show similar, moderately strong concordances. Recall that we are correlating opinions across pairs of individual respondents; so we might expect lower coefficients than if we were correlating different indicators of theism within individual respondents. Each of the theism items concerns God, but we believe they represent a general meaning system of

TABLE 17.1   *Opinion Concordances, 424 Pairs of Close Friends*

Index and Items	Concordance (gamma)
Theism	
1. I definitely believe in God.	.22
2. God or some other supernatural force has a very strong influence on my life.	.29
3. Suffering often comes about because people don't obey God.	.25
Individualism	
4. People usually bring suffering on themselves.	.07
5. The poor simply aren't willing to work hard.	.13
6. If one works hard enough, he can do anything he wants to.	.07
Social Science	
7. I believe forgotten childhood experiences have an effect on me.	.02
8. Suffering is greatly caused by social arrangements which make people greedy for riches and power.	.11
9. Man evolved from lower animals.	.29
Mysticism	
10. I have experienced the beauty of nature in a deeply moving way.	.03
11. It is good to live in a fantasy world every now and then.	.20
12. New insights about myself have had a very strong influence on my life.	−.06

conventional religion, rather than a narrowly theistic system, because other religion indicators in the questionnaire correlate with them and exhibit similar concordances. For example, the concordance on belief that biblical miracles actually happened is gamma = 0.34, exactly the same as the concordance on frequency of church attendance. The concordance on the question, "How important to you are your religious beliefs?" is 0.28, in the same range as the theism indicators.

The individualism indicators show an equally uniform but very different pattern: essentially no concordance. Apparently, as measured by Wuthnow's three items, individualism is not especially salient for social bonds between university students. Individualism may still be a meaning system, or at least a low level ideological cluster, but it does not appear to be a socially important one. The social science indicators do not seem to work as a unit at all. The item on evolution shows a concordance in the same league as the three theism statements, but the other two fail to do so. Similarly, the mysticism items go their separate ways, with the one about living in a fantasy world showing some concordance, but the others not.

The irregular pattern in Table 17.1 suggests the possibility that theism is a true meaning system and the others are nothing more than collections of unrelated questionnaire items. The fact is that Wuthnow's book does not contain a convincing demonstration that the 12 indicators really represent four distinct meaning systems. His main supporting evidence is the apparent power of these items to explain experimentation with new life-style alternatives, a subject we consider shortly. But this is at best indirect evidence about whether they actually represent meaning systems. Wuthnow does offer a massive factor analysis of 28 opinion items, including these 12, but it is not easy to interpret (Wuthnow, 1976a:229–230). For one thing, he followed the familiar convention of defining a solution that called for as many factors as had eigenvalues greater than 1.0. This gave ten factors. In discussing interpretations other than his favored meaning system analysis, he says, "It might be concluded, from a factor analysis of the data, for example, that the simplest way to reduce the data to some easily manipulable variables is to combine all the items having to do with religion, all the items having to do with social issues, and analyze the relations between the two" (Wuthnow, 1976a:190). He dismisses this alternative approach without criticism, apparently uninterested in considering it seriously. Yet, as we shall see, it has merit.

One way to evaluate the coherence of the alleged meaning systems is by looking at intercorrelations linking the three indicators of each. We see no reason why this method would be inappropriate for Wuthnow's 12 items. He properly argues that a given meaning system may guide some individuals, yet be unimportant to others. But if each is at least moderately popular, as Wuthnow says, tests of simple linear relationships should prove positive. Like Wuthnow, we found that factor analysis was a convenient way of reducing the data to manageable form. But, rather than let the eigenvalues determine the number of factors, we thought it more reasonable to test for the four meaning systems by inspecting solutions that called for four factors based on correlations linking the 12 items. If the four meaning systems are coherent and each moderately influential, then the indicators of each should cluster in separate factors. Table 17.2 reports factor loadings from one of these analyses, using data from 1,249 university students who responded to all 12 statements, assigning the numbers one through four to the four responses to each statement.

The first factor clearly represents theism. The three theism indicators have high loadings on factor one and, of course, not on the other factors. But the ninth statement, "Man evolved from lower animals," also loads highly, if negatively, on this factor. The statement is supposed to be an indicator of social science, but it seems to function as a fourth theism item, tapping conservative Christian opposition to Darwinian biology, as chapters 3 and 15 already found.

TABLE 17.2   *Factor Analysis of 12 "Meaning System" Indicators (N = 1249)*

| | Varimax Factor Loadings | | | |
| | Factor 1 | Factor 2 | Factor 3 | Factor 4 |
Indicator				
Theism				
1. I definitely believe in God.	.841	.022	−.051	−.099
2. God or some other supernatural force has a very strong influence on my life.	.872	.164	−.029	−.009
3. Suffering often comes about because people don't obey God.	.679	.037	.119	.262
Individualism				
4. People usually bring suffering on themselves.	−.002	.060	.407	.145
5. The poor simply aren't willing to work hard.	.013	−.086	.322	.005
6. If one works hard enough, he can do anything he wants to.	−.019	.092	.530	−.214
Social Science				
7. I believe forgotten childhood experiences have an effect on me.	−.070	.355	−.068	.119
8. Suffering is greatly caused by social arrangements which make people greedy for riches and power.	.080	.145	.025	.268
9. Man evolved from lower animals.	−.604	.115	.018	−.313
Mysticism				
10. I have experienced the beauty of nature in a deeply moving way.	.007	.550	−.038	.042
11. It is good to live in a fantasy world every now and then.	−.149	.172	.122	−.151
12. New insights about myself have had a very strong influence on my life.	.083	.524	.107	−.014

The three individualism items have moderate loadings on factor three, suggesting that they do represent a loose ideological cluster. The three social science indicators do not cohere at all well. Not only is the evolution item really part of the theism index, but the two others are most strongly loaded on separate factors. Two of the mysticism indicators, beauty of nature and new insights, load moderately on factor two, but the fantasy world item loads only weakly across the board. In sum, this factor analysis supports the existence of a theism meaning system (although it adds a fourth indicator to the measures), gives very weak evidence for an individualism meaning system, and offers no support at all for social science and mysticism meaning systems.

This particular factor analysis is not definitive. In scoring responses to the items with the integers one through four, we treated ordinal data as interval data. But other factor analyses, both dichotomizing our data (agree = one and disagree = zero) and using the 1973 data, gave very similar results. Table 17.3 lets us look at association matrices for the 12 items in both sets of data, with gamma as our measure. Coefficients above and to the right of the diagonal line come from our Seattle university students; coefficients below and to the left are from the youth sample in the 1973 San Francisco area survey. We have recorded only coefficients of .20 or greater, for the sake of clarity. When applied to data with a small number of categories, as is the case with the two surveys, gamma tends to produce much larger coefficients than do several other measures of association; and, in these data sets, a gamma of .20 really is quite small and unworthy of respect. The many blank spaces in Table 17.3, representing gammas closer to zero than .20, do not conceal any significant results. For example, there are five coefficients missing in the individualism, social science, and mysticism meaning systems for the San Francisco data. But far from representing suppressed gammas of significance lurking just under .20, they average only .09, and none is greater than an unimpressive .15.

In both sets of data, the three original theism items and the wayward evolution item correlate very strongly, with gammas ranging from .59 to .89. Again, as in the factor analysis, the individualism items show some cohesion, although the gammas do not exceed .32. The social science items do not cohere at all, and the mysticism items show a propensity to correlate with other items as strongly as with each other. On average, in the San Francisco data, the theism items correlate gamma = .73 with each other, compared with only .22 for the individualism items, .11 for social science, and .16 for mysticism. On average, the items in these two latter "meaning systems" correlate more strongly *across* these two groups, .18, than within them. Our verdict is the same as with the factor analysis: Theism may well be an influential, real meaning system. Individualism appears to be a weak ideological cluster. The other alleged meaning systems cannot be found in these data. When we performed the same computations using just the older people in the 1973 survey and using the entire weighted data set (see Table 17.8), we got substantially the same results.

Meaning Systems as Explanations of Life-style Experimentation

The chief empirical support for existence and significance of the four meaning systems is a master table in Wuthnow's book that tabulates respondents' attitudes toward a variety of aspects of liberal and experimental life-styles against involvement in the four systems (Wuthnow,

TABLE 17.3   Associations (gamma) Linking 12 Index Items in San Francisco and Seattle Data

	Theism			Individualism			Social Science			Mysticism		
	1	2	3	4	5	6	7	8	9	10	11	12
Theism												
1		.89	.73						−.60			
2	.81		.73						−.59	.21		.24
3	.69	.70							−.59			
Individualism												
4	.30				.20	.31						
5						.23						.27
6			.21	.32	.21		.28			.32		.26
Social Science												
7												
8		−.51										
9	−.59		−.52								.30	
Mysticism												
10							.22		.26			.46
11							.20		.43			.21
12				.23			.23		.22	.24		

San Francisco Youth Data (N = 565)
Seattle College Student Data (N = 1,439)

1976a:148). The master table runs complex indexes against complex indexes, appears to reveal very powerful effects, but is in fact very difficult to interpret. Wuthnow uses six "experimentation" indexes: political, economic, religious, family, leisure, and a summary of the first five. Seven indicators of political experimentation include being politically liberal or radical. Economic experimentation favors affirmative action, equal rights for women, taxes to prevent people from becoming wealthy, and a guaranteed minimum wage. Religious experimentation includes low church attendance and being attracted to one or more of the following Eastern religious movements: yoga, Zen, and Transcendental Meditation. Family experimentation includes acceptance of an unmarried couple living together, positive attitudes toward communes, and favoring more freedom for homosexuals. Leisure experimentation covers a wide range of attitudes and behaviors, including drug use and having participated in an encounter group.

Wuthnow does not simply correlate each of the experimentation indexes with each of the meaning systems; he uses a very different approach. To simplify slightly, he identifies four main subsets of respondents. Members of each score higher on one of the meaning systems than on any of the other three. Some mixed groups are also identified, containing those who score high on two meaning systems simultaneously. A slight complication is added when he counts a respondent as scoring high on "People usually bring suffering on themselves" only if they do not score higher at the same time on "Suffering is greatly caused by social arrangements which make people greedy for riches and power" (Wuthnow, 1976a:140). Wuthnow uses these groups as stages in a comprehensive meaning system index, which places theism at one end, followed by individualism, social science, and mysticism, in that order, with transitional mixed groups ranged in between.

Wuthnow's summary master table shows that theistic people score very low on the experimentation index; individualists score slightly higher; social science people score much higher; and mystics score highest of the four ideal types. A table in Wuthnow's (1976a:261–262) appendix shows how individual experimentation items vary by the different meaning systems, but we are never shown what happens inside the meaning systems, the contribution each of the 12 indicators makes toward explaining experimentation. Table 17.4 shows how some questions similar to Wuthnow's experimentation items are associated with the 12 indicators in our data.

Table 17.4 shows a consistent relationship between experimentation items and indicators of traditional religion — the three theism items and number 9 on evolution. Religion opposes life-style experimentation. Indicator 11, "It is good to live in a fantasy world every now and then,"

TABLE 17.4 Associations (gamma) Linking 12 Index Items with Selected Items (N = 1439)

	Theism			Individualism			Social Science			Mysticism		
	1	2	3	4	5	6	7	8	9	10	11	12
Number of times respondent has been high on drugs	-.27	-.25	-.23	.02	.04	.06	.12	-.03	.29	.03	.17	.01
Respondent gives a favorable preference rating to marijuana.	-.31	-.30	-.29	-.02	.01	.02	.09	.00	.34	.01	.21	.00
Respondent agrees "It is all right for an unmarried couple to have sexual relations."	-.52	-.57	-.56	-.04	-.09	.14	.12	-.06	.59	.01	.33	.01
Respondent is politically liberal (on NORC scale).	-.22	-.21	-.25	-.01	-.24	.00	.07	.05	.24	.07	.19	.13
Low church attendance	-.71	-.69	-.56	-.01	.04	.04	.06	-.05	.53	-.06	.17	-.11
Respondent agrees "Some Eastern practices, such as Yoga, Zen, or Transcendental Meditation, are probably of great value."	-.30	-.25	-.28	-.06	-.11	.09	.22	.05	.43	.14	.33	.13

shows a positive association with experimentation. A couple of stray associations appear elsewhere in the table, but none of the other indicators appears to have any consistent connection to experimentation. Again, we see strong evidence that theism is a meaning system that has the power to govern attitudes and behavior in many spheres of life. We see no evidence of other operating meaning systems.

Table 17.4 suggests what might really be happening in Wuthnow's master table. Theism is low on experimentation. Individualism is unrelated to experimentation, but, in tabular analysis such as Wuthnow used, people high on individualism but not high on other indicators will simply be about *average* on experimentation. The alleged social science meaning system actually contains an anti-theism item, "Man evolved from lower animals." Therefore, it will score higher than average on experimentation in the tabular analysis. Thus, individualism sits passively, and a religious factor places theism to one side and social science to the other. This, we believe, explains much of the apparent power of Wuthnow's meaning systems analysis in his master table.

Further research may be required on the mysticism meaning system. In fact, Wuthnow himself has gone further in this direction. His second book, based on the same data set, employs a new mysticism index, composed of seven items, including the beauty of nature but excluding fantasy world and new insights (Wuthnow, 1978:78–98, 205). In the master table of his first book, mysticism may score somewhat high on experimentation because of the fantasy world item. We do not pretend to understand what it means "to live in a fantasy world," what this single item is really measuring, or why mysticism scores slightly higher on experimentation than does social science in Wuthnow's master table. Our Table 17.4 shows that much, if not all, of the variation he reports in attitudes toward experimentation is really due to the single, familiar factor of traditional religion, not to the differential effects of four meaning systems.

Table 17.5 uses data from Wuthnow's 1973 youth sample to reexamine associations linking the four theism indicators, including the evolution item, and selected items that play roles in Wuthnow's analysis. For these gammas, we have dichotomized the four indicators along reasonable lines, distinguishing strongly religious responses from others of more ambiguous nature. For example, those who are sure that God definitely exists are scored one on this indicator, and all others, zero. According to Wuthnow, low church attendance is an indicator of religious experimentation; of course, persons who endorse the four traditional religious beliefs tend to take part in the activities of some religious group.

Respondents who score high on these religion indicators tend not to have been "high" on drugs. They believe it is important to live up to

TABLE 17.5 *Associations (gamma) Between Four "Theism" Items and Life-Style Variables, San Francisco Youth Respondents (N = 565)*

	Believe in God	God Has Influence	Obey God or Suffer	Man Did Not Evolve
Respondent takes part in the activities of a church, synagogue, or other religious group.	.61	.51	.44	.43
Respondent has been high on drugs.	−.42	−.39	−.40	−.27
Respondent feels it is important to live up to strict moral standards.	.40	.40	.41	.35
Respondent opposes an unmarried couple living together.	.56	.50	.63	.49
Respondent opposes more freedom for homosexuals.	.41	.31	.52	.51
Respondent likes the idea of living in a commune.	−.27	−.23	−.21	−.31
Respondent has taken part in an encounter group.	−.19	−.09	−.35	−.45
Respondent is attracted to Yoga, Zen, or Transcendental Meditation.	.31	.09	.31	−.49

strict moral standards. They tend to oppose an unmarried couple living together. They oppose more freedom for homosexuals. They do not like the idea of living in a commune. They are less likely to have taken part in an encounter group or to be attracted to yoga, Zen, or TM. Table 17.5 verifies that the religion items, by themselves, operate powerfully in the 1973 data. This, in turn, not only supports our critical evaluation of Wuthnow's master table, but also supports again the identification of theism as a true meaning system, influential in determining people's attitudes and behavior.

RELIGIOUS AFFILIATION

Throughout this book, we have stressed the importance of social exchanges and formal organizations in establishing and maintaining systems of attitudes, beliefs, and behaviors. Following the methods introduced in Chapter 15, Table 17.1 examines social relationships between pairs of individuals and finds some concordance on the theism items (and on "fantasy world"), but not on the others. We have shown that a simple religious factor appears to explain much of the variation in life-style experimentation, both in our survey and in the 1973 San Francisco research. We would naturally conclude that religious affiliation, member-ship in specific religious groups and categories of religious self-identification, will be a powerful force determining these attitudes and behaviors. Religion is a meaning system, sustained by religious organizations and transmitted through social relationships.

One question in our university survey asked, "What is your religious affiliation?" Respondents were first asked to check one of five boxes: Catholic, Protestant, Jewish, other, and none. Those who responded Protestant or other were also asked to write in their denomination. An-other very good question, used to great effect in Chapter 15, was the born again item taken from the Gallup poll, asking whether students had had a "turning point in your life when you committed yourself to Christ." Another question asked, "How important to you are your reli-gious beliefs?" Although these last two questions are about experiences and attitudes, rather than about affiliation itself, we feel they can be used as good indicators of involvement in the powerful wave of conser-vative, evangelical religion that has washed the campus.

Table 17.6 examines the effect of different religious affiliations on a variety of life-style experimentation indicators. The first four columns of figures are percentages of the four groups of respondents who make the indicated response. Jewish students were not numerous among our respondents, and "other" religious affiliations included many small groups; so we have omitted these two categories from our analysis. To get the four groups, we first removed all born again respondents, leav-ing 241 with no religion, 251 Catholics who were not born again, and 319 Protestants who were not born again. Because the born again ques-tion concerned an experience the students might have had in the past, we could not be sure it correctly described all of them at the present time. One student even wrote in that, after his born again experience, he had experienced its opposite, presumably some kind of irreligious insight. Therefore, we concentrated on the 245 respondents who had been born again and who said their religious beliefs were "very impor-tant" to them. The calculations of gamma in the fifth column are based on responses to the single born again question, to which 368 students out of 1,439 answered yes.

The first four questionnaire items are about religion itself. Not sur-prisingly, students who have no religion do not attend religious services once a week or more. Catholic students show the traditionally higher church attendance of their group compared with liberal and moderate

TABLE 17.6   *Religious Affiliation and Life-Style Experimentation Items*

	Percent of Each Group Giving the Indicated Response				Gamma with
N =	No Religion 241	Catholic 251	Protestant 319	Born Again 245	Born Again 368/1439
Respondent attends religious services once a week or more.	0.0	24.8	4.7	68.0	.67
Respondent agrees "Miracles actually happened just as the Bible says they did."	16.8	64.9	58.0	96.3	.77
Respondent agrees "Man evolved from lower animals."	92.6	74.2	75.9	19.9	−.68
Respondent gives a zero preference rating to religious literature.	59.3	21.2	23.8	1.2	−.72
Respondent gives a zero preference rating to marijuana.	33.3	32.3	37.1	81.2	.47
Respondent has been high on drugs at least once.	74.6	72.0	71.1	40.2	−.33
Respondent agrees "It is all right for an unmarried couple to have sexual relations."	96.3	85.8	86.8	28.6	−.64
Respondent saw *The Exorcist* and liked it (preference rating 4–6).	21.2	26.3	25.4	11.0	−.31
Respondent saw *The Rocky Horror Picture Show* and liked it (preference rating 4–6).	26.1	29.1	30.7	9.4	−.38
Respondent is politically liberal (1–3 on NORC scale).	57.8	47.8	46.0	29.0	−.25

Protestants; yet only a fourth of them attend church weekly. However, more than two-thirds of the born agains are this actively involved in religion. Belief in biblical miracles is almost universal among the born again group and rare at the opposite extreme; acceptance of the theory that humans evolved from animals shows almost exactly the opposite pattern. One section of our questionnaire consisted of preference items, asking respondents to indicate how much they liked each of a long list of things, using a seven-point scale from zero (do not like) to six (like very much). Although the majority of students with no religion gave the lowest possible rating to "religious literature," only 1.2 percent of the born agains expressed such dislike.

Marijuana was one of a number of consumables rated on the same preference scale, and we see a much higher rejection of it among born agains than among others. The question on whether the respondent has ever been high on drugs also reveals the importance of religious affiliation. These two drug questions show an intriguing pattern. The differences separating those with no religion, Catholics, and ordinary Protestants are very slight. The born agains stand out. Here the religion effect operates only at the extreme, although, at the extreme, it is powerful.

The question about an unmarried couple having sexual relations reveals a slight difference of about ten percentage points between the nonreligious and Catholics or Protestants, but a great majority in each of these groups registers approval of such sexual freedom. The born agains dissent strongly. Among the preference items were several motion pictures and television shows, among them two sex-and-horror films, *The Exorcist* and *The Rocky Horror Picture Show*, which had been seen by 43.4 percent and 46.6 percent of 1,439 respondents, respectively. Here, as with the drug items, the first three groups show very similar patterns of response. The born agains were both less likely to have seen either film and less likely to have enjoyed them if they did see them. These tendencies compound to produce the big differences in the table. Finally, we see a significant political effect, using a question from the annual NORC social survey.

The 1973 survey was designed to explore the "new religious consciousness," including experimentation with occult practices and cult movements. However, Wuthnow did not consistently offer the meaning systems as an explanation of such religious innovation. But Table 17.7 shows us that traditional religious affiliation has a strong influence, inhibiting acceptance of occult practices and cult movements. The one item connected with Wuthnow's index of religious experimentation, attitudes toward yoga, Zen, and TM, shows an extremely strong negative relationship with traditional religion. The differences between those with no

TABLE 17.7 Religious Affiliation and Occult Items

	Percent of Each Group Giving the Indicated Response				Gamma with Born Again 368/1439
N =	No Religion 241	Catholic 251	Protestant 319	Born Again 245	
Respondent agrees "Some Eastern practices, such as Yoga, Zen, or Transcendental Meditation, are probably of great value."	72.5	65.6	60.2	28.1	-.47
Respondent agrees "Some occult practices, such as Tarot reading, seances, or psychic healing, are probably of great value."	16.4	21.6	11.8	5.5	-.46
Respondent gives a zero preference rating to occult literature.	37.7	33.6	35.8	64.5	.32
Respondent gives a zero preference rating to his or her horoscope.	29.0	24.4	23.2	53.3	.27
Respondent agrees "There is much truth in Astrology — the theory that the stars, the planets, and our birthdays have a lot to do with our destiny in life."	21.7	22.7	12.8	8.6	-.39

religion, Catholics, or Protestants are not great, but the enthusiasm toward these cults from born agains is vastly less, as Table 15.5 predicts.

Small percentages of all groups are willing to express positive evaluations of tarot reading, seances, or psychic healing, and the trend is irregular. Once more, born agains have the lowest level of acceptance. Twice as many born agains as others reject occult literature, and the two questions about horoscopes and astrology also get unsympathetic responses from religious conservatives.

Table 17.7 reveals an interesting fact about the students who claim no religion. Rather than being secular rationalists who reject supernatural ideas, they show a high level of acceptance of cults and occultism, seldom lower than ordinary Catholics and Protestants and noticeably higher in several cases. Lack of formal religious affiliation is not equivalent to rejection of the supernatural, as we demonstrate in Chapter 4. Perhaps lack of religious affiliation, especially lack of involvement in highly conservative religious groups, frees the individual to contemplate radical supernatural and pseudoscientific alternatives.

This hypothesis, already mentioned and to some extent supported in earlier chapters, is the topic of the concluding section of this book. Before we leave the debate with Robert Wuthnow, however, we must respond to a few of his comments on the journal article on which this chapter is based.

A DEBATE ON VALIDITY

In a rejoinder to our initial essay on the consciousness reformation, Robert Wuthnow (1981) argued that the four "meaning systems" might show some kind of symbolic coherence, each within itself, apart from the consistency or inconsistency in people's responses to the triads of indicators. If we understand him correctly, he claims that the indicators are known to represent meaning systems on the basis of information other than that collected in his survey. As we see it, there are two ways Wuthnow could show us that the indicators are properly grouped in meaning systems, other than through consistent patterns of correlation in our two data sets. First, he could present us with a detailed analysis that shows the logical connections uniting triads of items. Second, he could show us formal statements of these meaning systems in the works of particular philosophers, ideological tracts, or the creeds of social movements, proving that some ideological tradition places a given triad of indicators together. He did neither of these things, however, either in the original book or in his rejoinder.

Perhaps this is a project for future research. At one point in his rejoinder, Wuthnow (1981:24) notes, "Studies in which religious symbols, rather than individuals, serve as the units of analysis have been relatively uncommon and have been conducted almost entirely outside the confines of quantitative sociology." He then mentions three qualitative studies that drew their data exclusively from religion texts and comments, "Examples of data drawn directly from the users of symbolism are virtually nonexistent outside of anthropology (one significant exception is Bainbridge's [1978c] valuable discussion of symbolism in a satanic cult)" (Wuthnow, 1981:25). A similar qualitative analysis of each of the four "meaning systems" named by Wuthnow is not offered in his book, and, with the exception of the theistic, we are left without a source to verify that the symbols are used *as a system* by *any* social group. Wuthnow (1981:25) says these four are "symbol systems that have enjoyed prominence in American culture," but he does not give his evidence for this claim or evidence that the triads of statements are good indicators.

The three items in the individualism triad seem logically connected, in our minds as in his. Indeed, they are practically related by syllogism. *Major premise*: "People usually bring suffering on themselves." *Minor premise*: "The poor suffer." *Conclusion*: "The poor bring suffering on themselves." How do they do this? Perhaps the poor fail to do what is necessary to avoid suffering: "The poor simply aren't willing to work hard." And if the objection is raised that working hard would not help the poor escape their suffering, the logical individualist could cite the third statement in the triad: "If one works hard enough, he can do anything he wants to." Thus, on logical grounds at least, there is some warrant for calling the three statements indicators of a meaning system. But the evidence from both surveys shows that the meaning system is not very salient for ordinary Americans. Although the three items correlate moderately, they have little influence on other attitudes, beliefs, and behaviors. Individualism, we grant, is a possible philosophical position, but we do not see evidence that many people are committed to it or that it provides meaning around which people could organize their lives.

The alleged indicators of social science do not show any logical connections. Further, we very much doubt that there is even a traditional connection between them. The item about forgotten childhood experiences is said to reflect Freudian theory (Wuthnow, 1976a:118), the scientific status of which remains in serious doubt. Certainly, we have not felt the need to draw heavily on Freudian conceptions for this book or for our other publications. The statement about suffering being caused by social arrangements is unclear, but smacks of vintage Rousseau rather than of the current contents of major social science journals. But perhaps this is meant as an indicator of popular Marxism. Although some social philosophers combine Freud and Marx in their writings, and this rare ideological blend may have been communicated to some ordinary young citizens (Roszak, 1969), the number of other variants of philosophical schools that have some currency outside academia is great, each by mathematical necessity influencing only the tiniest proportion of the general public. We would need very good ethnographic evidence before we could believe a combination of Freudianism and Marxism was an influential alternative despite the absence of confirming correlations.

We have already noted in chapters 3 and 15 that questions about Darwin's theory of evolution tap religious sentiments rather than scientific attitudes. Contemporary social science seems to have as much difficulty with the theory of evolution as does traditional religion. Until the much opposed emergence of sociobiology (E. O. Wilson, 1975), sociology seemed to have forgotten about Darwin, and even now the theory of evolution as applied to humans is a field of battle between political ideologies and scientific perspectives. Mortal combat between Darwinism and Marxism took place in a real, rather than metaphoric, sense in the Soviet Union (Medvedev, 1971), and we fail to see how the Darwin item can be part of the same "meaning system" as the Freud and Marx items.

Our discomfort with the typification of these items as representative of social science is echoed by the failure of any association in our student data between liking "the social sciences" and attitudes toward the three alleged social science statements. One item in our student questionnaire, one of a series of preference questions, asked students to indicate how much they like the social sciences, expressing their feelings on a seven-point scale from zero (do not like) to six (like very much). Preference for the social sciences achieved an insignificantly weak correlation with the Freud item (gamma = .09) and utterly invisible associations with the Marx item (gamma = .01) and the Darwin item (gamma = −.01).

We are much perplexed by the mysticism indicators. "I have experienced the beauty of nature in a deeply moving way" seems to tap aesthetic sentiments, but of what kind we cannot say. The concept "fantasy world" is ambiguous. Does this refer to psychosis or mere reverie? One of the preference items in our student survey was science fiction novels, and liking this kind of fantasy did not correlate significantly (gamma = .08) with feeling "It is good to live in a fantasy world every now and then." The association was even weaker between the fantasy world item and preference for spy and detective novels (gamma = .04) and best-selling novels (gamma = .03); so apparently this index item does not measure love of fiction. The statement "New insights about myself have had a very strong influence on my life" seems as likely to be a social science indicator as a mysticism indicator. Indeed, as Table 17.3 indicates, it does correlate with the Freud item in both the San Francisco and Seattle samples. If there exists a mysticism meaning system, we do not understand why these three items should be clear and unambiguous indicators of it.

In a footnote to his rejoinder, Wuthnow pointed out, quite correctly, that our published analysis rested on only the youth part of his San

TABLE 17.8   *Age and the 12 Index Variables (San Francisco Respondents)*

Index and Items	Gamma with Mature versus Youth Sample	Weighted Sample ($N = 1,000$)	
		Gamma with the First Index Item	Gamma with the Second Index Item
Theism			
1. I definitely believe in God.	.34		
2. God or some other supernatural force has a very strong influence on my life.	.23	.80	
3. Suffering often comes about because people don't obey God.	.15	.65	.67
Individualism			
4. People usually bring suffering on themselves.	−.07		
5. The poor simply aren't willing to work hard.	.15	a	
6. If one works hard enough, he can do anything he wants to.	−.19	.25	a
Social Science			
7. I believe forgotten childhood experiences have an effect on me.	−.20		
8. Suffering is greatly caused by social arrangements that make people greedy for riches and power.	−.19	a	
9. Man evolved from lower animals.	−.47	.28	a
Mysticism			
10. I have experienced the beauty of nature in a deeply moving way.	−.11		
11. It is good to live in a fantasy world every now and then.	−.13	.20	
12. New insights about myself have had a very strong influence on my life.	−.33	a	a

[a]The gamma is less than .20.

Francisco sample (Wuthnow, 1981:25). But the results were almost exactly the same when we used just his youth sample, just his mature sample, and the weighted combination of both. We agree that age is an important variable, and one reason for emphasizing the youth sample — in his research as well as our own — was to focus on respondents most likely to follow the new meaning systems. The youth sample was the larger part of the total sample; it permitted direct comparisons with our own data; and it could be employed without the confusing necessity of weighting the two samples before combining them. Table 17.8 shows the impact of age on responses to the 12 indicator items.

The first column of coefficients shows the gamma between agreement with each statement and whether the respondent was a member of the mature sample (coded one) or of the youth sample (coded zero). Traditional religious sentiments get somewhat stronger support among the older respondents, and there is a slight tendency for most other items to get a little stronger support from the young. Although age and traditional religiosity are related to some extent, this column in the table suggests there may be an age or generational dimension affecting responses to the statements, but not one that singles out one of the nonreligious triads and gives it the force of an age-based meaning system.

The second and third columns of the table repeat selected computations from Table 17.3, showing how coherent each of the four indexes is for the entire weighted sample of respondents from the San Francisco survey. Had we chosen to repeat Table 17.3 in its entirety, we would see essentially the same pattern of correlations *across* indexes. Here we do see the same failure of items in the three secular "meaning systems" to associate together as they should. Again, we have set a cutoff point (gamma = .20) below which coefficients do not deserve to be reported. With this very permissive standard, only three of the nine expected relationships appear, and these are exceedingly weak compared with the huge associations linking the three theism statements.

All evidence supports the view that religion really is a meaning system. It provides apparent coherence to human understandings of life and is influential in preventing experimentation in life-styles and exploration of alternative supernatural ideologies. We found little evidence in favor of the existence of an effective individualism meaning system, although logic does suggest the items fit together in principle. At most, Wuthnow's individualism items appear to represent a weak ideological cluster unimportant in explaining other attitudes or behavior patterns we examined. No evidence emerged in favor of social science or mysticism meaning systems.

CONCLUSION

A number of theoretical and empirical conclusions flow from our replication and reanalysis of Wuthnow's work. One ought not base theories on the assumption that people usually will possess meaning systems, defined as systematic, coherent, and comprehensive frames of reference. To do so is to overintellectualize humanity, a common failing of social scientists. To the extent that we could find only one meaning system—conventional religion—a large number of these respondents must not have one in that they did not score high in their acceptance of the religious measures. Indeed, the widespread religious experimentation and seeking going on in our society surely suggest that many people do not possess an adequate religious meaning system. What else could they be looking for? Moreover, decades of research should have made it clear that humans have the ability easily to hold mutually contradictory and logically incoherent beliefs and opinions. Even when we construct attitude scales of items that logically imply one another—perhaps like the individualism scale—error types abound.

We do not find it surprising that people often lack meaning systems. Our theoretical work suggests that such systems are difficult to construct and can be created and sustained only through specialized and organized social activities. In the case of conventional religion, these requirements are clearly met. For millennia, specialists have been honing religious meaning systems. For an equally long time, organizations have existed to inculcate and defend religious meaning systems. But one does not see such elites and organizations hard at work to create and sustain other meaning systems. Perhaps Leftist political parties would be an example, but, even in San Francisco, they have been singularly unsuccessful in establishing orthodox party lines that receive the solid faith of a significant number of people. There may be a Leftist political milieu in the United States, but there is no one, supreme ideology of the Left capable of asserting itself as a meaning system.

Where are the functional equivalents of priests and churches for the social science, individualism, or mystical meaning systems Wuthnow postulated? If they do not exist, how can these meaning systems exist?

If it is problematic whether individuals have meaning systems, surely it is not a *given* that "Societies are organized with reference to systems of ultimate meaning" (Wuthnow, 1976a:vii). Some may be, especially very small, preliterate societies. But there is no reason to take for granted that large, modern societies are organized by meaning systems. One thing is certain: Meaning systems do not hover above societies without visible means of support; meaning systems are not phenomenological smog banks. To exist, meaning systems must be the property of human beings and thus must be sustained through human interactions. If that is so, then the place to look for meaning systems is not in an ozone layer of literary criticism or philosophical speculation, but in the concrete opinions and behavior of individuals, in the ongoing interactions among humans (that is, their social networks), in the division of labor, and within formal organizations. It deprives the idea of meaning systems of all utility to postulate their existence in the face of data showing their putative elements are of little or no importance in social networks.

Our results reaffirm the importance of elementary methodological principles. Validity is always a crucial concern. When items do not have undeniable face validity, it is urgent to demonstrate that they nonetheless serve their intended purpose. It does not take a sociologist of religion to recognize that an item measuring support for Darwin's theory of evolution is a strong measure of Christian fundamentalism and therefore may not be a valid indicator of a social science meaning system.

Moreover, whenever one constructs an index, and surely when one seeks to index meaning systems that constitute "overarching symbolic frames of reference" (Wuthnow, 1976a:2), one ought to make some effort to check the coherence of each index. Do the relevant items go together? This brings us to our most fundamental conclusions.

Wuthnow was not wrong to suppose that meaning systems exist or that they may greatly influence other attitudes and behavior, such as experimenting with mildly deviant lifestyles or exploring novel supernatural (religious) ideologies. His error lay in supposing that such experimentation and exploration currently are produced by an interplay of *competing* meaning systems, for all we have been able to find is one meaning system: religion. And it is variation in the degree to which people are attached by acceptance of, and social bonds to, this meaning system that produces the variations in exploration and experimentation that Wuthnow found. Those firmly anchored socially in traditional religion reject such experimentation and religious exploration. Those more weakly attached are more prone to deviant social experimentation.

This seems to us a major confirmation of our position that culture can be sustained and transmitted only through social relationships and organizations. When people are not linked organizationally to a religious meaning system, their belief in, and conceptions of, that system tend to drift. Thus, they become available for recruitment to alternative meaning systems. But they will not cease drifting, will not become committed to an alternative meaning system until they encounter and are recruited by organizations that sustain such systems.

Interpreted thus, our understanding of both Wuthnow's data and our own is compatible with broader theoretical views and a wide variety of empirical findings. The finding that anchorage in conventional religion determines religious experimentation is wholly compatible with findings we report in Chapter 19 that cult movements flourish most in areas where the conventional churches are weak. The finding that conventional religion inhibits experimentation with mildly deviant life-style activities (such as using marijuana or engaging in premarital sex) is wholly supportive of new research showing that religion has powerful effects on crime and delinquency (Stark, Doyle, and Kent, 1980; Stark, Kent, and Doyle, 1982; Stark, Bainbridge, Crutchfield, Doyle, and Finke, 1983).

At the most basic level, of course, finding that meaning systems do not thrive apart from an intentional basis in the social structure is compatible with the mainstream of modern social thought. Gone are the days when sociologists could invoke the *Zeitgeist* as an adequate explanation of cultural change.

We are not prepared to argue that all meaning systems are religious. We are prepared to argue that the concept of *meaning system* is itself meaningless so long as it is a purely cultural construct. Meaning systems must have *social* meaning. Hence, if meaning systems exist, it must be possible to locate them within social networks and organizations.

18 *Who Joins Cult Movements?*

Although previous chapters emphasize the role of social networks in recruitment, it obviously is not the case that just *anyone* linked by social bonds to cult movement members is a high probability recruit. Hence, although the process of recruitment is quite normal, even ordinary, it does not necessarily follow that it primarily is "normal" people who join cults. In fact, it is widely believed by the general public and widely proclaimed by many social scientists that people who join cults are *not normal*—that they usually are marginal, deprived, disturbed individuals. If that is so, then cult movements have little hope of becoming significant new religions, for they will originate with followers who are so incapacitated and stigmatized that such groups will be forever limited to the fringes of societies. Yet, in times past, some cult movements have risen to be great world faiths. Were things different back then? Or is the perception that people who join cult movements are abnormal simply wrong?

In several previous chapters, we discuss some individual characteristics that define or limit the potential pool of cult recruits. In this chapter, we pursue these individual traits in greater detail and suggest why and how they influence recruitment. The chapter also serves as a necessary bridge to the final section of this book, where we return to the perspective of whole religious economies and explore questions such as when, where, and why new religious movements arise. All such macroanalyses rest on assumptions about individual behavior, for the fact is that populations do not form cults any more than they have babies.

Only individual people ever *do* anything. Hence, all statements about the behavior of social units (cults, churches, regions, and so forth) assume that certain individuals included in these collective nouns will act in certain ways for certain reasons.

We examine the characteristics of individuals who join cults in terms of three major factors: their religious condition, their social circumstances (emphasizing gender and education because good data are available), and their mental health. The discussion of mental health allows us to deal with the highly charged debate concerning "brainwashing" and "deprogramming." There also the theme of this chapter becomes most explicit: *Under present sociocultural conditions, cults can have great success recruiting persons who are fully normal in terms of almost any characteristic one wants to measure.*

This chapter presents much evidence that American cults, in the previous century as well as today, have recruited disproportionately from some of the more favored segments of the population. To put it simply, successful cults may skim more of the cream of society than the dregs.

But we do not pretend that the issue is a simple one. Clearly, the sort of persons recruited to new religious movements is a *variable*, dependent upon several identifiable factors. Already, in our discussion of the geography of American cults, we have noted great variation in the proportions of the population attracted to cults. In social environments where cultic deviance is rare and strongly punished, it may take special circumstances to get an individual to join a cult. Where cultism is common, almost anybody might participate.

Three factors might facilitate joining a cult when the surrounding sociocultural environment threatens to inflict heavy costs on such religious deviance. First, persons experiencing great strain and deprivation might join in a desperate search for solutions to their severe problems. Second, social isolates or small, encapsulated groups, unconnected to the conventional social order, might be free to join because they are beyond the social reach of those who might want to punish them. We have considered these ideas in earlier chapters. But there is an interesting third possibility: Certain segments of society's elite may have the power and other resources to do whatever they please, including indulging in novel religious experiences. If J. P. Morgan wishes to meditate at midnight in the Great Pyramid, who can stop him?

It may be that Western society has entered a phase in the history of religion in which the balance among these factors is shifting, and deprivation and isolation are playing less of a role in facilitating cult membership than they once did. Perhaps the real recruiting ground for cults is now among the relatively privileged —or at least among those with sufficient material and cultural resources to permit them to explore new styles of life and faith. Indeed, this may have already been the case in America many years ago, for, by their very definition, *cults are experiments in cultural innovation*. In many spheres of endeavor, the most educated classes promote cultural innovation.

Much attention has been given recently to innovations "from below" — to clothing styles and varieties of music developed by disadvantaged subcultures. But cultural diffusion often flows from the elite to the masses, even in some cases that superficially appear to demonstrate the opposite (Flugel, 1930), and innovations are adopted early among well-placed groups and individuals.

By 1960, two great traditions of sociological research had explored these questions in significant depth, moving along parallel tracks, although cultic innovation was not one of their topics (Katz, 1960). Rural sociologists, such as Everett M. Rogers (1960), had traced the diffusion of agricultural innovations, and mass communication researchers had found similar social patterns in the spread of innovations through urban social networks (Katz and Lazarsfeld, 1955). Both bodies of research support the hypothesis that cultural innovations generally spread first through relatively well placed, educated networks, diffusing from them to the rest of the population. This even may be true when the innovation in question is a delusion, a deviant belief similar to some that form the intellectual basis of cults (Medalia and Larsen, 1958).

Unfortunately, after 1960, the focus of sociological attention moved away from these issues, although a concern for networks of social influence has recently returned (Laumann et al., 1977). Only two main areas of sociology retained a primary interest in *culture*, and both emphasized the subcultures of deprived groups. Certainly, research on disadvantaged ethnic minorities did this. And the research on deviant subcultures — such as the drug culture — carried out by criminologists and sociologists of deviance emphasized the creation and diffusion of culture by nonelites. Sadly, much of the cultural innovation produced by elites over the past two decades went unstudied by sociologists. An important exception, which received at least some social scientific attention, was the politicocultural radicalism of the late 1960s, which seemed particularly attractive to children of the elite (Lipset, 1976; Gardner, 1978). Thus, our field has the prejudice that cultic innovation and recruitment take place within disadvantaged groups, but there is good reason to suspect the opposite.

Twenty years ago, Otto Larsen (1962), one of the mass communication sociologists, offered a suggestion we might find useful in our theorizing about cults, although the topic of his research was television, not religion. Larsen took from Rogers a model of innovation that distinguished several categories of person in terms of when they accepted a new innovation that had just begun to spread through the society. That tiny minority who first tried the new thing were called *innovators*. They were followed by a somewhat larger minority called *early adopters*. Because Rogers used a normal-curve model of diffusion, dividing the population in terms of standard deviations before or after the moment when the average citizen tried the new thing, innovators were somewhat arbitrarily defined as the first 2.5 percent and early adopters as the next 13.5 percent to participate in the diffusion process. Let us grant the distinction without accepting the exact percentages.

Innovators accept the new thing before it has established a place in the cultural repertoire of the society — at a time when it might be described as deviant (or at least ambiguous) with respect to current standards. As Larsen (1962:18) points out, "When a major technological innovation first appears, there is a period of active definition or norm formation in which the relationship of the innovation to the established features of the environment is worked out." The innovators participate actively in this process, even though by innovators Rogers and Larsen do not mean the persons who actually invented the new thing in the first place. Most important, Larsen (1962:33) suggests, "You *cannot* predict where innovators might emerge on the basis of status, ethnicity or family size." However, it is very possible to predict the social characteristics of early adopters. Compared with those who adopt the new thing later on, early adopters are above average in terms of education, income, social contacts, and attitudes favoring innovation in general.

Applied to cults, this conceptualization suggests that we may have difficulty predicting exactly who will join when cults are exceedingly rare and treated as intensely deviant. We previously suggested three possible factors that might facilitate recruitment under such otherwise unfavorable circumstances, but, in general, these three are pretty much independent of each other. In the ever changing flux of American social structure, almost anyone might suddenly become deprived, socially isolated, or, conversely, so rich and powerful that ordinary social constraints no longer operate. There will be some statistical regularities that permit prediction, but the job of identifying the sources of cult recruitment when cult membership is rare is not an easy one.

We assert that religious history has moved beyond the phase in which only those whom Rogers and Larsen would call innovators join cults. We think that the phase of early adopters is well advanced, at least in some regions of the United States and other Western nations, and the early adopters can be identified by the fact that they rather comfortably involve themselves in cultic activities as one aspect of life-style experimentation. They are people especially open to experimentation because of formal education and other experiences that make them particularly interested in novel ideas. Although we had cause to disagree with our colleague Robert Wuthnow in the previous chapter, here we are happy to report that his research has given us some of the best evidence in support of this important point (Wuthnow, 1976a, 1978).

The fact that we seem to be in a period of historic religious transition makes it difficult to answer such a general question as "Who joins cults?" As more and more early adopters, in addition to the innovators, participate, the social patterns will stabilize for a time, and cults will attract mainly persons above average in education and social contacts. At present, however, studies of recruitment to cults performed in different regions and social categories will have some tendency to give contradictory results because different phases of the evolutionary process are in effect.

This research situation is further complicated by the fact that many individual cults recruit from very narrow strata or from small, homogeneous categories of citizens. This is true in part because such specific recruitment may be the policy of cult leaders and because cult movements that remain active in the client cult business will tend to serve narrow categories of customers. It is true also because recruitment takes place primarily through development of new social bonds linking members with prospective recruits or through activation of existing interpersonal bonds, as we note in Chapter 14. And persons tend to have and to form enduring social relationships with persons very much like themselves. Thus, it is not surprising that the deprived members of the first Moonie cell in America tended to recruit other deprived persons (Lofland and Stark, 1965; Lofland, 1966). Nor is there any contradiction between this observation and the fact that the relatively elite members of The Process tended to recruit persons from above-average backgrounds (Bainbridge, 1978c). Therefore, it is important not to leap to conclusions from data on recruits to a single cult or in a single social milieu. Within the limits of data available, this chapter seeks evidence from many sources to ensure against such errors.

THE RELIGIOUS CONDITIONS OF CONVERSION

Persons truly dedicated to one religion are not ready converts to another. Viewed from the perspective of whole societies, that means that it will be difficult to found new religions to the extent that the conventional faiths are healthy and vigorous. Individuals with a firm religious affiliation are not free to embrace new religions, regardless of the overall condition of conventional religious organization. Such statements verge upon being true by definition. Yet close scrutiny of the religious backgrounds of those who join cult movements or even who entertain deviant religious beliefs provides important insights that are not entirely self-evident.

If secularization prompts cult formation, it ought to follow that people who are most subjected to the impact of secularization are the ones most likely to form and to join cult movements. Hence, persons lacking any religious background, and those affiliated with the most secularized conventional religious bodies, ought to be especially likely to join cults. In other chapters, we have noted that Spiritualism in the late 19th century drew mainly on unchurched socialists and intellectuals, on the one hand, and on large numbers of Universalists and Unitarians (clergy as well as laity), on the other. And the college student data we just considered suggest similar conclusions. Now we can examine contemporary data of greater scope.

In 1977, the Gallup poll asked a national random sample of 1,500 adult Americans whether they were involved in or practiced four "experiential religions" that seem reasonable indicators of cult involvement: yoga, Transcendental Meditation, Eastern religions, and mysticism. In Chapter 13, we use the data on TM and comment that far too many people claimed to practice it, considering the official TM statistics on how many had been taught this practice. Of course, it may be that many Gallup respondents who do some kind of meditation decided to say they did the TM brand as the closest approximation of the truth encouraged by Gallup's polling format. In any case, we found the regional variation made sense, and here we employ the data again with some confidence.

Fortunately for us, Gallup tabulated responses to these four cultism questions against two interesting religion questions. One simply asked whether the respondent was a formal member of a church; the other determined the respondent's denominational affiliation. We would predict that attraction to these cults would be greater among the unchurched and among members of the most secularized, "liberal" denominations. Among the gross denominational categories Gallup used, the contrast between Episcopalians and Baptists is probably the most clear. Although the Baptist category represents a collection of various styles of religion, on average, it suggests a much more conservative, traditional, unsecularized orientation than the very permissive Episcopalian.

Table 18.1 reveals that respondents lacking church membership are much more likely than church members to be involved in the four cultic activities. Similarly, Episcopalians are more likely than Baptists to be in-

TABLE 18.1   *Percent Involved in or Practicing Cult Activities*

Involved in or Practicing	Church Membership		Protestant Denomination	
	Yes	No	Baptist	Episcopal
Yoga	2	5	1	5
Transcendental Meditation	3	7	2	18
Eastern religions	1	3	1	2
Mysticism	1	2	1	6

Source: Gallup (1977), p. 52.

volved. The percentages are small, but the pattern is consistent. Church membership and membership in a conservative denomination are preventives against cultism. The unchurched and those affiliated with the more secularized denomination are more open to cult involvement.

True to our principle that data from a single source are insufficient to give us confidence that our theory is sound, we now examine data from good studies of actual members of six cults: Hare Krishna (Judah, 1974), Scientology (Church of Scientology, 1978), a gathering of witches (Melton, 1981), the Moonies (Melton, 1981), Ananda Cooperative Village (Nordquist, 1978), and the Satchidananda Ashram (Volinn, 1982). Table 18.2 examines the composition of these cult movements in terms of the members' religious origins. We are unable to explore denominational differences within Protestantism here, but we can compare five categories of religious affiliation. For ease of comparison, we have turned raw data into ratios reflecting larger or smaller proportions among cult members in contrast with the proportion present in the general public. Thus, for example, if the proportion of people from Jewish backgrounds were the same among Hare Krishnas as in the population at large, the ratio for Jews would be 1.0. Ratios larger than 1.0 reflect overrepresentation; smaller ratios reflect underrepresentation.

Table 18.2 clearly confirms predictions about who joins cults. Two of the studies, those of Ananda and Satchidananda, did not report a "no religion" category, although one respondent at Ananda said he was raised as an atheist. But for the four groups from which we have full data, "nones" are very heavily overrepresented. This is, of course, in full accord with findings in Chapter 17, where we see that nones were unusually prone to accept occult beliefs and to see value in cults such as TM. Here we find them extremely overrecruited by the Hare Krishnas and the Scientologists and least overrepresented among Moonies, who maintain great cultural continuity with Christianity.

TABLE 18.2   Religious Origins of Cult Members Proportional to the U.S. Population

| Cult | Parents' Religion (1.0 represents the proportion for the U.S. population who claim this affiliation) | | | | |
	Jewish	None	Protestant	Catholic	Other
Hare Krishna	7.3	12.5	.6	.7	1.8
Scientology	3.5	3.5	.7	1.0	1.0
Witches	3.1	1.7	.7	1.0	3.8
Moonies	2.7	1.2	.8	1.3	1.2
Ananda	15.4		.7	.9	1.0
Satchidananda Ashram	9.0		.8	.8	2.8

Note: Two cells are empty because the response category was not reported in the original study.

In similar fashion, Protestants are underrepresented in each of these groups, falling well below their proportion in the population. Were we able to examine variations within Protestantism, we would expect to find that the "immunity" to cult recruitment is based in the more orthodox and evangelical bodies, those with higher proportions of born again members. Chapter 17 shows how resistant the born agains are to occult beliefs and, in Table 18.1, we see a similar resistance to participation in cults on the part of Baptists. Overall, Catholics tend to be in cults about in proportion to their population numbers, as are those from "other" backgrounds. The latter do appear to be very overrepresented among the witches. However, the mystique of the witchcraft scene stresses ties with an unbroken, esoteric tradition going back to pagan times. Thus, there is a tendency (which we have observed in our field research) among witches to claim falsely to be from a family with a long tradition of magick. Examination of the original questionnaires confirmed that the "other" category was inflated by just such claims.

Perhaps the most stunning finding, however, is the extraordinary overrepresentation of Jews in these contemporary cult movements. Although they are least overrepresented among the Moonies, even here they are present in numbers nearly three times their proportion in the general population. The immense emphasis Moonies place on their Christian culture undoubtedly weakens their appeal to Jews, and we see much higher overrepresentation in the other groups.

Why are Jews so prone to join cults? An important clue is to be found in the data on witches. Melton's questionnaire was sufficiently detailed as to ask Jews their specific religious background. Not a single one reported having been raised in an orthodox home.

Jewish overrecruitment by cults would seem primarily to reflect that, in contemporary America, Judaism has been more greatly eroded than Christianity by the process of secularization. Evidence abounds. A smaller proportion of Jews than of gentiles has a formal religious affiliation. Furthermore, even those who do belong to a synagogue display low levels of commitment. For example, only 13 percent of *members* of Reform synagogues and only 24 percent of Conservative synagogue members attend services frequently (Lazerwitz and Harrison, 1979). Even the most liberal and declining Protestant denominations generate frequent attendance from a far higher proportion of their members (Stark and Glock, 1968). Of Jews without a denominational preference, only 1 percent were frequent attenders — nominal Christians have much higher participation rates than that.

For a variety of historical reasons, some having to do with Jewish involvement in radical politics in past decades (cf. Lipset, 1976), to have been born into a Jewish home has, for many years, meant a high probability of being raised in secularity, as only a cultural, not a religious, Jew. And this is only a short step from joining the "nones" or adopting a novel religious affiliation. One recent study, based on data from the General Social Survey, found that over 11 percent of respondents who had considered themselves Jewish at age 16 now had no religious preference (Chalfant et al., 1981). For Catholics and for the typical Protestant denomination, only about 5 percent abandoned religious affiliation altogether (although the figure for Episcopalians was nearly 17 percent). Jews have been especially overrepresented in organized irreligion, such as Ethical Culture Union, the American Humanist Association, and even the psychoanalytic movement (Aronson and Weintraub, 1968; Weintraub and Aronson, 1968). The result is an oversupply, compared with those of Protestant and Catholic backgrounds, of young Jews without religious socialization. Note, as a final datum on this point, the extreme overrepresentation of Jews at Ananda and Satchidananda, revealed in Table 18.2. Presumably, some of these nominally Jewish respondents would have checked a "no religion" box had it been offered them.

The fact that a young person grew up without religious training does not mean that religious interests and questions have been banished from his or her consciousness. One need not possess mystical gifts to recognize the great existential issues: Why am I here? What does life mean? Is death the end? Whence cometh justice? But lack of religious training does mean that people will discover these questions while lacking "standard brand" answers. Thus, Jews who have been raised as "nones" are as open to recruitment by a religious group as are persons who claim no religious affiliation at all. The centuries of conflict between Christians and Jews probably will make Jews more open to non-Christian religious options, as Table 18.2 strongly demonstrates. But even Christian options do draw them today — it seems unthinkable that Jews for Jesus would have arisen in the Orthodox Jewish communities of Eastern Europe in the last century.

The extreme overrecruitment of Jews by contemporary religious movements touches upon a very sensitive issue — the great energy various Jewish organizations and community leaders have devoted to recent anticult campaigns. Indeed, some recent legislative proposals, such as the Lasher Bill in New York State, seek to impose severe legal restrictions on all forms of religious recruitment (Richardson, 1980). But, as we discuss at length later in this chapter, it simply is not true that the cults are deceiving our children and stealing them from us. Our children join new religions to fill needs that we created, either by raising them without a religion we might prefer to one they could choose or by raising them within a highly secularized religious group. Here a contrast with England is instructive.

In her revealing surveys of the Moonies in England, Eileen Barker (1979, 1981, 1984) has found they are drawn from families with unusually *strong* religious convictions. But, once having left home, many young people in England have discovered that their faith was not much reflected by the churches they encountered. For example, many young Moonie converts in England were raised in a quite orthodox form of Anglicanism, only to discover later an Anglican church in which even many bishops scoff at the divinity of Jesus or the existence of a personal "God up There" (cf. Robinson, 1963). For these young people, the Moonies represent a Christian sect offering a restored, vigorous Christianity of the kind in which they were raised.

Returned Mormon missionaries report the same phenomenon, not just in Britain, but in Scandinavia and Northern Europe. Indeed, these parts of Europe abound in cults and are deficient in Christian sects. The health of evangelical Protestantism in the United States probably limits a similar turn to cults by those from highly religious homes here, thus leaving those with deficient religious backgrounds as the primary recruitment pool.

The data on the religious origins of cult converts display great congruity with the ecological data we examine in Part V, where we see that cults thrive where conventional faith is weak. Here we see that it is those most adrift from conventional faith who provide the primary source of cult recruits.

SOCIAL ORIGINS OF CULT MEMBERS

There exists an internal tension in religious organizations between those who desire to maximize the worldly dimension of religion and those who seek to maximize otherworldliness. The latter tend primarily to be persons who need religious compensation for their lack of scarce earthly rewards. Thus, sects are formed by and draw their members primarily from among the less powerful and more disadvantaged members of a society (although people at the very bottom may not participate in any kind of social movement, religious or political).

If this is the source of sectarians, who joins cults? To understand why people join cults, we must expand our view of the consequences of secularization. By becoming increasingly worldly, religions frustrate the poor and provoke revival. But as the cycles of secularization and sect formation continue, the fundamental plausibility of the whole religious tradition begins to erode. Too often have the dominant organizations turned away from their original otherworldliness. Too many charges and countercharges have been flung by and toward erupting sect movements. Even people with deep religious concerns begin to question: Who has the truth? Does any group have the truth?

This seems to have been the situation in the United States during the 19th century, especially in the aftermath of episodes of great religious fervor that, having passed, left the religious situation as unresolved as before — a cacophony of competing churches and sects (cf. O'Dea, 1957). Many efforts to restore and reunite Christianity were launched, from great revival campaigns to new organizations such as the Disciples of Christ. But Christianity was not united. In this tumult, religious innovation increased and began to make headway. Indeed, in a Yankee family with at least two generations of expressed disaffection from sectarian disputes, there appeared a son determined to set things right — Joseph Smith (cf. O'Dea, 1957; Brodie, 1971; Arrington and Bitton, 1979). Smith proclaimed that God had moved to restore all that had been lost, that the Age of Revelations had recommenced, and that a new time of dispensation had begun. Thus were born the Mormons in the midst of the "burned over" district in western New York.

This was not a new sect; it was a wholly new religion, albeit one that presented itself as the next stage of development in the conventional Christian-Judaic tradition. It was an effort to construct a faith unmarred by sectarian disputes and by past secularization — that is, to offer a vigorous and plausible faith. Moreover, it did not draw its recruits from the ranks of the impoverished and deprived. It arose in and drew its followers from the most "prosperous, and relatively sophisticated areas" of western New York, those rural areas with a high proportion of quite cosmopolitan Yankee residents that surpassed other areas in the proportions of children they sent to school (O'Dea, 1957:10). Those who accepted Smith's new revelations were better educated than their neighbors who did not and displayed considerable intellectualism. They were people interested in ideas, who read a lot and who discussed theological and social issues.

This ought to be no surprise. New religions involve *new ideas*. A substantial amount of novel culture must be understood and evaluated in order for a person to become a competent member. Where sect revivals drum the old culture — the ideas in which everyone has been steeped through normal socialization and everyday experience — cults necessitate the willingness and the ability to entertain the new and unfamiliar. Thus, sects are able to appeal to people of limited intellectual inclination or capacity, but cults find such people very difficult to reach. Cults in significantly secularized societies, therefore, tend to draw upon the middle classes, even to recruit persons having considerable social standing and privilege.

Why would they join? Recall the third dimension of religious commitment, the universal dimension. All persons, regardless of their power and privilege, are deprived of those intensely desired rewards that are not simply scarce, but that seem to be absolutely unavailable in this world. If a religious tradition is weakened, it is not only its ability to compensate for scarce rewards that suffers (the otherworldly dimension), but also its capacity to provide efficacious compensators of the universal variety. Thus, for example, today's liberal Protestant bodies not only fail to provide sufficient comfort for those losing out on life's bounty, but fail also to provide nearly so vivid and credible promises of everlasting life as once they did (cf. Stark and Glock, 1968). In such circumstances, even the more privileged may be motivated to seek a new, more efficacious faith. Moreover, it is these people who will be most aware of erosions in the plausibility of the conventional religious traditions, for this too is an intellectual perception requiring some awareness of history. Thus, it takes people of some degree of sophistication both to understand new religions and to recognize the need for them, and this generally means a high level of education.

EDUCATION

There is a growing body of evidence that this theoretical analysis of to whom cult movements ought to appeal is in fact correct. Not only did the Mormons begin with relatively educated members, but Mormon converts today come very disproportionately from the ranks of well-educated young men and women moving into professional, managerial, and technical careers (Stark, 1983). The same is true of the Moonies. Moon himself was trained as an engineer and always has sought educated followers. Moonies are much better educated, as a group, than the population from which they are recruited (Barker, 1981). Data on Scientologists also reveal an unusually well educated membership. Even though Scientology training is in many ways an alternate to ordinary formal education, one survey of 3,028 members found that 37.4 percent had attended universities and another 13.9 percent had received other kinds of higher education (Church of Scientology, 1978). Eighty-nine percent of those at Ananda (Nordquist, 1978) and 81 percent of those at Satchidananda (Volinn, 1982) had attended college.

Robert Wuthnow's analysis of experimentation with Eastern religions shows the important role played by intellectual sophistication. In Table 18.3, we show just a small part of his consistent findings, data on

TABLE 18.3   *Education and Percent Attracted to Eastern Cults*

Eastern Cults	Some College	No College
Attracted to		
Transcendental Meditation	17.3	5.9
Yoga	26.9	11.7
Zen	17.3	4.6
Actually took part in		
one of these cults	15.6	5.4

Note: Based on the responses of 1,000 residents of the San Francisco area. After weighting to compensate for oversampling of youth, an estimated 59 percent had attended college.

education and attraction to three cults, adapted from a more complex table published by Wuthnow (1978:21). The respondents were a random age quota sample of San Francisco area residents, and here the numbers have been weighted to compensate for oversampling of youth. For each of the four cult questions, respondents with at least some college education were two to three times as likely to express interest or involvement than were those with no college experience.

Table 18.4 gives us similar information from the Gallup poll (1977), augmented with remarkably consistent findings that support the wider theory from which we derived our prediction that cultic involvement should be positively associated with education. Most interesting is the fact that there is essentially no difference between the educated and the uneducated in whether they have had a religious or mystical experience. Yet confidence in organized religion is much more common among the uneducated, and lack of a religious preference is more common among the educated. Persons with college educations are more likely to have participated in yoga, TM, Eastern religions, or mysticism — cultic activities — and the pattern is uneven for the charismatic movement, a Christian phenomenon. Involvement in *faith healing,* a term that probably brings images of evangelical Christian magic to the minds of most respondents, is more common among those who never got as far as high school. Two questions tapping evangelical or fundamentalist Christianity, the one about being born again and one on the literal interpretation of the Bible, receive far fewer favorable responses from the college educated than from those with only a grade school education. Thus, cults are attractive to those with more education, and sects find their greatest strength among the less educated. But the need for religion exists in every social class, perhaps in equal measure, as suggested by the first item in Table 18.4. The educated are especially

TABLE 18.4   *Education and Openness to Religious Innovation—*
             Percent Giving Indicated Response

Questionnaire Item (Gallup Poll, 1977)	College (N = 450)	High School (N = 815)	Grade School (N = 230)
Respondent has had "a religious or mystical experience–that is, a moment of sudden religious insight or awakening."	29	31	30
Respondent has "a great deal of confidence in organized religion."	26	40	56
Respondent has no religious preference.	10	5	4
Respondent has been involved in or practices:			
Yoga	5	2	0
Transcendental Meditation	7	3	2
Eastern Religions	2	1	0
Mysticism	3	1	0
The Charismatic Movement	3	1	3
Faith Healing	6	7	11
Respondent has had the "born again" experience.	27	36	42
Respondent agrees: "The Bible is the actual word of God and is to be taken literally, word for word."	17	42	60

Source: Gallup (1977).

likely to have lost faith in the old traditions, to have little confidence in conventional organized religion, and to be ready recruits for cults.

Evidence abounds as well that better educated persons, more in touch with the sources of information about new cultural developments, are more apt to be familiar with the kind of cult that spreads through the entire society. For example, in July 1976, the Gallup poll reported on a survey that included brief questions about astrology. Although 85 percent of the college educated and 81 percent of those who had just attended high school claimed to know the sign under which they had been born, only 45 percent of those who had not gone beyond grade school claimed to know their sign. In 1977, the Gallup poll sought people's opinions of a number of denominations and religious leaders, including Reverend Sun Myung Moon of the Moonies. Although only 12 percent of the college educated had no opinion of this prominent cult leader, 31 percent of the high school educated and 49 percent of the grade school educated had no opinion. Thus, the better educated citizen is more likely to be aware of new cultural movements and of the cultural background from which they spring, as well as to be cut loose from the traditional compensator systems and thus open for recruitment.

These findings on the role of higher education suggest that the pools from which cults may draw members are much larger today than when the Mormons originated. Recall that Smith's movement arose not only among relatively educated Americans, but also out of the ashes of the "burned over" district. Thus, it came into being in a sociocultural environment that may have been the extreme for its day in secularization — or in the degree of disappointment in conventional religion. Thus, Mormonism may well have been the harbinger of things to come.

Today, one can hardly call the nation's universities a burned over district, because the flame of religion grew cold even in many colleges with nominal religious affiliations long ago. Such revival movements as the Campus Crusade for Christ will undoubtedly reignite enthusiasm for traditional religion from time to time. But religion in most universities seems so burned out rather than merely burned over that one can hardly expect these institutions to sustain for long a flame of traditional faith. Therefore, for many young people in future years, the colleges will be the ultimate experience of secularism, to be followed in early adulthood by affiliation with novel cults.

New religious movements will vary to the extent that they draw privileged followers. The more the emphasis is on ideas, on complex culture, the more that recruitment will be restricted to persons of considerable privilege and sophistication. Here Christian Science stands out. Its emphasis is on a highly abstract and counterintuitive doctrine. It eschews all emotionalism in its services, which more closely resemble a study session than a worship ceremony. Not surprisingly, it has appealed almost exclusively to people of considerable wealth and social standing. In his pioneering study of Christian Science, Wilson (1961) noted the unusual number of English Christian Scientists with titles and the abundance of well-known and aristocratic family names. He also noted that Christian Science practitioners in England tended to have home addresses in fashionable and prosperous neighborhoods, but that, in the ordinary working-class districts, Christian Science practitioners are conspicuous only by their absence. Analysis of American data support the same conclusion. Christian Scientists were recruited overwhelmingly from prosperous and genteel backgrounds (Stark, forthcoming).

New religions that emphasize otherworldliness and sacrifice may draw upon a less privileged population pool, as seems the case with the Hare Krishnas. Even then, recruitment will not be based upon the lower strata, but on persons who might well have aspired to success were it not for certain impediments. Thus, the Hare Krishnas, like many hippie communal experiments in the 1960s, are drawn from the sons and daughters of the middle class who are dropping out, and the same is true of the Children of God (Davis and Richardson, 1976). This observation suggests we should consider the role of drugs and of the psychedelic movement in providing recruits for contemporary cults.

DRUGS AND THE PSYCHEDELIC MOVEMENT

Evidence is overwhelming that the use of illegal psychoactive drugs and participation in the psychedelic movement of the 1960s contributed significantly to the growth of many cults in the 1970s. Robert Wuthnow (1976b:280) has demonstrated this fact using data from his survey of 1,000 residents of the San Francisco area. In one analysis, he employed the same kind of ratio we did in Table 18.2, examining whether persons who admitted ever being "high" on drugs were overrepresented among those who were attracted to various new religious movements. To get his ratios, Wuthnow divided the percentage of those attracted to each group who had been high by the percentage of the total sample who had been high. If there were no relationship between drug use and attraction to a particular group, the ratio would be exactly 1.0. The ratio happens to be 0.9 for the Campus Crusade for Christ, indicating that drug users are slightly underrepresented in this sect movement. But for seven cults, the ratios are above 1.5, indicating significant overrepresentation of drug users: Hare Krishna (1.6), Scientology (1.7), *est* (1.7), Zen (1.7), yoga (1.8), Transcendental Meditation (2.1), and Satanism (2.1).

Similar findings have been reported for persons who actually participated in cults. A very high proportion of Hare Krishnas, for example, claim considerable prior involvement with drugs (Judah, 1974). The same is true for the guru Maharaj Ji's Divine Light Mission (Downton, 1979). A survey of 3,028 Scientologists, carried out and reported by the cult itself, indicated that 62.3 percent had taken "nonprescription" drugs, other than alcohol and tobacco, before joining (Church of Scientology, 1978). Like many such groups, Scientology claims to offer not only a cure but a positive alternative to illegal drugs, and the same survey reported illegal drug use was currently below 1 percent among the members polled. A survey of 250 participants at the 3HO summer solstice "Sadhana" held in New Mexico in 1973 found that 95 percent had used "mind-affecting drugs" (Tobey, 1976:22).

Such findings are not limited to areas where cults are especially strong, such as California or New Mexico. A 1975 survey of adult college students in Montreal, Canada, discovered the same thing (Bird and Reimer, 1982). Respondents were asked whether they had ever participated in any of a list of 12 "new religious and parareligious movements" and whether they had used marijuana or LSD on three or more occasions. The 12 movements were mainly cults, including TM, Scientology, Divine Light, yoga, Baha'i, and Spiritualism. The parareligious movements, which did not overshadow the fully religious cults in participation rates, included martial arts and therapy groups, which may have a cultic quality, depending upon the particular martial arts master or therapist. Forty-five percent of those who had used marijuana frequently said they had participated in one or more of these movements, compared with 27.4 percent of the nonusers. The pattern was much the same for LSD (53.9 percent compared with 29.9 percent). Certainly, the respondents were a very atypical set of Montreal residents, a city our Canadian research for Chapter 20 found to be weak in cults. Yet the internal comparison between drug users and nonusers is valid and instructive.

In trying to explain the association between drug use and cult participation, we are faced with an embarrassment of intellectual riches. There are too many good ideas on why illegal psychedelic drugs might facilitate recruitment to cults! We already stated one idea: Some cults recruit heavily from the sons and daughters of the middle class who are dropping out of conventional society, and, in many cases, drugs may have contributed to dropping out. For one thing, both the pharmacological and the social consequences of taking these powerful and illegal chemical agents may prevent the individual from maintaining higher class status through achievement in a conventional career. Conversely, taking drugs may often be an act of defiance by somebody already in the process of dropping out. And there is no reason these two factors could not combine in many cases, each contributing to the other in a series of steps from full involvement in a conventional career to utter estrangement.

The psychedelic movement specifically urged people to "turn on, tune in, and drop out" — to find in psychoactive drugs a new vision of humanity and nature in many ways equivalent to a religious revelation. When Timothy Leary and Richard Alpert began experimenting with psilocybin and LSD at Harvard in 1960, they began a kind of ideological war against their social scientist and medical colleagues over the very nature of reality. There was absolute disagreement between two general explanations of the effect of the drugs. Where opponents saw chemical disruption of normal brain functions, Leary and Alpert saw higher consciousness and spiritual growth (Benson and Smith, 1967). The very word *psychedelic* (consciousness expanding) is a statement of superempirical faith, asserting the alleged transcendent value of mind-altering drugs (Goode, 1969).

At the opposite end of the continent, the leader of the psychedelic movement was probably Ken Kesey, a successful author who had tried LSD as an experimental research subject as early as 1960. By 1964, he had gathered around him a small group of followers known as the Merry Pranksters, half theatrical troupe and half religious cult, similar in many ways to The Process. The Pranksters made a vivid public show of their involvement with psychedelic drugs and did much to popularize the values and ideas that developed into a full-fledged social movement by the late 1960s (Wolfe, 1968).

Andrew Weil (1972) made one of the classic statements of the psychedelic ideology. Having experimented with drugs at Harvard alongside Leary and Alpert, Weil came to believe that meditation was somewhat better than chemical agents in producing a higher consciousness, but he argued that psychedelics could be useful tools of the mind if employed wisely. He disparaged what he called "straight thinking" and recommended "stoned thinking," whether achieved through drugs or through spiritual techniques. Straight thinking, Weil said, uses the rational intellect and the senses to understand physical reality and external things. He claimed that stoned thinking is a more direct, intuitive experience of inner reality. Weil argued that straight thinking, which includes science, is by nature pessimistic and leads inevitably to despair. He asserted that stoned thinking permits a person to achieve sensations of infinity and cosmic unity, thus gaining mystical optimism and joy.

When the psychedelic movement crashed shortly afterward, many of its leaders renounced drugs in favor of religious or philosophical concerns. Ken Kesey spoke vaguely of a new stage in the "psychedelic revolution." In an odyssey that took him in and out of many nations and jails, Timothy Leary developed a new mystical philosophy of outer space civilization (Leary, 1977). Richard Alpert visited India, seeking spiritual enlightenment, and was transformed into Baba Ram Dass, a drugless guru (Ram Dass, 1971). He became the patron of the Lama Foundation, a cult commune near Taos, New Mexico (Gardner, 1978). Psychoactive drugs became mere illegal recreation for a large subculture of deviant youth, stripped of the temporary, transcendent psychedelic ideology.

It might be too much to say that the psychedelic movement was itself a religious cult, although drug-based cults are fairly common. But, clearly, the psychedelic ideology that sought to interpret the larger meaning of the drugs was based on sweeping general explanations about the meaning of existence and the source of spiritual bliss. Thus, the movement depended upon general compensators, such as those that are the chief business of any religion. The main thing lacking was the social coherence that marks true religious organizations. Thus, we could describe the psychedelic movement as an instance of collective behavior, a Great Awakening that could flow into formal religion but was not sufficiently stable in itself to become a coherent religious establishment.

In taking drugs, movement participants certainly were violating secular norms and defying the opposition to drugs of conventional religious organizations (see Chapter 17). Associating with fellow deviants and detached from the institutions and social networks that enforce conventionality in most citizens, they were free to experiment with novel religious alternatives.

The psychedelic movement itself bordered on being a great cultic religious awakening, and it deposited many of its participants directly into numerous small cults. But, in following the psychedelic dream, young people of the late 1960s were fulfilling their middle-class culture as much as they were leaving it, for the psychedelic movement was a novel cultural development that spread through networks of the educated (including Harvard professors and students) like most other innovations of its kind, as explained earlier in this chapter. In so doing, it drew innovative youth from the same strata in society from which conventional careers draw their most prominent members and was in many ways an elite movement at the same time that it tore participants away from conventionality and helped recruit many of them to religious cults.

FEMALE RECRUITMENT TO CULTS

The abundance of middle-class dropouts in contemporary cult movements leads to another aspect of the social origins of converts. It is not only the poor who are deprived — serious relative deprivation can exist at virtually all levels of society. For example, in feudal societies, younger sons are a constant source of social friction because their future prospects are dim in contrast to their fathers and elder brothers. Women of the nobility have been a major source of cultural innovation, again in response to their relative deprivation vis-à-vis their husbands and brothers. A similar phenomenon would seem to account for the tendency for new religious movements to overrecruit females.

In Chapter 11, we note that nearly all cult movements in America in the 1920s were very heavily female. Of the 28 largest religious denominations at the time, Christian Science had the highest proportion female among its membership, 75 percent. A similar pattern exists in many new religious movements today, and the same is true for client cults and audience cults. Table 18.5 gives some evidence from client cult

TABLE 18.5   *Female Public Involvement in Cults*

Activity	Number of Cases	Percent Female
Occupational Data from the 1970 U.S. Census		
Professional, technical, and kindred workers	11,666,966	40
Religious workers	232,262	10
Clergymen	216,540	3
Client Cult Practitioners		
Who's Who in the Psychic World	400	48
International Psychic Register	666	58
Directory of New England Astrologers	62	63
Fate Magazine		
Letter writers, 1960–1969	954	77
Letter writers, 1970–1979	1,094	77
Respondents to Gaston's questionnaire, 1978	854	63

directories we consider in Chapter 10, along with *Fate* magazine statistics and comparative occupational data from the 1970 census of the United States (Bureau of the Census, 1973).

Clearly, one of the things that attracts particularly ambitious women to cults is the opportunity to become leaders or even founders of their own religious movements. By long tradition, low tension religious bodies have excluded women from leadership positions in churches, and it was left to both types of high tension religion to offer them such statuses. As the first part of Table 18.5 shows, although women represented 40 percent of the professional and technical workers in 1970, they were far less well represented in religion, one of the subclassifications under the professional category. Only 10 percent of all religious workers, and just 3 percent of the clergy who were the bulk of this occupational category, were women in 1970. The very fact that the occupation is called "clergy*men*" rather than just "clergy" underscores the male dominance of this field.

The denominations representing the majority of Americans refused to ordain women as clergy until quite recently, and it has been left to some very unusual religious organizations to provide the female clergy counted by the census. Indeed, the proportion female among the clergy has changed little as the 20th century passed. In 1930, women accounted for 2.2 percent of the clergy, compared with 2.9 percent 40 years later.

Jacquet (1979:266) estimates that, even in 1977, only 17.4 percent of female clergy were in "mainline Protestant denominations," 29.9 percent in "paramilitary denominations" (mainly the Salvation Army), and 31.8 percent in Pentecostal bodies. Among the large Protestant denominations, several permitted ordination of women only very recently: the United Methodist Church and the United Presbyterian Church in 1956, the Presbyterian Church in the United States and the Southern Baptist Convention in 1964, the American Lutheran Church and the Lutheran Church in America in 1970, and the Protestant Episcopal Church only in 1977. And, of course, the Roman Catholic Church shows no signs of admitting women to the priesthood. At the opposite extreme, the Salvation Army has ordained women since 1880. Such cults as Christian Science, Theosophy, and Spiritualism also offered women exceptional opportunities many years ago, and they still do.

In the middle of Table 18.5, we see high proportions of women among the professionals listed in three client cult directories. We introduce the first two in Chapter 10, but the *Directory of New England Astrologers* (Marks, 1978) was too narrow in scope to contribute to the national analysis of cult geography in that chapter. The total number of cases will differ from what we report in Chapter 10 because some of the listings we count there are for businesses that chose not to name their company president; others are for couples for which two names can be counted now. We went through these directories, carefully coding the names of client cult practitioners as male or female, often guided by first-name lists in the dictionary. Sometimes, never in more than 4 percent of the cases and often in as little as 1 percent, we were unable to determine the sex of the owner of the name. For each of the three directories, the proportion female is well above that among professional, technical, and kindred workers—and vastly above the proportion female among clergy or religious workers. For the *Psychic Register* and *New England Astrologers*, women represent more than half the client cult practitioners. Although it is common to find that women outnumber men among religious congregations, here we find them the majority among cult leaders and professionals.

The female overrepresentation among practitioners of astrology is mirrored by an overrepresentation among the clients of this cult service. In Chapter 15, we note that female college students are more interested in astrology than are males. The same is true for the national sample of citizens surveyed by the Gallup poll in 1976 and reported in Chapter 11.

That study found that female respondents show both greater familiarity with astrology and greater appreciation of it. Although 69 percent of the men professed to know the zodiac sign under which they were born, 83 percent of the women did so. Although only 16 percent of the men said they read an astrology column regularly, 29 percent of the women follow their stars through these mass media audience cult articles.

The bottom of Table 18.5 reports a gender analysis of over 2,000 of the letters sent to *Fate*'s "Proof of Survival" and "True Mystic Experiences" columns from 1960 to 1979, along with a result from a survey of *Fate*'s readership carried out for the magazine's editor (Gaston, 1978). As in Chapter 10, we count letters rather than letter writers, and it is possible that women might send repeated missives and male readers might be reluctant to write at all. Therefore, it is good to have Gaston's data for comparison, although there may be some differences in male or female tendencies to respond to his survey, which had a response rate of 28.5 percent. *Fate*'s readership is older than average for the population as a whole, 21.3 percent being 65 or older, compared with 15.4 percent for the population at large and 14.0 percent for subscribers to comparison magazines also polled by Gaston. This might contribute to the overrepresentation of females both because of male mortality and because *Fate* probably represents an older style of cult than represented by the youth-oriented organizations we emphasize in this chapter. In contrast, only 0.4 percent of Scientologists are 65 or older (Church of Scientology, 1978).

Overrecruitment of females is not universal to new religious movements. Indeed, this seems a major basis for distinguishing the few relatively successful movements from the others — that is, successful movements appear not to overrecruit females. This was very clear in the 1920s data with respect to the Mormons. They were and still are equally male and female, and they are far and away the most successful new religion to appear in the West in centuries (Stark, 1983). Of today's groups, the Moonies do not overrecruit women. Instead, they tend to attract and hold slightly more males than females (Barker, 1981). The same appears to be true for the Healthy-Happy-Holy cult (Tobey, 1976).

Groups that overrecruit women are likely not to achieve great success for a number of reasons. First, they will tend to be deficient in fertility; thus, as the mortality of first-generation converts rises, much conversion will be necessary simply to replace them, let alone for growth. This problem appears to have caused the sudden halt to the growth of Christian Science that occurred in the 1930s (Stark, forthcoming). The celibate Shakers, who perpetuated themselves through recruitment alone, are an extreme example. Increasing female overrepresentation after 1850 made the Shakers less attractive to potential recruits of both sexes

(Bainbridge, 1982). A second problem created by overrecruitment of women is that, so long as women enjoy less status than men, the movement will also suffer lower status. When movements draw only women, this is symptomatic of their failure to penetrate into the social mainstream wherein real success always lies.

Earlier we identified three factors that might facilitate joining cults when such novel religious movements are highly deviant — when participants might be called *innovators*, in the terminology of Rogers and Larsen. We have just pointed out that many women have suffered deprivation, compared to men, in the career and other public opportunities open to them. Furthermore, traditional restriction of women to the home, which often meant the near solitary confinement of the nuclear family, has made many women chronic social isolates quite against their wills (cf. Slater, 1970). As we have also just suggested, women who joined cults may often have been members of the societal elite, with many resources enabling them to experiment freely with cults. For women, but not for men, these three factors may often have gone together. Female members of the societal elite could easily be relatively deprived and socially isolated, all at the same time, and thus seek social involvement in cults.

However, today many cults seem to have equal numbers of male and female members. We think this is one further piece of evidence that our society has moved into a phase in which cults are far less deviant than before and when early adopters, drawn without sex bias from the upper classes, have begun to join in some numbers.

THE POPULAR THEORY OF BRAINWASHING

It has become fashionable among those who hate or fear cults to assert that these novel religions get new members by fiendish deceptions and by rapid frontal assaults on the minds of their victims, that is, by *brainwashing*. Although a lot was written about brainwashing in the 1950s, the concept by now seems to have lost whatever scientific status it temporarily acquired in the wake of Korean War prison camp stories. The term is a translation from the Chinese and certainly represents the attempt to turn unwilling prisoners into faithful followers. But even under the conditions of extreme pressure and control possible in the Communist prison camps, attempts at brainwashing were not commonly successful.

According to Webster, brainwashing is a forcible indoctrination to induce someone to give up basic political, social, or religious beliefs and attitudes and to accept contrasting regimented ideas. Because people are recruited to cults in the liberty of an open society, rather than in the confinement of a prison camp, and are free to reject religious appeals directed at them, the brainwashing theory implies that cults must be especially deceptive and must use overwhelmingly powerful techniques to kidnap the minds of their victims. Because brainwashing is a concept overflowing with extreme connotations and lacking in clear scientific standing, its use is likely to represent an attempt to influence public opinion through propaganda rather than a sober attempt at rational analysis of cult recruitment.

As Shupe and Bromley (1980:30) point out, the metaphor of brainwashing is in many respects a modernized form of the earlier notion of demonic possession: "What the brainwashing metaphor did was to provide a secular equivalent to this archaic religious theme, reshaping it into a form more acceptable to twentieth-century rational man and documented with 'scientific' evidence which would account for such radical individual changes in a fashion more consistent with dominant paradigms of human behavior."

The real meaning of both concepts is to be found in their tactical value for persons or groups who despise religious deviance and wish to destroy it. With this hostile view of recruitment to cults, there is not the slightest reason to grant ordinary civil rights to cults or their members. Both the concept of demonic possession and that of brainwashing urge the utter annihilation of the offending evil and the uninhibited use of the most heroic (or villainous) methods to "rescue" the alleged victims. As Anthony and Robbins (1981:267) note: "The application of brainwashing and mind control metaphors to members of a social movement implies that they are not acting or thinking voluntarily and are not therefore entitled to the freedom of religion and freedom from physical restraint which applies to rational individuals. The primary 'right' vouchsafed to 'brainwashed' converts is the right to be 'cured,' the right to be forcibly liberated from psychoslavery."

So the ideology of brainwashing immediately suggests and justifies the use of counterbrainwashing techniques to free the victims from cultic bondage. Thus, so-called *deprogrammers* such as Ted Patrick were proud to claim great success fighting fire with fire, using what they thought were effective brainwashing techniques to return cult members to their families (Patrick and Dulack, 1976). Of course, the coercive deprogramming bore little relationship to the processes by which people come to join cults in the first place, most especially because deprogramming seemed to depend on first depriving people of their liberty before changing their minds. Some deprogrammings appear to succeed — but the mere fact that some persons do not return to their cult is not proof of a successful deprogramming unless you firmly believe they were mind slaves while members and were not, as is so often the case, in a period of exploration and experimentation that would have taken them away from the cult eventually even without any heroic treatments. And many deprogrammings failed, as in the cases of two members of Seattle's Love Family cult. One was taken by force to Southern California, with a TV crew filming the whole thing, and the other was carried off to Israel, but both made their way back to the cult, despite the greatest efforts to prevent them. Although civil authorities tolerated deprogramming for a time, exposés and the complaints of angry cult members eventually brought the practice to a near halt.

A classic statement of brainwashing theory was provided by William Sargant (1959), who argued that religious conversion, especially when effected by high tension sects and cults, forces a collapse of the nervous system by inflicting intolerable stress. Religious ritual and other intensely emotional religious practices are supposed to overwhelm the individual's ordinary mental equilibrium, to produce bizarre behavior in suggestible persons, and to lead to a sudden, radical change in personality and beliefs. Indeed, Sargant's theory is very physiological — it is the *nerves* that give way under the pressure — thus granting the victim no responsibility for the results.

The idea that intense religion can assault the mind and weaken it to the point of madness is not new. Indeed, we were astonished to discover that the summary volume of the 1860 U.S. Census devoted several paragraphs to this very question, asserting that excessive sectarian religion had driven many hundreds of citizens literally mad and flung them into the mental asylums (Kennedy, 1864). Of course, mad people are entitled to their religion, too. And, in any population of several thousand Americans, a few hundred will belong to sects and sectlike denominations, professing in their madness the same faith held by more numerous sane sectarians. The old census compilers made no attempt to compute rates of madness for different denominations!

Freud and his followers frequently suggested that all religion was a mass delusion, a communal neurosis, or even a shared psychosis (Freud, 1927, 1930). Of course, Freud's circle consisted of well-educated, highly secular persons who prided themselves on their scientific attitudes. But we suggest that the main reason for this hostility to conventional religion was the fact that Psychoanalysis itself was a client cult, struggling to establish itself at the very border of religion. Surely, it offered a package of compensators, some of which were very general, totally outside the prevailing Christian culture. In attacking conventional religions, Psychoanalysis explicitly sought to replace them. For many of Freud's followers, indeed, for an embarrassingly prominent set of his most famous disciples, Psychoanalysis did develop into a religious cult (Rieff, 1968).

At one point in *The Future of an Illusion,* a tract against religion, Freud (1927:86) acknowledged the possibility that the "scientific findings" of Psychoanalysis might be errors:

> You will not find me inaccessible to your criticism. I know how difficult it is to avoid illusions; perhaps the hopes I have confessed to are of an illusory nature, too. But I hold fast to one distinction. Apart from the fact that no penalty is imposed for not sharing them, my illusions are not, like religious ones, incapable of correction. They have not the character of a delusion. If experience should show me — not to me, but to others after me, who think as I do — that we have been mistaken, we will give up our expectations.

If this is the test, then Freud's behavior and that of his disciples proves the point he denied. Orthodox Freudian Psychoanalysis persists, despite 75 years of failure to provide convincing empirical evidence in favor of its claims about the nature of the psyche and dismal data indicating the failure of the technique to cure (Eysenck, 1965; Rachman, 1971; Salter, 1972). This client cult continues to operate confidently, without the slightest interest in scientific evidence about the efficacy of the technique. This is the behavior of a band of the faithful holding tight to compensators. These observations lend some special credence to the hypothesis that the brainwashing theory of cult conversion, as supported by some psychotherapists, is a propaganda tactic that, in part, serves the interests of a competing client cult, Psychoanalysis.

Psychoanalysts call all religion neurotic — or worse — not just high tension brands. Yet careful studies have failed to show any hint of mental illness on the part of active churchgoers when compared with others of similar social standing. That the faithful are better adjusted than the faithless has yet to be proven, but religion certainly does not produce maladjustment (Stark, 1972). Some recent studies of cult members likewise fail to reveal distinctive pathology caused by cults (Galanter et al., 1979; Ungerleider et al., 1979).

We have both studied cults ethnographically, as participant observers — yet certainly we are not cultists ourselves. We have the testimony of our own senses to tell us that the brainwashing metaphor is wrong and that cult members are not recruited by turning them into zombies. Some cults may attract the mentally ill, but it is hard to incorporate such unfortunates into any social group, cults being no exception.

At this point, some well-informed readers may be saying to themselves, "But what about all the testimony by psychotherapists who have treated former cult members? Indeed, what about all the former cult members who claim they were the victims of brainwashing and mind control?" This is a valid question that requires an answer.

First, let us consider the therapists. Many of the most outspoken have treated few, if any, former cultists. Their highly publicized statements about mind control and cult-inspired neuroses are but expressions of their faith in psychological doctrines. Because all religion is "sick," they simply deduce that unusual or deviant religion must be extraordinarily sick. However, a number of those convinced of the mind control thesis have, in fact, treated former cult members and have found them to exhibit psychological problems. The difficulty here is that the only cult members they have examined are defectors who decided they needed therapy (cf. Kiev and Francis, 1964).

It would be surprising if the majority of those who seek psychiatric treatment, whatever their backgrounds, were not diagnosed as having problems. Moreover, all organizations, whether they be cults, churches, labor unions, political parties, service clubs, or fraternal lodges, will attract some proportion of members with less than ideal mental health. Indeed, many neurotics may be particularly drawn to cult movements because of the initial opportunity for human relationships, which the neurotic often lacks, and in hope of finding solutions to their problems. Ultimately, many of these people will fail to find fulfillment in the cult movement, in part because they will find trouble in maintaining firm bonds to others once they are no longer new recruits being showered with special attention. So they will drift on, seeking relief elsewhere. Encountering psychiatric therapists who encourage the view that joining a cult was indeed a symptom of abnormality, some will accept and ratify that view.

One does not accurately gauge the mental health of a cult movement by examining its dropouts who have sought therapy, any more than one would accurately conclude that members of the freshman class of Harvard University were all crazy on the grounds that all who had come to the student counseling service seeking psychotherapy were in fact disturbed (Nicholi, 1967).

What of the many ex-cultists who seek to publicize their claims to have been victims of brainwashing and mind control? Can we ignore their testimony? Let us examine their position more closely. Suppose one has broken one's ties to friends and relatives and greatly upset them by joining a very deviant religious movement. Suppose that later one decides to rejoin conventional society. One must now explain his or her deviant actions. Suppose one says, "Well, it seemed like the thing to do at the time; and the Moonies are really sensitive, dedicated, nice people. But I discovered I was not cut out to be a member." With such words, one gives notice that future deviance might be forthcoming. Conventional people want some guarantee that an episode of deviant behavior is over and that the person now is "cured" and deserving of trust and responsibility (Trice and Roman, 1970). If a person can convince others that the deviant behavior was involuntary, the problem is solved because no defect of character must be dealt with. The story that one was an innocent victim of the Moonies, was subjected to insidious mind control, but has now escaped that captivity, is a sure ticket back into conventional good standing. Moreover, for many angry former cultists, this option was carefully taught to them during a session of deprogramming when they were tormented and threatened to admit they were brainwashed by the cult.

In its general outlines, this situation is not new. During the medieval witchcraft crazes, tens of thousands of persons confessed to having been possessed by the devil and of flying off on broomsticks to horrible Satanic gatherings. Today we are certain that they did not do such things. But they did confess, and they did so because they were accused of these crimes and then interrogated and tortured until they confessed to the charges. Many sincere and even humane churchmen accepted these confessions, although they had been wrung from the accused, thinking that those possessed by Satan were stubborn liars until put to the extreme.

Today not even deprogrammers use the rack and thumbscrew. Yet, in order to prove that one has regained normal standing in conventional society, persons who have sojourned in deviant religion face strong social pressures to confess to mind control. These pressures are imposed by therapists and intimates, and they are reinforced by wild press accounts. In effect, the former cult member cops a plea of not guilty of craziness by reason of temporary captivity — or not guilty of fundamental craziness by reason of temporary craziness. If you joined a cult freely, without mind control or compulsion, how can we be sure you will not turn around and join another one?

The situation we have been describing is but one aspect of the tension with the sociocultural environment many cults experience. If some of these groups survive the persecutions and continue to attract mentally healthy sons and daughters of the upper classes, their tension may diminish greatly. The accusations from their opponents may also diminish because such accusations are not plausible when directed against a church publicly recognized as low in tension.

Cults vary. Therefore, there somewhere may exist cults that fit the brainwashing metaphor. But we have not seen them. There is no need for the notion of brainwashing — unless, of course, one is engaged in a propaganda war against religious novelty. Chapter 14 adequately explains recruitment to cults. Preexisting deprivations and emotional problems may play a role, and cults, like sects, may provide compensation for relative deprivation. But the crucial factor in recruitment is the development of strong social bonds with persons who already are members of the cult. This is a perfectly normal, healthy process. Indeed, it is mad people who find it difficult to form social bonds with others, and any cult that can establish enduring social relationships with the mad may have cured madness, not caused it. As the years pass, it seems easier and easier to draw numbers of perfectly ordinary or above-average people into many cults.

The world is changing. If ever it was necessary to break a person's spirit before he or she would join a novel religion, it is not so now. Gradual but unhalting secularization has weakened the "mainline" denominations. They lost legal secular power long ago; now they have lost much of their former ability to provide efficacious general compensators to their congregations. For many people, especially highly educated members of these faltering churches, the old religious traditions are no longer plausible. Many of these people continue to seek the answers to the enigmas of human existence — in new directions. And, through the medium of new friendships, they join cults.

Conclusion

If only pathetic, confused, "inferior" people join cult movements, then the world can justly scorn novel or exotic forms of religion. Considered from the perspective of persons and organizations that oppose religious innovation, the idea that cults appeal primarily to desperate or aberrant individuals is very useful because it suppresses a number of painful questions. If cultists are beneath contempt, then there is no reason to see in them evidence of the failure of traditional faiths, no necessity to take seriously their alien beliefs, and no need to grant them the freedom to proselytize in respectable society. Thus, opponents gain political power to use against cults from the myth that no reasonable person could ever be attracted to them.

But now that cult movements have touched millions of citizens, and hundreds of thousands actively participate in them, the obvious fact that some reasonable people are involved makes it difficult to dismiss novel religions as mere refuges for stupidity and psychopathology. More and more ordinary people in Western society have respected friends and relatives who have joined cults and thus have personal experience of the fact that cults now recruit many normal people from the more favored segments of society. Some opponents of cults have resorted to the theory that cults use fiendish "brainwashing" techniques to seduce unwitting normal people into joining, thus continuing to disparage novel religions while admitting that they may recruit ordinary citizens.

The evidence we present throughout this book is not compatible with the brainwashing theory. All humans seek explanations about how to gain the greatest rewards and avoid the greatest costs, and it is natural that most of them will come to accept general compensators based on supernatural assumptions. The process of secularization, which reduces the power of the most liberal denominations to provide efficacious compensators, has an especially strong impact on better-educated citizens, as well as upon the geographically mobile moving into and within those geographical areas where the standard denominations are organizationally weakest. The crucial factor leading to membership in a novel religion is the development of social bonds with persons who already are members, a process likely to be as wholesome as it is natural.

Were cultists inferior and cults pathogenic, there would be little reason to suppose that they will play important positive roles in the future of religion. But once we understand that many well-balanced, well-educated people seek the meaning of life in novel and exotic religious groups, we can predict that religious innovations will have significant influence in the coming years. New visions of the sacred will gain popularity while some traditional churches lose.

V Sources of Religious Movements

19 Secularization, Revival, and Cult Formation

Secularization is the dominant theme in modern assessments of the future of religion. According to Webster, the term *secular* means "of or belonging to the world and worldly things as distinguished from the church and religious affairs." Secularization, then, means to become worldly. More specifically, modern writers use the term *secularization* to mean the erosion of belief in the supernatural—a loss of faith in the existence of otherworldly forces.

At the start of this book, we argue that secularization is nothing new, that it is occurring constantly in all religious economies. Through secularization, sects are tamed and transformed into churches. Their initial otherworldliness is reduced and worldliness is accommodated. Secularization also eventually leads to the collapse of religious organizations as their extreme worldliness—their weak and vague conceptions of the supernatural—leaves them without the means to satisfy even the universal dimension of religious commitment. Thus, we regard secularization as the primary dynamic of religious economies, a self-limiting pro-

The major portion of this chapter is a revision of Rodney Stark and William Sims Bainbridge, "Secularization, Revival, and Cult Formation," *Annual Review of the Social Sciences of Religion*, 1980, 4, pp. 85–119. An earlier version of that paper was read at the 1980 annual meeting of the American Association for the Advancement of Science. The latter part of this chapter is a revision of Rodney Stark and William Sims Bainbridge, "Secularization and Cult Formation in the Jazz Age," *Journal for the Scientific Study of Religion*, 1981, 20:4, pp. 360–373.

cess that engenders revival (sect formation) and innovation (cult formation).

Most modern scholars, however, do not regard current trends of secularization as the harbinger of religious change, but as the final twilight of the gods. Many recognize that, in the past, secularization resulted only in the rise of new faiths, but they are convinced that a new factor has entered into and canceled the old equation: the rise of science. Science is expected to make religion implausible, and hence modern secularization will not produce new major religions, but an era of rationality in which mysticism can no longer find a significant place. Anthony F. C. Wallace (1966:264–265), among the most distinguished anthropologists of religion, spoke for the vast majority of modern social scientists when he wrote:

> . . . the evolutionary future of religion is extinction. Belief in supernatural beings and in supernatural forces that affect nature without obeying nature's laws will erode and become only an interesting historical memory. To be sure, this event is not likely to occur in the next generation; the process will very likely take several hundred years, and there will always remain individuals, or even occasional small cult groups, who respond to hallucination, trance, and obsession with a supernaturalist interpretation. But as a cultural trait, belief in supernatural powers is doomed to die out, all over the world, as a result of the increasing adequacy and diffusion of scientific knowledge . . . the process is inevitable.

Clearly, science is a new and potent cultural force, and it has had dramatic impact on many religious organizations. Indeed, a major element in modern secularization involves the retreat by religious bodies from supernatural explanations of various phenomena as science has revealed the natural causes of these phenomena. Moreover, the impact of science has undoubtedly created a period of unusually rapid and extreme secularization. Today, many of the leading religious organizations of Western civilization are so secularized that, to the extent they refer to God at all, it is to the most distant, indistinct, impersonal, and inactive entity.

Thus, the issue is posed. Is this the end of the era of faith? Is science the basis for the "final secularization" of societies? Or is this simply a very dramatic swing of the age-old pendulum? Will this wave of secularization also be self-limiting?

Our theory of religion forces the conclusion that religion is not in its last days. We think that most modern scholars have misread the future because they have mistakenly identified the dominant religious traditions in modern society with the phenomenon of religion in general. Most observers have noted correctly that major Christian-Judaic organizations are failing, but they have not seen or appreciated the vigor of religion in less "respectable" quarters.

Our confidence that religion will persist follows directly from our analysis of what religion is and does, which we outline in Chapter 1. We conclude that supernatural assumptions are the only plausible source for many rewards that humans seem to desire intensely. Only the gods can assure us that suffering in this life will be compensated in the next. Indeed, only the gods can offer a next life — an escape from individual extinction. Only the gods can formulate a coherent plan for life, that is, make meaningful in a fully human way the existence of the natural world of our senses. It can be easily demonstrated that, as long as humans persist in such desires, systems of thought that posit the supernatural will always have a competitive edge over purely naturalistic meaning systems (see chapters 1, 17, and 22).

We see no reason to suppose that the diffusion of science will make humans in the future less motivated to escape death, less affected by tragedy, less inclined to ask, "What does it all mean?" True, science can challenge *some* of the claims made by historic religions, but it cannot provide the primary satisfactions that have long been the raison d'être of religions.

Our theory permits us to understand the rise and persistence of intellectual elites who can live without feeling intense religious needs. But it cannot be made compatible with the eventual mass triumph of scientific rationalism over supernaturalism. This means either that our theory is deeply flawed or that projections of secularization toward a religionless future are simply wrong.

Of course, we believe the latter is the case. Moreover, throughout previous chapters, we have examined many signs that religion per se remains robust in the modern era. One such sign is that those who have abandoned a specific religious affiliation and who report their religion as "none" are hardly the scientific, secular humanists they often are thought to be. In Chapter 17, we find that "nones" often accept such deviant supernaturalism as astrology and are exceptionally attracted to yoga, Zen, and Transcendental Meditation. A second sign, mentioned in Chapter 1, is that the majority of Americans who grew up in irreligious homes ("none") today belong to a Christian denomination (more often a very traditional one). Secularity in one generation typically is followed by reaffiliation in the next. Third, we have noted the relative vigor of the more evangelical Christian denominations. Although the most secularized churches are crumbling, those least secularized still thrive. Finally, it is myopic to note only the weakening of once-potent religious organizations while dismissing the significance of the rise of hundreds of new religions.

THE SECULARIZATION PROCESS

We demonstrate in Chapter 1 that some very general explanations, about how humans can obtain valued rewards and avoid feared costs, can take the form only of compensators and also must postulate the existence of the supernatural. We define *religion* as a system of very general compensators based on supernatural assumptions. This permits a crucial distinction between magic and religion. Following Durkheim (1915), we characterize magic as offering only compensators for specific rewards. The most general compensators are beyond empirical test, but the same does not apply to very specific compensators. Thus, although religion may offer eternal life beyond the grave, a claim beyond evaluation, magic may offer to cure a specific ailment here and now. Indeed, magic competes with science in attempting to produce tangible results. Hence, magic often is very vulnerable to empirical disconfirmation. That magic is often disconfirmed empirically, although religion *need never* face such tests, provides the key to our arguments about science and secularization.

Religions that arise prior to the development of organized science will tend to include magic in their offerings. That is, they will deal not only in very general compensators (which are not subject to empirical evaluation), but will also offer some specific compensators that are subject to empirical evaluation. This will especially be the case for religions that attempt to monopolize a religious economy. As we point out in Chapter 5, monopoly faiths must offer a considerable amount of magic.

Science is simply the name for the development of systematic procedures for evaluating explanations. The process of evaluation will always tend to drive out empirically testable explanations that are false or at least less efficient than some other explanation. In consequence, as science is more widely practiced, it will tend to drive out magic. This is no more than an application of Malinowski's famous middle-range proposition about magic, which, as deduced in our theory, takes the form: People will not exchange with the gods when a cheaper or more efficient alternative is known and available. This simply means that magical explanations about how to gain a desired reward (or avoid a damaging cost) will tend to be discredited by scientific test and to be discarded in favor of scientifically verified explanations.

This tendency has serious consequences for religions that include a significant magical component. Consider the case of the lightning rod (White, 1896). For centuries, the Christian church held that lightning was the palpable manifestation of divine wrath and that safety against lightning could be gained only by conforming to divine will. Because the bell towers of churches and cathedrals tended to be the only tall structures, they were the most common targets of lightning. Following damage or destruction of a bell tower by lightning, campaigns were launched to stamp out local wickedness and to raise funds to repair the tower.

Ben Franklin's invention of the lightning rod caused a crisis for the church. The rod demonstrably worked. The laity began to demand its installation on church towers — backing their demands with a threat to withhold funds to restore the tower should lightning strike it. The church had to admit either that Ben Franklin had the power to thwart divine retribution or that lightning was merely a natural phenomenon. Of course, they chose the latter. But, in so doing, they surrendered a well-known and dramatic magical claim about the nature of the supernatural. Such admissions call into question other claims made by a religion, including even those that are eternally immune from empirical disconfirmation.

Thus, the rise of science meant a retreat by religions that, originating in prescientific ages, contained significant elements of magic. In this way, these religions became increasingly secularized — they made progressively fewer claims about the powers of the supernatural and the extent to which the supernatural was active in the empirical world. Each of these retreats was noted and recorded for posterity.

Meanwhile, because science resulted in more efficacious explanations than did magic (indeed, science is the selection of efficacious explanations), scientists increasingly possessed highly valuable exchange resources. Hence, scientists have tended to become an elite and thus able to withstand opposition from religious elites. Because it can never be clear a priori just where the boundary between magic and religion lies — what seems beyond verification in one time often is easily verified in another — science engenders skepticism toward religion. And, as an elite, scientists are rewarded for such skepticism, and their skepticism tends to permeate all intellectual elites.

As this occurred, a somewhat novel instance of the church-sect process took place. Secularization usually transforms religious groups to bring them into lower tension with their environments. With the rise of science, some low tension bodies found their environment moving away from them. That is, as the general culture was made less hospitable to traditional supernaturalism, major Christian and Jewish groups found themselves in greater tension with their environment. To hold tightly to Genesis, for example was to move from lower to higher tension. To regain (or retain) low tension with society, and thus to best serve the needs of their most dominant and privileged members, these denominations had to water down their doctrines concerning the supernatural — especially those, such as faith healing, that involved demonstrable magic. And, of course, these groups have jettisoned one traditional tenet after another in order to stay in low tension.

Granted that, in the beginning, religious elites fought against the challenge of science. But, being committed to empirically vulnerable positions and opposing a new culture with obvious and profound practical payoffs, they lost. In this century, it has been religious intellectuals, not scientists, who have done the recanting. In recent decades, religious intellectuals have outdone themselves in disparaging traditional supernaturalism in an apparent effort to seek respectability in the eyes of secular intellectuals (cf. Robinson, 1963; Cox, 1965; Kueng, 1976).

Obviously, this is a much oversimplified sketch of modern secularization. We think it does identify key processes, but clearly it omits the rich complexities of concrete historical events (cf. Martin, 1978). These details are beyond the scope of our present needs. We also have not explained the rise of science beyond noting that more efficacious explanations will tend to drive out the less efficacious. Some scholars have even suggested that religion of certain kinds may itself stimulate the growth of science, thus unintentionally accelerating its own decline (Westfall, 1958; Merton, 1970). This is not the place to assess social and historical processes of such magnitude. It is sufficient for present purposes to note the vulnerability of magical elements in religions to scientific disconfirmation. Therefore, let us turn our attention to modern times, when science is highly developed and the dominant religious organizations are severely eroded by repeated retreats from scientific disconfirmation.

When we examine these religious organizations, we find that today they offer only very weak general compensators. The conception of the supernatural they sustain has receded to a remote, inactive, almost nonexistent divinity. We see bishops and theologians denouncing as mere superstition the notion of a god "up there." Does a god who is not "up there" plausibly preside over heaven and offer triumph over death? Many of the most prestigious denominations offer mixed signals at best in answer to this question. Such religions have reached the point where they can no longer offer the quality of general compensators that has been the historic raison d'être of religions. They offer little solace to the bereaved, to the dying, to the poor, or to those who seek to understand the enigmas of existence (Stark and Glock, 1968; Kelley, 1972).

Simply because human societies have the blessings of advanced science does not mean that they are free from existential anxieties or from a desire for rewards that remain unobtainable. These desires persist because science cannot satisfy them. In similar fashion, radical politics ultimately fails to eradicate them. People may commit themselves to radicalism in hopes of satisfying desires for scarce rewards. But, should the revolution occur, relative scarcity (stratification) continues and unmet desires persist (in combination with those desires for unobtainable rewards that the revolutionary movement could not effectively address in the first place).

Given churches (and revolutionary regimes) that fail to meet the desires for efficacious compensators, faiths that effectively offer such compensators will have a most favorable market position. And, to the extent that religious innovation or dissent is possible, such faiths ought to thrive as a result of the secularization of the dominant religious organizations. This reaction against secularization is likely to take two primary forms: *revival* and *innovation*.

Revival

In response to an unmet demand for more efficacious compensators, movements will arise to restore the potency of the conventional religious traditions. This pattern is typified by the vigor of evangelical Protestantism and the growth of the Catholic charismatic movement in contemporary America. The tactic involved is simply to reassert the validity of the general compensators of traditional faith because these have not been (and cannot be) invalidated by scientific discovery.

However, such a reassertion raises the problems that led to the extreme secularization of the major denominations in the first place. Many elements of the Christian-Judaic tradition have, in fact, been disconfirmed by science. Not merely lightning, but the literal interpretation of creation and of the flood, indeed, the underlying astronomical and geological assumptions of the Bible clearly are discrepant with secular knowledge: The sun does not go around the earth and it seems incredible that it ever was stationary in the sky, no matter what God wanted to signal to His people. Thus, the trouble with revival is that it is heir to a whole cultural history, and this history is replete with defeats of doctrine by science. Moreover, as soon as this problem is dealt with by picking and choosing those parts of the tradition that remain invulnerable to disproof, secularization has been reintroduced as legitimate — science will dictate what doctrines can be accepted. Thus, revival seems to be chronically vulnerable to secularization and to lack long-term staying power, especially if there is an alternative. Such alternatives are created by the rise of new religious traditions.

Innovation

The dominant faiths of today arose a very long time ago and offered desired explanations unavailable from science. That is, they were well suited to the culture in which they arose — they did not make claims that were obviously false at that time. In consequence, the dominant faiths suffer from an ineradicable history of defeat because they were not designed for our present culture. But this is not necessarily so for new faiths — faiths that arise to meet the circumstances of *this* culture. A new faith can offer a set of general compensators invulnerable to secularization. Such a faith will have no history of futile holding actions and past defeats by science. It will not have to admit to picking and choosing among its tenets, for it has none at risk. Put another way, new faiths can be fully in harmony with the culture without having to be in any way subservient to it.

A case in point is Mormonism. Although it claims to be merely the next unfolding of the Christian-Judaic tradition, it appeared in the 19th century and was fully compatible with scientific knowledge of that time. Indeed, a major denunciation of the Book of Mormon made by 19th-century Christian theologians was its modernity. Unlike the Bible, which posits a tiny earth and seems to regard the Mediterranean as the whole of the oceans, the Book of Mormon, although claiming to be of ancient origins, bases its accounts on the existence of a large world and on knowledge of all the continents and oceans. Indeed, its primary setting is in the New World; thus, it is aware of the existence of the western hemisphere and of details of the cultures and peoples to be found there. "Unfair," charged the Christian clergy. "How easy to prophesy of the past or of the present time!" wrote Alexander Campbell (1832:13).

As a new faith, Mormonism is much less vulnerable to empirical disconfirmation (although too great reliance on empirical arguments rooted in 19th-century anthropology may be a source of trouble). More recent faiths may entirely eschew empirically vulnerable claims and thus be wholly accommodated to science. This does not mean that a new faith must accommodate itself to prevailing *moral* norms. To the contrary, it would probably be strengthened if it fostered a stricter morality — faiths can lose credibility by being too inexpensive.

Thus, new faiths would appear to have much better long-run chances than do old faiths for maintaining highly efficacious compensators in the midst of a culture that is corrosive to magic. Of course, our predictions depend upon the continuing social influence of organized science. Although a new dark age might restore traditional Christianity to its former throne (Miller, 1960), a collapse of civilization could as easily establish contemporary cults as the dominant churches (Sorokin, 1941).

The argument we have developed thus far is incompatible with the dominant view of the relationship between secularization and religious innovation. The prevailing wisdom, best expressed by Bryan Wilson (1975b) and Richard Fenn (1978), is that the prevalence of cults or "new religions" in the modern world is part and parcel of the process of secularization *as such*. Thus, Wilson (1975b:80) argues that the modern world produces "a supermarket of faiths; received, jazzed-up, home-spun, restored, imported and exotic. But all of them co-exist only because the wider society is so secular, because they are relatively unimportant consumer items." Wilson's evaluation of new religions as superficial and inauthentic is echoed by many others (Truzzi, 1970; Fenn, 1978).

This evaluation of cults is rooted in Christian-Judaic parochialism. That cults fall outside the dominant, respectable, religious traditions of Western civilization is taken as prima facie evidence of their fundamental inferiority. That, in the first century, Christianity was both deviant and unimpressive is ignored. New faiths are dismissed as inauthentic because they are new.

We suggest that anyone with a serious interest in empirically testing the worth of this judgment spend some time in one of the highly respectable denominations (Episcopalian, for example) and then spend some time with Mormons or Moonies. Then make a comparative judgment about the depth of commitment and the authenticity of these religious groups. It will be patent that Mormonism and the Unification Church are not "relatively unimportant consumer items." Furthermore, if we can demonstrate that cult movements are serving as alternatives to conventional faiths, what grounds remain for calling the one authentic and the other superficial? However, many modern cults do seem in many ways to be ill conceived and implausible. We expect that many of these will be short-lived and insignificant. But it takes only a *few* effective cults to serve as the vehicle for a massive religious renewal. Indeed, it might take only one.

Simply to equate cults with religious trivia and to make them a *symptom* of secularization is to miss the opportunity to investigate the link between secularization and religious innovation. Surely it is to deprive the concept of secularization of coherent meaning if we describe persons deeply engrossed in supernatural belief and worship as secularized. We therefore propose to examine cult formation as a religious reaction to secularization and to suggest that simply because some faiths retain little religious content is no reason to suppose that all faiths have been emptied of the power to satisfy fundamental human needs.

Another problem with the view that cults reflect secularization per se has been the failure to distinguish among cultic social phenomena. In Chapter 2, we point out that not all cults are full-fledged religions. There and in chapters 10 and 11 we suggest that only cult movements are religions. Client cults deal primarily in magic, not religion, and consequently cannot bind their clients into stable organizations. Audience cults deal primarily in myth and entertainment. Because they function primarily through the mass media, audience cults attract considerable attention and may well be the basis for judgment of all cults as unimportant consumer items. Surely such a blanket judgment is absurd in light of the deaths of 917 members of the Jim Jones cult. People do not commit mass suicide on behalf of unimportant consumer items.

Given our line of analysis, it follows that the weaker the established religions become, the more religious innovation ought to occur and the more such innovation will be sustained by a growing population in search of new religious alternatives. Daniel Bell (1971:474) expressed the idea succinctly:

> Where religions fail, cults appear. This situation is the reverse of early Christian history where the new, coherent religion competed with multiple cults and drove them out because it had the superior strength of a theology and an organization. But when theology erodes and organization crumbles, when the institutional framework of religion begins to break up, the search for a direct experience which people can feel to be religious facilitates the rise of cults.

Although the low tension denominations are threatened everywhere and the challenge of science is a worldwide antagonist, the organizational and social weakness of conventional religion is more pronounced in some places than in others. For example, wherever rates of geographical migration are especially high, a greater proportion of the population will be free to experiment in search of more efficacious systems of compensators because their social bonds to the old organizations are loosened. Thus, we can expect great geographic variations and can test our theory through a geographic hypothesis: *Cults will abound where conventional churches are weakest.*

To follow the logic of the dominant view of secularization leads to a contrary prediction. Secularization is seen as an unstoppable trend. If we mean by secularization a decline in the credibility of all systems of thought that postulate the existence of the supernatural, then it follows that secularization produces people who resist supernatural explanations. To the extent that occurs, there will not exist a clientele for religion, whether new or old, or for magic. People who have turned their backs on the rich variety available within the Christian-Judaic tradition are unlikely to take up with exotic cults. This leads to a hypothesis wholly opposite to the one we have advanced: *Cults will be weakest where conventional churches are weakest.*

We have argued that the conventional religious organizations have been eroded by centuries of conflict with science. We have *not* argued that this has caused masses of people to lose their belief in some form of supernatural or their interest in very general compensators based on supernatural assumptions. Rather, we have argued that the mainline churches in the United States are failing to offer such compensators in effective form because these organizations have adopted very vague conceptions of the supernatural. Thus, our primary concern is with *organizational weakness* of the religious bodies within the Christian-Judaic tradition. Indeed, the hypotheses to be investigated make contradictory predictions about the relationship between the strength of traditional religious organizations and the vigor of religious innovation — the formation of cults. Hence, the most appropriate of available measures of organizational weakness is the rate of membership in conventional churches (see Chapter 4).

Church Membership and Cult Movements in the 1970s

If our conclusions about the self-limiting character of secularization are correct, we ought to find that there is a significant *negative* correlation between the church membership rate and the cult movement rate (see Chapter 9). That is, the higher the church membership rate of a state, the lower its cult movement rate ought to be.

If others are correct that secularization is a process that leads to the demise of religion — that people drop out of the traditional churches comfortably to accept a nonreligious outlook — then the sign of the correlation ought to be *positive*. Cults ought to flourish where traditional religion is strongest — where large numbers of "religious" people are still to be found. Two so diametrically opposed hypotheses provide a rare opportunity to conduct a crucial test of two lines of argument.

Our first computation revealed an *r* of −.37 between the church membership rate and the cult rate using all 50 states as our units of analysis (see Table 19.1). This correlation is highly significant: .004. This is strong confirmation of our hypothesis that cult formation thrives in response to crumbling commitment to traditional religion. Cults do not flourish where traditional religion is strong, but in areas that, judging by membership in conventional religious groups, are the most secularized.

However, we were not satisfied that our initial analysis did justice to the real strength of the relationship. A major problem is a defect in our measure of the cult movement rate, which puts an artificial limit on the observed correlation. Nine states score zero on the index. This does not mean that they have no cult activity. Nor does it mean that they have the same amount of cult activity. It merely means that whatever level they have is unmeasured. Because these states differ considerably in terms of their church membership rates, they add a great deal of noise to the data and severely restrict the size of the potential correlation.

TABLE 19.1   *Correlations (r) Between the Church Membership Rate and Various Cult Rates for States*

Measure of Cult Activity	Correlation with Church Membership Rate	Significance
1a. Cult Movement Rate	−.37	.004
1b. Cult Movement Rate (with nine zero-rate states and New Mexico omitted)	−.61	.001
2. Cult Centers Rate	−.52	.001
3. "New Age" Stores and Restaurants Rate	−.33	.009
4. *Fate* Letter Writers Rate	−.58	.001
5. *Fate* Subscription Rate	−.68	.001
6. Psychic Practitioners Rate	−.45	.001
7. TM Initiation Rate 1970	−.42	.001
8. TM Initiation Rate 1975	−.51	.001
9. Astrologers Rate[a]	−.35	.007

[a]N = 47; all others, N = 50.

We therefore removed these nine states from the data. Recomputing r based on the remaining 41 cases, the correlation increased to −.49 and significance improved beyond .001. Considering that a number of additional states with extremely similar and low cult rates (probably also poorly measured) still remain in the data, this seems to us a very high correlation lending considerable plausibility to our analysis of secularization.

However, we felt justified in making one additional change in the data. New Mexico is an extremely deviant case, lying far out from the slope of the observed correlation and greatly influencing it. This is easy to see, given that New Mexico is second highest in terms of cults (with a rate of 9.1 per million residents) while standing twelfth from the top in terms of church membership: 640 per 1,000. Deviant cases can occur by chance, by measurement error, or for quite specific reasons. This led us to make a laborious county-by-county analysis of how New Mexico produced its high rates. States are not the ideal unit of analysis for our study because they are not always very homogeneous in terms of social and cultural patterns. Thus, for example, the very low church membership rate of California tends to mask somewhat higher rates in less populous counties well inland from the coast. We have utilized states as our unit of analysis simply because it was not possible to create cult rates for smaller ecological units.

In the case of New Mexico, use of state as the unit of analysis turned out to be extremely misleading. New Mexico contains many counties with extraordinarily high church membership rates and others with very low rates. Summed, these produce a quite high overall membership rate for the state. However, the cults that give New Mexico its high rate on that measure are located in those counties with extremely low church membership rates. That is, within New Mexico, the expected relationship between secularization and cult formation holds very clearly. But, when New Mexico is taken as a whole, these extreme internal variations produce a highly deviant case that reduces the correlation between church membership and cult formation. For these reasons, we omitted New Mexico from the data set and recomputed the correlation on the basis of 40 cases. This resulted in an r of $-.61$, significant beyond the .001 level.

We believe that we observed good methodological practices in dropping cases, as we have reported, and that the correlation of $-.61$ is the best of the three estimates of the extent to which the vigor of traditional religious bodies is negatively correlated with cult activity. Some readers, of course, may disagree. If so, we direct them to the highly significant correlation ($r = -.37$) observed when all 50 cases were used. If we take that as the most credible estimate, we are still in the position of having clearly eliminated one hypothesis and supported the other. Cults flourish where membership in traditional religious bodies is low. They are rare where membership in traditional religious bodies is high.

Further insight into this matter can be seen in data we reported in Chapter 4. Belief in the supernatural does not vary nearly so much across regions of the United States as do church membership rates. Although a smaller proportion of persons along the West Coast hold such beliefs than elsewhere (and this is also the region where church membership is lowest), levels of belief remain quite high — for example, the great majority of persons living in California, Washington, and Oregon believe in a personal God and may pray frequently. Thus, although some persons in this region are not members of established churches because they have embraced a secular outlook, the modal person in this region retains belief in the supernatural while being unchurched. Secularization has reduced the traditional churches to a minority status, but it has not created an irreligious culture, only an unchurched one. This is precisely the condition under which we theorize that cults are bound to arise (if they are not ruthlessly suppressed).

What we have argued is that centuries of secularization have made ruins of many of the traditional religious bodies. But the process of secularization has not caused people to reject the possible existence of supernatural forces or caused them no longer to desire things that are difficult or impossible to obtain in this world. A simple application of the laws of supply and demand would lead one to expect that such a vacuum would tend to be filled. Indeed, many cults are founded in a purely entrepreneurial fashion, as Chapter 8 notes. The data show that new religious movements are making many efforts to fill the vacuum being left by declining adherence to the traditional faiths.

OTHER CULT ACTIVITY MEASURES

We have noted several limitations to the data on cult movements, particularly the inability to measure variations across states that lack a cult headquarters. In consequence, we sought other means to measure cult activity within states. As we report in Chapter 10, we were able to secure a number of additional measures.

Our second measure is based on the *Spiritual Community Guide* (Singh, 1974). This guide does not list all the groups on which our cult movement rates are based, but it has the advantage of listing each of the centers or outposts of groups it covers, rather than just their headquarters. One section lists 1,345 centers and communities "devoted to the spiritual path, raising one's consciousness, transmitting higher knowledge or promoting universal love and unity," (Singh, 1974:110). Only three states failed to achieve at least one entry. Thus, in transforming these data into a rate of cult centers and communities per million residents for each state, we were able to distinguish among many states that were not differentiated by the cult movement rate. And the large number of cases probably helps distinguish among states with only one or two cult movements as well. The church membership rate is strongly negatively correlated with the cult centers rate: −.52 (significant at the .001 level). Again our hypothesis is sustained.

For a third measure of cult activity, we returned to the *Spiritual Community Guide,* which also provides a national list of "New Age" bookstores, foodstores, and restaurants offering magical nourishment for body and soul. The 1,023 stores and restaurants listed in the guide provided a new set of state rates for this very different indicator of cult activity. Again our hypothesis is confirmed by a correlation of −.33 with the church membership rate (significant at the .009 level). This measure is flawed because Vermont has a highly deviant rate, 60 per million, 3 times the second place state and 12 times the national average. When Vermont is removed, the correlation rises to −.56, significant well beyond the .001 level.

Our fourth measure of cult activity is based on coding 2,086 letters from readers published in *Fate* magazine from January 1960 through

September 1979. Although the *Spiritual Community Guide* is the result of great diligence on the part of its editors, the fact that it comes from California suggests a possible geographic bias; so it is worth remembering that *Fate* magazine is edited and published in Illinois. Again we transformed the data into state rates per million residents. As can be seen in Table 19.1, once again our hypothesis is confirmed. Church membership is correlated $-.58$ with the *Fate* letter writers rate (significant at the .001 level).

Our fifth measure also comes from *Fate*, the tabulation of subscribers to the magazine kindly provided by the publisher, Curtis G. Fuller. A total of 82,812 persons received the November 1979 issue through the mail, 79,907 of them residents of the 50 states. These data on the magazine's circulation do not merely duplicate our earlier count of stories submitted by readers because most subscribers may enjoy *Fate* privately without risking censure from friends and family, but published stories broadcast their authors' involvement with the occult. This measure also shows a strong negative correlation with the church member rate, $-.68$.

A sixth measure of cult activity is based on *The International Psychic Register* (McQuaid, 1979), published in Erie, Pennsylvania. This comprehensive guide lists 705 "psychic and metaphysical practitioners" in the United States, including aura readers, dowsers, psychic investigators, parapsychologists, past lives readers, and tarot readers. Converting these listings into state rates per million residents, we found the psychic practitioners rate was highly correlated with each of our other measures. As shown in Table 19.1, this rate also replicates our previous results: It is correlated $-.45$ with the church membership rate.

Our seventh and eighth measures are complete figures for urban initiates to Transcendental Meditation for the years 1970 and 1975, data we also report in Chapter 13. TM accepted the status of deviant cult movement in 1977, although it had previously presented itself as a relatively low tension client cult. The particular data set analyzed here lists the number of persons initiated each year whose homes were in 5,629 urban areas, a total of 16,066 in 1970 and 232,306 in 1975. In calculating rates, we divided each state's total initiates for a given year by the estimated urban population. We chose 1970 because it was the earliest single year for which we could calculate state rates and 1975 because it was the peak year for TM. Thus, we measured two different stages in the life cycle of one of the most popular recent cults. Again the correlations are significant and in the predicted direction, $-.42$ for 1970 and $-.51$ for 1975.

Our ninth and last measure is a tabulation of all 571 professional astrologers listed in all classified telephone directories for the nation's 277 standard metropolitan statistical areas. We found that this measure has a rather strong bias toward large cities compared with other measures, but, in a sense, this merely adds variety to what is, in toto, a very comprehensive set of indicators of cult activity. Unfortunately, two states lack metropolitan areas, and an anti-fortune-telling law in Pennsylvania prevents astrologers from advertising; so here we are reduced from 50 to 47 cases. But again we see an association that supports our hypothesis, $-.35$.

To sum up: Nine independent measures of cult activity yield identical results. Cult activity seems to be a *response* to secularization. Cults flourish where the conventional churches are weakest. Indeed, as already noted, the failure of the conventional churches to attract the majority of residents of West Coast states is not a symptom of the emergence of a population of atheists and agnostics; in that sense, secularization has made very little headway in American society. What organizational secularization has produced is a large population of unchurched people who retain their acceptance of the existence of the supernatural. They seem only to have lost their faith in the ability of the conventional churches to interpret and serve their belief in the supernatural. Hence, it should be no surprise that many of these unchurched believers are willing, perhaps eager, to examine new religions, to find a faith that can offer an active and vigorous conception of the supernatural that is compatible with modern culture.

SECULARIZATION AND REVIVAL

Because revival represents an effort to protect and maintain deep attachments to the traditional religions, rather than efforts to create new religions, we do not expect it to flourish where the traditional churches are weakest. To the contrary, we expect efforts at revival to be centered where the traditional churches are still reasonably vigorous. Put another way, if cult formation reflects the efforts of the unchurched to become churched, revival reflects the efforts of the churched to remain churched.

We conceive of religious revival primarily in terms of the emergence and growth of sect movements. As the traditional faiths move toward greater accommodation with secular society, they give birth to many groups that desire to retain or to reinstate more otherworldly versions of that faith. Sects are high tension, schismatic movements within a conventional (nondeviant) religious tradition.

Our analysis leads to the conclusion that cult and sect formation are not direct functional alternatives. Rather, we think they are quite different responses to secularization that predominate at different stages in the secularization process. Sect formation is, in part, a response to early stages of weakness in the general compensators provided by the conventional churches. Cult formation tends to erupt in later stages of church weakness, when large sectors of the population have drifted away from all organizational ties to the prevailing faiths.

Applied to cross-sectional data, this line of reasoning leads to the prediction that sect formation will be concentrated in areas with higher, rather than lower, church membership rates. But the situation is not as simple as with cults, and we might not expect as strong a relationship. For example, it might be that the relationship between the church membership rate and sect formation is slightly curvilinear, high in areas of moderate institutional decay of the low tension denominations and low where they are either well entrenched or very weak. Our data set, limited to a mere 50 cases (the states), does not permit sensitive statistical analysis to resolve all these complexities, but it is adequate for testing the main propositions.

In Chapter 6, we examine American-born sects and identify a list slightly shorter than that of cult movements. We tabulate them similarly and code each existing sect group in the nation according to the state in which its headquarters is located. As with cults, many sects are small and have all their members in one state. But although few cults have an extensive membership, many sects are quite large and have members in many states. Having been forced to code a sect in one state only leaves much to be desired in terms of measurement. However, lacking state-by-state membership data on most sects, we had no other choice. And, as with the data on cult movements, a number of states were essentially unmeasured in terms of their sect activity, having no sect headquarters located within their borders.

When we compared the data on cult and sect movements, we found that the average sect is much older than the average cult. Sixty-one percent of the cult movements we identified had been founded since 1959, but only 20 percent of sects were this new. If we are right about sects tending to occur at an earlier stage of the secularization process, this is the kind of difference we ought to find between cults and sects. These findings also indicate that, at present, many more cults than sects are being formed. However, it appears that sects have been better able to survive in the United States, especially in earlier eras; hence, some of the difference in the average age of cults and sects is caused by the greater longevity of sects. Because only existing sects and cults can be counted with any accuracy, we are not able to show that many more sects than cults were forming in the United States 50 or 100 years ago. Our data conform to such a conclusion but cannot fully sustain it.

However, when we examine the correlation between the church membership rate and the sect rate, we find additional support for our hypothesis. Although the cult movement rate was strongly negatively correlated with the church membership rate, the sect movement rate is positively correlated with church membership. The correlation is $+.25$, significant at the .02 level. Sects tend to thrive where the conventional churches are stronger. This is not merely a case of autocorrelation, because few of our sects were willing, able, or asked to provide state and county data to the survey by the National Council of Churches; hence, they are not included in the church membership rates. Thus, it seems reasonable to conclude that sects and cults are not simply interchangeable responses to secularization, but are relatively different.

An additional way to demonstrate that cult and sect movements are not basically the same is to examine the relationships between them. We expect to find the absence of a positive correlation, which would indicate they are indeed phenomena with distinctive social significance and causes, and perhaps a slight negative correlation. Table 19.2 shows the correlations between the sect rate and our nine measures of cult activity.

The findings are very persuasive. All nine measures of cult activity are negatively correlated with the sect rate, five of them significantly. None shows a significant positive correlation. Two factors account for the lack of a significant negative correlation between cult and sect movement rates. First, both rates suffer from a lack of differentiation among a number of states having no cult and/or no sect headquarters.

TABLE 19.2 *Correlations* (r) *Between the Sect Movement Rate and Various Cult Rates for States*

Measure of Cult Activity	Correlation with Sect Movement Rate	Significance
1. Cult Movement Rate	$-.03$	.42
2. Cult Centers Rate	$-.40$	.002
3. "New Age" Stores and Restaurants Rate	$-.37$	.004
4. *Fate* Letter Writers Rate	$-.17$	.12
5. *Fate* Subscription Rate	$-.30$	.02
6. Psychic Practitioners Rate	$-.17$	.12
7. TM Initiation Rate 1970	$-.43$	.001
8. TM Initiation Rate 1975	$-.52$	.001
9. Astrologers Rate[a]	$-.17$	.13

[a] N = 47; all others, N = 50.

Many other states are virtually not differentiated on one or both measures because their rates are extremely low and hence about the same. (To remove all these cases would eliminate so many states that there are too few left for adequate analysis.) Because a lack of cult or sect headquarters tends to be associated with having a small population, some pressure toward a positive correlation is produced by many small states with artificially similar low scores on both cult and sect headquarters rates. A second problem is that there is a modest tendency for cult and sect headquarters to be located in regional urban centers as a matter of convenience. This tendency will also cause some positive correlation between the two rates. The net result is no correlation at all because negative and positive tendencies cancel out.

The other eight measures of cult activity do not suffer from these problems—each gives a somewhat more sensitive measurement of interstate differences in cult activity. Although three of the eight correlations fall short of the .10 level of significance, the remaining five are individually significant, and the entire set adds up to a very convincing rejection of the null hypothesis. If Vermont is removed from the New Age stores and restaurants rate, its correlation with the sect movement rate strengthens to $-.39$, significant at the .003 level. Of course, our theory would have been confirmed merely by the lack of a positive correlation. These negative correlations give powerful confirmation that cults and sects are responses to very different stages in secularization.

We have worked with the best data available, but none of these measures is as good as might be desired. The best data can be produced only by a census or an extremely large survey study that would permit us to examine actual membership rates in all the various cult and sect movements in existence. Such data do not exist and probably never will.

Despite the limits of our various measures, the findings offer reasonably substantial support for our fundamental thesis. The weakening of the traditional churches does not seem to portend the sudden demise of religion. Secularization seems instead to be prompting its own religious solutions. While the mainline denominations discard their traditional confessions, clash over the ordination of women and homosexuals, and often seem to regard the governance of South Africa as the central religious matter of the day (and, in so doing, alienate thousands more of their current members), other movements, both sects and cults, are dealing in a far richer expression of the supernatural.

Given that our rates are based on 501 current cult movements and 417 active sects, the nation does not lack for religious alternatives. These data lead to the conclusion that the current wonderment over the present wave of deviant religion and mysticism is misplaced. The current vitality of deviant religion is amazing only on the assumption that religion in general is being overwhelmed by secularization. If we see that only particular religious organizations, albeit those with the longest history and the highest social standing, are crumbling, not religion in general, then it should be no surprise that new organizations are moving in on the market no longer effectively served by the old ones.

Cult Activity in the Roaring Twenties

Based on current data for the United States, we have found strong confirmation for our thesis that secularization is a self-limiting process that produces religious innovation. The trouble is that, when a test of a very general theory must rest on data from one nation and one time, many ad hoc counterarguments can be constructed. Thus, we must seek tests from many times and places.

Ideally, we would like empirical data far distant in time and place. What we would not give for a set of data from ancient China! Perhaps, with it, we could demonstrate how the progressive secularization of Confucianism (which came to be as empty of supernaturalism as is modern Unitarianism) was closely followed by the explosion of Buddhism and Taoism. We can, however, seek to replicate our work within more modest variations in time and place. The following chapter crosses the border into Canada; here we look back in time. The 1926 data we report in Chapter 11 permit examination of smaller units of analysis than do our contemporary U.S. data. Earlier in this chapter, we could not work with units smaller than states for lack of reliable cult rates for smaller units.

Using states caused us some concern, for many states are very heterogeneous culturally. Recall that we were forced to exclude New Mexico from the analysis because it combined a very high church membership rate (sustained by extremely high rates in more rural Catholic counties) with a very high cult movement rate (based on rapidly growing counties with very low church membership rates). For the Roaring Twenties, we can analyze cities as well as states and thus guard against findings influenced by intrastate variations.

The cult data reported in Chapter 11 come from a marvelous set of surveys carried out by the U.S. Bureau of the Census. The best of these, done in 1926, gathered good data on over 200 denominations and permits the calculation of valid church membership rates for each state and for each city of over 25,000 population (Bainbridge and Stark, 1981). Table 19.3 shows the correlations between the church membership rate and rates for five cult movements, using both states and cities as units of analysis. Here we focus on the cults that proved to be the best

TABLE 19.3   *Church Membership and Cult Membership Rates for States and Cities, 1926*

Cult Movements	Correlation (r) with Church Membership Rates			
	States[a]	Significance	Cities[b]	Significance
Christian Science	−.54	.001	−.59	.001
Theosophy	−.52	.001	−.52	.001
Liberal Catholic	−.31	.01	−.38	.001
Divine Science	−.28	.02	−.20	.04
Baha'i	—	—	−.30	.004

[a]N = 48 states.
[b]N = 79 cities with 100,000 or more population.

indicators of local receptivity to novel religions, as identified in Chapter 11, and consider just the 79 largest cities with the most reliable rates. Overall, the findings strongly confirm our results from contemporary data, and there is very high concordance between data based on the cities and on the states. For clearer discussion, we consider the results for each cult movement.

Christian Science

In Chapter 11, we conclude that Christian Science membership data offer the best single measure of a city's or a state's receptivity to cult movements. We cite a number of reasons. First, Christian Science is a native-born faith and well suited to American culture. Second, by 1926, it was large, reporting more than 200,000 members nationally. Size is important because it tends to smooth out idiosyncratic effects such as the impact of one very effective missionary going to one particular place — a factor that can easily distort membership patterns for small cults. Third, by 1926, Christian Science had been in existence for 50 years and had spread to every state and had time to establish itself. Finally, and most important, Christian Science was not subject to any substantial migration effects. It grew by local recruitment and thus offers a measure of local receptivity to a novel faith.

Table 19.3 shows a very large and highly significant negative correlation (r = −.54 and −.59) between the church membership rate and the Christian Science membership rate for both states and cities. Christian Science did not flourish where the conventional churches were strong, but where they were weak. Indeed, looking at specific state rates illustrates this very clearly. Christian Science was founded in Boston and has remained headquartered there. Yet, by 1926, Massachusetts and other

New England states were not the focus of Christian Science success. Instead, Christian Science was much stronger on the West Coast — in California, Oregon, and Washington — than anywhere else. These also were states with among the lowest church membership rates.

Theosophy

The Theosophical Society is a blend of European occultism and Eastern mysticism. It was founded in New York in 1879 by Helena Petrovna Blavatsky, a Russian who lived for many years in India. Today many Theosophical groups exist in the United States, most of them small. The 1926 religious census included the largest group, the American Theosophical Society, with more than 7,000 members in 223 lodges, and the schismatic Theosophical Society of New York, with only 55 members in 1 lodge. Our analysis combines these groups.

Table 19.3 shows that Theosophy also was stronger where the conventional churches were weaker. Across the states, the correlation between church membership and Theosophical membership rates is −.52, and the correlation is the same with large cities as the unit of analysis. Thus, although Theosophy had only a fraction of the members attracted by Christian Science, it also provides clear evidence that cults flourish where churches lag.

Liberal Catholics

Theosophy attracted considerable attention among Old Catholic and Anglican clergy. In a process that depicts our theory of cult formation in miniature, clergy who had rejected most of the supernatural elements of Christianity found themselves in need of an active conception of the supernatural. Unable to reembrace the old, they embraced the new. In 1915, a group of these clergy broke away from their churches to form a new cult movement that combined the traditional Christian high mass with the esoteric supernaturalism of Madame Blavatsky.

The secularization of churches does not mainly produce secularized people, but people who lack adequate means to meet their religious needs. The fact that clergy who had rejected the literal divinity of Jesus and doctrines of salvation were eager to adopt Theosophy's elaborate fabric (ascended masters, an active spirit world, and communication with the dead) reveals that they had not become secular humanists. The group they formed was a novel organization dedicated to supernaturally based general compensators, and they named it somewhat ambiguously the Liberal Catholic Church. In 1917, the movement was brought to the United States by Bishop James Wedgwood, who traveled the country and ordained priests. In the 1926 census, only nine years after the cult began in this country, the Liberal Catholics had 39 congregations and 1,799 members.

Given smaller numbers of members, the correlations for Liberal Catholics in Table 19.3 are somewhat depressed, for some states and cities have a zero membership rate in this cult. Yet, highly significant correlations obtain ($r = -.31$ and $-.38$). Once again our hypothesis is confirmed.

Divine Science

Divine Science originated in the United States and belongs to the New Thought family of cult movements. It began as two independent movements, one formed by Malinda Cramer in San Francisco in 1885 and the other by Nona L. Brooks and her sister Fannie James in Denver in 1888. Both groups stressed healing and theological monism. A visit by Cramer to Denver in 1889 resulted in a merger, and the group slowly began to spread across the nation. The 1926 census reported 22 congregations and 3,466 members of Divine Science.

Once again, the small number of cases limits the strength of possible correlations. But, once again, significant correlations obtain and support our hypothesis ($r = -.28$ and $-.20$).

Baha'i

Baha'i is a Persian (Iranian) cult movement that began in the mid-19th century. In 1893, a world parliament of religions was held in Chicago and Baha'ism was represented. This soon led to the founding of a group in Chicago and the launching of a national effort at conversion. Today there are 980 local Baha'i assemblies in the United States. In 1926, the census found only 44 assemblies with a total of 1,247 members.

Because of Baha'i's small number of members and their concentration in large cities, correlations based on states are meaningless (and nonsignificant) — 31 states have a zero rate of Baha'i membership. However, this problem is overcome when data on cities of 100,000 or more are examined. As can be seen in Table 19.3, the correlation between the church membership rate and the Baha'i membership rate is $-.30$ and significant beyond .004.

Thus, we have found powerful confirmation for our hypothesis. Using membership for five independent cult movements, we have found that, in 1926, as today, cults flourish where the churches are weak. Secularization does seem to prompt religious innovation.

Using partial correlation techniques, we examined the relationships between the cult membership rates and the church membership rates while holding constant a number of other variables. The variables that made a significant difference were all measures of population turnover. For example, there is a correlation of .58 between proportion of the population born in the same state where they currently reside and the church membership rate for the 79 big cities. The correlation between this measure of population stability and the Christian Science membership rate is. −.45, but using partial correlations to control for this variable leaves the correlation linking the Christian Science rate and the church membership rate highly significant, reducing it only from −.59 to −.45.

Population turnover is a major factor in reducing church membership. We discuss this at length in Chapter 4. Rapid population turnover weakens the social networks by which all voluntary organizations are maintained. People deficient in social bonds, such as recent arrivals in a city, will tend to seek relationships with other persons and with formal organizations, and some of them will be recruited to deviant religious organizations through new friendships they form. Thus, it is possible that social disorganization, not the weakness of the churches in itself, is the cause of cult recruitment. However, with this factor controlled, significant correlations remained between church membership and cult membership.

CLIENT CULTS

Some of our contemporary data are about cults that deal primarily in magic, not fully developed religion. These cults do not bind members into a social movement, but consist of short-term exchanges involving specific compensators — an exchange best characterized as that between consultant and client. For this reason, we have identified such cult phenomena as *client cults*. Our concern is to identify magical practitioners and their customers because our theory shows the connection as well as the difference between magic and religion and because magical cults often evolve into fully developed cult movements, a process we examine in chapters 8, 12, and 13.

Client cults were not included in the 1926 religious census because they do not maintain churches. Hence, astrologers, water dowsers, fortune-tellers, and the like cannot be found by an enumeration of religious congregations. However, the regular U.S. Census does yield useful data on some client cult practitioners. Examination of the detailed occupational categories used by the census shows at least three that belong in the client cult category: healers, chiropractors, and inventors.

In Chapter 11, we give extended attention to the validity of these occupational titles as measures of client cult practitioners. Table 19.4

TABLE 19.4   *Church Membership and Client Cult Practitioners for States and Cities, 1926*

| Client Cult Practitioners | Correlation (r) with Church Membership Rates | | | |
	States[a]	Significance	Cities[b]	Significance
Healers	−.34	.01	−.62	.001
Chiropractors	−.60	.001	−.57	.001
Inventors	−.13	NS	−.27	.01

[a]N = 48 states.
[b]N = 79 cities with 100,000 or more population.

shows the correlations between rates of these three client cult occupations and the church membership rates for 1926. Although the occupational data come from the 1930 census and thus are four years later than the church membership data, there is no reason to suppose this matters. Church membership rates for cities and states are extremely slow to change. Indeed, the correlation between the 1926 and 1971 church membership rates for states is .75, as measured by Pearson's *r*.

Looking at the table, we see that all six coefficients are negative, as our theory predicted. For healers (persons who attempt to cure disease outside the conventional medical professions), the correlations are −.34 for states and −.62 for cities. Chiropractors (practitioners of a pseudoscience founded by an Iowa grocer) achieve very powerful negative associations with church membership, −.60 and −.57. We grant that the category of inventor is not as clean a measure of client cult activity as healer or chiropractor, although we think most legitimate inventors were listed under other occupations, such as "engineer." But inventors tend to be where the churches are weak. The correlation for cities is −.27, significant beyond the .01 level, although the correlation for states falls short of significance.

By basing our analysis on data that are more than 50 years old, we have tried not merely to replicate other tests of our theory, but also to place the phenomenon of cult formation in a historical perspective. Specifically, we have meant to reveal the inadequacy of most recent work on cults that has mistakenly emphasized the uniqueness of recent developments. The most novel aspect of cult formation in the past decade has been the attention given it by journalists and social scientists. A few unusual events have attracted attention to the fact that many movements that are new to the United States have recently appeared and many others have formed that are entirely new. This has led many to the false conclusion that the phenomenon of cult formation in this country is itself something new — that we are living in novel times. The consequence of this view is to encourage a search for unique features of the present to account for the current outburst of religious innovation.

But cult formation in the United States is not a recent outburst; it has had a relatively high and constant rate of occurrence. Cults have been forming in this nation since the earliest days of settlement, and others have arrived regularly from Europe and Asia over the same period. This phenomenon cannot be explained by a search for unique aspects of the 1960s and 1970s. What is needed is a much more general conception of why and how new religions form.

We have isolated some important, general processes that prompt the formation and subsequent fate of new religions. By basing our analysis in this section in the 1920s, we escape the grasp of trendy explanations. Our basic premise is that cults will form in all societies, but that they will tend to flower to the extent that religions operate under free market conditions. Given that religions in this country have long been relatively free to seek followers, new groups have been a consistent element of the religious scene. Most new groups have failed; some have done very well. To understand how cults gain a following, we must examine the overall dynamics of the market within which they operate, not merely look at aspects of a given group. And we should not mistake momentary disturbances in the market (such as a few abnormally large birth cohorts) for basic features.

CONCLUSION

Secularization, even in the scientific age, is a self-limiting process. This theoretical proposition is supported by consistent correlations linking cult activity with low rates of church membership. Whether we look at cult formation, represented by the cult movements rate, or at client cult offices and occult magazine readers, we see the same thing. The statistical associations hold steady over a span of five decades and are based on thousands of cases. Cults do abound where the conventional churches are weakest.

We are *not* suggesting that cult movements are currently filling the gap left by the weakness of conventional religion. It is clear in our American data that, even with all the cult members added in, the Pacific region still has a very low religious membership rate. Indeed, for our 1926 calculations, the cults were all included in the church member rate; yet the positive autocorrelation produced by this fact was swamped by the negative associations between conventional church membership and receptivity to cults.

We do not posit a steady-state religious economy in which cults immediately make up deficits in conventional religious affiliation. We argue only that, to the degree a population is unchurched, there will be *efforts* to fill the void. Most such efforts will be abortive, for most cults are ill conceived and badly led or lose heart as even a high rate of annual growth produces only a small absolute number of members over the first several decades of recruitment efforts. Thus, most cults will have no impact on the void left by secularization. Only once in a while will an effective, rapidly growing cult movement appear. We cannot predict accurately *when* that will happen. But we think we can say *where* this is apt to happen and *why*.

Until effective cult movements appear, an area may remain indefinitely low in church membership — indeed, the Unchurched Belt along the West Coast of the United States has persisted for a century. Hundreds of cult movements have arisen there, as our theory predicts. When one of them will achieve real success, we cannot say. We notice, however, that the Mormons have greatly increased their membership each decade during this century. Should their growth continue for only a few more decades, the Pacific region may no longer be low in religious affiliation. Or perhaps the new religion for the Pacific region has but 50 members today.

However, we do not expect any single new religious movement to rise to the dominant position so long enjoyed by Christianity. As we have argued in Chapter 5, pluralism is the natural state of religious economies, and even the limited success of Christianity in achieving a religious monopoly depended on enlisting the coercive powers of the state. Hence, unless a massive cultural shift enables a new religion to gain an exclusive franchise, no one religion will ever again even appear to be universal. Rather, we anticipate that the future will more closely resemble the Roman Empire than the Holy Roman Empire. A number of vigorous religious traditions will coexist.

Most cults in America do not conform to our expectations of what a really successful faith of the future would be like. Many current cults, such as the various witchcraft and pagan groups, have reacted to secularization by a headlong plunge back into magic. They reject the whole scientific culture as well as Christian-Judaic religious traditions. They succeed in gathering a few members because they claim to offer extremely efficacious compensators. They unblushingly promise to give the individual the power to harness supernatural powers to manipulate the natural world. In our judgment, these cults are reactionary and have little future. They are utterly vulnerable to the same forces of secularization that have corroded much better organized and accommodated faiths. They will not thrive unless the modern world itself collapses.

Other current cult movements have reacted to secularization by adopting a scientific facade. TM used this tactic for a considerable time, and Scientology remains an outstanding example. The problem with these groups is that their "science" is very vulnerable to empirical evaluation and most likely will be revealed as magic if and when such evaluations are made. But that may not do them real harm so long as true science is unable to offer the specific rewards for which these cults offer mere compensators. There is an immense literature exposing the scientific inadequacy of Psychoanalysis, but it remains a very lucrative profession (Eysenck, 1965; Stuart, 1970; Rachman, 1971; Salter, 1972).

In our judgment, faiths suited to the future will contain no magic, only religion. This will not, of course, allow them to escape the long run forces of secularization — all successful faiths are fated to be tamed by the world. But faiths containing only religion will be immune to scientific attack and thus will avoid the accelerated secularization in effect during recent centuries.

Perhaps all contemporary cult movements contain too much magic to become really successful mass movements. But simply because we cannot point to an apt example does not mean that none exists or that one will not be born tomorrow. Contemporary observers also failed to notice earlier great world religions during their formative periods. As the poet William Butler Yeats asked,

> And what rough beast, its hour come round at last,
> Slouches towards Bethlehem to be born?

20 *Church and Cult in Canada*

Our theoretical conclusion that secularization prompts cult formation is meant to apply to all religious economies. A philosopher of science would observe that universal statements such as this never can be verified fully. Even if it were possible to examine all past and present cases to which the statement applies, the future holds an infinite set of instances in which the theory could fail. Science proceeds by posing as many opportunities as possible for a theory to fail. As these tests increase in number and the theory is supported, our confidence in the theory grows. We begin to assume that the theory is correct despite our awareness that it could fail in its next application.

In the previous chapter, we make many tests of the hypothesized link between conventional religion and cults. Each sustains our prediction that cults will flourish where the conventional churches are weak. In this chapter, we test our theory on a different religious economy. Moving north to Canada, we once again expect to find cult activity concentrated where conventional religion is weakest.

The Canadian Religious Economy

Social commentators are free to emphasize either the differences or the similarities between Canada and the United States. The greatest differ-

The original version of this chapter was given as a paper at the 1981 meeting of the American Sociological Association, held in Toronto, Canada, and was published as William Sims Bainbridge and Rodney Stark, "Church and Cult in Canada," *Canadian Journal of Sociology,* 1982, 7:4, pp. 351–366.

ences probably are to be found in the religious sphere. Canada, like the United States, has known religious diversity since the beginning (Oliver, 1930; Clark, 1948), and Canada is divided by religion and language into the two "solitudes" of French and English. But the separation between church and state is narrower in Canada, and religion may more often play the conservative role of supporting traditional secular culture and socioeconomic structures (Porter, 1965; cf. Cheal, 1978). As Lipset (1964:183) has put it, "Because of the strong tie between church and state in Canada, religious development there, in contrast to religious movements in the United States, has been less prone to fundamentalism and experimentalism."

In a survey of small religious groups, including Christian Science and a number of sects, Harry W. Hiller (1978:192) noted, "while the North American continent has been a breeding ground for religious experimentation and innovation, the Canadian frontier was less so than the American frontier because of the presence of institutional controls in which alliances between the state and established religious institutions deliberately sought to discourage religious experimentation." Canadian conservatism and the greater scale of the United States meant that small Canadian religious groups often are mere outposts of U.S. organizations, having "to look south of the border for direction, sustenance and social support as head office, publishing facilities, dynamic orators, educational institutions, and large local congregations provided models to inspire" (Hiller, 1978:191; cf. Fallding, 1978).

Unlike the United States, where the government today is separated even from systematic knowledge about the churches, Canada includes a question on religious affiliation in its national census. Thus, a trove of exceedingly valuable data lies in Canadian census publications, and it is possible to trace denominational strengths all the way back to 1871 with a high degree of precision. For the first time in 1971, the census question offered a "no religion" response category, and 4.3 percent took this opportunity to declare no religious affiliation. Of course, the Canadian census question measures only *nominal* religious affiliation, and levels of formal church membership and participation are much lower. But the "no religion" response undoubtedly is a good measure of weakness in religious organizations, just as the proportion without church membership is in the United States.

Table 20.1 shows the regional distribution of Canadians with no religion, along with other data from the 1971 census and from studies by Reginald Bibby (1980) and Werner Cohn (1976). Canadian irreligiousness displays much the same geographic pattern as that for the United States. The westernmost province, British Columbia, has by far the

TABLE 20.1 *Regional Variation in Religious Affiliation (percent)*

Affiliation	British Columbia	Prairie Provinces	Ontario	Quebec	Atlantic Provinces	Canada
None	13.1	5.2	4.5	1.3	1.7	4.3
Catholic	18.7	25.2	33.3	86.7	41.8	46.2
United Church	24.6	27.9	21.8	2.9	18.4	17.5
Anglican	17.7	10.7	15.8	3.0	17.3	11.8
Migrant (1966–1971)	34.6	24.1	25.0	20.3	18.6	23.9
Weekly Church Attendance	18	28	27	35	52	31
Proportion of Jews Who Married Non-Jews	47	23	16	8	—	15

Note: The empty cell indicates too few cases for a reliable rate.

highest percentage declaring no religion (13.1 percent). British Columbia has 10.1 percent of the nation's population, but it has 30.9 percent of those without even nominal religious affiliation. The prairie provinces (Alberta, Saskatchewan, Manitoba) show a slight excess of irreligiousness above the national norm; Ontario, the most populous province, is very close to the rate for all of Canada (4.5 percent compared with 4.3). Quebec shows the lowest proportion who claim no religion (1.3 percent), but it is rivaled in religiousness by the Atlantic provinces (New Brunswick, Nova Scotia, Prince Edward Island, Newfoundland).

Figure 20.1 presents these facts on a map of the Canadian provinces. Here we show each region's "no religion" rate as a percentage of the national rate, rounded off to the nearest 10 percent. Thus, the 4.5 rate for Ontario is 104.7 percent of the national rate of 4.3, which rounds down to an even 100 percent. This map shows vividly the western superiority in "no religion" and the wide range of variation across the country, a factor of ten to one from British Columbia to Quebec.

The second through fourth lines in Table 20.1 show the percentage claiming affiliation with the three largest Canadian denominations. American readers will know that Quebec is largely Catholic, but the actual percentage, as well as the Catholic pluralities in the regions bracketing Quebec, may surprise them. To be Catholic in Canada generally means far more than to be Catholic in the United States (Westhues, 1978). When the English seized French Canada, they were faced with a nearly impossible problem of administration, vastly outnumbered as they were. The Quebec Act of 1774, designed to secure support for England from

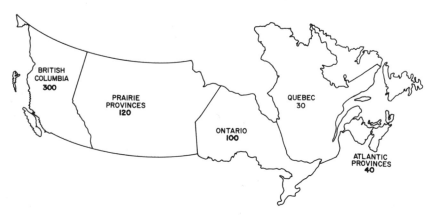

FIGURE 20.1   *Regional Proportions with "No Religion," Indexed to the National Proportion*
(National rate = 100)

the French Canadians, essentially recognized Catholicism as the established church of Quebec. It has functioned as such ever since.

The principle of separation of church and state, so dear to Americans, has had far less influence in Canada, and the Canadian Catholic schools receive some measure of formal or informal support from every province but British Columbia. Catholicism in Canada has a greater influence on its adherents because of the geographical concentration of Catholics. As Kenneth Westhues (1976:216) notes, "While 91 percent of American Catholics live in dioceses where they constitute a minority, only 33 percent of Canadian Catholics do so; on the other hand, almost 60 percent of Canadian Catholics live in an overwhelmingly Catholic milieu, as compared to 1 percent of their coreligionists in America."

The United Church of Canada was formed in 1925 through a union of Methodist, Congregationalist, and Presbyterian groups. About 4 percent of Canadians claim affiliation with Presbyterian groups that remained independent of the United Church (Silcox, 1933). Although Baptists are the largest Protestant category in the United States, only about 3.1 percent of Canadians claim this affiliation, slightly less than the 3.3 percent who are Lutherans.

It has often been pointed out that Canada shows less religious diversity than the United States. Together, the three largest denominations comprise 75.5 percent of the population in census reports, or 78.9 percent of those claiming any affiliation. If one considers only official statistics from those religious groups that report membership, the Roman Catholic, United Church, and Anglican denominations constitute 87 percent of the total. To achieve the same 87 percent of church members in official U.S. reports, one must add together the 21 largest denominations, seven times as many as the three required in Canada (Westhues,1976; Jacquet,1979).

Each of the three largest Canadian denominations has much the quality of an established church. The Anglican Church is an extension of the established church of England, and the United Church lays some claim to being the Canadian national Protestant denomination. Geographically concentrated as it is, Catholicism approaches the status of fully established church in many areas. A recent study of the variable power of religion to prevent women from achieving high status careers showed that religion is a force for conservatism in Canada, but not in the United States (Bainbridge and Hatch, 1982). Thus, when we turn to Canada to replicate our American cult findings, we look at a very different religious economy with significantly higher concentration in a few denominations and therefore a greater power of old traditions.

The fifth row of Table 20.1 shows the proportion of residents in each of the regions who moved into their current municipality between 1966 and 1971. For Canada as a whole, 14.0 percent moved within the same province; 4.3 percent came from another province and 4.2 percent, from outside the country. Comparing the migration statistics with those for no religious affiliation, one sees an apparent correlation, one we document more precisely later in this chapter. The region with the highest rate of migration, British Columbia, also has the largest proportion of those with no religion. These facts support our frequent observation that social bonds are important for sustaining religion and that the rupture of social bonds through migration will weaken religious organization (cf. Veevers and Cousineau, 1980).

Also shown in Table 20.1 are data on weekly church attendance taken from a national survey of Canadians conducted in 1975 by Reginald Bibby (1979a, 1979b, 1980). Weekly church attendance is somewhat influenced by the denominational makeup of an area because weekly attendance is given greater stress by Roman Catholics, but attendance is also a measure of the strength of conventional religions. Here we see the familiar westward tilt, with high attendance in Quebec and the Atlantic provinces reflecting both Catholicism and stronger churches; the very low level of attendance in British Columbia reflects both Protestantism and weak churches.

The final line of Table 20.1 provides further confidence in the fundamental weakness of conventional religion in the West. These data are from Werner Cohn's (1976) study and show the proportion of Jews who married non-Jews in 1971. The propensity of Jews to marry non-Jews would seem to be a double measure of the weakness of traditional faiths. On the one hand, it signals the great weakness of Judaism in British Columbia, where almost half the Jews entered "mixed marriages." On the other hand, it signals the relatively low salience of their religion for the non-Jews who married Jews. On both counts, we see the relative weakness of conventional faiths in western Canada. Therefore, according to our theory, western Canadians should be especially open to new religious affiliations, and cults should flourish in the Canadian West.

CULTS IN CANADA

Despite the differences between the Canadian religious market and that found in the United States, Canada, too, has experienced an invasion of cults of all kinds. The 1901 census counted 2,644 Christian Scientists already in Canada, a number that rose to 20,260 over the next 40 years. Unfortunately, the 1971 census did not list Christian Science membership separately, but the number remained very nearly constant from

1941 to 1961; so we can guess that there still are about 20,000 Christian Scientists in the country. Today, this mature cult claims more than 80 congregations in Canada, as well as student organizations at 14 colleges and universities (Walters, 1981).

William E. Mann estimated that the province of Alberta contained at least 3,485 cult members in 1946, half of them Christian Scientists. Nine other groups also were represented: Church of New Jerusalem, Church of Truth, Consumers' Movement, Divine Science, I Am, Rosicrucians, Spiritualism, Theosophy, and Unity Truth (Mann, 1955:39). Two groups that we do not consider cults for purposes of this chapter, yet that have many novel qualities, show strength both in size and rapidity of growth. The 1971 census counted 66,635 Mormons, an increase of 32 percent from the 1961 census compared with an 18 percent increase in national population. In 1971, some 174,810 Canadians considered themselves members of the Jehovah's Witnesses, a phenomenal increase of 157 percent over 1961.

In his survey of religious attitudes, Reginald Bibby (1979a:7) found that 28 percent of his Canadian respondents had some degree of interest in yoga, and 21 percent were at least mildly interested in Transcendental Meditation. Of course, both of these represent relatively nondemanding client cults, and one might expect far less interest in highly deviant cult movements. Ten percent expressed some interest in the Children of God, 8 percent in Zen, 5 percent in some kind of guru, 4 percent in Hare Krishna, and just 2 percent in Satanism. Bibby also asked two questions about astrology. Five percent claimed to be firm believers, and another 44 percent felt the ideas of astrology were "perhaps possible." Fourteen percent read their horoscopes daily, and another 63 percent did so occasionally.

To get a general overview of cult movements in Canada, we secured copies of classified telephone directories for the 22 census metropolitan areas (CMAs) identified in the 1971 census and tabulated cults listed under "churches," "church organizations," "religious organizations," and their French equivalents. As we had found in our tabulation of astrologers in American SMSA telephone books, it was necessary to secure a number of directories for the larger cities and to exercise some care in tracing the boundaries of the CMAs so we could calculate proper rates.

We found several listings for single-center religious organizations of uncertain nature and were guided by the *Encyclopedia of American Religions* (Melton, 1978) and by similar publications in deciding which small groups to consider cults, counting only those we could be sure were novel or exotic religious organizations. Thus, we may have missed a few very small and new groups, including some of indigenous Canadian ori-

TABLE 20.2   *Cults in Census Metropolitan Areas*

Cult	Centers Listed in Classified Telephone Directories	
	Number	Percent
Christian Science	49	32
Baha'i	19	12
Scientology	15	10
Spiritualist	10	7
Unity	8	5
Eckankar	5	3
Iskcon (Hare Krishna)	5	3
Others	42	27
Total	153	100

gins. Table 20.2 tabulates by cult the 153 cult centers we were able to identify with confidence.

Seven international organizations, each with at least five centers, account for 73 percent of the total. The "other" groups are Ahmadiyya, Aquarian Truth, Church of the Truth, Dharmadhatu, independent Dianetics, Emissaries of Divine Light, Foundation Faith, Holy Order of MANS, I Am, Infinite Way, Liberal Catholics, New Thought, Oahspean Faithist, Psychic and Spiritual Advancement, Religious Science, Science of Mind, Seicho, Self Realization Fellowship, Spiritual Science, Sri Chinmoy, Subud, Swedenborgians, Theosophy, Unification Church, Universal Buddhist, Zen, and Zoroastrian. In compiling this list, we tried to avoid including any groups that simply were tiny, exotic ethnic religions, as some Buddhist groups are and Zoroastrians might have been. Although a couple of these are of unknown origins, we cannot safely identify a single one as of Canadian birth. All appear to be import cults, most having been introduced from the United States, whatever their ultimate origins.

Another good source of Canadian cult data is the 1974 *Spiritual Community Guide* (Singh, 1974), the directory of cult movement and client cult centers we used to good effect in previous chapters. We counted 2,470 American listings, for a national rate of 11.8 per million, and were able to find 237 listings for Canada, for a national rate of 10.9 per million. Because the guide is produced near San Francisco, California, one might think it would miss a number of potential Canadian listings. In any case, the rates for the two nations are very similar.

Table 20.3 compares the distribution of listings among the guide's six classifications. Clearly, the distributions are very similar, although Can-

TABLE 20.3　*The 1974* Spiritual Community Guide

Type of Listing	Canada		United States	
	Number	Percent	Number	Percent
Centers	149	62.9	1,271	51.5
Communities	7	3.0	84	3.4
Bookstores	20	8.4	253	10.2
Foodstores	43	18.1	635	25.7
Restaurants	11	4.6	135	5.5
Other	7	3.0	92	3.7
Total	237	100.0	2,470	100.0

ada has a higher proportion of the largest category, "centers" (a difference that just reaches the .05 level of significance as measured by chi square). We suspect that the guide editors simply were better informed about Canadian "centers" because many of them are branches of international organizations. If this interpretation is correct, then the rates of potential listings may in fact be identical in both nations. Many of the centers do appear to be recruiting stations for cult movements, including nine I Am ashrams, seven Eckankar offices, six Ananda Marga centers, and at least two each for Dharmadhatu, Arica, TM, Church of the New Jerusalem, Sri Chinmoy, Ruhani Satsang, Gestalt, Divine Light, International Meditation Society, Rosicrucians, Theosophy, 3HO, and Anthroposophy.

Thus, despite the great differences in its religious economy, like the U.S., Canada does possess cults. Our theory would certainly predict that this great modern nation would have its complement of novel and exotic religious groups. A significant percentage of the population lacks traditional religious ties, and some among these people should be recruited to nontraditional alternatives. Because Canada shows marked geographic variation in the strength of religious organizations, we further predict that, like the United States, Canada will have an excess of cults where the churches are weak — in western parts of the country and wherever high rates of migration tear people away from the standard churches.

Geography of Canadian Cults

In addition to the CMA telephone directory tabulations and *Spiritual Community Guide* listings, we have collected several other sets of cult data for Canada. Table 20.4 reports the variation across Canada in five cult rates and the proportion who claimed no religion on the 1971 census.

The first column reveals considerable variation in no religion across

TABLE 20.4   *Geography of Canadian Cults*

| Province | 1971 Census: Percent with No Religion | 1974 *Spiritual Community Guide* | Rate per Million Population | | | |
			1979 *Fate* Subscribers	1951–1980 *Fate* Letter Writers	1980 Telephone Directory CMA Cult Centers	1961 Christian Scientists
Newfoundland	0.4	0	14	6	7	109
Prince Edward I.	1.0	0	25	0		382
Nova Scotia	2.4	1	61	16	11	282
New Brunswick	1.9	0	26	2	17	437
Quebec	1.3	8	16	3	3	299
Ontario	4.5	13	48	11	11	1,293
Manitoba	4.3	2	54	6	7	1,276
Saskatchewan	3.7	0	75	9	10	790
Alberta	6.7	5	75	16	20	1,339
British Columbia	13.1	31	94	34	31	3,414
National	4.3	11	47	11	12	1,067
Total Number	929,575	237	1,125	210	153	19,466

the ten provinces, as presaged in Table 20.1. Alberta, westernmost of the prairie provinces, falls second in the proportion of those without even nominal religious affiliation, echoing the low rates of church membership found in some parts of America's Mountain region. In population, Ontario and Quebec are close rivals, reporting 8 and 6 million inhabitants, respectively, on the 1976 census; British Columbia came in a distant third with 2.5 million. We should expect higher rates of cultural innovation not only from Toronto, but from the other cities of Ontario, and greater conservatism in Quebec's Montreal, of equal size. Thus, on purely historical and cultural grounds, we should not be surprised if Ontario has rates of cult activity at or above the national average and Quebec has rates considerably below the national average.

The second column in Table 20.4 reports the rate of *Spiritual Community Guide* listings per million population in each of the provinces. British Columbia leads the nation, with 31 per million; Ontario, the modern cultural center, has a rate of 13 per million, just above the national rate of 11. One would expect these cultic businesses to establish themselves in the largest cities, where there are the greatest pools of potential customers, and, indeed, Toronto has 71 of them, compared with 56 for Vancouver. Third place is held by Montreal, with 41 listings, and fourth by Ottawa, the national capital, with 23. But in terms of rates per million, Vancouver holds first place (at 50), with Victoria, B.C., tied for second with Ottawa (at 35). The rate for Toronto is 26 per million, and Montreal, despite its size advantage, has a rate of just 15 per million.

The third and fourth columns report Canadian data on *Fate* magazine, the leading American occult periodical we found so revealing in previous chapters. *Fate* went on sale in Canada with the August-September 1951 issue, about three years after its founding in the United States. In November 1979, there were 1,125 *Fate* subscribers in Canada, a national rate of 47 per million, just 13 percent of the American rate. This lower rate undoubtedly reflects the difficulties of distributing specialty magazines across the border.

As we explain in Chapter 10, since the beginning, *Fate* readers have contributed little stories of contact with the supernatural — "True Mystic Experiences" and "Proofs of Survival." We tabulated letters from Canadian readers in the 321 issues we were able to obtain through February 1980, including ordinary letters to the editor as well as these reader stories. In the fourth column of Table 20.4, we show the distribution of 210 different letter writers, discounting repeated missives from the same person. Nova Scotia surpasses the national rate in both measures, and we have no knowledge of the cause. We might think the 12 letter writers who lived in Nova Scotia represented an active occult subculture also responsible for the elevated subscription rate, but these 12 had their homes in ten different towns. The low Quebec rate may be due in part to the language barrier (*Fate* is published in English), but these Quebec rates are comparable to those from other cult measures. The two *Fate* rates are based on individual subscribers and letter writers and need not be sustained by large urban centers, as are cult businesses. Alberta is free, therefore, to leap into second place behind British Columbia, which, as usual, leads all the rest.

The fifth column reports the distribution of cult listings in classified telephone directories, the same data reported in Table 20.2. Because the phone books cover only census metropolitan areas, the divisors for these rates are the CMA populations of the provinces. Lacking a CMA, Prince Edward Island cannot be included. Based on a small number of cases, the rates in this column jump around considerably, but, as usual, British Columbia leads the list.

Censuses prior to 1971 report data on Christian Science; so, in the final column of Table 20.4, we translate these numbers into rates per million population. In Chapter 11, we find that Christian Science was the best single cult measure for the United States in 1926. The same factors that make it a good indicator of local receptivity to cults in the United States ought to apply in Canada as well. Certainly, we have seen that Christian Science had established itself fully six decades before the 1961 census and had time to spread across the nation.

Again we see that British Columbia has the highest rate, with Alberta second. Because Christian Science is a healing cult (England, 1954), we may interpret the very low rate for Quebec not only in terms of traditional religious opposition to experimentation with religious novelties, but also in terms of the competition healing cults receive from Quebec Catholicism. Elsewhere (for example, in Chapter 5) we note the Catholic ability to absorb its own sects and speak of the competition between churchly and extrachurchly magic. Catholicism, it seems, also has the ability to absorb its own cults, for just outside the city of Quebec lies the healing shrine of Ste. Anne de Beaupre, where one of us years ago observed devout Catholics congregating in search of church magic to cure a variety of ailments. With Saint Anne just next door, who needs to import Mary Baker Eddy from Boston?

Four minor measures of cult activity are shown by region in Table 20.5. Because these rates are based on very small numbers of cases, we have not attempted to give rates for the smaller provinces, and one should expect a high level of random variation. The 1979 *Spiritual Community Guide* (Singh, 1978) was very different in format from the one published in 1974, and it contained far fewer classified listings. For the United States, the 1979 guide contained only 38 percent as many entries

TABLE 20.5   *Minor Cult Measures by Region*

Region	Rate per Million Population			
	1978 *Spiritual Community Guide*	1979 *Psychic Register*	1975 *Organic Traveler*	1975 *Occult Directory*
Atlantic	1	0	0	0
Quebec	2	0	1	2
Ontario	3	2	1	3
Prairies	1	1	2	2
British Columbia	9	3	4	9
National	3	1	1	3
Total Number	70	33	33	68

as the 1974 edition, and for Canada, the reduction was even greater, to only 30 percent. *The International Psychic Register* (McQuaid, 1979) is a directory of psychic and metaphysical practitioners published in Erie, Pennsylvania. *The Organic Traveler* (Davis and Tetrault, 1975) is a guide to organic, vegetarian, and health food (read: magical) restaurants published in Syracuse, New York.

The only directory of cults and occult services we have found published in Canada is *Occult Directory*, compiled by Ken Ward, a resident of Saskatoon. This is a fairly amateur, mimeographed catalog of "Occult, Religious, Magical, Metaphysical and Esoteric Organizations, Book Stores and Individuals; many of them claiming a different Path to the Truth concerning Life and Happiness" (Ward, 1975:ii). Ward himself represents the Canadian branch of the Ordo Templi Orientis Antiqua and appears to be of Crowleyite cultic persuasion (cf. Symonds, 1958). The 1975 edition of the directory and the ten supplements to it issued by December 1979 contain hundreds of American references and quite a number from Great Britain, but only 68 with Canadian addresses.

Although the statistics in Table 20.5 are based on perilously few cases, they present a familiar distribution. In each column, the rates for British Columbia are two or three times as high as for any other region of Canada. Thus, all the distributions fulfill our prediction that cults will flourish where the churches are weak, which, for Canada as for the United States, means the West. But the quality and quantity of Canadian data mean we need not stop with simple distributions; we can safely go on to examine correlations among our best measures of cult activity and correlations linking them with explanatory variables.

Correlational Analysis of Cult Activity
We were able to develop rates for four of our best cult measures for each of the 22 census metropolitan areas identified in the 1971 census.

TABLE 20.6   *Cult Activity in 22 Census Metropolitan Areas*

| | 1974 Spiritual Community Guide | Correlation (r) with | | |
		1951– 1980 Fate Letter Writers	1980 Telephone Directory Cult Centers	1961 Christian Scientists
CMA Population	.40	−.20	−.17	.00
Percent who moved since the previous census	.46	.41	.43	.49
CMA Longitude	.41	.56*	.65**	.77**
Percent with no religion	.69**	.59*	.75**	.83**
1961 Christian Scientists	.63**	.80**	.79**	
1980 Telephone Directory Cult Centers	.58*	.60*		
1951–1980 *Fate* Letter Writers	.28			

*Significant at the .01 level.
**Significant at the .001 level.

One does not ordinarily think of running correlations for such a small number of cases as 22, but there is no reason to avoid using Pearson's *r* to summarize relationships, as long as we keep in mind the nature of our data. Table 20.6 shows correlations linking four cult rates with each other and with four interesting variables taken from the 1971 census.

The Christian Science rates deserve comment. Because the 1971 census failed to report the number of Christian Scientists in any geographic area and the 1961 census did not tabulate religion statistics for CMAs, we had to simulate CMA rates using tabulations for Canadian towns and cities of 10,000 population or greater. For large CMAs, we had to add together several of these smaller units, a somewhat hazardous operation, and we were never able to duplicate the precise boundaries of CMAs. However, the numerators and denominators for these rates are coordinated; so the rates probably are not bad estimates, undoubtedly as good as the other cult measures that are based on far fewer cases.

The table reveals that only one of the four cult measures, the businesses listed in the *Spiritual Community Guide,* is associated with city size, these operations enjoying larger potential clienteles in big cities. We see a constant association between cult activity and the migration rate, a measure of weakness in the social control that might otherwise prevent cultic deviance. Migration also is an indirect measure of low church membership, a fact we are reminded of by the huge correlation ($r = .70$) between the percent that had moved since the previous census in 1966 and the percent with no religion. We use the longitude of the CMA as a measure of western region, because longitude increases as one moves west. With longitude, the correlations get so strong that some of them achieve a high level of statistical significance with only the 22 cases!

The biggest correlations are with the percent claiming no religion, three of them significant at the .001 level. Again, we see powerful evidence that cults abound where the churches are weak. In the previous chapter, we verified that this is so for two periods in American history. Now we have verified that the same principle holds in Canada, a nation with a distinctly different religious economy. Thus, our theory is supported.

Despite the difficulties in estimating Christian Science rates for the 22 CMAs, the correlations are higher for Christian Science than for any of the three other measures, as well as from each of them to the four explanatory variables, except city size (which we conclude does not matter). The quality and detail of the published Christian Science statistics for 1961 demand closer analysis. This great cult provided our best single measure for 1926 America, and it does also for 1961 Canada.

Figure 20.2 maps the relative strength of Christian Science across the five regions, providing a comparison for Figure 20.1, which similarly mapped "no religion." Again, we have divided the regional rates by the national rate and expressed the result as a percentage. Of course, the two distributions are not identical, but a close correspondence can be seen.

In Table 20.7, we focus on much finer units of analysis, reporting correlations based on a total of 14,306 Christian Scientists who lived in 209

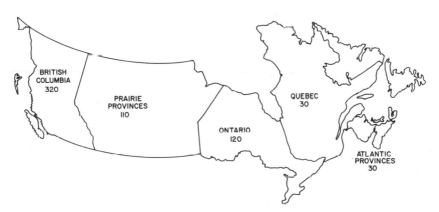

FIGURE 20.2   *Regional Rates of Christian Science, Indexed to the National Rate*
(National rate = 100)

TABLE 20.7   *Christian Science in Canadian Urban Areas, 1961*

| | Correlation (r) with Percent Christian Scientist | | |
	209 Urban Areas	168 Urban Areas East of Alberta	59 Quebec Urban Areas
Population	.05	.08	−.02
Percent Catholic	−.48*	−.56*	−.66*
Percent Born in the Same Province	−.57*	−.58*	−.66*
Region	.57*	.51*	
Percent with No Religion	.67*	.69*	.65*

*Significant at the .001 level.

urban areas. The census actually reports figures for 241 urban areas, but we wanted to employ the 1971 measure of "no religion" and therefore had to limit ourselves to the urban areas that remained relatively constant in name, boundaries, and statistics reported over the decade. If the 22 CMAs do not seem a sufficient number of cases for convincing results, then replicating at least some of the findings with nearly ten times the number of cases will add great strength to our conclusions.

As in the previous table, we see no correlation between the population of the urban area and the proportion that is Christian Scientist. Certainly, the two variables fluctuate enough to produce correlations if, in fact, there were any connection between them. About a tenth of the urban areas had zero rates of Christian Science. The urban area with the largest number of Christian Scientists is central Vancouver (1,538 for a rate of 4,000 per million). Toronto has the second largest number (1,244 for a rate of only 1,840 per million). Calgary and Winnipeg are tied for third place with 567. The highest rate is 14,000 per million (or 1.4 percent) in the municipal subdivision of West Vancouver, which has 356 Christian Scientists. Population of the urban areas varies from 10,054 to 1,191,062, a ratio of more than a hundred to one.

To underscore the importance of Catholicism in Canada, where the proportion Catholic is a much more potent variable than in the United States, we have included percent Catholic in Table 20.7, using as our divisor the total population minus the Christian Scientists to avoid any problems of autocorrelation, unimportant though they may be. For the 209 urban areas, Christian Science is associated more strongly with population stability, measured here by the percent born in the same province in which they were polled, than with percent Catholic.

For the variable called *region*, we have grouped the provinces in the five familiar categories shown on our two maps (1 = Atlantic provinces, 2 = Quebec, 3 = Ontario, 4 = prairie provinces, 5 = British Columbia). As with longitude in the previous table, we see a strong western effect. The question about religious affiliation in the 1961 census did not have a response category of "no religion," so we used the 1971 proportion, knowing that rates of church membership are rather stable over time.

For the 209 urban areas, there are very powerful effects of population stability, region, and percent with no religion, outweighing the Catholic effect. Despite the gap of ten years between the Christian Science rate and the "no religion" rate, the association between them is by far the strongest. One might suspect that region is the real determinant of Christian Science and that the culture of British Columbia is mainly responsible. Of course, a counterargument can be found in the facts that the world headquarters of Christian Science is in Massachusetts, one of America's "Atlantic provinces," and that the Canadian national headquarters is in Toronto (Jacquet, 1979). Further, the interesting associations in Table 20.7 are quite robust, resisting attempts to reduce them to insignificance by controlling for other variables. And the variables are indeed tightly linked. For example, the correlation between percent born in the same province and percent with no religion is overwhelming ($r = -.76$), providing yet another proof of the importance of social bonds in supporting religious affiliation.

The second and third columns in Table 20.7 examine the possibility that Christian Science is explained by a British Columbian religious subculture by focusing only on parts of the country remote from B.C. Of course, region and variables correlated with it lose variation in the second column, and region disappears in the third column, based only on Quebec cities. But the explanatory variables remain of essentially equal strength all across the table. Apparently, both regional culture and the stability of social bonds play roles in determining local receptivity to cults such as Christian Science. To be sure, culture and social structure are powerfully interrelated, each in great measure determining or supporting the other. High rates of migration produce an open religious market, and an open society attracts in-migration.

The data show that, for Canada as a whole as well as for Canada east of Alberta, Christian Science is strongest where the proportion with no religion is highest. Moreover, Table 20.7 shows an even more dramatic test of our thesis. Quebec is a bastion of conventional religion. Only 1.3 percent reported they had no religious affiliation, and Quebec also is low in cults. Yet, using the 59 urban areas of Quebec alone, we find the correlation between Christian Science membership and no religion unchanged from that of Canada as a whole — a highly significant .65.

CONCLUSION

We have successfully put our theory at risk for a third time. Indeed, some would say we have done so for a fourth time as well — that Quebec is a separate religious economy from the rest of Canada. Yet even here, where nine-tenths of the population is affiliated with one established church, cults thrive in the nooks and crannies where the church is slightly weaker. This greatly increases our confidence in our theory and our desire to see it tested in a greater variety of settings.

21 *Europe's Receptivity to Cults and Sects*

If sociological rumors are to be believed, our theory fails when applied to modern Europe. Secularization appears to be even more advanced in many European nations than in the United States or Canada. One can hardly escape the reports of empty churches and declining faith in Britain and in northern Europe. But where are the cults? Our theory requires that, other things being equal, these nations ought to have produced or attracted even more cult movements than have the United States and Canada. But "other things" are *not* equal. Later in this chapter and in the next, we note the impediments to religious movements imposed by established churches, repressive states, and substantial left-wing parties. However, to invoke mitigating circumstances in defense of theories inevitably seems like special pleading. Our theory must be subject to considerable doubt if America and Canada abound in cult and sect movements, but Europe shows little receptivity to them.

We faced this challenge, mindful of the weight of intellectual authority in opposition. A series of distinguished European visitors has marvelled at the grass roots vitality of American religion and the immense variety it sustains. And each, like Max Weber (1946), has assured us that nothing like this does, or could, go on back in Europe. European scholars, from Sigmund Freud (1927) to David Martin (1978), have

The original version of this chapter was published as Rodney Stark, "Europe's Receptivity to Cults and Sects," in Rodney Stark (ed.), *Religious Movements: Genesis, Exodus and Numbers.* New York: Rose of Sharon Press, 1984.

dominated scholarly work on how religions die, but Americans, from H. Richard Niebuhr (1929) to Charles Y. Glock (1964), have focused on how religions are born. This transatlantic division of labor has been thought to reflect differences in local conditions.

Yet, there are contradictory signs. Perhaps the most important of these is that, all the while reports of empty cathedrals and widespread religious indifference flow from Europe, scores of American-based religious movements annually report great success in their European missions. If the Mormons, Jehovah's Witnesses, Seventh-Day Adventists, Assemblies of God, and varieties of Baptists, to say nothing of the Scientologists, Moonies, and Hare Krishnas, all are making headway in Europe, why do we hear of it almost exclusively from them? Can it be that there is a whole lot of religion going on in Europe, but that European scholars fail to see it, or give it no importance?

We think this is the case. Consider David Martin's (1978) study of secularization, the best current attempt to characterize religious trends and conditions in Europe nation by nation. It does not escape his notice that the Netherlands and Switzerland, for example, abound in varieties of deviant religious movements, from Tibetan Buddhism to counterculture Jesus freaks, or indeed that the Jehovah's Witnesses are active everywhere in Europe. To him, however, these are but ephemeral symptoms of the crumbling of faith, not to be taken seriously. Moreover, Martin is so particularly interested in how major Christian bodies interplay with the politics of European nations (a theme he pursues with great insight) that he is not inclined to attend to any movements that seem not (or not yet) deeply involved in the political process or whose effects are unimportant.

All observers will note new religions once they have waxed powerful, but our theory tells us to look for the beginnings of such movements in the form of early stirrings, when a host of "trivial" movements will be clustered in places of potential opportunity. That means, of course, that we must attend to all manner of religious novelty, some of it seemingly silly, much of it fated to amount to little.

We are uneasy about the reliability of reports of the decline of religion from sources who seem too eager for the "postreligious era" to begin. Indeed, comparisons of "secularized" Europe with "still-pious" America too often seem intended primarily to reaffirm European claims to greater cultural maturity and enlightenment. Surely, this raises the possibility that reports on religion in Europe ought not be taken at face value.

If Americans have tended to pay more attention to the formation of new cults and sects because they are close at hand, why is the center of such scholarship not at one of the California universities instead of at All Souls College, Oxford? The most important recent contributions to cult and sect literature, particularly case studies of specific groups, have been made by Bryan Wilson (1961, 1970, 1975a, 1982) and his circle of students (cf. Wallis, 1975). This is true even for groups that originated in the United States. Thus, Wilson's student, Roy Wallis (1976), wrote the first major scholarly study of Scientology. Although Americans did the first important work on the Moonies (Lofland and Stark, 1965; Lofland, 1966), the more sustained study has been by Eileen Barker (1979, 1981, 1984) of the London School of Economics. These scholars did not need to fly to America to do their work; they found these groups well developed close at hand.

In this chapter we attempt to show that expert opinion is in error. It is true that in much of Europe the long-dominant and established denominations have fallen on bad times, as have the highest status and most liberal Protestant bodies in America. However, fully in accord with our theory, secularization produces religious revival and innovation, in Europe as well as in North America. We shall see that the United States is not especially prolific of cult and sect movements; many European nations are even more receptive to such movements than is America. Indeed, many distinctively American cult and sect movements are doing better across the Atlantic (and the South Pacific as well) than they ever have done back home.

Statistics on Cult Movements

Lacking the resources to undertake a major research project, we are necessarily restricted to somewhat crude efforts to assess the prevalence of cults and sects in Europe. We could not simply go to the library and find material on cults and sects in Europe even slightly comparable with such works as J. Gordon Melton's *Encyclopedia of American Religions* (1978), with its more than 1,200 entries. Indeed, not even the telephone books for most of Europe offer the resources to be found in the American Yellow Pages. Therefore, we have used a hodgepodge of sources, many of indifferent quality and none of which attempted to be complete. Many were compiled by believers who listed groups they liked and did not list those they did not like. We discuss these biases when we use each source.

Taken together, the inadequacies of our sources work *against* our conclusions, for the result surely is an undercount of deviant religious movements in Europe. If, despite this problem, we still can demonstrate that parts of Europe are more receptive to cults and sects than is the

United States, we will take this to be very strong support of our theory.

A second bias that also works against us is that often, because of the greater availability of good data, we shall be examining American-born religious movements in Europe. These groups usually have had much longer to build a following in America than abroad, and it also seems reasonable to suppose that movements tend to thrive more in their native habitats than in overseas missions. However, these data will be very useful to make comparisons among European nations — to draw conclusions about their relative receptivity to sects and cults.

A third possible bias is that persons leading novel religious movements may accept expert opinion and thus believe that the United States is more fertile soil than is Europe. Therefore, they may direct more effort into building a movement in America. For example, the Moonies and the Hare Krishnas seem to have placed initial emphasis on their American operations, and The Process moved from its birthplace in London to America especially because it believed the opportunities were greater in the new land (Bainbridge, 1978c).

It is impossible to be an expert on each case utilized in studies based on a number of societies. Hence, to undertake such research is always to risk error. Moreover, comparative studies always place sociologists in conflict with specialists. The latter are rewarded for particularizing, for stressing how different their case (society) is from others. The sociologist is required to emphasize similarity and comparability. Thus, a specialist might, for example, stress how the Haugian movement has made Norway's Lutheranism very different from that of Sweden, but our task as sociologists is to note the deterioration of Lutheran state churches all across Scandinavia. This is in no way to suggest that details such as Haugism are trivial, merely that they are not pertinent to the larger generalizations we seek here.

English and Welsh Cults

Ideally, we would like to be able to compute a cult movement rate for every nation of Europe, similar to the rate for the United States we present in Chapter 9. For the United States, as of the late 1970s, we computed that there were 2.3 independent cult movements in existence for every million Americans. It was possible to produce this rate only because of the immense previous work done by others, especially by Melton, to identify, locate, and list cult movements. For lack of similar source material, we are unable to compute a general cult movement rate for nations on the European continent, but we were able to do so for England and Wales.

Our most valuable source was a compilation of cult movements prepared by Stephen Annett (1976). Although it is an admirable work, Annett's sympathies seem to lie with New Age and Eastern religions, and he failed to include a substantial number of groups in other cult families, especially the magick and witchcraft groups. We built upon Annett's work from a number of additional sources. One of these is a mimeographed *Occult Directory* compiled by Ken Ward (1975), the North American corresponding secretary of the Ordo Templi Orientis Antiqua (in the Crowley tradition of magick), who lives in Canada. We introduced this source of data in the previous chapter. Ward's directory understandably concentrates on American and Canadian groups, but includes a number of English groups as well. An additional source was *The Aquarian Guide to Occult, Mystical, Religious, Magical London and Around* (Strachan, 1970). We also made much use of Singh (1981), which we describe fully in the next section. We compiled our list of cult movements in England and Wales by cross-checking these sources to eliminate the transitory and trivial. We also drew on Melton's immense resources to determine where American-based groups had significant overseas branches.

Admittedly, a count of cult movements is not a count of cult members. Although some of these groups are large and well established (Spiritualists, Theosophists, Mormons), having branches in many locations, others are very small, consisting of but one group meeting in one place. Some of the groups are led by sincere believers; others are led by cynical entrepreneurs. Most of these groups will never amount to much, but some already do.

Despite these great variations, close examination of all such groups reveals considerable commitment among their adherents. It is for this reason that we disagree with scholars who would dismiss cult movements as mere pseudoreligions, as superficial and insignificant. Indeed, one would reach rather an opposite impression from comparing the salience of their faith among, for example, Anglicans and Hare Krishnas. In any event, we have used the same criteria in selecting cult movements in England and Wales as we did for the United States. The two sets of data contain a reasonably similar mix of types and sizes. Indeed, the data for England and Wales underscore our conclusion, based on American and Canadian data, that, where one finds the bigger and older cults, there also one finds a host of smaller and newer ones.

Our final list consisted of 153 cult movements operating in England and Wales. We are certain that this is a serious undercount. For one thing, we have no Black movements on the list, such as the many forms of Vudon (we have very few of these in our American data either). We failed to find any UFO-based cult movements, but we are certain some exist, and we are equally sure that we have missed the greater proportion of the magick and witchcraft groups. These groups are extremely secretive, and it took Melton years to win sufficient trust among them in the United States so that he could secure good data.

Nevertheless, even with all these deficiencies, the rate for England and Wales is 3.2 cult movements per million population, which is substantially higher than the American rate of 2.3. There is almost one more cult per million in England and Wales than in the United States.

It was this result that encouraged us to push on and to try to assess other parts of Europe to the extent that we could obtain data. Rather than presenting our theory with a problem, the state of religious deviance in England and Wales is as the theory would predict. The well-publicized weakness of conventional faith in Britain is producing many efforts to create or adapt new faiths.

Of course, this is not to say that cult movements have taken up all the slack left by the secularization of conventional faiths. Our theory does not predict just when a new religion well suited to the market will arise and attract a mass following; it merely tells us where to look for such a new movement and why. When we look at England and Wales, we see many current efforts to found and build such movements. Is the same true across the channel?

Indian and Eastern Cults

We already have mentioned the potential bias of comparing Europe and America on the basis of religious movements that originated in the latter. But the reverse also could be biasing. That is, the United States would appear more receptive to deviant religion if Scientology membership were examined, but Europe could appear much more receptive if Anthroposophist membership were used. The most unbiased comparisons would be based on novel religious movements native neither to Europe nor to the United States. The recent influx of new religious movements from India and the East presents such a standard of comparison. Fortunately, we were able to obtain the most comprehensive international data on these particular groups.

For the past ten years, a group calling itself Spiritual Publications, located in San Rafael, California, has been producing lavish guides to New Age groups, centers, services, communities, bookstores, foodstores, and restaurants. In previous chapters, we make good use of data from two editions of the *Spiritual Community Guide* published by this group. The very high correlations between rates derived from the guide and many other cult rates gave us confidence of the worth of the data. In 1981, this same group produced a new edition of its international directory, *A Pilgrim's Guide to Planet Earth* (Singh, 1981). This thick book provides the same kinds of lists for Europe and some other parts of the world.

The publishers of these guides are devotees of a variety of Hindu religious movements. In constructing their listings, they gave primary emphasis to such groups, but they also paid considerable attention to other Eastern faiths: Buddhism in its many forms, Jainism, and the like. In contrast, they seldom list groups in the Moslem tradition and have been very hit-or-miss in their coverage of new religions based on Western culture. Thus, for example, they list Theosophy, noting its links to the East, but seldom list the Unification Church, despite its Korean origins, perhaps because of its strongly Christian emphasis.

Because it is clear that listings outside the Eastern and Indian traditions were inconsistent and incomplete (more so for Europe than for the United States), it was appropriate to edit all the listings to count only groups within the Eastern and Indian traditions. We also chose to ignore occult bookstores, health food restaurants, and other client or audience services and to count only real *religious* organizations: centers where cult members regularly gather and communities (primarily communes) organized on the basis of common religious practice.

Some of the centers listed are branches of a single cult organization such as 3HO, but many have no actual ties to a larger organization and are independent, local, cult organizations. However, whether independent groups or branches of a larger organization, the simple density of these centers and communities clearly indicates an area's receptivity to cult movements imported from India and the East. As we note in previous chapters, these are *not* simply ethnic, immigrant churches, and hence a function of the size of immigrant populations. Whatever the national origins of the leader and beliefs, the members of these groups typically are persons of European stock.

Having edited the listings for each nation, we then computed rates, dividing the number of listings by the population to produce the number of these centers and communities per million. We were forced to omit Norway and Portugal from these computations because it was obvious that the Spiritual Community people had failed to cover them adequately. Table 21.1 gives numbers of listings and rates per million for the nations we covered.

Many interesting comparisons appear in Table 21.1, but of most significance is the American-European comparison. Europe's rate is significantly higher! Given that the *Spiritual Community Guide* editors had devoted more resources to developing their American data, through more

TABLE 21.1   *Indian and Eastern Cult Centers and Communities per Million Population*

Area	Number	Rate per Million
Denmark	16	3.1
Sweden	21	2.5
Finland	13	2.8
England and Wales	146	3.0
Scotland	18	3.2
West Germany	85	1.4
Netherlands	28	2.0
Austria	16	2.1
Switzerland	23	3.8
France	133	2.5
Belgium	10	1.0
Italy	38	.7
Spain	23	.6
Europe[a]	573	1.8
United States	290	1.3
Canada	35	1.5
Australia	77	5.3
New Zealand	16	5.2

[a]Total population based only on nations listed above.

editions of several kinds of catalogue, and had the advantage of geographic proximity to the U.S. centers and communities, the undercount of Europe ought to be greater and the true difference even larger.

Moreover, the European rate is depressed by inclusion of Spain and Italy, very populous nations that we would expect to be much lower in cults than the United States. In fact, the truly revealing comparisons are nation to nation. Only three nations of Western Europe (Italy, Spain, and Belgium) have rates lower than the United States. Most of the others have considerably higher rates — and the rates tend to rise the farther north the nation. Switzerland has the highest rate (later in this chapter, we devote a section to Switzerland as a deviant case), followed by Scotland and Denmark. We expected England and Wales to surpass the U.S. rate, as they do, but we were surprised to see France also well above America. This reminds us of the waves of occultism in French history (Darnton, 1970; McIntosh, 1972) and the intimate connections between the occult and revolutionary traditions in France and, indeed, in Europe more generally (cf. Billington, 1980).

At the bottom of the table, we show the other "English-speaking democracies." The Canadian rate is close to that of the United States, but Australia and New Zealand far surpass all other nations for which we have rates. Although this surprised us, it did not surprise the editors of the guide. Of Melbourne, they wrote: "Generally accepted to be the 'yoga capital of the world,' Melbourne houses more yoga schools per capita than any other city on the planet" (Singh, 1981:258). But it is not simply yoga mania that gives Australia its high rate. All manner of Indian and Eastern faiths abound there—a pattern confirmed in the other data to be examined. New Zealand is much the same.

Looking within Europe, we see that the three nations with the lowest rates are overwhelmingly Catholic countries in which the church remains very vigorous (unlike Catholic France, where the church is much weaker). Impressionistically, at least, the data pattern is in accord with what are believed to be greater and lesser degrees of secularization. Great Britain and Scandinavia are higher; southern Europe is low (Martin, 1978). That Spain has the lowest rate prompts mention of the fact that, until 1967, it was illegal for any non-Catholic religion to operate openly in Spain, and the 1967 act of religious tolerance was not actually implemented until 1970. Prior to this time, only the most militant non-Catholic groups attempted to operate in Spain, primarily the Jehovah's Witnesses and the Pentecostals. Yet, in only a decade, Spain has caught up with Italy in terms of Indian and Eastern cult centers—a "catch up" that will be seen in other tables as well.

Overall, these data do much to dispel the notion of America as the land of novel religious movements, while Europe leads the way into an "enlightened" future. Imported faiths from Asia seem to be doing even better in much of Western Europe than in the United States. We think these data justify our unwillingness to accept learned opinion. Rather than a lack of cults in Europe calling our theory into question, it appears that our theory accurately has called into question the notion that there are but few cult movements in Europe.

Scientology

As we explain in Chapter 12, Scientology is an American-born movement, the creation of L. Ron Hubbard, a science fiction author with a background in the occult. It operates out of many small centers, but these are subordinated to Scientology "orgs" (churches), rather as parish churches are subordinated to a cathedral. As of 1979, there were 51 Scientology churches worldwide. Of these, 23 were in the United States, 14 in European nations, and 14 in Canada, South Africa, New Zealand, and Australia.

TABLE 21.2   *Scientology Churches and Full-Time Staff Members per Million Population*

Area	Scientology Churches		Full-Time Staff
	N	Rate per Million	Rate per Million
Denmark	3	.59	50.0
Sweden	3	.36	16.4
United Kingdom	5	.09	10.5
West Germany	1	.02	4.5
Netherlands	1	.07	2.5
Austria			2.7
Switzerland			14.3
France	1	.02	2.7
Belgium			2.0
Europe	14	.07[a]	6.9[b]
United States	23	.10	17.9
Canada	4	.17	18.3
Australia	4	.27	13.9
New Zealand	1	.32	17.7

[a]Population of Europe based only on nations having a church.
[b]Population of Europe based only on nations having a staff person.

Table 21.2 reports the distribution of Scientology churches in terms of rates per million population. Also shown are the number of Scientology staff members in each nation, also computed as rates per million (Church of Scientology, 1978). The data on churches are based on very small numbers of cases and thus potentially subject to considerable random fluctuation, but the staff data represent a very large number of cases, 1,527 staff members in Europe alone, and thus will be very reliable statistically. As it turned out, the rates based on churches are reliable, too, for both sets of data tell precisely the same story ($r = .95$). Denmark, Sweden, and the United Kingdom are high, as they were on Indian and Eastern cults, and France, Belgium, the Netherlands, and Austria are low.

The American origins of Scientology do show up in the higher overall rates for the United States as compared with Europe. However, Denmark and Sweden surpass the United States in receptivity to Scientology, and Canada, Australia, and New Zealand also equal or surpass America. Once again we see that the popular image of the United States as the land of cults is inaccurate. Other nations, including some in Europe, are just as hospitable.

Hare Krishna

Appearances to the contrary, Hare Krishna is essentially an American-born movement, founded in 1965 by A. C. Bhaktivedanta Swami Prabhu-pada. Although Bhaktivedanta developed his religious ideas in India, it was only after coming to the States that he recruited a following and launched his now-familiar movement. Still, the movement presents itself as of ancient Hindu lineage and indeed has diverted substantial resources to establishing itself back in India. Despite the irony of American converts teaching Hinduism to Hindus, the movement has, in fact, been rather successful in attracting an Indian following. Moreover, the movement has made strides in becoming a worldwide phenomenon, now having temples on every inhabited continent (Shinn, 1983).

As with Scientology churches, rates based on Hare Krishna temples suffer from the small number of cases involved. That the Scientology church rates correlated almost perfectly with the rates based on staff lend credibility to the Hare Krishna data as well. We also recognize that rates based on organizations and staffs might not reflect true differences in membership. However, we think that religious movements usually will build temples and station staff in places where they are strong and spurn places where they are weaker. Certainly, in Chapter 19 and Chapter 20, all the various cult measures tell the same story. Moreover,

TABLE 21.3   *Hare Krishna Temples per Million Population*

Area	N	Rate per Million
Denmark	1	.20
Sweden	3	.36
United Kingdom	3	.05
West Germany	3	.05
Netherlands	1	.07
Austria	1	.13
Switzerland	1	.16
Belgium	2	.10
Italy	2	.04
Europe	17	.08[a]
United States	33	.15
Canada	7	.29
Australia	6	.41
New Zealand	2	.65

[a]Population of Europe based only on nations having a temple.

for some groups we examine later in this chapter, we had data on actual membership as well as on congregations, and the two kinds of rate gave nearly identical results. Finally, the many quite different cult movement rates we examine in this chapter correlate very highly, thus lending credibility to each other.

Once again, in Table 21.3, the same nations stand out for being high and low. Although the overall U.S. rate for the America-based Hare Krishna cult is significantly higher than the rate for Europe, Denmark and Sweden noticeably exceed the American rate. Switzerland and Austria have about the same rate as the United States, and Italy and Spain are low. New Zealand has the highest rate of all, and Australia also is very high.

Christian Science

In earlier chapters, we make considerable use of data on Christian Science to assess cult receptivity, and we had anticipated doing so in this study of Europe as well. But, when we obtained current data on Christian Science, we discovered it was too late. Everywhere, Christian Science is a movement in rapid and serious decline. Indeed, close examination revealed that Christian Science peaked by the start of World War II and ever after has been receding. Stark (forthcoming) gives extended attention to the rise and decline of this important new religious movement. Here we simply point out that ruins can reveal very important facts, but only about the past and only by careful reconstruction. This is not the place for so demanding an undertaking, and Europe's residual Christian Science congregations do not reflect current religious conditions with any clarity.

Mormons

The Mormons are the most successful and significant of all the novel religious movements produced by America. They have maintained a substantial growth rate for 150 years. Their high fertility offsets both mortality and defection; meanwhile, they continue to attract many new converts. Mormon data are not useful for assessment of local receptivity to cult movements within the United States because the Mormons are highly concentrated in the West through massive migration, not through local recruitment (see Chapter 11). A reverse problem mars the comparison of Mormonism in Europe and America. Until after World War I, converts to Mormonism were assisted in immigrating to the United States. Thus, despite high rates of recruitment by Mormon missionaries in Europe (especially in Britain), few local Mormon congregations sprang up. Instead, European Mormonism remained a scattering of missionaries as the waves of converts boarded ships headed West. Following World War I, Mormons ceased urging immigration upon European converts and in recent decades have discouraged it. Still, European congregations are of deceptively recent vintage and are much smaller than they would be had early converts stayed home. Indeed, Mormonism spreads most effectively from family to family, not via missionary contacts, and this too long impeded European Mormonism (see chapters 14 and 16). By sending convert families off to the American West, the movement left too few Mormon families in Europe to recruit others.

Nevertheless, by 1977, there were more than 150,000 Mormons in Europe. Table 21.4 converts these statistics into national rates per million population. The findings are very like those for Indian and Eastern cult centers and movements. Indeed, the two sets of rates are highly correlated ($r = .77$, based only on the European nations and excluding Switzerland, for reasons we take up later). The United Kingdom and Scandinavia are quite high in their Mormon rates, and the rates fall the farther south the nation in Europe. Canada and Australia also have quite high rates, and New Zealand actually surpasses the United States. Much of the Mormon success in New Zealand is among the Maori population. Indeed, Mormons are doing extremely well in the whole South Pacific, especially in Samoa.

We did not expect to find Mormonism more successful in Europe than in America, and, in fact, the European rate is much lower. But we think the Mormon data are valid as a gauge of the relative receptivity of various nations of Europe to novel religious movements. Indeed, where the exotic religious movements of India and the East abound, where Scientology and Hare Krishna also cluster, there one finds the higher rates of Mormon membership.

Seventh-Day Adventists and Jehovah's Witnesses

At least 33 American religious bodies can be traced back to the Great Disappointment of October 22, 1844, when the millennium failed to occur. It was the second time that year that thousands of followers of William Miller had gathered, many garbed in white ascension robes, to greet the Second Advent. When nothing happened, the Millerites splintered into many groups, most of them intent on converting the faithless (Festinger et al., 1956).

The first major group to emerge in the aftermath of the failed prophecy were the Seventh-Day Adventists. They were led by Mother Ellen G. White, who claimed divine inspiration for greatly reforming Christianity in order to usher in the Second Coming. Today this group

TABLE 21.4   *Mormons per Million Population*

Area	Rate per Million
Denmark	786
Sweden	700
Finland	775
Norway	845
England and Wales	1,353
Scotland	1,678
West Germany	423
Netherlands	531
Austria	361
Switzerland	770
France	204
Belgium	356
Italy	105
Spain	67
Portugal	108
Europe	481
United States	11,001
Canada	3,036
Australia	2,327
New Zealand	11,725

has 3.4 million members worldwide in 21,327 congregations. Only 17 percent of members and of congregations are in the United States.

In 1879, Charles Taze Russell, who had reworked Miller's original calculations, launched a new movement to prepare for the Second Coming in 1914. Adopting the name Jehovah's Witnesses, the group aimed to convert a band of "elect" Christians who would ascend in glory. In 1914, the world did not end, but World War I was interpreted as the onset of the Apocalypse. By war's end, Russell was dead. His followers evolved a new doctrine concerning the start of an invisible rule of Christ in 1914 and began extremely intense missionizing under the slogan, "Many now living will never die." Today the Jehovah's Witnesses have 2.2 million members, 25 percent of them in the United States.

These groups pose a problem of classification: Are they sects or cult movements? Each claims full membership in the Christian family — indeed, each tends to claim to be *the* Christian church. Yet many cults also claim direct Christian descent. The Mormons, Moonies, and Christian Scientists do not reject the Old and New Testaments. They are cults, however, because they add a significant amount of deviant culture to the Christian tradition — in effect, each has added a third testament and recent revelations. The Seventh-Day Adventists and the Jehovah's Witnesses do not possess "third testaments"; yet each has added a good deal of novel, modern prophecy to traditional Christian doctrine, and each remains ardently premillennial (although now each prohibits "date setting"). Moreover, both groups are markedly and very visibly deviant. Seventh-Day Adventists observe extremely strict norms of Sabbath keeping and have moved the Sabbath back to Saturday. They also stress vegetarianism. The Jehovah's Witnesses refuse military service, will not swear oaths or salute flags, reject blood transfusions, and are highly visible as door-to-door and street corner missionaries.

Thus, both of these groups are near the borderline between sect and cult. At issue here is not merely a matter of labels, for our theory makes different predictions for cults and sects. What is cult and what is sect is not decided by scholars, but by societies. That is, what groups are regarded as still within a conventional religious tradition and which lie beyond it is a matter of public perception and may differ from society to society and over time. In Chapter 3, we examine ways to measure these perceptions, but none of these means is available to help us here. The problem is especially acute when nations are the unit of analysis, for a group may be a cult in one and a sect in another.

On balance, we suspect that the Jehovah's Witnesses are regarded as more cultlike than sectlike. The *Mission Handbook* we discuss later in this chapter does not include Jehovah's Witness data, as it does not include the mission activity of Mormons, Christian Scientists, Scientology, or the Hare Krishnas. Conversely, we suspect that the Seventh-Day Adventists tend to be seen as more sectlike than cultlike. They are listed in the *Mission Handbook*, for example. Generally, then, we would expect the Jehovah's Witnesses to be doing better where other cults are doing better but the Seventh-Day Adventists to follow the pattern of cult success less closely.

Table 21.5 gives some support to this expectation. The Seventh-Day Adventists are doing slightly better in Scandinavia than elsewhere in Europe, but they are doing relatively poorly in the United Kingdom and relatively better in the Germanic region. Overall, the American rate is considerably higher than that for Europe, but the combined rate for Australia and New Zealand is much higher than that for the United States.

In contrast, the Jehovah's Witness data more closely follow the pattern for the cult movements. The differences between Scandinavia and the rest of Europe are very great. A major departure to be seen here is that the Jehovah's Witness rates do not fall greatly for the Catholic nations of southern Europe. In part, this testifies to the ability of the Jehovah's Wit-

TABLE 21.5   *Seventh-Day Adventist and Jehovah's Witness Congregations per Million*

Area	Seventh-Day Congregations per Million	J.W. Congregations per Million
Denmark	10.78	44.90
Sweden	6.59	37.11
Finland	11.49	53.40
Norway	18.25	45.50
United Kingdom	2.68	20.84
West Germany	6.37	23.43
Netherlands	3.33	20.21
Austria	5.47	28.80
Switzerland	9.37	36.19
France	} 2.14	22.28
Belgium		28.67
Italy	1.26	23.02
Spain	1.19	20.03
Portugal	5.05	40.10
Europe	3.67	25.28
United States	16.46	34.16
Canada	10.71	43.74
Australia	} 24.43	36.83
New Zealand		38.39

nesses to persist in climates of repression and in the face of still potent state churches. Jehovah's Witnesses willingly risk imprisonment to spread their faith — many were in Spanish jails until the late 1960s. They claim nearly 4,000 illegal congregations in Soviet bloc nations, despite intense persecution. Although the European rate is not as high as the American, the difference is not so great as for Seventh-Day Adventists.

As Table 21.7 shows, the Seventh-Day Adventist and Jehovah's Witness rates are negatively correlated. Although the latter's rates correlate with those for other cult movements, the Seventh-Day Adventist rates do not.

Combined with data already examined, these data discredit the possibility that Australia and New Zealand are high on Indian and Eastern cult centers simply because of proximity. They also are high on these American-based movements. The latter cannot be attributed to common language, however, because these groups do not do nearly as well in Britain, but they do exceptionally well in Scandinavia. Instead, the findings suggest that some nations have religious economies very receptive to religious novelty and innovation and that the spectrum of their receptivity is broad.

But where are the sects? Our theory suggests that sect and cult movements will *not* be clustered in the same locales. There should, instead, be a tendency for cults to do best where the conventional faiths are weakest but for sects to do best where these faiths are somewhat stronger. In effect, we argue that cults reflect efforts by the unchurched to become churched, and sects reflect efforts by the churched to remain churched. To pursue these aspects of our theory, we now consider data on the European mission efforts of North American evangelical Protestants.

MISSIONARIES TO EUROPE

The Christian missionary is a major historical figure. As the West spread its political and cultural influence around the globe, the missionary often was in the lead, spreading the Gospel. By the late 19th century, Americans played the leading role in the mission fields, as all of the major American Protestant denominations devoted large budgets to overseas mission efforts (Bainbridge, 1882).

Today many of these same American denominations have greatly deemphasized their missionary programs. Indeed, to many of them, missionizing now seems in poor taste — to smack of ethnocentrism and colonialism. Where once the touring returned missionary was a figure of great public interest and respect, today it would appear that the missionary impulse has all but vanished. But this is illusory. The big liberal denominations have all but abandoned the mission fields, but the conservative, evangelical Protestant bodies, both large and small, have more than taken up the slack. In 1979, more than 650 American and Canadian mission organizations spent well over $1 billion to support more than 40,000 missionaries abroad. The primary emphasis is on missions to Africa, Latin America, and Asia (there are more than 10,000 mission congregations in Korea alone). But there has also been a remarkable shift from earlier mission days. Today a substantial missionary effort is devoted to Europe.

Even in the 19th century, some of the more radical American sects gave high priority to European missionizing (Wilson, 1970), thus reversing the historic flow of religious novelty from Europe to America. But, in recent times, Europe has become a major mission field even for very conventional and well-established evangelical Protestant bodies such as the Southern Baptist Convention, the largest Protestant denomination in the United States.

Data from all American and Canadian Protestant overseas missions are collected by World Vision of Monrovia, California, and published every several years in the *Mission Handbook*. We consulted the most recent (12th) edition, where we found not only annual budgets and the number of personnel assigned to each nation by a given group, but also the number of mission-supported congregations in each nation. These provide a firm basis for assessing the full impact of North American Protestant sects overseas. Of course, the *Mission Handbook* was not created especially for the purpose of giving us data, and therefore the listings required careful editing. We had to remove groups that merely provide services to local congregations, such as distributors of tracts and audiovisual materials. We removed the Seventh-Day Adventists because we already examined their rates separately. World Vision does not collect data on Jehovah's Witnesses, Christian Scientists, or Mormons. We dropped one group because their data obviously were not believable, just as we do with the Spiritualists in earlier chapters. This group, which shall remain unnamed, reported exactly 100 churches in each of three nations, exactly 50 in four others, 30 in two, 10 in two, and 5 in two — never a deviation from perfect units of five. The world is not that neat. In the end, we were able to compute rates that ought to be very accurate: the number of U.S. and Canadian evangelical Protestant mission congregations per million population. These are shown in Table 21.6.

TABLE 21.6   *North American Evangelical Protestant Mission Congregations per Million*

Area	N	Rate per Million
Denmark	3	.59
Sweden	1	.12
Finland	0	.00
Norway	0	.00
United Kingdom	213	3.89
West Germany	266	4.34
Netherlands	68	4.82
Austria	57	7.60
Switzerland	272	43.17
France	1,143	21.31
Belgium	64	6.53
Italy	1,624	28.49
Spain	225	6.00
Portugal	400	41.24
Australia	128	8.76
New Zealand	21	6.77

Here we can see a dramatic shift in the data. America's Protestant sects are not making their greatest inroads in the same places as are the cult movements. They are virtually absent from Scandinavia. Because the data are based on such a large number of evangelical missions, which have established a huge number of churches in some European nations, the zero rates for Finland and Norway are extremely meaningful, as are the near zero rates for Denmark and Sweden. North American sects also are obtaining some success in the United Kingdom, West Germany, the Netherlands, and Austria. Once again Switzerland exhibits a huge rate — 43 mission congregations for every million Swiss. As we move south, the reverse trend is obvious. France has a high rate of mission congregations. Overall, North American evangelical missions are doing much the best in the solidly Catholic Latin nations — Portugal and Italy are numbers two and three in terms of mission congregations per million. Even Spain, long difficult for foreign faiths to penetrate because of government restrictions, shows a substantial number of mission congregations and exceeds 7 of the 14 European nations included in the table. Similarly, although New Zealand and Australia have consistently displayed high cult rates, they show only medium level mission rates.

Another way to look at these data is that Denmark, Sweden, and Finland have many more Indian and Eastern centers and communities than they have mission congregations. (We could not compute this cult rate for Norway, but, because Norway is known to have some of these cults, the same generalization holds.) For other nations of Europe, the reverse is true.

We must caution against overinterpreting these data. They certainly do not show that there are no sect movements active in Scandinavia. We know that many vigorous sects are to be found there (cf. Mol, 1972). What the data do show is that, although American evangelical groups continue to send missionaries to Scandinavia (55 to Sweden and 43 to Finland, for example), they have failed to have significant results in terms of founding congregations. Even the Assemblies of God, who have hundreds of congregations in Western Europe and who even have large numbers in Eastern Europe, have none in Scandinavia. But where the sects have failed, the cults have thrived.

MEASURES OF CULT STRENGTH

We have examined a variety of measures of cult activity in Europe. Some seem better measures than others. The Indian and Eastern centers rate overcomes the bias of American origins. The Mormon data are better than those for Scientology and Hare Krishna simply by being based on

TABLE 21.7 *Correlations (r) Among Cult Measures (Europe Only)*

	Indian and Eastern Centers	Mormons	Scientology Churches	Scientology Staff	Hare Krishna	Jehovah's Witnesses	Seventh-Day Adventists
Indian and Eastern Centers	1.00	.77**	.55**	.54**	.33	.53**	−.13
Mormons		1.00	.37*	.37*	.24	.30	−.22
Scientology Churches			1.00	.95**	.75**	.32	−.39*
Scientology Staff				1.00	.60*	.30	−.29
Hare Krishna					1.00	.15	−.22
Jehovah's Witnesses						1.00	−.27
Seventh-Day Adventists							1.00

*p < .05.
**p < .10.
Note: N varies from 11 to 13, depending upon missing data. Units of analysis are Denmark, Sweden, Finland, Norway, United Kingdom, West Germany, Netherlands, Austria, France, Belgium, Italy, Spain, and Portugal.

large numbers of cases, lending statistical reliability. The Jehovah's Witness rates, and especially those for Seventh-Day Adventism, suffer from ambiguity over the status of these groups as cults or sects.

Table 21.7 permits examination of the correlations among these seven sets of rates. The data are limited to European nations, and Switzerland is excluded (as we discuss later). The correlations support our judgments about the relative worth of various rates as measures of cult activity. The Indian and Eastern cult rates are very highly correlated with the Mormon rates. The Indian and Eastern rates also are highly correlated with those for Scientology and Jehovah's Witnesses, but fall short of significance with the Hare Krishna rates. The Seventh-Day Adventist rates are negatively correlated with *all* others. Clearly, this latter group does not measure cult strength, and we shall drop it from further analysis. Given the small number of cases with which we can work, we think these are powerful results.

CHURCHES, SECTS, AND CULTS

Our theory suggests that cults will thrive where conventional religions are weaker, and sects will be more active where conventional religion is stronger. In previous chapters, we find that a variety of cult rates for the United States and Canada are very strongly negatively correlated with rates of membership in conventional churches. But the correlation reverses for sects.

Does the same hold in Europe? On impressionistic grounds, it would appear so. It is widely believed that the Scandinavian churches suffer from advanced secularization and those of southern Europe retain considerable vigor. But impressions can be wrong. Indeed, one purpose of this chapter is to show that the impression of America as unusually prone to sects and cults is wrong.

In 1968, the Gallup poll published the results of surveys taken in a number of nations (Sigelman, 1977). One item asked, "Do you attend church in a typical week?" Eight of the nations included in our present study were among those Gallup polled. Comparable data could be located for four others (Mol, 1972). These confirm the impressions of differential secularization. Church attendance is very low in Scandinavia (Norway's 14 percent reporting weekly attendance is much the highest), substantially higher in the Germanic nations, and higher again in the Catholic south.

Table 21.8 reveals stunning support for our major hypotheses. Each of the cult measures is very strongly negatively correlated with rates of church attendance. Indeed, despite the small number of cases, five of the six are highly statistically significant. Because this represents six independent tests of the hypotheses, the multiplication rule is applicable, which means that the odds that these are chance results are extremely small. Clearly, in Europe, as in the United States and Canada, the cults cluster where the churches are weakest. Keep in mind that we are measuring the weakness of the conventional religious *organizations,* not widespread rejection of religious ideas and beliefs. Gallup also asked about belief in God. In all of these nations a very large majority expressed belief in God, and international variations were minor, especially in contrast with differences in church attendance. Thus, in Scandinavia, the bulk of the population is effectively unchurched but continues to credit the existence of the supernatural. What better potential converts to a new religion?

Below the broken line in Table 21.8 we see data bearing on our second major hypothesis: that sects will cluster where the churches remain stronger. This, too, is strongly supported by a large, significant, positive correlation between rates of Protestant mission congregations and church attendance.

In addition to weekly church attendance, we also have available an inferential measure of the strength of conventional religion: of all new books published in a year, the proportion that is on religious topics. Robert Wuthnow (1977) first suggested using these figures (which are published annually in the United Nations' *Statistical Yearbook*) as a cross-national indicator of religious commitment. By basing the rate on all new books published per year, rather than on population, we can over-

TABLE 21.8   *Correlations* (r) *of Cult and Sect Rates with Rate of Weekly Church Attendance*

	r	Significance
Cult Measure		
Indian and Eastern Cult Centers	−.82	.002
Mormon Membership	−.69	.009
Scientology Churches	−.55	.04
Scientology Staff	−.53	.05
Hare Krishna	−.27	NS
Jehovah's Witnesses	−.71	.006
Sect Measure		
Rate of North American Protestant Mission Congregations	.69	.009

Note: The number of cases varies from 10 to 11, depending on missing data. Units of analysis are the same as for Table 21.7, except that Spain and Portugal are not included.

come extreme variations across nations in the number of books they publish (smaller nations tend to have much higher per capita publication rates). However, this measure leaves much to be desired. It does not tell us how many people read these books or the relative sales of religion books vis-à-vis others. Nor do we know anything of the contents of these books beyond their designation as "religious." Thus, many could be cult movement books. If so, this would work against our hypothesis.

We chose to examine this measure in our study because it permits the inclusion of several nations for which we do not have church attendance statistics and because it lets us assess the potential use of the measure in other research. Thus, Table 21.9 reexamines the findings shown in Table 21.8, with religious books substituted for church attendance. The findings are weaker but sustain the same conclusions. Cults cluster in nations with proportionately low rates of religious book publishing, and the reverse is true for sects. Had this been the only measure of secularization available to us, we would have confirmed our hypotheses, albeit with less statistical power. This is particularly interesting because the correlation between the church attendance rates and the religious publication rates is not especially strong ($r = .26$) and, on so few cases, falls well short of statistical significance. We cautiously conclude that we can use this inferential measure of national religious commitment in cross-national research, but because it is a somewhat weaker measure than church attendance, we must take care about rejecting hypotheses that more adequate data might well support.

Our theory also suggests that cult and sect rates will be negatively

TABLE 21.9   *Correlations (r) of Cult and Sect Rates with Religious Book Publication Rate*

	r	Significance
Cult Measure		
Indian and Eastern Cult Centers	−.58	.03
Mormon Membership	−.26	NS
Scientology Churches	−.40	.10
Scientology Staff	−.38	.13
Hare Krishna	−.51	.05
Jehovah's Witnesses	−.03	NS
Sect Measure		
Rate of North American Protestant Mission Congregations	.21	NS

Note: The number of cases varies from 11 to 13, depending on missing data. Units of analysis are the same as for Table 21.7.

TABLE 21.10   *Correlations (r) of Cult Rates with the Sect Rate*
(North American Protestant Mission Congregations)

	r	Significance
Cult Measures		
Indian and Eastern Cult Centers	−.45	.08
Mormon Membership	−.62	.01
Scientology Churches	−.34	.12
Scientology Staff	−.32	.14
Hare Krishna	−.37	.10
Jehovah's Witnesses	−.17	NS

Note: The number of cases varies from 11 to 13, depending on missing data. Units of analysis are the same as for Table 21.7.

correlated. Table 21.10 strongly supports this prediction. All correlations are in the right direction; most individually achieve significance; and once again the multiplication rule is applicable, producing a very high level of overall significance. Thus, data for Europe support our fundamental view that church and sect coexist and cults challenge where both church and sect are weakening.

SWITZERLAND: EXPLORING A DEVIANT CASE

Nations are not ideal units for analysis, for they are often so heterogeneous. For example, the rates presented here for the United States and Canada obscure the vast internal variations that have been the subject of previous chapters. Had it been possible, we would much have preferred to have used European cities, or at least provinces, as our units of analysis in this chapter—thus working with units of relatively equal area and population and having some degree of cultural unity. But we could create rates only for nations. We therefore are comparing some tiny and relatively homogeneous societies (for example, Denmark and Finland) with some that are very large and often diverse. Diversity can produce misleading averages. Thus, for example, in our study of the United States, New Mexico turned up as a highly deviant case having both a very high cult rate and a very high church membership rate. Looking inside New Mexico, county by county, revealed that the hypothesized correlation existed: Counties high in church membership lacked cults; the few counties with very low church membership rates had the cults. Summed up, however, New Mexico distorted the correlations across states.

A similar problem arose in this study because of Switzerland. Switzerland excels on all our measures. It is number one in its rate of publishing religious books, has a high level of church attendance, has the highest rate of sect congregations, stands first on Indian and Eastern centers, and stands high on Jehovah's Witnesses, Seventh-Day Adventists, Mormons, and Hare Krishna temples. With Switzerland included, the correlations shown in tables 21.7 through 21.10 are changed substantially, for Switzerland always sits far from the slope of the correlation, badly distorting it. Had we large numbers of cases, we could ignore some such anomalies, for they would have less impact. With no more than 14 cases available, one extremely deviant case has ruinous effects. We therefore have excluded Switzerland from these analyses.

We think this decision would be justified even if we lacked all insight into why Switzerland is so deviant. But, in fact, we have some indications that Switzerland is the New Mexico of Europe — that its extraordinary heterogeneity produces strange averages. Switzerland is, in many vital ways, several nations. It is about equally divided between Catholics and Protestants and into four distinctive language groups: German, French, Italian, and a form of Latin. Moreover, language and religion combine to form geographical units of considerable solidarity. Indeed, if any nation is likely to be too heterogeneous to serve as a useful unit of analysis, it is Switzerland.

Overall, however, Switzerland seems a nation in which the conventional Protestant and Catholic churches are still relatively vigorous. Campiche (1972) reports levels of church attendance that are substantially higher than those reported for most of Northern Europe and Scandinavia (cf. Mol, 1972; Sigelman, 1977). But why, then, does Switzerland score so high on all the cult measures? To answer that question, we sought means to examine internal variations in Switzerland's cult rates. We could obtain few adequate data, but those we have tell a clear and convincing story.

Returning to our data on Indian and Eastern cult centers, we determined the city in which each of Switzerland's 23 cult centers is located. We found 10 of them in Geneva. This is an extraordinary number, given that Geneva is a rather small city, having only about 175,000 people in the 1970 census (and it since has gotten smaller). Translated into a rate, this produces the astonishing figure of 57.5 cult centers per million. We know of no other city with anything like this level of cult receptivity. For the sake of comparison, San Francisco, America's cult capital, has a rate of 19.8 Indian and Eastern centers per million, and Los Angeles has a rate of only 5 per million. London has a rate of only 6.9; Copenhagen's rate is 16 per million; and Stockholm's is 19.9.

Geneva is truly off the scale in terms of cult centers. If we simply exclude Geneva from the Swiss data, the nation's Indian and Eastern cult center rate drops to 2.1 per million. This is not a remarkable rate;

indeed, it is the same as that of Austria. Thus, one city raises Switzerland's rank among European nations from the lower half to the top of the list. It might be argued that Geneva's rate is mere artifact, that, for some reason, the Spiritual Community people simply were much more thorough in discovering Geneva's cult centers than they were elsewhere. This seems unlikely, however, because the same finding turns up when we examine Mormon data.

Because the boundaries of Mormon congregations do not always conform to Swiss political boundaries, we could not compute membership rates for each canton or for each major city. Fortunately, we could do so for Geneva and for several other major Swiss cities. The Mormon data are gathered and reported with great care (and are subject to audits), and thus can be taken as very reliable. Once again we find the national rate greatly inflated by Geneva. Although Geneva has little more than 2 percent of the population of Switzerland, it accounts for *12 percent of the nation's Mormons.* Geneva has 2,406 Mormons per million; Zurich, the largest city in Switzerland, has only 1,573 Mormons per million. Keep in mind that Zurich is *not* a bastion of Swiss resistance to religious innovation. In terms of Indian and Eastern cult centers, Zurich ranks number two among major Swiss cities, with a rate of 11.8 per million. Thus, it is not that Zurich is so low in cult centers or in Mormons, but that Geneva is so extraordinarily high.

Because two independent measures reveal that it is Geneva that is greatly inflating Switzerland's apparent receptivity to new religious movements, it seems appropriate to examine more closely John Calvin's old stronghold. What makes Geneva so receptive to cult movements? Table 21.11 offers some suggestive answers. There we show data for the nine major cities of Switzerland, all having populations of 50,000 or more.

Of particular interest is the column reporting the percent with "no religion." Overall, 1.1 percent of the Swiss reported their religion as "none" in the 1970 census. Another 0.4 percent gave no answer, which also is taken to indicate no religious affiliation. And 0.1 percent gave their religion as "other." Published data for individual cities lump these three categories together. Examination of these data for each canton, however, suggests that the mix in each is about the same — that is, about 1 "other" for every 11 "nones" and 4 "no answers." Thus, what is being measured here is almost wholly a lack of religious affiliation. According to our theory, cults should be clustered where the defection from conventional religion is highest. In our study of Canada, we found that the proportion reporting no religious affiliation to the census was an excellent measure of secularization. The same relationship can be seen in Table 21.11. Geneva greatly excels, not just in cult centers, but in the

TABLE 21.11 *Comparing Swiss Cities (50,000 and Larger)*

City	Indian & Eastern Cult Centers per Million	Percent No Religion	Percent Protestant	Percent German Speaking	Jews per Million
Geneva	57.5	8.0	37.8	11.3	79,551
Zurich	11.8	3.6	55.0	82.7	12,947
Basel	9.4	5.1	51.3	81.8	9,723
Lausanne	7.2	4.1	54.8	8.7	10,175
Bern	0.0	2.5	71.3	82.3	3,463
Biel	0.0	1.7	62.2	56.5	2,781
Lucerne	0.0	1.7	20.8	87.8	5,866
St. Gallen	0.0	2.0	42.2	86.3	3,346
Winterthur	0.0	2.8	62.8	83.4	892

proportion of the population without religious affiliations. The correlation between these two rates is .92, significant beyond the .001 level.

The table also shows that Calvin's Geneva is no longer a Protestant city, being predominantly Roman Catholic. Catholicism, however, has no overall connection with cult activity when all nine cities are examined. Geneva also is a French-speaking city (64 percent) and two of the top four Swiss cities in terms of cult centers are French speaking. But, like Catholicism, French seems unrelated to cults overall.

However, the proportion of Jews is extraordinarily related to cult activity ($r = .99$). The four cities with cult centers greatly exceed the other five in terms of their Jewish populations, and Geneva has more than six times the proportion of Jews as the next city. Once again we see evidence of the special susceptibility of Jews to new religious movements, especially to ones outside the Christian tradition, as is the case here.

To sum up: Geneva is a secularized city, out of step with the levels of religious commitment prevailing in other parts of Switzerland. It has such high cult rates that it inflates the national rate greatly. In effect, Switzerland is the New Mexico of Western Europe. However, our internal analysis of Swiss data replicates our other findings. Secularization of the conventional faiths does prompt much religious experimentation.

CONCLUSION

Cults do abound in the most secularized parts of Europe, as our theory predicts. Moreover, sect activity seems clustered where the conventional churches remain strongest. But we hardly suggest that secularization is the only factor affecting the amount of religious variety or novelty in societies. Other factors also bear on religious economies.

The case of Spain shows that state repression can strongly limit at least the public activities of deviant religious movements. To the extent that religious dissent is forced underground, recruitment will be impeded. If it is risky to admit to others that one is committed to an illicit faith, it will thereby be more difficult to recruit others. Of course, no amount of state repression will eliminate all religious deviance. The medieval state could not, nor could Franco's Spain. Although Spanish jails housed many Jehovah's Witnesses, they still gathered a significant following, which burst forth into public view in 1970, when it became legal to establish Kingdom Halls. Nor have the secret police in the Soviet bloc stamped out religious dissent. The Jehovah's Witnesses do not publish nation-by-nation figures on congregations and members behind the Iron Curtain, but they admit having 3,896 illegal congregations. The Assemblies of God report truly substantial numbers of congregations in

Poland (5.7 per million), Czechoslovakia (6.0), Bulgaria (24.1), and Romania (37.4). In contrast, they report only 2.4 for West Germany and 13.3 for Italy. This logically leads to a discussion of the influence of left-wing politics.

Left-wing politics often serve as a functional alternative to sect and cult movements (cf. Stark, 1964; Martin, 1978). To the extent that nations have serious left-wing political movements, some of the energy that might otherwise have been channeled into religion will be diverted. To the extent, then, that the Left is far stronger in many European nations than in Canada and the United States, comparisons of sect and cult rates will be influenced — without as much radicalism, the more secularized European nations ought to be even higher than they are on cults, and southern Europe ought to be even more receptive to sects.

But, as we suggest in the next chapter, this pattern changes dramatically if radical regimes come to power. The facts of relative deprivation persist. The zeal and sense of purpose that once found outlet in efforts to make the revolution now find no effective secular expression. Thus, although left *politics* divert potential religious impulses, left *regimes* reanimate them. This can be read in the data on Jehovah's Witnesses in Eastern Europe and the high rates of Assemblies of God congregations. Note also that the rates are lowest in the two Eastern European nations that are most restive under their Communist regimes (Poland and Czechoslovakia) and where it would appear that the Catholic church retains greater integrity and independence. The Assemblies of God rates are very high in Romania and Bulgaria, in comparison. There, we suppose, it could be argued that religion is substituting for political resistance — or indeed that religion is the form political resistance takes.

Established state-supported churches also influence the variety within religious economies, even if they do not invoke the repressive powers of the state to limit competition. For one thing, they can continue to appear dominant despite serious defection, for their funding is not via voluntary contributions. Thus, in Germany, for example, the Lutheran and Catholic clergy are civil servants. This easily can encourage widespread notions that religion is "free," a sort of welfare mentality of faith. This is precisely what Weber noted when he expressed his amazement upon learning that a group of German immigrant lumberjacks in America were each contributing $80 a year to their church out of an annual salary of $1,000. "Everyone knows," Weber (1946:302) wrote, "that even a small fraction of this financial burden in Germany would lead to a mass exodus from the church." To the extent that Weber was correct, competition with state-supported faiths is made more difficult, for competitors will have to be financed by voluntary contributions.

Offsetting this may be a tendency for people to value religion in terms of what it costs. Cheap state churches would not fare well in this comparison. But, money aside, established churches will dominate the public forum. To get the religious implications of various issues, for example, the press will turn to the state church. The existence of an established church or churches helps define the legitimate sphere of religious options very narrowly. That is, where it is somewhat exotic to be a Protestant, or even a different major brand of Protestant, it will be extremely deviant to belong to a Christian sect, let alone to a cult movement. Put another way, the more faiths that are seen as legitimate, the more easily a new faith can escape serious stigmatization.

Aside from the matter of established churches is the matter of religious homogeneity. In and of itself, homogeneity depresses religious variety, and not only in the obvious statistical way that, if nearly everyone belongs to the same faith, there will be few left over to sustain other faiths. Rather, to the degree that people pursue one faith, it will be increasingly costly and deviant to pursue *any* other faith — at the extreme, people will not believe that there are any other faiths. This tendency for homogeneity to limit variety will be especially marked when people live in relatively stable, small communities with high individual visibility. As Claude Fischer (1975) has argued, the larger and denser a population, the greater the tendency for deviant subcultures to form and the easier they are to maintain simply because individuals are protected by (and more weakly tied to the normative culture by) their anonymity.

Great novelty can appear in a religious economy because of crises that overtax the conventional religions. Collisions between groups having different levels of technology typically prompt great religious innovation in the less advanced groups — these are the well-documented culture shock religions (cf. Wallace, 1956). Plague, war, famine, flood, and economic collapse all may reveal serious weaknesses in the conventional faiths and encourage innovation (cf. Cohn, 1961; Wilson, 1975a).

Many pressures bear upon religious economies. But, in the final analysis, only by examining the operation of *whole religious economies,* not simply the behavior of a few "firms" in these economies, can we understand religious change. The rate at which new firms enter an economy and their relative success are determined by the extent the established firms are permitting market opportunities to exist. When the conventional faiths are young, vigorous, and not yet greatly secularized, competition is difficult. When these firms have lost vigor and no longer provide a product satisfactory to many, new faiths will move into the gap. Those that offer the superior product will grow. And this, of course, shorn of historical detail and theological rhetoric, is the fundamental story of the rise of Christianity, of Buddhism, of Islam, of all today's great world faiths. They came at the right time, when the conventional faiths no longer satisfied demand, and they offered the better product. More recently, this also is the story of Mormonism — although we are still in the first chapters. Are the Mormons on the way to being a great world faith? Or does the more dramatic future success lie with one of the obscure groups included in our cult rates?

As with the theories of physics, so with those of sociology. It takes a great deal of engineering and empirical trial and error to bridge the gap between general theories and specific empirical applications. Our theory cannot pick winners out of a pool of new religious movements. It cannot even say *when* a really effective new movement will begin. But it can tell us when and where to *look* for such a movement and why that movement will gain momentum. And, once again, when we look closely where the theory tells us to look, we see a great deal of innovative religious activity taking place.

22 *Rebellion, Repressive Regimes, and Religious Movements*

On February 25, 1534, in the German town of Münster, Anabaptist zealots staged an armed uprising and installed a radical dictatorship. All who refused to undergo rebaptism into the new faith were driven from the city without food or belongings during a snowstorm. The regime impounded all food, money, and valuables and canceled all debts. Mobs burned the financial records of all local merchants. Housing was reassigned. Former beggars capered in the streets, decked in plundered finery.

The religious positions of the new regime were equally radical. Under the new moral order it imposed, all books other than the Bible were burned. All "sins," including swearing, backbiting, complaining, and disobedience, were to be punished by instant execution. Soon the regime instituted polygamy. Unmarried women were ordered to marry the first man who asked them — and 49 women were executed and their bodies hacked into quarters for failing to comply.

Before long, however, the outside world reacted. Münster was soon besieged by its bishop, who had recruited an army of mercenaries. Surrounded and cut off, the city was beset by growing confusion. Then, out of the rebel ranks, there arose a new and absolute leader—John Beukels (or Bockelson), who assumed the name of John of Leyden and claimed he had been appointed by God to be king of the last days. A this-worldly rebellion now became firmly otherworldly. The rebels did not need to win victory over their temporal rulers, for all was now in the hands of

God. These were the last days. God was coming soon to hold the Last Judgment.

Encircled by the bishop's forces, the city slowly starved. As conditions worsened, Beukels proclaimed a series of revelations. The most important of these predicted that God would come before Easter 1535 and would raise the citizens of Münster to a glorious sovereignty in a redeemed and cleansed earthly kingdom. But Easter came and went. Beukels explained that his prophecy referred to "spiritual salvation" only.

The siege continued and starvation was rife. The regime held power through increased terror. Those who wavered in their commitment were executed; their bodies were quartered; and they were nailed up on walls, gateways, and convenient trees to serve as a reminder to others.

On June 24, 1535, it ended. The bishop's troops made a surprise assault in the night and took the city. Many inhabitants were slain by the rampaging troops, but John of Leyden was taken alive. Over the next few months, he was led by a chain from town to town and "exhibited like a performing bear" (Cohn, 1961:306). In January 1536, John of Leyden was led back to Münster. There, in front of a large crowd, he was tortured to death with red hot irons. Then his body was put in an iron cage and suspended from the church tower. The cage still hangs there today.

There was nothing very unusual about the rebellion that occurred in Münster, or that it took the form of a religious movement. Similar events were commonplace in medieval Europe, especially in the growing commercial towns of the Rhine Valley (Cohn, 1961). In this chapter we explore the tendency for political protest and hope to be channeled into religious expressions and for there to be a great deal of magic combined with such religions. Then we examine these same elements from the reverse point of view: Why can even the most repressive totalitarian states not stamp out religion? Why are antireligious regimes chronically vulnerable to religious challenge?

MAGICAL AND RELIGIOUS REBELLIONS

To discover the conditions that cause political discontent to take magical and religious form, we must examine more closely the situation of the rebels at Münster. It is not important that we understand fully why they were embittered by their conditions of life. As Norman Cohn (1961) has pointed out, European feudalism was fundamentally rural. As commercial towns developed, they raised questions of authority, such as to whom a city belonged. Population mobility and economic upheavals aggravated the confusions. The towns of medieval Europe were chronic sources of political unrest. Such rebellions as that at Münster were frequent. The interesting question is why these rebellions nearly always erupted as *new religious movements*. Why did medieval rebellion depend upon or produce messianic leaders? The answer lies in two aspects of the situation faced by all medieval rebels. One of these problems is peculiar to only certain times and places; the other is general.

Impact of Monopoly Religions

The peculiar problem faced by all political dissenters in medieval Europe was the existence of a religious monopoly. There was only one legal religion, the state church. For centuries, the monopoly religion throughout Europe was the Roman Catholic Church. Following the Reformation, many nations established monopoly Protestant state churches.

No religion can achieve a monopoly out of its own resources alone. No faith can inspire universal, voluntary acceptance, except, perhaps, in tiny, primitive societies. As we see in chapters 5, 6, and 7, to the extent that a religious organization serves the need for effective compensators among the powerless, it poorly serves the religious needs of the powerful, and vice versa. Thus, unmet religious needs will prompt competing religious groups in a society as long as a free market exists. Religious monopoly can be achieved only by reliance on the coercive powers of the state. Neither Roman Catholic nor Protestant clergy could prevent religious dissent (heresy). Only the king's soldiers, or the threat of the king's soldiers, could suppress religious dissent (and then only to a degree, for even at the height of Catholic dominance of Europe, dissent flourished in all the cracks and crannies of society and constantly burst forth). Sometimes, of course, the state permitted the church to recruit its own troops and deploy them against religious deviants—as occurred at Münster. But this was only a limited delegation of the state's ultimate control of coercion.

In order for a religious organization to have the backing of the state to create a religious monopoly, it must offer something of value to the state. Other things being equal, the state will prefer a free religious marketplace, thereby to keep all religions weak and to risk no challenges from a too strong religious center of power. What can a religion offer the state in exchange for monopoly? It can offer supernatural sanctions of the state's authority. Thus, all challenges to the state will be classified as sins — political dissent will be identified with sacrilege, for the state rules with divine right (Frankfort, 1948; Stark, 1964; Glock and Stark, 1965).

Thus, wherever there is religious monopoly, political dissenters necessarily must deal with religious opposition. They must expect not only to meet the power of the state, but also to have the power of the gods invoked against them. To rebel against the medieval nobility was, therefore, also to rebel against God.

Only three solutions to the problem seem possible, in addition to the option simply to endure. The first of these has been the most common historically. As in Münster and many other areas of medieval Europe, political dissent is combined with religious dissent. As the movement proposes an alternative to secular power, it also proposes an alternative to sacred power. Thus, the political movement is also a fully developed religious movement capable of providing its followers with an uninterrupted supply of general compensators, a supply threatened with interdiction by the monopoly faith. Hence, the frequent medieval tocsin against king *and* pope.

The second possibility is alliance between a political movement and a suppressed religion. The two are not fused into a single movement, but complement each other—the political movement deals with the worldly forces of coercion, and the religious movement guards its flanks against the forces of otherworldly coercion. The alliance between Martin Luther and the German princes is a famous example. For a long time, the German nobility had smarted under the rule of the Holy Roman Emperor, finding it impossible to maintain a political challenge in the face of potential excommunication by the church. Meanwhile, a long line of religious dissenters had been crushed for lack of means to overcome state coercion in service to the church. By backing Luther, the German nobles gained the means for liberation from the pope's threats and Luther gained the military protection required to build the great sect movement called Protestantism.

The third alternative is rather new in history. The political dissenters adopt an explicitly antireligious doctrine and promise to supply rewards now instead of the compensators offered by religion. As we see later in this chapter, this tactic is often very successful before a radical movement gains control of the state, but it suffers a chronic inability to withstand religious challenges after it has taken power.

These, then, are the only options available to political dissenters when they face a "united front" between church and state. Even where less than a religious monopoly exists, to the degree that the dominant religious organizations support the status quo, political dissent is driven to adopt one of these three options.

Impossible Goals

The rebels at Münster faced a second problem, one that political dissenters frequently face, whether or not there is militant religious support of political authority. Political protest often has no realistic hope of success. This can be due to two factors. First, the coercive power arrayed against the political dissenters simply is irresistible. Second, the group's political aims are simply not possible in this world. Frequently, both factors press upon political dissent. Under such conditions, political dissent becomes plausible only on the basis of magical assumptions, and these must be extremely credible magical assumptions. Such cannot be gained from mere magicians. They require a grand rationale, a conception of active supernatural forces that will intervene to make an objectively hopeless situation manageable — and that will supply the potent magic. Such magic can be underwritten only by fully developed religions. For these reasons, radical political energy often sustains the evolution of magical religious movements.

It is hard to know just what military judgment the Münster rebels had. Clearly, one small city had no objective possibility of withstanding the military might that would be brought to crush their rebellion against secular rule. But, no matter how badly they may have misjudged beforehand, it was obvious to everyone in the city just how matters stood once the bishop's troops had surrounded their city. Retribution stood at their gates, and it would not be kept at bay for long. In these circumstances, John of Leyden took power because he offered the only plausible solution: God will save us. God sees the justice of our cause and will come and trample on our oppressors. Had someone arrived via time machine with the actual rewards the rebels desired, perhaps a company of tanks and a regiment of mechanized infantry, John of Leyden and his system of compensators probably would have been ignored. But objective means of deliverance were not at hand. Here was a vacuum in which only magical means, sustained by religion, were available. When tested, of course, the magic failed. But it was the *only* hope.

MALINOWSKI'S THEORY OF MAGIC

Bronislaw Malinowski (1948) is justly famous for his anthropological studies of the Trobriand Islands, which he carried out while interned in the First World War. For sociologists of religion, the centerpiece of his work is the theory of magic. The culture of the Trobriands was rich in magic. But, Malinowski noticed, magic was not associated with all native activities; it seemed reserved for only certain kinds of activities. For example, the islanders used little magic in preparation for fishing within the calm lagoon off the island, but they employed a great deal of magic when preparing for dangerous fishing expeditions out onto the high seas. Such selective use of magic led Malinowski to propose that magic is utilized as a substitute for science and technology — that magic is employed to give people the hope of control, or even the sense of actual control over important activities whose outcome they cannot control by more direct means. Magic, therefore, thrives where the need for control is great and the means for control are lacking.

A most important point here is that Malinowski dismissed the common, but unenlightening, belief that people use magic simply because they are superstitious or irrational. To the contrary, he argued, people use magic in a highly rational manner (cf. Lewis, 1963; Henslin, 1967). The "primitive mind" is not irrational. Primitives never resort to magic when there is a better choice. Thus, for example, a primitive does not try to substitute magic for work when it comes to gardening:

> He knows as well as you do that there are natural conditions and causes, and by his observations he knows also that he is able to control these natural forces by mental and physical effort. His knowledge is limited, no doubt, but as far as it goes, it is sound and proof against mysticism. If the fences are broken down, if the seed is destroyed or has been dried or washed away, he will have recourse not to magic, but to work guided by knowledge and reason. (Malinowski, 1948:28)

But, Malinowski argued, many factors *are* beyond the control of the primitive agriculturist, who cannot control the weather or prevent swarms of insects from eating the crops. These thwart the agriculturist's efforts and exceed his knowledge. "To control these influences *and these only* he employs magic" (Malinowski, 1948:29 [italics added]).

It *is* more efficient to pull weeds than to pray for food. It is *not* more efficient to spit on fields than to pray for rain. We stress this point because we wish to make clear that we conceive of both magic and religion as rational human activities, not as the bursting forth of deep, irrational impulses. That is, religious compensator systems arise out of the same processes of reasoning, and of trial and error, as do other aspects of human culture. Even a primitive people's religious rites have been subjected to as much thought and evaluation as have their gardening techniques. That we may be in a position to demonstrate that rituals to ensure good crops do not work in no way suggests that primitive farmers ought to recognize this fact or that such beliefs about the effect of rituals are irrational.

No one has made this point more clearly than Melford Spiro (1964:105):

> A religious system then, is first of all a cognitive system, *i.e.*, it consists of a set of propositions, explicit or implicit, about selected aspects of the world which are asserted to be true. Undeniably, many of these propositions, when transmitted to actors, evoke their assent because, among other reasons, they

would like them to be true. . . . Others, however, evoke the assent of the actors despite the fact that they would prefer that they not be true. Nevertheless, the pleasant and the unpleasant beliefs alike continue to be held because, in the absence of other explanations, they serve to explain, *i.e.*, to account for, give meaning to, and structure, otherwise inexplicable, meaningless, and unstructured phenomena. They are assumed to be true because in the absence of competing beliefs, or disconfirming evidence, there is no reason to assume that they are false.

Elsewhere, Spiro (1966:113) points out that merely because the "premises" on which a religion might be based "are false does not render them irrational — until or unless they are disconfirmed by evidence." The point is that it is the human reaction *against* irrationality that gives rise to religious and magical beliefs. Such beliefs make rational things that otherwise would be irrational. It therefore is no surprise that people engage in rational behavior when they deal with the gods. When they know a cheaper or better way to gain rewards, people tend not to seek them from the gods.

BLOCKED ASPIRATIONS

In Chapter 8, we examine the tendency of modern psychotherapy movements to evolve into cult movements. We argue that, when humans commit themselves to attaining truly immense goals, such as becoming transformed and effective beings, there will be a tendency for them to shift from naturalistic to supernaturalistic methods. This is a direct application of Malinowski's theory of the use of magic among primitives.

The best documented of groups that have followed the path from psychotherapy to magic and religion is The Process, which we discuss in chapters 8 and 14. As their group therapy sessions failed to produce the aims of total self-realization, the group slowly became magical and then began to undergird its magic by constructing a novel and complex theology. Soon it was a new cult movement (Bainbridge, 1978c). And, of course, Transcendental Meditation moved some distance toward the supernatural when it began to falter as a mild client cult.

Striking similarities can be found in the case of Synanon, as analyzed by Richard Ofshe (1980). Synanon began as an organization that aimed to cure drug addiction and gained rapid fame when its unwarranted claims (irresponsibly confirmed by professional social scientists) of a high cure rate were widely publicized. The actual low rate of success was apparent inside the group, however. In an effort to achieve better results, the group moved toward a communal, lifelong membership model, meanwhile upping its aims to levels that can be described only as utopian. As time passed and these aims, too, proved elusive, mystical experimentation set in. The ouija board was introduced into Synanon encounter sessions, and messages from the dead gave religious significance to Synanon's mission and to the founder's authority (Lang, 1978). Soon the mysticism became dominant. Synanon declared itself a religion, and its founder, Charles E. Dederich, was declared the highest spiritual authority of the group.

In both these instances, an overtly secular psychotherapy group found itself reaching for those vast and utterly scarce rewards that always have exceeded the human grasp in this world. Rather than pull back from these desires, the group evolved a novel compensator system to sustain them.

Scientology also displays this pattern (Wallis, 1976). It, too, started as a secular therapy, Dianetics, which attracted literally tens of thousands of followers in the 1950s. And it, too, committed itself to impossible goals of human fulfillment. Specifically, L. Ron Hubbard promised that his new therapy would enable people to become "clears," to erase all their psychological scars and blocks and thus gain superhuman powers, including total recall, an extraordinary IQ, and freedom from ailments such as the common cold — in short, that they would be to normal people as normal people are to the severely insane. As we see in Chapter 12, the failure to achieve these aims caused a number of departures and innovations. Chief among these was the introduction of supernaturalism in the ideology and the construction of a host of compensators for the rewards the therapy itself could not deliver. Although some Scientologists continue to believe that their organization is a science posing as a religion for legal reasons, the truth is that Scientology long has been a religion posing as a science.

A list of therapy movements that have been transformed into religions could be extended to great length. A movement toward mysticism seems to characterize the human potential movement generally. Like Jung, whose pursuit of the psyche led him to the supernatural, *est* and other leading human potential cults seem fated to evolve into religions (Rieff, 1968; Fodor, 1971).

Modern psychotherapy groups are rather tepid enterprises when compared with the rebels at Münster and other such groups that seek to overturn temporal political authority. Although groups such as Scientology or Synanon may run afoul of laws governing medical practice, their path to success is not barred by the armed might of the state. Yet, that their blocked aspirations so often do lead into magic and religion makes it the more understandable that groups facing the threat of overwhelming coercive force will, like Malinowski's Trobriand Islanders, seek to accomplish by magical means what is hopeless in any other fashion.

MAGIC, RELIGION, AND REBELLION

The rebels at Münster followed a familiar pattern when they turned to a prophet to deliver them from the hands of their enemies. Not only was this pattern extremely common in medieval Europe, it has characterized rebellions of the oppressed as far back as our historical accounts can take us. Norman Cohn, whose *The Pursuit of the Millennium* (1961) is the classic study of revolutionary messiahs, has found the common themes of these religious and magical solutions to the problem of military weakness well developed in the Book of Daniel. This portion of the Bible was composed about 165 B.C., when Israel suffered under the political repression of the Syro-Greek dynasty of the Seleucids. The "dream" in the Book of Daniel spells out why and how divine liberation will soon occur. Indeed, it is

> the paradigm of what was to become and to remain the central phantasy of revolutionary eschatology. The world is dominated by an evil, tyrannous power of boundless destructiveness—a power moreover which is imagined not as simply human but as demonic. The tyranny of that power will become more and more outrageous, the sufferings of its victims more and more intolerable—until suddenly the hour will strike when the Saints of God are able to rise up and overthrow it. Then the Saints themselves, the chosen, holy people who hitherto have groaned under the oppressor's heel, shall in their turn inherit dominion over the whole earth. This will be the culmination of history; the Kingdom of the Saints will not only surpass in glory all previous kingdoms, it will have no successors. It was thanks to this phantasy that Jewish apocalyptic exercised, through its derivatives, such a fascination upon the discontented and frustrated of later ages—and continued to do so long after the Jews themselves had forgotten its very existence. (Cohn, 1961:21)

It was this religious vision of magical triumph in the Book of Daniel that made credible the Maccabean revolt of the Jews. This same vision, augmented with the expectation that God would send the messiah to lead the Jews to victory, made successive Jewish revolts against Rome seem rational. We need not concern ourselves here with the debate about the historical role of Jesus, whether he meant to lead a this-worldly revolt and failed or whether his message from the start was concerned wholly with the Kingdom of God. It is clear that many Jews rejected Christianity because they continued to expect a messiah who would overthrow the Roman oppressors. Indeed, the Jews rose many times against Rome, culminating in their dramatic and remarkable rebellion in about 132 under the leadership of Bar-Kokhba, whose early successes were seen as proof that he was the promised messiah (Yadin, 1971). This legacy lived on in medieval messianic rebellions.

However, such magical, religious solutions to military weakness are not confined to societies possessed of the Judeo-Christian tradition. They abound in all corners of the globe. They are most commonly found where technologically less advanced societies confront those with advanced technology.

American Indian Messianic Movements

One of the greatest works of American anthropology is James Mooney's (1896) monumental study of the role of messiahs in prompting American Indian resistance to the encroachments of White settlement. The government commissioned the work in 1890 to investigate the outbreak that year of Ghost Shirt dancing, an intense religious movement, among the Plains Indians.

Mooney went among many Plains tribes from 1890 until 1894 in an effort to record the rituals and doctrines of the Ghost Shirt movement and to understand its underlying meaning. What he discovered sent him to the library to study documents concerning prior Indian messianic movements, for he found the cult of 1890 was but the last of a long line of similar movements. Thus, his great book includes a lengthy account of prior movements.

Mooney's thesis was simple but profound. Messianic movements among the Indians were an attempt to drive out alien invaders and recover pre-Columbian autonomy. They took religious, rather than only military, form because the latter had failed. Repeated wars upon the Whites had ended in heavy losses, defeat, and worsened conditions. Victory thus depended upon finding means to overcome irresistible White military supremacy. Such means could come only from the gods. Thus, a long series of prophets came forward to preach that deliverance was now at hand.

These were prophets of new religions, not merely magicians, for what is involved here are not the understandable desires to control the dangers inherent in "normal" military engagements. Rather, the need is to master the risks of wholly "abnormal" warfare — wars that seem hopeless. Bryan Wilson (1975a:221) noted this important distinction: "There is usually a role for the shaman or the magician in warfare: the war-dance and war-paint are themselves heavily endowed with magic as a mystical underwriting of military enterprise. But new magical claims, more powerful than those made in the past, become necessary if military activity against enemies with superior weapons is to be effectively encouraged."

War-paint no longer sufficed for the American Indians. What was needed was potent intervention by supernatural powers, and thus a compensator system so general and ramified that it constituted a religion.

According to Mooney, one of the earliest of the Indian prophets to offer means to overcome the White enemy appeared among the Delaware Indians in Michigan in 1762. The name of this prophet is lost, but his message was well recorded. He preached tribal unity and total rejection of all elements of White culture and technology. Only by returning absolutely to native Indian ways could the Great Spirit be enlisted in behalf of the Indians. This meant not only the rejection of liquor, woolen clothing, and medical techniques. It meant abandonment of firearms. If this were done, and if the Indians addressed the Great Spirit with new, special rites and prayers, they would vanquish the White invaders by the use of their traditional spears and bows.

This new cult stirred great excitement among the Indians. Eventually, the great chief of the Algonquins, Pontiac, embraced it. He established a confederation of tribes, and, in 1763, he launched a war against the Whites. The Indians were totally defeated and Pontiac was killed. But the messianic message did not die with him, for the conditions that gave it urgent relevance persisted.

Again a prophet came forward — Tenskwatawa, a Shawnee. On the basis of a vision he received in 1805, he founded a new cult movement aimed at Indian liberation. His brother, the famous chief Tecumseh, built the cult movement into the greatest Indian federation in history. In 1811, Tecumseh was beaten by troops commanded by General William Henry Harrison. The next year Tecumseh tried again, this time joining in an alliance with the British in the War of 1812. But the British lost and so did the Indians.

Again and again such cults occurred. Each time there was defeat. Toward the latter part of the 19th century, the promise of deliverance through military victory began to disappear. Now the promise was of direct action by the supernatural. Thus arose the Ghost Shirt dances under the influence of the prophet Wodziwob. He preached that a great cataclysm would soon ravage the earth. The White man would disappear forever. The Indians, too, would be swept away. But those who faithfully embraced the new religion and who engaged in the Ghost Shirt dancing would return to earth after a few days. This would be a heavenly era of peace and plenty, and the Great Spirit would dwell on earth among his devoted followers.

This doctrine avoided the severe empirical tests that had led earlier movements to disaster. It did not suggest military adventures or promise protection against bullets. And it survived into the 20th century.

Similar examples of the rise of magical religious movements can be found wherever indigenous populations have been overwhelmed by

Western technical might. Countless cases have been recorded in Africa, in Latin America, and in Asia: The famous Boxer Rebellion in China was based on an ideology virtually identical to the messianic movements among the American Indians. Bryan Wilson has analyzed an amazing number of these movements in his indispensable *Magic and the Millennium* (1975a).

Magical religious responses to powerlessness are not limited to primitive or technologically inferior groups. Similar movements can be found in the most advanced industrial societies. In Chapter 11, we sketch the frequency with which leading socialists and small utopian socialist communes embraced Spiritualism at the turn of the century. An element in this transformation of means was the growing realization that, at least in the United States and Great Britain, there was no likelihood of mounting a successful revolution. A second element, especially for those involved in concrete efforts to enact a socialist commune, may have been the discovery that socialist theory is incapable of producing socialism. Instead, it produces a substantial loss in productivity without resulting in the hoped for equality. Indeed, efforts to impose even material equality (equality of power and status cannot be achieved even in tiny, experimental communes) quickly demonstrate that equality is not *equity*. That is, those who work harder, work more effectively, or bear heavier responsibility quickly perceive that it is unfair for them to receive no more than the least able and productive, as has been found in studies of Israeli kibbutzim (Yuchtman, 1972). But things, apparently, were different in the spirit world. Many socialists and socialist groups discovered during seances that socialism truly exists in the next world; so they contented themselves with messages from beyond while waiting until they, too, would "pass over."

The Manson Family

The youth counterculture of the 1960s passed through a period of political militance. Some gave their energy to campus disturbances and political demonstrations; some turned to terrorism; and some turned their backs on "corrupt," "materialistic" society and formed utopian communes. Then suddenly the intense political concerns of many gave way to equally intense and exotic mysticism. Magic flourished as sales of the I Ching, ouija boards, tarot cards, astrology books, and other such occult paraphernalia boomed. Religious movements boomed, too, as Jesus freaks, Hare Krishnas, Moonies, Scientologists, and missionaries from a host of cult movements crowded public places, seeking donations and converts. Then, on the night of August 9, 1969, five prominent people, including actress Sharon Tate and heiress Abigail Folger, were brutally murdered in a house nestled in the hills above Hollywood. The murders were bizarre executions, and strident political slogans were smeared in the blood of the victims.

Several months later, the police swept down on a rural hippie commune and arrested Charles Manson and some of his followers for these and other sensational murders. A shocked nation discovered that "flower children" are not always gentle and that religious movements are not necessarily pacifist. Indeed, the Manson family, as the group was known, closely resembled the militant messianic movements of the American Indians.

Charles Manson was a school dropout with a long juvenile and prison record. Back on the streets in the middle 1960s, he scuffled around in the hippie scene in San Francisco, trying to become a rock star and encountering many of the new cult movements, including Scientology and perhaps The Process (Sanders, 1971; Bugliosi, 1974). Moving among the hippies, Manson discovered that his jail-learned skills in encounter sessions were a potent means for gathering a committed following of young drifters and runaways, kids whom he once poignantly described as "garbage nobody wanted" because he found them abandoned along the highways.

Soon Manson moved his "family" to Southern California and settled on an isolated ranch out in the desert. The family began to grow more rapidly. Most of his recruits were women in their late teens and early twenties. Many were pregnant or had infants, and most were into dope.

Through a process of social implosion very similar to that experienced by members of The Process, Manson began constructing a religious doctrine fed by his intense hatred of conventional society and reinforced by his followers' similar feelings. They began to collect guns and to practice military tactics in the desert. But, like the American Indians, the Manson family could pose no believable military challenge to the larger society. Then came Manson's messianic vision of "Helter Skelter," based on a line from a Beatles' recording in which Manson detected deep and hidden messages.

Helter Skelter was an apocalyptic prediction in the full tradition of the Book of Daniel and the great Indian prophets. Supernatural forces would produce a worldwide race war. Blacks and Whites would kill each other off. And, near the end, the Black Muslims would come out of hiding and kill the remaining survivors on both sides. Then the Black Muslims would begin to clean up the mess, to build back the cities and the factories. But, according to Manson, "Blackie" would not be able to handle running the world. At that point "Blackie" would come to the Manson family, who would have lived through the war by hiding in Death

Valley. "Blackie" would beg the family to show him how to run the world (Bugliosi, 1974:333).

Manson's followers accepted his vision of the future, especially because he was able to "prove it" by passages in the Bible and in the Beatles' White Album. Many members also believed Manson was the new Christ. But Manson's vision did not inspire only passive waiting. As Pontiac and Tecumseh knew that the Great Spirit would only work *through* them and that they had to commit their forces into battle, so, too, Charlie Manson knew that sparks were needed to set off Helter Skelter. The murders began in the belief that they would be blamed on Blacks and would stir White attacks on Black neighborhoods. Perhaps there were thousands of young dropouts wandering America in the late 1960s who were filled with hate, but they lacked Charlie Manson's religious vision to make armed rebellion a credible option.

From Militant Lesbianism to Witchcraft

In Chapter 9, we mention the activities of a militant coven of witches in Seattle, Washington. This group exhibited a classic transformation from direct political action to magical religious activities. Neither of us was able to study this group directly; we depend instead on secondhand and third-hand reports. But a primary source of information is direct because the leader of this group is a compulsive spray-can slogan painter with a very distinctive hand. When we first began to notice her proclamations in the mid-1970s (they festoon many buildings and underpasses along routes we routinely travel, and one of us lived close to their headquarters), they reflected purely secular, lesbian feminism. The slogans proclaimed the superiority of women and of exclusive feminine association. As time passed, the slogans became more strident. A common one was a target circle and, in the bull's eye, the line: "Put all men and boys here. Is that clear enough for you?" Other favorites were "Amazons will win" and "Kill for a World Without Men." Strong stuff indeed.

Reports we obtained on this group indicated they were a lesbian commune. Members reportedly were convinced that very soon thousands and then millions of women would flock to their banner—that Amazons *would* win. Of course, very little happened. As frustration grew, these women might have evolved a doctrine similar to Charlie Manson's and taken up terror tactics, but they did not. Instead, they evolved in a different, magical religious, direction. This was clear when the slogans changed dramatically: "Off Jesus, Up the Mother," "The Blood of Witches is on Christian Hands," "Wicca Will Win," "Amazons of Wicca." We first noticed these sprayed wildly all over the walls of a nearby Protestant church. Since then, they have become abundant in the usual places. The word *Wicca* refers to witchcraft. Thus, what can be read on the walls of Seattle is the transformation of a group of militant lesbians, who once filled their nights with brutal talk of castration and of armed regiments of women, and who held boundless aspirations for triumph, into a coven of witches. Now, apparently, they worship the Divine Mother. Like the late stages of the Ghost Shirt cult, they pose no serious threat to their neighbors while clinging to their hopes for victory.

Committee for the Future

Groups need not be composed of "misfits" in order to transform their political aims into religious solutions. These evolutions can occur among the wealthy, famous, and privileged, even among intellectuals who initially profess contempt for all magic and religion. It is all a matter of reaching too hard for goals of immense value that cannot be obtained through direct action, for then, our theory predicts, humans will tend to create and exchange compensators — a proposition that is no more than a more general statement of Malinowski's theory of magic.

One of us devoted portions of 1972 and 1973 to observing the transformation of an elite group devoted to spaceflight into a magical, religious cult. When it began in 1970, the Committee for the Future was a secular organization made up of wealthy and prominent people whose aim was to inspire support for the colonization of the solar system. By the end of 1973, they had largely abandoned this goal and had shifted to encounterlike conventions, the elaboration of mystical visions of the future, dabbling in occultism and pseudoscience, and the creation of a humanistic religion (Bainbridge, 1976).

The initial goal of the CFF was to establish a demonstration colony on the moon, using surplus Saturn V launch vehicles for the trip. They hoped that such a demonstration would spur support for the group's truly ambitious hopes: immediate colonization of the moon and the planets, which, in turn, would usher in a new era in which the human field of activity would be the entire universe. Thus, rather transcendent goals lurked within the CFF program from the start. Yet the group's initial aims were within the realm of technical possibility, and the prestige of the members encouraged them to hope they could bring their plans to fulfillment. For two years, the CFF lobbied and propagandized on behalf of their colonization scheme, but high costs, lack of support from NASA or the public, and uniformly negative evaluations from aerospace experts blocked their efforts.

The CFF members were dedicated amateurs, not space scientists or engineers. Early in the history of the spaceflight movement, the 1920s and 1930s, amateur groups made effective contributions. Indeed, the prominent space scientists of recent times had as youths been active in amateur rocket societies, in the Soviet Union as much as in the United States. But by the 1970s, the time for amateurs was past. The spaceflight movement has been institutionalized in great bureaucratic organizations such as the National Aeronautics and Space Administration, the American Institute of Aeronautics and Astronautics, and the aerospace companies.

As part of its efforts to press forward the plan of space colonization, the CFF initiated a series of open conventions, but the interplanetary interest quickly slid from view. Convention participants spent their time collectively developing grand schemes for utopia. Their initial aims blocked, they evolved rapidly in the direction of magic, following the subculture-evolution model of cult innovation that we describe in Chapter 8. Convention seminars degenerated into encounter groups. In these, mysticism and parapsychology replaced spaceflight as the topics of concern. Psychic fusion rituals were enacted to religious music. Soon complex theological systems began to surface (for example, Wescott, 1969).

At the early signs of occultism, the once friendly aerospace companies and agencies dropped all connections with the CFF. Free of specific practical focus and unfettered by ties with conventional organizations, the Committee for the Future was able to pursue unhindered its mystical speculations and religious experiences (Bainbridge, 1976).

REPRESSIVE REGIMES AND RELIGIOUS MOVEMENTS

As the countless messianic rebellions like that at Münster demonstrate, medieval regimes were not able to stamp out religious deviance. The universality of the universal Church was always somewhat illusory, as we note in Chapter 5, a veneer beneath which all manner of exotic faiths were practiced on the sly. Whenever the power of the state weakened or the ruling elite was lax in backing up the monopoly faith, these movements burst into lush growth.

But it was not only in medieval Europe that the state could not crush religious deviance and dissent. Nowhere has that ever been accomplished. Immediately following World War II, vast numbers of new religions appeared in Japan (McFarland, 1967; Morioka, 1975). This caused much scholarly speculation on how social dislocations and culture shocks produce new religions. These arguments have great merit, but they neglect an important fact. Many, probably most, of these new Japanese religions were not *new*. Most had been in operation for decades, some for centuries. But until the American occupation of Japan, these faiths had been illegal. Laws granting religious freedom merely brought them out into public view.

Religion and Politics

Most sociological discussion of the political role of religion is not merely misleading, but pernicious. The standard view, enshrined in dozens of textbooks, is that religion sustains the political status quo — that religion serves as a conservative, even reactionary, force in human societies. Clearly, such claims apply at best to only some religions and only in special social circumstances. Unfortunately, too many sociologists have paid attention to only a few notable instances in recent Western history. Many also have misstated the case because of their particular theoretical commitments (to say nothing of their personal antagonisms toward religion).

One such theoretical commitment that has led to misstating the political impact of religion is *functionalism*. Following the tradition of Durkheim, many functionalists simply assert that religion provides the unifying value systems of societies (indeed, that is their definition of religion) and therefore it legitimates state norms and institutions (cf. Parsons, 1957). There is something to be said for this proposition; yet it is wholly irrelevant to much that goes on in the world. One supposes that the bishop of Münster, camped outside the city with his army, would have turned away in disgust at the statement that religion sustains the state. He and his religion were busy in that service, but the Anabaptists inside the city surely were not. Thus, although it is true that religions that have entered into a monopoly agreement with the state usually will support existing social arrangements, it is equally true that countless movements aimed at overthrowing the state and radically altering existing social structures also act in the name of religion. Only if we eliminate from the definition of religion all groups that do not integrate whole societies and thus legitimate the status quo can the functionalist generalization be saved. But such a generalization would be empty, and most societies would be without religion, so defined.

That numerous religions have struck against the state reveals the inadequacy of the Marxist analysis of religion, too. The characterization of religion as an "opium of the people" is as partial and ill founded as the functionalist position. For many of the groups we examine in this book, particularly those we consider in this chapter, it would be more apt to describe religion as the "amphetamines of the people." Marx and Engels reached their famous conclusion from their argument that all culture is only a "superstructure" of "illusions" that grows out of the underlying material conditions in society. Thus, religion, like everything else, is a creation of the ruling class and, as such, is designed to advance and protect their interests. This leads to a conclusion identical with that reached by functionalists, that there will always be a mutuality of interests between religion and the state. Marxists can, of course, explain some religious divisions within societies as reflections of class conflicts. But what can they make of religious conflicts that cross-cut class lines or seem to occur wholly within a class — as when competing faiths divide a ruling elite?

The solution to this matter is to be found in the nature of religious economies and in the nature of the state. The two are, of course, closely linked. Religious monopoly can exist only if it is backed by the coercive forces of the state. In such circumstances, political and religious deviance are one. Heresy is against the law; rebellion is a sin. We examined the three possible solutions for movements faced with combined religious and political opposition. In the first of these, political dissent is embedded in a religious movement. In the second, political dissent makes common cause with religious dissent. Both strategies present a united front of opposition to the united front of the monopoly religion and the state.

We also mentioned a third strategy: not only to challenge political authority, but to reject religion per se, to dismiss it as an "opium" and offer compensators to be redeemed in this world in contrast with compensators to be redeemed in another world. This has been the common strategy followed by radical movements at least since the French Revolution. Smash the state *and the* church. Or, as the French firebrand Diderot proclaimed, "And with the guts of the last priest let us strangle the last king." Ever since, radicals have urged us not to be content with religious comforts; let us, as Nikita Khrushchev put it, create "a paradise on this planet, unlike Christianity, which promises a paradise after death."

There are probably many reasons why modern leftists embraced "scientific atheism." Major among these was the existence of established state churches, many still claiming monopoly status, in Europe during the formative period of modern radical doctrines. These religions did rally to the state. In a free market religious economy, it is more likely that political radicals would simply have left religious questions alone because religious opposition would not necessarily arise against them.

A second reason is that modern radicalism is the creation of intellectuals who aspired to a science of society. Thus, their religious views were shaped by the rapid secularization that set in during the 18th and 19th centuries and the bitter struggles between traditional religions and developing science (see Chapter 19). Indeed, the leading role played by nonpracticing Jews in shaping modern radical thought deserves mention. Men such as Marx and Trotski had abandoned the Jewish faith and were cut off from the Jewish community. Yet they were not assimilated into the gentile community either. Anti-Semitism cut them off from

Christians and confirmed them in their bitterness against both church and synagogue (cf. Marx, 1844).

A third reason was that movements focused on direct political action do tend to compete with religious movements, especially sects, for adherents. People who find satisfaction in religious compensators tend not to be moved to embrace political movements. Indeed, studies based on national samples of Great Britain, France, the Netherlands, and the United States have found significant incompatibility between religion and radicalism — people tend to support either one or the other, not both (Stark, 1964; Glock and Stark, 1965).

Our concern here is not to explain why modern left radicalism embraced atheism and is militantly opposed to faith. Our primary interest is the inability of radicalism to supplant religion, especially its inability to crush religion even when radicals control the vast power of the modern police state. This inability displays the unique power of supernatural compensator systems and is why religious movements continue to form and to grow under repressive radical regimes.

Radical versus Religious Compensators

Our analysis hinges on our conception of compensators and that the most general compensators are credible *only* if they are based on supernatural assumptions. While antireligious radical movements are out of power, they can issue credible compensators for many *scarce* rewards. They can promise that, after the revolution, relative deprivation will be eliminated — that workers will enjoy the full fruits of their labor in a land of plenty. For many, the fact that the party cannot promise the truly vast rewards, such as eternal life, will be overshadowed by the hope of many direct rewards and by the sense that they sacrifice in the name of history, justice, and virtue and will be honored by a grateful posterity.

Then comes the revolution, but the new day does not dawn. In post-revolutionary societies, marked social stratification remains. There are rich and poor, powerful and powerless. Relative deprivation persists. For the vast majority of people, many rewards continue to be so scarce that they have much less than they desire and much less than many others actually have. With revolution proclaimed and the party in control of the state, its compensators rapidly lose credibility.

For a time, the people may be content to wait until the great work of the revolution is complete. But this will not suffice for too long. Soon there is a major demand for, and market opportunity for, credible, effective compensators. Moreover, from the beginning, the party, not being a religious movement, lacked the means to offer plausible compensators for the greatest rewards, those not directly available to anyone on this earth. And these are the core of religion. Indeed, they are the exclusive features that not only define religions, but account for their existence. Only religions can supply these compensators. In this confrontation, all purely naturalistic, nonsupernatural movements are overmatched. In the long run, they simply lack the means to satisfy the needs religions meet so well.

The radical regime can, of course, resort to coercion to make it costly to practice religion or to found or join religious movements. Indeed, they all have done so, but they failed. This is not to suggest that religious movements will be able to overthrow repressive atheist states. We do suggest that the most such repressive states can accomplish, however, is a standoff. They may be immune to overthrow, but they will be unable, finally, to root out religion as a mass phenomenon. The harder they try, the more intense religion and religious opposition they generate. As Kowalewski (1980a:281) has put it: "repression of religion is comparable to driving a nail: the harder one hits, the deeper it goes."

The Soviet Union

Once the Communist party took power in the Soviet Union, it declared "scientific atheism" to be official state policy. Although the party did not absolutely outlaw the major religious organizations, it placed them firmly under government control and attempted to prevent the spread of religion to new generations. The schools began universal indoctrination of atheism; seminaries to train new clergy were prohibited; religious proselytization was outlawed; and aggressive policies were carried out to root out the "prerevolutionary remnants" of religion (Committee on the Judiciary, 1964–1965).

For six decades now, the regime has attempted to accomplish this aim. The police and state security agencies often have resorted to terror tactics to force atheization. Yet the regime has utterly failed to crush religion. Not only do the great masses of citizens still cling to the old religions, but, in recent years, even the government press has acknowledged a wave of religious revival sweeping the country as well as the growing strength of sects and cults (London and Poltoratzky, 1957; Glezer, 1976; Mihajlov, 1976; Beeson, 1977; Ellis, 1978; Kowalewski, 1980a, 1980b).

Despite discrimination in housing and employment against persons too clearly identified with religion, the Soviet people persist in religious activity. In recent years, the government has deployed huge numbers of police, troops, and members of the youth branch of the party to turn back people attempting to attend Christmas and Easter church services — allowing only elderly, regular attenders to enter. The important point is that such efforts are necessary and such huge crowds must be turned back. Despite the probability of having their names taken, and despite knowing their way may be barred, many people try to go to church. It seems reasonable to assume that, for everyone who turns out on such occasions, scores of others remain religious in more circumspect fashion.

The *samizdat* (or dissident literature) that now abounds in the Soviet Union has a very high content of religious expression. The dissident writers often blame the evils of the Communist state on its fundamental godlessness, in addition to expressing personal faith. These writers are not uneducated zealots, remnants of times past. They include world famous writers, such as Solzhenitsyn, scholars, scientists, even major military figures. Consider the words of Major General Pyotr Grigorenko, published in 1978:

> I am no longer a communist, although I professed this teaching almost my entire conscious life. . . . I see no communist state system which has not stifled its people, deprived it of its human rights, liquidated freedom and democracy, established full lordship of a party-state bureaucracy. . . . And if I must call myself anything, I would agree simply to take the name "Christian." (Quoted in Kowalewski, 1980a:282)

The state-controlled press acknowledges the *samizdat* claims of a great religious revival. Articles deploring Christian weddings and christenings admit that the number has long been rising.

The Western press fully reports the repression of Soviet Jewry and the tenacity with which the Jews have maintained their faith. Unfortunately, no similar attention has been given to the draconian state measures frequently imposed on Baptists, Pentecostals, and even on the Orthodox. Nor has the press dealt with the *militance* of these groups. Yet, in an important study, David Kowalewski (1980b) has managed to gather quite detailed information on nearly 500 serious religious protest demonstrations staged in the Soviet Union over a 13-year period. The vast majority of these mass protests resulted in injury, detention, and prison sentences for demonstrators. Yet they continue to erupt, and, for every public demonstration, there are large numbers of clandestine protests — anonymous leaflets, posting of slogans and banners, and the like.

Elsewhere in the Soviet-controlled nations of Eastern Europe, the strength of religion is even more open and public. The Polish strikers did not bedeck their factories and mines with Marxist-Leninist slogans, but with banners of Our Lady. Little wonder that Pope John Paul II scares all the regimes of the Soviet bloc. Religion may be defined as "antirevolutionary" and "antiparty," but it is alive and well.

China

China, too, presents clear evidence of the failure of a repressive state to root out religion. Here massive repression and education were utilized to cleanse the masses of "religious superstition," but the regime recently has acknowledged failure. In fact, it has relaxed restrictions on religious organizations in the face of the unwavering commitment of the masses to China's traditional faiths. The case of Chinese Christianity is of unusual interest.

Over the past several decades, fashionable historical revisionists have fostered the notion that not only were Christian missionaries in China agents of imperialism and of Western ethnocentrism, but they were also unsuccessful. The charge is that they attracted only "rice Christians," that they were fooled by poor Chinese who espoused Christianity only in return for the material benefits provided by the missions. If this is so, what are we to make of recent reports in the official Chinese press that many churches have been reopened and that many more and larger meeting places are needed because hundreds of thousands, perhaps millions, of Chinese persist in being Christians? Thirty years without contact with outside Christians; yet Christianity persists in China.

The reasons for this seem clear enough. Throughout this book, we have argued that religions possess a unique resource: access to the supernatural. Not even the powers of the modern state can match this as a potential source of plausible compensators for the immense needs most people feel. The party may ape the ritual trappings of religions, but it is no match for the real thing. Lenin's body may be displayed under glass and inspire the reverence given to national heroes, but no one supposes that he has ascended to sit on the right hand, or even on the left hand, of Marx. And hydroelectric dams along the Volga do not illuminate the meaning of the universe.

Repressive states increase individual suffering and, in so doing, add even greater fuel to the religious impulse. In making faith more costly, the Soviets probably have made it both more necessary and valuable. Perhaps religion is never so potent as when it is an underground church, for then its compensators bear no taint of worldliness and are of maximum potency. Unless or until communism turns supernatural and becomes a religion, it always will be overmatched in long-term conflicts with real religions.

CONCLUSION

In the future, as in the past, religion will be shaped by secular forces but not destroyed. There will always be a need for gods and for the general compensators which only they can plausibly offer. Unless science transforms humans into gods or annihilates humanity, people will continue to live lives hemmed by limitations. So long as we exist, we shall yearn for a bounty of specific rewards, rewards that in the mundane world are too scarce to be shared by all, and we shall ache for those general rewards of peace, immortality, and boundless joy that have never been found this side of heaven. Secularization has unchained the human spirit, not stifled it in a rationalized bureaucratic outbox. As King Arthur wisely commented about his own passing, "The old order changeth, yielding place to new; and God fulfills himself in many ways."

As in ancient days, magic is free again to broadcast a riotous tumult of specific compensators, unrestricted by religious monopoly. Nobody can be sure which of the potions sold in pharmacies are effective medications and which are snake oil, but we guess the proportion of magic is high. With greater confidence we class the vast majority of psychotherapies and self improvement schemes among the specific compensators. Surely the great political and social ideologies that have battled for control of civilization for more than a century are based on unfounded hopes and untested explanations. Social science has been capable of serious testing of theories for hardly more than a generation, yet all the politically powerful social ideologies committed themselves to models of reality long before that. Modern magic pretends to be science or common sense, and thus is seldom recognized for what it is; mainline religious denominations are well rid of it.

In some repressive states today religion is suppressed, while in others the old alliance between the political elite and the priests has been renegotiated. Neither relationship to the state is good for religion, but it will survive both. In officially atheistic societies, religion can be the focus of organized opposition, and through supernatural hopes it can offer general compensators for the personal freedom many citizens desire but cannot find in secular society. Client cults may flourish in atheistic repressive societies, if they avoid the label of religion and if the state has not been able to eliminate every last vestige of entrepreneurship from the healing professions. When conditions change and the state becomes less repressive, then religion can expand from the limitations placed on it by the state, evolve from client cults, and immigrate from other societies.

Repressive states that forge an alliance with religion give great power to whatever denomination they select as their partner, but they suppress other denominations and stimulate antireligious feelings among many of their political opponents. The course of religious history for such a society will depend on the duration of the repressive state and the vitality of competing religions it seeks to eradicate. If the rival religions are quickly destroyed, then opposition to the state will take on a completely antireligious character. If the repressive government falls, then religion may not regain its former popularity until memory of the time of repression is dimmed. But if the state slowly evolves toward liberalism, then religion may suffer only mild loss of popularity before regaining its position, as seems to be the case in much of western Europe today.

The scholars in the heart of Christendom who proclaim the death of God have been fooled by a simple change of residence. Faith lives in the sects and sectlike denominations, and in the hearts of the overwhelming majority of individual persons. New hopes enter the marketplace of religion with every new cult movement, and a comprehensive census would probably reveal a birth rate of potential messiahs higher than one an hour. Far from marking a radical departure in history and an era of faithlessness, secularization is an age-old process of transformation. In an endless cycle, faith is revived and new faiths born to take the places of those withered denominations that lost their sense of the supernatural. Through secularization, churches reduce their tension with the surrounding sociocultural environment, opening fields for sects and cults to grow and, in turn, themselves to be transformed.

Secularization has meant a decisive change in the religious life of liberal democracies, however. We doubt that any religious organization will ever enjoy the degree of monopoly held by the state churches of Europe generations ago, or even the hegemony achieved by some denominations for a time in the United States. Final separation of church and state will be healthy for religion, for what it loses in coercive power it will gain in spiritual virtue. When the religious market is fully free, people will still be at liberty to commit themselves utterly to one particular religion and join the community of a permanent congregation. But many will prefer lives of spiritual quest and sacred adventure, paralleling careers of secular mobility, experiencing one religious involvement after another. It would be wrong to imagine that all such folk are unsuccessful chronic seekers or trivial dabblers and false to conclude the religions that serve them are nothing but inconsequential consumer items. Only nostalgia for the lost certainty of the universal Church that never existed can prevent us from seeing the nobility and genuineness that express themselves in an open-ended sacrament of discovery.

"Quo vadis?" Jesus asked himself (John 16:5); his disciples had not the insight to know the question, let alone the answer. This book has asked: Whither goest thou, Religion? The answer is the same Jesus gave. "A little while, and ye shall not see me: and again, a little while, and ye shall see me, because I go to the Father." Religion dies, to be reborn. "Ye shall weep and lament, but the world shall rejoice; and ye shall be sorrowful, but your sorrow shall be turned into joy." Secularization, revival, and cult formation are the future of religion. "These things I have spoken unto you, that in me ye might have peace. In the world ye shall have tribulation: but be of good cheer; I have overcome the world."

Bibliography

Ackerknecht, Erwin H.
1943   "Psychopathology, Primitive Medicine and Primitive Culture," *Bulletin of the History of Medicine* 14:30–67.

Adler, Alfred
1927   *Understanding Human Nature.* Greenwich, Connecticut: Fawcett (1954).
1929   *Individual Psychology.* Totowa, New Jersey: Littlefield, Adams (1968).

Akers, Ronald L.
1977   *Deviant Behavior: A Social Learning Approach.* Belmont, California: Wadsworth.

Allen, Don
1979   "TM at Folsom Prison: A Critique of Abrams and Siegel," *Criminal Justice and Behavior* 6:9–12.

Allen, William Sheridan
1965   *The Nazi Seizure of Power.* Chicago: Quadrangle.

Allport, Gordon W.
1960   *Religion in the Developing Personality.* New York: New York University Press.

Almond, Gabriel
1954   *The Appeals of Communism.* Princeton, New Jersey: Princeton University Press.

Annett, Stephen
1976   *The Many Ways of Being.* London: Sphere Books.

531

Anonymous
  1975   *Fundamentals of Progress.* Fairfield, Iowa: Maharishi International
            University.
Anthony, Dick, and Thomas Robbins
  1981   "New Religions, Families, and 'Brainwashing.'" Pp. 263–274 in *In
            Gods We Trust,* edited by Thomas Robbins and Dick Anthony. New
            Brunswick, New Jersey: Transaction.
Anthony, Dick, Thomas Robbins, Madeline Doucas, and Thomas E. Curtis
  1977   "Patients and Pilgrims: Changing Attitudes Toward Psychotherapy
            of Converts to Eastern Mysticism," *American Behavioral Scientist*
            20:861–868.
Arendt, Hannah
  1958   *The Origins of Totalitarianism.* New York: Meridian.
Aronson, H., and Walter Weintraub
  1968   "Social Background of the Patient in Classical Psychoanalysis," *Jour-
            nal of Nervous and Mental Disease* 146:91–97.
Arrington, Leonard J., and David Bitton
  1979   *The Mormon Experience.* New York: Knopf.
Azzi, Corry, and Ronald G. Ehrenberg
  1975   "Household Allocation of Time and Church Attendance," *Journal of
            Political Economy* 83:27–56.
Back, K. W., and L. B. Bourque
  1970   "Can Feelings Be Enumerated?" *Behavioral Science* 15:487–496.
Bainbridge, William Folwell
  1882   *Around the World Tour of Christian Missions: A Universal Survey.* New
            York: Blackall.
Bainbridge, William Sims
  1970   "The Scientology Game." Unpublished thesis, Boston University.
  1976   *The Spaceflight Revolution.* New York: Wiley-Interscience.
  1978a   "Biorhythms: Evaluating a Pseudo-Science," *Skeptical Inquirer* 2
            (Spring-Summer):40–56.
  1978b   "Chariots of the Gullible," *Skeptical Inquirer* 3 (Winter):33–48.
  1978c   *Satan's Power: Ethnography of a Deviant Psychotherapy Cult.* Berkeley:
            University of California Press.
  1979   "In Search of Delusion," *Skeptical Inquirer* 4 (Fall):33–39.
  1981   "Comment on Daniel Bell's 'The Return of the Sacred,'" *Free Inquiry*
            1(4):26–29.
  1982   "Shaker Demographics 1840–1900: An Example of the Use of U.S.
            Census Enumeration Schedules," *Journal for the Scientific Study of Re-
            ligion* 21:352–365.
  1984   "Cultural Genetics." In *Religious Movements: Genesis, Exodus, and
            Numbers,* edited by Rodney Stark. New York: Rose of Sharon Press.
  FORTH-   "Science and Religion: The Case of Scientology." To be published in
  COMING   a volume edited by David Bromley and Phillip E. Hammond.
Bainbridge, William Sims, and Laurie Russell Hatch
  1982   "Women's Access to Elite Careers: In Search of a Religion Effect,"

Journal for the Scientific Study of Religion 21:242–254.

Bainbridge, William Sims, and Rodney Stark
1981   "Suicide, Homicide, and Religion: Durkheim Reassessed," *Annual Review of the Social Sciences of Religion* 5:33–56.

Balch, Robert W., and David Taylor
1977   "Seekers and Saucers: The Role of the Cultic Milieu in Joining a UFO Cult," *American Behavioral Scientist* 20:839–859.

Balswick, Jack O., and Gary L. Faulkner
1970   "Identification of Ministerial Cliques: A Sociometric Approach," *Journal for the Scientific Study of Religion* 9:303–310.

Bandura, Albert
1969   *Principles of Behavior Modification.* New York: Holt, Rinehart and Winston.

Barker, Eileen
1979   "Whose Service is Perfect Freedom." In *Spiritual Well-Being*, edited by David O. Moberg. Washington, D.C.: University Press of America.
1981   "Who'd Be a Moonie?" Pp. 59–96 in *The Social Impact of New Religious Movements*, edited by Bryan Wilson. New York: Rose of Sharon Press.
1984   "The Ones Who Got Away." In *Religious Movements: Genesis, Exodus, and Numbers*, edited by Rodney Stark. New York: Rose of Sharon Press.

Barrett, David B.
1968   *Schism and Renewal in Africa.* Nairobi, Kenya: Oxford University Press.

Barrow, Logie
1980   "Socialism in Eternity," *History Workshop* 9:37–69.

Bassett, T. D. Seymour
1952   "The Secular Utopian Socialists." Pp. 153–211 in *Socialism and American Life*, vol. 1, edited by Donald Drew Egbert and Stow Persons. Princeton, New Jersey: Princeton University Press.

Beeson, Trevor
1977   *Discretion and Valour: Religious Conditions in Russia and Eastern Europe.* Glasgow, Scotland: Fount.

Bell, Daniel
1971   "Religion in the Sixties," *Social Research* 38:447–497.
1980   *The Winding Passage.* Cambridge, Massachusetts: ABT.

Bellah, Robert N.
1970a   *Beyond Belief.* New York: Harper & Row.
1970b   "Christianity and Symbolic Realism," *Journal for the Scientific Study of Religion* 9:89–96.

Ben-Yehuda, Nachman
1980   "The European Witch Craze of the 14th to 17th Centuries: A Sociologist's Perspective," *American Journal of Sociology* 86:1–31.

Benson, J. Kenneth, and James Otis Smith
  1967 "The Harvard Drug Controversy." Pp. 115–140 in *Ethics, Politics, and Social Research*, edited by Gideon Sjoberg. Cambridge, Massachusetts: Schenkman.
Berger, Peter L.
  1967 *The Sacred Canopy*. Garden City, New York: Doubleday.
Berkower, Larry
  1969 "The Enduring Effect of the Jewish Tradition Upon Freud," *American Journal of Psychiatry* 125:1067–1073.
Bibby, Reginald W.
  1979a "Religion and Modernity: The Canadian Case," *Journal for the Scientific Study of Religion* 18:1–17.
  1979b "The State of Collective Religiosity in Canada: An Empirical Analysis," *Canadian Review of Sociology and Anthropology* 16:105–116.
  1980 "Religion." Pp. 387–427 in *Sociology*, edited by Robert Hagedorn. Toronto, Canada: Holt, Rinehart and Winston.
Billington, James H.
  1980 *Fire in the Minds of Men*. New York: Basic Books.
Bird, Frederick, and Bill Reimer
  1982 "Participation Rates in New Religious and Para-Religious Movements," *Journal for the Scientific Study of Religion* 21:1–14.
Blau, Peter M.
  1964 *Exchange and Power in Social Life*. New York: Wiley.
Bloomfield, Harold H., Michael Peter Cain, Dennis T. Jaffe, and Robert E. Korey
  1975 *TM—Discovering Inner Energy and Overcoming Stress*. New York: Dell.
Boas, Franz
  1940 "The Ethnographical Significance of Esoteric Doctrines." Pp. 312–315 in Franz Boas, *Race, Language and Culture*. New York: Free Press.
Boling, T. Edwin
  1973 "Sectarian Protestants, Churchly Protestants and Roman Catholics: A Comparison in a Mid-American City," *Review of Religious Research* 14:159–168.
Bouma, Gary D.
  1973 "Recent Protestant Ethic Research," *Journal for the Scientific Study of Religion* 12:141–155.
Breggin, Peter Roger
  1971 "Psychotherapy as Applied Ethics," *Psychiatry*, 34:59–74.
Briggs, Catherine, et al.
  1967 *Scientology and the Bible*. East Grinstead, Sussex, England: Department of Publications World Wide.
Brodie, Fawn M.
  1971 *No Man Knows My History*. 2nd edition. New York: Knopf.
Bromley, David G., and Anson D. Shupe, Jr.
  1979 *"Moonies" in America*. Beverly Hills, California: Sage.

1980   "Financing the New Religions: A Resource Mobilization Perspective," *Journal for the Scientific Study of Religion* 19:3.

Brown, H. G.
1943   "The Appeal of Communist Ideology," *American Journal of Economics and Sociology* 2:161–174.

Brown, J. A. C.
1967   *Freud and the Post-Freudians*. Baltimore: Penguin.

Brownsberger, Carl N.
1965   "Clinical Versus Statistical Assessment of Psychotherapy: A Mathematical Model of the Dilemma," *Behavioral Science* 10:421–428.

Bugliosi, Vincent
1974   *Helter Skelter: The True Story of the Manson Murders*. New York: Norton.

Bureau of the Census
1910   *Religious Bodies: 1906*. Washington, D.C.: United States Government Printing Office.
1919   *Religious Bodies: 1916*. Washington, D.C.: United States Government Printing Office.
1930   *Religious Bodies: 1926*. Washington, D.C.: United States Government Printing Office.
1933   *Fifteenth Census of the United States: 1930*. Washington, D.C.: United States Government Printing Office.
1941   *Religious Bodies: 1936*. Washington, D.C.: United States Government Printing Office.
1973   *Census of Population: 1970*. Washington, D.C.: United States Government Printing Office.

Burgess, Robert L., and Ronald L. Akers
1966   "A Differential Association Reinforcement Theory of Criminal Behavior," *Social Problems* 14:128–147.

Campbell, Alexander
1832   *An Analysis of the Book of Mormon*. Boston: Benjamin H. Greene.

Campiche, Roland J.
1972   "Switzerland." Pp. 511–528 in *Western Religion*, edited by Hans Mol. The Hague: Mouton.

Carden, Maren Lockwood
1969   *Oneida: Utopian Community to Modern Corporation*. Baltimore: Johns Hopkins University Press.

Catton, William R.
1957   "What Kind of People Does a Religious Cult Attract?" *American Sociological Review* 22:561–566.

Cavan, Ruth Shonle
1971   "Jewish Student Attitudes Toward Interreligious and Intra-Jewish Marriage," *American Journal of Sociology* 76:1064–1071.

Chalfant, H. Paul, Robert E. Beckley, and C. Eddie Palmer
1981   *Religion in Contemporary Society*. Sherman Oaks, California: Alfred.

Cheal, David
    1978   "Religion and the Social Order," *Canadian Journal of Sociology* 3:61–69.

Church of Scientology
    1978   *What is Scientology?* Los Angeles: Church of Scientology.

Clark, Elmer T.
    1937   *The Small Sects in America.* Nashville, Tennessee: Cokesbury.

Clark, Samuel Delbert
    1948   *Church and Sect in Canada.* Toronto, Canada: University of Toronto Press.

Cohen, Albert K.
    1955   *Delinquent Boys.* New York: Free Press.

Cohen, Daniel
    1975   *The New Believers.* New York: M. Evans.

Cohn, Norman
    1961   *The Pursuit of the Millennium.* New York: Harper & Row.
    1975   *Europe's Inner Demons.* New York: Basic Books.

Cohn, Werner
    1976   "Jewish Outmarriage and Anomie," *Canadian Review of Sociology and Anthropology* 13:90–105.

Cole, John R.
    1980   "Cult Archeology and Unscientific Method and Theory," *Advances in Archaeological Method and Theory* 3:1–33.

Coleman, James S.
    1956   "Social Cleavage and Religious Conflict," *Journal of Social Issues* 12:44–56.

Committee on the Judiciary, United States Senate
    1964–   *The Church and State Under Communism.* Eight Volumes. Washington,
    1965   D.C.: United States Government Printing Office.

Cooper, Joel, and Edward E. Jones
    1969   "Opinion Divergence as a Strategy to Avoid Being Miscast," *Journal of Personality and Social Psychology* 13:23–30.

Cooper, Paulette
    1971   *The Scandal of Scientology.* New York: Tower.

Cox, Harvey
    1965   *The Secular City.* New York: Macmillan.

Currie, Eliot P.
    1968   "Crime Without Victim: Witchcraft and its Control in Renaissance Europe," *Law and Society Review* 3:7–32.

Curtis, Russell L., Jr., and Louis A. Zurcher, Jr.
    1971   "Voluntary Associations and the Social Integration of the Poor," *Social Problems* 18:339–357.

Darnton, Robert
    1970   *Mesmerism and the End of the Enlightenment in France.* New York: Schocken.

Davis, Maxine W., and Gregory J. Tetrault
1975   *The Organic Traveler*. Syracuse, New York: Grasshopper Press.
Davis, Rex, and James T. Richardson
1976   "The Organization and Functioning of the Children of God," *Sociological Analysis* 37:321–339.
Demerath, N. J. III
1965   *Social Class in American Protestantism*. Chicago: Rand McNally.
Denniston, Denise, Peter McWilliams, and Barry Geller
1975   *The TM Book — How to Enjoy the Rest of Your Life*. New York: Warner.
De Santis, Sanctus
1927   *Religious Conversion*. London: Routledge and Kegan Paul.
Devereux, George (ed.)
1953   *Psychoanalysis and the Occult*. New York: International Universities Press.
Dittes, James E.
1971   "Typing the Typologies: Some Parallels in the Career of Church-Sect and Extrinsic-Intrinsic," *Journal for the Scientific Study of Religion* 10:375–383.
Dodd, Stuart C.
1961   "Can Science Improve Praying?" *Darshana* 1:22–37.
Doherty, Robert W.
1967   *The Hicksite Separation*. New Brunswick, New Jersey: Rutgers University Press.
Dohrman, H. T.
1958   *California Cult*. Boston: Beacon.
Dominion Bureau of Statistics
1953   *Ninth Census of Canada — 1951*. Ottawa, Canada: Queen's Printer.
1962   *1961 Census of Canada*. Ottawa, Canada: Queen's Printer.
Downton, James V.
1979   *Sacred Journeys: The Conversion of Young Americans to Divine Light Mission*. New York: Columbia University Press.
Duncan, Otis Dudley, Archibald O. Haller, and Alejandro Portes
1968   "Peer Influences on Aspirations: A Reinterpretation," *American Journal of Sociology* 74:119–137.
Durkheim, Emile
1897   *Suicide*. New York: Free Press (1951).
1915   *The Elementary Forms of the Religious Life*. London: Allen and Unwin.
Dynes, Russell R.
1955   "Church-Sect Typology and Socio-Economic Status," *American Sociological Review* 20:555–560.
1957   "The Consequences of Sectarianism for Social Participation," *Social Forces* 35:331–334.
Eaton, Joseph W., and Robert J. Weil
1955   *Culture and Mental Disorders*. Glencoe, Illinois: Free Press.

Eberhard, Ernest
  1974   "How to Share the Gospel: A Step-by-Step Approach for You and Your Neighbors," *Ensign* (June):6–11.
Eister, Allan W.
  1967   "Toward a Radical Critique of Church-Sect Typologizing," *Journal for the Scientific Study of Religion* 6:85–90.
  1972   "A Theory of Cults," *Journal for the Scientific Study of Religion* 11:319–333.
Ellis, Jane
  1978   *Letters from Moscow: Religion and Human Rights in the USSR*. San Francisco: Washington Street Research Center.
England, R. W.
  1954   "Some Aspects of Christian Science as Reflected in Letters of Testimony," *American Journal of Sociology* 59:448–453.
Evans, Christopher
  1973   *Cults of Unreason*. New York: Dell.
Evans-Pritchard, E. E.
  1937   *Witchcraft, Oracles, and Magic Among the Azande*. New York: Oxford University Press.
Eysenck, Hans J.
  1965   "The Effects of Psychotherapy," *International Journal of Psychiatry* 1:99–144.
Fagerstrom, Mary F.
  1973   "A Descriptive Study of Beginning Transcendental Meditation." Unpublished master's thesis, University of Washington, Seattle.
Fallding, Harold
  1978   "Mainline Protestantism in Canada and the United States of America: An Overview," *Canadian Journal of Sociology* 3:141–160.
Faris, Ellsworth
  1928   "The Sect and the Sectarian," *American Journal of Sociology* (special edition) 60 (1955):75–89.
  1929   "Some Phases of Religion that are Susceptible of Sociological Study," *American Journal of Sociology* (special edition) 60 (1955):90.
Fenn, Richard K.
  1978   *Toward a Theory of Secularization*. Ellington, Connecticut: Society for the Scientific Study of Religion.
Festinger, Leon, H. W. Riecken, and S. Schachter
  1956   *When Prophecy Fails*. New York: Harper & Row.
Finch, William J., and Elizabeth Finch.
  1971   *Who's Who in the Psychic World*. Phoenix, Arizona: Psychic Register International.
Finkel, Norman J.
  1976   *Mental Illness and Health*. New York: Macmillan.
Fischer, Claude S.
  1975   "Toward a Subcultural Theory of Urbanism," *American Journal of Sociology* 80:1319–1341.

Flammonde, Paris
  1975   *The Mystic Healers.* New York: Stein and Day.
Flugel, J. C.
  1930   *The Psychology of Clothes.* New York: International Universities Press.
Fodor, Nandor
  1971   *Freud, Jung and Occultism.* New Hyde Park, New York: University Books.
Forem, Jack
  1973   *Transcendental Meditation.* New York: Dutton.
Fortune, Reo F.
  1932   *Sorcerers of Dobu.* New York: Dutton.
Frank, Jerome
  1961   *Persuasion and Healing.* Baltimore: Johns Hopkins University Press.
Frankfort, Henri
  1948   *Kingship and the Gods.* Chicago: University of Chicago Press.
Frazer, Sir James G.
  1922   *The Golden Bough.* New York: Macmillan.
Freud, Sigmund
  1927   *The Future of an Illusion.* Garden City, New York: Doubleday (1961).
  1930   *Civilization and Its Discontents.* New York: Norton (1962).
  1946   *Totem and Taboo.* New York: Random House.
Furst, Peter T. (ed.)
  1972   *Flesh of the Gods: The Ritual Use of Hallucinogens.* New York: Praeger.
Gaede, Stan
  1976   "A Causal Model of Belief-Orthodoxy: Proposal and Empirical Test," *Sociological Analysis* 37:205–217.
Galanter, Marc, Richard Rabkin, Judith Rabkin, and Alexander Deutsch
  1979   "The 'Moonies': A Psychological Study of Conversion and Membership in a Contemporary Religious Sect," *American Journal of Sociology* 136:165–170.
Gallup Opinion Index
  1976   "32 Million Look to Stars for Help in Conducting Daily Affairs," report number 132 (July): 25–27. Princeton, New Jersey: American Institute of Public Opinion.
  1977   *Religion in America 1977–78.* Princeton, New Jersey: American Institute of Public Opinion.
Gans, Herbert J.
  1962a   "Urbanism and Suburbanism as Ways of Life." Pp. 625–648 in *Human Behavior and Social Processes,* edited by Arnold M. Rose. Boston: Houghton Mifflin.
  1962b   *The Urban Villagers.* New York: Free Press.
Gardner, Hugh
  1978   *The Children of Prosperity.* New York: St. Martin's.
Gardner, Martin
  1957   *Fads and Fallacies in the Name of Science.* New York: Dover.

Gaston, Jerry
    1978   "Readership Study." Unpublished report prepared for the editor of
            Fate magazine.
Gilfillan, S. C.
    1970   *The Sociology of Invention.* Cambridge, Massachusetts: M.I.T. Press.
Glasser, William
    1976   *Positive Addiction.* New York: Harper & Row.
Glezer, Alexander
    1976   "Religion and Soviet Non-Conformist Artists," *Religion in Commu-
            nist Lands* 4:16–19.
Glick, Rush G., and Robert S. Newsom
    1974   *Fraud Investigation.* Springfield, Illinois: Thomas.
Glock, Charles Y.
    1959   "The Religious Revival in America?" Pp. 25–42 in *Religion and the
            Face of America,* edited by Jane Zahn. Berkeley: University Exten-
            sion, University of California.
    1962   "On the Study of Religious Commitment," *Religious Education* (spe-
            cial issue).
    1964   "The Role of Deprivation in the Origin and Evolution of Religious
            Groups." Pp. 24–36 in *Religion and Social Conflict,* edited by Robert
            Lee and Martin E. Marty. New York: Oxford University Press.
Glock, Charles Y., and Robert N. Bellah (eds.)
    1976   *The New Religious Consciousness.* Berkeley: University of California
            Press.
Glock, Charles Y., and Rodney Stark
    1965   *Religion and Society in Tension.* Chicago: Rand McNally.
    1966   *Christian Beliefs and Anti-Semitism.* New York: Harper & Row.
Goode, Erich
    1967   "Some Critical Observations on the Church-Sect Dimension," *Jour-
            nal for the Scientific Study of Religion* 6:69–77.
    1969   "Marijuana and the Politics of Reality," *Journal of Health and Social
            Behavior* 10:83–94.
Goody, Jack
    1961   "Religion and Ritual: The Definitional Problem," *British Journal of
            Sociology* 12:142–164.
Granovetter, Mark
    1973   "The Strength of Weak Ties," *American Journal of Sociology* 78:1360–
            1380.
    1978   "Threshold Models of Collective Behavior," *American Journal of Soci-
            ology* 83:1420–1442.
Greeley, Andrew M.
    1975   *The Sociology of the Paranormal: A Reconnaissance.* Beverly Hills, Cali-
            fornia: Sage.
    1977a   *The American Catholic: A Social Portrait.* New York: Basic Books.
    1977b   *An Ugly Little Secret: Anti-Catholicism in North America.* Kansas City:
            Sheed, Andrews and McMeel.

1981   "Religious Musical Chairs." Pp. 101–126 in *In Gods We Trust*, edited by Thomas Robbins and Dick Anthony. New Brunswick, New Jersey: Transaction.

Greenberg, Joel
1979   "Close Encounters — All in the Mind?" *Science News* 115:106–107.

Gurr, Ted Robert
1970   *Why Men Rebel*. Princeton, New Jersey: Princeton University Press.

Gustafson, Paul
1967   "UO-US-PS-PO: A Restatement of Troeltsch's Church-Sect Typology," *Journal for the Scientific Study of Religion* 6:64–68.

Hadden, Jeffrey K.
1969   *The Gathering Storm in the Churches*. Garden City, New York: Doubleday.

Hadden, Jeffrey K., and Charles E. Swann
1981   *Prime Time Preachers: The Rising Power of Televangelism*. Reading, Massachusetts: Addison-Wesley.

Hall, Manley Palmer
1928   *An Encyclopedic Outline of Masonic, Hermetic, Qabbalistic and Rosicrucian Symbolic Philosophy*. Los Angeles: Philosophical Research Society (1945).

Hardyck, Jane Allyn, and Marcia Braden
1962   "Prophecy Fails Again: A Report of a Failure to Replicate," *Journal of Abnormal and Social Psychology* 65:136–141.

Harrison, Michael I.
1974   "Sources of Recruitment of Catholic Pentecostalism," *Journal for the Scientific Study of Religion* 13:49–64.

Heirich, Max
1977   "Change of Heart: A Test of Some Widely Held Theories about Religious Conversion," *American Journal of Sociology* 83:653–680.

Henslin, James M.
1967   "Craps and Magic," *American Journal of Sociology* 73:316–330.

Herberg, Will
1955   *Protestant, Catholic, Jew*. Garden City, New York: Doubleday.

Hiller, Harry
1978   "Continentalism and the Third Force in Religion," *Canadian Journal of Sociology* 3:183–207.

Hirschi, Travis
1969   *Causes of Delinquency*. Berkeley: University of California Press.

Hirschi, Travis, and Michael J. Hindelang
1977   "Intelligence and Delinquency: A Revisionist Review," *American Sociological Review* 42:571–587.

Hobsbawm, E. J.
1959   *Primitive Rebels*. Manchester, England: Manchester University Press.

Homans, George C.
1950   *The Human Group*. New York: Harcourt, Brace and World.

1961   *Social Behavior: Its Elementary Forms.* New York: Harcourt Brace (2nd edition, 1974).

Horner, Jack
1970   *Dianology.* Westwood Village, California: Association of International Dianologists.

Hostetler, John A.
1968   *Amish Society.* Baltimore: Johns Hopkins University Press.
1974   *Hutterite Society.* Baltimore: Johns Hopkins University Press.

Houriet, Robert
1972   *Getting Back Together.* New York: Avon.

Hubbard, L. Ron
1950a   "Dianetics: The Evolution of a Science," *Astounding Science Fiction* 45 (May):43–87.
1950b   *Dianetics, the Modern Science of Mental Health.* New York: Paperback Library.
1951   *Science of Survival.* Los Angeles: Publications Organization World Wide.
1958   *Have You Lived Before This Life?* East Grinstead, Sussex, England: Department of Publications World Wide.
1959   *Ceremonies of the Founding Church of Scientology.* East Grinstead, Sussex, England: Department of Publications World Wide.
1965   *Scientology Abridged Dictionary.* Copenhagen, Denmark: Scientology Publications Organization.
1968a   *Level 0 PABs.* Edinburgh, Scotland: Publications Organization World Wide.
1968b   *Scientology Basic Staff Hat Book.* East Grinstead, Sussex, England: Publications Organization World Wide.
1979   "Executive Directive 17 December 1978," *The Auditor* 16, L157:6–8.

Jacquet, Constant H. (ed.)
1979   *Yearbook of American and Canadian Churches, 1979.* Nashville, Tennessee: Abingdon.

James, William
1902   *The Varieties of Religious Experience.* New York: Longmans, Green.

Jencks, Christopher
1972   *Inequality.* New York: Basic Books.

Johnson, Benton
1957   "A Critical Appraisal of the Church-Sect Typology," *American Sociological Review* 22:88–92.
1963   "On Church and Sect," *American Sociological Review* 28:539–549.
1971   "Church and Sect Revisited," *Journal for the Scientific Study of Religion* 10:124–137.

Johnson, Douglas W., Paul R. Picard, and Bernard Quinn
1974   *Churches and Church Membership in the United States.* Washington, D.C.: Glenmary.

Johnson, Paul
1979   *A History of Christianity.* New York: Atheneum.

Judah, J. Stillson
1974 *Hare Krishna and the Counterculture.* New York: Wiley.
Jung, Carl G.
1969 *Psychology and Religion.* Princeton, New Jersey: Princeton University Press.
Kandel, Denise B.
1974 "Inter- and Intragenerational Influences on Adolescent Marijuana Use," *Journal of Social Issues* 30:107–135.
Kandel, Denise B., Donald Treiman, Richard Faust, and Eric Single
1976 "Adolescent Involvement in Legal and Illegal Drug Use: A Multiple Classification Analysis," *Social Forces* 55:438–458.
Kanter, Rosabeth Moss
1972 *Commitment and Community.* Cambridge, Massachusetts: Harvard University Press.
Katz, Elihu
1960 "Communication Research and the Image of Society: The Convergence of Two Traditions," *American Journal of Sociology* 65:435–440.
Katz, Elihu, and Paul F. Lazarsfeld
1955 *Personal Influence.* Glencoe, Illinois: Free Press.
Kay, D. W. K.
1978 "Assessment of Familial Risks in the Functional Psychoses and Their Application in Genetic Counselling," *British Journal of Psychiatry* 133:385–403.
Keim, Albert N. (ed.)
1975 *Compulsory Education and the Amish.* Boston: Beacon Press.
Kelley, Dean
1972 *Why Conservative Churches Are Growing.* New York: Harper & Row.
Kennedy, John G.
1967 "Nubian Zar Ceremonies and Psychotherapy," *Human Organization* 26:185–194.
Kennedy, Joseph C. G.
1864 *Population of the United States in 1860.* Washington, D.C.: United States Government Printing Office.
Kerr, Howard
1972 *Mediums, Spirit Rappers, and Roaring Radicals.* Urbana: University of Illinois Press.
Kieckhefer, Richard
1976 *European Witch Trials.* Berkeley: University of California Press.
Kiev, Ari (ed.)
1964 *Magic, Faith, and Healing.* New York: Free Press.
Kiev, Ari
1972 *Transcultural Psychiatry.* New York: Free Press.
Kiev, Ari, and John L. Francis
1964 "Sabud and Mental Illness," *American Journal of Psychotherapy* 18:66–78.

King, Francis
  1970   *The Rites of Modern Occult Magic.* New York: Macmillan.
King, Morton
  1967   "Measuring the Religious Variable: Nine Proposed Dimensions,"
            Journal for the Scientific Study of Religion 6:173–190.
Kluckhohn, Clyde
  1962   "Values and Value-Orientations in the Theory of Action: An Ex-
            ploration in Definition and Classification." Pp. 388–433 in *Toward
            a General Theory of Action*, edited by Talcott Parsons and Edward
            Shils. New York: Harper & Row.
Kluegel, James R.
  1980   "Denominational Mobility," *Journal for the Scientific Study of Religion*
            19:26–39.
Knudsen, Dean D., John R. Earle, and Donald W. Shriver, Jr.
  1978   "The Conception of Sectarian Religion: An Effort at Clarification,"
            Review of Religious Research 20:44–60.
Kornbluth, Jesse
  1976   "The Fuehrer Over est," *New Times*, March 19, pp. 36–52.
Kornhauser, William
  1959   *The Politics of Mass Society.* Glencoe, Illinois: Free Press.
Kowalewski, David
  1980a   "Religious Belief in the Brezhnev Era: Renaissance, Resistance, and
            Realpolitik," *Journal for the Scientific Study of Religion* 19:280–292.
  1980b   "Trends in the Human Rights Movement." Pp. 150–181 in *Soviet
            Politics in the Brezhnev Era*, edited by Donald R. Kelley. New York:
            Praeger.
Kueng, Hans
  1976   *On Being a Christian.* Garden City, New York: Doubleday.
La Barre, Weston
  1969   *They Shall Take Up Serpents.* New York: Schocken.
  1972   *The Ghost Dance.* New York: Dell.
LaMore, George E.
  1975   "The Secular Selling of a Religion," *Christian Century* 10:1133–
            1137.
Lang, Anthony
  1978   *Synanon Foundation: The People Business.* Cottonwood, Arizona: Way-
            side Press.
Lang, Larry
  1979   "Woman Awarded $2 Million in Scientology Suit," *Seattle Post-Intelli-
            gencer*, August 16, pp. A1, A16.
Langer, Walter C.
  1972   *The Mind of Adolf Hitler.* New York: Basic Books.
Larsen, Otto N.
  1962   "Innovators and Early Adopters of Television," *Sociological Inquiry*
            32:16–33.

Larson, Richard F.
    1964   "Clerical and Psychiatric Conceptions of the Clergyman's Role in the Therapeutic Setting," *Social Problems* 11:419–428.
    1968   "The Clergyman's Role in the Therapeutic Process: Disagreement Between Clergymen and Psychiatrists," *Psychiatry* 31:250–263.

Lasswell, Harold D.
    1930   *Psychopathology and Politics*. New York: Viking (1960).

Laumann, Edward O., Peter V. Marsden, and Joseph Galaskiewicz
    1977   "Community-Elite Influence Structures: Extension of a Network Approach," *American Journal of Sociology* 83:594–631.

Lazerwitz, Bernard, and Michael Harrison
    1979   "American Jewish Denominations: A Social and Religious Profile," *American Sociological Review* 44:656–666.

Leary, Timothy
    1977   *Exo-Psychology*. Los Angeles: Starseed and Peace Press.

Lederer, Wolfgang
    1959   "Primitive Psychotherapy," *Psychiatry* 22:255–265.

Lee, Robert
    1960   *The Social Sources of Church Unity*. New York: Abingdon.

Lemert, Edwin
    1967   "Paranoia and the Dynamics of Exclusion." Pp. 246–264 in *Human Deviance, Social Problems and Social Control*. Englewood Cliffs, New Jersey: Prentice-Hall.

Lévi-Strauss, Claude
    1963   "The Sorcerer and His Magic." Pp. 161–180 in *Structural Anthropology*. New York: Basic Books.

Lewis, Gordon R.
    1966   *Confronting the Cults*. Grand Rapids, Michigan: Baker.

Lewis, Ioan M.
    1971   *Ecstatic Religion*. Baltimore: Penguin.

Lewis, Lionel S.
    1963   "Knowledge, Danger, Certainty, and the Theory of Magic," *American Journal of Sociology* 69:7–12.

Lewis, Oscar
    1965   "Further Observations on the Folk-Urban Continuum and Urbanization." Pp. 491–503 in *The Study of Urbanization*, edited by P. H. Hauser and L. Schnore. New York: Wiley.

Lindsey, Robert
    1983   "Fight Over Funds Divides Scientology Group," *New York Times*, January 6, pp. A1, B18.

Linton, Ralph
    1943   "Nativistic Movements," *American Anthropologist* 45:230–240.

Lipset, Seymour Martin
    1964   "Canada and the United States: A Comparative View," *Canadian Review of Sociology and Anthropology* 1:173–195.

1976   *Rebellion in the University.* Chicago: University of Chicago Press.
Lofland, John
1966   *Doomsday Cult.* Englewood Cliffs, New Jersey: Prentice-Hall.
Lofland, John, and Rodney Stark
1965   "Becoming a World-Saver: A Theory of Conversion to a Deviant Perspective," *American Sociological Review* 30:862–875.
London, Ivan D., and Nikolai P. Poltoratzky
1957   "Contemporary Religious Sentiment in the Soviet Union," *Psychological Reports* (monograph supplement) 3:113–130.
Longino, Charles F., Jr., and Jeffrey K. Hadden
1976   "Dimensionality of Belief Among Mainstream Protestant Clergy," *Social Forces* 55:30–42.
Luckmann, Thomas
1967   *The Invisible Religion.* New York: Macmillan.
Lynch, Frederick R.
1977   "Toward a Theory of Conversion and Commitment to the Occult," *American Behavioral Scientist* 20:887–907.
1979   "'Occult Establishment' or 'Deviant Religion?' The Rise and Fall of a Modern Church of Magic," *Journal for the Scientific Study of Religion* 18:281–290.
MacDougall, Curtis D.
1958   *Hoaxes.* New York: Dover.
Malinowski, Bronislaw
1948   *Magic, Science and Religion.* Garden City, New York: Doubleday.
Malko, George
1970   *Scientology: The Now Religion.* New York: Delacorte.
Mandelbaum, David G.
1966   "Transcendental and Pragmatic Aspects of Religion," *American Anthropologist* 68:1174–1191.
Mann, William E.
1955   *Sect, Cult and Church in Alberta.* Toronto, Canada: University of Toronto Press.
Marks, Tracy
1978   *Directory of New England Astrologers.* Natick, Massachusetts: Sagittarius Rising.
Martin, David
1978   *A General Theory of Secularization.* New York: Harper & Row.
Marty, Martin E.
1959   *The New Shape of Religion.* New York: Harper & Row.
Marx, Karl
1844   "On the Jewish Question." Pp. 40–97 in Karl Marx, *Selected Essays.* Freeport, New York: Books for Libraries Press (1968).
May, Philip R. A.
1971   "For Better or for Worse? Psychotherapy and Variance Change: A Critical Review of the Literature," *Journal of Nervous and Mental Disease* 152:184–192.

McCall, Robert B.
    1977   "Childhood IQ's as Predictors of Adult Educational and Occupational Status," *Science* 197:482–483.

McCleary, Richard, Andrew C. Gordon, David McDowall, and Michael D. Maltz
    1979   "How a Regression Artifact Can Make Any Delinquent Intervention Program Look Effective," *Evaluation Studies Review Annual* 4:626–652.

McConaghy, N., and S. H. Lovibond
    1967   "Methodological Formalism in Psychiatric Research," *Journal of Nervous and Mental Disease* 144:117–123.

McCready, William C., and Andrew M. Greeley
    1976   *The Ultimate Values of the American Population.* Beverly Hills, California: Sage.

McFarland, H. Neill
    1967   *The Rush Hour of the Gods: A Study of New Religious Movements in Japan.* New York: Macmillan.

McIntosh, Christopher
    1972   *Eliphas Levi and the French Occult Revival.* New York: Weiser.

McQuaid, Donald A.
    1979   *The International Psychic Register.* Erie, Pennsylvania: Ornion Press.

Medalia, Nahum Z., and Otto N. Larsen
    1958   "Diffusion and Belief in a Collective Delusion," *American Sociological Review* 23:180–186.

Medvedev, Zhores A.
    1971   *The Rise and Fall of T. D. Lysenko.* Garden City, New York: Doubleday.

Melton, J. Gordon
    1978   *Encyclopedia of American Religions.* 2 vols. Wilmington, North Carolina: McGrath (A Consortium Book).
    1981   "The Origins of Contemporary Neo-Paganism." Paper presented at the meetings of the Popular Culture Association, Detroit, Michigan.

Merton, Robert K.
    1970   *Science, Technology and Society in Seventeenth-Century England.* New York: Harper & Row.

Messing, Simon D.
    1958   "Group Therapy and Social Status in the Zar Cult of Ethiopia," *American Anthropologist* 60:1120–1126.

Meyer, John W., David Tyack, Joane Nagel, and Audri Gordon
    1979   "Public Education as Nation-Building in America: Enrollments and Bureaucratization in the American States, 1870–1930," *American Journal of Sociology* 85:591–613.

Midelfort, E.H.C.
    1972   *Witch Hunting in Southwestern Germany, 1562–1684.* Palo Alto, California: Stanford University Press.

Mihajlov, Mihajlo
    1976   *Underground Notes.* Kansas City: Sheed, Andrews, and McMeel.

Miller, Patricia Y., and William Simon
 1974　"Adolescent Sexual Behavior: Context and Change," *Social Problems* 22:58–76.
Miller, Walter M., Jr.
 1960　*A Canticle for Leibowitz.* Philadelphia: Lippincott.
Mol, Hans (ed.)
 1972　*Western Religion.* The Hague: Mouton.
Mooney, James
 1896　*The Ghost Dance Religion and the Sioux Outbreak of 1890.* Fourth annual report of the Bureau of Ethnology to the Secretary of the Smithsonian Institution. Washington, D.C.: United States Government Printing Office.
Morioka, Kiyomi
 1975　*Religion in Changing Japanese Society.* Tokyo, Japan: University of Tokyo Press.
Moroto, Aiko
 1976　"Conditions for Accepting a New Religious Belief: A Case Study of Myochikai Members in Japan." Unpublished master's thesis in sociology, University of Washington, Seattle.
Nelson, Geoffrey K.
 1969　*Spiritualism and Society.* New York: Schocken.
Nelson, Mary
 1975　"Why Witches Were Women." Pp. 335–351 in *Women: A Feminist Perspective,* edited by J. Freeman. Palo Alto, California: Mayfield.
Newman, William M., and Peter L. Halvorson
 1979　"American Jews: Patterns of Geographic Distribution and Change," *Journal for the Scientific Study of Religion* 18:183.
Nicholi, Armand M., Jr.
 1967　"Harvard Dropouts: Some Psychiatric Findings," *American Journal of Psychiatry* 124:651–658.
Niebuhr, H. Richard
 1929　*The Social Sources of Denominationalism.* New York: Henry Holt.
Nordhoff, Charles
 1875　*The Communistic Societies of the United States.* London: John Murray.
Nordquist, Ted
 1978　*Ananda Cooperative Village.* Uppsala, Sweden: Borgstroms.
Noyes, John Humphrey
 1870　*History of American Socialisms.* Philadelphia: Lippincott.
O'Dea, Thomas F.
 1957　*The Mormons.* Chicago: University of Chicago Press.
 1966　*The Sociology of Religion.* Englewood Cliffs, New Jersey: Prentice-Hall
Ofshe, Richard
 1980　"The Social Development of the Synanon Cult," *Sociological Analysis* 41: 109–127.

Oliver, Edmund Henry
  1930   *The Winning of the Frontier.* Toronto, Canada: United Church Publishing House.
O'Neil, Mary
  1981   "Discerning Superstition: Trials of Clerics and Exorcists in 16th Century Italy." Paper presented at the International Congress on Medieval Studies, Kalamazoo, Michigan.
Orrmont, Arthur
  1961   *Love Cults and Faith Healers.* New York: Ballantine.
Pagano, Robert R., Richard M. Rose, Robert M. Stivers, and Stephen Warrenburg
  1976   "Sleep During Transcendental Meditation," *Science* 191: 308–310.
Parsons, Talcott
  1957   "Motivation of Religious Belief and Behavior." Pp. 380–385 in *Religion, Society and the Individual,* edited by J. Milton Yinger. New York: Macmillan.
Patrick, Ted, and Tom Dulack
  1976   *Let Our Children Go!* New York: Ballantine.
Peters, Victor
  1965   *All Things Common.* New York: Harper & Row.
Phillips, Derek
  1967   "Social Participation and Happiness," *American Journal of Sociology* 72:479–488.
Pinard, Maurice
  1967   "Poverty and Political Movements," *Social Problems* 15:250–263.
Podmore, Frank
  1902   *Modern Spiritualism: A History and Criticism.* London: Methuen.
Pollin, William, Martin G. Allen, Axel Hoffer, James R. Stabenau, and Zidnek Hrubec
  1969   "Psychopathology in 15,909 Pairs of Veteran Twins: Evidence for a Genetic Factor in the Pathogenesis of Schizophrenia and its Relative Absence in Psychoneurosis," *American Journal of Psychiatry* 126:597–610.
Pope, Liston
  1942   *Millhands and Preachers.* New Haven, Connecticut: Yale University Press.
Porter, John
  1965   *The Vertical Mosaic.* Toronto, Canada: University of Toronto Press.
Quinley, Harold E.
  1974   *The Prophetic Clergy.* New York: Wiley-Interscience.
Rachman, Stanley
  1971   *The Effects of Psychotherapy.* Oxford, England: Pergamon.
Ram Dass, Baba
  1971   *Be Here Now.* San Cristobal, New Mexico: Lama Foundation.
Randi, James
  1975   *The Magic of Uri Geller.* New York: Ballantine.

Regardie, Israel
    1971   *My Rosicrucian Adventure.* St. Paul, Minnesota: Llewellyn.

Richardson, Herbert (ed.)
    1980   *New Religions and Mental Health: Understanding the Issues.* New York: Edwin Mellen Press.

Richardson, James T., and Mary Stewart
    1977   "Conversion Process Models and the Jesus Movement," *American Behavioral Scientist* 20:819–838.

Rieff, Philip
    1968   *The Triumph of the Therapeutic.* New York: Harper & Row.

Roberts, Bryan R.
    1968   "Protestant Groups and Coping with Urban Life in Guatemala City," *American Journal of Sociology* 73:753–767.

Roberts, Edward B.
    1969   "Entrepreneurship and Technology." Pp. 219–237 in *Factors in the Transfer of Technology,* edited by William H. Gruber and Donald G. Marquis. Cambridge, Massachusetts: M.I.T. Press.

Robinson, John A. T.
    1963   *Honest to God.* Philadelphia: Westminster Press.

Rogers, Everett M.
    1960   *Social Change in Rural Society.* New York: Appleton-Century-Crofts.

Rogler, Lloyd H., and August B. Hollingshead
    1961   "The Puerto Rican Spiritualist as a Psychiatrist," *American Journal of Sociology* 67:17–21.

Roheim, Geza
    1955   *Magic and Schizophrenia.* Bloomington: Indiana University Press.

Rokeach, Milton
    1973   *The Nature of Human Values.* New York: Free Press.

Roszak, Theodore
    1969   *The Making of a Counter Culture.* Garden City, New York: Anchor.

Rowley, Peter
    1971   *New Gods in America.* New York: David McKay.

Russell, Gordon W.
    1975   "The View of Religions from Religious and Non-Religious Perspectives," *Journal for the Scientific Study of Religion* 14:129–138.

Salter, Andrew
    1972   *The Case Against Psychoanalysis.* New York: Harper & Row.

Sanders, Ed
    1971   *The Family: The Story of Charles Manson's Dune Buggy Attack Battalion.* New York: Dutton.

Sargant, William
    1959   *Battle for the Mind.* New York: Harper & Row.

Schanck, Richard Louis
    1932   "A Study of a Community and Its Groups and Institutions Conceived of as Behaviors of Individuals," *Psychological Monographs* 43:2.

Schelling, Thomas C.
1960   *The Strategy of Conflict.* London: Oxford University Press.

Schoeneman, T. J.
1977   "The Role of Mental Illness in the European Witch Hunts of the 16th and 17th Centuries: An Assessment," *Journal of the History of the Behavioral Sciences* 13:337–351.

Schuman, Howard, and Michael P. Johnson
1976   "Attitudes and Behavior." Pp. 161–207 in *Annual Review of Sociology,* vol. 2. edited by Alex Inkeles, James Coleman, and Neil Smelser. Palo Alto, California: Annual Reviews.

Scott, John Finley
1971   *Internalization of Norms.* Englewood Cliffs, New Jersey: Prentice-Hall.

Selznick, Gertrude J., and Stephen Steinberg
1969   *Tenacity of Prejudice.* New York: Harper & Row.

Selznick, Philip
1960   *The Organizational Weapon.* Glencoe, Illinois: Free Press.

Shinn, Larry
1982   "The Many Faces of Krishna." Pp. 113–135 in *Alternatives to American Mainline Churches,* edited by Joseph Fichter. New York: Rose of Sharon Press.

Shupe, Anson D., Jr., and David G. Bromley
1980   *The New Vigilantes.* Beverly Hills, California: Sage.

Sigelman, Lee
1977   "Multi-Nation Surveys of Religious Beliefs," *Journal for the Scientific Study of Religion* 16:289–294.

Silcox, Claris Edwin
1933   *Church Union in Canada.* New York: Institute of Social and Religious Research.

Silverman, Julian
1967   "Shamans and Acute Schizophrenia," *American Anthropologist* 69:21–32.

Simmel, Georg
1905   "A Contribution to the Sociology of Religion," *American Journal of Sociology* 11:359–376.

Simon, William, and John H. Gagnon
1976   "The Anomie of Affluence: A Post-Mertonian Conception," *American Journal of Sociology* 82:356–378.

Singer, Burton, and Seymour Spilerman
1976   "The Representation of Social Processes by Markov Models," *American Journal of Sociology* 82:1–54.

Singh, Parmatma (Howard Weiss)
1974   *Spiritual Community Guide, 1975–76.* San Rafael, California: Spiritual Community Publications.
1978   *Spiritual Community Guide, 1979.* San Rafael, California: Spiritual Community Publications.

1981   *A Pilgrim's Guide to Planet Earth.* San Rafael, California: Spiritual
        Community Publications.
Slater, Philip
    1970   *The Pursuit of Loneliness.* Boston: Beacon Press.
Smelser, Neil J.
    1962   *Theory of Collective Behavior.* New York: Free Press.
Smith, M. Brewster, Jerome S. Bruner, and Robert W. White
    1956   *Opinions and Personality.* New York: Wiley.
Sorokin, Pitirim A.
    1941   *The Crisis of Our Age.* New York: Dutton.
Spiro, Melford E.
    1964   "Religion and the Irrational." Pp. 102–115 in *Symposium on New Ap-
            proaches to the Study of Religion,* edited by June Helm. Seattle: Uni-
            versity of Washington Press.
    1966   "Religion, Problems of Definition and Explanation." Pp. 85–126 in
            Anthropological Approaches to the Study of Religion, edited by Michael
            Banton. New York: Praeger.
Stark, Rodney
    1964   "Class, Radicalism and Religious Involvement in Great Britain,"
            American Sociological Review 29:698–706.
    1965a   "Social Contexts and Religious Experience," *Review of Religious Re-
            search* 7:17–28.
    1965b   "A Sociological Definition of Religion." Pp. 3–17 in *Religion and
            Society in Tension,* edited by Charles Y. Glock and Rodney Stark.
            Chicago: Rand McNally.
    1965c   "A Taxonomy of Religious Experience," *Journal for the Scientific Study
            of Religion* 5:97–116.
    1971   "Psychopathology and Religious Commitment," *Review of Religious
            Research* 12:165–176.
    1972   "The Economics of Piety: Religious Commitment and Social Class."
            Pp. 483–503 in *Issues in Social Inequality,* edited by Gerald Thielbar
            and Saul Feldman. Boston: Little, Brown.
    1980   "Estimating Church-Membership Rates for Ecological Areas," Na-
            tional Institute of Juvenile Justice and Delinquency Prevention,
            LEAA, U.S. Department of Justice. Washington, D. C.: United States
            Government Printing Office.
    1983   "The Mormon 'Miracle': How New Religions Succeed," *Sociological
            Analysis.*
    FORTH-
    COMING "The Rise and Decline of Christian Science."
Stark, Rodney, and William Sims Bainbridge
    1980   "Towards a Theory of Religion: Religious Commitment," *Journal
            for the Scientific Study of Religion* 19:114–128.
Stark, Rodney, William Sims Bainbridge, Robert Crutchfield, Daniel P. Doyle,
            and Roger Finke

1983   "Crime and Delinquency in the Roaring Twenties," *Journal of Research in Crime and Delinquency* 20: 4–23.

Stark, Rodney, Daniel P. Doyle, and Lori Kent
1980   "Rediscovering Moral Communities: Church Membership and Crime." Pp. 43–52 in *Understanding Crime*, edited by Travis Hirschi and Michael Gottfredson. Beverly Hills, California: Sage.

Stark, Rodney, Daniel P. Doyle, and Jesse Lynn Rushing
1983   "Beyond Durkheim: Religion and Suicide," *Journal for the Scientific Study of Religion* 22: 120–131.

Stark, Rodney, Bruce D. Foster, Charles Y. Glock, and Harold E. Quinley
1971   *Wayward Shepherds.* New York: Harper & Row.

Stark, Rodney, and Charles Y. Glock
1965   "The New Denominationalism," *Review of Religious Research,* 7(1): 8–17.

1968   *American Piety.* Berkeley: University of California Press.

Stark, Rodney, Lori Kent, and Daniel P. Doyle
1982   "Religion and Delinquency: The Ecology of a 'Lost' Relationship," *Journal of Research in Crime and Delinquency* 19:4–24.

Statistics Canada
1974   *1971 Census of Canada.* Ottawa, Canada: Queen's Printer.

Steinberg, Stephen
1965   "Reform Judaism: The Origin and Evolution of a Church Movement," *Journal for the Scientific Study of Religion* 5:117–129.

Stonequist, Everett V.
1937   *The Marginal Man.* New York: Scribner's.

Strachan, Francoise
1970   *The Aquarian Guide to Occult, Mystical, Religious, Magical London and Around.* London: Aquarian Press.

Stuart, Richard B.
1970   *Trick or Treatment: How and When Psychotherapy Fails.* Champaign, Illinois: Research Press.

Swanson, Guy E.
1960   *The Birth of the Gods.* Ann Arbor: University of Michigan Press.

Symonds, John
1958   *The Magic of Aleister Crowley.* London: Muller.

Thomas, Keith
1971   *Religion and the Decline of Magic.* New York: Scribner's.

Thrasher, Frederic M.
1927   *The Gang.* Chicago: University of Chicago Press.

Tiryakian, Edward A.
1972   "Toward the Sociology of Esoteric Culture," *American Journal of Sociology* 78:491–512.

Tobey, Alan
1976   "The Summer Solstice of the Healthy-Happy-Holy Organization." Pp. 5–30 in *The New Religious Consciousness*, edited by Charles Y.

Glock and Robert N. Bellah. Berkeley: University of California Press.

Torrey, E. Fuller
1972 "What Western Psychotherapists Can Learn from Witchdoctors," *American Journal of Orthopsychiatry* 42:69–76.

Trevor-Roper, H. R.
1969 *The European Witch-Craze of the Sixteenth and Seventeenth Centuries.* New York: Harper & Row.

Trice, Harrison M., and Paul Michael Roman
1970 "Delabeling, Relabeling, and Alcoholics Anonymous," *Social Problems* 17:538–546.

Troeltsch, Ernst
1931 *The Social Teaching of the Christian Churches.* New York: Macmillan.

Truzzi, Marcello
1970 "The Occult Revival as Popular Culture: Some Random Observations on the Old and Nouveau Witch," *Sociological Quarterly* 13:16–36.

Ungerleider, J. Thomas, and David K. Wellisch
1979 "Coercive Persuasion (Brainwashing), Religious Cults, and Deprogramming," *American Journal of Psychiatry* 136:279–282.

Veevers, J. E., and D. F. Cousineau
1980 "The Heathen Canadians," *Pacific Sociological Review* 23:199–216.

Vernon, Glenn M.
1968 "The Religious 'Nones': A Neglected Category," *Journal for the Scientific Study of Religion* 7:219–229.

Volinn, Ernest
1982 "Lead Us from Darkness: The Allure of a Religious Sect and Its Charismatic Leader." Unpublished doctoral dissertation, Columbia University.

Wallace, Anthony F. C.
1956 "Revitalization Movements," *American Anthropologist* 58:264–281.
1966 *Religion: An Anthropological View.* New York: Random House.

Wallace, Robert Keith
1970 "Physiological Effects of Transcendental Meditation," *Science* 167:1751-1754.

Wallace, Robert Keith, and Herbert Benson
1972 "The Physiology of Meditation," *Scientific American* 226 (February):84–90.

Wallis, Roy
1975 *Sectarianism.* New York: Wiley.
1976 *The Road to Total Freedom.* New York: Columbia University Press.

Walters, Susan (ed.)
1981 *Canadian Almanac and Directory.* Toronto, Canada: Copp Clark Pitman.

Ward, Ken
1975 *Occult Directory.* Saskatoon, Canada: Ward.

Weber, Max
1946   *From Max Weber: Essays in Sociology.* New York: Oxford University Press.
1949   *The Methodology of the Social Sciences.* Glencoe, Illinois: Free Press.
1963   *The Sociology of Religion.* Boston: Beacon Press.
Weil, Andrew
1972   *The Natural Mind.* Boston: Houghton Mifflin.
Weingarten, Henry
1977   *The NASO International Astrological Directory.* New York: National Astrological Society.
Weintraub, Walter, and H. Aronson
1968   "A Survey of Patients in Classical Psychoanalysis: Some Vital Statistics," *Journal of Nervous and Mental Disease* 146:98–102.
Welch, Kevin W.
1981   "An Interpersonal Influence Model of Traditional Religious Commitment," *Sociological Quarterly* 22:81–92.
1983   "Community Development and Metropolitan Religious Commitment: A Test of Two Competing Models," *Journal for the Scientific Study of Religion* 22:167–181.
Welch, Michael R.
1977   "Analyzing Religious Sects: An Empirical Examination of Wilson's Sect Typology," *Journal for the Scientific Study of Religion* 16:125–139.
Wescott, Roger W.
1969   *The Divine Animal.* New York: Funk and Wagnalls.
Westfall, Richard S.
1958   *Science and Religion in Seventeenth-Century England.* New Haven, Connecticut: Yale University Press.
Westhues, Kenneth
1976   "Religious Organization in Canada and the United States," *International Journal of Comparative Sociology* 17:206–225.
1978   "Stars and Stripes, the Maple Leaf, and the Papal Coat of Arms," *Canadian Journal of Sociology* 3:245–261.
Westoff, Charles F.
1979   "The Blending of Catholic Reproductive Behavior." Pp. 231–240 in *The Religious Dimension,* edited by Robert Wuthnow. New York: Academic Press.
Westoff, Charles F., and Elise F. Jones
1977   "The Secularization of U.S. Catholic Birth Control Practices," *Family Planning Perspectives* 9:203–207.
White, A. D.
1896   *A History of the Warfare of Science with Theology in Christendom.* Gloucester, Massachusetts: Peter Smith (1978).
White, Harrison C., Scott A. Boorman, and Ronald L. Breiger
1976   "Social Structure from Multiple Networks," *American Journal of Sociology* 81:730–780.

White, Harrison C., and Ronald L. Breiger
    1975   "Pattern Across Networks," *Society* (July–August): 68–73.
White, John
    1976a   "A Critical Look at TM," *New Age Journal* (January):30–35.
    1976b   "Second Thoughts: What's Behind TM?" *Human Behavior* (October):70–71.
Whitworth, John McKelvie
    1975   *God's Blueprints.* London: Routledge and Kegan Paul.
Whyte, William Foote
    1943   *Street Corner Society.* Chicago: University of Chicago Press.
Wilson, Bryan
    1959   "An Analysis of Sect Development," *American Sociological Review* 24:2–15.
    1961   *Sects and Society.* Berkeley: University of California Press.
    1966   *Religion in Secular Society.* London: C. A. Watts.
    1970   *Religious Sects.* New York: McGraw-Hill.
    1975a   *Magic and the Millennium.* Frogmore, England: Paladin.
    1975b   "The Secularization Debate," *Encounter* 45:77–83.
    1979   "The Return of the Sacred," *Journal for the Scientific Study of Religion* 18:268–280.
    1981   *The Social Impact of New Religious Movements.* New York: Rose of Sharon Press.
    1982   *Religion in Sociological Perspective.* New York: Oxford University Press.
Wilson, Edward O.
    1975   *Sociobiology–The New Synthesis.* Cambridge, Massachusetts: Harvard University Press.
Winter, J. A.
    1951   *A Doctor's Report on Dianetics.* New York: Julian Press.
Wirth, Louis
    1938   "Urbanism as a Way of Life," *American Journal of Sociology* 44:3–24.
    1940   "Ideological Aspects of Social Disorganization," *American Sociological Review* 5:472–482.
Wolfe, Tom
    1968   *The Electric Kool-Aid Acid Test.* New York: Bantam.
World Vision
    1979   *Mission Handbook.* Monrovia, California: World Vision.
Wrigley, E. A.
    1969   *Population and History.* New York: McGraw-Hill (World University Library).
Wuthnow, Robert
    1976a   *The Consciousness Reformation.* Berkeley: University of California Press.
    1976b   "The New Religions in Social Context." Pp. 267–293 in *The New Religious Consciousness,* edited by Charles Y. Glock and Robert N. Bellah. Berkeley: University of California Press.

1977   "A Longitudinal, Cross-National Indicator of Societal Religious Commitment," *Journal for the Scientific Study of Religion* 16:87–99.

1978   *Experimentation in American Religion.* Berkeley: University of California Press.

1981   "Two Traditions in the Study of Religion," *Journal for the Scientific Study of Religion* 20:16–32.

Wuthnow, Robert, and Kevin Christiano

1979   "The Effects of Residential Migration on Church Attendance in the United States." Pp. 257–276 in *The Religious Dimension,* edited by Robert Wuthnow. New York: Academic Press.

Yadin, Yigael

1971   *Bar-Kokhba.* New York: Random House.

Yinger, J. Milton

1970   *The Scientific Study of Religion.* New York: Macmillan.

1977   "Countercultures and Social Change," *American Sociological Review* 42:833–853.

Young, Michael, and Peter Willmott

1957   *Family and Kinship in East London.* Baltimore: Penguin.

Yuchtman, Ephraim

1972   "Distribution and Work-Role Attractiveness in the Kibbutz — Reflections on Equity Theory," *American Sociological Review* 37:581–595.

Zablocki, Benjamin

1971   *The Joyful Community.* Baltimore: Penguin.

Zellman, Gail L.

1975   "Antidemocratic Beliefs: A Survey and Some Explanations," *Journal of Social Issues* 31:31–53.

Zweig, Stefan

1932   *Mental Healers.* New York: Viking.

Index

Designer:	Sandy Drooker
Compositor:	Innovative Media, Inc.
Printer:	Vail-Ballou Press
Binder:	Vail-Ballou Press
Text:	10/12 Baskerville
Display:	Helvetica Black and Baskerville